HEROES IN A GLOBAL WORLD

THE HAMPTON PRESS COMMUNICATION SERIES
Mass Communication and Journalism
Lee B. Becker, supervisory editor

HEROES IN A GLOBAL WORLD

edited by

Susan J. Drucker
Hofstra University

Gary Gumpert
Communication Landscapers

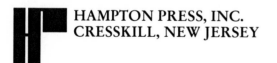

HAMPTON PRESS, INC.
CRESSKILL, NEW JERSEY

Printed in the United States of America

Heroes in a global world / edited by Susan J. Drucker, Gary Gumpert
      p. cm. -- (The Hampton Press communication series)
  Includes bibliographic references and index.
  ISBN 978-1-57273-694-8 (hardbound) -- ISBN 978-1-57273-695-5 (paperbound)
1. Heroes in mass media. 2. Heroes. 3. Civilization, Modern--21st century.
I. Drucker, Susan J. II. Gumpert, Gary
  P96.H46H47 2007
  302.2308--dc22

                 2007025682

Hampton Press, Inc.
23 Broadway
Cresskill, NJ 07626

"As you get older, it is harder to have heroes,
but it is sort of necessary."

Ernest Hemingway

This book is dedicated to our personal heroes
who are there quietly doing all that is necessary to keep us going.

Susan Drucker and Gary Gumpert

CONTENTS

Chapter 1

THE GLOBAL COMMUNICATION ENVIRONMENT OF HEROES

Susan J. Drucker
Hofstra University

Gary Gumpert
Communication Landscapers

TIMES AND THE HERO

This is a confusing time for heroes. It is a confusing time for those of us who need heroes. It is even a more confusing time for those who write about heroes. The headlines and the newscasts are full of performers, political opportunists, national opponents, constructions, adventurers, plotters, and assassins. It has been 10 years since *American Heroes in a Media Age* was published and it seems as if the world is going through a period of upheaval and turmoil unlike previous eras of confusion and mayhem. It may just be the common myopia of those of one age looking back at previous times. As one judges from the present, an aura of romantic clarity hovers over and divides one period from another. The past seems clearer than the present, the players bolder and more distinct.

These are times of extraordinary circumstance accompanied by rapid and innovative developments in communication technology. The circumstances and the technology are intertwined. We are who we are because we are able to speak and listen to each other, to watch and read about the other without the restrictions of time and place. With the ability to preserve and distribute words and images we seek to transcend the margins of location. It took 500 years to move the letters of Gutenberg electronically. It has taken less than a century to progress from the most rudimentary pioneering attempt at television to television imbedded in the Internet and the mobile telephone. It is a time when mass media have been augmented and redefined by the information dissemination capabilities of cyberspace. It is now a time when the tale of the hero, the stories so essential to the creation and maintenance of the hero, can be told in traditional fora or posted to a Web site or blog.

Since 2001, we have faced the horror of 9/11, the U.S. involvement in Afghanistan and the Iraq war, the rise of worldwide terrorism, genocide in Africa, the continuation of division and conflict in the Middle East, increased religious polarization, and the awareness globally of Muslim fundamentalism. Since 1994, the world has witnessed the rise of the European Union, the growth and influence of China and India as economic powers, and the fractionalization of the Soviet Union.

Concurrently, the past decade has witnessed the convergence of communication technology, the miniaturization and mobility of that technology, the acceleration of the Internet and the increased impact of the World Wide Web on our daily lives. Community has been extended past the confines of immediate home and location. Our local orientation has been augmented by a shift to a global perspective or *glocalization*—the process in which distant sites become localized and part of our virtual community.

In the acceleration of information and communication opportunities, with a transition of individual access to worldwide connection, with the conversion of the consumer into potential publisher, both the conception and creation of celebrities and heroes has been transmogrified—a transition slightly tainted by the grotesque. Where are the large, boldly sculpted heroes of the past? What has happened to the regal but good person who falls from the heights of greatness to the depth of despair because of a flaw in character? Those great figures have, in all probability, been set aside as academic relics reserved for literary appreciation and intellectual fascination. Oedipus, Hamlet, and Othello a part of the Western literary canon—to be appreciated and learned from, but they do not serve as daily mentors of behavior and morality. They have joined the fairy tale as benign companions of growing up. It was in the good old days that there was a link between the fairy tale and community, between legends, heroes, and culture. It is that link of immediacy and relevancy to specific cultures that has been radically altered particularly in relationship to heroes. There is no dearth of celebrities, those figures that are manufactured and disseminated by media outlets seeking to attract large audiences in order to sell brands and products. Their appeal is short-lived and their claim to fame is neither cerebral, nor rejected or embraced along a scale of values running from good to evil. They may be immoral, heroic, daring, or gallant—what counts is their public façade and their notoriety. In that sense, there is little to distinguish one from the other—they are interchangeable and only notable as mass-produced icons. They are consumable, disposable, and "exportable" products. When longer fashionable, they recede into the background and are replaced with what is current, hip, and in . . . at least for the moment.

This is not to suggest that we no longer have a need for heroes. We have greater access to the hero-like figures than ever before and we probably have a greater need for them as the larger than life, symbolic, incontrovertible figures shrink back in their relevance and significance. The celebrity has become the contemporary "erzatz" hero. The performer; the actor, singer, musician, and artist, even some fictional characters, assume larger than life proportions blown up and designed by a committee of communication specialists using the palette of digital technology. With the morphing of actors and animation Spider Man, the Terminator, the Hulk are transformed into comic characters with heroic pretensions.

For some of us, as we search into the not so long ago experienced past, larger than life heroes once existed. Perhaps it is part of growing older that contemporary figures never appear to achieve the dimensions of greatness that we associate with heroes. Perhaps some would argue the larger than life impressions and accomplishments of Napoleon, Mahatma Gandhi, FDR and JFK, Martin Luther King, and Mother Theresa. Looking about it becomes apparent that the hero is a culturally relative concept, that the other side embraces its heroes. The antithesis of those we recognize as the great man or woman must have also have been someone else's hero, some one identified with a fanatical cause or passion abhorrent to us. It is hard to reconcile Hitler, Mussolini, Stalin, or Osama bin Laden, in all of their incarnate evil, as heroes, but they did and do manage to capture the zeal and blind adoration of a mass of people willing to sacrifice their lives for them. With its celebrity and hero assembly plant globally available to individual, organization, and government, the national and cultural relativity of the products become sharply self-evident. Osama bin Laden is a case in point—a placeless nomadic enemy distributed and disseminated by a worldwide network of radio and television stations, satellite transmission, e-mails, blogs, instant newspapers, national and governmental news organizations, xeroxes, audio- and videotapes available, and competing with all.

Whereas the original intent of *American Heroes in a Media Age* was to focus on the concept of *the hero* as a communication phenomenon, the significance of the celebrity emerged eclipsing the significance of "hero." In that volume, the examination of the hero led to the conclusion that there was an increasing ambiguity between modern hero and celebrity. Celebrities were identified as heroes, heroes were celebrified. The media machines used in the celebrity creation process were at the heart of many case studies of so-called heroes and pseudo-heroes. Perhaps heroes meet personal and societal needs in times of insecurity, anxiety, change, and war in ways celebrities cannot. Perhaps hero worship is more satisfying than a celebrity–fan relationship. Perhaps the curtain has been pulled aside providing enough of a glimpse of the celebrity-making process to reveal the operation of formulaic media creations. Fame for the sake of fame has become an art form with the stars of reality TV subjecting themselves to situations in which they engage in activities ranging from the embarrassing and unpleasant to the sickening and revolting. Not satisfied with heroes or celebrities alone we have seen the rise of the "Idol" phenomenon.

Internationally the television formula for turning the old talent show into an "idol-making machine" has succeed in garnering huge audiences with a dedicated following. The chosen "idol" (and sometimes runners up too) are transformed in a journey through the celebrity-making machine. (It should not be forgotten that one association with the term *idol* was that of "sham or pretender.") From British *Pop Idol* through the wildly popular *American Idol* we search for our "perfect embodiment" and anoint someone who can be adored blindly and excessively all while delivering good television ratings.

In the intervening years between these two volumes, a renewed interest and need for heroes has emerged. The line between hero and celebrity continues to blur, particularly because of the accessibility to the hero/celebrity apparatus to *all*. The chapters in this volume reveal that at the same time the unique features distinguishing hero and celebrity have become less clear, less distinguishable. On the one hand, the distinction between the two, once characterized by the larger-than-life dimension of the hero, has narrowed. The more traditional hero required distance and perspective, qualities not easily attainable in today's communication climate because the machinery penetrates and unravels any protective veneer that separates the extraordinary from the ordinary. The contemporary process emphasizes the prosaic, the imperfections, those average traits that we share rather than the transcending and the unusual that sets us apart. Bringing the hero closer to us, magnifying both the physical and psychological facets of the great person, destroys the aesthetic distance that heroes require for self-protection. Remove that space or sense of remoteness and the hero is chained to the ordinary. Without the protection of space the nonheroic dimensions of the hero are exaggerated. He or she has no place to hide. Joseph Campbell (1972) suggested that we are all potential heroes. At a time when media accessibility increases the opportunities for fame (even if only by virtue of a webcam or blog), we are all potential celebrities more than potential heroes.

THE IMPACT OF SEPTEMBER 11

The mortal, real-life hero has become a rarity—or is transformed by the myth-making apparatus. The firefighting hero rushing to rescue those trapped in the World Trade Center towers, emerged from the tragedy of 9/11. The brave, the courageous, and the doomed became heroes, through no fault or decision of their own. The victims of 9/11 became instant heroes to be mourned and honored, amplified by the enormity of the horror of those moments. This is a different sense of the hero, the accidental hero, the victim of circumstances beyond control. This is the ordinary, the commonplace hero who is thrust into momentary fame.

The ashes and rubble of 9/11 revealed another variation epitomized by the role and contribution of New York City Mayor Rudolph W. Giuliani, a polarizing figure as mayor, adored by some and reviled by others, but who stepped back into the public arena at a time when a symbolic figure was urgently needed by shocked citizens grasping for some understanding of the cataclysmic events. It was a unifying, reassuring, humane, nonpolitical Giuliani who answered the call representing the city for both New Yorkers and the international community. The message was clear and unambiguous: New York would endure and rise out of the ashes. And for that moment, Rudolph W. Giuliani became a global hero signaling to the entire world that New York would persist and a national leader on whom the entire nation could measure the precarious moment. But such a moment must be understood, because it represents one of those rare points in time in which the entire focus is concentrated and served by all operational communication technology. It is a moment in which all else ceases to operate and the center of attention is riveted on the catastrophe. It is the quintessential mediated moment where the communication system links the world's participants together.

VARIATIONS ON A THEME OF HERO

The Celebrity Spokesperson

The intersection of heroism and celebrity has become increasingly complex when one considers the ever-growing phenomenon of celebrity activist or celebrity spokesperson, the celebrity who uses fame to do good deeds. From Princess Diana's campaigns for AIDS babies and against land mines to anti-smoking and anti-drunk driving public service announcements (PSAs), celebrities are the popular spokespeople for diseases and treatments. Jerry

Lewis' dedication to the Muscular Dystrophy Association, Elizabeth Taylor and AIDS, Michael J. Fox and Parkinson's disease, and Tour de France champion cyclist Lance Armstrong, a cancer survivor, are examples of celebrities in public health education and advocacy. Bono, lead singer of the Irish rock group U-2, has become an acknowledged leader campaigning for humanitarian aid for Africa and third-world debt relief. Bono has become a credible voice and enjoys access to presidents, prime ministers, and popes. The Katie Couric Effect is studied with regard to the positive impact a celebrity spokespersona can have on preventive health behavior. Ms. Couric, former anchor for the *Today Show* became an advocate of colon cancer prevention. Ms. Couric's colon cancer screening campaign is linked with a statistically significant increase in the use of colonoscopy in the demographics represented by her audience (The Couric Effect, 2004).

Even a superhero became a "real hero." Christopher Reeve, best known for his role as Superman, was recognized and ultimately eulogized as having gone from "on screen superhero to real-life hero." A horseback riding accident rendered Reeve a quadriplegic, confined to a ventilator and a wheelchair. Although he died in 2004 at age 52, never having achieved his goal of walking again, he served as a symbol of resolve against insurmountable odds. He became an activist for stem cell research, using his celebrity status to get publicity and give voice to the needs of those with spinal cord injuries. He lobbied Congress for legislation to fund research, and regularly spoke to schools and national groups. Fame used to sell more than products may turn a celebrity into a hero.

The Child as Hero

In sharp contrast, that same period has a concurrent hero of a very different nature—the heroic child, the fictional protagonist, the innocent warrior. When Harry Potter was introduced in 1997. There was little indication the boy wizard would conjure up a global phenomenon. But within a few short years, Harry's adventures at Hogwart's School of Witchcraft and Wizardry have sold more than 265 million books worldwide with a global distribution in more than 200 countries. The series has been translated into 62 languages, including Classical Greek. The fifth book of the series, *The Order of the Phoenix*, sold 5 million copies within 24 hours of publication. The Harry Potter series has been a money-making machine. Record-setting book sales have been supplemented by three major Hollywood blockbusters, computer games, and inspired Potter paraphernalia, including toys, making J.K. Rowling the first billion-dollar author. The first movie grossed almost $1 billion worldwide, making it the second-highest grossing movie of all time after *Titanic.* Potter has become a phenomenon perhaps unparalleled in the publishing industry—and the entertainment business as a whole. Parents and educators find magic in Harry's ability to make children (along with adults) want to read a 750-page book. Harry Potter fever has been credited with getting hundreds of thousands of kids excited about reading. Critics demonize Rowling for her use of witchcraft in the Potter series as a literary device. Sermons, books, articles, and Web sites warn that "Harry Potter is a Dangerous Hero for Our Children" (Norris, 2004), suggesting that Harry Potter makes sorcery and witchcraft enticing, which is inconsistent with a Christian worldview. Prior to his elevation to Pope, Cardinal Joseph Ratzinger denounced the books, noting that it "deeply distort[s] Christianity in the soul, before it can grow properly" (Malvern, 2005, p.).

Harry Potter serves as a child-hero and or role model for his readers worldwide. He struggles in school, with his friends, with his relationships. Although not physically strong, he is good, kind, selfless, humble, but imbued with talents. The young wizard tracks the path of many heroes before him: an extraordinary birth, a childhood spent in exile, adventure, descent, and triumph. His weapon is a wand. He can fly like Superman with the aid of a broomstick, and he is brave. J.K. Rowling uses many hero archetypes found in mythology following a very human journey filled with imperfections, yet we are still able to look up to Harry for his bravery and extraordinary magical powers. He confronts his fears, although he is often scared in the situations he must face.

The return of the hero has taken many incarnations. There are many types of heroes from the traditional literary, military, and unsung to the intellectual, animal, and super variety. The Web site www.myhero.com, a not-for-profit educational web project is dedicated to an ever-growing assortment of hero types.

> MY HERO is a not-for-profit educational Web project that celebrates the best of humanity. Our mission is to inspire people of all ages with an ever-growing Internet archive of hero stories from around the world. From peacemakers such as Nelson Mandela to scientific visionaries such as Albert Einstein, visitors can explore historical heroes, contemporary heroes and hometown heroes.

> MY HERO invites you, your family, school or organization to take part. By publicly honoring your hero on this award-winning project, you reward those who have made a difference, and bring new hope to the online global community. (www.myhero.com)

The myhero.com directory of heroes suggests categories including *angel* heroes, *animal* heroes, *artist* heroes, *business* heroes, *child* heroes, *community* heroes, *earthkeeper* heroes, *explorer* heroes, heroes of *faith*, *family* heroes, *freedom* heroes, *hero's* heroes, *lifesaver* heroes, *literary* heroes, *musician* heroes, *mythological* heroes, *peacemaker* heroes, *philosopher* heroes, *poet* heroes, *science* heroes, *sports* heroes, *teacher* heroes, *women* heroes, and *writer* heroes. Features are available on "heroes of faith" and "heroes working for human rights."

The Public Intellectual Hero

From mainstream media to academic conferences, the subject of "heroes" is back. It is a time when we question the very existence and role of the "public intellectual hero," the "cultivated mind," those "men of the mind," described by Ayn Rand in *Atlas Shrugged* who were, heroes of a more advanced intellectual nature. Christopher Hitchens (2004) comments on Susan Sontag's death are important in his consideration of the public intellectual as hero/heroine.

> The 20th century was perhaps unusual in the ways in which it forced such people to quit their desks and their bookshelves and to enter the agora. Looking over our shoulders, we do not find that we have much respect or admiration for those who simply survived, or who kept the private life alive. We may owe such people more than we know, but it is difficult to view them as exemplary. Our heroes and heroines are those who managed, from Orwell through Camus and Solzhenitsyn, to be both intellectual and engaged. (This combination of qualities would also be true of a good number of our fools and villains, from Celine to Shaw, with Sartre perhaps occupying the middle position.)

The Sports Hero

Sports heroes are elevated to ever greater heights in terms of salaries, media exposure, and marketability. Multimillion dollar packages and celebrity product endorsements beckon. Name recognition and respect for on-field accomplishments have lead to careers in acting and to elected office. It is debatable whether sports figures are genuine heroes or pseudo-heroes (Drucker & Cathcart, 1994). In 1994, Drucker and Cathcart argued that "the modern sports hero is actually a misnomer for the sports celebrity. On the surface professional sports seem to offer a natural source for heroes, but on closer examination they offer celebrated sports figures shaped, fashioned, and marketed as heroic" (p. 93). If sports hero is the correct term, today our sports heroes are increasingly revealed as flawed. Doping scandals rock many sports from professional to amateur sports, from high schools to the Olympics. With the rise of sports as big business, new scandals appear, casting suspicion not only on players but even on the sporting events themselves, as evidence by the site-selection bribery scandal of the 2002 Winter Olympic Games in Park City, Utah. Performance-enhancement drugs abound. Barry Bond's pursuit of the coveted major league baseball homerun throne has been tainted by his alleged connection to the steroid scandal.

Sports figures are implicated in cases of domestic abuse, charged with rape, driving under the influence, tax evasion, illegal gambling, betting on sports, and even murder. News media cover the stories; entertainment media dramatize, fictionalize, and further propagate the flaws of the modern sports "hero."

The international fame and adoration increasingly enjoyed by sports figures has grown in the past decade. The local sports hero has, in part, given way to the nonlocal global sports figure. Local sports available and marketed internationally has created sports heroes (or pseudo-heroes) recognized around the world. NBA basketball and the New York Yankees franchise merchandise is ubiquitous, especially the knockoffs. Foreign audiences started tuning into American pro-sports, especially basketball, in previously unheard of numbers. Teenagers snapped up player jerseys and stayed *until all hours of the night* to watch games on live television. They began imitating moves on their own courts and fields. According to *David Goldiner* (2004), *a reporter for the New York Daily News*:

> More than any single athlete, Jordan, the magnetic and charismatic Chicago Bulls superstar, transformed American sports into a global phenomenon. Jordan's soaring dunks and graceful athleticism made him a worldwide poster child for the American dream. Starting in the late 1980s, he drew hundreds of millions of dollars into the sport and became one of the most recognized persons in the world.

American sports are beamed around the world. At the same time, foreign stars have been welcomed onto the fields, courts, and rinks of the U.S. professional leagues. Chinese basketball centers Yao Ming, high-scoring forward Dirk Nowitzki from Germany, and Brazilian Nene Hilario have emerged as stars in the NBA. Satellite radio and television, along with coverage provided via the Internet, mean following one's "home team" does not depend on remaining home. Immigrant communities around the world retain home team allegiance, religiously following their sports legends. The sports club or café that offers a live satellite feed often serves as a central meeting point in immigrant enclaves.

> Some sports have been exported creating international sports heroes. The adoption of baseball in Japan, though not a recent innovation has changed with the exportation of legends to U.S. franchises. Player/ "heroes" are both welcomed in their new homes and followed faithfully by fans "back home." Ichiro, Hideo Nomo, Hideki Matsui, Hideki Irabu, Sasaki Kazuhiro, Masato Yoshii, to name a few.

It wasn't until 1964 when a player exchange between the San Francisco Giants and the Nankai Hawks brought Murakami to the Majors but since the 1990s the exchange has had a more noticeable impact. The global media environment enables up to the minute fan following. In Japan, legions of fans tune in at odd hours each day to watch their chosen hero take on North American adversaries. For example, with Suzuki on the Seattle Mariners, Japan's NHK network broadcasts each Mariners game back to Japan and, between innings, focused on Suzuki as he jogs, stretches, tosses a warm-up ball (Pearlman, 2001).

America's "national pasttime" has become internationalized. By 2000, both top rookie honors went to foreign-born players (Seattle Mariner's Kazuhiro Sasaki from Japan and Dominican Republic-born shortstop Rafael Furcal of the Atlanta Braves). Chan Ho Park joined the Los Angeles Dodgers in 1994, becoming the first Korean player in major league history. By 2003, major league players in the United States came from 31 different nations (Vass, 2003). For decades a few Latin American stars excited U.S. baseball fans and ignited interest at home epitomized by Mexican pitcher Fernando Valenzuela and Dominican curveballer Juan Marichal but now more than a quarter of all Major League Baseball players were born outside the United States (Goldiner, 2004). Today baseball has global all-stars with players from all over Latin America, including Cuba. The "beisbol" players from Venezuela, Panama, and, especially, the Dominican Republic *supply sports "heroes," for the U.S. game.* Volumes have been devoted to not only the significance in terms of sports but the cultural importance of the export-ed sports "hero" exemplified by Robert Whiting' s (2004) book, *The Meaning of Ichiro,* which focuses on Japanese playing baseball in the American Major Leagues.

Global sporting events enjoy increased media coverage. No longer lim-ited to traditional broadcasts and the available print press, international sporting events produce global sports heroes. From Lance Armstrong's dominance in the Tour de France in the world of cycling to Tiger Woods in golf, professional athletes perform in international competitions on a global media stage. Amateur athletes, from Olympic to little league champs, engage in international contests accessible by fans irrespective of location.

A PREVIEW OF THE VOLUME

The array of topics associated with heroes is vast in this global, post-September 11, modern media environment. By necessity, this volume is lim-ited in scope, its aim modest. This volume provides a survey and hopefully stimulates consideration of continuity and change with regard to heroes.

The book could have gone in many other directions. The internationalization of sports and the reconsideration of the sports hero is a rich area, as illustrated in the brief discussion just presented. Interesting research is now being conducted into the rise of the celebrity as spokesperson for social issues. Both advertising and communication research has confirmed the power of celebrities to influence attitudinal and behavioral change in audience members and the cultural significance of celebrity power (Duff, 2003). The importance of blogs, chatrooms, listservs, and Web sites, as online presence creates new communities in search of heroes, offers tantalizing possibilities. High-profile cases of conflict over the creation of public memorials abound. From the appropriate use of the space at Ground Zero to the appropriate commemorative space in Berlin for victims of the Nazi era, to questions of safety at the Princess Diana memorial in London, the act of commemoration and the attendant debate and conflict over memorials in public spaces reveal a great deal about the relationship of public to hero.

The mass media relentlessly search out those who satisfy the public's appetite for super-status and just as relentlessly portray their human faults and failings. The means of telling the story and keeping it in the public eye determines what is heroic and who is to be celebrated. Joshua Gamson (1992) provided a chronology of celebrity linked to the publicity industry and asserts that the celebrity phenomenon became systematized by the early 20th century. From developments in newspaper distribution, telegraphy, photography, through the early stages of sound recording, motion picture, and ultimately television celebrity creation evolved into a powerful, professionalized ultimately visible industry. Although these continue to be the forces of celebrity formation, heroes are not untouched or beyond reach. In *American Heroes in a Media Age*, the relationship of celebrity and heroes was explored. In *Heroes in a Global World,* it is the condition of hero in the media environment of the celebrity that is under consideration.

The chapters that follow explore many variations on a theme of hero from martyr hero, anti-hero, superhero, and the "controversial hero" who is an anti-hero or villain to some, thereby becoming a hero to others. Many distinctions and questions emerge. Is there a difference between a leader and hero? Must the impact of a hero's deeds be public? Is there a difference between a hero and a heroine? Is there a difference between a male and female hero? Are the media creating both heroes and anti-heroes? Can heroes profit from their deeds? Does the hero fall to celebrity when he or she profits or seeks compensation? Is there a globalized hero? Is there a universally recognized hero?

Heroes in a Global World is concerned with the role communication processes, practices, and technologies play in developing the contemporary hero. The first section is composed of chapters that place the hero (and celebrity) into general contexts of the communication, intercultural, and media worlds in which we live. In Chapter 2, Lance Strate traces the historical evolution of the hero from orality to literacy and then to the postliterate electronic culture, and considers how the nature and function of the hero is dependent on the dominant medium of communication. In Chapter 3, Brown and Fraser focus on the relationship of hero and celebrity and the rise of the "international" celebrity hero. The social influence of the celebrity hero is discussed with regard to economics, politics, media, and culture.

In a rich and broad-ranging examination, John Dean considers the historical antecedents of the modern hero and examines the unique societal imprint heroes carry by comparing U.S. and European conceptions of heroism. In Chapter 4, Dean offers a concise survey of the concept of *hero* itself from the very derivation of the word, through eight historical stages identifying phases through which heroes have progressed from the Homeric Age to the Renaissance to the Industrial Age. Intertwining concepts of fame, information, propaganda, advertising among the myriad themes considered amidst diverse historical and literary illustrations. Dean examines how heroism is the result of a process of social construction and examines the essential nature of that process.

Joshua Meyrowitz analyzes the nature of the mediated relationship between audience members and media "friends." In Chapter 5, he considers the sense of intimacy created by modern media cultivating a sense of attachment to those in the mass media including celebrities, newscasters, actors, singers, sports figures, and even politicians. Unlike the distance associated with hero worship, he explains that these relationships become part of an extended network of social ties providing friendships and a genuine sense of loss and grief with the death of media friends.

In a chapter that first appeared in *American Heroes in a Media Age,* Gary Gumpert traces the evolution of the heroic fall and the flawed hero and the relationship of various media in either elevating or bringing low the hero. In Chapter 6, "The Wrinkle Theory: The Deconstruction of the Hero," Gumpert examines the role of media technologies and institutions in the process of demythification of the hero. It is the technology and organization of the media of communication that promote scrutiny and that deter, alter, and facilitate the relationship with the hero. An audience nurtured by penetrating media comes to expect the elimination of the public face and demands insight into the private. He argues that heroes cannot withstand such scrutiny.

Part II focuses on the hero and the events of the September 11. Overnight the term *hero* seemed to become omnipresent. Photos of missing victims were transformed into images of lost heroes. Firemen, police, and emergency workers took center stage as heroes. Military response to the "war on terrorism" led, in some circles, to the revitalization of the military hero. There was an apparent surge in the need for heroes. The next grouping of chapters consists of more specific case studies and comparisons of diverse cultural and national approaches to heroes, particularly framed by the tragedy of 9/11. Mahmoud Eid distinguishes the Muslim/Arab world from the Western world. In Chapter 7, a case study of Osama bin Laden as *controversial hero,* Eid demonstrates how the hero to some may epitomize the villain to others. Noting that bin Laden is controversial both within and outside the Arab world, he compares the media use and media coverage of bin Laden as a means of constructing him as hero, celebrity, or enemy

Is there a difference between a heroine and a female hero? Fayer (1994) argued that male heroes and heroines are not functional equivalents. The role of gender in the heroes of September 11 is considered by Valerie Smith in Chapter 8. Historically, the notions of hero and heroism were associated with the male domain. Smith argues that in the aftermath of September 11, the reporting on the heroes at Ground Zero was primarily male-oriented. She explores hero gender differences using the case of two female New York City police officers who were part of the rescue mission. Next, Susan Duffy considers folkloric and mythic formulae for hero construction and maintenance that have endured across historical eras, geography and religions. Applying these formulae, she examines current heroes of 9/11 and war to explore diverse types of heroes and anti-heroes from the perspective of storytelling. Rounding out this section is Chapter 10, which shifts the examination of heroes to a specific hero–worshipper or fan relationship, that of the relationship between heroes and children. Cheryl Harris and Alison Alexander seek to identify the characteristics children view as heroic. They assert that in the post-September 11 period, superheroes have re-emerged in significance. Children consume media superheroes that possess special powers alongside mediated messages of heroes who embody other qualities including courage and self-sacrifice. Through interviews with children, the authors identify characteristics of those figures that attain hero status for children.

Part III provides diverse case studies of heroes in different cultural contexts. In Chapter 11, Susan Swan and Timothy Walters, Americans living in the Arab world, describe and consider the heroic in a context of Arab-Islamic values focusing on the through a case history of the recently deceased Sheikh Zayed bin Sultan al Nahyan of the United Arab Emirates.

Encompassing another distinct cultural or religious view of the hero, Eva Berger considers modern Israeli heroes, connecting them with their antecedent Biblical counterpart. In Chapter 12, Berger explores how heroes become famous through the dominant medium of communication of their culture. She examines heroes created through the spoken word, through Old Testament hero narratives that offer understanding of the nature of "oral heroes." A comparison of cultural and religious differences in oral heroes is offered by contrasting the heroes of Ancient Greece with Jewish Biblical heroes.

Sondra M. Rubenstein and Adam Ehrlich examine a distinct type of hero, the political hero, based on a theory of charisma. In Chapter 13, Israel's Menachem Begin provides a vivid case study. The authors suggest that although other types of heroes may be associated with one great deed, a political hero does not emerge from a single feat or event although in the modern media world it is only when a particular event or act attracts media attention does the act of heroism appear. However, the resulting attention to an event often overlooks the political hero.

The hero and communication of an organized religious leader is considered in the case study of the pope as hero in Chapter 14. Maria Way provides a survey of media developments mirrored in the history of the Catholic Church, the papacy in particular. She argues that the late Pope John Paul II, skilled in the use of the Vatican as a worldwide media center, created a pope who was not only hero but celebrity. In the days leading up to the selection of Pope Benedict XVI in April 2005, pundits publicly considered whether media proficiency had been added to criteria when considering qualifications for any pope.

The significance of religious ethos vis-à-vis the elevation of the hero continues to emerge with the examination of the case study of the hero in Japan. The influence of Shintoism in the conception of heroism in Japan is examined by T.J.M. Holden, who explores diverse incarnations of heroes in Japan (Chapter 15). From mythic hero to fantasy to mundane hero, Holden considers the role of the samurai as hero. He considers the nature of "Asian heroes" and the significance of globalization on Asian hero creation.

Some heroes resonate with both children and adults. The motion picture *Shrek* has an appeal that has crossed generations as well as cultures, proving highly successful at the box office worldwide. Steven Combs (Chapter 16) uses *Shrek* as a vehicle through which to consider Joseph Campbell's concept of the archetypal hero. He considers how culture-specific the hero may be, given that a hero reflects and reaffirms values of a specific community. To illustrate this point, he contrasts Western views and Eastern views by applying Daoist teaching.

In Chapter 17, Drucker re-visits the ever growing phenomenon of the sports hero. In a piece that appeared in the *American Heroes* volume, it was argued that the modern sports hero is actually a sports celebrity or pseudo-hero. This original chapter is reprinted with a prologue in which questions are raised as to what have become of sports heroes within the context of the internationalization of sports.

In this global economy the hero is big business and Part IV introduces several economic and legal dimensions for consideration. If heroes are culture-specific, then the global exportation and availability of these figures raises questions about the changing functions of heroes. In Chapter 18, Phillip Drake examines how global celebrities have been able to co-opt qualities traditionally associated with heroes. Through the perspective of political economics, he examines how celebrities have fought for a stronger right of control over their image through the right of publicity. The underlying assumptions and significance of intellectual property rights issues are examined. Drake demonstrates that political, economic, legal, and cultural discussions are interdependent.

The degree to which heroes can survive scrutiny becomes a central controlling factor. The relationship of paparazzi and medium is important and fascinating. It represents a love–hate relationship in which each requires the other. In the media coverage of heroes and celebrities, the line between public and private life has become indistinct. Laws have been passed in numerous countries to protect the famous and new measures. In Chapter 19, Susan Drucker surveys the U.S. legal landscape and the delicate balance between the right and desire to be let alone and the indispensable role of media feeding the status of hero or celebrity. Specifically, the legal issues associated with the right to privacy, defamation, trespass, false imprisonment, and so on, are considered.

Each of us approaches hero and celebrity from our own cultural perspective. In our efforts to present an international or global view on the subject we remain shaped by our own cultural boundaries. This volume is edited by two Americans attempting to provide the reader a more global perspective. If anything, September 11 and its villains and heroes of terror give pause us to think about the relativism of heroism.

The studies in this volume support certain common, perhaps universal conclusions about heroes: All cultures have them; all cultures need them; who or what is considered heroic may vary from culture to culture; the heroes of a culture reflect or define culture values. Communication is at the heart of hero creation and maintenance. Even in an age of globalization, individuals may be globally famous but not globally heroic. In a global age, an individual may be a worldwide celebrity but the status of hero is more local or culturally determined.

We hope this volume adds to an understanding of the age-old and global phenomenon of the hero. This book is offered in the hope that Mohammad was right that "The ink of a scholar is more sacred than the blood of the martyr."

REFERENCES

Campbell, J. (1972). *The hero with a thousand faces*. Princeton, NJ: Princeton University Press.

Couric Effect. (http://www.eifoundation.org/national/nccra/pdfs/um couric_effect .pd).

Drucker, S., & Cathcart, R. (1994). The hero as a communication phenomenon. In S. Drucker & R. Cathcart (Eds.), *American heroes in a media age* (pp. 1–11). Cresskill, NJ: Hampton Press.

Duff, D. (2003, November). *The effective celebrity spokesperson for a health issue: Experiencing Michael J. Fox, spokesperson for Parkinson's Disease.* Paper given at the National Communication Association Convention, Miami Beach, FL.

Fayer, J. M. (1994). Are heroes always men? In S. Drucker & R. Cathcart (Eds.), *American heroes in a media age* (pp. 24–35). Cresskill, NJ: Hampton Press.

Gamson, J. (1992). The assembly line of greatness: Celebrity in twentieth-century America. *Critical Studies in Mass Communication, 9,* 1-24.

Goldiner, D. (2004). *Games for the whole world.* http://usinfo.state.gov/journals /itsv/1203/ijse/goldiner.htm

Gumpert, G. (1994). The wrinkle theory: The deconsecration of the hero. In S. Drucker & R. Cathcart (Eds.), *American heroes in a media age* (pp. 47–61). Cresskill, NJ: Hampton Press.

Hitchens, C. (2004, December 29). Remembering an intellectual heroine. *Slate.* Retrieved January 3, 2005, from http//:www.slate.com/id/2111506/

Malvern, J. (2005, July 14). Harry Potter and the vatican enforcer. *Times Online.* Retrieved July 15, 2005, from http://www.timesonline.co.uk/article/0,,2-1693365,00.html

Norris, M. (2004). Harry Potter a dangerous hero for our children. Retrieved January 21, 2005, from http://www.swordofthelord.com/archives/potter.htm

Pearlman, J. (2001, June 11). Ichiro the hero: U.S. baseball fans are now on a first name basis with the Japanese outfielder who is tearing up the league. *Time Asia; 157(23).* http://www.time.com/time/asia/arts/magazine/0,9754,129011,00.html

Vass, G. (2003). The wide world of baseball: Foreign-born players are filling major league rosters, showing the true measures of global talent in the American pastime. *Baseball Digest.* http://www.findarticles.com/p/articles/mi_m0FCI/is_2_ 62/ai_95915320/pg_2

Whiting, R. (2004). *The meaning of Ichiro: The new wave from Japan and the transformation of our national pastime.* New York: Warner Books.

Part I

HEROES IN A WORLD
OF GLOBAL CONNECTION

Chapter 2

HEROES AND/AS COMMUNICATION

Lance Strate
Fordham University

The hero is a representation of self and a product of the extant media. This chapter provides a media history of the hero and takes the position that the only way to study the evolution of the hero is to study communication about the hero. This chapter is a media ecologist's journey and examination of hero development from pre-typographic to typographic, to electronic media ages.

✧ ✧ ✧

Heroes are our ideal selves, the selves that inspire us, the selves that we aspire to, the selves that we desire. Whether they take the form of archetypes, role models, or manikins, our heroes shape our sense of self, and color the ways that we interpret our identities. They teach us how to be the heroes of our own life-stories, how to live heroically. And we desperately need to live heroically, as psychoanalyst Ernest Becker (1971, 1973) explained, because of the heavy price we pay for the unique gift of human consciousness. Alone among the animals, through our capacity for self-reflexiveness brought on by language and symbol use, we human beings are aware of our own mortality, and we must find a way to live with this awful knowledge. We must find a way to deal with the dread that the thought of our own extinction evokes, to defend our ego against collapse in the face of our inevitable descent into nothingness. Our heroes teach us how to make something out of nothingness, how to live our lives in defiance and denial of the fear of death, how to live heroically and become heroes ourselves. Joseph Campbell noted that the very act of living one's life is in its own way a hero's adventure. As we embark upon a hero's journey from birth to death, "we have not even to risk the adventure alone, for the heroes of all time have gone before us. The labyrinth is thoroughly known. We have only to follow the thread of the hero path" (Campbell & Moyers, 1988, p. 123). Our heroes show us the way.

The hero's journey cannot be undertaken without the prior existence of a hero's geography. Heroic acts performed by heroic agents require heroic scenes (see Burke, 1945). And as Becker (1971) put it, "Culture-heroes have to have available to them some kind of heroic action system in which to realize their ambitions, and this symbolic system is what we call 'culture'" (p. 78). Becker defined *culture* as "a structure of rules, customs, and ideas, which serve as a vehicle for heroism" (p. 78). Culture, then, is the hero's medium, as it is the medium of our own heroic selves:

> The fact is that this is what society is and always has been: a symbolic action system, a structure of statuses and roles, customs and rules for behavior, designed to serve as a vehicle for earthly heroism. Each script is somewhat unique, each culture has a different hero system. What the anthropologists call "cultural relativity" is thus really the relativity of hero-systems the world over. But each cultural system is a dramatization of earthly heroics; each system cuts our roles for performances of various degrees of heroism: from the "high" heroism of a Churchill, a Mao, or a Buddha, to the "low" heroism of the coal miner, the peasant, the simple priest; the plain everyday, earthly heroism wrought by gnarled working hands guiding a family through hunger and disease. (Becker, 1973, pp. 4-5)

Cultures are hero-systems, and heroes are a universal component of human culture. Every people and every era has its heroes. As Chaim Potok (1973) said, "heroes are the inevitable concomitant of a system of value and thought that has been embraced by an aggregate of men" (p. 71). Heroes serve as the anchors of human culture, the condensation of collective identity, the personification of our values, beliefs, and knowledge. They are our sources of authority and legitimation, our models for socialization, as well as our guides for psychological development. They give culture a human face and a human voice. But heroes are not human beings, at least not insofar as they are heroes. For example, in his classic work, *The Hero With a Thousand Faces*, Campbell (1968) explained:

> We do not particularly care whether Rip van Winkle, Kamar al-Zaman, or Jesus Christ ever actually lived. Their stories are what concern us: and these stories are so widely distributed over the world—attached to various heroes in various lands—that the question of whether this or that local carrier of the universal theme may or may not have been a historical, living man can be of only secondary moment. The stressing of this historical element will lead to confusion. (pp. 230-231)

To Campbell, the hero is a narrative element within a story, and a symbol whose meaning needs to be interpreted. From other perspectives, the hero can be seen as a text that is written and read, as information that is transmitted and received, and as a cultural form that is constructed and commemorated. Simply stated, the hero is a product of communication. That heroes are born of human communication should come as no surprise, for insofar as we human beings love to talk, our favorite subject matter is ourselves, including our idealized versions of ourselves. And insofar as "culture is communication" as Edward T. Hall (1959, p. 97) maintained, then what Becker (1973) called hero-systems, and the heroes that arise within them, are communication phenomena as well.

Communication is always associated with some type of relationship (Watzlawick, Bavelas, & Jackson, 1967), and hero relationships are generally understood to be hierarchical (Meyrowitz, 1985). Hierarchy has it roots in the parent–child relationship, no doubt, but it also comes naturally to human beings, as it does to all social species from ants and bees to wolves and chimpanzees, the difference being that our social order is maintained through symbolic interaction (Burke, 1950; Duncan, 1962, 1968). Therefore, culture understood as a hero-system can also be understood as a *heroarchy*, as our heroes help us to learn how we fit into the social order (Becker, 1971, 1973). But the hero relationship also involves identification (as does communication in general; see Burke, 1950), which transcends hierarchy. It is therefore possible for the hero relationship to be one of equality, or even in some instances to see the hero as inferior, as in the anti-hero, the scapegoat, and the ironic hero (Burke, 1950; Frye, 1957). Neither are all hero relationships hierarchical, nor are all hierarchical relationships heroic in character. What distinguishes hero relationships are their symbolic character, the meaning they hold, especially for the hero's admirers.

We might go so far as to say that the hero exists in the eye of the beholder. Every hero must be a hero *to* someone. Is Osama Bin Laden a hero? Are Mohamed Atta and the other 9/11 hijackers? To even pose the question would offend the sensibilities of most Americans, but can we deny that they are in fact heroes to a great many Arabs and Muslims? Or that Adolf Hitler was a hero to millions at one time, and sadly remains a hero to some today? Hero relationships are relative, and therefore need to be viewed in terms of cultural relativism and subjectivity. This is not to deny the possibility of discussing the hero in the abstract, and setting up criteria by which to evaluate heroes, such as Sidney Hook's (1943) argument that the only true heroes are individuals who alter the course of history, for good or ill. But Hook's historical heroes are still heroes because they are heroes *to* scholars such as Hook, even if the relationship is rooted in the rational rather than the emotive.

The hero is not a human being, but the hero can be a response to a human being, an image of a human being that we hold internally (see Boulding, 1956), the meaning that we give to a particular individual or historical figure. In the case of the fictional character, Hamlet or Superman for example, it is easiest to see that the hero is a product of communication. When the hero is seen as a real human being, however, it is possible to get the hero and the human confused. It is important to understand that the real person is simply the raw material for the hero, raw material that is processed via narrative, textuality, information transmission, human symbolic communication and the making of meaning. In this sense, there are no heroes in reality, there is only communication about heroes. And the only real way to study heroes is to study communication about heroes. We can study how communication about heroes is produced, how heroic characters are created, how real individuals are presented or present themselves as heroes. And we can study how admirers create their heroes. But it would be a mistake to consider the hero to be nothing more than a human fabrication, socially constructed entirely out of whole cloth, nothing but a subjective phenomenon. Rather, the form that the hero takes is very much influenced by the type of communication that produces the hero.

Different modes of communication will yield different types of heroes. Culture heroes are the result of societal, public, or mass communication. Some fictional heroes may become culture heroes, but typically culture heroes are considered *real*: Even mythical heroes are real to the people who worship them (Eliade, 1975). Culture heroes can be distinguished from organizational heroes (e.g., the company founder, the CEO), who are the outcome of organizational communication. Small groups can have their heroes as well (e.g., the group or community leader), based on small group communication. And our personal heroes (e.g., parents, teachers, clergy, etc.) are the result of interpersonal communication. When asked to name our heroes, we may respond with any one or a combination of these types, but it is useful to recognize that these are very different types of heroes. Culture heroes are entirely different from interpersonal heroes, as Napoleon understood when he remarked, "No man is a hero to his valet." Without distance, there can be no culture heroes. As a general rule, members of a society are separated from their culture heroes by time, space, and social class, and therefore know their heroes only through stories, images, and so on.

Admirers perceive their culture heroes to be distant in some way, and distance enhances their hero status. But there is a dialectic between distance and presence that is governed by the available means of communication. To extrapolate from Hall (1959), the culture hero is a communication hero. The culture hero is never an *unsung hero*, an oxymoron that implies that a hero who ought to be well known remains unknown, through some injustice. The unknown hero may possess certain qualities deemed *heroic*, may exemplify *heroism*, in other words, may be like unto a hero. But can there really be a hero without an admirer, without someone to sing his or her praises? By the same token, terms such as "sung hero," "known hero," or "famous hero" are redundant. To be a culture hero is to be famous by definition, to be known to the members of an entire culture. Fame itself has become the subject of study (e.g., Braudy, 1986; James, 1993), and can be defined as a communication phenomenon, the state that exists when information about a subject is widely disseminated among a group of people. And therefore, to fully understand the phenomenon of the hero, we need to ask questions about *how* that information is disseminated, about the means through which a society communicates about its heroes, about the media of heroic communication. For as the media that we use change, so does our communication about heroes, and consequently, so does our cultural conception of the hero.

BOORSTIN'S DILEMMA

Daniel Boorstin was the first to clearly identify the relationship between heroes and media in a work originally entitled *The Image: Or What Happened to the American Dream* (1962), later revised under the title *The Image: A Guide to Pseudo-Events in America* (1978). In this influential book, Boorstin pointed to a variety of factors affecting contemporary American culture, but pays particular attention to what he calls the graphic revolution, a revolution in the production of images, and in audiovisual communications. It begins in the early 19th century with photography and the application of steam power to typography to create high-speed printing, and culminates in the mid-20th century with the widespread adoption of television. In general, Boorstin argued that technology has given us the ability to replace authentic experiences with manufactured ones; ultimately, we have come to prefer the artificial in place of the real, he argues, and have lost the ability to distinguish between the two. Out of touch with reality, we now have extravagant expectations concerning the world, and ourselves. And whereas we once pursued the American dream, we are now distracted by American illusions. We have substituted images for ideals. And we have replaced real events with pseudo-events (i.e., media events), false events manufactured to provide our media with content; as journalists shifted from newsgathering to newsmaking, this in turn gave rise to the pursuit of publicity, the public relations industry, and the press agent.

Paralleling these developments, Boorstin (1978) argued that we have also replaced genuine heroes with human pseudo-events, otherwise known as celebrities. Boorstin (1978) famously defined the celebrity as "a person who is known for his well-knownness" (p. 57), and therefore a self-fulfilling prophecy produced by publicity: "The hero was distinguished by his achievement; the celebrity by his image or trademark. The hero created himself; the celebrity is created by the media. The hero was a big man; the celebrity is a big name" (p. 61). Celebrities "simply seem great because they are famous," whereas real heroes, according to Boorstin, "are famous because they are great" (p. 48). Greatness, then, is the defining quality of the hero, from Boorstin's perspective, and traditionally, fame and greatness went hand in hand. The graphic revolution gave us the ability to isolate fame from greatness, and to make individuals famous without even the slightest indication of talent or accomplishment. This, Boorstin acknowledged, has changed our cultural conception of the hero:

> In the last half century the old heroic human mold has been broken. A new mold has been made. We have actually demanded that this mold be made, so that marketable human models—modern "heroes"—could be mass-produced, to satisfy the market, and without any hitches. The qualities which now commonly make a man or woman into a "nationally advertised" brand are in fact a new category of human emptiness. Our new mold is shaped not of the stuff of our familiar morality, nor even of the old familiar reality. (Boorstin, 1978, pp. 48-49)

The new mold of celebrity constitutes a false hero in Boorstin's eyes, even though they are admired as if they were true heroes. "Celebrity-worship and hero worship should not be confused. Yet we confuse them every day, and by doing so come dangerously close to depriving ourselves of all real models" (p. 48). Celebrities are false idols, and the sin in worshipping them is not that we are turning from good to evil, but that we are making something from nothing:

> Perhaps what ails us is not so much a vice as a "nothingness." The vacuum of our experience is actually made emptier by our anxious straining with mechanical devices to fill it artificially. What is remarkable is

> not only that we manage to fill experience with so much emptiness, but
> that we manage to give the experience such appealing variety. (p. 60)

In the face of this emptiness, we are left only with the echoes of greatness, and with what amounts to the worship of the self. Thus, Christopher
Lasch (1978) diagnosed celebrity as a symptom of a narcissistic culture.

Boorstin's dilemma is that the heroes that dominated American culture
in the late 20th century were not heroes. They were not heroes because they
did not measure up to the traditional standards of greatness. But they *were*
heroes insofar as they were heroes *to* many Americans. Without discounting
the validity of his criticism of the celebrity, Boorstin's dilemma and the
hero–celebrity dichotomy are reminiscent of the high–low debates concerning culture and the arts. Boorstin argued from an elitist position from which
he (and others) can judge which heroes are worthy of the epithet, based on
particular criteria (i.e., greatness). Ultimately, however, such critical analysis
comes down to aesthetics or value judgments. Is setting an athletic record
heroic? Is making a great deal of money a kind of greatness? Would donat-
ing to charities and supporting causes be a form of heroism? We can debate
these points endlessly, which is why I think it best to frame the issue differently. Rather than telling people that their heroes are not really heroes, I
would rather begin from a (relatively) objective and neutral position, and try
to determine who their heroes are, and what constitutes their cultural conception of the hero. And rather than employing a two-valued, either/or orientation to heroes and celebrities, I think it is more effective to regard
celebrities as contemporary heroes, understanding that this constitutes a
major change in our cultural conception of the hero. This is a point that
Boorstin himself acknowledged:

> Our age has produced a new kind of eminence. This is as characteristic
> of our culture and our century as was the divinity of Greek gods in the
> sixth century BC or the chivalry or knights and courtly lovers in the
> middle ages. It has not yet driven heroism, sainthood, or martyrdom
> completely out of our consciousness. But with every decade it overshad-
> ows them more. All older forms of greatness now survive only in the
> shadow of this new form. This new kind of eminence is "celebrity." (p.
> 57)

Boorstin also implicitly acknowledged here that this is not the first
time that cultural conceptions of the hero have changed. The traditional
hero that Boorstin defended is the historical hero, and the historical hero
was once an upstart and usurper too, having replaced the mythical hero.
As Campbell (1968) explained, "whenever the poetry of myth is interpreted as biography, history or science, it is killed. The living images become

only remote facts of a distant time or sky. Furthermore, it is never difficult to demonstrate that as science and history mythology is absurd" (p. 249).

The shift from mythic to historical hero is at least as dramatic as the shift from historical hero to celebrity. And both are shifts that are connected to changes in dominant modes of communication, the first involving the literate revolution, the second the graphic revolution. Theorists working from the media ecology perspective, such as Marshall McLuhan (1962, 2003), Neil Postman (1979, 1982, 1985), Eric Havelock (1963, 1982), Harold Innis (1951, 1972), Walter Ong (1967, 1982, 2002), Elizabeth Eisenstein (1979), Gary Gumpert (1987), and Joshua Meyrowitz (1985) have established that changes in media and methods of communication lead to changes in the content that is communicated, the relationships formed by communicators, and the culture that is created through communication. Thus, technological innovations such as writing, print, and electronic communications have changed the way in which we talk about heroes, tell stories about heroes, and experience heroes, and thus have altered our conceptions of the hero. Communication technologies also exert an indirect influence, through their impact on the ways in which we think and organize ourselves, as our way of life is then reflected in our heroes. Clearly, there are factors other than media that influence a particular culture's conception of the hero, but I believe that the most significant characteristics of the hero are related to communication technologies. And the most dramatic shifts in conceptions of the hero have been associated with innovations in communication such as the invention of writing and printing, and the development of the electronic media (see Harvey & Strate, 2000; Strate, 1985, 1989, 1993, 1994, 1995).

FROM ORAL HERO TO LITERATE HERO

In oral cultures, speech is the dominant mode of communication, and the preservation of information over time is dependent on collective memory. Culture heroes become known and are remembered through oral poetry and song, the Homeric epics being a well-known example. Without a storage medium outside of human memory such as written documents provide, economy is the rule. This means that, relative to literate cultures, oral cultures can only carry a limited number of heroes. If new heroes are adopted, older heroes will be forgotten, or identities will be merged. Oral heroes often become composite figures, where the actions of many are attributed to one hero. This cannot help but make the oral hero larger than life. Of course, exaggeration comes into play as well, and is unchecked by any recourse to written records that provide more accurate accounts of the hero's deeds.

Moreover, the more unusual and bizarre the hero's adventures, the more memorable the story, so in this way too oral cultures favor the extraordinary and supernatural hero. The story of the oral hero is typically one involving adventures and journeys, as Campbell (1968) noted, one that includes contests, combat, and quests. Here too, the more dramatic and agonistic the narrative, the more memorable it is. The result is that oral heroes are known for their acts or actions. In the end, what counts is not the name of Hercules, Gilgamesh, Beowolf, or King Arthur; it is their actions that are worth remembering, that carry valuable information for the culture, that model behaviors that are worthy of emulation.

Oral heroes tend to be impersonal, generic or type characters, as details relating to individual idiosyncrasies would tax the limited storage capacity of collective memory, and are not essential for cultural survival. They are predictable, and characterized by clichés and formulas (e.g., clever Odysseus, brave Achilles). Oral composition consists of managing a limited number of oral formulas, and stitching them together to form a song. The concept of the hero is contained in the formulas, and the singer simply plugs the specific hero's name into an otherwise formulaic composition—hence Campbell's (1968) monomyth. As Milman Parry (1971) explained

> Homer . . . assigned to his characters divinity, horsemanship, power, and even blond hair, according to the metrical value of their names, with no regard to their birth, their character, their rank, or their legend: except in so far as these things were common to all heroes. Except, that is to say, in so far as these things are interchangeable. If being "divine," for example, has about the same value as being "king" or "horseman" or "blameless" or "strong" or any of the other qualities indicated by the generic epithet, then the poet was led by considerations of metre to stress one of these qualities for a given hero more than another. (p. 150)

In other words, Parry essentially said that the meter is the message. Moreover, meter and formulas are mnemonic devices, but the heroes themselves are memory aids that help members of oral cultures retain knowledge. As Walter Ong (1967) explained,

> the figures around whom knowledge is made to cluster, those about whom stories are told or sung, must be made into conspicuous personages, foci of common attention, individuals embodying open public concerns. . . . In other words, the figures around whom knowledge is made to cluster must be heroes, culturally "large" or "heavy" figures like Odysseus or Achilles or Oedipus. Such figures are essential for oral culture in order to anchor the float of detail which literate cultures fix in script. These figures, moreover, cannot be too numerous or attention

will be dissipated and focus blurred. The familiar practice sets in of attributing actions which historically were accomplished by various individuals to a limited number of major figures (Rome's complex early history is seen in the biography of Aeneas or as the story of Romulus and Remus); only with writing and print could the number of characters in a modern history book or in fiction such as *Finnegans Wake* be possible at all.

Thus the epic hero, from one point of view, appears as an answer to the problem of knowledge storage and communication in oral-aural cultures (where indeed storage and communication are virtually the same thing). (pp. 204-205)

Because of the need for economy, any given hero may become associated with knowledge pertaining to a wide variety of subjects, including science (explanations for natural phenomena), geography, religion, ethics, warfare, politics, economics, psychology, and practical matters (e.g., navigation of ships, farming, carpentry). This also includes the singing of tales itself, as communication professionals in all types of cultures tend to celebrate their own activities and occupations, be they singers of tales, writers, or media entertainers. Unlike other types of heroes, however, oral heroes are masters of all trades, as a consequence of the need for economy and the necessary mnemonic function that is performed, and this also contributes to their superior stature. In sum, oral heroes are mythical or legendary heroes because the communication characteristic of oral cultures favors this conception of the hero.

When writing is introduced, the conditions that support the oral hero begin to erode, as Mircea Eliade (1975) noted:

Through *culture*, a desacralized religious universe and a demythicized mythology formed and nourished Western civilization. . . . There is more here than a triumph of *logos* over *mythos*. The victory is that of *the book* over oral tradition, of the document—especially of the written document—over a living experience whose only means of expression were preliterary. (p. 157)

Writing does not automatically eliminate the oral hero, but literacy allows individuals to separate themselves from their traditions, and to view them reflectively and critically, as we may view and review our words once they are written down. In this way, the oral hero may be undermined and delegitimized. This process can be seen in the historical writing of Herodotus, for example, as he begins to question the superhuman feats of Hercules and Greek genealogies that trace their descent back over 15 generations to the gods (Momigliano, 1977; Scholes & Kellogg, 1966). Once written records are accepted as authoritative, oral memory becomes questionable, and with it the oral hero.

Writing allows for much greater numbers of heroes to be celebrated and remembered than oral tradition, and sheer numbers alone make the individual culture hero less unique, and more human. With the presence of a means to store information outside of collective memory, the heavy figures of myth and legend are no longer needed, and lighter heroes become the norm. These new literate heroes are still exceptional, but they are no longer supernatural or superhuman, nor are they formulaic. They are realistic figures, the object not of worship so much as admiration. The increased storage capacity made possible by writing means that more information about each hero can be retained, so that heroes become individualized. The literate hero is tied to a specific historical context, and tales of the hero's exploits are replaced by biographies that cover the entirety of the hero's life. Character, virtue, and inner quality become part of the new concept of the historical hero. Campbell's monomyth shifts from an outer odyssey to an inner trip as we move from orality to literacy. The oral hero must confront and conquer a hostile natural environment, one that is often expressed in concrete, anthropomorphic terms. The literate hero is on a journey of self-discovery, self-mastery, and self-actualization, the conflicts then being more or less psychological and spiritual in nature. Also, the oral hero's exploits are expressed in episodic format (Ong, 1982; Scholes & Kellogg, 1966), as a series of relatively disconnected adventures, with no need to determine chronological order or eliminate inconsistencies. Writing and print make possible linear narratives, and favor closure and consistency, so that the historical hero is presented in terms of a complete life story, in which the events are connected and logical (e.g., hard work in youth leads to success as an adult). The result is a kind of characterization that is complex but consistent, yielding a conception of the hero as a unique and homogenous individual or subject, and as Boorstin (1978) maintained, uniformly characterized by greatness.

The introduction of the printing press extended the development of the literate hero. According to Eisenstein (1979), typography "made it possible to supplement tales of great men teaching by example and the lives of saints and saintly kings, by biographies and autobiographies of ordinary people pursuing more variegated careers" (p. 229). Greater numbers of heroes and greater amounts of information were related to the emergence of more specialized types of heroes, first in the literate cultures of antiquity, later in the print culture of early modern Europe. Thus, we get military heroes who are distinct from political heroes, who are distinct from religious heroes, and so on. Ultimately, every vocation and avocation generated its own set of heroes. And as the oral hero incorporated the poet or singer of tales, the literate hero introduces the specialized category of writer. Thomas Carlyle, lecturing in 1840, showed an awareness of this development:

> Hero-Gods, Prophets, Poets, Priests are forms of Heroism that belong
> to the old ages, make their appearances at the remotest of times; some
> of them have ceased to be possible long since, and cannot any more
> show themselves in this world. The Hero as *Man of Letters* . . . is alto-
> gether a product of these new ages; and so long as the wondrous art of
> *Writing*, or of Ready-writing which we call *Printing*, subsists, he may
> be expected to continue, as one of the main forms of Heroism for all
> future ages. He is, in various respects, a very singular phenomenon. (p.
> 383)

Clearly, the author is a type of hero that could not exist without literacy, but writing and print made possible many other new types of heroes,
such as scholars, scientists, inventors, artists, musicians, and so on. These
new literate heroes are known for their ideas, their intellectual and creative
production. Action may still be present, but it is the mental, not the physical, that is emphasized. As much as the man of letters, the leader of men is
also known for ideas, as a strategist, not a warrior. Napoleon and
Washington are celebrated not for fighting prowess, but for military and
political achievements. Columbus, unlike Odysseus, is not remembered for
the events of his quest, but for the idea behind his voyage.

In oral cultures, there is no clear dividing line between fiction and nonfiction, and it is not until after the printing revolution that a distinct category of fictional narrative is introduced (Scholes & Kellogg, 1966). The new
fictional heroes of the novel and short story are entirely unreal, and yet
decidedly realistic, paralleling the historical hero in significant ways, and
thereby reinforcing the prevailing literate conception of the hero.

FROM TYPOGRAPHIC HERO
TO ELECTRONIC HERO

The printing revolution is predicated on the development of moveable type,
but historians argue that the printing press was in fact a double invention,
one that included both typography and engraving (Eisenstein, 1980; Ong,
1982). Although engraving could not match the amount of visual detail conveyed through portrait painting, enough information could be reproduced
to make the subject recognizable, and this information could be disseminated quite widely. This is in contrast to coins, which functioned as a mass
medium and included images of actual individuals since the time of
Alexander the Great, but lacked the necessary detail to make the subject
truly distinct. As Eisenstein (1979) related:

> The difference between the older repeatable image which was stamped on coins and the newer by-product of print is suggested by one of the more celebrated episodes of the French Revolution. The individual features of the emperors and kings were not sufficiently detailed when stamped on coins for their faces to be recognized when they traveled incognito. But a portrait engraved on paper money enabled an alert Frenchman to recognize and halt Louis XVI at Varennes. (pp. 84-85)

As Walter Benjamin (1968) made clear, mechanical reproduction has a democratizing effect on the work of art and the visual image, and therefore on the hero. And although this technology made face recognition a possibility, it is not altogether clear to what extent it was a reality. Consider the fact that the Frenchman had to compare Louis XVI to his printed image in order to verify his identity. How many Americans living today would need to make this type of comparison were they to encounter George W. Bush under similar circumstances? Writing of the United States in the 18th and 19th centuries, Neil Postman (1985) stated: "Public figures were known by their written words . . . not by their looks or even their oratory. It is quite likely that most of the first fifteen presidents of the United States would not have been recognized had they passed the average citizen in the street. This would have been the case as well of the great lawyers, ministers and scientists of that era" (p. 60). The election of our 16th president coincided with the widespread diffusion of photography (which was also used to document the Civil War), and it is no coincidence that Lincoln was the first president to be criticized for his looks. He was assassinated before the invention of the phonograph, however, so Lincoln is not remembered as having a high-pitched voice, but instead imagined to have a deep voice that matches the gravity of his image.

Each new medium has been accompanied by further mutations of the hero. The motion picture gave us the movie star, larger-than-life like traditional heroes, but only on the surface, otherwise lacking in their intrinsic qualities, and relying on gossip columns and fan magazines. The heroes of the silent film were known for their faces, gestures, and body movements, and many did not survive the transition to talkies, which emphasized both voice and less grandiose, more realistic acting. Photography and printing have given us the fashion model, superior in appearance but seemingly inferior in most other qualities (Harvey & Strate, 2000). Sound recording made heroes out of musical performers, eventually resulting in the new category of recording artist. The microphone gave us crooners such as Frank Sinatra and Bing Crosby, who were adored for their amplified whispers, while electronic amplification gave us the guitar heroes of rock and roll. Radio made heroes out of disembodied voices who gave us the illusion of intimacy, while "video killed the radio star," in the immortal words of The Buggles. And more than any other medium, it is television that has undermined the typo-graphic hero in favor of the celebrity, or electronic hero (precipitating Boorstin's critique in *The Image*, 1962).

Each new medium that has been introduced over the past two centuries has expanded the amount of information that is transmitted within our cul-ture, thereby allowing for greater numbers of heroes than ever before. The result is a kind of hero inflation that gives us even lighter figures than the heroes of print culture, figures so light that Boorstin argued they are not truly heroes at all. Electronic telecommunications also favors rapid turnover of information, the new and the up-to-date over the old and traditional; thus, the electronic hero tends to be a contemporary, rising to stardom overnight and fading from view just as rapidly. In the words of Andy Warhol: "In the future everyone will be famous. For fifteen minutes." Or as David Bowie and John Lennon wrote: "Fame—what you get is no tomor-row." In the past, biographies and autobiographies were not written until after the subject was dead, or at least not until the end of the subject's career; now they appear at the first hint of widespread fame. By the time his or her career is over, the electronic hero may be long forgotten, and the biography of little interest. Rapid turnover is the rule, and as Boorstin (1978) noted, this is in contrast to traditional heroes who gradually become famous and gain in stature over the generations. Properly managed, however, the elec-tronic hero can go through the celebrity mill more than once, the comeback constituting a new cycle of fame (Rein, Kotler, & Stoller, 1997). And by carefully avoiding overexposure, a few celebrities may retain their hold on public consciousness over the long term.

Some electronic heroes may transcend the turnover altogether and gain immortality on the strength of their images. Certainly, there seems to be a more or less permanent place in our culture's memory bank for the perform-ances of movie stars such as Charlie Chaplin and Marilyn Monroe; the look and sounds of popular musicians such as Frank Sinatra, Elvis Presley, and the Beatles; the appearances of television personalities such as Lucille Balle and Jackie Gleason; and the audiovisual recordings of other types of heroes such as John F. Kennedy, Martin Luther King, Princess Diana, and Pope John Paul II. It may be that Boorstin's (1962, 1978) criticism of the celebri-ty as always being a contemporary was premature. When he first wrote about celebrity in the early 1960s, motion pictures and sound recordings had only existed for a generation or two, not long enough to adequately gauge how audiovisual media would affect our ability to communicate over time. Although it is still too early to draw conclusions, it seems reasonable to con-clude that certain electronic heroes will stand the test of time, whereas oth-ers may make periodic posthumous comebacks, following the cycle of turnover into posterity. Unlike previous hero molds, however, the electron-ic heroes of the past will retain their immediacy, and continue to foster a sense of intimacy as they are brought back to life by the audiovisual media. As electronic heroes of the past come to dominate our perception of history, this will further delegitimize the historical heroes of typographic culture. After all, how can a written account compare to the moving image and sound recording as a means of preserving the past? How can the historical hero help but appear unreal in contrast to electromagnetic recreation of the individual? For literate and typographic heroes of the past to remain culture heroes in an electronic media environment, they need to be brought to life through the dramatic performance of actors appearing on television, in movies, or the like.

Information presented in an audiovisual format is more generally accessible than information encoded in writing as it does not require any degree of literacy or specialized knowledge (Meyrowitz, 1985). And this reinforces the fact that the electronic media increase the amount of information that can be transmitted, thereby increasing the amount of information about any given hero that is made accessible. Rapid turnover also contributes to the tendency to seek out information about celebrities, and disseminate that information, whether it is important or not. And generally it is not. Electronic communication trivializes heroes. We learn about their health and family problems, about the food they eat, the cars they drive, the persons they are sleeping with. For example, Bill Clinton was unable to keep the fact that he had an affair with a White House intern from the media, and this all but ruined his presidency, while conferring on Monica Lewinsky a significant degree of celebrity, as she became famous for an act of fellatio. Clinton had long since tailored his image to the television camera by appearing on a talk show wearing sunglasses and playing saxophone, answering the "boxers or briefs" question on MTV, and holding intimate "electronic town meetings." His success was based on the celebrity strategy of sacrificing dignity in favor of intimacy, but the scandal revealed too much information about Clinton's human weaknesses, disrupting his performance as president (although many Americans apparently felt that it was "just sex," and not inconsistent with Clinton's "Elvis-like" star persona).

Unlike the heavy figure of oral culture who is qualitatively greater than us, or the typographic hero characterized by significant achievement in a specialized sector, the light figure of electronic culture is ordinary, just like us. Electronic heroes may even have less control over their lives than we do, making them ironic figures. We, therefore, have seen the introduction of the victim as hero, not a martyr to a cause like Lincoln, but merely a casualty of senseless violence, like Kennedy, or survivors who have done nothing more than endured an ordeal, such as the Americans embassy personnel who made it through the Iranian hostage crisis. Moreover, taking on the role of victim, and admitting to a psychological or physical problem can be part of a celebrity's comeback strategy, guaranteed to at least secure an appearance on a daytime talk show. But every celebrity who loses control of his or her image, or is unable to cope with the demands of fame, ultimately becomes an ironic hero, the most extreme version being the celebrity suicide. And as one press agent commented upon hearing of Elvis Presley's fatal overdose, death is a good career move.

Being ordinary or ironic, the electronic hero is not worthy of our worship as was the oral hero, nor of our admiration as was the literate and typographic hero. Thus, the hero worshipper or admirer is replaced by the fickle fan. The celebrity's quick rise to fame can generate hysteria, hence the origin of the *fan* as a shortened form of *fanatic*. But *fans* follow *fads*, and the large number of heroes to choose from and their rapid turnover work against any long-term loyalty the admirer might feel toward a hero. The ordinariness of the electronic hero means that celebrities and fans are more or less equals, and more or less interchangeable. The result is a feeling of entitlement, as we come to believe that we deserve our fifteen minutes of fame too, or failing that, that the celebrity owes us 15 minutes of his or her time in return for our devotion. The lack of distance between fan and hero results in an illusion of intimacy on the fan's part (Horton & Wohl, 1982), so that we relate to the celebrity as familiar, as a friend or lover. In the world of celebrity, it is possible to become famous for being a fan, and it is of course possible to cross over from fan to celebrity. Indeed, some successful celebrities become famous for continuing to act like fans, as did Rosie O'Donnell on her talk show. Groupies sometimes become famous for their activities, crossing over either as celebrity-groupies or by way of more stable romantic relationships with stars. At its most extreme, the celebrity–fan relationship gives way to the pathology of celebrity assassins such as John Hinckley and Mark David Chapman, who gain a fame of their own through attacks on electronic heroes.

All this leads to confusion as to what constitutes a hero, leading Becker (1971) to argue that our hero systems underwent a crisis of belief during the 1960s: "Our own national hero-systems are themselves suffering the discredit that primitive tribes had suffered earlier; our drop-out youth are the newly detribalized. With the breakup of agreed patterns of heroism, you see the emergence of all kinds of special heroics by sub-groups, and private heroics by individuals—everyone decides to be heroic in his own way" (p. 126). No wonder that more recently, when individuals are asked to name their heroes, the lists include historical heroes, celebrities, fictional heroes, and even interpersonal heroes. There has been a confusion about what constitutes a hero, which is either a result of being in the midst of a shift in conceptions of the hero, or perhaps reflects the establishment of a new, more heterogeneous concept of the hero. Either way, we still retain our traditional notions of the heroic and heroism, much as the content of a medium is another, often older medium (McLuhan, 2003). But the concept of the literate hero has been undermined, in this case not so much directly delegitimized as overshadowed and ignored. For example, in 1979, *Scholastic Magazines* surveyed their youthful readership, asking them to name their heroes. The top five choices were Steve Martin, Erik Estrada, Burt Reynolds, John Wayne, and Jerry Lewis ("Heroes," 1980). But what I find especially striking is the wisdom expressed in the following commentary from *Scholastic Action*:

> Yes, all of the top five heroes named are men. They are also movie or TV celebrities. There are no politicians. There are no religious leaders. There are no people from history.
>
> Some people find that strange and sad. "In order for anything to be real to young people," they say, "it must be on TV."
>
> But 14-year-old Kurt, a Southern Hills student, explains it this way:
>
> "Times have changed," he said. "People like George Washington and Abe Lincoln are still respected for what they did. But that's a different kind of hero." ("Heroes," 1980, p. 13)

A different kind of hero indeed! On television, it is neither actions nor ideas that are emphasized, but appearance and personality. Ideas can occupy an individual for a lifetime; images can be presented and digested in a matter of seconds. Even when ideas are presented on television, they are overshadowed by images, creating an image of ideas, but no substance. Actions may be a component of the image, for television is a dramatic medium, but unlike the oral hero, the electronic hero's actions are not memorable. We are left only with an image of action, an image of the hero as a man or woman of action, whereas the specific deeds are forgotten. Compare, for example, the often bizarre labors of Hercules to the hundreds of ultra-violent but otherwise unexceptional actions of movie stars such as Sylvester Stallone and Arnold Schwarzenegger. In short, electronic heroes are known for images, not actions or ideas. In an oral culture, the hero lives and dies by the sword. In a print culture, the pen is mightier than the sword. But in an electronic culture, the deciding factor is neither arms nor pen, but appearance and personality. And whereas literate heroes were the subject of biographies, and therefore known for their lives, electronic heroes are the subject of gossip columns, magazines like *People*, and programs like *Entertainment Tonight*, where they are know not for their *lives*, but for their *lifestyles*.

Moreover, just as the pen and printing press created new kinds of heroes, so does the electronic media. Typically, the new kind of hero otherwise known as the celebrity is an entertainer: the television and movie star, the recording artist, and the disk jockey. Others are media professionals such as the newscaster, sportscaster, and fashion model. These new types of heroes have all but eclipsed the older forms, and even serve as authority figures. As John Phelan (1977) said: "To produce a movie, get a star. To cure diseases, get a star. To sell soap, get a star. To save souls, get a star. To be heard, be a star" (p. 64). But when celebrities promote products and when they promote charities, they also promote themselves. And when they seek publicity for causes, they cannot help but gain publicity for themselves (Sudjic, 1990). The most altruistic and selfless public acts, when performed by celebrities, are indistinguishable from action that is entirely calculated and self-serving. Call it the Celebrity Uncertainty Principle, after Heisenberg, or the First Axiom of Celebrity, that celebrities cannot not self-promote, after Watzlawick and his colleagues.

As entertainers and media professionals constitute the new heroic mold, more traditional types of heroes become famous by being transformed into celebrities. Thus, politicians now routinely appear on talks shows and situation comedies, or they host *Saturday Night Live*; they might even pitch products in advertisements; of course, the fact that entertainers may become politicians is not longer considered extraordinary, even outside of California. Politics has always had much in common with entertainment, but other sectors are not immune to the lure of celebrity. Religious leaders now obtain their own television programs and become talk and variety show hosts, and sometimes inadvertently, soap opera stars. Lee Iacocca made appearing on television commercials part of the job description for running a major corporation, while Donald Trump now demonstrates that gaining a starring role on a television program is the true bottom line in business. Authors such as Truman Capote, Norman Mailer, Jerzy Kosinski, and Kurt Vonnegut become television and movie actors, artists since Andy Warhol have understood and appealed to the culture of celebrity, as have classical musicians such as John Cage, Yo-Yo Ma, Lucianno Pavarotti, and Itzhak Perlman. Scientists have not been immune to this phenomenon, as Rae Goodell (1977) explains in *The Visible Scientists*. Whereas Newton and Einstein were specialists known for their ideas, today's celebrity-scientists become famous by latching onto "hot topics" that attract media coverage due to their relevance and controversial nature, even if they are outside of the scientist's area of expertise: "Visible scientists are a product of media fads. . . . Timing is important not only in getting on the bandwagon but also in getting off. Deliberately or instinctively, scientists with lasting visibility and influence have moved from one issue to another with shifts in public interest" (Goodell, 1977, p. 19). Carl Sagan, who demonstrated the power of celebrity through his appearances on the *Tonight Show*, his own TV series *Cosmos*, and his involvement in the controversy concerning nuclear winter, was one of the most visible of visible scientists, a category that Goodell applies to psychologists and social scientists as well as the hard sciences. Academics of all stripes yearn for visibility, and a chosen few become public intellectuals by virtue of their on camera punditry; Marshall McLuhan was one of the first to find fame with frequent television appearances and a cameo in Woody Allen's film, *Annie Hall*; more recently Cornell West took a role in *The Matrix Reloaded*. The ivory tower itself has fallen before the onslaught of celebrity, as universities seek out visible academics, and nonacademic celebrities for their faculty. Nor is this phenomenon limited to the United States. In France, where intellectuals had been literate heroes in a class of their own, Regis Debray (1981) argued that they too have turned into celebrities: "The members of the high intelligentsia are dependent on their image, and the dependence often becomes an obsession. For the professionals of the idea, 'Is my image good or not?' is a much more pressing (and frequent) question than 'Are my ideas correct or not?'" (p. 146).

Ultimately, all of the specialized heroes characteristic of print culture disappear, as occupations are transformed into roles to be played in front of the camera, roles that are easily discarded in favor of others. John Lahr (1984) put it succinctly: "Politicians become newscasters; newscasters become movie actors; movie actors become politicians. Celebrity turns every serious endeavor into a performance. Everything that rises in America must converge on a TV talk show" (p. 218). The electronic hero is not a master of all trades, but an actor of all trades. But it is not acting in the traditional sense that is called for. It is commonly noted that although actors play roles, stars play themselves, and celebrity takes this characteristic to its extreme. The only thing required of a celebrity is self-display, to make a spectacle of one's self. This naturally places a high premium on attractive appearance, which is why celebrity culture has revolutionized a number of industries, including fashion, cosmetics, hair styling, prosthetics (e.g., shoe lifts), and plastic surgery. Postman (1985) argued that in the age of television it is impossible for an unattractive individual to be elected president, and although good looks are a tool that can be used to gain high visibility in any occupation, more generally electronic heroes are characterized by a distinctive appearance. Jay Leno's chin and David Letterman's gap between his front teeth become their trademarks; similarly, being overweight becomes part of the image for Rosie O'Donnell, Roseanne Barr, and Oprah Winfrey. Of course, nudity can enhance the distinctiveness of one's image, so posing for magazines such as *Playboy*, *Penthouse*, or even *Hustler* becomes an option that is given serious consideration for female celebrities, and not just for the monetary payoff, but for the very high visibility it affords; neither would it be inconsistent with the notion of self-display. The one value that celebrities trumpet is honesty, but it is not honesty in the traditional sense of ethical conduct (as in the apocryphal story of George Washington and the cherry tree, or Lincoln's epithet, Honest Abe). Rather it is honesty in self-display, using self-disclosure as the basis for celebrity performance, on talk shows, in interviews in fan magazines, in stand-up comedy routines. The sense that all one needs to do to be famous is to get in front of a camera and be one's self reinforces our sense of the ordinariness of electronic heroes, and feeds out desire to take our place alongside them. No wonder that reality television is all the rage in recent years. *Survivor*, *Big Brother*, *The Bachelor*, *The Apprentice*, even *American Idol* all are celebrations of our new hero system in which we are all implicated.

On television, the performance is the only reality, so that the distinction between fact and fiction becomes meaningless. When characters are experienced only through the printed word, there are accepted procedures for determining whether they are fictional or real-life heroes. This is not the case when a fictional character is brought to life on television. Actors who play fictional roles appear to be as real, or unreal, as those who play themselves. They are both performers, both performances, both forms of self-display. In many ways, the fictional character seems more real that the person who plays the part. For example, the characters of Captain Kirk, Archie Bunker, Buffy the Vampire Slayer, and Tony Soprano all become better known than William Shatner, Carroll O'Conner, Sarah Michelle Gellar, and James Gandolfini, the actors who portrayed them. The distinction between fictional and nonfictional heroes, a product of literacy, becomes increasingly irrelevant in an electronic culture, even among the well-educated. Thus, Robert Young, the actor who played Marcus Welby, has been called on to address the American Medical Association, and an ad for an over-the-counter medication features an actor endorsing the product, saying "I'm not a doctor, but I play one on TV." Alan Alda has delivered commencement addresses at medical schools, and Raymond Burr at law schools, as has Judge Joseph Wapner of television's *The People's Court* (at least Wapner did once serve as a judge, albeit an undistinguished one). The distinction is further eroded on programs such as *Seinfeld*, where Jerry Seinfeld the comedian played himself, but as a fictional character named Jerry Seinfeld, who at one point is the star of a fictional sitcom named *Jerry*, where he played himself playing himself as a fictional character.

Computer media have extended and intensified many of the characteristics of the electronic hero. Certainly, computers have introduced new kinds of heroes, such as programmers and various types of hackers. Also, the Internet has introduced new forms of fame (e.g., net presence, downloadable images, Web site hits, etc.), thereby further increasing the number and lightness of heroes. There is a strongly democratic element to the online hero, as participation in discussion lists and chatrooms, creation of Web sites, and installation of webcams, can makes celebrities of us all. At the same time that digital technologies have amplified the electronic hero's reach, they have further blurred boundaries through their capacity to remix and reposition audiovisual content, as, for example, when Tom Hanks was seamlessly inserted into old news footage in *Forest Gump*. The electronic hero's image may also be used for gaming purposes, becoming a puppet subject to the whims of a multitude of players. Artificial intelligence programming and expert systems have already begun to record some of the thought processes of distinguished individuals in a variety of fields; further work may succeed in recreating some semblance of the individual's personality as well. Coupled with further developments in our ability to capture and recombine voice and images, and the time cannot be too far off when synthetic performances supplement and even substitute for more traditional types of acting. Whether or not it is a good career move, death may no longer signal the end of a celebrity's career. Moreover, simulations of historical figures such as Lincoln or Plato may turn such literate heroes in interactive electronic personalities. No doubt this would contribute to the celebrity–fan relationship, as one could own one's own interactive simulation of one's hero, but it also further blurs the line between fact and fiction, reality and illusion. Moreover, the digital hero may be a complete and utter computer simulation, a descendent of the computer programs Eliza and Racter, much like the computer generated movie star depicted in the film *Simone*. There is at once something utterly ironic about these digitized heroes, being so much less than human. But as Frye (1957) suggested, when pushed to its extreme, the ironic hero flips into a mythic hero (as is the case for the scapegoat hero), and there is something indeed mythical about computer simulations. And the electronic hero's journey may involve a confrontation and reconciliation with a social environment filled with our technological extensions, just as Campbell's monomyth emphasized coping with the natural environment in oral culture, and with the internal environment of mind and spirit in literate culture (see Rushing & Frentz, 1995).

HEROES IN POST-9/11 AMERICA

The basic thesis that I have put forth here, that our cultural conceptions of the hero are based on the dominant modes of communication that we employ, was put to the test in the wake of the tragic events of September 11, 2001. For a brief moment, it seemed as if we might abandon our devotion to celebrity in favor of the more traditional type of heroism exhibited by the firefighters, police officers, and rescue workers who sacrificed their lives on that day, and their colleagues who put their lives at risk on a regular basis. We also looked to the heroes of United Airlines Flight 93 who sacrificed themselves while preventing a fourth terrorist attack, and to those who risked or gave their lives as they tried to help others during the disaster. Soon afterward, we could add the traditional heroism of the men and women serving in our armed forces, as they were sent to Afghanistan, and more recently to Iraq. But after all was said and done, while recognizing the heroic qualities of "the heroes of 9/11," most Americans are hard put to name specific individuals, or to point to specific faces from the thousands of these genuine heroes. In other words, they remain unsung heroes, and therefore cannot be considered culture heroes, however much we might want to believe them to be.

Perhaps the best known hero of 9/11 is Todd Beamer, one of the heroes of United Flight 93, which crashed in rural Pennsylvania; Beamer and his fellow passengers are credited with rising up against the hijackers and preventing a fourth attack on the White House or Capitol building. We know about Beamer through the medium of the cell phone, through which he communicated his determination to stop the terrorists, his faith in God, and his final transmitted words, "Let's roll!" This quote was repeated by Tom Hanks in the telethon *America: A Tribute to Heroes*, by Neil Young as the chorus and title of a song about 9/11, by George Bush in his speech to the nation the week after 9/11, and on a number of subsequent occasions, and by many others as it became a rallying cry for the nation. His widow, Lisa Beamer, was introduced by Bush during his speech, gained a great deal of visibility in the aftermath of the attack through numerous interviews and television appearances, and authored a book (with Ken Abraham) entitled, *Let's Roll: Ordinary People, Extraordinary Courage* (2002). This has made Lisa Beamer something of a hero and celebrity herself, leading some to question her motives (the Celebrity Uncertainty Principle at work once more). But there is no doubt that Todd Beamer along with the somewhat lesser known hero of Flight 93, Jeremy Glick, are known for their final cell phone messages (Flayhan, 2003) as much as for their actions, of which we can only surmise.

Otherwise, the figure who emerged as the most visible hero of 9/11 was New York City Mayor Rudy Giuliani. Of course, this was essentially on the strength of his symbolic leadership. Whether he achieved greatness in crisis management is unclear at best. But what does stand out is the brave face he put on for the television cameras, and his ability to speak for New York City and our nation. In fact, Giuliani's image had become somewhat negative prior to 9/11, and had the attack not occurred, he would have remained one more in a long line of controversial New York mayors. Instead, 9/11 revitalized his image and gave him a celebrity he had never enjoyed before, to the extent that *Time* magazine named him its Person of the Year for 2001. This selection was not without controversy, because Osama bin Laden was the obvious choice given *Time*'s selection criteria—the person of the year is supposed to be the individual or individuals who had the greatest impact on the news, for good or ill. In 1980, the editors of *Time* stayed true to their standards and selected the Ayotollah Khomeini, and lost a significant portion of their subscribers. And although many criticized them for putting profits over journalistic integrity in their selection of Giuliani, it is worth recalling that *Time* instituted its "Man of the Year" in 1935 as a gimmick to increase sales and subscriptions. It is therefore part of the world of celebrity, even as it seems to celebrate traditional heroism (again, the content of the medium being in effect an older medium).

The war on Iraq, which began on March 20, 2003, afforded much better opportunities for celebrating the heroism of soldiers, due to the presence of embedded journalists. But it was the embedded television reporters, especially those associated with 24-hour cable news channels, that gained the most attention. The only soldier to become truly famous from Operation Iraqi Freedom was Private Jessica Lynch, who was initially presented in relatively traditional terms: She fought back against overwhelming odds after being ambushed, was wounded in combat and taken prisoner by the enemy. As a POW, she then became a heroine and damsel in distress, aided by a kindly Iraqi lawyer, and dramatically rescued by American forces in a raid that was captured on video via nightvision. We later learn that her weapon jammed and she never fired a shot, that her injuries were exaggerated, and that her rescue operation was far less perilous than we were led to believe. Critics condemned the Pentagon for producing blatant propaganda, but if this was a deliberate attempt it reflected a great ignorance of the most basic principles concerning propaganda established decades ago (Ellul, 1965). The more likely explanation, in my opinion, is that the logic of celebrity has now penetrated the military's warrior culture, and the Pentagon could not help but get swept up in it. The basic story was exciting, and her appearance, an attractive blonde, added to her appeal. Moreover, the military had already become familiar with the phenomenon of celebrity among their high-ranking officers (e.g., Oliver North, Norman Schwartzkopf, Colin Powell, and the many retired colonels and generals performing as pundits for the news programs).

Lynch's celebrity as a common soldier was intensified by the ambiguities surrounding the circumstances of her being taken prisoner, including her captivity (was she threatened, raped, tortured?), her rescue, her criticism of the government's initial portrayal of her story, and the fact that she was too busy to meet the Iraqi lawyer who helped her when he came to the United States for a visit. And true to celebrity form, she became the subject of a TV movie, *Saving Jessica Lynch*, a title that alludes to the film, *Saving Private Ryan*, a connection that was frequently made in the media previously and serves to blur the boundaries between reality and fiction. The film debuted on NBC on November 9, 2000, while *The Elizabeth Smart Story* was broadcast at the same time on CBS, further intensifying the sense of celebrity overkill. Lynch also is associated with a book, *I Am a Soldier Too: The Jessica Lynch Story* (Bragg, 2003), and nude photographs of her taken before she went to war have surfaced (purchased by Larry Flynt, editor of *Hustler* magazine, who says he will not publish them, although the possibility remains open). In the meantime, numerous acts of courage and heroism on the part of other soldiers (including Specialist Shoshana Johnson, an African-American woman who was also a POW) have received little or no media attention.

If there is any doubt that the traumatic events of 9/11 have had little effect, if any, on the dominance of celebrity in American life, consider the fact that 2003 was dominated by images of Madonna kissing Britney Spears and Christina Aguilera, Arnold Schwarzenegger taking over as governor of California, scandals involving Michael Jackson and basketball player Kobe Bryant, and the performances of celebrity heiress Paris Hilton, first in an X-rated home video that circulated on the internet, and second in a new reality series on television, *The Simple Life* (co-starring Nicole Ritchie, daughter of music star Lionel Ritchie).

Just as the oral hero was delegitimized while writing and print gained ascendance, so today the literate and typographic hero is disappearing, replaced by the electronic hero. There is much that is disturbing about this development, and Boorstin (1978) was correct to remind us that the older types of heroes provided us with inspirational models of human greatness that cannot be replaced by celebrities. We have gained a more democratic and egalitarian conception of the hero, but whether this is adequate compensation for the loss of the old heroic mold is debatable. At the very least, we should be aware of what we have given up in the bargain, and consider what might yet be lost as our concept of the hero continues to mutate in response to innovations in our media of communication.

REFERENCES

Beamer, L., with Abraham, K. (2002). *Let's Roll: Ordinary people, extraordinary courage*. Wheaton, IL: Tyndale House.

Becker, E. (1971). *The birth and death of meaning: An interdisciplinary perspective on the problem of man* (2nd ed.). New York: The Free Press.

Becker, E. (1973). *The denial of death*. New York: The Free Press.

Benjamin, W. (1968). *Illuminations* (H. Zohn, Trans.). New York: Harcourt, Brace & World.

Boorstin, D. J. (1962). *The image: Or what happened to the American dream*. New York: Atheneum.

Boorstin, D. J. (1978). *The image: A guide to pseudo-events in America*. New York: Atheneum.

Boulding, K. E. (1956). *The image: Knowledge in life and society*. Ann Arbor: University of Michigan Press.

Bragg, R. (2003). *I am a soldier, too: The Jessica Lynch story.* New York: Knopf.

Braudy, L. (1986). *The frenzy of renown: Fame and its history.* New York: Oxford University Press.

Burke, K. (1945). *A grammar of motives.* Berkeley: University of California Press.

Burke, K. (1950). *A rhetoric of motives.* Berkeley: University of California Press.

Campbell, J. (1968). *The hero with a thousand faces* (2nd ed.). Princeton, NJ: Princeton University Press.

Campbell, J., & Moyers, B. (1988). *The power of myth.* New York: Doubleday.

Carlyle, T. (1840/1940). *Sartor resartus; On heroes, hero-worship and the heroic in history.* London: J.M. Dent & Sons.

Debray, R. (1981). *Teachers, writers, celebrities: The intellectuals of modern France* (D. Macey, Trans.). London: NLB.

Duncan, H. D. (1962). *Communication and social order.* New York: Bedminster Press.

Duncan, H. D. (1968). *Symbols in society.* New York: Oxford University Press.

Eisenstein, E. L. (1979). *The printing press as an agent of change: Communications and cultural transformations in early modern Europe* (2 vols.). New York: Cambridge University Press.

Eliade, M. (1975). *Myth and reality* (W. Trask, Trans.). New York: Harper Colophon Books.

Ellul, J. (1965). *Propaganda: The formation of men's attitudes* (K. Kellen & J. Lerner, Trans.). New York: Vintage.

Flayhan, D. (2003). From slave ships to to September 11 to the Russian theater siege: The human voice, connection during tragedy, and a transformation in sudden death experience with cell phone technology. *Explorations in Media Ecology, 2*(1), 35-41.

Frye, N. (1957). *Anatomy of criticism: Four essays.* Princeton, NJ: Princeton University Press.

Goodell, R. (1977). *The visible scientists.* Boston, MA: Little, Brown.

Gumpert, G. (1987). *Talking tombstones and other tales of the media age.* New York: Oxford University Press.

Hall, E. T. (1959). *The silent language.* Garden City, NY: Doubleday.

Harvey, D., & Strate, L. (2000). Media, celebrity, and commercialism: The rise of the supermodel. In R. Andersen & L. Strate (Eds.), *Critical studies in media commercialism* (pp. 203-213). London: Oxford University Press.

Havelock, E. A. (1963). *Preface to Plato.* Cambridge, MA: The Belknap Press of Harvard University Press.

Havelock, E. A. (1982). *The literate revolution in Greece and its cultural consequences.* Princeton, NJ: Princeton University Press.

Heroes. (1980, January 10). *Scholastic Action,* p. 13.

Hook, S. (1943). *The hero in history: A study in limitation and possibility.* Boston: Beacon Press.

Horton, D., & Wohl, R. R. (1982). Mass communication and para-social interaction; Observations on intimacy at a distance. In G. Gumpert & R. Cathcart (Eds.), *Inter/media* (2nd ed., pp. 188-211). New York: Oxford University Press.

Innis, H. A. (1951). *The bias of communication.* Toronto: University of Toronto Press.

Innis, H. A. (1972). *Empire and communications* (rev. ed., M. Q. Innis, Ed.). Toronto: University of Toronto Press.

James, C. (1993). *Fame in the 20th century*. New York: Random House.

Lahr, J. (1984). *Automatic vaudeville: Essays on star turns*. New York: Alfred A. Knopf.

Lasch, C. (1978). *The culture of narcissism: American life in an age of diminishing expectations*. New York: W. W. Norton.

McLuhan, M. (1962). *The Gutenberg galaxy: The making of typographic man*. Toronto: University of Toronto Press.

McLuhan, M. (2003). *Understanding media: The extensions of man* (Critical edition, W. T. Gordon, Ed.). Corte Madera, CA: Gingko Press. (Original work published 1964)

Meyrowitz, J. (1985). *No sense of place: The impact of electronic media on social behavior*. New York: Oxford University Press.

Momigliano, A. (1977). *Essays in ancient and modern historiography*. Middletown, CT: Wesleyan University Press.

Ong, W. J. (1967). *The presence of the word: Some prolegomena for cultural and religious history*. Binghampton, NY: Global.

Ong, W. J. (1982). *Orality and literacy: The technologizing of the word*. London: Routledge.

Ong, W. J. (2002). *An Ong reader: Challenges for further inquiry* (T. J. Farrell & P. A. Soukup, Eds.). Cresskill, NJ: Hampton Press.

Parry, M. (1971). *The making of Homeric verse: The collected papers of Milman Parry* (A. Parry, Ed.). Oxford: Clarendon Press.

Phelan, J. M. (1977). *Mediaworld: Programming the public*. New York: Seabury Press.

Postman, N. (1979). *Teaching as a conserving activity*. New York: Delacorte.

Postman, N. (1982). *The disappearance of childhood*. New York: Delacorte.

Postman, N. (1985). *Amusing ourselves to death: Public discourse in the age of show business*. New York: Viking.

Potok, C. (1973). Heroes for an ordinary world. In *Great ideas today, 1973* (pp. 71-76). Chicago: Encyclopedia Britannica,.

Rein, I., Kotler, P., & Stoller, M. (1997). *High visibility: The making and marketing of professionals into celebrities*. Lincolnwood, IL: NTC.

Rushing, J. H., & Frentz, T. S. (1995). *Projecting the shadow: The cyborg hero in American film*. Chicago: University of Chicago Press.

Scholes, R. E., & Kellogg, R. (1966). *The nature of narrative*. New York: Oxford University Press.

Strate, L. (1985). Heroes, fame, and the media. *ETC: A Review of General Semantics, 42*(1), 47-53.

Strate, L. (1989). The concept of the hero in the era of electronic communication. *Hed-Hagan, 2*, 139-142. (Hebrew translation)

Strate, L. (1993). *Who Framed Roger Rabbit* and the reinvention of myth. In M. T. Newman (Ed.), *A rhetorical analysis of popular American film* (pp. 44-72). Dubuque, IA: Kendall/Hunt.

Strate, L. (1994). Heroes: A communication perspective. In S. Drucker & R. Cathcart (Eds.), *American heroes in a media age* (pp. 15-23). Cresskill, NJ: Hampton Press.

Strate, L. (1995). The faces of a thousand heroes: The impact of visual communication technologies on the culture hero. *The New Jersey Journal of Communication, 3*(1), 26-39.

Sudjic, D. (1990). *Cult heroes: How to be famous for more than fifteen minutes.* New York: Norton.

Watzlawick, P., Bavelas, J. B., & Jackson, D. D. (1967). *Pragmatics of human communication: A study of interactional patterns, pathologies, and paradoxes.* New York: Norton.

Chapter 3

GLOBAL IDENTIFICATION WITH CELEBRITY HEROES

William J. Brown
Regent University

Benson P. Fraser
Regent University

The relationship of celebrity and hero is a complicated issue. But the global impact of global heroes and celebrities is self-evident. In this chapter, the authors define the celebrity hero and the international social and economic impact of this type of hero. The authors explore the notion of the "pseudo-hero" and the psychological involvement, through the phenomenon of the "parasocial relationship" and "identification" of audience and celebrity/ hero.

The global influence of international celebrities in postmodern culture presents communication scholars with a fascinating phenomenon. Despite the plethora of media effects studies and academic works on media criticism, media scholars have provided only a limited understanding of the central place of the celebrity in society and the appeal of celebrities across cultural, political, social, and economic boundaries. The ubiquitous reach and proliferation of entertainment media has prompted a renewed interest in how media persona influence the values, beliefs, and behavior of the world's diverse and complex audiences who daily consume potent mixtures of entertainment, information, and persuasion.

In this chapter, we discuss the global appeal of international celebrity heroes. We first discuss important influences of celebrities in the world and explain how certain celebrities have become heroes to many people. Second, we provide a theoretical framework for investigating the social influence of celebrity heroes through the process of identification. Third, we discuss the global influence of several international celebrity heroes. Finally, we examine important implications of the role that celebrity heroes play in today's world and consider how their influence can be used for prosocial purposes.

THE GROWING INFLUENCE OF CELEBRITIES

The proliferation of communication technology throughout the world since the 1960s, has given rise to a new social, cultural, and economic entity: the international celebrity. In June 1998, when the Chicago Bulls were desperately fighting for their sixth NBA championship against the Utah Jazz, officials in the city of Chicago debated how many millions of dollars of revenue Michael Jordan annually attracted to the city's economy. Many concluded Jordan's 1-year salary of $34 million was a profitable investment for Chicago given the attention and revenue he had generated for the city.

Although many of the world's media consumers do not follow the NBA as closely as other sports such as soccer, Jordan's international recognition was pervasive. Jordan generated an estimated $10 billion of revenue annually at the height of his career (Johnson & Harrington, 1998), not solely because of his remarkable basketball skills, but because he was an international celebrity. Substantial good will could be created by using the currency of celebrity to reach out across cultural and geographical boundaries. Perhaps bringing celebrity memorabilia as gifts to Kim Jong Il from his favorite film stars will not solve the nuclear crisis with North Korea, but it would certainly contribute to entering into a constructive dialog. The U.S. military could have used truckloads of Michael Jordan T-shirts, preferably signed, when they entered Baghdad in April 2003.

We are purposefully facetious here to drive home an important concept: The appeal of the international celebrity crosses economic, political, and cultural boundaries. Successful athletes, film stars, musicians, fiction writers, and a host of other entertainment careers produce powerful media persona whose scope of persuasive influence is extensive.

Consider the economic power of celebrities, an attribute that has long been recognized by product advertisers. Celebrities not only earn some of the highest incomes as reported annually by *Forbes* magazine, they also generate an extraordinary amount of revenue for those companies that employ them (Kafka, 2001). The increased exposure to celebrities through both news and entertainment media has provided advertisers with a powerful means of persuasion. Salaries and endorsement contracts for entertainers have risen dramatically since the 1990s. At age 24, Tiger Woods signed a 5-year endorsement contract with Nike for $100 million, spurring some financial analysts to predict that Woods would become sports' first $1 billion man (Ferguson, 2000). Woods' father predicted Tiger's net worth to eventually exceed $5 billion. After just 10 years on the PGA tour, Woods' net worth had already exceeded half a billion dollars (Sirake, 2006).

Advertising research indicates celebrities can effectively promote product sales by creating more consumer awareness and favorable attitudes of the products they endorse (Atkin & Block, 1983; Friedman & Friedman, 1979; Kamins, 1990; Tripp, Jensen, & Carlson, 1994). Marketing studies have documented the persuasive influences of celebrities such as actor Al Pacino (Friedman, Termini, & Washington, 1977), singer and songwriter Johnny Cash (Kamens, Brand, Hoeke, & Moe, 1989), and actress Mary Tyler Moore (Friedman & Friedman, 1979) for a variety of products. By seeking to match endorsers' public exposure, attributes, and lifestyle with the type of product or service being promoted, celebrities have been shown to be effective influencers of purchasing behavior (Erdogen, Baker, & Tagg, 2001; O'Mahony & Meenaghan, 1997/1998; Till & Busler, 2000).

Corporations that employ celebrities as spokespersons also tend to increase their profits (Agrawal & Kamakura, 1995; Mathur, Mathur, & Rangun, 1997). This may be because celebrity endorsers are perceived as more trustworthy and competent as compared with noncelebrities, enhancing product image and increasing product use (Atkin & Block, 1983). Since the 1990s, advertisers have turned to dead celebrities to promote product sales (Goldman, 1994; Miller, 1993). Albert Einstein, W.C. Fields, Marilyn Monroe, James Dean, Steve McQueen, John Wayne, Humphrey Bogart, Louis Armstrong, Groucho Marx, James Cagney, Greta Garbo, and Babe Ruth have all sold products after their deaths; and, unlike living celebrities, they do not get themselves into trouble, a major concern of companies who hire celebrities to endorse their products.

The income-generating power of celebrities can extend long after their deaths. In 2002, one of the world's highest paid entertainers was Elvis Presley, whose estate earned $37 million, 25 years after his death. Other dead celebrities who also fared well were singer-songwriter John Lennon and NASCAR legend Dale Earnhardt, who each earned $20 million (Schiffman, 2002).

Revenues generated by American-born celebrities are not restricted to the United States. Leonardo DiCaprio, for example, celebrity king of *Titanic* fame (which grossed nearly $5 billion in total sales worldwide), appeared in a series of television advertisements in Japan in the late 1990s to increase the sales of Orico credit cards and Suziki wagons (Jacobs, 1998). *Titanic's* big splash in Japan made DiCaprio a wealth generator for Japanese companies. The marketability of other celebrities extends to places they have never visited. The largest Elvis Presley fan club exists in London, where all kinds of Elvis memorabilia is sold, yet Elvis never visited London. Nike sports stars like Jordan and Woods receive their lucrative endorsement contracts because of the worldwide distribution of Nike products.

When the advertising agency for the Nike Company, J. Walter Thompson (JWT), designed its original Nike campaign for China, it employed Chinese basketball stars, including Wang Zhizhi of the Houston Rockets. Although Michael Jordan was Nike's most powerful pitchman, JWT thought that Chinese consumers would purchase more from Chinese players. However, the campaign failed because "Chinese kids wanted to be like Mike, not like Wang" (Walsh, 2002). Now Visa and Apple Computer are using Houston Rocket's center Yao Ming from China to promote their products in the United States.

The NBA is making a concerted global effort to market its products. By 2003, there were 65 NBA players from outside the United States representing 34 different countries and territories (Eisenberg, 2003). In the 2003 NBA All-Star Weekend featuring the sport's best new players, one third came from overseas. An estimated 20% of all NBA merchandise is now sold overseas (Eisenberg, 2003), most with the help of the league's most popular international celebrities.

In addition to economic influence, celebrities can influence political processes and outcomes. The intersection of celebrity, politics, and culture was embodied in John F. Kennedy Jr.'s magazine *George*. Before Kennedy's tragic airplane crash, the magazine featured famous politicians with celebrity appeal and celebrities who became political leaders. Aptly published by the son of John F. Kennedy, a U.S. president well known for his celebrity status and interaction with certain celebrities, *George* appealed to upper income mass audiences captivated by celebrity and power.

The election of Ronald Reagan to the presidency, Sony Bono and Fred Grandy to the U.S. House of Representatives, Fred Thompson to the U.S. Senate, Clint Eastwood as mayor of Carmel, and Jesse Ventura to the governorship of Minnesota, and Arnold Schwarzenegger to the governorship of California provide several examples of entertainers who have become political leaders. The potential political influence of entertainers is powerfully illustrated by the work of Paul Hewson of Ireland, otherwise known as Bono. The lead singer for rock band U2, Bono is not an elected official. Instead of pursuing political office, Bono is using his celebrity status throughout the world to raise money for African famine relief, promote AIDS awareness and prevention, inspire investment in Africa, and influence church organizations and U.S. government policy to help meet the needs of the poor in Africa (Falsani, 2003).

The rise of the celebrity in society has also affected the legal profession. The 1932 Lindbergh trial provided one of the best examples of the international attention drawn to a legal case involving a celebrity. Charles Lindbergh's 19-month-old son had been kidnapped and murdered. Bruno Hauptmann, a German-born carpenter, was arrested, tried for the murder, found guilty, and executed. Yet, controversy existed as to whether he was the real villain. In October 1994, Hauptmann's widow, who fought for 62 years to clear her husband's name by exposing several legal questions in the case, died still claiming his innocence and bias against her husband. Lindbergh's fame appeared to have provided the prosecution with a great advantage against Hauptmann.

Celebrities accused of crimes often have a great advantage in the legal system because of their appeal to jurors. The famous comic Roscoe (Fatty) Arbuckle was tried three times for the rape and murder of starlet Virginia Rappe in 1921, in San Francisco. After two hung juries and intense media coverage, a third jury, consisting of several members reputed to have received bribes, acquitted Arbuckle after 6 minutes of deliberation (Kirkpatrick, 1994).

The trials of Patricia Hearst and Claudine Longet in the 1970s, Claus von Bulow in the 1980s, and William Kennedy Smith, Christian Brando, Calvin Broadus (Snoop Doggy Dogg), O.J. Simpson in the 1990s, and Michael Jackson's trial in 2004 and 2005, all exemplify how celebrities can benefit from their celebrity status. In none of the cases mentioned here were the celebrities found guilty of the original charges made against them. As exemplified by the O.J. Simpson criminal trial, which was followed throughout the world, it is difficult for the public to convict popular celebrities of the original crimes for which they were brought to trial, regardless of the evidence against them (Brown, Duane, & Fraser, 1997).

In addition to the socioeconomic, political, and legal influences of celebrities, they also can have a profound influence on culture in general that crosses geopolitical boundaries. The international chain of Planet Hollywood restaurants, despite their recent financial struggles, provides another example of how celebrities appeal to people across cultures. Once found in 70 cities worldwide, including Acapulco, Amsterdam, Barcelona, Bangkok, Berlin, Buenos Aires, Cancun, Cannes, Cape Town, Dublin, Helsinki, Hong Kong, Jakarta, Johannesburg, Kuala Lumpur, London, Manila, Melbourne, Moscow, Munich, Paris, Prague, Rio De Janeiro, Rome, Singapore, Sydney, Tel Aviv, Toronto, Vancouver, and Zurich, Planet Hollywood restaurants still operate in 18 countries (see http://www.planethollywood.com on the Internet). Based on the international appeal of international film stars, Planet Hollywood draws its customers with celebrity memorabilia.

The influence of celebrities on news media is substantial. Public interest in celebrities has increased the production of celebrity-based media. Television programs like NBC's *Entertainment Tonight* and *Access Hollywood* focus almost exclusively on providing news about celebrities. Even A & E's *Biography* regularly features the lives of celebrities. In June 1998, CNN/U.S., the flagship U.S. broadcast news network of the CNN News Group, teamed up with the popular news magazine *Entertainment Weekly*, to produce a new weekly television news program, *NewsStand: CNN and Entertainment Weekly*. Executives of *Entertainment Weekly* described the program as filling the void that exists in "hard-hitting entertainment-industry reporting on television" (Squires & Seymore, 1998).

The international focus on celebrities that grew during the 1990s affected many areas of journalism, including coverage of business, politics, and culture (Shenk, 1996). Neimark (1995) claimed that a culture saturated with celebrity news provides the public with "more and more information about people who are less and less real" (p. 57). Celebrities have been featured as the primary focus of many print publications, especially tabloid newspapers and magazines such as *Entertainment Weekly, Rolling Stone, Vanity Fair, Cosmopolitan,* and *People Magazine.* The demand for journalists who cover the lives of celebrities, or what some refer to as the "celebro-journalist," has increased during the past decade to satisfy the public's seemingly insatiable desire for celebrity news.

In summary, the growing influence of celebrities can be seen in the worlds of economics, politics, media, and culture. Their international influence is extensive owing to the pervasive reach of entertainment media, which continues to increase throughout the world. The conglomeration of media companies and vertical integration of the industry has brought music, print, television, and film production under the control of single, multinational companies whose distribution outlets span across the world. At the heart of marketing media products internationally is the creation of media stars, or persona, who attract large audiences. The most powerful media personas are those who fill the role of heroes and role models in our lives. Although international audiences do distinguish between celebrities and traditional heroes, we now discuss how certain celebrities can become heroes for many people, thus becoming what we call the *celebrity hero*.

FROM CELEBRITY TO PSEUDO-HERO

Boorstin (1961) was one of the first scholars to recognize the rise of the celebrity in popular culture. He accurately predicted the powerful international influence of popular media on society and culture through the lives of celebrities. The unprecedented expansion of multinational media corporations such as Disney, Viacom, Newscorp, AOL–Time–Warner, GE and others has made rock musicians, recording artists, television and film stars, and athletes internationally known in a way that was impossible when Boorstin wrote his visionary work more than 45 years ago.

Discussing the transition from traditional heroes to celebrities, Boorstin (1961) regarded the hero as a person who was distinguished by achievement and self-created, whereas he regarded the celebrity as an image or persona created by the media and distinguished by his or her trademark. He observed that "the hero was a big man, the celebrity a big name" (p. 61). Traditional heroes are known for great acts of courage or outstanding accomplishments requiring exceptional skill and fortitude. They often are reluctantly thrust into the public spotlight. In contrast, celebrities become known for their self-promotion and media exposure, often relishing the public spotlight. The status of traditional heroes usually grows slowly and endures over a long time period; but celebrities are given status by the amount of media coverage they attract, which often occurs rapidly but is seldom enduring. In the highly mediated culture in which we now live, many of those who are most famous and idolized are not necessarily those who have demonstrated moral courage or heroism, but those who have garnered the greatest amount of media attention (Loftus, 1995).

Vogler (1998) traced the root idea of hero to the concept of self-sacrifice on behalf of others. The requirement of self-sacrifice is no longer a necessary qualification to be considered a hero today. People treat certain celebrities like they would treat heroes. We provide two examples. Mark McGwire, a retired major league baseball player, was considered to be an American hero when he broke Roger Maris' 37-year-old home-run record in 1998. McGwire's celebrity status was so great at the time that many people who followed his pursuit of the record became more concerned about child abuse prevention and more interested in the anabolic steroid androstenedione (Brown, Basil, & Bocarnea, 2003a). Although McGwire's feat was a great athletic accomplishment, his status attained heroic proportions beyond the achievement of setting a new sports record, subsequently influencing important health issues.

Another example is illustrated by public reactions to the tragic death of renown racecar driver Dale Earnhardt. Many NASCAR fans and observers of the sport considered Earnhardt to be a hero, even those who rooted for other drivers to beat Earnhardt. Certainly, a degree of courage is needed to compete in car races, but Earnhardt did not sacrifice himself to protect or help others. When celebrities become so popular and well-liked that people began to look to them as heroes, they are regarded as pseudo-heroes.

FROM HERO TO CELEBRITY

Sometimes traditional heroes become celebrities, even against their wishes. Although many heroes do not receive much media attention, the September 11, 2001 terrorist attacks and war against international terrorists reintroduced traditional heroes to the U.S. public. These new heroes included New York City emergency workers, the former mayor of New York, and the passengers on board United Airlines Flight 93 (Brown, Basil, & Bocarnea, 2003c). Jessica Lynch, the 19-year-old women who was wounded, captured, and interrogated by an Iraqi paramilitary squad and later rescued by Special Forces on April 2, 2003, behaved heroically during her ordeal. Mohammed, a 32-year-old Iraqi lawyer who risked his life to help save her, is also a hero. Yet, because of the intense media in the United States, Jessica was eventually given so much public exposure that she became a short-term celebrity. Mohammed, in contrast, will most likely remain a hidden hero unknown to the U.S. general public.

The case of Virginia Beach, Virginia resident Rudy Boesch, the most popular contestant of the first year of the CBS television series *Survivor*, illustrates another type of hero to celebrity transition. Rudy was a Navy Seal for more than 30 years and one of the most distinguished officers of the original SEAL (Sea-Air-Land) Team TWO. He completed dozens of missions in Vietnam, earning a Bronze Star for his valor (Adel, 2000). Rudy was considered to be a hero by his family, friends, and fellow Navy SEALS long before his participation on *Survivor*. Yet, the headlines of his hometown newspaper, *The Virginian-Pilot*, announced Rudy's return to his home after he finished filming *Survivor* with the headline "Hometown Fans Get a Chance to Honor Their Hero" (Bonko, 2000). A large celebration was prepared for Rudy with extensive media coverage to commemorate his making the final group of four *Survivor* contestants, and the mayor of Virginia Beach proclaimed a Rudy Boesch Day. Reacting to all the attention given to Rudy, one local resident wrote,

> People seem to think that participating on the show somehow qualifies Rudy as a hero. Rudy Boesch is a true American hero, but not for participating on *Survivor*. He is a hero for his devoted service to his country and ensuring our survival as a free country. I wonder if Rudy or any of his fellow Navy SEALs made the front page of the newspaper after returning from a mission. (Hall, 2000)

This resident made an important observation. Rudy Boesch was a strong positive role model in one of the most respected elite fighting forces in the United States, yet he did not receive public recognition until he appeared in a television reality show. After thousands of people from

Virginia and North Carolina came to greet Rudy with signs such as "Rudy for President" and "Rudy, You Rock," Rudy exclaimed, "Now I know how Elvis felt" (Sinha, 2000).

A second example involves the case of Mother Teresa of India. The Albanian Catholic nun established a remarkable ministry to the poor that gained international acclaim. Her influence extended far beyond the realm of her life's work and vocation. Although Mother Teresa would never consider herself as important or someone with great status and influence, she met with popes, prime ministers, and presidents. The organization she founded, the Missionaries of Charity, serves the poor in 80 countries around the world. During her lifetime, Mother Teresa received numerous awards and citations, including the Nobel Peace Prize.

In a study conducted after Mother Teresa's death, about two thirds of the 233 respondents to an open survey question said that they were saddened by Mother Teresa's death, many mentioning that the world had suffered a great loss by her passing (Evanski, Bocarnea, Rowe, & Fraser, 1998). She has been honored throughout the world as one of mankind's greatest role models. In the case of Mother Teresa, she was clearly a national hero to India whose social influence transcended culture.

A third example is the internationally known wildlife conservationist, Steve Irwin, affectionately known as "The Crocodile Hunter," the name of the popular television series he hosted on *Animal Planet*. Irwin, who became director of the Australia Zoo in Queensland in 1991, taking over the zoo's management from his parents, burst onto the international scene in 1992 with a one-hour documentary entitled *Crocodile Hunter*. The hundreds of television programs and several films produced by Steve and his wife Terri have been seen by more than 500 million people. By the time of his tragic death on September 4, 2006, from a Stingray barb that penetrated his heart, Irwin had already established himself as a celebrity hero, having won international acclaim as a role model for wildlife education and conservation. No longer were the popular Australian phrases "crickey," "no worries mate," and "good on ya" exclusively Australian. Irwin had made them known throughout the world as well as the cause of protecting our planet's amazing creatures. In a 2006 study we conducted immediately after Irwin's death, more than 1,900 people from around the world completed our online web survey in a 5-day period to share how Irwin had influenced their lives.

Celebrity heroes have become public role models for thought and action. Sometimes the public knows very little about the moral character of media persona who are publicly emulated. For every true hero like Mother Teresa, there are pseudo-heroes whose character and integrity are woefully lacking, yet they are still emulated. The carefully constructed media images of popular celebrities commonly blend historical facts with entertaining fiction. The mythic celebrity heroes of today attract the attention and involvement of the world's global media consumers.

IDENTIFICATION WITH CELEBRITY HEROES

The social influence of celebrity heroes can be explained by two theories first proposed in the late 1950s and early 1960s: parasocial interaction theory and the theory of identification. In 1956, two psychologists published an article about the sense of intimacy that television viewers can develop with television personalities through repeated exposure to television programs. They called the imaginary relationship between a television viewer and television personality or "personae" a *parasocial relationship* and the process of developing a pseudo-relationship with a television personae *parasocial interaction* (Horton & Wohl, 1956). Levy (1979) also observed that repeated exposure to media celebrities through the mass media create a sense of friendship or intimacy in media users.

Parasocial relationships form when audiences look to media personalities as "friends" and as those with whom they feel "comfortable," thus contributing to the audience's enjoyment during media consumption. Parasocial relationships have been observed between television viewers and newscasters, talk show hosts, and soap opera stars (Babb & Brown, 1994; Brown & Cody, 1991; Levy, 1979; Rubin & Perse, 1987; Rubin, Perse, & Powell, 1985; Rubin & McHugh, 1987).

Brown and colleagues (see Brown & Basil, 1995; Brown, Basil, & Bocarnea, 2003a, 2003b, 2003c; Brown et al. 1997; Fraser & Brown, 2002) extended the concept of parasocial interaction beyond television personalities and television viewers, demonstrating that the general public establishes these relationships with sports celebrities through a variety of media. For example, audiences develop parasocial relationships with sports celebrities through their exposure to sports events, televised sports, movies, and commercials featuring sports celebrities.

Parasocial interaction can produce powerful effects on audiences across cultural boundaries. Viewers' parasocial relationships with the stars of *Hum Log* (*We People*), India's first television soap opera, promoted the status of women and family harmony throughout India, including the Hindi regions in the north, Marathi-speaking regions in the west central part of the country, and Tamil region in the south (Brown & Cody, 1991). Many thousands of television viewers joined literacy programs throughout Latin America through *parasocial* relationships with the popular soap opera character "Maria," star of the Peruvian *telenovela Simplemente Maria* (*Simple Mary*) (Singhal, Obregon, & Rogers, 1994). The public's strong parasocial relationship with Magic Johnson had a positive impact on HIV prevention with both Caucasians and African Americans (Brown & Basil, 1995).

Five years after Horton and Wohl (1956) theorized about parasocial relationship, Kelman (1961) introduced his theory of identification. He viewed identification as a persuasion process that occurs when an individual adopts behavior of another individual or group based on a "self-defining" relationship. Kelman observed that people imitated others as a way of maintaining a desired relationship to another person or group. Kelman explained:

> By saying what the other says, doing what he does, believing what he believes, the individual maintains this relationship and the satisfying self-definition that it provides him. (p. 63)

In the identification process described by Kelman (1958), a person adopts the attitudes and behaviors of another because he or she actually believes in the other person, and it is not necessary that the object of identification be aware that this process is taking place. Thus, a person can identify with a celebrity by adopting the attitudes and behaviors of the celebrity without any real interaction with that person (Basil, 1996). Although the process of identification commonly occurs in interpersonal relationships, it also can occur through prolonged exposure to celebrities through the media.

Although Kelman's theory of identification and Horton and Wohl's theory of parasocial interaction are very similar and conceptually overlap, there are two notable distinctions. First, a parasocial relationship is conceived of as a psychological state of involvement with a media personality through an imagined or perceived friendship. The relationship is an entity in itself, not a means of persuasive influence. Second, parasocial interaction does not require adopting another person's attitudes or behaviors. Adopting the behaviors of others can occur in close friendships but is a consequence of a friendship, not a condition of friendship. Parasocial interaction and identification as two closely related forms of involvement with a celebrity, and in many cases, parasocial interaction leads to identification.

There are a number of other important conceptions of identification. Freud (1922) defined identification as "the earliest expression of an emotional tie with another person" (p. 29). Lasswell (1965) also discussed this concept in the context of group behavior, referring to mass identifications such as nationalism. Johnson, Johnson, and Heimberg (1999) drew their conception of identification within organizations from both Freud (1922) and Lasswell. Organizational communication scholars also draw on the work of Burke (1969), who wrote extensively about this process (see Cheney, 1983; Cheney & Tompkins, 1987; Johnson et al. 1999).

According to Burke, identification occurs when one individual shares the interests of another individual or believes that he or she shares the interests of another. Burke noted that two individuals could be joined and still be distinct. In a pragmatic sense, identification is simply the common ground held by people in communication (Rosenfeld, 1969). Although Burke focused on the efforts of speakers to identify with their intended audiences, identification is also a way in which an audience member can say to a communicator, "I am like you" or "I have the same interests as you" (Cheney, 1983, p. 147).

Hoffner (1996), drawing on the work of Feilitzen and Linne (1975), explored the concept of "wishful identification" of children, described as "the desire to be like or behave in ways similar" to a mass-mediated character (p. 53). Other scholars have regarded the identification experienced by children as a wishful imitation and desire (Albert, 1957; Noble, 1975; Williams, LaRose, & Frost, 1981). Hoffner's (1996) study of children supports the link between parasocial interaction and identification proposed by Brown, Basil, and Bocarnea (2003a).

A number of media scholars have explored audience identification. Adams-Price and Greene (1990) confirmed that adolescents do identify with celebrities to whom they are exposed through media. Basil (1996) found that those who most identified with sports celebrity Magic Johnson were more likely to respond positively to Johnson's HIV/AIDS prevention message. Brown et al. (2003c) found that those who identified with baseball great Mark McGwire were more willing to try the muscle-enhancing drug androstenedione. Stack's (1987, 2000) study of suicides suggests identification with celebrities may even promote the imitation of destructive behaviors.

In summary, research indicates that people who are repeatedly exposed to celebrities develop psychological relationships with them as demonstrated by parasocial interaction. Often, these attachments become strong and audience members began to regard celebrities as a type of hero, which we designate as celebrity heroes. Eventually, parasocial interaction with celebrity heroes leads to identification, a process in which audience members adopt the values, beliefs, and practices of those with whom they identify. We now illustrate this social influence process through our discussion of four celebrity heroes, three of whom we regard as pseudo-heroes.

EXAMPLES OF GLOBAL CELEBRITY HEROES

In order to comprehend the scope of influence of global celebrity heroes, we briefly discuss the lives of Diana, Princess of Wales, American singer Elvis Presley, Argentina soccer sensation Diego Maradona, and Saudi-born Al Qaeda leader Osama bin Laden.

It is difficult to describe the incredible outpouring of international grief that occurred when Princess Diana tragically died. More than 1 million mourners lined the 3-mile funeral route in London to pay their respects to

Diana. People who had never met the former princess and who had no personal contact with her traveled to England from around the world just to be one of the millions who placed flowers along the funeral route. Two thousand celebrities from a variety of professions attended Diana's memorial service. These included fashion designers, film and television stars, political leaders, musicians, and writers such as: Donatella and Santo Versace, Hillary Clinton, Luciano Pavarotti, Tom Cruise and Nicole Kidman, Steven Spielberg, Henry Kissinger, Tom Hanks, and hundreds of members of royal families from around the world (Kantrowitz, Pedersen, & McGuire, 1997). An estimated 2.5 billion people watched the worldwide satellite transmission of the funeral to 200 countries in 44 languages, from small villages in Iceland to giant screens in Hong Kong (Blowen, 1997), making it the most watched event in history (Payne, 2000, p. x).

Princess Diana is the quintessential celebrity hero. Relatively unknown nationally before her marriage to Prince Charles, Diana rose to unmatched celebrity status. However, her battle through personal problems, including her struggle with bulimia and her failed marriage, and her involvement with a number of social causes, including the reduction of land mines and HIV/AIDS prevention, made her a hero to many people. Those who followed Diana's life established a strong degree of identification with her and sought to adopt the values she emulated (Brown et al. 2003c)

Elvis Presley is another excellent example of a celebrity hero. Thirty years after his death in August 1977, he is still at the center of one of the world's most lucrative entertainment franchises. Elvis is closely associated with traditional American values: He was patriotic, risked his career to serve his country in military service, respected his father and deeply loved his mother, was generous to the poor, was strongly religious, never disassociated himself with the lower income sociodemographic, and never despised his roots growing up poor in the south (Amarin, 1988; Lhamon, 1992). Despite his fame and fortune, Elvis kept his home in Memphis, did not project himself more important than those with less income and notoriety, and never forgot his origins in the working class (Stomberg, 1990).

Rodman (1996) gave three explanations for Elvis' tremendous posthumous career: (a) the cultural mythologies disseminated about the life of Elvis; (b) the permanent "Elvis space" in *Graceland* and Tupelo, Mississippi, visited by millions of people (only the *White House* receives more annual visitors than Elvis' home); and (c) the ongoing perpetration of "Elvis culture" (p. 24). Based on the hundreds of Elvis Presley Internet sites that exist today in many different countries, we agree with Rodman's conclusion that Elvis was and still is an international icon.

Elvis Presley impersonators, which number some 50,000 people, are also seen performing in many different countries. We have interviewed or otherwise documented Elvis impersonators in Canada, England, France,

Italy, Spain, Austria, Thailand, China, India, Taiwan, and Australia, and these are just some of the countries where we have conducted research. Most impersonators exhibit strong identification with Elvis. Some of the most successful impersonators include a Black Elvis, a Latino Elvis known as El Vez, a female group called the Elvettes, and a pre-teen boy who has impersonated Elvis since age 5 (Fraser & Brown, 2002).

Diego Armando Maradona is considered by many to be the greatest soccer player who ever lived. Maradona provides another example of a global celebrity hero. A review of the numerous Web sites on the Internet dedicated to Maradona provides insight into the power of his celebrity appeal. Some 75 poems and 10 songs have been dedicated to Maradona, who played most of his career in Italy, Spain, and Argentina. One Web site in Naples (www.vivadiego.com) has logged more than 1 million visitors since September 1996. Marcela Martuviak (personal communication, April 2, 2003), an Argentinian communication scholar who is studying Maradona, reported that pseudo-churches have arisen to form a type of Maradona cult worship.

Not only is Maradona a hero in Italy and Argentina for leading his teams to World Cup victories, he is a hero to soccer fans worldwide who identify with his disadvantaged upbringing in the slums of Buenos Aires. Maradona did for soccer what Michael Jordan did for basketball and what Tiger Woods is doing for golf.

The last example of a celebrity hero may be a curious one to those in the West who have not traveled to Muslim countries, but he certainly qualifies as one of the most important ones to consider. Osama bin Laden became a local hero in Afghanistan when he left his privileged lifestyle in Saudi Arabia to fight with the Mujahideen against the Russians.

In contrast to Princess Diana, Elvis, and Maradona, bin Laden was a traditional hero to many Muslims until his reputation became international through his terrorist activities.

The 9/11 terrorist attacks against the United States, which were orchestrated by bin Laden, gave him the fame of an international celebrity. Bin Laden's picture can be found in news magazines, on posters, and on T-shirts throughout the world. His fight against two of the world's most powerful nations, Russia and the United States, on the basis of his Muslim beliefs, has made him a hero to millions of Muslims. Like David was to the Israelites when he faced down Goliath, bin Laden is admired and emulated throughout the world.

Bin Laden's role as a celebrity hero should not be overlooked. Those who identify with him will be motivated to adopt his values, beliefs, and behavior. This is evident by the international influence he has had in motivating and recruiting other terrorists. As with the case of other celebrities whose moral character fails, it is difficult to break their powerful influence over people. The fact that more than 900 people would commit suicide on behalf of their flawed hero, Jim Jones, showed us in the Guyana tragedy in 1978 how strong and potentially destructive this form social influence can be.

CELEBRITY HEROES FOR PROSOCIAL INFLUENCE

There are many examples of celebrity heroes who use the currency of celebrity for good. Mother Teresa did not shy away from her plea for the protection of all children, including the unborn, when she met with former President Clinton at the White House. Bono has not been afraid to challenge America's involvement in the AIDS crisis in Africa. Christopher Reeve and Michael J. Fox testified before Congress for more medical research with stem cells. Dozens of celebrities have promoted fundraising for many different types of diseases, exemplified by the three decades of work by Jerry Lewis on behalf of muscular dystrophy. Celebrities can be very effective persuaders in health communication campaigns (Brown, Basil, & Bocarnea, 2003a).

The potential power of celebrity heroes is enormous. The ability of popular celebrities like Magic Johnson and Elizabeth Taylor to promote HIV/AIDS prevention, or actress Mary Tyler Moore and 1999 Miss America Nicole Johnson to promote diabetes research, or entertainer Jerry Lewis' long-term efforts to cure muscular dystrophy, or *Crocodile Hunter's* Steve Irwin to promote wildlife conservation, or actor George Clooney's efforts to stop the genocide in southern Sudan, illustrates the important role celebrities can play in promoting prosocial messages. There are a number of social needs and international problems in which celebrity heroes could help by using their social influence for good. Every society is going to have its celebrities and heroes. Those whose influence is global should be encouraged to use their celebrity currency to build bridges across the cultural divides that often keep us from finding solutions to critical problems. As has been demonstrated by Bono and bin Laden, celebrity heroes can use their fame to be powerfully constructive or powerfully destructive.

REFERENCES

Adams-Price, C., & Greene, A. L. (1990). Secondary attachments and adolescent self-concept. *Sex Roles, 22,* 187-198.

Adel, D. (2000, September 1). One for the money. *Entertainment Weekly*, pp. 30-37.

Albert, R.S. (1957). The role of mass media and the effect of aggressive film content upon children's aggressive responses and identification choices. *Genetic Psychology Monographs, 55,* 221-285.

Agrawal, J., & Kamakura, W. A. (1995). The economic worth of celebrity endorsers. *Journal of Advertising Research, 23,* 57-61.

Amarin, J. (1988). *He never got above his raising: An ethnographic study of a working class response to Elvis Presley.* Unpublished doctoral dissertation, University of Pennsylvania, Philadelphia.

Atkin, C., & Block, M. (1983). Effectiveness of celebrity endorsers. *Journal of Advertising Research, 23,* 57-61.

Babb, V., & Brown, W. J. (1994, July). *Adolescents' development of parasocial relationships through popular television situation comedies.* Paper presented to the International Communication Association, Sydney, Australia.

Basil, M. D. (1996). Identification as a mediator of celebrity effects. *Journal of Broadcasting & Electronic Media, 40,* 478-495.

Blowen, M. (September 7, 1997). With grace and depth, ABC ruled. *Boston Globe,* p. A32.

Bonko, L. (2000, August 29). Rudy has eye on space. *The Virginian-Pilot,* pp. E1-E2.

Boorstin, D. J. (1961). *The image: A guide to pseudo-events in America.* New York: Atheneum.

Brown, W. J., & Basil, M. D. (1995). Media celebrities and public health: Responses to "Magic" Johnson's HIV disclosure and its impact on AIDS risk and high-risk behaviors. *Health Communication, 7,* 345-370.

Brown, W. J., Basil, M. D., & Bocarnea, M. C. (2003a). Celebrity identification in entertainment-education. In M. J. Cody, M. Sabido, A. Singhal, & E. M. Rogers (Eds.), *Entertainment-education and social change: History, research, and practice* (pp. 97-115). Mahwah, NJ: Erlbaum.

Brown, W. J., Basil, M. D., & Bocarnea, M. C. (2003b). *Exploring the boundaries of heroes, celebrities and role models after 9/11: Lessons from Shanksville.* Paper presented at the International Communication Association, San Diego, CA.

Brown, W. J., Basil, M. D., & Bocarnea, M. C. (2003c). The influence of famous athletes on public health issues: Mark McGwire, child abuse prevention, and androstenedione. *Journal of Health Communication, 8,* 41-57.

Brown, W. J., & Cody, M. J. (1991). Effects of a prosocial television soap opera in promoting women's status. *Human Communication Research, 17,* 114-142.

Brown, W. J., Duane, J. J., & Fraser, B. P. (1997). Media coverage and public opinion of the O.J. Simpson trial: Implications for the criminal justice system. *Communication Law and Policy, 2,* 261-287.

Burke, K. (1969). *A rhetoric of motives.* Berkeley: University of California Press.

Cheney, G. (1983). On the various and changing meanings of organizational membership: A field study of organizational identification. *Communication Monographs, 50,* 342-362.

Cheney, G., & Tompkins, P. K. (1987). Coming to terms with organizational identification and commitment. *Central States Speech Journal, 28,* 1-15.

Eisenberg, D. (2003, March 17). The NBA's global game plan. *Time Magazine,* pp. 59-63.

Erdogan, B. F., Baker, M. J., & Tagg, S. (2001). Selecting celebrity endorsers: The practitioner's perspective. *Journal of Advertising Research, 41*, 39-48.

Evanski, J., Bocarnea, M. C., Rowe, J. B., & Fraser, B. P. (1998, July). *Responding to the death of Mother Teresa: Involvement across cross-cultural boundaries.* Paper presented to the National Communication Association and the International Communication Association joint summer conference, Consiglio Nazionale delle Ricerche, Rome, Italy

Falsani, K. (2003, March). Bono's American prayer. *Christianity Today*, pp. 38-44.

Feilitzen, C.V., & Linne, O. (1975). The effects of television on children and adolescents: Identifying with television characters. *Journal of Communication, 25*, 51-55.

Ferguson, D. (2000, September 15). Tiger Close to $100 million Nike deal. *The Associated Press.*

Fraser, B. P., & Brown, W. J. (2002). Media, celebrities, and social influence: Identification with Elvis Presley. *Mass Communication & Society, 5*, 185-208.

Freud, S. (1922). *Group psychology and the analysis of ego.* New York: Norton.

Friedman, H. H., & Friedman, L. (1979). Endorser effectiveness by product type. *Journal of Advertising Research, 18*, 63-71.

Friedman, H. H., Termini, S., & Washington, R. (1977). The effectiveness of advertisements using four types of endorsers. *Journal of Advertising, 6*, 22-24.

Goldman, K. (1994, January 7). Dead celebrities are resurrected pitchmen. *The Wall Street Journal*, p. B-1.

Hall, K. (2000, September 9). Rudy's a hero, but not for "Survivor." *The Virginian-Pilot*, p. B6.

Horton, D., & Wohl, R. R. (1956). Mass communication and parasocial interaction: Observations on intimacy at a distance. *Psychiatry, 19*, 215-229.

Hoffner, C. (1996). Children's wishful identification and parasocial interaction with favorite television characters. *Journal of Broadcasting & Electronic Media, 40*, 389-402.

Jacobs, A. J. (1998, June 5). Leo ads up. *Entertainment Weekly*, p. 17.

Johnson, R. S., & Harrington, A. (1998, June 22). The Jordan effect. *Fortune*, pp. 124-138.

Johnson, W. L., Johnson, A. M., & Heimberg, F. (1999). A primary and second-order analysis of the organizational identification questionnaire. *Educational and Psychological Measurement, 59*, 159-170.

Kafka, P. (2001, March 19). Star dollars star power. *Forbes.com*. Retrieved on April 11, 2001, from http://www.forbes.com/forbes/2001/0319/113.html.

Kamins, M. A. (1990). An investigation into the "match-up" hypothesis in celebrity advertising: When beauty may be only skin deep. *Journal of Advertising, 19*, 4-13.

Kamins, M. A., Brand, J. J., Hoeke, S. A., & Moe, J. C. (1989). Two-sided versus one-sided celebrity endorsements: The impact on advertising effectiveness and credibility. *Journal of Advertising, 18*, 4-10.

Kantrowitz, B., Pedersen, D., & McGuire, S. (September 15, 1997) The day England cried. *Newsweek*, pp. 30-36.

Kelman, H. (1958). Compliance, identification, and internalization: Three processes of attitude change. *Journal of Conflict Resolution, 2*, 51-60.

Kelman, H. (1961). Process of opinion change. *Public Opinion Quarterly, 25*, 57-58.

Kirkpatrick, C. (1994, June 27). Tales of celebrity babylon. *Newsweek*, p. 26.

Lasswell, H. D. (1965). *World politics and personal insecurity*. New York: The Free Press.

Levy, M. (1979). Watching television news as parasocial interaction. *Journal of Broadcasting, 23*, 69-80.

Lhamon, W. T. (1992). Elvis lives! *American Quarterly, 44*, 481-486.

Loftus, M. (1995, May). The other side of fame. *Psychology Today*, pp. 48-53, 70-80.

Mathur, L. K., Mathur, I., & Rangan, N. (1997). The wealth effects associated with a celebrity endorser. *Journal of Advertising Research, 37*, 67-73.

Miller, C. (1993). Some celebs just now reaching their potential—and they're dead. *Marketing News, 27*(7), 2-4.

Neimark, J. (1995). The culture of celebrities. *Psychology Today*, pp. 54-57, 84, 87, 90.

Noble, G. (1975). *Children in front of the small screen*. Newbury Park, CA: Sage.

O'Mahony, S., & Meenaghan, T. (1997/1998). The impact of celebrity endorsements on consumers. *Irish Marketing Review, 10*(2), 15-24.

Payne, J. G. (2000). Preface. In G. Payne (Ed.), *An era of celebrity and spectacle: The global rhetorical phenomenon of the death of Diana, Princess of Wales*. Boston, MA: Center for Ethics in Political and Health Communication, Emerson College.

Rodman, G. B. (1996). *Elvis after Elvis: The posthumous career of a living legend*. London: Routledge.

Rosenfeld, L. B. (1969). Set theory: Key to understanding of Kenneth Burke's use of the term "identification." *Western Speech, 33*, 175-183.

Rubin, A. M., & Perse, E. M. (1987). Audience activity and soap opera involvement: A uses and gratifications investigation. *Human Communication Research, 14*, 246-268.

Rubin, A. M., Perse, E. M., & Powell, R. A. (1985). Loneliness, parasocial interaction, and local television viewing. *Human Communication Research, 12*, 155-180.

Rubin, R. B., & McHugh, M. P. (1987). Development of parasocial relationships. *Journal of Broadcasting and Electronic Media, 31*, 279-292.

Schiffman, B. (2002, August 12). Top-earning dead celebrities. *Forbes.* Retrieved April 4, 2003, from http://www.forbes.com/2002/08/12/0812deadintro_print.html

Shenk, J. W. (1996, June). Star struck. *The Washington Monthly*, pp. 12-18.

Singhal, A., Obregon, R., & Rogers, E. M. (1994). Reconstructing the story of "*Simplemente Maria*": The most popular *telenovela* in Latin America of all time. *Gazette, 54*, 1-15.

Sinha, V. (2000, August 30). "Rudypalooza!" draws crowd of thousands for homecoming. *The Virginian-Pilot*, pp. A1, A9.

Sirake, R. (2006, February). Golf's first billion dollar man. *Golf Digest.com.* Retrieved on April 11, 2007, from at http://www.golfdigest.com/features/index.ssf?/ gd200602top50.html.

Squires, J., & Seymore, J. W. Jr. (1998, June 12). EW on the tube. *Entertainment Weekly*, p. 4.

Stack, S. (1987). Celebrities and suicide: A taxonomy and analysis, 1948-1983. *American Sociological Review, 52,* 401-412.

Stack, S. (2000). Media impacts on suicide: A quantitative review of 293 findings. *Social Science Quarterly, 81,* 957-971.

Stromberg, P. (1990). Elvis alive?: The ideology of American consumerism. *Journal of Popular Culture, 24,* 11-19.

Till, B. D., & Busler, M. (2000). The match-up hypothesis: Physical attractiveness, expertise, and the role of fit on brand attitude, purchase intent and brand beliefs. *Journal of Advertising, 29*(3), 1-13.

Tripp, C., Jensen, T. D., & Carlson, L. (1994). The effects of multiple product endorsements by celebrities on consumers' attitudes and intentions. *Journal of Consumer Research, 20,* 535-547.

Vogler, C. (1998). *The writer's journey* (2nd ed.). Studio City, CA: Michael Wise Productions.

Walsh, B. (2002, November 11). Mixed messages: Advertisers are learning that if you want to sell products in China, you have to understand the people—all 1.3 billion of them. *Time Magazine.* Retrieved April 2, 2003, from http://www.time.com/time /asia/features/china_cul_rev/advertising.html.

Williams, F., LaRose, R., & Frost, F. (1981). *Children, television and sex-role stereotyping.* New York: Praeger.

Chapter 4

U.S. AND EUROPEAN HEROISM COMPARED

John Dean
University of Versailles

Do Europeans and Americans have a different conception of the hero? This chapter is a European perspective of the hero as seen through the scholarly eyes of an American teaching in France. Not only does the chapter present contrasting views, but it outlines eight historical stages of the hero from the Homeric Age to the Industrial Age.

✧   ✧   ✧

INTRODUCTION: INTO THE FRAY

Do heroes still exist? Has the traditional value of *hero*, a force that held sway for at least 3,000 years, disappeared? Heroes customarily embodied civilization's constant values, ideals with a human touch across time. The hero was *conservative* — not in the small, political sense, but as a gigantic verb of holding and regeneration; conservative in the oldest sense of keeping intact that which is of constant value.

But has the conservative power of heroes gone down the drain of time? Could it be—more profound, more subtle than "the end of history"—that Western culture has experienced the end of this age-old convention of a pantheon of exalted standards? That we have devolved into a time of hard necessities and brutal self-defense, people bound more by cold systems rather than the hot blend of heroes that once pumped through civilized veins?[1]

The crux of the problem is to explore these questions, to find out who heroes were, what they meant, what happened to them across millennia, and who or what they are now. Vast argumentative generalizations must be made and cross-cut movements taken to consider as many levels as possible, to look at, into, and to compare the wealth of meanings that *hero* has within a distinctive culture area, Western Europe, and a nation, the United States. To do this, we must enter into a fray of controversies, go back to when an exalted continuity of great men and women gave life purpose.

The analysis presented here has three parts: (a) what *hero* has meant, (b) how this meaning has been achieved, and (c) who has embodied these figures of extreme admiration. Truth be told: My main concern is with *hero* in the English language, in Anglo-American civilization. Although the English word *hero* as now used does not itself bridge the cross-cultural gap that separates the word from its historical beginnings, it goes in the right direction.

Homeric Hero

The great word tree *hero* starts at the root-cap of the ancient Greeks. *Hero* was first of all Homeric, used in the *Iliad* (c. 850 BC)—*hrws*—as a title of honor for the Greeks before Troy, for the warrior who was free and brave. But how so? They could be exceedingly devious at times, sulky and almost craven as well as courageous. All could die by sword thrust or arrow's bite. Worse, as the opening lines to the *Iliad* exclaim: these men had "strong souls / of heroes, but gave their bodies to the delicate feasting / of dogs, of all birds" (*Iliad*, I, 3-5). Heroes could also wind up as refuse devoured by scavengers.

The free, brave warriors: Odysseus who was like Zeus in counsel; Telamonian Ajax; Menelaos of the great war cry; Agamemnon, the shepherd of the people; even swift-footed, brilliant Achilles were none of them squeaky-clean, shining knights in white armor. They affirmed Shakespeare's lines: "They say, best men are molded out of faults / And, for the most, become much more the better / for being a little bad" (*Measure For Measure*, V.1. 437–439). Homeric heroes were not distinguished by mere warriorhood or valor. Life was a battle in a passionate, whimsical, god-driven universe. Life was not perfect. So be it. They fought. To win. And the fact that they won made each the protector and progenitor of their tribe.

Reality and word "hrws" were immensely human; *hero* in its Homeric genesis was not a person immaculately protected by the armor of divinity, did not equal "demigod." This is an ordinary misconception, easily available in the second or third-hand knowledge of most dictionaries, encyclopedias, and reference books. Heroes as originally understood in Western civilization were glorious by virtue of the risks that are known and taken by human flesh and blood. They lived at a peak of human strength and vulnerability, embodied a rallying cry for their people—which thrilled people to their spine.

They had an intense presence that no one doubted. As the scholar Carl Kerényi (1960) insisted, in its original Homeric Greek sense *heroes* were not willowy phantoms. They were "marked by their substantiality, by a remarkable solidity" (p. 2). Equally close to the original truth would be Emerson's (1983), reading, that "the hero is he who is immovably centered" (p. 1096). They were vigorous, helpful egotists.

Striking from heroism's beginning in the Homeric environment was how *hero* could also refer to women defended by the gods, as Medea, wronged wife of Jason, or Penthesilea, the Amazon heroine who fought at Troy and who, legend has it, Achilles fell in love with as he killed her. This gender-free usage would extend into the Hellenistic period in works such as the prose romance Heliodorus' *Aethiopica* (c. 3rd century AD). Regardless of gender, the word *hero* in its Homeric inception had about it a quality of weight and integrity, an aura of tragedy and the generous human essence of the sacred among the secular. The ancient Egyptians, in comparison, had very few heroes. Their pharaohs had a virtual monopoly on glory, divinity, and exalted chicanery.

Demigod Hero

Second, after Homer came *hero* as demigod in classical Mediterranean myth, legend, and history with heroism's extension into the works of Hesiod (fl. 8th century BC), Pindar (c. 518–c. 438 BC), Herodotus (c. 484–c. 425 BC), Virgil (70–19 BC), and Ovid (43 BC–18 AD) and the likes of Herakles and Aeneas, the preservation and transformation of the Greek heritage for Roman use—specially in the period of Hellenistic civilization (c. 300 BC–275 AD).[2] Altered from the Homeric standard, this later stress on hero as demigod made heroes into shadows of a god or goddess, a greater father or mother. Hero as demigod has been the moral fantasy of victory over death. The demigod is lighter than the hero. As Friedrich Nietzsche (1966) wrote in *Beyond Good and Evil*: "around the hero everything turns into a tragedy; around the demigod, into a satyr play" (p. 83)—that is, into comedy.

The Greek philosopher Heraclitus (c. 535 BC–c. 475) was quick to note this enigma from the start. He stressed how the demigod was a prickly paradox, however much believed. He wrote in one of his epigrams, so much like zen koans, about the supernatural force supposedly embodied in demigod heroes. How could men be so blended? "The sea is the purest and the impurest of all waters," wrote Heraclitus. "For fish it is drinkable and very healthy—but to men undrinkable and deadly" (Heraclitus, Fragment 61) How could divine elixir coarse through man's veins?

No matter, the human need was there—is there—to conceive of demigod heroes. And when the demigods died they did not die as men and women, but became the beacons of the constellations, a place never gained by Homeric heroes. They are there still, the demigod men, women, animals, monsters, and household goods: Orion, Pleiades, Hercules, Pagasus, Centaurus, Aquila, Cassiopeia.

This half-human, half-god growth of meaning would see the word introduced into the English language in the Middle-English of Ranulf Higden's renowned universal history the *Polychronicon*, translated from Latin into English by John of Trevisa in 1387, who noted that Sibylla Erythrea [*sic*.]: "wroot moche of Criste, and hat openliche, as in his verse of heroes" (Higden, Trevisa, II, 401). Thus the word *hero* became a canonical mantle that wrapped Jesus Christ, demigod, born of woman, son of God in Christian mythology.

The word *heroine*, in contrast, would take some time to appear in English—not till the Neoclassical Period and the Restoration Age of the 1650s–1660s (with the influence of Queen Henrietta Maria and Henrietta of England): first, as a female intermediary between a woman and a goddess; second, as a woman of exalted courage; and third, by the early 1700s, *heroine* became the neologism for a work of literature's principal female character.[3]

Women's secondary status in Western culture as *heroine* would not be overcome until the late 20th century—when American English achieved this progress. It came about first by women as equal to men, as heroes, in the U.S. counterculture of the 1960s, and then its general acceptance in the post-war popular culture of the 1970s. First, in U.S. political culture with women members of the radical *Weathermen* movement; second with Marvel comics' male and female *X Men* heroes. And, by the 1990s, *hero* had gained general acceptance as a gender-neutral term in the sense of a person of any gender noted for his or her courageous action.

Noble Gentleman Hero

Third, to root and trace again, that same period of Middle English and then of the early Renaissance made of hero a contrast with the *vyleyn*—the villain: the low-born, base-minded rustic of ignoble ideas and instincts, and thus exalted the hero as the noble gentleman. Sir Thomas Mallory's *Le*

Morte D'Arthur (1485) about King Arthur and his Round Table knights, many French medieval *chansons de geste* about the likes of Roland or the *chevalier* Bayard, and the bumptious, battling knights, royal lovers and hardy monsters of Ariosto's *Orlando Furioso* (1532), personified this adventurous, chivalric type in contrast to the peasant, the knave, the scoundrel.

Reality and word *hero* now had about it an ivory shell of class and aristocracy—those of long lineage and purple blood—which it would never forfeit in European civilization. Noble gentleman hero was greatly discredited in the Euro-American Revolutionary period (1765–1815). Very important in this respect for the United States is the sacred law of its *Constitution* (1787) that: "No title of nobility shall be granted by the United States" (I, 9, 8). Common man and woman are not to be lorded over. But the noble gentleman hero returned with a vengeance in the Victorian period—a rapscallion Tory brilliantly embodied by Baroness Orczy's Scarlet Pimpernel figure (in plays, novels, movie: 1905-1935), whose direct lineal descendant was no other than that charming, ruthless upholder of The Establishment: James Bond, created by British journalist and secret service agent Ian Fleming (1908–1964).[4]

Renaissance Hero

Fourth, come to the Renaissance and one had rebirth into heroism. It is pervasive in the political, military, and artistic life of the time. Giorgio Vasari's *Lives* (1550), dedicated to Cosimo de' Medici, is a catalogue of heroic artistic achievements—especially Italian. The potency of national identity has ever been affirmed by heroism (the absence of pan-European heroes is a vacuum at the center of the current European monetary and bureaucratic union). European life of Renaissance times, beginning in the north of Italy, was peopled with larger-than-life men and women: Dante Alighieri (1265–1321), at the cusp where Medieval touched Renaissance, Alfonso the Magnanimous of Naples (1396–1458), Boccaccio (1313–1375), Lorenzo the Magnificent (1449–1492), Machiavelli (1469–1527), Pope Alexander VI (ruled 1492–1503)—to name a few.[5] European civilization underwent a seismic change from one phase to another, one that would also result in European settlement of the Americas, fueled by heroic individualism.

In the Middle Ages, as the German cultural historian Jacob Burckhardt (1818–1897) wrote: "man was conscious of himself only as a member of a race, people, party, family, or corporation—only through some general category" (Burckhardt, 1950, p. 81). But, come the Renaissance, and this veil "melted into air" and man's "*subjective* side . . . asserted itself . . . man became a spirited *individual,* and recognized himself as such"—as a free spirit (Burckhardt, 1950, p. 263). Not without cost. Michelangelo's gigantic sculpture *David* (1501) remains an iconic embodiment of the Renaissance heroic ideal. David was a deifier, a giant killer, the boy who would be king, heroic in a sense that involved "a contempt for convenience and a sacrifice of all those pleasures that contribute to what we usually call civilized life," as Sir Kenneth Clark noted of this sublime piece of unrest. The Renaissance appearance of the heroic transcended the mundane pleasures of security and well-being. "It's the enemy of happiness. And yet we recognize that to despise material obstacles and even to defy the blind forces of fate is man's supreme achievement" (Clark, 1969, p. 97).

The heroism of the European Renaissance was an audacity fueled by the sentiment of honor. Burckhardt insisted on the deep, human relation between honor and heroism; honor that "enigmatic mixture of conscience and egotism which often survives"—even in modern man—"after he has lost, whether by his own fault or not, faith, love, and hope" (Burckhardt, 1950, p. 263). Honor does not guarantee virtuous or noble qualities. But it can be a wellspring, a fountain, which, like the hero, exists as source and rallying force when all else appears lost.[6]

Novel Hero

Fifth, when the novel started to appear in Europe as a widespread form, which began with the most significant of the early novels, Cervantes' *Don Quixote* (1605), *hero* was then applied to the chief character in a work of literature, equivalent to *protagonist*. The great word tree—root and bole, branch and leaf—extended outward as heroism expressed a high level of sentiment and exaltation for ordinary efforts that alternately celebrated and satirized the extraordinary amid the ordinary. As exemplary hero, The Knight of the Sad Countenance, Don Quixote, is a tangle of idealism and realism, knight and squire, head-in-the-clouds madness and feet-on-the-ground sanity.

With Cervantes the generic soil of the novel enriched the hero as a person within modern, democratic reach. Medium was the message. Without the novel, there was no equivalent central-character hero. The epic, romance, and drama—the other long narrative forms of their time favored by the literate power elite—did not allow the reader the private, extensive attention which the novel gave to incident, plot form, point of view, complex motives, and character.

The social function of the novel was crucial. In Europe and the United States, from approximately the 1740s through the First World War I, the novel was *the* imaginative mirror and secular purveyor of values for the middle class. In a world without electricity, yet of revolutionary cultural, economic, and political changes along with ever-increasing literacy, people reflected on and came to understand their own world through a world of word and print communication. *Hero* as a novel's chief character was not merely fictive, but the protagonist of contemporary conflicts—a reflective relationship subsequently taken over by the storied events of movie, radio, television, and eventually the computer game hero.

Revolutionary Hero

Following the Renaissance, the sixth great heroic figure is the revolutionary hero. Here Europe and America part ways, establish different heroic traditions. America's revolutionary heroes start first with the nations Founding Fathers and Mothers, John and Abigail Adams, George and Martha Washington, of the late Colonial through Federalist periods (1760s through the late 1820s). Europe's revolutionary heroism was born of the French Revolution (1789–1795) more than any other single event. Out of the treasure chest of comparisons one could make here, one stands out above all others: Europe established the *moral* revolutionary prototype—whereas America established the *litigious* revolutionary prototype.

Objectively defined, a revolution is the right of the citizens of a society to violently overthrow incompetent or unjust rulers in order to establish a better government. But America's first prototypical set of heroic leaders, subsequently monumentalized in everything from the principle of original intent through the paintings of Gilbert Stuart (1755–1828), John Copley (1738–1815), Benjamin West (1738–1820, and John Trumbull (1756–1843), established revolution in the United States as a fundamental alteration of a peaceful, procedural nature uniquely allowed by the *U.S. Constitution*—for example, in the 1791 Bill or Rights or the 1964 Civil Rights Act.

Was this not odd considering the dominant role of violence in U.S. culture? No, because violence was established as an individual right, guaranteed by the gun ownership law of the U.S. Constitution's Second Amendment. While revolution was to be worked out by the lawyers, not the guns—this the great gift of the heroic founders.

In contrast, Europe's royal institutions of government and church-state union created national institutions of mystical authority. Europeans had the two bodies of the king, the royal-religious and individual-state "We"—royal sovereignty; which the United States had brazenly replaced with "We, The People"—popular sovereignty. Moral power, ideology, and claims to spiritual transcendence were needed in Europe to change regimes, in order to decapitate the old leadership. America's revolutionaries figuratively committed patricide when they broke from King George III. But French revolutionary heroes George Danton and Maximillien Robespierre on one level *actually did* kill their father and mother when they executed King Louis XIV and Marie Antoinette.

In all cases, a great moral force was needed both to justify and energize this killing of the parents by their "subjects," their children. European civilization has subsequently been a much more morally obsessive environment than the United States. This has been a mixed blessing and has resulted in many extremes, from Europe's federal legitimization of heroic fascism in the 1930s and 1940s, through the removal of the death penalty by the late 20th century.

Industrial Age Hero

Moving onto the seventh stage of the development of *hero* — one comes to the industrialism of the 19th and 20th centuries. This brought new forms and diffusions of literacy and information, of uncommon art and common levels of news reporting, achieved the new enrichment of naturalism, realism, the facts and figures of the modern workaday man and woman. When *hero* moved into this era of industrial transformation it entered "the triumph of a society which believed that economic growth rested on competitive private enterprise," as E. J. Hobsbawm (1975/1979) wrote in *The Age of Capital*, "on success in buying everything in the cheapest market (including labor) and selling in the dearest." The driving engine and sound foundations of this system was the growing middle class, the "bourgeoisie composed of those whom energy, merit, and intelligence had raised to their position and kept there" (p. xvii). Middle-class heroes, and lower, arrived, thrived, and multiplied.

Hero underwent a radical shift of tone and content in the new industrial age. It came to express a horizontal range of values rather than vertical. Heroism extended among the people, spread at the vernacular level. Heroism was no longer exclusively a top–down matter of king versus serf. This new horizontal emphasis was increasingly present in literary works ranging from the bestselling fiction of Balzac, Zola and Maupassant, Defoe and Dickens in Europe, to the writings of Walt Whitman, Frederick Douglass, Stephen Crane, Edith Wharton, Sherwood Anderson, Hemingway, Faulkner, Sinclair Lewis, and John Hersey in America.[7]

Visually, it was at the very heart of Gustave Courbet's and Honoré Daumier's paintings and graphics in 19th–Century France. This new sympathetic gaze, which saw the brilliance of the typical spread into American painting by way of Winslow Homer (1836–1910) and Thomas Eakins (1844–1916), flourished in the first all-American school of "The Eight," New York City's "Ashcan School" of the late 19th and early 20th centuries. Photography and then cinema captured the heroism of the every day, especially the insightful records of portraiture, of war photography and photojournalism, the cinema of social realism, the brilliance of the documentary form. What had been prosaic became poetic.

The mass diffusion and refinement of genre stories in both visual and written forms allowed for the development of common male and female heroes under the safe cover of westerns, science fiction, fantasy, crime, and detective stories. Pulp was poetic. The heroism of the common man and woman finally spread spectacularly across the United States in the news stories, news syndicates, and mass media empires run by William Randolph Hearst, Joseph Pulitzer, C. L. Sulzberger, Henry R. Luce, William S. Paley, Phil and Katharine Graham, along with the Gannett newspaper chain and down to the present-day communications empire run by Rupert Murdoch.

The sum total of this diffusion and consumption of a new, horizontal sensibility for heroes exposed and fixed respect for people in Western, social democracies who before had been comic—the little man or woman, the housewife and the peddler, the bar maid or the laborer, "the forgotten man."[8] In the United States, politically and culturally, the epic pivot for this change was the person and policies of President Franklin Delano Roosevelt, who was the first national leader to effectively disassociate quality from money in the American mind.

Parenthetically, two other key processes also took place in the transition of *hero* into modern, industrialized times. First, the glory gauge was progressively pumped up. The great wars—social, cultural, military, economic, domestic, and international—of the 19th, 20th, and 21st centuries fed this need. For bittersweet reasons. Sweet: the genuine achievements of warriors and reformers. Bitter: because the creation of glorious heroes obscured the great buying, selling, and whoring of war, the waste and cannibalism of the human spirit practiced in the "dark Satanic mills" of factory and workshop.[9] Both realities demanded monuments of heroic glory to commemorate or obscure their activities.

Second, key processes in the transition of heroes into modern times was a cultural choice of values that posed Europe against the United States. The principal contrastive element in the Old World versus New World respect for *hero* has been the difference between a spiritual, elitist emphasis in the European hero versus a material, popular emphasis in the American hero. In Europe, heroic status has mostly belonged to a chosen few; in America, it became a right. In Europe, it was a given genius (a force of nature); in America, it was an achieved goal (aspiration). Class and quality as opposed to identity and selfhood. The chosen one versus the engineer: think France's Charles de Gaulle versus America's Charles Lindbergh; Rastignac or Julien Sorel versus Huck Finn or Sister Carrie.[10]

The Copious Hero

Eighth and last of the intertwining veins of essential traits across time has been the contemporary dilemma of *hero*—its embarrassment of riches, the copious hero. By the late 20th and 21st centuries the term *hero* had inflated into as many parts and apparent types as Mickey Mouse had busy brooms to deal with in Disney's *Sorcerer's Apprentice*. Western mass media and audience consumption from the time of the Franco–Prussian War in Europe (1870–1871), the Civil War (1861–1865), and the Spanish–American War in the United States (1898), took reality and concept of *hero* by storm.

Like a set of rogue magicians inebriated with their own powers, and aided by economies of scale, producers and consumers made of *hero* a copious heaven of popular constellations. The electric web of mass media and telecommunications that charged and shaped the 20th and now the 21st centuries have stretched *hero* to lengths undreamed of by sane Cervantes or mad Don Quixote.

Read through all the encyclopedias, dictionaries, and thesauruses you can find. Soak in all the mass media you can bear. And out of the English-language cornucopia of the Information Age bursts out for *hero* the linguistic nightmare:

1. *The brave person.* The adventurer, combatant, daredevil, warrior, soldier, the brave heart, the paladin.
2. *The risk-taker.* The explorer, pioneer, pathfinder, voyager, wanderer, fortune-hunter, gambler, speculator, entrepreneur, inventor, innovator, the doer, the *macher*, businessman, pirate, rogue, romantic, swashbuckler.
3. *The dignitary.* The big cheese, big deal, big gun, big name, big shot, big stuff, big banana, big cahunah, bigwig, big momma, big guy, the heavyweight, hot dog, hotshot, the luminary, mighty mahatma, major leaguer, the personality, the somebody, the someone, the V.I.P., the fearless leader.
4. *The champion.* The winner, the victor, the ace, the champ, the defender, endorser, exponent, the victor, the worthy one, the lord and master, number one, the best, numero uno, the titleholder, top dog, guardian, the protector, vindicator, the white knight, the good samaritan, the ordinary guy hero, a Lenny Skutnick.[11]
5. *The defeater.* The successful challenger, the odds low winner, the conquering hero, the subjugator, the activist, the remaker, the hate buster, the truth teller, the crusader, the reformer, the good cop, police officer, detective, crime fighter, fireman, firewoman, the rescue worker.
6. *The worshiped one.* The adored, apotheosized one, the martyr, the saint, the prophet, the visionary, the canonized, the sanctified one, the inspired one, minister, priest, nun, rabbi, elder, *sheikh*, *mullah*, *imam*, doctor, the lifesaver, helping hand, exalted one, glorified one, the one whom people are mad about, are daffy about, look up to, deify, dote on, are nuts about, wild about.
7. *The example.* The epitome, the role model, lodestar, the paradigm, the archetype, the quintessence, those who are the real

thing, who have the right stuff, the best, who are the standard by which others are measured, the touchstone, the alchemist, the culture hero, the local hero, the anti-hero, gone but not forgotten, the last hero.

8. *The celebrity.* The big name, big gun, big guy, the famous one, the diva, prima donna, the luminary, the personality, somebody who is somebody, the heavy, the lionized one, the living legend, the one in the spotlight, the leading lady, the leading man, the star, the movie star, the hollywood star, the star of stage and screen, the celebrity, famous one, the superstar, matinée idol, pop idol, pop star, pop hero, the notorious one, the headliner, woman or man most admired, the actor, actress, the leading lady, the big wig, man or woman of the hour, the big name, big cheese, Mr. Big, Mrs. Big, Ms. Big.

9. *The commodity.* The hero sandwich, the trademarked, *TM*, Wrangler brand of "hero socks" for men, hero life insurance ads, hero issues of *Time*, *Newsweek*, *Sports Illustrated*, the merchandising of hero figures from Buster Brown in the early 20th century down through the latest, blockbuster, hero-soaked movies, TV shows and video games by, about, and for the sake of selling heroes, the Pennsylvania Goodyear Commercial Truck Tires "Highway Hero Award," Houston's texasrecycles.org H-E-B© "Go Home A Hero"™ ecological plastic bags, WRQ's internet technology campaign: "In the Information Integration World You Can Be the Hero,"© and the "Heroes Aren't Hard to Find"© Web site on the internet. And so it goes.

All of which amounts to what? Too much of a good thing? A stretch from the noble to the ridiculous? A clash of lightning storms with smoke and mirrors? Is there a pattern of relationships amid this turmoil of meanings that firmly, clearly delineates *hero*?

Hero has come full circle from its earliest days of Homeric assertion and egotism, glory, gender-free usage, superb imperfection, need to relate to and serve a group—from the ninth century BC to the present day. We are now at a sum point of people molded out of their faults, the demigod hero, chivalric hero, renaissance individualistic hero, revolutionary hero, central character hero, popular hero, the embarrassment-of-riches, modern cornucopia of heroes. Altogether the meanings for *hero* have accrued like the make-up of Russian dolls, one over the other, each inside the other—all together as one.

The structure of heroism is the result of social construction. People build their heroes. The essential processes we now seek.

First the noun, now the verb of the thing. For both western Europe and the United States share a key set of formative elements that structure the hero. But each culture area has used these molding forces in different ways. It is in the anthropological nature of culture to be both universal and particular. Everyone eats. But how and what people eat varies greatly among cultures.

To reduce the shape-giving set to its essentials, the most important for the social construction of *hero* are story; collective representation; archetypes; lightning; charisma; fame; propaganda, advertising, and information; nexus; role model; gender; leadership; the natural.

Story

There must be a *story*. Men adjust to their environment through the medium of stories that reconstruct their common concerns on the logic of a narrative model. A story is a rhyme of events that makes a hero's life memorable. The best stories beat out a primal, complementary rhythm: like sea waves and blood throb—and the audience feels echoes in themselves.

Plus a story is an open explanation. It shows better than it tells. It is portrait rather than caricature, art rather than criticism. Sequential narrative, the force of the mimetic, evokes natural patterns—tree grows from acorn, summer follows spring, "but when I became a man, I put away childish things"—which draws the audience in closer to the camp fire where the story is told.

The audience is at least half of the story. The great teller is a bard who sings the song of the tribe. The basic triumphs and conflicts of the hero are rooted in the society and culture to which our hero belongs. There is no such thing as a disembodied hero, an abstract hero. They are fruit of the soil, nurtured by a real environment. The hero impresses their audience with personal recognition; the hero is surrogate.

Collective Representation

Collective representation is a superb idea that was first conceived by the Alsatian-French social scientist Emile Durkheim (1858–1917). Applied to story, it means the totemic power of narrative and the talisman force of hero. In plain language: a familiar pattern that is believed to be lucky. This familiar pattern does not have to be a story: It could be a flag (Union Jack, le *Tricolore*, Old Glory), an animal with a certain character (bull dog, cock rooster, bald eagle), a sacred place, monument, building, or sculpture (London's St. Paul's Cathedral, *L'Arc de triomphe* in Paris, or the Capitol building in Washington, D.C.).

The hero's life collects the problems and challenges with which his or her people are most concerned. They give their heartfelt attention, concentrate their spiritual energy, on the events of the hero's life. They charge them with meaning. The hero is magnified with belief. Faith in the hero creates sacredness; and thus the group composes belief in itself. The hero—an embodied totem—is not sacred in and of him or herself. The hero is an organic creation, nurtured into existence, or extinguished, by the group which he or she collectively represents.

Archetype

Some psychologists, cultural historians, and literary criticism readers have taken the phenomenon of collective representation so far up another notch that the hero has been termed an *archetype*. At which point, it seems to me, the shape-giving force of collective representation shades off from social science into mysticism. Faith is belief in things unseen, but known to be there. An archetype is an original pattern or model of which all things of the same type are copies or representations of C. G. Jung (1875–1961) championed archetypes as an inherited idea or mode of thought derived from the experience of the race—the collective unconscious, and thus present in the unconscious of the individual. The continuity and vitality of archetypes allows the cultural translation from the language of the past into the speech of the present.

The archetype is an awfully satisfying idea, but totally unprovable. Each hero is not what they used to be; they reflect an original light. As such, through Jungian thinking, an archetype offers each attentive observer an individuation process wherein they may discover themselves. Archetype offers the ultimate spiritual role model. With hero as archetype, a proto-type—be it the good mother, the evil mother, the trickster, the first hunter, warrior, savior, beauty, she-cat or fertility giver—an anthropomorphic, spiritual absolute returns again and again. Which you will subconsciously *know*; dowse into and discover yourself with—so Jungian reasoning goes.

The hero as archetype is the eternal return of a magnificent DNA pattern that will not stop. So it goes beyond the life of any one generation. The archetype break the bonds of time. To know them is to love them, be in awe of them, to drink that eternal elixir.

Lightning

Much of the reflections on heroes is heady stuff. Where, for example, does a hero's force come from? Archetype isn't the only spiritual solution. An older, traditional response is that the hero sprang from Promethean fire. This is the hero as *lightning*, an idea luminously employed by the most influential 19th-century Anglo-American thinker in heroism studies, Thomas Carlyle (1795–1881). In his rhapsodic harangue *On Heroes, Hero-*

Worship and the Heroic in History (1899), Carlyle claimed [*sic*]: "The Great Man was always as lightning out of Heaven; the rest of men waited for him like fuel, and then they too would flame" (p. 71).

Hero as lightning turned history into biography, into personal spirit. This was dangerous thinking. Lightning is beautiful, capricious, and cruel. As political reasoning, Carlyle's effect was both exhilarating and stifling. Following his line of belief about the hero: What happens to the social community? What happens to the ideas, customs, and skills of the group? They get sizzled away by the dominating Big Burning One. Carlyle authored the biggest cliché ever to come out of heroism studies [*sic*]: "The History of the World is but the Biography of great men" (Carlyle, 1899, p. 27).

Welcome The Emperor, *Der Fuhrer*, *Il Duce*, Evita Peron, Lincoln the Messiah, the Apotheosis of George Washington, Kingfish Huey Long, Father Charles Coughlin, Malcolm X (before his visit to Mecca), down to John F. Kennedy's shabby eternal flame and Joe Dimaggio's eternal rose laid at the mausoleum of Marilyn Monroe.[12] The truths of the past are the clichés of the present. But cliché is thought and language half-dead, thus half-alive, still lingering. Carlyle's lightning hero opens the way to the hagiography, the fearless-leader worship of authoritarianism, totalitarian rule, the demagogue. Demagogue is demigod. (Asked what it was like to kiss Marilyn Monroe, Tony Curtis replied: "Like kissing Adolf Hitler".)[13] In Western civilization, these authoritarian heroes are much diminished from what they were. But does not the power ever threaten to return?

Charisma

What brings the authoritarian hero back time and again is their *charisma*. Charisma extended from Carlyle's idea of a power of uncompromising force that equally "rejects all rational economic conduct" and "makes a sovereign break with all traditional or rational norms" (Weber, 1946, pp. 247, 250). As theorized by sociologist Max Weber (1864–1920) with regard to institutional power, charisma is a unique, magical quality evident either in an individual or in an office (such as the president or the presidency), which can dangerously destabilize social order.

Charisma entertains. It is evident in the political force which evokes an immediate personal assent from a crowd or in movie star magnetism which charms the audience into pleasant voyeurism. British musical producer George Martin (1996, in McCabe-Bippart, part 3) defined charisma with regard to the Beatles: "They had charisma. They were the kind of people you actually felt better for being with." Prior to the 20th century, charisma was not machine-produced, but by the 1920s *charisma* came to be enhanced and equated with *photogenic, mediagenic, entertaining*. And froth replaced drink.

Fame

Fame is the logical extension of heroic glory into the present time. In modern, mass-mediated times it has become inordinately important, disproportionate to heroism itself. Again, a key to understanding lies at the root-cap. In Homeric Greek "glory" or "glorious" was *klutos*—a term applied to gods and men. Thus, Zeus was "glorious shaker of the earth" (*Iliad*, IX, pp. 361-362). Listen up. Reference to glory was usually to things heard, hearkened to—which implied obedience. Like thunder or lightning.

Fame devolved in the 20th and 21st Centuries into *celebrity*—a force that threatens to cheapen and end heroism (or else force heroism into finding different ways in which to be expressed). Celebrity displaces the heroic because it provides form without content, the narcissism of heroic attraction, the two-way opiate of audience and entertainer, as an end in itself. Froth becomes drink. Insubstantial image replaces substantial discourse.

The celebrity is the new eminence of our contemporary Information Age, this "person who is known for his well-knownness . . . a new substitute for the hero" (Boorstin, 1961/1987, p. 57), media figments with short, shiny shelf lives who help sell TV—such as: Donna Rice, Gennifer Flowers, Paula Jones, Monica Lewinsky, Alexandra Polier—who detract from more serious issues of public policy.[14] "The hero was distinguished by achievement; the celebrity by his image or trademark" (p. 60). "The hero created himself; the celebrity is created by the media. The hero was a big man; the celebrity is a big name" (p. 61).

What is worse, celebrity heroism produced well-knownness that could be harnessed to sell products. After her affair with U.S. Senator Gary Hart in 1987, Donna Rice did lucrative MTV commercials endorsing No Excuses jeans: "I make No Excuses—I only wear them" (Slansky, 1989, p. 212). Or consider the fate of Charles Lindbergh, whose life took on a lower, monetary meaning in the late 1920s when Lindbergh sold the $37.50 Bulova "Lone Eagle" wrist watch in magazine and billboard endorsements; one of many spectacular cases of mercantile degradation (Atwan, McQuade, & Wright, 1979, pp. 282-324).

Propaganda, Advertising, Information

Or was it? To tout the hero's name and fame is an old tradition, and not without respect. Enter here the snappy triplets *propaganda, advertising,* and *information.* Heroic actions told in story have great power to convince and lead. During World War II Americanism was defended by a bastion of Hollywood movies. One of the most popular movies of all times, *Casablanca* (1942), is probably the greatest U.S. propaganda movie ever made champions propagate the faith (the literal definition of propaganda).

The movie's champions propagate the faith (the literal definition of propaganda). Rick–Bogart in *Casablanca* affirmed America's wartime commitments. Americanism triumphed over the two other great "isms" of the 20th century—communism and fascism—significantly by virtue of the propaganda charm and power of its mass media and popular culture.

Advertising, the commodity propaganda of our common mass-mediated life in the United States and Western Europe, assaults its audience with the monologue of the beautiful product endorsed by astonishing people. Heroic charisma has been harnessed. It was done with women's rights advocate Elizabeth Cady Stanton (who endorsed Fairy Soap), William McKinley (whose face and signature sold Waterman pens), King Edward VIII of Great Britain (endorsed Angelus Player pianos), Ty Cobb (Tuxedo tobacco), Amelia Earhart (Lucky Strike cigarettes), Eleanor Roosevelt (the Zenith hearing aid), Ernest Hemingway (Ballantine ale). And so it goes. Rare is the public personality, the hero of modern times, who has not succumbed to the siren call, to this traditional marriage, of income and publicity. Certainly more so in the United States than elsewhere (Atwan et al., 1979).[15]

George Plimpton (1997) told a story at the end of the documentary *When We Were Kings* how once, at the end of a graduation speech at Harvard University, Muhammad Ali was called upon by a cheering audience to give a poem. So he pointed to himself and said: "Me." He pointed to his audience and said: "We." The crowd roared.

For the audience is at least half the story. Of their hero, they want more. One reason for endorsements of the celebrated has been public thirst for heroic relics. Public approval by someone who is famous or respected, when product or personality match, thus allows people to buy a little bit of that original aura. Even more so with art and politics in our age of reproductions.

Cultural historian Walter Benjamin (1892–1940) first put this issue on the map of the sociology of mass media in his "The Work of Art in an Age of Mechanical Reproduction" (1936). Benjamin showed how we increasingly live in a world that's all copies, without an original. In which the magic is for sale. It's foolish, of course; but so weren't the relics and indulgences of the middle ages as purveyed by the ecumenical church. Except we have no Luther. Moreover, if Benjamin was right, does culture—and heroes—have an independent inertia? Is culture *not* organically handed down from generation to generation; but reproduced? So the key to any subject of cultural concern is not so much the subject—but who chooses what is manufactured and sold. Who buys and why.

We not only live in the Market Age, but the Information Age. In which an endorsement of the right product by the right person at the right time to the right target audience is crucial—no doubt about it, marketing, branding, and advertising are an art; as they say at Young & Rubicam advertising agency: "The product tells you who you are"—the product offers enlightenment, knowledge, inside dope (Marlowe, 2001, interview). When done well, whether it's Elizabeth Cady Stanton selling Fairy Soap or Michael Jordan selling Nike Sneakers, it works. "Utility is the proof of success," said Edison (1931, p. 37). The magnetism of heroism has been successfully industrialized.

Nexus

The hero's approval supplies a need. A great illness of the modern world has been *anomie*—an increasing lack of norms, purpose, a coherent frame of values secured by individuals together in society and culture. The high visibility of a hero sells more than one value at a time. Hero is *nexus*, a concrete analogy drawn from science and mathematics. Nexus is specially needful in the United States. Heroes function as a connection or tie between people. Those linked by heroes can themselves be alone, group members, or groups connected.

In America, the otherwise isolated achieve union by point in common, binding place, intersection of heroic nexus, however short term or long lived, by virtue of Oprah Winfrey, Harry Truman, or Forrest Gump, because of New York City's 9/11 firemen, Mayor Rudi Giuliani, or by rallying round the flag with President George W. Bush. The phenomenon of heroic nexus gives joining and rallying point in an otherwise spectacularly lonesome society. The United States: where more than 25% of the population lives alone, which suffers one of the highest divorce rates in the world and one of the highest prison incarceration rates. Such a friendly land and such a locked-up world. Common heroes provide temporary place of valued agreement, momentary solace. They help create a nation of common myths, common cause, historical memories, and a public culture.

Role Model

Heroes are important as *role models*, very important for young people everywhere and Americans in particular. The hero as role model, an idea pervasive in U.S. social psychology and everyday American life, is greatly reduced in importance in Europe. It is less evident in advertising (or seen as an "Americanization"). Although European social scientists see less free will and far more socioeconomic determinism as decisive shaping factors, the world in which culture critics live gives bias. Role model makes great sense in the individualistic, performance-oriented American culture, much less in the authoritarian, bureaucratic societies of modern Europe.

Gender

In the 20th and 21st centuries the potency of the hero as role model was increased in the United States by the intense focus in everyday life and throughout the media on the politics of *gender* identity. In the Western tradition, if character is fate—then gender has traditionally both expanded and limited that fate, leads the willing or drags the reluctant. Neither Prometheus nor Pandora, or Adam and Eve, are interchangeable in their stories. What they do and the values they represent must be achieved by a man or a woman. Their gender-defined heroism cannot be rewritten.

Or can it? Gender has alternately surfaced and disappeared as a prominent issue in American life from the days of Anne Hutchinson (1591–1643) and Abigail Adams (1744–1818) down to African-American author and educator Bell Hooks (b. 1955, a.k.a.: "bell hooks") and longtime cyber-hero Lara Croft. Since the late 1960s, in particular, gender reality and concept has been most visibly, adroitly, and politically contested in the United States.

Of particular note for the American context of the woman as hero are three elements.

First, *special-interest groups*: the intellectual terrain of literary and social critics and cultural historians—notably the special interest studies of feminism, gay studies, queer theory, male studies, and minority studies that have flourished in the groves of academia since the 1970s—have each attempted to regain heroic values for their group. These schools of U.S. thought laid claim to democratic universalism, to the same heroic rights as other Americans. Their primary objective has been to do away with the double standard, create gender equity, to convince American students, politicians, and business leaders that a level playing field should be provided for all sexes, all minorities. That they too are admirable.

By 1982, this group of public intellectuals had almost helped create an Equal Rights Amendment for the U.S. Constitution, had been very influential in the construction of affirmative action. But American debate in this area has been profound and unsettling, with special interest studies often as biased as a religious crusade. Although this movement has certainly helped to fundamentally improve equal pay for equal work and the advancement of women in various professions.

Ironically, in the process, the gender identity of the hero has become more important by supposedly being less important. Gender, as heroine became hero, became conspicuous by virtue of its absence. Gender has not been overcome. Social and economic expediency has been served. Get more women into all sorts of workplaces, increase consumer spending, get more players into the market culture. As sexual problems, prominence, and debate in American public and private life. Europe, in contrast, has had no Anita King and Judge Thomas, Monica Lewinsky and Bill Clinton scandals in modern times. They do not have the same need to debate sexual values—heroes and villains—as Americans do.

Second, has not the attention given to both ethnic identity and gender in the United States since the 1960s greatly diminished the worry and attention once given to *class*? Whereas gender is shouted from the roof tops, headlines the newspapers, luridly laces the visual culture of movies, TV, Internet telecommunications—class has become a "non dite": something known about but not discussed.[16] America's dirty little secret. The nation's heroes prior to World War II had strong class identity—Franklin Delano Roosevelt: that "betrayer of his class"; Clark Kent–Superman: adopted son of the yeoman, midwestern farmer; Paul Robeson, Billie Holiday: outspoken middle- or lower class Blacks.[17]

Open, vociferous debates about class—amid the historical amnesia of America—was subsequently taboo, offset by the attention given to gender and rights, obscured as a betrayal of the U.S. right to the pursuit of happiness. And class became taboo because of shame. As 34-year-old playwright and culture hero Adam Rapp (c.1969- ; author of *Nocturne* 2000, *Blackbird*, 2002) noted recently about his own poverty-stricken childhood: *normal* was equated with *middle class*, and "when you're poor, you don't want anyone to know you're poor" (McKinley, 2003, p. 1). Losers are the trailer park people, which spells death in a culture of winners.

Third, one result of the movement for gender rights was to remove the romance from heterosexual fidelity and sentimentalism, to create an intensified battle of the sexes in American life, to underline wedding vows with marriage contracts, and specially to intensify both in the popular culture and the U.S. military the role and profession of the warrior woman. To affirm *women's heroic status*, Americans returned to Western culture's Homeric roots. The strong woman warrior hero has become steadily visible in video-game vixens like Lara Croft and Trinity, in best-selling games like *Cy Girls* or *Brute Force*, and in action-adventure movies: *X2: X-Men United*, *The Matrix Reloaded,* and *Charlie's Angels: Full Throttle*. And, with each new American war, in the U.S. military itself. No more "our boys in the field"; now it's: "our fighting men and women."

Leadership and The Natural

Which leads to the last and final shape-giving forces in the social construction of hero—the creation of *leadership*, the belief in and search for the *natural*, which are givens in America and in much of the heroic tradition. Leaders, and the gifted ones, are equally made as well as found, a matter of training and opportunity along with ability and native gifts.

The natural aspect of the hero is just that: They "do what comes naturally." Lincoln read law books as a teenager. Amelia Earhart was born with a blissful sense of taking high risks and escaping. Elvis Presley asked for a guitar for Christmas—not a bike (and got the guitar). Pocahontas naturally had conversations with trees or animals. King Arthur easily loosened the sacred sword from the stone. Legend has it that, from childhood, Cochise was a leader within his tribe of obstreperous Chiricahua Apache. Each a hero based on an innate sense, in accord with and predetermined by nature (and therefore expressing a force of nature); altogether possessed of winning, ingenuous ways. In the United States, the national argument goes, these natural powers are released because the hero exists in a political environment that guarantees the principle of "Life, Liberty, and the pursuit of Happiness." The principle that in each American there is some great kernel waiting to burst out and bloom.

But should heroism be equated with leadership? Heroic examples may provide moral leadership. Management, or the charisma of high office, can provide the driving force of leadership. Employees obey the boss. But people in leadership positions act out roles of great power more by virtue of chance, circumstances, and election rather than by spectacular ability. Most U.S. presidents were more like James Buchanan than Abraham Lincoln. If and when one individual combines leader and hero—this phenomenon permanently reinforces the charisma of the position, activates the process of leader, follower, situation, objective, and leaves behind a heritage which redefines the circulation of elites (as Martin Luther King did in America or Nelson Mandela did in South Africa—but singer and social activist Paul Robeson failed to do in the United States).

In the final analysis, could it be that leadership is a position of authority; heroism is monumental? Leadership: focus of coordination, unification of activities, information, decision making? Heroism: dominance and prestige accrued through self-sacrifice for the greater good? Leadership has place; heroism brands memory?

TYPOLOGY OF U.S. AND EUROPEAN HEROES

To wrap up, I suggest a final typology of the hero in the United States and Europe. Typology of heroes is important not to locate averages, but to find the repertoire of distinguished personalities who continuously encourage their culture to flourish, to be itself.

Culture is a pattern of relationships. It is process. It is not a static list of traits. Heroes are among the repertoire of organic elements which give individual, cultural definitions. Like a divine force, they are life giving. They are a choice of self offered in the cultural context.

Heroes can fruitfully be understood in the Weberian sense of ideal types derived from components. They are empirically observable, historically recognized, heuristic, problem-solving constructions that provide their users with both ways to develop and ways to belong; builders and building blocks both. Heroes are far more coherent than the wild scattershot goods that fly from encyclopedias, dictionaries and thesauruses, mass media and the Internet.

Heroic Types: American

The Pathfinder. Here is the prototype of the American hero: the ground breakers, those who find the path that lead others forward. This is a high-risk profession. Many set out, many die without having achieved their goal. Here is an explorer, a road builder. Here is road as sacred object in American culture: a material expression of hope, of opportunity; potentially accessible to everyone. Examples include Sacajawea, Squanto, Daniel Boone, Charles Lindbergh, Amelia Earhart, Neil Armstrong and Christa McAuliffe.

The Reformer. Here are those who stake their all in order to morally improve the nation, The People, to better the values people live by — often whether their fellow man or woman want them improved or not. A delicate task and an explosive heroism. Often religious, even if they are atheist; with a faith in something unseen, but believed, a bible. The reformers are most prone of all popular heroes and heroines to become a martyr to a cause. Examples include Patrick Henry, Susan B. Anthony, John Brown, Frederick Douglass, Franklin Delano Roosevelt and Eleanor Roosevelt, Martin Luther King, Cesar Chavez, and Rosa Parks.

The Salesman. These figures deal best with the interchange of material goods, money, and profit. They live for the dream and art of buying and selling, give and take, advantage that is sometimes win–win, sometimes win–loose. And the need to sell, stop, then sell again. Salesman or woman do not merely sell socks; but hope. They conjure, entertain, perform. They possess the gift to release the magic from the mundane. Here the high risk is to walk a knife edge between the material and the spiritual, money and its opposite, Eldorado and The City on a Hill. Examples include P.T. Barnum, Andrew Carnegie, Charles F. Kettering, Henry Kaiser, Willy Loman, Michael Jordan, and Bill Gates.

The Outcast. These people are rejected from the mainstream or are those who rejected it. Conspicuous figures who could not deny what they are, who refuse self-denial, and are cast out. The outcast lives a life of values in contrast with middle-class, commonplace norms. Outcasts may begin inside the regular norms, then move out. Yet many outcasts are gradually integrated into the mainstream, will eventually become representative of the mainstream itself. Odd becomes even, out becomes in. Examples are: Anne Hutchinson, Thomas Paine, Billy the Kid, John Reed, Emma Goldman, Margaret Sanger, Eugene Debs, Helen Keller, Harry Hopkins, and Betty Friedan.[18]

The Thinker. The thinkers who have received the most praise and worship in America have been the engineers, inventors, mechanical wizards, problem solvers who strike it rich for themselves and improve everyday life with their marvelous achievements. Are they "intellectual"? If so, they are generally quarantined to schools. Americans are traditionally uneasy with their abstract thinkers; "intellectual" equals "ineffectual." As President Eisenhower defined the term: someone "who takes more words than necessary to tell more than he knows" (Levinson, 1967, p. 123). Examples of America's heroic thinkers, are Benjamin Franklin, Eli Whitney, Samuel Morse, Henry Ford, Thomas Edison, Rachel Carson, Edward R. Murrow, and Thomas Watson ("Think": IBM's original motto).

The Politician. What is the politician? It is an expression of civic needs, a necessary evil, an acrobat who remains consistently perpendicular while sustaining equal pressure from all sides? The greased pig in the game of American politics is the president, who tries to be everything to everyone, to lead where most will follow, who is created, destroyed, and recreated again. Presidents come and go; the *presidency* remains. Examples include George Washington, Abraham Lincoln, Teddy Roosevelt, John F. Kennedy, Ronald Reagan—and the nations spectacular, spotty history of city mayors (from James Couzens in Detroit to James Curley in Boston).

The Military. This group is the soldier, the warrior, that personification of power that extends and enforces justice and security for the nation-state. They serve under government control, although they possess their own codes of law and honor. They often get squeezed between deep lines of conflict within the nation-state. Strangest of all in the United States: deep respect for the military, but the curious absence of fascism. Miles Standish, Tecumseh, Cochise, Andrew Jackson, Robert E. Lee, Sergeant Alvin York, Dwight D. Eisenhower, Audie Murphy, Charles Yeager, and Norman Schwarzkopf are some good examples.[19]

Time and space forbids extended analysis of these American types—but certain patterns are clear: The overall gender, numerical superiority of women as reformers, but a minority of women as salesmen (with similar "on and off" pattern for pathfinders vs. politicians). Sports figures alternate from reformers to salesman (e.g., Muhammad Ali vs. Michael Jordan). There are wheels within wheels: the figure, the type within the type—such as the U.S. immigrant in their first generation or the Okies of the Great Depression as outcast. It is also very curious in the United States how the big-time American salesmen have learned to take the edge off their greed with the sharing device of philanthropy, which keeps the money, ups the glory, shares the wealth.

Heroic Types: European

Is there such a thing as Europe? It exists geographically as a culture area with broad patterns. As contended by Professor Terry G. Jordan (1988) in his classic *The European Culture Area—A Systematic Geography*, Europe's first defining trinity of characteristics is a religious tradition of Christianity, people who speak one of the numerous related Indo-European languages, and are of the Caucasian race. The second defining set is: that modern Europe is also a well-educated, healthy, well-fed population with birth and death rates far below the world average, with an average annual per capita income far above the world average. Its population is dominantly urban, with an industrial-oriented economy, a market-oriented agriculture, an excellent transport system, and stable, freely elected governments.

But so what? That is: so what for heroes? In March 2003, three European associations surveyed six, key European nations in order to identify the great figures whom Europeans cherished. That is, who are their great heroes? If Europeans could choose anyone, they were asked, who would they spend an hour with? The results: each nation chose people of their own nationality, mainly the present leaders of their own country. Europe may, in many ways, be a state (with one currency) but, fundamentally, it is *not* a nation. Coins of their new pan-European currency try to mark out their identity, but not with unity, with difference: the iconography of a pointy German eagle, a flamboyant French Marianne, and DaVinci's trademark, splayed-out Italian Renaissance man. A hero is a symbolic dimension of vital social identity—which they lack. There are *national* typologies, but no firm European heroic typologies as yet.

Since the 1990s, a lot of time and money has been invested by European cultural organizations mining for common heroes. This has been evident in magazine ads, parades, television programs and radio talk shows, the creation of pan-European theme parks, the reinforcement of older sacred cultural sites. Particularly striking was how in the year 2000 Paris' Museum of National Arts and Folklore held a highly produced show called *Popular Heroes*, which meant the common heroes of Europe. This was one of the closest approximations to a European heroic typology yet created.

This exhibition began with the holy, medieval crusader figure versus the unholy warrior, Count Dracula in particular. Choice then moved to the puppets and dolls most often played with by children across Europe. The major figure here was Punch-Punchinello, the cruel, thick-headed, lying puppet.[20]

Then came the naval hero, particularly Jean Bart (1650–1702)—decidedly, as well, an heroic builder of colonies. Followed by the romantic, tragicomic figure of Cyrano de Bergerac; and the blatantly absurd fool, like Wilhelm Busch's Max and Moritz. Next in line was the adventurer-explorer hero: Christopher Columbus, Robinson Crusoe, Saint-Exupery—whose adventurous life sometimes led to the rebirth of his nation: such as Garibaldi or Napoleon.[21] The curators then stretched their compass eastward and included the Ukrainian Cossack Mamai, warrior and wise guy, joker, philosopher, *bandura* player and singer.

The exhibit then turned to the common, tragic figure of the fallen soldier, along with the helpful figure of the doctor. Finally, the typology culminated with a threefold crescendo of the celebrity hero (from Che Guevara to Marilyn Monroe); a selection of comic book heroes not well known in the United States (Bécassine, Mr. Vieux Bois, Corto Maltese);[22] and finally an international selection of what the museum's curators termed "guitar heroes": ranging from Hank Marvin and Jeff Beck through Jimi Hendrix and Eddie Van Halen—modern Orpheus' of jazz, blues, and rock and roll. With a few notable exceptions—Joan of Arc, Krimhilde, the figure of the leftist, mainly Russian female worker type, with Marie Curie and Sarah Bernhard—women were absent from this rich visual and textual survey of European heroes. When I asked the curator about this, she replied half-jokingly, half-seriously: "Because women have more common sense than men." And, as the collection's introduction noted: *Pas de héros sans une part de folie*—no heroes without some madness (Groshens, Rannai, & Cdardelle, 2001–2002, p. 15).

Outstanding here as types among this chosen European pantheon at Paris' Museum of National Arts and Folklore, in contrast to the United States, would be Europe's ambivalent warrior; the benevolent healer; the ordinary, unredeemed fallen soldier; the enshrinement of values on the basis of class and privilege (from proud Lord Roland of Charlemagne's medieval court down through the hearty Soviet-socialist worker figure of the late 1940s). Outstanding here as characteristics would be the relative closeness of the distant past (in America we could not begin with our crusader heroes); an affection for cruelty; deep respect for the reality of class; and a decisive sense of gender difference—where mainly men take the risks, gain the glory, play the fool.

CONCLUSION

Civilizations use repertoires of heroes in order that their members might identify themselves individually and as a group. An ocean of difference exists between America and Europe which is not bridged by the hero. Yet we are in sight of one another due to a common heritage. It is in the anthropological nature of culture to be both universal and particular. Everyone eats. How and what people eat varies greatly.

Women and certain ethnic and religious minorities have been freer to join the heroic pantheon in the United States than in Europe, which holds to the enshrinement of values on the basis of class and privilege evident in as elemental an activity as hunting; an aristocratic activity in Europe down to this day, as opposed to its blue-collar character in the United States.

America has its own limitations. U.S. civilization suffers from a profound case of historical amnesia. Recent mainstream U.S. childrens' books about national heroes, such as *First Facts About American Heroes* (King, 1996), omit George Washington as an important player in the American Revolution. Since World War II, the heroism of America's individual soldier has been steadily replaced by the force of the killing machine. Technology and military culture fused. Marksman was replaced by atomic bomb, individual physical skill in battle by Apache helicopter expertise. The machines are the foundation of a new, 21st-century pantheon of heroes. The U.S. military is aware of the limitations here. There's a current U.S. army joke: You know you're going overboard when there's a 1-800 tech support number that comes with your fighting vehicle.

Many questions remain about the social construction of heroes in both culture areas. Has heroic achievement been trivialized in the United States because of mass media treatments, such as the embarrassing soap opera *Holocaust* (1978) or Spike Lee's quasi-musical *Malcolm X* (1992)—or did the opposite happen? People learned history and heroes they otherwise never would have known about? If "news is only the rough draft of history," as Phil Graham, publisher of *The Washington Post* once said, have movies and TV shows become the final draft? At least as far as popular knowledge is concerned.

Social institutions in the United States and western Europe unquestionably determine the wide-scale visibility of heroes. The basic edition of the U.S. *National Standards for History* (1996) stressed the need to educate K–4 children about "ordinary people who have believed in the fundamental democratic values such as justice, truth, equality, the rights of the individual"— at the expense of omitting the "traditional biography of great men" as "a very disabling notion," as project co-director Gary B. Nash declared (Nash, 1996, p. 1).

Closer to home has been the role of the family. A significant study done in the United States in the early 1990s (Patterson & Kim, 1991) tried to show how Americans did *not* look to popular heroes as moral authorities. That their top four choices for moral authorities, for heroes, were: spouse/lover, parent, grandparent, best friend. Heroic leadership by public figures rated low on the scale, beginning with the president of the United States (who ranked as 19th on this U.S. list).

However, all is not as it seems. What the Patterson and Kim study did not answer at all is why individuals respect certain people in the circle outside their family and close friends, certain people who mirror family members, who supplement their inner circle. That is, isn't Bill Cosby or Michael Jordan a dad or big brother you wished you could have had? Chavez, King, or Rosa Parks: didn't they give off emulative power? Even big bumptious Roseanne or the late great Lady Di—the funny mom or elegant big sister you missed? The simple and the serious. You lacked. They gave. Something was still missing.

An example here would be Roger Kahn's remarkable 1973 autobiography *The Boys of Summer*, about the author's great admiration for the Brooklyn Dodgers of the 1950s, his boyhood and adulthood heroes, an autobiography which was equally about that stupendous Brooklyn Dodgers team of Jackie Robinson, Leo Durocher, and Pee Wee Reese and about this baseball team as common ground between Roger Kahn and his father. The aching love he had for his father. And for the Dodgers. His dad was basically a failure—but a winner too: like the Dodgers. Because "that's the hell of it. That's the rottenest thing in this life, isn't it? The best team doesn't always get to win" (Kahn, 1973, p. 179).

And what about "celebrity"—the famous one? By the end of the 20th century, "celebrity" was given in many a dictionary as synonymous with "hero."[23] Are they the same? This chapter has already attempted to answer this question. But who has the final answer? As interpreted herein, hero has been equated with "ideal"—with strong moral overtones from Homer's courageous warriors through regular guy, champion Lenny Skutnick. And celebrity?

Truth is in the nuances. Isn't celebrity immensely visual? Celebrity is equated with *star, star power*. A thing more seen than thought. Its language is photojournalism: *People* magazine and its endless ilk. The lifeblood of celebrity is gossip. The hero exemplifies a cause. With celebrity surface meets surface. They offer a look, a style, form rather than content. Authenticity is not a key factor for a celebrity—but performance is. And performance not in the heroic sense of achieving a noble deed. The celebrity *performs*: entertains, executes a spectacle.

In movie, TV, sound recording, or "live" concert performance "perfection is more desirable than authenticity"—where the willing audience enters the opium den of the product itself, which is all "about spectacle and sheer star proximity, not the miracle of live . . . production" (Nelson, 2004, p. 8). The audience accepts media enhancement of their celebrity pop icons from Einstein to Eminem, Jacqueline Kennedy Onassis to Halle Berry, Madonna to Bruce Springsteen to pop princess Britney Spears.

Of course there are exceptions—many a celebrity has infused their life with a cause (Muhammad Ali to Superman, Princess Diana to Michael J. Fox). But the cause does not the celebrity make. Cause is icing on the celebrity's cake. Unquestionably, "hero" is in transition and "celebrity" is the major contender for its territory of meaning. But does this obliterate the higher value of hero? Follow the drug metaphor for celebrity. People consume it and know what they're doing; the pantheon of heroes versus the pharmacy of celebrities.

The hero remains very personal and very public. Answering our needs. Leaving us hungry for more. Heroes break from all their contours. They see you. And me. And mark the absence we have in common. Tell us as a group what we need. How we must alter if we are to improve.

ENDNOTES

1. The "end of history" idea refers to the bestseller *The End of History and The Last Man* by Francis Fukuyama (1992) which argued, in very tortured prose, that after the Cold War (1945-1991) history might end. He was wrong.

2. "Herakles" is the original Greek version of the mythical hero Hercules; "Aeneas" is the hero of the great Roman national epic the *Aeneid*, written by Vergil c. 29 BC.

3. Queen Henrietta Maria (1609-1669): Roman Catholic queen consort of Charles I of England, very active in foreign policy. Henrietta of England (1644-1670): wife of Philippe I, duc d'Orléans, famous for negotiating the Treaty of Dover in 1670, and then probably poisoned by her husband.

4. Baroness Emmuska Orczy (1865-1947): Hungarian-British playwright, author of romantic novels and detective short stories. Orczy's most famous character, The Scarlet Pimpernel, appeared in a number of novels about the French revolution, and a wildly successful 1934 movie, *The Scarlet Pimpernel* staring Leslie Howard.

5. Dante Alighieri (1265-1321): Italian poet, author of *The Divine Comedy* (c.1307-1321); Alfonso the Magnanimous of Naples (1396-1458): King of Aragon, Sicily, Naples, great patron of arts and letters; Boccaccio (1313-1375): Italian writer and humanist, author of *The Decameron* (1348-1353); Lorenzo the Magnificent (1449-1492): towering figure of Italian Renaissance, patron of arts, literature, learning, ruler of Florence as city-state; Machiavelli (1469-1527): Florentine statesman and political philosopher, author of *The Prince* (1513); Pope Alexander VI (Pope: 1492-1503): made Rome a brilliant Renaissance capital.

6. Jacob Burckhardt (1819-1897): Swiss historian, founder of the modern discipline of cultural history, author of *The Civilization of the Renaissance in Italy* (1860).

7. Honoré de Balzac (1799-1850): French novelist; Emile Zola (1840-1902): French novelist, journalist, social critic; Henri René Albert Maupassant (1850-1893): French short-story writer and novelist; Daniel Defoe (1660-1731): English novelist, pamphleteer, journalist; Charles Dickens, (1812-1870): English novelist; Walt Whitman (1819-1892): U.S. journalist, poet, essayist; Frederick Douglass (c.1817-1895): Afro-American orator, journalist, abolitionist; Stephen Crane

(1871-1900): U.S. short-story writer, poet, war journalist; Edith Wharton (1862-1937): U.S. novelist, social critic; Sherwood Anderson (1876-1941): U.S. novelist, short-story writer; Ernest Hemingway (1899-1961): U.S. novelist, short-story writer; William Faulkner ((1897-1962): U.S. novelist, short-story writer; Sinclair Lewis (1885-1951): U.S. novelist, critic of middle America; John Hersey (1914-1993): U.S. journalist, novelist.

8. "The Forgotten Man": title of a famous 1883 essay by William Graham Sumner of the U.S. Progressive era about the perpetual U.S. economic underdog. See: William Graham Sumner "The Forgotten Men" in: Anders Breidlid et al., *America Culture—An Anthology of Civilization Texts* (New York: Routledge, 1996) pp. 213-215.

9. "dark Satanic mills": reference to the famed, opening lines to *Jerusalem* by British poet and mystic William Blake (1757-1827), which notes the malignant spread of factories across the blessed land of England: "And did the Countenance Divine / Shine down upon those clouded hills; / And was Jerusalem builded here / Among those dark Satanic mills?" Blake's *Jerusalem* is also the Labor Party's signature song in the United Kingdom.

10. Rastignac: Eugene Rastignac, a gifted social climber, is the most famous recurring character in *La comédie humaine* (1842-1848; translated as *The Human Comedy*, 1895-1900) by Honoré de Balzac (1799-1850); Julien Sorel: hero gifted in passion and power, protagonist of *The Red and The Black* (1830) by French novelist Stendhal (1783-1842); Huck Finn: self-aware, youthful protagonist of *The Adventures of Huckleberry Finn* (1884) by Mark Twain (1835-1910); Sister Carrie: covetous, ambitious, but admirable main character of *Sister Carrie* (1900) by Theodore Dreiser (1871-1945).

11. Lenny Skutnick: common man or woman as risk-taking Good Samaratine—named after the Washington, D.C., office worker Lenny Skutnick who dove into the Potomac River amid snow and freezing weather to save victims of a crashed Air Florida airplane in 1982.

12. Figures least likely to be known in this list: "The Emperor"—title given to Napoleon I (1769-1821); *Il Duce*—title given to Benito Mussolini (1883-1945) Italian dictator and leader of the Fascist movement; Evita Peron—a.k.a.: Eva Duarte de Peron (1919-1952), Argentine political leader; Kingfish Huey Long— Senator Huey Pierce Long (1893-1935), American political leader, Southern demagogue; Father Charles Coughlin (1891-1979): Canadian Roman Catholic priest in U.S. residence, famed "radio priest" of the U.S. 1930s, pro-Nazi and anti-Semitic.

13. Attributed Curtis quote made during the filming of the movie *Some Like It Hot* (1959). See: "Screen Kiss Secrets" by Kevin Lewin; page 1; online at http://www.women.com/celebs/celebspecial/articles/0,,592831_600493,00.html

14. Figures least likely to be known in this list: Donna Rice: would-be Miami model with whom would-be presidential candidate Senator Gary Hart was caught having an extramarital affair in Spring 1987; Gennifer Flowers: U.S. night club singer who surfaced amid the 1992 presidential campaign and claimed a long-time sexual liaison with William Jefferson Clinton, subsequently denied by the Clintons on CBS' program *60 Minutes*; Alexandra Polier: the supposed DC "intern" who supposedly had worked for Senator John Kerry and had a sexual

liaison with him—news as spread by Internet muckraker Matt Drudge in February 2004.

15. Elizabeth Cady Stanton (1815-1902); William McKinley (1843-1901), U.S. president; King Edward VIII of Great Britain (1894-1972), Ty Cobb (1886-1961), Amelia Earhart (1898-c.1937), Eleanor Roosevelt (1884-1962), Ernest Hemingway (1899-1961).

16. *non dite*: modern French colloquialism, literally means the "not said"—whatever is unspoken or taboo among people, often in a suppressed, unhealthy way.

17. Paul Robeson (1898-1976): African-American actor, singer, social activist; Billie Holiday (1915-59): African-American singer, original name: Eleanora Fagan.

18. Helen Keller (1880-1968): blind and deaf from childhood, internationally known U.S. promoter of the disabled, subject of Pulitzer Prize play *The Miracle Worker* (1959; movie: 1962), autobiography: *The Story of My Life* (1903). Harry Hopkins (1890-1946): social reformer, close friend and assistant of Franklin Delano Roosevelt (1882-1945), head of Work Progress Administration in the New Deal, U.S. Secretary of Commerce: 1938-1940.

19. Cochise (c.1823-1874): Chiricahua Apache war chief, successful in his decade-long war against whites in Arizona; Sergeant Alvin York (1887-1964): the most highly decorated U.S. soldier of World War I; Audie Murphy (1924-1971): the most highly decorated U.S. soldier of World War II, subsequent Hollywood movie star.

20. Punch-Punchinello: the British and the Italian name for this traditional figure of European folklore, famed for the "Punch and Judy" puppet shows in which Punch is a cruel, hunchback husband always punching his nagging, betraying, Judas-like wife Judy.

21. Max and Moritz: comic strip about two young children by German painter and poet Wilhelm Busch (1832-1908); Antoine de Saint-Exupery (1900-1944): French aviator and writer, authored the *Little Prince* (1943), among other works.

22. Mr. Vieux Bois: comic strip authored by Swiss novelist Rodolphe Topffer (1799-1846) in 1823, considered by some to be the first modern comic strip. Bécassine: French comic strip (bande dessinée) begun in 1905, authored by many famous artists, such as M. Languereau et J. Pinchon, about the life and times of a Brittany servant girl: Annaïck Labornez. Corto Maltese: a comic strip for all ages begun in 1970s by Hugo Pratt, about a Joseph Conrad type of sailor—with adventures in foreign lands reminiscent of *Lord Jim* (1900).

23. As in, for example, *The American Heritage Dictionary of the English Language*, 3rd ed. (Boston: Houghton Mifflin, 1992) 308.

REFERENCES

Atwan, R., McQuade D., & Wright, J. W. (1979). *Edsels, luckies, & fridgidaires*. New York: A Delta Special—Dell Publishing Co.

Benjamin, W. (1936/1968). *The work of art in an age of mechanical reproduction*. First published in Berlin as *Das Kunstwerk im Zeitalter seiner technischen*

Reproduzierbarkeit. In W. Benjamin (Ed.), *Illuminations*, with an Introduction by H. Arendt (H. Zorn, Trans.) (pp. 219-254). London: Fontana-Collins.

Boorstin, D. J. (1987) *The image: A guide to pseudo-events in America.* New York: Vintage-Random House. (Original work published 1961)

Bradlee, B. (1995) *A good life: Newspapering and other adventures.* New York: Touchstone-Simon & Schuster.

Brunel, P. (Ed.). (1992). *Companion to literary myths, heroes and archetypes.* London: Routledge.

Burckhardt, J. (1950). *The civilization of the renaissance in Italy* (S.G.C. Middlemore, Trans.). New York: Phaidon.

Clark, K. (1969). *Civilisation: A personal view.* London: Penguin.

Emerson, R. W. (1983). "Considerations By the Way" in his collection *Conduct of life; essays and lectures.* New York: The Library of America.

Fukuyama, F. (1992). *The end of history and the last man.* New York: The Free Press.

Gast, L. (Dir.) (1997). *When we were kings* with Muhammad Ali, George Foreman, George Plimpton, Norman Mailer.

Getty, A. (1990) *Goddess mother of living nature.* London, New York: Thames & Hudson.

Goffman, E. (1959). *The presentation of self in everyday life.* New York: Anchor Books.

Groshens, M-C., Rannou, K., & Colardelle M. (2001–2002) *Héros populaires— Musée national des Arts et Traditions populaires.* Paris: Editions de la Réunion des Musées Nationaux.

Higden, R. (1874). *Polychronicon Ranulphi Higden, monachi Cestrensis: Together with the English translations of John Trevisa and of an unknown writer of the fifteenth century.* London: Longman.

Hobsbawm, E. J. (1979). *The age of capital, 1848-1875.* New York: Mentor–NAL. (Original work published 1975.)

Hobbes, T. (1968). *Leviathan.* London: Penguin Books. (Original work published 1651)

Jones, F. A. (1931). *The life story of Thomas Alva Edison.* New York: Grosset & Dunlap.

Jordan, T. G. (1988). The *European culture area—A systematic geography.* New York: Harper & Row.

Kerényi, C. (1960). Introduction. In C. Kerényi (Ed.), *The heroes of the Greeks* (H. J. Rose, Trans.). New York: Grove Press.

Kahn, R. (1973). *The boys of summer.* New York: Signet-New American Library.

King, D. C. (1996). *First facts about American heroes.* Woodbridge, CT: Blackbirch Press.

Martin, G. (1996). As quoted in "So You Want to be a Rock 'n Roll Star," part 3. In *Dancing in the Street*, a ten part series, WGBH Boston, Daniel McCabe, Vicky Bippart, directors, Elizabeth Deane Executive Producer.

McKinley, J. (2003). Writer's youths in pain have the will to survive; Adam Rapp parlays the angst of his childhood into plays and novels. *The New York Times*, Sec. E, p. 1.

Nash, G. B. (1994, October 31). As quoted in Joe Urschel, "History without heroes?" *USA Today*, p. 7A.

National Standards for History—Basic Edition. (1996). Online at: http: //www.ssc-net.ucla.edu/nchs/standards.

Nelson, C. (2004. February 4). Pop music's new etiquette: Faking it. *International Herald Tribune-New York Times*, p. 8.

Nietzsche, F. (1963/1966). Epigrams and interludes. In W. Kaufmann (Trans.), *Beyond good and evil*. New York: Vintage Books-Random House.

Patterson, J., & Peter, K. (1991). *The day America told the truth*. New York: Prentice-Hall.

Slansky, P. (1989). *The clothes have no emperor: A chronicle of the American 80s*. New York: Fireside-Simon & Schuster.

Summer, W. G. (1996). The forgotten men. In A. Breidlid, F. C. Brogger, O. T. Gulliksen, & T. Sirevag (Eds.), *American culture: An anthology of civilization texts* (pp. 213–215). New York: Routledge.

Weber, M. (1946). The sociology of charismatic authority. In H. H. Gerth & C. Wright Mills (Trans. and Eds.), *Max Weber: Essays in sociology*. New York: Oxford University Press.

Chapter 5

FROM DISTANT HEROES
TO INTIMATE FRIENDS

Media and the Metamorphosis of Affection
for Public Figures

Joshua Meyrowitz
University of New Hampshire

In this chapter, Meyrowitz analyzes the new sense of intimacy with strangers that has been created by those modern media that simulate the sights and sounds of real-life interactions. This sense of intimacy drives the attachment to "media friends"—those celebrities, actors, newscasters, politicians, talk-show hosts, singers, sports figures, and so on, who become part of an extended network of social ties. Meyrowitz explains how new technologies reduce the distance between us and our media friends, blurring our response to their skills and talents with our response to their personalities. He suggests that the "unreal" relationships with media friends are, ironically, often deeper and longer lasting than many real-life ties. He then explores these "intimate" relationships to the point of loss and shows how new forms of grief have been developed to cope with the death of media friends.

✧   ✧   ✧

At the time they split up, I too broke away from my family, my friends, the places I had known all my life, to attend school in California. As I drove over the hills into the Los Angeles basin, a new song by John

99

Lennon crackled on the car radio, as if the Beatles were saying, "We're with you. You haven't left us behind."

—Schaumburg (1976, p. 3)

Because we were so used to the way he thought, the habits, the turns, the surprises of his mind, we can enter him as we remember his last moments, to let it be us in the car, pulling up to the curb, opening the door, stepping out, breathing the night. Someone said he was happy that night, and we somehow know what his happiness felt like, and we can imagine ourselves resurgent, electric with energy.

—Spencer (1981)

Four days after . . . when I woke up to find . . . the story off the front page, that process by which the mind struggles with a fact it will not accept was still working. I scanned the front page again to see if I'd missed anything. . . . Nothing. Does this mean, I thought, that it's over? That he's not dead anymore?

—Marcus (1981, p. 27)

"John Lennon Killed by Stranger" screamed the headlines in December 1980. But for assassin Mark David Chapman, John Lennon was no stranger. Although Chapman had never come within 100 miles of the former Beatle until that winter, he knew him very well, so well that he often seemed to believe that he *was* John Lennon.

As a teenager, Chapman wore his hair like Lennon's, learned to play the guitar, and joined a rock group. He played and sang Lennon's songs over and over again. Chapman, like Lennon, married an older Japanese woman. At his last job, as a security guard at a Honolulu condominium, he even taped Lennon's name over his own on his identification tag. And on the day Chapman quit, he signed out as "John Lennon" in the logbook (Clarke, 1980; Mathews et al., 1980).

Yet, Chapman must have been acutely aware of the gap between himself and his alter ego. The last stroke of his pen in the logbook crossed the name out. Within a few weeks, Chapman was on his way to New York City to close the open psychic circle. First, he played the adoring fan, asking for and receiving an autograph outside Lennon's apartment building, the Dakota, at 72nd Street and Central Park West. Then he returned later in the day to empty his gun into Lennon's body, thereby defining the rest of his own life in relation to the life he ended.

In a sense, John Lennon was killed by the sinister side of the same force that makes millions of people still mourn him and other dead media heroes: a new sense of personal connection to selected strangers. This sense of connection is fostered by media that simulate the sights and sounds of real-life interactions.

We are still lacking in the terminology and conceptual frameworks to understand fully these strange bonds. In their seminal 1956 essay on this topic in *Psychiatry*, Donald Horton and R. Richard Wohl use the term *parasocial interaction* to analyze how mass media can provide audiences with the illusion of face-to-face interactions with performers. John Caughey (1984) uses the term *media figures* to describe the contemporary celebrities, historical figures, and fictional characters who inhabit our "imaginary social worlds." Richard Schickel (1985) writes about celebrities as "intimate strangers" who exist in a confused realm that inappropriately blurs public and private life. Jib Fowles (1992) analyzes how we have become "starstruck" by a relatively small group of celebrities who substitute for the neighbors in the villages in which most of us no longer live. Joshua Gamson (1994) analyzes the culture of "celebrity" in the United States as growing out of the conflicting American values of equality and distinction. In this volume, and in its forerunner edited by Susan Drucker and Robert Cathcart (1994), the evolution in conceptions of "heroes" and "media heroes" is explored from a communication perspective.

My analysis is relevant to most of these terms, including *celebrity* and *media hero*, but I focus primarily on an elaboration of my concept of *media friend* (Meyrowitz, 1985). Each of these three terms addresses an aspect of the complex relationships with contemporary media figures. The term *celebrity* captures the fact that modern media enhance the possibility that someone could be widely known for being widely known (Boorstin, 1961). The term *media hero* embraces the sense of awe that one may feel concerning the accomplishments of a person one knows about through the media. To my thinking, however, the concept of *media friend* addresses the strangest and most significant dimension of these relationships: the sense of intimate knowledge and empathic connection. We feel a direct, one-to-one tie to a media friend that exists apart from, and almost in spite of, how widely known the person is. Furthermore, as with real-life friends, we feel bound to the person, not simply because of what he or she can *do*, but based on a more personal set of feelings about who the person is—and how his or her "presence" makes us feel.

What we expect from heroes is often different from what we expect and accept from media friends. Great heroes may make boring or awkward friends, and media friends may make poor heroes in the traditional sense. Indeed, a revelation that would destroy heroic aura may only deepen the sense of intimate connection with a media friend. The natural mental space for a hero is at a distance and on some sort of pedestal. The imagined space for a media friend is at our sides—hanging out together at home, riding in the car, sharing an adventure. The multifaceted role that John Lennon and others have played in our lives has all these dimensions: celebrity, hero, and friend.

Unfortunately, Mark David Chapman is not the only unbalanced person to push the media relationship to extreme ends. There have been many other similar attempted or realized assassinations that have grown from this new form of intimacy. John Hinckley, Jr. attempted to assassinate Ronald Reagan in order to impress actress Jodie Foster. "You'll be proud of me, Jodie," he wrote to her. "Millions of Americans will love me—us" ("An innocent life," 1989, p. 64). Robert John Bardo, obsessed with actress Rebecca Schaeffer, star of the TV sitcom *My Sister Sam*, shot and killed her in 1989. Dozens of other celebrities have been threatened, stalked, or attacked. Actor Michael J. Fox received more than 5,000 letters and death threats from one fan who was upset about his marriage, and actress-singer Olivia Newton-John was followed twice to Australia by an Illinois mental patient ("An innocent life," 1989). In the late 1980s and early 1990s, TV talk show host David Letterman's home was broken into at least four times, and his sports car was taken for drives by a woman who called herself "Mrs. Letterman" (Gilatto, 1998; Toufexis et al., 1989). In December 1999, Michael Abram, who "nursed an irrational obsession with the Beatles" and believed them to be witches, broke into former Beatle George Harrison's estate and stabbed Harrison repeatedly, seriously wounding him (Lyall, 1999).

Fan reaction to the sudden death of a media friend can be equally strong. Following John Lennon's murder, a teenage girl in Florida and a 30-year-old man in Utah killed themselves. Their suicide notes spoke of depression over Lennon's death (Cocks, 1980).

Because simulated intimacy drives the attachment, celebrities who present the kindest personae to the public are, ironically, the ones most prone to violent threats and acts on the part of obsessed fans. These celebrities appear more approachable, more seductive. Performers who present harsher fictional or nonfictional personae may receive more hate mail, yet are less likely to be stalked and killed by those who see themselves as jilted lovers (Toufexis et al., 1989).

One does not have to be mentally unbalanced, however, to feel a close bond to celebrities. Except for the attempts to hurt these media heroes or to demand that they return the personal attention and affection, the behavior of these "obsessed fans" is often not that different from the behavior of ordinary fans. (Indeed, the word *fan* itself is derived from the word *fanatic*.) When Chapman was a teenager, for example, he was only one among millions who felt devoted to Lennon and emulated aspects of his appearance and behavior. Harrison's attacker was not alone in believing that the Beatles held mystical powers. Beatle fandom persists to this day, shaping the actions and perceptions of hundreds of thousands of people, many of whom view Liverpool as a kind of mecca (Leonard, 1999). Each year, more than 600,000 Elvis fans still make pilgrimages to Graceland, the late singer's home in Memphis, Tennessee (Elvis Presley Enterprises, 2004). About 4 million people visit President John Kennedy's grave each year (Grunwald, 1991). And the growth of the World Wide Web has spawned the development of thousands of personal Web sites, newsgroups, chatrooms, and "shrines" devoted to particular celebrities, both living and dead.

EVOLUTION OF THE MEDIA RELATIONSHIP

Over the last century, the evolution of communication media has fostered an increasingly intense sense of intimacy with those who would otherwise be strangers. Every era has had its heroes, and people still visit the graves and homes of famous artists, writers, politicians, soldiers, actors, and poets from prior centuries. But until the eve of the 20th century, "special people" were experienced primarily through abstract or distancing media: oral or written stories, statues, images on coins, or painted portraits. On rare occasions, a hero could be seen in the flesh, but generally only from a great distance, for a short time, and by only a small minority of the population.

A new relationship between the adored and the adoring was born with the rise of the film industry. Audiences could see the facial expressions and body movements of performers with greater clarity than from a front row seat at a live performance, and individual performers could quickly gain a following much larger than would be humanly possible through a lifetime of live appearances. Early filmmakers were taken by surprise by the strong emotional attachment that developed between performer and audience. At first, film companies, such as Biograph and Bison, did not even bother to share the names of the performers with the public. But when audience members wrote fan letters to the "Biograph girl" and their other favorites, film producers quickly realized the economic value of "stars" (Sklar, 1975).

The nature of media relationships changed again with the addition of sound to film, which reduced some of the mystery surrounding movie stars. In some cases, this demystification destroyed careers; in others, it enhanced the closeness of the relationship between star and fan. In both silence and sound, however, film fostered a relatively distant closeness. Performers were seen sporadically, from afar, and as literally much "larger than life" on a big screen in an oversized room in the public sphere. Such settings generated awe along with a new sense of personal bond. Indeed, many early U.S. movie theaters were designed as splendid palaces for Hollywood-created royalty.

The radio era also fostered its own unique media relationships. Radio personalities were close in aural space and often entered people's homes daily, but their "presence" during these visits had no visual dimensions except in the listener's imagination. Media performers who were experienced through the radio were like friends at a pajama party who arrived after the lights were turned off and left before daybreak. With radio, there was an odd mix of intimacy and distance, of knowledge and mystery.

LIFE-LONG VICARIOUS INTIMATES

Compared to the film and radio eras, our own time is characterized by a greater intimacy, encouraged by the closeness and smallness of the audio speakers and video screens in our homes and cars and by the many media through which we experience the same performers. As a result, a broader array of social performers has more fully entered our personal spaces on a more regular basis. Additionally, because children do not have to leave home to watch television, such media friendships now begin very early in life. When Fred Rogers died in February 2003, newspapers filled with letters from his former viewers who essentially described how he helped to raise them. As family researcher David Finkelhor has noted, Mr. Rogers "was a major and explicit promoter of the idea that you could be 'friends' with someone you simply saw repeatedly on television," thus priming a very young and highly impressionable audience for a lifetime of media friendships (personal communication, June 5, 2003).

Through media experiences, we come to feel that we really know a John Kennedy or a John Lennon, a Magic Johnson or a Woody Allen, a Peter Jennings or a Lady Diana. We feel we have spent time together, that we have met some of their family members and friends, that we understand something about who they are as people.

The more we see and hear them, the more actors, sports figures, newscasters, singers, politicians, and talk show hosts become part of our extended network of social ties. Some of them are there to say "Good morning" to us, others to whisper "Good night." Our media buddies are cheerful with us at breakfast, and they solemnly and reliably fill us in on the day's news over dinner. We can find reflective or playful media friends to hang out with in the evening. And there is always a media pal who will sing for us as we jog. The voices and faces of our media friends often provide a backdrop even to the most intimate scenes of our lives, including lovemaking.

There are obvious surface differences among our relationships with different types of media friends—presidents, rock stars, sports heroes, actors, and news anchors, for example—but there are also some important underlying commonalities. We often feel that our media friends share themselves with us more easily than other people do and that we know them better than most of the people we see in our daily lives. Because of the unidirectional nature of most of the media through which we experience them, we can closely watch and listen to our media friends without being distracted by concerns over how we look, what we say in return, or what they think of us. Media-friend relationships offer a sense of intimacy without the risk of embarrassment or physical harm.

We follow celebrities through various phases of their personal lives and public activities, and their life stages often become some of the key signposts we use to mark and recall the different periods of our own lives. With the help of television programs such as *Entertainment Tonight* and publications such as *People, Us, In Touch*, and many others, we keep up with their romances and problems, their good years and bad years, their changing hairstyles and different phases of dress, the birth of their children and the death of their family members, their successful and unsuccessful plastic surgeries, their addictions and recoveries. With some performers, such as Cher, we have been allowed to see new tattoos. We even saw John and Yoko naked.

There is, of course, a great deal of variation in how significant a role media friends play in the lives of media audiences. As Rosengren and Windahl (1972) describe, media relationships may merely "supplement" relatively full social lives, "complement" live relationships that do not fulfill an individual's need for social interaction, or "substitute" for social interaction among those who are socially isolated. The individual's degree of involvement with media figures also varies, note Rosengren and Windahl, from "detachment" to "para-social interaction" to "solitary identification" to "capture" (both interaction and identification).

Given how many celebrities there are to choose from, it is likely that most people do not care deeply about most media figures. As in real-life interactions, the degree of attachment to those experienced through the media varies from one "relationship" to the next and ranges from positive to neutral to negative. In addition to emotionally significant media friends, there are mere "media acquaintances"; one is aware of them, but there is no sense of strong connection. There are also those performers whom one finds annoying. They could be called "media pests." And there are those one cannot abide ("media enemies"). Moreover, given the growing overload of media outlets, there are those who are simply "media non-entities" from a given person's perspective; although they may appear in some public media forum, their existence does not impinge on one's consciousness.

Yet, in a mediated society, almost everyone seems to feel a close connection to at least one, or some, media friends. For many fans, the distant intimacy with celebrities spawns detailed fantasies about relationships with them, including imagined courtships, rescues, even fights (Caughey, 1984). Media figures appear in many people's dreams, where "they are more likely to do so as a friend, collaborator, or associate rather than in their 'real life' role as celebrity" (Alperstein & Vann, 1997, p. 149).

Make-believe characters portrayed in various media have also spawned media friendships. Fans exhibit connections to fictional characters in action movies, soap operas, situations comedies, dramatic series on TV, and even cartoons, such as *The Simpsons.*

Our relationships with media personae frequently outlast our relationships with many of our neighbors, co-workers, lovers, and real-life friends. Indeed, our permanent relationships with media friends often form part of the shared experience that binds us to our temporary real-life friends. Conversely, a lack of sharing of similar media friendships can immediately terminate negotiations for friendship with people we meet (such as when a Sinead O'Connor fan discovers that the guy sitting next to her is humming Tammy Wynette tunes; or a Barry Manilow fan dismisses the notion of becoming close to a devoted David Bowie fan). On the Internet, such mismatches are often avoided, as fans "gather" at Web sites and chatrooms dedicated to particular celebrities. Some of these virtual interactions among fans eventually build into embodied encounters at festivals devoted to the celebrity or in more private physical interactions.

For many fans, relationships with living and dead media friends become a way to engage with various social issues that the celebrities come to embody. Over the last 30 years in the United States, these personality-linked issues have included patriotism (John Wayne), radicalism (Abbie Hoffman), reincarnation (Shirley McLaine), liberalism (Ted Kennedy), conservatism (Ronald Reagan), feminism (Gloria Steinem), the right to bear arms (Charlton Heston), and international peace (John Lennon). Richard Schickel (1985) fears that such personifications weaken our ability to think abstractly and thereby undermine democracy. Jib Fowles (1992), on the other hand, believes that the same trend democratizes the culture by expanding the number of citizens who confront social issues. In either case, it is clear that many of us use celebrities to develop our "positions" in the culture and to align with, or against, other real-life acquaintances.

Relationships with media friends partially compensate for the impermanence of many interpersonal relationships. But they may also increase the instability of real-life connections by making it easier to end them. As difficult as it remains to leave one's home, get divorced, or travel to another part of the country or world, each of these changes is now made simpler by the fact that not all our social relationships are severed. Wherever we are, whether living alone or with others, we may continue to enjoy the company of our media friends. How can we feel completely alone when we are offered companionship by the likes of Bill Cosby, Bruce Springsteen, Oprah Winfrey, Leonardo DiCaprio, Michael Jordan, Paul McCartney, Jennifer Lopez, Howard Stern, Paul Simon, Cyndi Lauper, Jerry Seinfeld, Tom Brokaw, Puff Daddy, Willie Nelson, Jay Leno, and scores of other fascinating and talented people, both living and dead? Similarly, young children in the United States always live near Mister Rogers' neighborhood (even if now only in reruns) and just down the block from their friends at Sesame Street.

SELECTED PERSONALITY FACETS

Of course, we see only selected dimensions of the personalities of our media friends and heroes. Those who watched talk show host Johnny Carson's first program after the death of his son realized how much of Carson's personality and emotional life had remained hidden even after thousands of late-night chats. Similarly, David Letterman, Jay Leno, and Conan O'Brien, for all their irreverent humor over many hours each week, reveal very little about their personal emotional lives. As Horton and Wohl (1956) suggested in the 1950s, talk-show hosts "play themselves." That is, what we see is often a genuine dimension of a media friend's personality, but it must be "played" to the extent that other dimensions of his or her personality remain purposely hidden. Indeed, the general consistency of our media friends' behaviors may be what often makes them seem to be more trustworthy and reliable than the people we interact with in everyday life. Unlike real family and friends, our media friends let us into their personal spaces (however constructed or controlled) and entertain us with high energy, without making any reciprocal demands on us. In fact, one of the factors that seems to separate "normal" fans from the "crazed" ones is that the latter often react as if some personal demand on them *were* being made, only to become angry and violent when they feel themselves ignored or rejected.

In addition to selected dimensions of personality, media friends' performances often rely on other means of "staging" as well. When we watch a singing performance "taped live" in front of a studio audience, for example, we are rarely told that what we are watching may actually be the best takes from two or more sequential performances. Similarly, national politicians now typically arrange to speak in front of largely supportive audiences so that "live and unrehearsed cheering" can contribute to an upbeat media performance. In May 2003, White House staff asked the men to be photographed behind President George W. Bush to take off their ties, so that they would appear to be the "ordinary folk" the president claimed would benefit from his tax cut (Bumiller, 2003). In such situations, the pictured audience members are not actually those for whom the performances are designed; rather, they function as "extras" in a drama constructed for a mediated audience of millions.

Media production variables are also manipulated to shape a celebrity's image. Soft filters or special "skin-contouring" cameras are used to hide lines on faces and to create a warm, glowing feel (not only for actors and actresses, but even for male and female news anchors). Camera angles and distances are selected to establish the desired image: low-angle medium shots for power and level close-ups for intimacy, for example, with shot framings simulating interpersonal distances and perspectives (Meyrowitz, 1986, 1998). Journalists are usually shown in level medium shots, suggesting that they are neutral and objective reporters ("on the level" and not personally involved in the story). Other visual and aural techniques are used to add dynamism, enhance positive features, and mute negative characteristics.

Most members of the public may be unaware of the specifics of image manipulation, yet the general awareness that a media friend may be "performing for us," rather than simply "being with us," leads to a lively trade in anecdotes about celebrities' offstage behaviors. That is, stories circulate about how media friends behave in situations in which the cameras and microphones are off—or in which the media friends *think* that they are off. These behaviors, it is often believed, reveal or confirm the media friend's true personality. One hears about the performer with the caring public persona who is abusive toward an airplane attendant, about the "sensitive" actor who is charged with beating his wife, about the politician who condemns others for using bad language but is then exposed in his or her own cursing (as happened with President Richard Nixon and the discovery of his White House tapes), and so on. Erving Goffman (1981, p. 267) recounts the classic story of "Uncle Don" who, after closing his children's radio program and mistakenly thinking the microphone was off, said: "I guess that will hold the little bastards." Such incidents can weaken or destroy a media friendship. But there are also frequent tales about offstage behaviors that confirm a public persona and thereby strengthen fans' devotion.

Ironically, media performers are often so aware of the power of offstage behavior to enhance onstage personae that they may work hard at shaping their seemingly unshaped behavior. Talk-show host Jay Leno, for example, not only reportedly shakes hands and signs autographs almost everywhere he goes, he also chats with other drivers through his car window and even telephones some of the people who write him letters of complaint. Leno, it is said, believes in President Lyndon Johnson's dictum that "every handshake is worth 250 votes" because, as Leno notes, "each person then goes and tells someone else you're a good guy and then they go and tell more people" (cited in Stengel, 1992, p. 58).

THE SHIFT FROM RESUMÉ CRITERIA
TO DATING CRITERIA

Although it is clear that media friends reveal themselves to us only in selective ways, it would be a mistake to miss the increase in personal revelation that has been fostered by changes in media. In the past, if national figures were seen at all, it was usually from afar, where facial expressions were invisible. In newspaper quotes or transcripts, the flesh-and-blood person was absent. Even still photographs did not commonly replace engravings in newspapers until the threshold of the 20th century (Sandman, Rubin, & Sachsman, 1982). At first, motion pictures were missing the key component of sound, and even early sound movies required a cooperative subject who was willing to move into the light and step up to the microphone.

Today, smaller and more sensitive cameras and microphones create less disruption of ongoing occurrences and thereby encourage greater revelation of what was once part of the behind-the-scenes aspects of *all* social performances (Meyrowitz, 1985). Changes in media have thereby altered the dividing lines between what sociologist Erving Goffman (1959) described as "front regions" and "back regions" (or "onstage" and "backstage," in more common terms for these concepts within Goffman's dramaturgical perspective). Even the most formal of our media friendships have become more intimate as media have entered many social arenas from which they were once banned — presidential press conferences, Senate hearings, and courtrooms, to name a few. And the pictures and sounds have become more revealing: President Nixon shoving his press secretary, President Ford tripping over words and down stairs, President Carter collapsing while jogging, President Reagan falling asleep in an audience with the Pope, the elder President Bush passing out after vomiting at a Japanese state dinner, President Clinton nervously answering questions about his sexual activities, and the younger President Bush smirking and mangling the English language by using such non-words as "misunderestimate" and nonsensical sentences such as "Not over my dead body will they raise your taxes."

As Lance Strate (1994) notes, "different kinds of communication will result in different kinds of heroes" (p. 15). As awareness has increased regarding the behavioral styles that work best on television, we have seen a general shift in the conception of which people have the appropriate personalities to fill various public roles. Stiff, wooden styles rarely make a good impression on television, regardless of the accomplishments, credentials, or other capabilities of the individual. Such considerations seem to have influenced the success and failure of a wide array of performers, including newscasters, rock stars, presidential hopefuls, and recent Supreme Court nominees. As I have detailed elsewhere, there are even indications that the

Catholic Church took into account a good "television personality" in elect-
ing Popes John Paul I and John Paul II (Meyrowitz, 1985).

Citizens once knew the people in the public, political realm primarily
through their words. Words can be used to talk about anything, distant or
close, abstract or concrete. But the images and sounds in modern "presentational" media are always, in basic ways, about the performers themselves
(Meyrowitz, 1985). As a result, our culture has been increasingly moving
away from abstract, word-based "résumé criteria" in evaluating public figures toward concrete, image-based "dating criteria." Rather than ask "What
does he know?" or "What has she accomplished?" we increasingly ask
"What is he like?" and "Do I like her?" By these criteria, the young and not
very well-educated Lady Diana easily triumphed over the older, more
accomplished, and well-educated Prince Charles. To the camera's eye and
ear, Diana was warm, likeable, and engaging, whereas Charles seemed cold
and aloof. Similarly, the charming and handsome John F. Kennedy, Jr. had
more hopes attached to his imagined political future than his professional
résumé could easily support (especially when contrasted with the richer
political experiences of his less photogenic cousins).

A common response to the reading of a speech in a newspaper is to ask
whether the statements are logical, whether the facts mentioned are true, and
whether we agree with the arguments. But a typical response to a similar
speech viewed on television is to think about the personality and performance of the speaker: "Does he seem nervous?" "Is she forceful?" "Is he sincere?" "Is she losing her cool?" Thus, it somehow makes sense that polls of
voters in television-era presidential elections have found that people will vote
for someone they disagree with on the issues, or vote against someone they
agree with, based on whether they "personally like" the candidate (see, e.g.,
Clymer, 1982). Television gives us that feeling of personal connection.

Caughey (1984) notes that despite the absence of real face-to-face contact with media figures, audiences describe them—both positively and negatively—in the language of interpersonal interaction. Rather than imperson-
ally describing celebrities as "talented," "entertaining," "not well trained,"
for example, most of Caughey's informants used personal terms such as
"sweet," "shallow," "kind," "phony," and "manipulative." The same sense
of personal knowing can be seen in the media tributes to Ronald Reagan
after his death in 2004. The "real Reagan legacy," wrote the editors of one
magazine tribute, was that he was "self-deprecating, self-effacing, a nice
guy" (Gold Collector's Series, 2004, p. 7).

In the 2004 political campaign, the sense of intimate interaction provided the context for the undoing of the Howard Dean campaign. After his
third-place showing in the Iowa caucuses in January, Dean tried to rally the
spirits of thousands of his volunteers. Struggling to be heard over a roaring
crowd, he shouted into a hand-held microphone. But the microphone he

used was designed to filter out background noises, with the result that what could barely be heard by people in the room sounded like an ugly outburst of emotion to the much larger TV audience (ABC News, 2004). The "Dean scream" was played and replayed on cable and broadcast TV nearly 700 times in a few days. It was set to music on numerous Web sites and was mocked by late-night TV comedians. Dave Letterman's staff modified the videotape to show Dean's head exploding at the end, and Letterman summarized the situation as "The people of Iowa realized they didn't want a president with the personality of a hockey dad" (Morrison, 2004). Howard Dean's wife felt compelled to join her husband for the first time in a TV interview with ABC's Diane Sawyer, and she and her husband were confronted with 90 questions, by the *LA Times*' count, about personality and temperament, including whether Howard could control his anger. In this and other media contexts, Judy Steinberg Dean also had to endure comments and questions that essentially framed her as an odd "media date," who didn't care enough about courting the public to wear makeup or fancy clothes. The Dean campaign never recovered, and John Kerry captured the Democratic nomination. One bumper sticker summarized the situation as, "Dated Dean, Married Kerry." (Kerry has not been considered the perfect "media mate" either, of course. He has had to address the perception that he is arrogant and aloof.)

The sense of personally knowing our media friends may explain why the public is now rather tolerant of ghostwriters and of the openness with which they are relied on. In a newspaper era, an explicitly ghostwritten speech would have seemed rather odd, even insulting to the public. After all, the public could know a national figure only through his or her printed words. Today, the person who *performs* the words is more important than whoever might have written them. It would be unacceptable for a contemporary president to follow President Thomas Jefferson's approach to his State of the Union addresses: He crafted the words himself, but had the speeches read aloud to Congress by a clerk. Yet, the public does not seem at all disturbed by the fact that media friends Katie Couric, Charles Gibson, and Brian Williams typically perform news scripts that are written by others (as did the legendary news anchor Walter Cronkite). Newspaper reporters, in contrast, are expected to write their own material, and small scandals erupt when newspaper articles are shown to contain passages written by someone other than the bylined reporter.

Even when President Reagan's speechwriters had him reading a letter from a little girl within a speech that was itself ghostwritten—and thus speaking words two steps removed from his own—Reagan's performance appeared to tell the public a great deal about his personal being, beliefs, and passions. We saw tears well up in his eyes, we heard the catch in his voice. Some of us sensed personal conviction; others sensed deceit. With such a rich conveyance of personal attributes, it did not seem absolutely necessary for the words to be his alone, any more than Frank Sinatra and Elvis Presley fans insisted that the singers perform only songs they had written on their own. Similarly, we rarely insist that our real-life friends tell us only those jokes they themselves have crafted. In these real and vicarious associations, we seem to crave the intimacy of interaction more than the artistry of invention.

Of course, the sense of intimate knowing can be even greater when the content of the performance is also created by our media friends. There was a special deepening of the relationship with the Beatles, for example, when they moved to recording only their own songs. Similarly, fans' devotion to singer-songwriters such as Bob Dylan and Phil Ochs in the 1960s had very little to do with their skill as musical performers. Those music critics who could not understand why these songwriters did not license their songs to technically superior singers and musicians missed the whole point.

As we come to know new media friends or deepen our relationships with old ones, we also come to know ourselves in new ways. The self, after all, is not simply an essence that resides *within* each of us. Although we often prefer to think of ourselves as autonomous individuals who march to our own drummers and shape our own destinies, when we try to define who we are, most of the concepts we use are relative and social. When we think of ourselves as being short or tall, hesitant or daring, smart or dumb, kind or harsh, we implicitly engage in comparison to others. Each of us develops a social self as we begin to see ourselves and judge our actions as they would be viewed by "significant others" (Mead, 1934). Our sense of self is changed, then, as we gain new significant others—live or mediated—from whose vantage points we can view our own actions. When Mark Chapman experimented with drugs, for example, he knew that his parents would be horrified. But he must have also sensed that John Lennon would understand.

BLURRING OF PERSONALITY AND SKILL

We become emotionally tied to our media friends as *people*, apart from our reactions to their artistic skill or professional activities. Or perhaps it is more accurate to say that it often becomes difficult to separate the personal and the professional dimensions of the relationships, especially when media friends push their art to service the media relationships themselves.

After the Beatles broke up, for example, the individual members of the group, particularly John Lennon, recorded songs that were increasingly personal in nature. One such song called to his mama "don't go" and to his daddy "come home." Thus, Lennon's own art began to comment on the biographical details known to every dedicated fan: After Lennon's father abandoned the family, his mother left him to be raised by an aunt, and then, just as mother and son began to become reacquainted, his mother was killed by a drunken driver (an off-duty policeman) while she waited for a bus. Other songs commented on publicized feuds with Paul McCartney and on Lennon's devotion to his wife, Yoko (who was not well liked by Lennon's ex-partners and was scorned by many Beatles fans).

Fans' evaluation of the "quality" of Lennon's musical artistry, then, was difficult to separate from their sense of intimate knowledge of his life, loves, and traumas. What in other contexts might be considered an unpleasant scream on a song, could be cherished as an invitation to share the emotional discoveries of the primal therapy through which a close friend was passing. Indeed, the excesses and experiments of some of our media friends can be as endearingly annoying to us as the sounds of one of our children learning to play a musical instrument.

Perhaps the most ironic paradox arose when Lennon's later songs tried to puncture the myths that surrounded him and the Beatles. Through his critiques of his superstar status, Lennon increased his intimacy with fans by ridiculing the intimacy that had been previously established and developed. What would otherwise seem absurd comes to make some sense when one realizes that media friends tend to promote the relationship with their fans by speaking to millions of us at once as if they were speaking to each of us alone (Horton & Wohl, 1956). Lennon, then, could seem to be saying to each one of us that his relationship with all the *other* faceless fans was somewhat silly and overblown.

With the media's primary focus on personality, we see an increasing overlap of entertainment, sports, journalism, and government. Actors become politicians (Ronald Reagan, Clint Eastwood, Sonny Bono, Arnold Schwarzenegger), and politicians become part-time actors. (Reverend Jesse Jackson, Congressman Tip O'Neill, Mayor Ed Koch, Mayor Rudy Giuliani, and others have all played themselves on TV comedy programs.) Sports figures turn to acting in advertisements, TV shows, and movies, and famous actors participate in celebrity sports competitions and in shows such as *The Circus of the Stars*. Similarly, TV journalists, including Mike Wallace, Ted Koppel, Tom Brokaw, Dan Rather, and Brian Williams have appeared as celebrity guests on talk shows. Five high-profile newswomen—Katie Couric, Faith Daniels, Joan Lunden, Mary Alice Williams, and Paula Zahn—appeared as themselves in the baby-shower episode of the situation comedy *Murphy Brown*. The talk-show circuit has been playing an unprecedented role in U.S. presidential elections, especially since appearances on CNN's *Larry King Live* launched the "Perot for President" drive in 1992. Of course, major media stars, such as presidents and popes can create their own "talk shows" at any time and in any place by granting exclusive interviews or creating other media events.

The TV-induced blurring of news, entertainment, fiction, and reality was captured in *K Street*, the 10-part series that HBO aired in 2003. The series starred political operatives James Carville and his wife Mary Matalin, and it featured a number of Washington insiders, including *Washington Post* reporter Howard Kurtz and Senators Barbara Boxer, Charles Schumer, and Rick Santorum—all playing themselves in a kind of fictional documentary that seemed more real than much of what is usually aired on television. In the opening episode, for example, Governor Howard Dean is shown getting advice from Carville and Democratic consultant Paul Begala. Later, when a segment from an actual TV broadcast is shown, Dean tells the joke that Carville was earlier shown advising him to tell.

Most print journalists are unknown to their readers. Yet because we experience TV journalists' gestures, tone of voice, and facial expressions, we now often feel as close to them as we do to the public figures they report on. After revealing the personalities and homes of many world leaders and celebrities, Barbara Walters apparently felt it only fair and sensible that she do a television program on her *own* home and personal life. Similarly, Walter Cronkite's retirement from the *CBS Evening News* and Dan Rather's initially troubled attempts to fill the role played by "Uncle Walter" were themselves major news stories. Ironically, Cronkite was considered "the most trusted man in America" and was viewed as a viable presidential candidate, even though no one knew—until years after his retirement from the nightly news—what his political views were.

CALCULATED INTIMACIES

The degree to which our sense of intimacy with media friends is coincidental or calculated varies tremendously. As noted previously, early filmmakers seemed genuinely surprised by the personal attachments to the "hired help." Later, however, film studios devoted much energy to courting and shaping the emotional attachments of fans. Beatles' manager Brian Epstein probably helped make the Beatles more acceptable by softening their rough edges before introducing them to the world. Yet, Beatlemania ultimately relied as much on what Epstein could not control about the quartet's irreverent behavior as on the aspects he could shape to his liking.

Although the media-induced bonds with Elvis, President Kennedy, and the Beatles were planned, there remained a sense of innocence and freshness to those relationships. They were among the first of their kind, and the nature and scope of such media friendships were unanticipated by the performers, their handlers, and the public. Subsequent relationships seem more familiar, and more calculated.

Now, those media friends who trade on the mystique of their "offbeat, creative personalities" more willingly expose dimensions of their lives that could remain private. Madonna did this in the movie *Truth or Dare*. A very different sort of media friend, filmmaker Francis Ford Coppola, released a revealing "home movie," *Hearts of Darkness: A Filmmaker's Apocalypse*, about the personal and professional problems he endured during the making of *Apocalypse Now*. In a similar revelatory vein, Lady Diana stunned the British Royal Family with a 1995 TV interview in which she admitted to having an eating disorder, engaging in adultery, and attempting suicide. The even bigger shock for Diana's in-laws, however, was that these revelations, rather than destroying Diana's public image, only deepened most of the public's affection for her. Yet although Lady Diana clearly learned to use the media to her advantage in a public relations war with Prince Charles and his family, the difficulty she had escaping the cameras when she wanted privacy made it almost impossible for her to have any "offstage" life.

The spread of DVD technology has added another means for performers and producers to manage and deepen the public's relationships with media friends. DVDs of movies and other performances now typically include a host of "extras," such as outtakes, sequences on "the making of" the production, interviews with the performers and the directors, and so on. These special features encourage audience members to feel as if each of them is being allowed to enter the "backstage" as a quasi-member of the performance team. Yet, what the audience is allowed to see of the backstage is generally carefully selected and controlled.

Relationships with media friends have also been calculatingly fostered or suppressed for ideological reasons. During the McCarthy era, the off-the-record Hollywood blacklist, for example, made it almost impossible for performers who held certain political beliefs to establish, maintain, or enhance media friendships with the public. Politically driven selective focus did not end with the decline of McCarthyism. The U.S. news media have historically made a strong effort to foster posthumous media friendships with the victims of terror and aggression committed by enemies of the United States, while downplaying or ignoring victims of the United States or its allies. For example, there was more U.S. press coverage of the 1984 murder of Polish priest Jerzy Popieluszko by communists than the combined coverage of the murders of 100 religious figures in U.S.-supported countries in Latin America between 1964 and 1985, including the assassination of Archbishop Romero and four U.S. churchwomen raped and murdered by members of the Salvadoran National Guard (Herman & Chomsky, 1988). Similarly, there has been a great imbalance in coverage of the victims of the September 11, 2001 terrorist attacks on the World Trade Center and Pentagon (who were individually pictured and briefly profiled over many weeks in *The New York Times*, for example) in contrast to the much larger number of innocent men, women, and children killed in the U.S. "war on terror" in Afghanistan and Iraq. Moreover, because of policies that were not reported on in the mainstream media and because of innocent victims who were rarely described, let alone pictured, few Americans can fathom the hostility toward the United States that has spread in the Arab world as a result of the thousands of Iraqi children who died every month from 1991 to 2003 in the wake of the U.S.-led sanctions against Iraq (Simons, 2004, p. 382) and the U.S. government's intentional destruction of the Iraqi water supply (Nagy, 2001).

Besides great variations in the amount of coverage, there are also significant variations in the style of coverage. Those killed by official enemies are resurrected in images and in emotional accounts by family and friends, and descriptions of their murders include details of wounds, torture, and abuse—which enhance sympathy for the victims and hostility toward the murderers. Such details are generally muted or suppressed for the victims of "our" actions and those of our government's official friends (Entman, 1991; Herman & Chomsky, 1988). Indeed, so unaccustomed is the American public to hearing the details of the suffering and death caused by U.S. actions or the actions of U.S. allies, that the rare report that describes them, let alone pictures them graphically, is often labeled as "biased," "propaganda," or "anti-American." For this reason, perhaps, CNN's Chair Walter Isaacson wrote in a 2001 memo to his staff that it "seems perverse to focus too much on the casualties or hardship in Afghanistan." The head of CNN's standards and practices, Rick Davis, then offered more detailed instructions about how to "balance" reports of civilian casualties with images or verbal descriptions of the carnage at the World Trade Center (FAIR, 2001). Those experts who would likely talk about U.S.-caused suffering—such as Noam Chomsky, Howard Zinn, and Michael Parenti—are routinely excluded from mainstream media in the United States. They have become, instead, cult media friends through alternative media. Non-mainstream fandom has also developed for some independent journalists, such as Amy Goodman, whose daily news program, *Democracy Now!* (aired on Pacifica Radio and Free Speech TV), routinely reports outside mainstream news narratives about the United States and the world.

A NEW GENRE OF GRIEF

It is when a media friend such as John Lennon, Elvis, or Princess Diana dies unexpectedly, that the unusual nature of the relationship is most evident. For unlike the loss of a real friend or relative, the mourning for a media friend is not eased by traditional rituals or clear ways to comfort the bereaved.

Attempts to attend the actual funeral or to speak to the dead person's family are, after all, intrusions by strangers.

In order to banish the demons of grief and helplessness, thousands of people spontaneously gather in the streets or parks, or hold vigils near the media friend's home or place of death. Instant shrines are created. Within 2 hours of Lennon's 11p.m. murder, for example, nearly 1,000 people gathered outside John and Yoko's apartment building (Mayer et al., 1980).

> By morning, the gates of the Dakota looked like the wall of a Mexican church, or an instant Lourdes, covered with a collage of flowers, messages, photographs, drawings. The crowd had been brought together as if to some new Holy Place, expressing a deep primitive need to mourn. (Hamill, 1980, p. 39)

Others gathered in Dallas' Lee park, the Boston Common, San Francisco's Marina Green, the ABC entertainment complex in Los Angeles, and similar locations around the country (Mayer et al., 1980).

The sudden death of a media friend often leads real friends—new, old, and half forgotten—to telephone or e-mail each other to mourn their shared media friend. Strangers embrace and cry. Crowds stand in silent witness or chant the dead hero's words or songs. The pain is paradoxical: It feels personal, yet it is strengthened by the extent to which it is shared with the crowd.

On October 9, 1985 (John Lennon's birthday), a permanent memorial site for Lennon, Strawberry Fields, was established in a section of Central Park near where he had lived. One can go there any day to meet fellow Lennon devotees. Crowds gather there annually on Lennon's birthday and on the day he was killed (December 8), surrounding the mosaic that bears the title of one of his most famous songs, "Imagine." Beatles fans spontaneously assembled there again when the news of George Harrison's death from cancer was reported in November 2001.

Just as media friendships develop over national borders more easily than place-based friendships, the feelings of mourning for a media friend may be surprisingly deep in distant lands. The assassination of President John Kennedy spawned torchlight processions in Berlin and Berne, moments of silence in Tokyo department stores, crowds gathered around radios and television sets in Paris, and other spontaneous rituals of mourning from Nairobi to Seoul (United Press International & American Heritage Magazine, 1964, pp. 48-51). Similarly, Lennon's murder led to an outpouring of emotion around the globe. Even in Warsaw—for 1 day at least—newspapers gave more coverage to Lennon's death than to the Soviet troops massing on the border ("Sharing the grief," 1981). One hundred and twenty three countries contributed to the establishment of the Strawberry Fields gardens in Central Park. The international attachment to Lady Diana was testified to by the presence at her funeral of 2,000 celebrities and hundreds of members of royal families from around the world. The funeral, transmitted by satellite television to 200 countries in 44 languages, reached an estimated 2.5 billion viewers, making it the most-watched event in history (Brown, Basil, & Bocarnea, 2003).

Millions of mourners, scattered as they may be across vast territories, draw on a stock of shared intimacies and "secrets" that bring similar spontaneous worries, concerns, and shattered dreams. With Lennon, these included the pain that stemmed from the knowledge that he had played the key parenting role for his five-year-old son, Sean, and would not be able to fulfill the comforting promise in his just-recorded lullaby, "Beautiful Boy" ("have no fear . . . your daddy's here"). There was empathy for Lennon's teenage son Julian (named after John's mother, Julia), from his first marriage, who was just getting to know his father and, now, like John, had lost the same parent twice. There was the sadness felt for John's Aunt Mimi, who had raised him from the age of 3. There was also every die-hard Beatles fan's hope—often unexpressed (John, after all, would not approve) and now meaningless—that the Beatles would somehow, sometime, someplace perform together again. There were even sillier shared notions, such as that we would never get to see if John would indeed come to look like the spirited old man pictured in artist Michael Leonard's well-known picture of the aged Beatles, an illustration for their song "When I'm Sixty-Four."

Ironically, but appropriately, the media that give birth to these relationships also provide the most ritualized settings for mourning a media friend's death. Radio and television present specials, retrospectives, and commentaries. Following John Kennedy's assassination, U.S. television networks suspended their regular programs and commercials for 4 days. After Lennon's murder, many radio stations throughout North America and Europe played nothing but Beatles music and Lennon songs and interviews, or opened their phone lines to grief-stricken callers. Even Radio Moscow, in then Communist Russia, devoted 90 minutes to Lennon's music (Flippo, 1981; Mayer et al., 1980). Other media friends guide us through our grief by hosting the media memorials. The ultimate tribute to a widely loved media hero, however, is the rare suspension of all media-friend magic—a minute or more of media silence.

To be prepared for their important role in mourning the heroes they have helped to create, media professionals must always be ready to turn their growing collections of the sounds and images of a living media friend into an instant memorial. The media stalk some celebrities almost constantly, not only to capture the ongoing stream of their lives, but also to be near when the end comes. Ever since the news media had to rely on an amateur movie (the Zapruder film) to replay the assassination of President Kennedy, network news cameras have kept what is grimly called a "death watch" on the president and major presidential candidates whenever they are in public (Mankiewicz & Swerdlow, 1979, p. 108).

The case of Princess Diana offers a tragic irony on this point: The drive to photograph her every move is widely seen as having contributed, at least indirectly, to her untimely death in a car that was speeding through the streets of Paris to escape the pursuing paparazzi. In a similar vein, John F. Kennedy, Jr.'s hunger to pilot the type of small airplane in which he, his wife, and sister-in-law were killed was stimulated in part by his desire to avoid the commotion and media intrusions that accompanied his travel through public spaces, including airports.

In a more humorous incident in June 1998, members of the U.S. Congress eulogized comedian Bob Hope in an impromptu memorial service televised by C-SPAN before it was realized that the Associated Press had mistakenly posted an "advance obituary" of the still-living Hope on its Web site. As the embarrassed news service explained, many major news organizations prepare obituaries of celebrities ahead of time so "copy can be moved quickly when they die" ("Bob Hope laughs," 1998). When Hope did, in fact, die 5 years later, the news media were well prepared.

Media friends are not allowed to rest even after their deaths. Unlike most of us, media friends often perform at their own memorial services. In media specials, public vigils, and private rituals, the mourned media friend's "live" image and voice are played and replayed as if to revive the dead. As television cameras focused on President John Kennedy's flag-draped casket in St. Matthew's Cathedral in 1963, for example, the images of the ending of a relationship with a president were contrasted with the sounds of its inauguration: "Ask not what your country can do for you; ask what you can do for your country" (Barnouw, 1990, p. 337). "Family album" images of Kennedys—both living and dead—were displayed again in 1999 during the media coverage of the JFK, Jr. plane crash and funeral. Similarly, familiar images of Princess Diana were broadcast as part of her 1997 funeral as the visual accompaniment to media friend Elton John's eulogistic adaptation of his song "Candle in the Wind" (originally written about another media friend, Marilyn Monroe).

The final irony is that, in many ways, the media friend never dies. After all, the only means through which most people came to know him or her—records, films, tapes, and discs—remain available forever. Dead media friends' images and voices continue to live all around us. Even 10 years after his death, Lennon was still with us to perform his song "Imagine" to 1 billion people simultaneously over radio stations in 130 countries, in celebration of what would have been his 50th birthday ("Lennon broadcast," 1990). Lennon was there again on New Year's Day 1992 to mark a peace accord in El Salvador by singing "Give Peace a Chance" on the rebels' radio station

(Mine, 1992). Long-dead comedians Gilda Radner and John Belushi still visit us and make us laugh on reruns on cable TV's *Comedy Central*. Months after his death, actor Michael Landon was in my living room trying to sell me a program to help my children do better in school. And Marilyn Monroe and Humphrey Bogart maintain an embodied presence in our media experiences, long after their real bodies have turned to dust. Advances in digital technology now allow dead media friends to add performances to their professional résumés, as their images are inserted into new advertisements, situation comedies, and variety shows.

When a media friend dies, the relationship is embalmed rather than destroyed. In a sense, nothing that we actually have had is taken away from us, but the sense of loss is profound nevertheless. Perhaps it is the potential and hope for increased intimacy that dies, and the never-to-be face-to-face consummation of the relationship that is most mourned.

LIVING WITH THE LOSS

The feelings of loss after a media friend's death and the dashed hopes for a potential deepening of the relationship are partially addressed through a variety of avenues. There is a steady stream of "never-before-published" photos, "rare footage" of personal moments, bootlegged tapes of performances that were thought to have gone unrecorded, and reprocessed and remastered versions of old recordings. There are even a few "new" performances, such as when John Lennon sang his "Free as a Bird," accompanied by the other three former Beatles, 15 years after his murder. There are interviews with people who knew the media friend personally. There are impersonators who recreate the live performance style of the media friend for audiences who want to experience it again and for those who are saddened by having missed the real thing when the opportunities were still available. There are other media friends, new and old, who write and sing tributes to the deceased. Sometimes, there is growing fame and affection for those who lived with them. The successful acting career of Elvis' ex-wife Priscilla Presley, for example, seemed to keep alive a part of Elvis' youth; he saw something special about her when she was only 14. Similarly, Yoko Ono's prestige and appeal grew after she became John Lennon's widow (for examples from immediately after the killing, see Brownmiller, 1981, and "Sharing the grief," 1981). The loss of future facets of the media friendship, then, is offset partially by adding dimensions and depths to the past.

For those who are more patient, there is the fascination with the offspring of deceased media friends and the hope that they will grow up to carry forward their parents' names and characters. Julian Lennon, for example, rocketed to fame in 1984 with a debut album in which he sounded eerily like his father. Fourteen years later, Lennon fans' eyes and ears turned to Julian's younger half brother, Sean, as he launched his recording career. The decades of glimpses of Lisa Marie Presley's slightly crooked smile and drooping eyelids, inherited from her father, were enough to give Elvis fans some small solace, and they set the stage for a warm reception for her debut rock album in 2003. The children of John and Robert Kennedy are scrutinized for hints that they may have within them some of the greatness of their fathers (which explains part of the intensity of the sadness surrounding JFK, Jr.'s untimely death). And death seems to take a holiday when modern recording technology allows for such feats as singer Natalie Cole accomplished in 1991 when she recorded a duet with her father, Nat King Cole, who had died 26 years earlier, when Natalie was only 15.

As popular as media friends are in their lifetimes, they tend to be even more widely accepted after they are dead. Many political differences dissolved in the face of the growing JKF legend. (It is difficult now to imagine, for example, that Kennedy had taken his fateful trip to Dallas, Texas, in part because he had significant concerns about not being re-elected in 1964.) Elvis' death stimulated an interest in his music among those too young and too old to embrace him when he was alive. And, after his death, Lennon — who lived on the radical side of the pop-culture spectrum — was praised by conservatives (such as William Buckley) and by high-culture institutions. The Tate Gallery in London, for example, broke precedent and mourned him even though his work was not represented within its walls (Mayer et al., 1980).

For long-time fans of the media friend, the wider cultural embrace of their dead hero is both upsetting and pleasing. On the one hand, there is a negative feeling of the relationship being diluted and co-opted: "He was my friend, not yours, while he was alive." On the other hand, there is the positive sense of vindication for believing in the importance of the media friend before others came to the same realization: "Now the whole world understands."

Fans may also hope to gain some solace by sharing their relationship with the media friend with their own children. Yet, given the origin of the strongest emotional bonds between fan and media friend — in vicarious interactions over real time in the lives of both parties — the deep mourning for a media friend is often specific to the members of the age cohort or subculture who have spent the most time "with" the media friend. Even in the case of those figures who have transcended specific ages and subcultures — such as John Kennedy and John Lennon — the sense of loss is not easy to convey to those who were very young or not yet born when the media friend died. Each generation has its own media experiences and special media friends. In this sense, media friendships not only emotionally bind strangers together, they also create new emotional rifts between generations growing up in the same household.

Nevertheless, because of the continued existence of the actual means through which the media friendship grew—technologically produced images and sounds—the current media environment also allows for new means of sharing these experiences across generations. Perhaps even more than in traditional societies, we are able to have our children see and hear exactly those things that we saw and heard before they were born. Our children may follow in the same footsteps of discovery, watching early performances and then later ones, or they may work backward, or, more typically, they may follow a random pattern.

Of course, the contexts that gave some of the original performances their cultural impact and meaning are usually gone. What teenager of today could understand the outrage and sensation over the way that Elvis Presley moved his legs, for example (leading him to be disparagingly labeled "Elvis the pelvis")? What person not yet at the age of consciousness at the time could fathom the disgust and excitement generated by the short bangs on the Beatles' foreheads (which were then seen as shaggy "long hair")? Most of all, the titillating anticipation of a new relationship of uncertain future is missing, and the often tense negotiations over the media friend's place in the culture are largely over. Yet, some of the magic may remain. My children, born in the 1980s, have been enchanted by the early Elvis' sad eyes and crooked smile, by the Beatles' irreverent humor and cheeky demeanor, by Martin Luther King's powerful oratory, and by President John F. Kennedy's youth, charm, and dynamism.

Fans' sense of loyalty to the memory of a media friend may make them angry over the seeming disloyalty of the media friend's family and real friends, who often refuse to play and replay the roles set for them in the media images from the days immediately following the media friend's death. "How could Jackie remarry?" "How could Yoko seem so cheerful?" "How could Diana's sons appear to be so happy?"

In addition to placing constraints on survivors, the sense of intimate personal knowledge of media friends also places new limits on artistic and scholarly work. Even in nonfiction and history, there has always been dramatic reconstruction of dead heroes' presentational styles. We omit some things about people and invent others. Thomas Jefferson's speech impediment or Abraham Lincoln's high, squeaky voice are rarely mentioned or portrayed. And many of the stories about young George Washington—such as the one where he, unable to tell a lie, confesses to the chopping down of a cherry tree—were created from thin air. But such omissions and inventions depend on not having a detailed visual/aural record of people. By giving us realistic visual/aural memories, modern media have been narrowing the range of believable and acceptable dramatization. When the lives of dead media friends are portrayed, most audiences now expect the directors and actors to reproduce as closely as possible the look, sound, and feel of the media images they have already experienced and of those that have been discovered after the media friend's death. Thus, the power of the movie *JFK* derives partially from director Oliver Stone's careful recreation of the scenes so familiar from news and documentaries. In *The Buddy Holly Story,* it was important that actor Gary Busey look and sing like Buddy Holly. Val Kilmer was praised for his capturing the appearance, stage presence, and singing style of Jim Morrison in *The Doors.* And it is difficult to imagine John Lennon being successfully portrayed by an actor who does not generally look and sound like him.

New technologies raise the question of how much time fans will devote and how far back they will go to maintain a lifelong relationship with a dead media friend. Image scanners and digital audio already allow for easy reproduction, customized manipulation, and the posting of available sights and sounds on personal web sites. Over the coming years, the potentially obtainable documentary material is likely to increase. Rather than having only a limited number of still photographs or brief silent home movies of the childhoods of our adult media friends, we are increasingly likely to have hundreds of digital photos and hours of camcorder-produced videos shot by parents, neighbors, friends, babysitters, and relatives. We may be able to observe our politicians, newscasters, and artistic performers when they were whiny children, fighting with their siblings, making a mess at dinner, or desperately in need of a nose-wiping. (An unsettling trend may be heralded by the publicly available hardcore home videos of figure-skater Tonya Harding's wedding night, actress Pamela Anderson and rock musician Tommy Lee's sexual escapades on their honeymoon, and a night of sex between heiress Paris Hilton and her ex-boyfriend Rick Salomon.) These kinds of material are likely to change our perceptions of our media friends while they are alive, as well as narrow the range of artistic license in *re*-presenting their lives to us after their deaths.

Because of a sense of personal knowledge, many fans would prefer to watch a documentary with the "real" images and voice of the media friend rather than see a play or movie in which an actor portrays the media friend (just as many people would find greater satisfaction in looking through old photographs, films, and tapes of a deceased relative than in seeing an actor portray the relative). Ironically, the images of media friends are in one sense a step closer to reality than the images of real friends or relatives: They constitute the media friend's existence in our lives. That is, one of the reasons it is difficult not to watch the television set when dead media friends appear is that these are the actual images and sounds of our own emotional life experiences. These recordings more closely resemble the outcome of a successful séance than the recollections stimulated by a moving eulogy.

CONCLUSION: UNREAL, BUT REAL

There are, in short, many things that are odd and fabricated about attachments to media friends. At the same time, these relationships have features
that are very human, very warm, and very caring.

Unlike face-to-face relationships, we have limited control over media
friendships. We can rarely influence our media friends directly and personally. Furthermore, we cannot create the friendships on our own; we can only
select from those that are offered to us. Moreover, the array of widely accessible media friendships is often limited by powerful political and economic
forces that are directed toward maximizing corporate profits and narrowing
political discourse. Nevertheless, there are many media friends from which
to choose, and they generally enrich our lives while placing few, if any,
demands on us.

Although some fans are driven to try to see, touch, and influence their
media heroes, most other fans do not seek to experience media friends in a
close face-to-face encounter. For the latter, perhaps, the spell of vicarious
intimacy would be weakened or broken by a media friend's real-life blank
stare, or a look of annoyance or fear. It is through their media performances, after all, that most media friends create the greatest sense of comfort and
intimacy with each of us.

One can think of the spread of media friendships as a sad commentary
on an impersonal society, a world where, as Baudrillard (1988, p. 167) warns,
we have substituted "signs of the real for the real itself." Or, more reassur-
ingly, we can view the feelings toward media friends as part of a broadening
of human caring across a wider field. Media now expand the sphere of empathy that was once restricted primarily to those who shared the same physical spaces. Even brief TV-fostered relationships—with starving Ethiopian
children, with a teacher chosen to travel into space, with Chinese students
protesting for democracy, or with the victims of a bombing in a television
war—have potent emotional impact. It is almost as if we, as a species, are
hard-wired to react in a personal way to those whose faces we can see in
detail. When the camera moves from long shot to close-up, our emotions are
engaged.

Even with the selected people we are permitted to see through the mainstream media, the age-old ability to dehumanize physically distant others—
one of the bases of war—may be growing weaker. Moreover, to the extent
that the Internet continues to flourish largely beyond direct government and
corporate control, it will promote new links and relationships between a
wider range of celebrities and their fans, as well as new forms of media
friendships among noncelebrities, regardless of physical distance. Such
media undermine the power of place to define communities, while fostering
new forms of kinship and communion (Meyrowitz, 1985, 1997).

In the world of media friends, the sacred and profane blend—in style, location, and conversation. Talk show hosts and rock stars develop devoted followings that are the envy of religious leaders, while religious leaders increasingly adopt the informal behavioral styles of other media friends. Formerly distinct settings blur; the Pope and Madonna share the same airwaves. The two extremes of the sacredness spectrum collide in humor by and about media friends—"John Paul Elected Pope; George Ringo Pissed," ran one mock newspaper headline.

For those who hound, stalk, or kill their media friends, the relationship is often an all-consuming passion. Even among the general population, however, the array of media friendships takes an important place among daily live interactions with family, friends, and colleagues. Real friends and associates often discuss the antics of their media friends. For many members of society, celebrity gossip is a game that ties real-life friends to each other and that is not necessarily accompanied by reverence for, or deep emotional ties with, the celebrities being discussed (Gamson, 1994). For many others, however, as uncomfortable as it can be to admit, the death of some media friends may hurt more deeply than the deaths of some of our acquaintances or relatives.

In the final analysis, no theoretical discussion of these unreal, but real relationships can explain them away or weaken their emotional power. We may never have seen them in the flesh, and they would not have taken note of our deaths, but when our media friends die or are killed, we feel pain. We worry about their widowed spouses and fret over their children who have lost a parent. We dwell on ways the tragedy could have been avoided. Sometimes, we even feel partly responsible, as if we could have saved or warned them.

I understand the absurdity of many aspects of the relationships with media friends, yet I have also felt all these things. When a TV program airs a clip of President John Kennedy, I am riveted to the screen. The negative information I have learned about Kennedy's backstage behavior somehow coexists with, rather than mutes, the positive feelings engendered by his media persona. As for John Lennon, I continue to find it difficult to listen to the last music album he released before his death. Although almost three decades have passed since Lennon was murdered, my emotions remain raw. Yes, I never really knew him. Yes, he was not even aware of my existence. But I still miss him.

ACKNOWLEDGMENTS

Earlier versions of this chapter appeared in Drucker and Cathcart (1994) and Le Guern (2002). The author thanks Candice Leonard, Renée H. Carpenter,

REFERENCES

ABC News/WABC/abc12 (2004, February 17) The Dean scream: The version of reality that we didn't see on TV. Viewed September 2004 at http://abclocal. go.com/wjrt/news/012904_NW_r2_group_deanscream.html.

Alperstein, N.M., & Vann, B. H. (1997). Star gazing: A socio-cultural approach to the study of dreaming about media figures. *Communication Quarterly, 45*(3), 142-152.

An innocent life, a heartbreaking death. (1989, July 31). *People Weekly*, pp. 60-62, 64.

Barnouw, E. (1990). *Tube of plenty: The evolution of American television* (2nd rev. ed.). New York: Oxford University Press.

Baudrillard, J. (1988). Simulacra and simulations. In M. Poster (Ed.), *Jean Baudrillard: Selected writings* (pp. 166-184). Stanford, CA: Stanford University Press.

Bob Hope laughs at report of his "death." (1998, June 6). *Foster's Daily Democrat* (AP), pp. 1, 14.

Boorstin, D. (1961). *The image: A guide to pseudo events in America*. New York: Harper & Row.

Brown, W.J., Basil, M.D., & Bocarnea, M.C. (2003). Social influence of an international celebrity: Responses to the death of Princess Diana. *Journal of Communication, 53*(4), 587-605.

Brownmiller, S. (1981, January 22). Yoko and John. *Rolling Stone*, p. 25.

Bumiller, E. (2003, May 16). Keepers of Bush image lift stagecraft to new heights. *The New York Times*, pp. A1, A20.

Caughey, J.L. (1984). *Imaginary social worlds: A cultural approach*. Lincoln: University of Nebraska Press.

Clarke, G. (1980, December 22). A lethal delusion. *Time*, p. 29.

Clymer, A. (1982, January 31). Poll finds Reagan popularity rating misleads. *The New York Times*, p. 22.

Cocks, J. (1980, December 22). The last day in the life. *Time*, pp. 18-24.

Drucker, S. J., & Cathcart, R. S. (Eds.). (1994). *American heroes in a media age*. Cresskill, NJ: Hampton Press.

Elvis Presley Enterprises. (2004). EPE History and Structure. Viewed September 6, 2004 at http://www.elvis.com/corporate/elvis_epe.asp.

Entman, R. (1991). Framing U.S. coverage of international news: Contrasts in narratives of the KAL and Iran Air incidents. *Journal of Communication, 41*(4), 6-27.

FAIR, CNN says focus on civilian casualties would be 'perverse.' (2001, November 1). Action Alert. Viewed online August 26, 2004, at http://www.fair.org/ activism/cnn-casualties.html.

Flippo, C. (1981, January 22). Radio: Tribal drum. *Rolling Stone*, p. 19.

Fowles, J. (1992). *Starstruck: Celebrity performers and the American public.* Washington, DC: Smithsonian.

Gamson, J. (1994). *Claims to fame: Celebrity in contemporary America.* Berkeley: University of California Press.

Gilatto, T. (1998, October 26). Fade to black. *People*, pp. 133, 136.

Gold Collector's Series. (2004). *A tribute to Ronald Reagan.* Ambler, PA: London.

Goffman, E. (1959). *The presentation of self in everyday life.* New York: Anchor.

Goffman, E. (1981). Radio talk: A study of the ways of our errors. In E. Goffman (Ed.), *Forms of talk* (pp. 197-327). Philadelphia: University of Pennsylvania Press.

Grunwald, L. (1991, December). Why we still care. *Life*, pp. 34-36, 38, 40, 42-44, 46.

Hamill, P. (1980, December 22). The death and life of John Lennon. *New York*, pp. 38-50.

Herman, E. S., & Chomsky, N. (1988). *Manufacturing consent: The political economy of the mass media.* New York: Pantheon Books.

Horton, D., & Wohl, R. R. (1956). Mass communication and para-social interaction: Observations on intimacy at a distance. *Psychiatry, 19,* 215-229.

LeGuern, P. (Ed.). (2002). *Les Cultes médiatiques: Culture fan et oeuvres cultes.* Rennes: Presses Universitaires de Rennes.

Lennon broadcast is beyond imagination. (1990, October 5). *Portsmouth Herald* (AP), p. D8.

Leonard, C. (1999, March 7). Liverpool: You will never lose affection. *Boston Sunday Globe*, pp. M1, M19.

Lyall, S. (1999, December 31). George Harrison stabbed in chest by an intruder. *New York Times*, pp. A1, A10.

Mankiewicz, F., & Swerdlow, J. (1979). *Remote control: Television and the manipulation of American life.* New York: Ballantine Books.

Marcus, G. (1981, January 22). Life and life only. *Rolling Stone*, pp. 26-27.

Mathews, T., with Abramson, P., Morris, H., & Maier, F. (1980, December 22). Lennon's alter ego. *Newsweek*, pp. 34-35.

Mayer, A. J., with Agrest, S., & Young, J. (1980, December 22). Death of a Beatle. *Newsweek*, pp. 31-36.

Mead, G. H. (1934). *Mind, self, and society: From the standpoint of a social behaviorist* (C. W. Morris, Ed.). Chicago: University of Chicago Press.

Meyrowitz, J. (1985) *No sense of place: The impact of electronic media on social behavior.* New York: Oxford University Press.

Meyrowitz, J. (1986). Television and interpersonal behavior: Codes of perception and response. In G. Gumpert & R. Cathcart (Eds.), *Inter/Media: Interpersonal behavior in a media world* (3rd ed., pp. 253-272). New York: Oxford University Press.

Meyrowitz, J. (1997). Shifting worlds of strangers: Medium theory and changes in "them" vs. "us." *Sociological Inquiry, 67*(1), 59-71.

Meyrowitz, J. (1998). Multiple media literacies. *Journal of Communication, 48*(1), 96-108.

Mine, D. G. (1992, January 2). Salvadoran guns to fall silent. *Foster's Daily Democrat* (AP), p. 7.

Morrison, B. (2004, January 21). Dean scream gaining cult-like status on Web. *USA Today*. Viewed September 6, 2004 at http://www.usatoday.com/news/politicse-lections/nation/2004-01-22-dean-usat_x.htm.

Nagy, T. J. (2001, September). The secret behind the sanctions. *The Progressive*, pp. 22-25.

Rosengren, K. E., & Windahl, S. (1972). Mass media consumption as a functional alternative. In D. McQuail (Ed.), *Sociology of mass communications* (pp. 166-194). London: Penguin.

Sandman, P. M., Rubin, D. M., & Sachsman, D. B. (1982). *Media: An introductory analysis of American mass communication* (3rd ed.). Englewood Cliffs, NJ: Prentice-Hall.

Schickel, R. (1985). *Intimate strangers: The culture of celebrity*. New York: Doubleday.

Sharing the grief. (1981, January 22). *Rolling Stone*, pp. 20, 73-75.

Schaumburg, R. (1976) *Growing up with the Beatles*. New York: Pyramid.

Simons, G. (2004) *Iraq: From Sumer to Post-Saddam* (3rd ed.). Houndmills, UK: Palgrave.

Sklar, R. (1975). *Movie-made America: A cultural history of American movies*. New York: Random House.

Spencer, S. (1981, January 22). John Lennon. *Rolling Stone*, p. 13.

Stengel, R. (1992, March 16). Midnight's mayor. *Time*, pp. 58-61.

Strate, L. (1994). Heroes: A communication perspective. In S.J. Drucker & R.S. Cathcart (Eds.), *American heroes in a media age* (pp. 15-23). Cresskill, NJ: Hampton Press.

Toufexis, A., with Lafferty, E., & Sachs, A. (1989, July 31). A fatal obsession with the stars. *Time*, pp. 43-44.

United Press International & American Heritage Magazine. (1964). *Four days: The historical record of the death of President Kennedy*. New York: American Heritage Publishing Co.

Chapter 6

THE WRINKLE THEORY

The Deconsecration of the Hero

Gary Gumpert
Communication Landscapers

"See the hero run, look for the flaws, watch the hero fall, look for another hero." In this chapter Gumpert asks why our contemporary heroes become so quickly tarnished and why we seem to have a growing preference for desecrated heroes. He examines the public confusion over celebrity and hero and offers an explanation for the rise of the anti-hero. His position is that the fascination with the flawed and contaminated hero is related, in part, to the Aristotelian notion of the tragic hero and, in part, to the transformation of the tragic flaw by our contemporary media. He describes how the comic book hero has shifted from the all powerful to the vulnerable, how radio brought the hero into the living room, and how the motion picture and TV screen brought us close enough to the hero to be able to detect physical and emotional flaws. He offers his "wrinkle theory" to explain the present shift in allegiance from the protagonist to the antagonist.

✧   ✧   ✧

PROLOGUE:
DEWRINKLING THE WRINKLE

Since writing this chapter, the technologizing of the superhero has continued to accelerate. The premise remains—that the wrinkled attire of the hero is not conducive to their depiction. Although the television camera revealed the flaw, the wrinkle, the blemish—never a problem in the airbrush and ink world of daily comic strip and comic book—it became the sartorial flaw that did them in. But the continuing convergence of flaw eradicating technology results in the flawless hero created and controlled through the convergence of animation and human actor, the morphing (the controlled transformation) of one image into another. The process of digitalization results in the fusing of photography, graphic arts, animation, and the human being. The result is a hybrid form in which the human body is both transformed and controlled.

Television has never been the medium of the superhero—it is too penetrating, too small, too revealing. Even the scope of the motion picture is reduced to unheroic dimensions when broadcast within the confines of a 4x3 aspect ratio. How wide-screen high-definition television will shape the superhero is difficult to forecast, but certainly there will be an impact. The dewrinkling of the superhero has taken a curious path—from the airbrush virtuosity of the comic book to the cruel video destruction of actors attempting to assume the uniform of heroism to Matrix morphing magic to the video game and the consumer-controlled destiny of the subjects and on to Botox magic and plastic surgery. The postproduction wizards are able to transform, erase, and mask the signs of mortality and the scars of surgery. The digitalization process dewrinkles the mundane and transforms the ordinary into the façade of the heroic.

CONTEMPORARY HEROES

Hero . . . Antiq. A name given to men of superhuman strength, courage, or ability, favored by the gods; regarded later as demigods, and immortal. 2. One who does brave or noble deeds; an illustrious warrior 1586. 3. A man who exhibits extraordinary bravery, firmness, or greatness of soul, in connexion with any pursuit, work, or enterprise; a man admired and venerated for his achievements and noble qualities 1661. 4. A man who forms the subject of an epic; the chief male personage in a poem, play, or story 1697. (*Oxford Universal Dictionary*, 1955, p. 895)

Despite this antediluvian sexist explication, the definition is cited to serve as a barometer, a yardstick, to gauge and measure the vagaries of the word. The use and application of *hero* is complex and bewildering. What is a hero? Who are our heroes? This chapter contrasts our conflicting notions of the hero and shows that our relationship to the phenomenon is linked to the intrinsic properties that define the media that are used to disseminate the legends of heroes.

The heroes of the past are generally vivid two-dimensional figures whose persona and portraits appear to have been painted with broad bold strokes. They are figures whose deeds inspire, awe, and overshadow the simple ordinary human folk. Each culture has a set of heroes of the past who represent virtue and sacrifice, whose determination against a host of forces serves as symbols of courage. These are the symbols of morality transmitted from one generation to the next. They are the nondebatable images of the past that persist and guide. But the unquestionable nature of such heroes seems to have vanished in the contemporary quest for larger-than-life individuals with whom to identify. The hero business is not what it used to be. It has descended into the nether world of the celebrity.

Russell Baker (1990) suggested that Marion Barry's achievements as a Mississippi civil rights activist and his election as mayor of Washington, DC, placed him on a potential hero path from which temptation and greed would successfully entice him.

> Heroes are pretty well all washed up in the United States these days. In place of heroes, we now have celebrities, which is to say, junk people.
>
> The celebrities' social mission is to have their frailties, peccadilloes and vices lavishly recorded by press and television to keep the uncelebrated mass titillated. Their purpose to keep us happy with our anonymity.
>
> Saving yourself from becoming a celebrity is hard once you acquire a taste for seeing your name in headlines. (p. A27)

Women, drugs, and corruption undid the good mayor. Baker suggests that Mayor Barry failed heroism because he succumbed to the less than noble enticements of celebrity status.

Writer Fred Bruning (1990) contrasted the hero worship of Nelson Mandela, as he was released from prison and returned to Soweto, with John Gotti, who returned to his admirers after being acquitted (in the 1989 trial) on charges of hiring assailants to assault and batter a fellow gangster. Bruning, like Baker, expressed a concern about the shortage of heroes.

> Americans may feel they have no choice but to entertain applications from just about anyone-killers, thugs, and hijackers included. We have

the peculiar luxury of choosing our heroes badly and elevating the least worthy beyond their fondest dreams. To a prosecutor in New York, John Gotti may be "a badly articulate lowlife, a thug by even Mafia standards." To those easily dazzled, however, Gotti is irresistible—a strutting and disdainful dandy in slick suits who waves to admirers from behind the windows of a burgundy Cadillac, who sneers at the law and those who enforce it, a movieland character as apt to spend his hours in local hangouts as in the city's finest restaurants, a smoothie who three times in four years has faced criminal charges and all three times beaten the rap, a consummate practitioner of streetsmanship who proved with his swagger and style that only suckers settle for the legal limit. (p. 13)

Then there is the tale of Toyohiro Akiyama, "A Japanese Innovation: The Space Antihero" (Sanger, 1990). For a number of years in the late 1960s and early 1970s, the space program and its astronauts captured the imagination of many people. After all, to be propelled into space and weightlessness, to orbit the earth and walk on the moon, are feats of courage that require adventurers larger than life. It was the hope of the Japanese Television System that having the first television journalist to orbit the earth would boost its ratings. So, they paid the Soviet Union $12 million to have Toyohiro Akiyama accompany Soviet astronauts in space.

> Struggling through the first of his nightly live broadcasts from the heavens, Mr. Akiyama spent a lot of time describing the uglier details of space sickness. A chain smoker, he repeatedly longed for a cigarette. His brain, he complained, felt as if it was "floating around in my head." Told to pack light, he failed to bring along enough underwear . . .
>
> At dinnertime he mused, "I wish I had brought some natto," the smelly, fermented soybeans that even many Japanese say they cannot bring themselves to swallow . . .
>
> Mr. Akiyama seems like a man who wants nothing more than a chance to get back home, open a beer, and light up. He worries that his children are spending too much time in front of the television, even if it is to watch their father bounce into his astronaut colleagues. (pp. 1, 5)

What do Marion Barry, John Gotti, and Toyohiro Akiyama have in common? Probably very little, except the consensus that somehow their stature and nobility does not measure up to the larger-than-life dimensions of the likes of Mahatma Gandhi, Abraham Lincoln, Jeanne D'Arc, George Washington, and Thomas Becket.

Reporter Charles Leerhsen (1990) asked teenagers in a military academy in Indiana, in a girls' school in Dallas, in a high school in the midwest, and on an Indian reservation to list their heroes. The number one choice by consensus of all the students was Chicago Bulls' basketball star, Michael Jordan. The group of eclectic achievers selected by Culver Academy students included, perhaps predictably, a military array of Ulysses S. Grant, Robert E. Lee, Alexander the Great, Chuck Yeager, Audie Murphy, and Sergeant York, in addition to the noncombative roster of Mother Teresa, Martin Luther King, Jr., Houdini, Winnie the Pooh, Lucille Ball, Margaret Thatcher, Superman, and Jane Goodall. Students at the Hockaday School for girls in North Dallas mentioned Martin Luther King, Jr., Michael Jordan, Superman, James Dean, Anne Frank, Oliver North, and Sineaed O'Conner. Pupils at a high school in the Bronx mentioned fashion model Elle MacPherson, Bart Simpson, God, Arsenio Hall, Michelangelo, Larry Bird, Mayor Dinkins, and Public Enemy. The Indian reservation students included Native American heroes such as Fools Crow and Chief Red Cloud, but Michael Jordan got the most votes. In addition, Donald Trump, Michael Milken, and Maury Povich were mentioned.

The Leerhsen survey reveals a tendency to select individuals who are often less noble and more ordinary, but with characteristics more commonly shared by most of the teenagers than the individuals who are generally associated with heroes. Leerhsen mirrored his fellow journalists' observation that the contemporary heroes chosen are a somewhat tarnished and often tawdry group.

> Thanks to TV and celebrity journalism, kids all over the country are choosing from the same menu of celebrities—and rarely with any great enthusiasm. The problem is not that fame comes, these days, to those who don't deserve it. The shortage of really inspiring heroes probably has more to do with the dearth of pure fans. So many kids today are so informed about pop culture-and about who's cheating on their mate and who's cheating on their taxes; who's been to Betty Ford and who still hasn't-that it's as if they have one foot in the audience and one behind the scenes. Such familiarity must inevitably breed at least a little contempt. (p. 47)

Although the confusion between *hero* and *celebrity* is self-evident (they serve different functions), one is struck by an increasingly different perception of the role model as expressed by the polled teenagers from previous periods in time. The loss of the untarnished, traditional hero is the critical and mystifying issue that needs to be explored.

The position taken in this chapter is that the rise of the celebrity, the fascination with a flawed and contaminated hero, and the strange appeal of the villain as hero is related to the effect of contemporary media developments on the Aristotelian notion of those necessary characteristics that constitute the tragic hero.

THE TRAGIC HERO

The nature and status of the hero became an important dramatic theory issue in theater several years ago as scholars debated whether contemporary playwrights could create a modern protagonist with whom the audience would identify in the heroic sense. Can today's playwright emulate the heroic tragedies of Aeschylus, Sophocles, Euripides, and Shakespeare? In the late 1940s, the debate was stimulated by the production of Arthur Miller's *Death of a Salesman.* In response, Joseph Wood Krutch, the dramatic critic for the *Nation,* wrote "Me Tragic Fallacy." For those who claimed that salesman Willy Loman was a contemporary tragic hero, Krutch dissented stating that there could be no common tragic hero without the requisite fall from heights of grandeur; the modern-day hero does not have the necessary eminence to accompany the great fall which evokes our pity and fear (Krutch, 1947).

The original and primary work which articulated the nature of the tragic hero was Aristotle's *Poetics* (1954) in which the hero of Greek drama is described as a great person who falls from "reputation and prosperity" through "some error in judgment," a flaw in his or her character.

> The perfect Plot, accordingly, must have a single, and not ... a double issue; the change in the hero's fortunes must be not from misery to happiness, but on the contrary from happiness to misery; and the cause of it must lie, not in any depravity, but in some great error in his part. (p. 239)

Aristotle's protagonist is a person of such stature and nobility that his or her fall arouses in the audience the "tragic pleasure of pity and fear" (p. 240) (referring to the process of catharsis or purgation that purifies the spirit of that audience as they witness and learn from the downfall of that grand and majestic figure). For the Greek audience the tragedy mirrors reality.

The question posed by contemporary critics is whether for a 20th-century audience this extraordinary sense of a dramatic relationship can ever exist. The Greek and Elizabethan tragedies can be appreciated as works of art, but Krutch (1947) maintained that their therapeutic nature is diminished because the social and psychological structure of modern times is radically different from those early periods in history. "For while to us the triumphant voices come from far away and tell of a heroic world which no longer exists, to them they spoke of immediate realities and revealed the inner meaning of events amidst which they still lived" (p. 518).

Instead of "tragedy" the contemporary theater achieves the "tragic," an experience quite different from the elevation of spirit which characterized earlier dramatic experience.

The term [*tragedy*] is a misnomer since it is obvious that the works in question have nothing in common with the classical examples of the genre and produce in the reader a sense of depression which is the exact opposite of that elation generated when the spirit of a Shakespeare rises joyously superior to the outward calamities which he recounts and celebrates the greatness of the human spirit whose travail he describes. (p. 518)

Krutch used as a basis for his argument the Aristotelian view that tragedy is the "imitation of noble actions," contending that contemporary society has no real conception of a noble action. An action that is considered noble depends on an understanding of nobility; it relies on believing oneself capable of having a grand and heroic nature.

If the plays and the novels of today deal with little people and less mighty emotions it is not because we have become interested in commonplace souls and their unglamorous adventures, but because we have come, willy-nilly, to see the soul of man as commonplace and its emotions as mean. (p. 519)

The tragic fallacy is the assumption or illusion that an individual's soul is an integral part of the universe, that for the moment we detach ourselves from a pessimistic view of the nature of human beings in order to empathize with the dramatic hero.

Whether it is possible to have a tragic hero in a contemporary age may be somewhat of an esoteric question, but its answer provides some clues about an age in which Toyohiro Akiyama, Freddy Krueger, and Darth Vader join Abraham Lincoln, Moses, and John F. Kennedy as either role models or heroes.

THE COMIC BOOK HERO

Heroes are not the same to all people at all times in their lives. Cultural history and diversity shape the portraits of heroes. They serve different functions and needs at particular periods in time and during stages of individual growth and maturation. It seems that during childhood and adolescence especially, a cadre of heroes is required, perhaps to satisfy inner frustrations, perhaps to provide secret visions and dreams in contrast to the external pressures imposed by growing up in an adult world. Therefore, the heroes of youth act as fascinating barometers of attitude. One area in which the dynamics of change can be seen is in the world of comic strips and books.

Stan Lee, one of the impresarios of the comic book, realized in the early 1970s that economics and the times required a change in the persona of the comic book hero. With this in mind he created a number of comic book heroes, all bordering on the edge of the heroic and pathetic. Marvel Comics and Stan Lee produced the Fantastic Four: "The Invisible Girl," "The Human Torch," "Mr. Fantastic," and "The Thing" (later they become "Iron Man," "Thor," "Spiderman," and "Ibe Thing"). Lee's reasoning behind the creation of these strange characters is extremely revealing.

> Let's let them not always get along well; let's let them have arguments. Let's make them talk like real people and react like real people. Why should they all get superpowers that make them beautiful? Let's get a guy who becomes very ugly. That was the "Thing." I hate heroes anyway. Just because a guy has superpowers, why couldn't he be a nebbish, have sinus trouble and athlete's foot? (cited in Braun, 1971, p. 43)

The most successful of Lee's anti-heroes is Spiderman, an immediate hit. "Spidey," as he is known to his fans, is actually Peter Parker, a teenager who has the proportionate strength of a spider and yet, in Lee's words, "can still lose a fight, make dumb mistakes, have acne, have trouble with girls and have not too much money." Someone says to Spiderman, "Don't you feel like a jerk parading around in public in that get-up?" Spiderman questions himself, "Can they be right? Am I really some sort of crackpot wasting my time seeking fame and glory? Why do I do it? Why don't I give the whole thing up?" (p. 43). So, this strange hero has an identity crisis—one that was symptomatic of an age of anxiety—the strange 1960s.

In an earlier period, the comic book hero was a character of a vastly different sort, responding to a differently woven cultural tapestry. One shift in comic strip history occurred in the 1930s when the adventure strip first appeared. Prior to that time, the comic strip primarily celebrated the comical, rather than the serious narrative of adventure. Of the 22 comic strips that originated in the 1920s, only two—"Buck Rogers" and "Tartan"—stressed the power of the main character. In contrast, 21 strips were begun in the 1930s, and 12 of them were about powerful people including: "Joe Palooka," "Dick Tracy," "Terry and the Pirates," "Flash Gordon," "The Lone Ranger," "Alley Oop," and "Superman." One explanation of this trend was offered by Sales (1972), writing in *Psychology Today:*

> When we are afraid . . . we turn to strong leaders who can protect us. We become intolerant of outgroups and of those who differ from us. We admire power and those who wield power; we come to despise weak-

ness and ambiguity. We are cynical about mankind, and we become superstitious. In short, when we are threatened, we become authoritarian. (p. 94)

What is particularly significant in the Marvel Comic shift is the transformation of the traditional comic book hero from the "all-powerful" to the "vulnerable somewhat-powerful" character. Suddenly, instead of superheroes who make no mistakes, superheroes emerge with flaws in their character.

In 1970, Denny O'Neil revived the adventures of two superheroes, "Green Lantern" and "Green Arrow." The revival took place at a time of social turmoil in the United States, at a time when activism, protest, and disillusionment had become commonplace.

FOR YEARS HE HAS BEEN A PROUD MAN! HE HAS WORN THE **POWER RING** OF THE **GUARDIANS,** AND USED IT WELL, AND NEVER DOUBTED THE RIGHTEOUSNESS OF HIS CAUSE .... [The box of narrative accompanies the image of the muscular masked hero in green swooping over a crowed urban street full of cars and trucks.]

IN THE NEXT **DOZEN SECONDS,** AN EVENT WILL OCCUR WHICH WILL SIGNAL THE END OF HIS GRANDEUR, AND THE BEGINNING OF A LONG TORMENT ...

THERE WILL BE NO HAPPY ENDING FOR THIS IS NOT A HAPPY TALE ... NOR A SIMPLE ONE, BUT WHAT WE ARE ABOUT TO WITNESS IS, PERHAPS INEVITABLE. —HIS NAME, OF COURSE, IS **GREEN LANTERN** [in bold green large letters]— AND OFTEN HAS VOWED—NO **EVIL SHALL ESCAPE MY SIGHT!** [in large bold red letters silhouetted in yellow] ...

HE HAS BEEN FOOLING HIMSELF. (*Green Hornet/Green Lantern,* 1970, p. 1)

That is the introduction to the April 1970 issue that traces the journey of the superheroes from the all-powerful to the doubting to the superhero social activist status. It is a questioning hero who must face the realization that he has defended a middle-aged man being attacked by a mob, only to find out that he rescued a slum lord. In that issue's epilogue, the Green Arrow berates his friend the Green Lantern: "YOU CALL YOURSELF **A HERO!** CHUM ... YOU DON'T EVEN QUALIFY AS A MAN!" (p. 21).

THE CELEBRATION OF THE FLAW

Apparently, the time of the superhero has passed and perhaps Krutch was correct in suggesting that the distance between hero and audience has grown so far that a frame of reference, a required ingredient for the assessment of greatness, has virtually disappeared. Yet the need for heroes persists. Meyrowitz (1985) stated the following:

> Still we hunger for heroes, and perhaps our search beneath social masks is filled with the hope of finding people whose private selves are as admirable as their public ones. But since most of the people who make enduring contributions to our culture remain under our scrutiny too long to remain pure in our eyes, we have also begun to focus on people who make one grand gesture or who complete a single courageous act that cannot be undermined by scrutiny. (p. 311)

Heroes are useful only as long as they are icons with whom an audience can identify, when one's social and psychological needs are not fulfilled elsewhere. The unemployed hero is one who does not survive scrutiny, either because his or her persona is out of date and too remote, or because familiarity has bred contempt. The audience is too close to the former superstar. Instead of the traditional noble hero, the contemporary champion, even if he or she is not one of the average folks, must now exhibit some ordinary traits.

There is yet another aspect of the deconsecration of the hero that is linked to the traditional depiction of the hero. Aristotle described the tragic hero as someone who, through "some error in judgment," a flaw in his or her character, falls from prosperity and stature to destruction and despair. The flaw, in this case, is the pivotal attribute around which the circumstances of the fall revolve. It is the flaw that connected audience and hero and that facilitated the complex emotional relationship in the "tragic pleasure of pity and fear" between audience and hero. The result of that relationship was spiritual and psychological elevation, the celebration of the moral order. The shift in the contemporary approach to the hero requires that not only must the hero share in our ordinariness, but that we discover the less-than-virtuous traits with which we can identify. In short, the flaw is the thing, the trait to be discovered and, perhaps, to be celebrated.

Yet, why should this strange disenchantment with the grand and noble hero emerge at this time? Certainly, time and circumstances change attitudes and perspectives, but additional factors have been instrumental in altering the psychological distance between hero and audience. Assuming that the potential of the heroic is still a part of contemporary society, the extent to which the public has access to heroes or, as Meyrowitz suggested, the degree to which heroes can survive scrutiny, becomes a central controlling factor. This chapter maintains that it is the technology and organization of the media of communication that promote scrutiny and deter, alter, and facilitate the heroic relationship.

THE MEDIUM AND THE HERO

The materials of heroes are legends: tales passed from one generation to the next, surviving the coloration of time, that are eventually gathered and chronicled by masterful tellers of tales. The medium of the traditional hero was memory. Havelock (1963) pointed out the form of the tale was directly connected to the nature of the medium:

> The psychology of oral memorization and oral record required the content of what is memorized to be a set of doings. This in turn presupposes actors or agents. Again, since the content to be preserved must place great emphasis on public and private law, the agents must be conspicuous and political people. Hence they become heroes. All non-human phenomena must by metaphor be translated into sets of doings, and the commonest device for achieving this is to represent them as acts and decisions of especially conspicuous agents, namely gods. (p. 171)

Just as memory is a determinant of heroic form, the very nature of the hero would be transformed over time, along with the evolution and development of media technology.

Each medium is defined by the intrinsic properties, the technical and scientific components, that determine transmission and artistic potential. The sensory components of a medium establish a relationship between audience member and event, based on the nature of that which is transmitted, the actual distance bridged, and the psychological distance that exists between them. Thus, the reader of a book can achieve a level of intimacy with writer, character, and scene because the auditory and visual components of the literary experience are created by words that are decoded from the printed page. The radio listener stimulated by the creative manipulation of sound generates an auditory and visual theater of the mind, based on the absence of the visual. As the comic strip relied on a nonphotographic visual mode, it stylized the visual into either comedic or heroic genres because it could transcend the realistic. Still photography isolates and magnifies detail and stimulates the imagination by freezing details in time. In contrast, the motion picture, with both auditory and visual components, is particularly defined by both the large dark auditorium and the size of the screen on which the images are projected. Therefore, spectacle, pageantry, and the hero are particularly connected with the cinema because of its potentially larger-than-life capability. In contrast, the relatively small television screen miniaturizes spectacle and emphasizes intimacy and detail. There is an obvious connection between the small television screen and cameras, lenses, and the editing system used to capture minute details magnified and transmitted on that screen.

In *I Am A Camera: The Mediated Self* (1986), Cathcart and I pointed out that media technology altered the interaction of individuals and groups. We argued that "not only are the media substantively altering the relationship among individuals, but that the formulation of the individual's *self image is,* in large part, media dependent" (p. 90). Similarly, the sensory components of a medium increase or decrease the psychological distance between the mediated event and the auditor of that event. Thus, the intrinsic properties of each medium determine an ideal aesthetic relationship that is imposed on the content being transmitted. The "star" system of the motion picture can be related to the scope and proportions of the screen and the necessary cameras, film, lenses, and projector simultaneously developed. Television would, however, reduce cinemascopic legends into 17-inch neighbors. It is this transformation of magnitude that is examined in Langer's (1981) analysis of television's "personality system." "What is the significance of the fact that whereas the cinema established a 'star system,' television has not? There are stars of stage, screen and television, but no stars of television alone. Instead we encounter what television calls its 'personalities'" (p. 351).

If familiarity can breed contempt, intimacy may erode nobility. Ong (1977) noted that with the electronic age, "when the possibility of storing detailed verbalized knowledge becomes virtually infinite, the hero has almost vanished as a major conservator of culture" (p. 205). Yet, the details are not only cumulative. Magnified minutia are the essence of intimate media. Sociologist Richard Sennett (1974) wrote that "intimacy is a field of vision and an expectation of human relations" (p. 338). It is an intimacy that is, in some part, based on the defining ability of media technology to bridge distance, either by saturating us with cascades of data or by confusing the public and the private as the camera invades and places the subject under scrutiny, revealing the ordinariness that is shared with others. Although Langer (1981) distinguished between "star" (rather than hero) and "personality," there is a link between the larger-than-life attributes of the "star" and the grandeur and nobility of the "hero."

> Whereas the star system operates from the realms of the spectacular, the
> inaccessible, the imaginary, presenting the cinematic universe as "larger

than life," the personality system is cultivated almost exclusively as "part of life," whereas the star system always has the ability to place distance between itself and its audiences through its insistence on "the exceptional," the personality system works directly to construct and foreground intimacy and immediacy; whereas contact with stars is unrelentingly sporadic and uncertain, contact with television personalities has regularity and predictability; whereas stars are always playing "parts" emphasizing their identity as "stars" as much—perhaps even more than—the characters they play, television personalities "play" themselves; whereas stars emanate as idealizations or archetypal expressions, to be contemplated, revered, desired and even blatantly imitated, stubbornly standing outside the realms of the familiar and the routinized, personalities are distinguished for their representativeness, their typicality, their "will to ordinariness" to be accepted, normalized, experiences as *familiar.* (pp. 354-355)

No medium operates in isolation. Individuals function with, react to, and think in terms of multiple media. We telephone, listen to the radio, work with a computer, watch television, fax a letter, listen to audio discs, watch video discs, and remember when once, not so long ago, records were sold instead of cassettes and discs. The psychological influence of media is both cumulative and interconnected. The point is that one functions in one medium with an awareness of others. Each person perceives the world through a mediated sensorium—a sensory collective created by an awareness and dependency on all operative forms of communication.

Similarly, mass media content influences programming concurrently and over time. Thus, radio, television, motion pictures, and the print media of books, magazines, and newspapers are interconnected in terms of subject matter, content, and treatment. The content featured in one medium often is adapted to the technical and social needs of another.

THE TRANSMOGRIFICATION
OF THE HERO

Nowhere is that interconnection of media forms more clearly demonstrated than in that former world of the hero celebrated in the late 1930s, 1940s, and early 1950s. Batman, Superman, the Lone Ranger, Tarzan, the Green Hornet, Wonderwoman, Terry and the Pirates, Dick Tracy, and Flash Gordon were some of the protagonists who captured the imagination of young children and teenagers who believed in the adventures of their heroes as they loyally followed their exploits in comic strips, comic books, radio serials, and motion pictures (sometimes in animated form, other times in realistic serial form). Most of the heroes began their strange careers as comic strip or book adventurers who would simultaneously display their deeds in radio and film. By the end of 1938, six serials featuring comic book characters were on the national radio networks: Dick Tracy, Don Winslow of the Navy, Jack Armstrong, Little Orphan Annie, Terry and the Pirates, and Tom Mix (Barnouw, 1968).

Many more joined that group before the rise of television in the late 1940s would alter the form and shape of all the other mass media and, in many cases, displace radio programming. Some of the superheroes would attempt the trauma of television (and later, for some, a return to the motion picture medium) adaptation, but few would succeed in the transition without major adaptation and alteration—genre and persona could not escape radical redefinition. It does seem strange that the panoramic setting of the west would so easily be accommodated to the television screen, but it was primarily the western genre that migrated successfully from motion picture to television screen (Hopalong Cassidy, Gene Autry, Roy Rogers, Tex Ritter, Wild Bill Hickok, Wyatt Earp, etc.). Perhaps this was because the western hero was more grounded in limited combat, requiring less heroic (spectacular) deeds, or because the producers understood that the artistic and economic demands of television required a different variation on the theme of heroism.

Several of the original comic book heroes were revived from wherever the remains of superheroes are placed to rest to become curious dopplegangers of their earlier selves. *Batman,* with Adam West, would become a popular television series and would later be produced as a major motion picture starring Michael Keaton. Superman (Parts I, II, III, and IV), with Christopher Reeves as superhero, became a box office hit beginning in the late 1970s. In the summer of 1990, *Dick Tracy* appeared with Madonna and Warren Beatty. Did this renaissance signal the possible return of the superhero genre to the motion picture and television screens? The answer is "no"! Whereas the success of the earlier Batman, Dick Tracy, and Superman characters was based on a naive belief that evil could be confronted and disarmed by the extraordinary, often fantastic (in the literal sense) deeds of individuals who transcended simple mortality, the college students who flocked to the all-night showings of the old **reissued** *Batman* film serials celebrated the joy of camp. The Adam West television series was a spoof, a satire, not necessarily intended for children, but meant for adults who revered the old ghost of a hero. Superman took form in many media—as a radio serial (successful), a motion-picture cartoon (moderately successful), a television serial (uninspired boredom), and as a major motion-picture spectacular. The motion picture was a Hollywood extravaganza in special effects, which reduced Superman to enduring the experience of such ordinary base emotions as love and passion. At the same time, the antagonists of those films achieved new heights of revelry.

THE WRINKLE THEORY

The medium did them in. The medium was not only the message, but it was the culprit, the force that inadvertently unmasked the superhero by revealing the hero's lack of perfection. Comic book superheroes were painted in grand bold strokes, articulated muscles stretched out and held in by luminous uniforms which accentuated sleekness, power, and cut down on wind resistance as they glided from deed to deed. These were the heroes who did not sweat, whose hair was never out of place, whose omnipotence reassured fragile young minds that rescue was always just around the corner, that anything could be overcome if you believed. Superheroes could not withstand the scrutiny of the all-seeing television lens that revealed not major culpability, but minor corporeal disarrangement. Superman probably could withstand the devastating revelation of his double identity, but not the wrinkles that marred his uniform and suggested that perhaps behind that frayed exterior could be found a torn and tattered soul—someone closer to us.

In an age in which even the average mortal can jog down the street in an unwrinkled spandex outfit, in which basketball star Michael Jordan can swoop, glide, and remain suspended in mid-air for what seems like minutes, with athletic skill once thought impossible, the superhero's survival was threatened by the photographic resolution of the television medium. It is the combination of photographic acuity, media's ready access (particularly newspapers, magazines, radio, and television) to event and persona through miniaturization and mobility of equipment, and the extraordinary amount of programming that is required by media organizations and devoured by the American public that dissolved the distance that protects heroes from an invasion of privacy. The aura of necessary invincibility cannot withstand constant and penetrating visibility. The role of heroes has changed. It is not catharsis that the audience seeks, but rather revelation. Most persons, even heroes, would like to protect their wrinkles from public exposure, but it is the collective medium that has created a national pastime—the revelation of the wrinkle. An audience nurtured by penetrating media comes to expect the elimination of the public face and demands insight into the private. Heroes cannot withstand such scrutiny.

One alternative is to transform the hero into a more human and believable force, to transform that symbol of the impossible into something more probable. The results are often comedic with superheroes such as Superman and Batman becoming caricatures of their former selves—to be enjoyed, but never taken seriously as they were when an audience suspended their disbelief and believed.

Another, somewhat bizarre, alternative is to shift one's dramatic allegiance from the protagonist to the antagonist (or for the protagonist to take on the features of the antagonist). This is exactly what began to happen in television and film and even in the comic book. In major motion-picture releases the almost comic/grotesque antagonists such as the Joker, Penguin, Flattop, and Lex Luthor vie for the affections of the fans and replace and dominate the nominal hero. The syndrome is evident in the James Bond films in which high-tech destruction and incarnate evil oppose the predictably debonair James Bond character. Goldfinger and Dr. No, although doomed, charm the audience. It is difficult to explain why and how an audience develops a fascination with two-dimensional representatives of evil, rather than identifying with the agents of morality and virtue. It is the flaw that grips the imagination instead of the ideal of unblemished virtue. It is the blemish and imperfection (often a combination of physical and psychological defects) exemplified in such characters as Darth Vader *(Star Wars)* that dominates the screen.

In Superman III the hero experiences a personality crisis induced by exposure to Kryptonite. The "man of steel" is reduced to a common beer-guzzling destructive low-life. Kael's (1983) review of that film is revealing about the state of heroes:

> So when the soul-sick superman is being prankish or surly—putting out the Olympic torch or straightening the Leaning Tower of Pisa or punching a hole in a tanker and causing an oil spill—we don't know how to react to this lecher with stubble on his chin and a soiled-looking cape. A funky, sexy sheik Superman could have audiences squealing with pleasure, and a Superman with a vendetta against the world could be awesomely neurotic, but the movie has no sooner suggested the possibilities than it drops them. When he sits alone in a bar, boozing and exploding bottles by flicking roasted almonds at them, we get more of a sense of how dangerous—*and attractive*—Superman could be than at any other time. The bad superman has burning dark eyes; he looks like an Etruscan warrior. (p. 90, italics added)

Superman does recover and in the end virtue conquers evil, but Kael's reaction that the evil Superman is potentially more interesting and attractive than either the immaculate good Superman or the wimpy Clark Kent supports my contention that the attraction of the flaw outweighs simplistic righteousness. Whether Superman as antihero is more attractive because the role is more believable, or because we are fascinated by the darker side of human behavior, is difficult to determine, but certainly the character and appeal of the protagonist has changed.

CONCLUSION

Marvel Comic fans have grown up and perhaps also have their heroes. In *Modern Comix: Goodbye, Superheroes and Innocent Mirth. Hello, Angst, Bent Humor and Post-Modernism*, Mernit (1989) reported that about 20% of the 20 million Americans who regularly read comics are older than 25. The average comic book customer is a college-educated 20- to 25-year-old male, who buys six comics a week. The interconnectedness of media and the coming of age of the superhero is succinctly articulated by Mernit:

> Modern comics have even begun to devour their own sources. Winter 1987 saw the appearance of a book-length comic novel called *The Dark Night Returns* . . . featuring none other than Batman. However, this Batman, written by Frank Miller, was utterly unlike the noble crime-fighter you may remember from childhood. He is tired, close to burn-out, and he's become the kind of violent vigilante that Charles Bronson often portrays. He not only kills his enemies, he occasionally misses and kills innocent bystanders. The book's tone is cynical and bleak with more in common with Raymond Chandler and *film noir* than with the rosy optimism of bygone superheroes. Obviously, comics can now be just as ruthless in exploiting and reworking their sources, as any other kind of post-modern art. (p. 20)

The new superhero is not someone you would care to bring home to mother. The new superhero is not someone whom you will emulate when you grow up. The superheroes of our childhood are no longer what they once were. It is not only that the superhero has changed, we all have. There is no one definitive cause that explains the fall of the superheroes and the rise of the flawed, if not corrupted and disillusioned, prototype antiheroes. However, there certainly has been an escalation of the vigilante (*Death Wish, Death Wish II, Rambo, Rambo II*), the unsavory, anti-administration police officer (*Dirty Harry, Dirty Harry II, Shaft, Shaft II*), and the postnuked, devastated Earth and alien warrior (*Road Warrior, Mad Max, Beyond Thunderdome, Terminator 1, Terminator II*) genres.

It is a long way from the Aristotelian hero as a person "not preeminently virtuous and just, whose misfortune, however, is brought upon him not by vice and depravity but by some error of judgement" (Aristotle, 1954, p. 238) to the vigilante. The audience learned from the hero of old that a moral system governed the universe. The vigilante, the self-appointed representative of law and order, also teaches—and the lesson is alarmingly clear—that when authority is no longer capable of governing lawlessness and disorder, any means necessary is sanctioned for the restoration of law and order. All heroes are linked to their times.

A number of interrelated factors can be cited for this national preoccupation with the flaw and the descent of the traditional Mr. Clean superhero from the pantheon of greatness. There are a host of complex social, psychological, and economic elements that influence and alter the need for, the relationship with, and the function of heroes. The argument that media technology is somehow linked to the fall of the hero is seldom offered as another variable, but in our contemporary world, values and beliefs are filtered through a media screen, and the impact is not fully understood. Ralph Waldo Emerson once said that "every hero becomes a bore at last." In a media age, the life of a hero lasts only until all but boredom is revealed.

REFERENCES

Aristotle. (1954). The poetics (I. Bywater, Trans.). In *Rhetorics and poetics*. New York: The Modern Library.

Baker, R. (1990, August 15). The loss of a hero. *The New York Times*, p. A27.

Barnouw, E. (1968). *Tube of plenty: The evolution of American television*. New York: Oxford University Press.

Braun, S. (1971, May 2). Shazam! Here comes the captain relevant. *The New York Times*, pp. 32-33, 36, 38, 41, 43-46, 48, 50, 55.

Bruning, F. (1990, March 5). Contrasts in hero worship. *MacLean's*, p. 13.

Cathcart, R., & Gumpert, G. (1983). Medicated interpersonal communication: Toward a new typology. *Quarterly Journal of Speech, 69*, 267-277.

Cathcart, R., & Gumpert, G. (1986). I am a camera: The mediated self. *Communication Quarterly, 34*(2), 89-101.

Green Hornet/Green Lantern. (1970, April). No. 76. Sparta, IL: National Periodical Publications.

Havelock, E. (1963). *Preface to Plato*. Cambridge, MA: Belknap Press of Harvard University Press.

Kael, P. (1983, July 11). The current cinema: Time-warp movies. *The New Yorker*, pp. 90, 93, 95.

Krutch, J. (1947). The tragic fallacy. In B.H.Barrett (Ed.), *European theories of the drama* (pp. 517-526). New York: Crown Publishers. (Original work published 1929)

Langer, J. (1981). Television's personality system. *Media, Culture and Society, 4*, 351-365.

Leerhsen, C. (1990, Summer/Fall). This year's role model. *Newsweek*, pp. 280-294.

Mernit, S. (1989, June/July). Comix. *Express*, pp. 16-20.

Meyrowitz, J. (1985). *No sense of place: The impact of electronic media on social behavior*. New York: Oxford.

Ong, W. (1977). *Interfaces of the word: Studies in the evolution of consciousness and culture*. New York: Cornell University Press.

Oxford Universal Dictionary. (1955). Oxford: The Clarendon Press.

Sales, S. (1972, November). Authoritarianism. But as for me, give me liberty, or give me, maybe, a great big, strong, powerful leader I can honor, admire, respect and obey. *Psychology Today*, pp. 94-98, 104-143.

Sander, D. (1990, December 7). A Japanese innovation: The space antihero. *The New York Times*, pp. 1, 5.

Sennett, R. (1974). *The fall of public man*. New York: Knopf.

Part II

HEROES AND SEPTEMBER 11

Chapter 7

THE TWO FACES OF OSAMA BIN LADEN

Mass Media Representations as a Force for Evil and Arabic Hero

Mahmoud Eid
University of Ottawa

Osama bin Laden is certainly one of the most notorious, galvanizing figures to emerge in recent years. The embodiment of evil to some, hero to others, he is considered a "controversial hero" to Mahmoud Eid. In this chapter, Eid compares the media use and media coverage of bin Laden as a means of creating bin Laden as a hero of celebrity or evil enemy. He places bin Laden within a larger context of Islamic heroes distinguishing the Muslim/Arab world. This controversial hero is positioned as a distinctive type of Muslim hero who is despised by others.

✧ ✧ ✧

To millions of people in the western world, [Osama bin Laden] has come to be viewed as the personification of evil. On the streets of Cairo, in the mountains of northern Pakistan, and even in the air-conditioned luxury of his native Saudi Arabia, he has many admirers, both open and secret.

— "Special report" (2001, p. 17)

> A follower: We will take revenge from America and its president. They should not think we are weak. We will emerge as heroes of Islam like Osama bin Laden.
>
> —Reeve (1999, p. 202)

Osama bin Laden will live in modern history longer than any American or Arabic political or religious leader, not because of his heroic religious character recognized by some Muslims, his rejection by the vast majority of Arabs and Muslims all over the world, nor the terrible consequences of his militant actions against Western societies, but rather for all of them collectively: hence a new and unique heroic personality bursts on the scene in the 21st century—a *controversial hero.*

RECONCEPTUALIZATION OF THE HERO

Since the September 11, 2001 attacks, many debates have been raised about a number of issues, particularly terrorism. The Arab and Muslim countries disagree with the American definition of terrorism and consider it very selective. Central to this issue is the conception of the *hero.* The September 11 attacks, attributed to Osama bin Laden and his organization, al-Qaeda (the base), have opened a new dimension in the conceptualization of the hero. Who is the hero of the 21st century? Is there any kind of general global agreement about the hero of a specific time and place? Or, are contemporary heroes seen only from the perspective of one adversary or another?

What is new in these times is that the same personality, who is strongly believed to be a hero by one group of people, is simultaneously seen in the opposite way (i.e., as a force for evil) by another large community. This personality, who burst into prominence on September 11, 2001, is Osama bin Laden. What distinguishes bin Laden as a hero (to some Muslim people) from other Islamic heroes who have been compared to him, is that those heroes of old were not despised by their enemies, but bin Laden is vilified by his. Even when enemies confronted one another in battle, they were aware of the heroic personalities among them and dealt with them as heroes. For example, history tells us that Salah ad-Din's (Saladin's) heroic personality was recognized not only by Arabs and Muslims but also by other Arab religions and, most importantly, by his enemies. But in bin Laden's case, only one party, his believers or followers, uphold his heroic qualities, whereas his adversaries strongly reject this idea and, more significantly, brand him as the opposite—a force for evil. It is argued here that the two opposing faces of Osama bin Laden currently in the mass media, the "evil one" in

America's eyes and the "hero" in the eyes of some Arabs and Muslims, are products of the historically unique characteristics of our daily lives. In complicated societies, Browne (1983) explained, heroes wear many faces because of their many responses to the numerous needs of individuals, groups of people, and national purposes.

Mass media play the key role here, as they cannot be separated from their social context, in reflecting this social change. Mass media also use their new features and functions in our modern society to represent the hero in a new form. It is argued here that mass media do not create a hero: They create a celebrity. However, as long as all heroes are celebrities, it is argued that mass media's sophisticated and advanced representation of the contemporary hero gives rise to a new type of hero. As Fishwick (1983) reminded us, "History is not meaningful without people, and people are ineffective without leaders. The search for paragons is inherent in human nature" (p. 10). At the same time, people's needs are changing rapidly and in unprecedented ways in this century, and the available leaders or heroes do not gratify or inspire all populations. The ongoing opposition and conflicts of interests and needs among various groups of people gives rise to a new type of hero. This chapter takes Osama bin Laden as an example of a unique type of hero, the type of the 21st century—the *controversial hero*.

No matter what his political, religious, or ideological persuasion, the hero used to receive universal admiration and respect from his or her followers or the society at large and at the same time from other societies, even those with completely different ideologies. "Controversial nature" here does not mean that the anti-hero or villain becomes a hero to the enemy, but rather that there is no common ground for recognition of the heroic character among the various communities on their respective sides of the conflict, or even within the society from which the hero arose in the first place. In the case of bin Laden, we see a personality who fulfills the heroic dream for a large group of people but at the same time is rejected by many other groups, including those who share his ideology and religion.

bin Laden's personality inspires only one sector of the worldwide population of Muslims, not necessarily all of them are Arabs like he is. They admire him because he satisfies their religious expectations with the carelessness of his ways and tools of achievement. In Pakistan, the headmaster of a large religious school said that bin Laden is a "hero because he raised his voice against the outside powers that are trying to crush Muslims" (Bergen, 2001, p. 31). For the majority of Muslims, bin Laden is considered neither as a political nor a religious hero because he has neither official political affiliation nor popular approval. The wide majority of Arabs and Muslims see paradoxes in bin Laden's actions and ways of serving Islam. For instance, although killing oneself, or suicide, is *Haram* (forbidden) in Islam, bin Laden's men believed their martyrdom would take them to Paradise and saw themselves as *Shuhadaa* (martyrs). Also, according to Islamic rules, it is forbidden to attack women and children, but Osama bin Laden expresses little sorrow for the many innocents killed on September 11.

Significantly, what increases the controversy regarding the heroic nature of bin Laden's personality is the fact that he became a celebrity in the eyes of both sides of Arabic-Muslim world and the West while at the same time being regarded as a hero by a specific group of followers. Therefore, it is argued here that even if "the praise and media attention made bin Laden a sought-after celebrity" (Bodansky, 2001, p. 28), they did not make him a hero; instead, his personal characteristics, deeds and Islamic principles that fulfill the heroic expectations for some Muslim people did. Some of these expectations are voiced in bin Laden's speeches, which include a clear emphasis on basing the confrontation with the United States on more than resistance to the presence of American troops in some Arab countries.

> We as Muslims have a strong feeling that binds us together. . . . We feel for our brothers in Palestine and Lebanon. . . . When 60 Jews are killed inside Palestine (in suicide bombings earlier this year), all the world gathers within seven days to criticize this action, while the deaths of 600,000 Iraqi children (after U.N. sanctions were placed on Iraq) did not receive the same reaction. Killing those Iraqi children is a crusade against Islam. We as Muslims do not like the Iraqi regime but we think that the Iraqi people and their children are our brothers and we care about their future. (bin Laden, cited in Bodansky, 2001, p. 191)

CONCEPTION OF THE HERO

> *Heros* (from the Greek) means superior man, directly related to the social and religious structure of his society. A gift of heaven, the *Heros* is a force sent by destiny. (Fishwick, 1983, p. 8)

Heroes are not eternal. They appear within a dominant discourse among specific groups of people at specific times, then disappear or at least are forgotten. As Fishwick (1983) said, "Heroes light up the heaven; and like the moon, they wax and wane" (p. 5). Similarly, Browne (1983) said, "Heroes, somewhat like fads though of longer life, come and go. They are 'in' and they are 'out'" (p. 96). Heroes also vary from era to era or from time to time. The concept of heroism itself changes. Characteristics of the hero in one century or time vary from those in others. As long as there are continuous changes in the societal structures, in ways of thinking, in technologies, and in needs and demands, the concept and characteristics of the hero will also change. The quality that people are looking for, or respond to, in a hero may be charisma—but not only that.

In their interesting study "What is a Hero?", White and O'Brien (1999) sought to determine how young students conceive of the hero and the basic characteristics of the hero. They noticed that, across age levels, there was an emphasis on the action taken by the person identified as a hero. For younger students, the focus was on saving someone, whereas for older students the focus was on helping others. Students aged 5 to 6 years and 8 to 9 years defined a hero as someone who saves or helps others. Also, the students' responses indicated the importance of the hero as a protector/giver. Another significant idea common to most students' conception of the hero was the notion of a hero either as unique, or capable of performing an extraordinary feat. The students seemed to consider at least one of four characteristics as essential to the definition of a hero: good, courageous, nice, and trustworthy. Finally, a hero set an example that was worthy of respect and admiration. Students in the 11- to 13- and 15- to 16-year age levels began to conceive of a hero not only as someone who helps others, for example, but also as a person whom they wanted to emulate.

In general, people are obsessed with heroes and anti-heroes. In the Arabic culture, for example, Salah ad-Din Yusuf ibn Ayyub, Sultan of Egypt and Syria, known in the West as Saladin, achieved the status of a great hero during his lifetime for his battles to liberate al Qudss (Jerusalem). The movie *al Nasser Salah ad-Din* (Victorious Saladin), directed by the famous Egyptian director Youssef Shahin, is regarded by Arabs as one of the all-time best Islamic movies. In this movie, Salah ad-Din manifests many Islamic values that constitute his heroic character, such as justice, strong faith in Allah, and forgiveness. America's obsession with heroes and anti-heroes, Blythe and Sweet (1983) explained, is reflected in the unique American genre, the comic book. The superhero is the staple of the comic book industry, and the situation of each superhero story is essentially the same; "Society is threatened by a powerful menace . . . the stakes are high . . . only a super-powered hero can stop the threat, and the resultant battle will be simplified into a war between good and evil" (p. 180). Ray Browne (1983) explained the role of heroes in society. He claimed that heroes serve as models and leaders for people and nations because they reflect the projections of the dreams, fantasies, self-evaluations, and needs of individuals and of the society itself. To a large extent, modern heroes are developments, although not inventions, of the technological media simply because the mass media are the dominant means of communication. To many observers the media create celebrities, not heroes.

Roger Rollin (1983) distinguished five different types of heroes: the *super hero*, the *supreme hero*, the *leader hero*, the *everyman hero*, and the *subordinate hero*. Super heroes, for him, are "superior in kind" to human beings, to those who populate their mythic world and who comprise their audience; they are different. They are with us but not of us; their weaknesses, if they have any, are not our weaknesses; their powers are ours but extraordinarily enhanced or of a different order from ours. Super heroes then are superior to the laws of nature as the makers of nature, the gods, are. Supreme heroes are "superior only in degree" to other humans. But so great is that degree of superiority that they function as demigods. Although they are not beyond natural law (e.g., not able to leap tall buildings in a single bound), they scale tall buildings rather readily. If superior in degree to other humans, but not to the physical environment, the hero is a leader. He or she has authority, passions, and powers of expression far greater than ours, but is subject both to social criticism and to the order of nature. Leader heroes are in several senses much closer to their fellow characters and to their audiences than are super and supreme heroes. They tend to be represented as thoroughly human. Everyman heroes are men and women whose powers, like ours, are limited, and who are noteworthy neither for their virtues nor their acquirements: They tend to be ordinary human beings thrust by chance or circumstance into extraordinary situations. However, unlike most humans, they do not back off. They accept the challenge, rise to the occasion, and thereby raise themselves above the multitudes. Therefore, they embody and evoke everybody's daydream, and as such, they should logically be the most popular and populous heroes in popular culture. But this may not, in fact, be the case. For the last type, a variety of factors, such as age and economic or social status, can make a hero figure subordinate both to other characters and to an audience. Initially, audiences are more likely to have sympathy for such characters than they are to identify with them. Or they may look down on figures so obviously deficient. As in the case of everyman heroes, subordinate heroes are more likely to figure in popular comedy and satire than in more mythic forms. Rollin (1983) claimed that all heroes are celebrities (i.e., no hero is not a celebrity) in the sense that celebrities are not just known, they are well known. At the same time, however, he emphasized that "all heroes are self-made," and disparaged the idea that the mass media can make a celebrity a hero. That power, he said, is reserved for the individual members of the audience who, in violation of all definitions or terms, consensus and even common sense, do so for reasons of their own. The mass media merely bring exceptional individuals to our attention.

People differ among themselves in their conception of their heroes and their expectations of them. But the consensus among scholars is that people cannot live without heroes. By nature, people are always looking for heroes: "The search and need for heroes is inherent in human history. . . . Throughout the inhabited world, in all times and under every circumstance, the myths of man have flourished. . . . The hero's story is a monomyth—and it has endless variations" (Fishwick, 1983, p. 9). In one age, many heroes may arise, but not all last. Some live in story and song, carried through to the following age by fathers and grandfathers. But in the third age, remote beyond memory, the hero becomes a mythic figure. Fishwick (1983) explained that heroes differ among the ages or centuries. From the classical age through the Middle Ages, the Renaissance, and the 18th century, to the 19th century, heroes varied from god-men to God's men, universal men, gentlemen, and self-made men. In the 20th century, heroes are the common men and women and the outsiders. The common attribute of heroes is that they act according to their historical time and place.

At this point, we have to ask ourselves: Who would be our heroes in the 21st century? What would their characteristics be? In other words, for whom are people now searching to be their heroes or what kind of hero do they really need? Mass media play an essential role in answering such questions. Given that mass media are key participants in redefining our attitudes, opinions, lifestyles, consumption habits, priorities, and so on; and given their expansive functions in the modern society; they may effectively participate in changing our ways of thinking about heroes and actually redefine the concept. However, it is important here to distinguish between celebrity and hero in terms of the role that mass media play in the portrayal of each.

For Arab-Muslims, the heroic character stems mainly from the teachings and values of Islam. In the Qur'an, many humanitarian values are safeguarded and encouraged, such as truthfulness, forgiveness, freedom of the individual, equality, justice, debt remission, honesty, goodness, and so on. Justice, for instance, is an essential value in Islam that is honored among Muslims and implemented by Islamic leaders. What draws some Muslims to Osama bin Laden and inspires them to view him as an Arabic Hero is what he has done to cause many of these qualities to be attributed to him. Basically, with a focus on "justice," bin Laden, through his continuous fight against Western oppression and injustice has come to embody all those religious values that strengthen his position as a leader and a defender of the faith and the interests of Muslims. By following the example and rules of historic Islamic militant leaders, bin Laden has opened a door through which he welcomes supporters and followers.

Misunderstanding of the roles of Islamic militant leaders has led some observers to regard bin Laden's open invitation to President George W. Bush, a few days after the tragic events of September 11, to convert to Islam (the message was publicized in the Israeli newspaper *Ha'aretz* on September 23, but unacknowledged by the American press), as "a joke" and attribute it to a collective hatred: "Obviously, such an appeal, if noticed at all, can simply be regarded as a joke. However, I do not believe that bin Laden would have invoked the name of Islam if he had not been serious. If we take his fantasmatic call to convert to Islam seriously, we can learn a great deal about the hidden workings of hatred" (Yanay, 2002, p. 54). Instead of looking superficially and easily at this "call for conversion" as hatred, it is recommended here that we investigate it deeply in terms of the Muslim expectations of an Islamic leader or hero. What bin Laden did is fully consistent with what Islamic leaders or heroes did during the historic Islamic conquests at the beginning of the spread of Islam. It is not expected that those who carried out that horrible event of September 11 in the name of defending Islam would joke, or at least appear to, but rather, to complete the picture, that they would invite the *Kuffar* (unbelievers) to convert to Islam. In this way, bin Laden proves to his followers that he is able to conquer the greatest enemy of Islam, damage it severely, frighten it, and, applying the historic Islamic rules of such events, ask its people, represented in the personality of their president, to convert to Islam. Nothing more is needed from an Islamic leader to be considered a hero in the eyes of his followers.

Therefore, understanding the role of the religious leader is a key point here. In seeking to understand the root causes of the events of September 11, Norris and Inglehart (2002) explained, many have turned to Samuel Huntington's controversial thesis of a "clash of civilizations," arousing strong debate. In a comparative analysis of the beliefs and values of Islamic and non-Islamic publics in 75 societies around the globe, the first claim in Huntington's thesis was confirmed: Culture does matter, and indeed matters a lot. However, some considered Huntington to be mistaken in assuming that the principal clash between the West and Islamic worlds concerns democracy. Alternatively, they suggest that there are striking similarities in the political values held in these societies. It is true that Islamic publics differ from Western publics concerning the role of religious leadership in society, but this is not a simple dichotomous clash—many non-Islamic societies side with the Islamic ones on this issue. They find significant cross-cultural differences concerning the role of religious leaders in politics and society, but these attitudes divide the West from many other countries around the globe, not just Islamic ones. "The major political disagreement between Western and Islamic societies was found in attitudes towards the role of religious leaders, where Islamic nations proved far more favorable" (Norris & Inglehart, 2002, p. 251).

No one except bin Laden, in our current times, has reached such a high degree of achieving what is seen by some Arab and Muslim groups as heroism. No one else compares with him, although there are some who show similarity in their actions. Saddam Hussein, for example, was not recognized by his Iraqi people as a hero even though he stood up to the world's superpower in two wars, in 1990/1 and 2003. In the Arabic context, the majority of Arabic newspapers described Saddam Hussein for his 1990 invasion of Kuwait in negative terms, calling him, for instance, "the treacherous" and "the dictator." On the global level, he has been compared to the most hated political leaders. For example, responding to Iraq's 1990 invasion of Kuwait,

President George Bush and Britain's Prime Minister Margaret Thatcher looked at Saddam Hussein as another Hitler and were determined not to repeat the mistakes of the Western response to the rise of the Axis in the 1930s or of the Vietnam War. "The prompt use of overwhelming force in the Gulf would succeed, Bush and Thatcher believed, just as the use of force had succeeded in the Falklands crisis, and just as such a policy, they believed would have deterred the Axis in the early 1930s" (MacDonald, 2002, p. 29). President George W. Bush and Britain's Prime Minister Tony Blair applied this same policy against Saddam Hussein with more determination and force in 2003.

What distinguishes bin Laden from Hussein and others is that he openly brought about extensive damage to Western societies, the enemy of Islam from his point of view, in the name of Islam. Despite Hussein's strong and aggressive personality that makes him, perhaps, a unique militant leader, he has never acted openly against Western societies in the name of Islam; and even though he has frequently voiced strong anti-American rhetoric, he has never carried out an aggressive anti-Western action. Saddam was seen as a political leader but not a religious one, therefore his image is not a heroic one. However, if his political leadership had succeeded, it might have worked indirectly for the benefit of Islam, and consequently he might have received the heroic honor. As for other religious leaders in Arab and Muslim countries, although they uphold religious values, they are not honored as heroic personalities to the same degree as bin Laden in the eyes of their people, because they have not achieved the same level of losses in the lines of their enemies. bin Laden alone accomplishes what political and religious leaders could not do, and consequently becomes a hero for those who were seeking such ends.

THE MEDIA POWER IN CONFLICT SITUATIONS

The mass media have a unique power in our social system that stems from our dependence on them for the majority of the information we receive in our daily lives and their multiple functions in society. Also, studies of media effects have demonstrated the enormous influence of mass media on the audiences' attitudes, opinions, and behaviors. With the complexity of societies, speed of events, and enormous diversity of information and news, and the limited ability of audiences to follow up on information provided by the media, the media have the power to formulate our understanding of the world. Analyzing the functions of mass communication, Rivers and Schramm (1969) explained that the media watch the horizon for us, much as the ancient messengers once did, and help us to correlate our response to the challenges and opportunities which appear on the horizon, to reach consensus on social actions, and to transmit the culture of our society to new members. Many other scholars have examined the political power of the media.

Another dimension of the media's power relies on the relationship between media and government. Richard Davis (2001), looking at the relations between the media and American politics, claimed that the role of the press in American politics has become a major source of discussion and controversy in recent years, and that the influence of the media is much more pervasive now than it was three decades ago. In general, Americans perceive the media as extremely powerful.

During a crisis situation, one of the obvious signs of whether mass media are playing a positive or a negative role is the degree to which they affect the escalation or de-escalation of the situation. Either they decrease tensions and violence or they fuel rumors and provoke the public to further conflict. In this respect, when mass media are used rationally and responsibly as an important means to effect de-escalation during a crisis situation, they become key players in helping opponents to manage their crisis.

When it comes to a controversial event between two parties, states, and/or organizations, mass media of both sides adapt sly techniques during the coverage of the controversial events where they indirectly diffuse their biases, attitudes, and beliefs through two-sided coverage. Journalists sometimes claim that "criticisms of the news from 'both sides' of divisive political issues in effect absolve them from allegations of 'bias': they are simply 'playing it down the middle'" (Karlberg & Hackett, 1996, p. 1). Perhaps it is true that "the American media do not play a direct role in the formulation of foreign policy but continue to have a growing influence in its implementation, explanation and articulation" (Mowlana, 1997, p. 31), and this is more dangerous. The Gulf War is an example of the nonresistible bias of the media, where the event was related to domestic issues. "The Gulf War presents a unique opportunity to observe the tensions between globalization and domestication of news because it allows researchers to compare national newscasts about a single world event" (Carrier, 1997, p. 179). Additionally, it is important to consider that "journalists, like scientists, usually had hypotheses in mind in working a story" (Stocking & LaMarca, 1990, p. 295).

However, true representation of events by the media is particularly important because "the goal of reading a news report is not just to understand it, that is, to build a meaning representation of it in memory, but to get to know and understand the events the news reports are about" (van Dijk, 1991, p. 229). It is too common that we have an event in which two persons, institutions, or states are contrarily involved and we have two different explanations or meanings to the same event. This may be intensified during crises, conflicts, or disasters.

The mass media are not only important channels for the transmission of ideas, thoughts, norms, and values within societies, but are also key participants in the representation of specific issues, including religion. Edward Brawley (1983) clearly outlined the importance and deep influence of the mass media in our lives: "The mass media constitute a powerful and pervading force in our lives. We are exposed daily to a bombardment of media messages. Most of the information we receive about our community, our state, the nation, and the world comes to us through newspapers, magazines, television, and radio" (p. 11). Moreover, using different approaches and techniques, the mass media mix news stories—"facts"—with their interpretation in the representation of any specific issue: "News stories, like myths, do not 'tell it like it is', but rather, 'tell it like it means'" (Bird & Dardenne, 1988, p. 71).

Mass media represent the world for us by portraying it through language, features, comments, pictures, and audio/visual materials, and in doing so they give meaning to events. For this reason, true representation by the media is extremely important, especially in transnational reporting, because audiences understand and remember information and the meaning of events according to the way they are constructed and represented by the mass media. Although the mass media are responsible for representing factual reality, this is nevertheless a difficult task: "Journalists know that events seem more real to readers when they are reported in story form; when they do this they find themselves slipping into the mire of 'fiction' and hauling out the lifebelts of objectivity and fact" (Bird & Dardenne, 1988, p. 82).

One should not separate media from their social environment. This relationship has been viewed by many theorists in the field of media and communication studies, among them Jeffery Alexander (1981), who suggested a possible and powerful effect of mass media, that is, the creation of some new forms of social activities within the society. He justified this suggestion by saying that because of the modernization and development in societies, mass media become key players in not just transmitting information but producing their own effects on people's lives: "The mass media produce symbolic patterns that create the invisible tissues of society on the cultural level" (p. 18).

"Myth" controls the way media personnel think, analyze, and represent events, disasters, and crises. It does not differ from developed to developing media or even differ from one civil society to another. This control by myth is needed, to a great extent, for audiences to react positively to the media. "Myths are stories that attempt to provide an understanding of the real world at the time they are conceived" (Ferrell, 2000, p. 5). This influence of prevalent myths on the media occurs during the process of researching solutions, explanations, or justifications for the story. In most controversial events, mass media of both sides use strategies of representation and construct forms of discourses with the support of some socially constructed myths. Both sides are influenced by a specific myth or group of myths, which controls their behaviors, beliefs, and attitudes toward the "Other." Despite the fact that each side's myth is probably rejected on the global level, opposed in the universal narrative and inconsistent with the other side, each side is strictly influenced by its own myth, even if indirectly.

During most conflictual or controversial incidents between the Arab World and the United States, the Arabic side is always influenced by the myth that every violent action against any Arab country is definitely supported by Israel. In the eyes of Arabic peoples, the strong relationship between Israel and the United States is the basis of conspiracy against them. This myth makes the Arabic side cautious when regarding American's explanations and investigations of the event and suspicious of every single procedure. On the other hand, the American side is influenced by the myth that Islam is a base for terrorism and violent actions:

> The renewed image of Islam as enemy has developed in dominant global discourses despite the military cooperation between the U.S. and governments of countries with Muslim majorities like Egypt, Turkey, and Indonesia, and even that with conservative states such as Saudi Arabia and Kuwait. (Karim, 2000, p. 136)

The Internet, representing new media, has certain unique features that distinguish it from other media of today, particularly the global nature of access and reach, speed of communication, capability for concealment of source and identity, and unregulated environment. Terrorist events are stress situations that give rise to conflict, crisis, or even war. For parties involved in a terrorist event, the Internet provides incomparable communication facilities. In text and visual communication through e-mails, chatrooms, or cellular messaging, Internet users across the globe are influenced by the nature of the Web—the ease, speed, and freedom of communication. Issues of ethics and responsibility, however, which are still being debated in the context of the old media, are becoming increasingly more significant and necessary for the Internet.

In Arab countries, the adaptation of new technologies and telecommunications is faster and at a higher rate of increase than traditional media. Internet use is growing rapidly after a slow start. Today, all countries except Libya, Iraq, and Syria allow the public to access the Internet through a local service provider. There are clear cultural constraints on the use of the Internet in a group of Arab countries, given that the 22 Arab countries are not equal in accessing or using the Internet. This group suffers from some restrictions that put them in an unequal situation not only with other Arab countries but also and more significantly with the rest of the world. Some of these constraints come from religious conservation and others from social norms and traditions. For online freedom of expression, many Arabic governments control access to sensitive political and religious discussions.

Communication technologies and new media, most significantly the Internet, have brought about political awareness that was never before possible under censored media and, as a result, have generated a desire for political participation among groups that were previously silent or disinterested. A study conducted by Declan Barry (2001) examines the acculturation experiences of Arabic immigrants and assesses the utility of the Internet as a data collection tool. The Internet proved to be an effective method for soliciting a relatively large, geographically dispersed sample of Arabic immigrants. Barry suggested that the Internet may be an important method to assess culture-relevant variables in further research on Arab immigrant populations.

In the September 11 attacks, the Internet was used by both sides of the conflict—terrorist groups and global governments alike, especially the United States—with each side aiming to achieve its own specific goals. The patterns and consequences of Internet use were, however, unexpectedly different from what would have been expected with the old media. The terrorist groups, blindly or not, were more successful in using the Internet to achieve their goals than they would have been with the old media. The anti-terrorist side, on the other hand, was unable to control anti-propaganda web messages or to achieve global response to its messages or support for its decisions in the same way as it might have done with the old media. These differences in communication and response can be attributed to the unique nature of the Internet that works globally within a multicultural diversity.

Arabic and Western sides of Internet Web sites have used this medium as a tool for reflecting their cultures and public opinions and attitudes toward the September 11 attacks. Interestingly, and in addition to the various usages and contents of the Internet, both Arabic and Western Web sites were full of jokes. On the Arabic side, Web sites such as Maktoob.com, Ajeeb.com, Masrawy.com, Arabia.com, and so on, showed jokes about bin Laden, Bush, Blair, Arabic leaders, and Israel's Sharon in the context of the attack event. On the Western side, there is an interesting study about the joke cycle of bin Laden's attack. Kuipers Giselinde (2002) considered the joke cycle about bin Laden and the attack on the World Trade Center as the first cycle of Internet disaster jokes. He argued that although both traditional oral jokes and visual Internet jokes are best understood as a reaction to media coverage of disasters, for Internet jokes, this connection with media culture is even stronger than for oral jokes. He justified that Internet jokes are visual *collages*, assembled from phrases and pictures from popular media, which derive their humorous effect from a combination of elements of innocuous genres from media, commercial or popular culture with references to disaster. Giselinde (2002), after collecting and analyzing 398

Internet jokes in October and November 2001 from five Dutch Web sites, found that the jokes were highly personalized, and nearly 70% were about bin Laden. In summary, in the cases of both sides, even jokes, which have the irrelevant mood of the consequences of the attack event, have been used through the Internet, and not only in the oral style, to reflect on the clash of cultures and conflicting attitudes toward the event.

SPONTANEOUS REACTIONS TO SEPTEMBER 11

Immediately after the September 11 attacks, U.S. government officials fingered bin Laden as the prime suspect and attributed these horrendous acts to members of his organization (al-Qaeda). September 11, 2001 is considered the worst single day, in terms of causalities and damages, in the United States since the American Civil War. Nineteen persons, suspected of having been authorized and funded by al Qaeda, boarded four U.S. commercial passenger jets in Boston, Newark, and Washington, DC, hijacked the aircrafts minutes after takeoff, and crashed them into the Twin Towers of the World Trade Center in New York, the Pentagon in northern Virginia, and the Pennsylvania countryside.

bin Laden was born in Riyadh in 1957, the 17th of the 52 children of Saudi Arabia's most successful building magnate. His father, Mohammed bin Oud bin Laden, emigrated from southern Yemen in 1932, when the Saudi kingdom's new dynasty was installed, and rose from humble beginnings to become the favored building contractor to the royal house. The bin Laden group still controls the kingdom's biggest construction business, with a turnover of tens of billions of dollars. Its latest projects include airport facilities in Kuala Lumpur, a runway in Cairo, and a huge new mosque in Medina. Among recent investments are a marble factory in Italy and a share in Iridium, a troubled satellite consortium. Unlike many members of the Saudi elite, Osama bin Laden was never educated in the West, nor at a Western-run college in the Middle East. His only exposure to a cosmopolitan, Western way of life was the 2 years he spent in the hedonistic atmosphere of Beirut after leaving school in 1973. Although his brothers studied abroad, he took his degree in engineering in his home city of Jeddah (Special report, 2001).

Mustafa al Sayyid (2002), director of the Center for the Study of Developing Countries at Cairo University, described the spontaneous reactions of the Arab and Muslim countries after the September 11 attacks. Responses of government officials and ordinary people to the news were varied. In general, the Arab and Muslim governments condemned the attacks and expressed sympathy for the American people. Even Iraq's then president, Saddam Hussein, deputy prime minister, Tariq Aziz, and permanent representative to the UN, Mohammed al-Douri deplored the attacks and expressed sympathy for the victims and their families. Aziz in particular, appearing in both Arabic and American mass media, firmly rejected any link between Iraq and the perpetrators of the attacks. The Jordanian government offered to send troops to participate in a future peacekeeping force in Afghanistan. Jordan's King Abdullah, standing next to President George W. Bush at the White House in mid-September 2001, was eager to announce Jordan's total solidarity with the American people. Also, Algerian president Abdul-Aziz Bouteflika took a forceful stand in support of U.S. actions. Many other countries in the Arab and Muslim world expressed their support for the United States in its political and military campaign against both bin Laden and al Qaeda, as well as the Taliban regime, as clearly indicated in statements issued by the Organization of the Islamic Conference at its Doha summit in October 2001. At the same time, certain Arab and Muslim countries—particularly Egypt and Saudi Arabia—although condemning the terrorist attacks on the U.S. and willingly sharing intelligence with U.S. authorities, were critical of certain aspects of the U.S. response to the attacks. *The Washington Post* and *The New York Times,* among other U.S. newspapers, have accused these countries of not providing the United States with sufficient support in its battle against terrorism. Other voices in the Muslim world were critical of the U.S. military campaign. For example, Iran's then president, Muhammad Ali Khatami rejected the two choices that Bush put to the world—"Either you are with the United States, or you are with the terrorists"—arguing that Iran was neither with the United States nor with the terrorists. Nonetheless, although the Iranian officials condemned the use of military force against the Afghan people, the Iranian government did not take any steps to prevent U.S. military actions in Afghanistan.

However, as is always the case in the Arab countries, the official position did not express the great majority of the people's opinions. Many Arab intellectuals and commentators believed that it was unlikely that bin Laden alone could have carried out such a well-orchestrated attack with such extraordinary consequences. Indeed, many Arab people were confused when bin Laden declared his support for the attacks in later statements transmitted to the Arab world through Qatar's al-Jazeera television network. The Arabic public sphere continued to be divided between those who believed that bin Laden had organized the attacks and condemned him for it, and those who thought that the attacks were the work of the enemies of Arabs and Muslims—most significantly Israel. Later, people began to think that their enemies wanted to undermine the relationship between the Arabs and Muslims and Western people to distort the image of Islam. These people see bin Laden as a hero, not for killing innocent people, but rather for fighting against the enemies of Islam.

Media labeling is a common activity conducted by mass media most significantly in times of conflicts and tension. In discussing the September 11 attacks, both sides of mass media framed and labeled each other through specific contexts. The Arabic side, representing the ideology of the only suspected actor, was influenced by its major enemy "Israel" and therefore described the terrorist acts as well planned and managed by intelligence agencies, most probably the "Musad." On the other side, Americans labeled the acts in context of terrorism. On both sides, the media coverage is best described here as a war of labels and accusations. Although Western media tend to label those individuals involved in terrorist activities "Muslim terrorists," Arab and Muslim states reject this idea. As al Sayyid (2002) stated, "These individuals cannot, by any stretch of the imagination, be considered representative of approximately one billion Muslims" (p. 179). The Arabic media have covered various groups of people representing the attitudes and opinions of Arab and Muslim people that are at odds with the official views of their pro-American governments. Among these were an elderly lawyer, the father of Mohammed Atta (the pilot who crashed the first plane into the World Trade Center) who expressed his great sympathy for the American people: "I love the American people. They're good people. I mourn for them—for anyone, American, Russian or Indian, who died. These are all people" (*Cairo Times*, September 27, 2001). Atta's family believed that their son's identity had been stolen as part of a conspiracy carried out by Israeli and American officials. Moreover, Abdullah Awad Aboud bin Laden, the head of Osama bin Laden's family, who has disowned him, in a statement to the Saudi press *Middle East Times* (September 27, 2001), declared: "We reaffirm what we announced in February 1994, namely that the bin Laden family has nothing to do with his actions and behavior. . . . We extend our condolences to the families of the innocent victims. . . . (All members of the family) strongly condemn and deplore this painful act which resulted in the death of many innocent men, women and children, and which contradicts our religion and is rejected by all religions and humanity." Above all, Sheikh Mohammed Sayyid Tantawi, the Grand Imam of al-Azhar in Cairo, the world's foremost center for Islam, stated: "Many Muslims deny that the martyrs of 11 September were Muslims" (Wikan, 2002, p. 125). For al-Ahram, the most widespread official Egyptian newspaper, Tantawi asserted that the killing of innocent men, women, and children is a horrible and ugly act that is against all religions and against rational thinking.

As a representative of the American Muslims' reaction, Riad Abdelkarim (2001) directed a message to bin Laden and his followers: "Don't do us any favors" (p. 72). Abdelkarim was much influenced by speeches of bin Laden and Suleiman Abu Gheith he had heard through the al-Jazeera television network when he narrated this:

I had just returned from an outing with my children when I heard the latest words to emanate from one of Osama bin Laden's henchmen. My wife, who dons the hijab [Islamic head covering], . . . relayed to me the chilling words of Suleiman Abu Gheith, which she had just seen on an Al-Jazeera broadcast. I shuddered when I heard of his warning to Muslims and children in the United States and Great Britain not to fly on any airplanes or live or work in any tall building. What does he think we will do—betray our fellow Americans . . . ? So that they can avoid killing any Muslims in any of their future treacherous plans? It is too late for that, Mr. Abu Gheith. Among the 6,000 [The latest count is under 4,000] or so innocent men, women, and children who were slaughtered on Sept 11 were several hundred Muslims. . . . What bin Laden, Abu Gheith and their ilk do not understand is that the estimated seven million American Muslims are just that—Americans and Muslims. There is no oxymoron in the use of this term, no contradiction, no paradox. Our children recite the pledge of allegiance at school every morning, and we also teach them to read from the Qur'an and live by the example of our great Prophet, Muhammad (may God's peace and blessings be upon him). . . . As American Muslims, we . . . deeply resent the fact that he has hijacked our faith . . . Osama bin Laden has no more legitimacy in his claim to be the "poster boy" for the Palestinian cause than did Saddam Hussein a decade ago. . . . So, Mr. bin Laden and Mr. Abu Gheith, if you were hoping to do us any favors, don't bother. Thanks, but no thanks. I will be flying aboard our American planes and encouraging all of my fellow American Muslims to do the same. And we will all continue to live and work in our nation's skyscrapers. Because we are Americans and Muslims. (p. 72)

In their first reactions to the attacks, and even now, Arab and Muslim governments do not feel any more responsibility than other countries in the war against terrorism. Instead, they condemn the United States and the United Kingdom as more responsible. Arab and Muslim governments have previously warned against the dangers of terrorism as they have been engaged in the fight against terrorism for many years. They have asked for support from the United States and the United Kingdom but received little help. Al Sayyid (2002) explained that, at different times during the 1980s, Egypt, Algeria, Jordan, Syria, Saudi Arabia, and even Iraq and Libya were engaged in fighting against Islamic organizations that were using armed struggle to overthrow or destabilize their governments. Consequently, leaders of these countries, such as Mubarak of Egypt, have called on Western governments not to provide easy asylum to well-known key figures in militant Islamic organizations who are wanted for trial for their involvement in terrorist acts. Sheikh Omar Abdel-Rahman, for example, as the spiritual leader of the Islamic Group, or *al-Jama'a al-Islamiyyah,* who calls on members to launch armed attacks to oust the Egyptian government, was given an entry visa to the United States, where he stayed and continued to stir up anti-Egyptian government sentiment until he was arrested for his role in the 1993 attempt to blow up the World Trade Center.

It is widely argued that these acts and the U.S. responses to them are acts of war, not of terrorism, by some terrorists and revenge takers. In any case, the consensus is that well-timed and well-synchronized attacks, killing 3,000 people, mostly civilians, from 87 different countries in a few hours' time, is not consistent with the previously experienced acts of terrorists. Wedgwood (2002) claimed that the psychological sense that this was an act of war is founded on the extraordinary destructiveness of the act: "Had the emergency evacuation of the World Trade Center towers not run efficiently, as many as 25,000 more might have died" (p. 328). On the American side, the air campaign in Afghanistan dropping thousands of tons of bombs seems to be a war as well. The United States regarded the September 11 incidents as comparable to a military attack. In the week following the attacks, Bush declared a national emergency and called to active duty the reserves of the U.S. armed forces. Additionally, he signed into law a joint resolution of Congress that states that "the President has authority under the Constitution to take action to deter and prevent acts of international terrorism against the United States" (Murphy, 2002, p. 242).

MASS MEDIA OF THE AMERICAN SIDE

A few hours after the attacks on the World Trade Center in New York and the Pentagon in Washington, DC, President Bush delivered his speech addressed to the American people. The first caption on CNN was "America under attack." Two days later it was changed to "America is at war," and soon after bin Laden was declared as the prime suspect and enemy number 1, the caption in CNN's reporting changed to "America's New War." From the beginning, American politicians blamed Islam and Muslims, using expressions such as "Islamic terrorists," "fundamentalism," "war against terrorism," "extremist Muslims," "militant Muslims," "Muslim terrorist groups," and so on. "The image of the "Islamic terrorist" has become a staple in coverage of Muslim societies. Whereas terrorism perpetrated by certain Muslim groups should indeed be of concern, similar depictions of Christians, Jews, or followers of other religions carrying out violence in the names of their respective faiths are rarely carried out" (Karim, 2000, p. 175). Then, bin Laden's picture started to appear in situations such as shooting a gun or in training camps of militant Muslims. Western media tended to misconstrue the relationship between Islam and terrorism significantly, often using the term *Jihad* to convey the notion of an armed struggle launched by

Muslims against people of other religions in order to compel them to renounce their religion and adopt Islam.

CNN was a good representative of its ideological context. al-Jazeera represented, although indirectly, the Arab public sphere after the attack. CNN presented the American standpoint on bin Laden and was much affected by the number of victims and the disastrous event in the United States and covered bin Laden news stories extensively. From September 12, 2001, bin Laden was the first and only prime suspect for the American politicians and public, and therefore the American media. CNN emphasized unusual aspects of the bin Laden's life, such as being the 17th of "52" children of construction magnate Muhammad Awad bin Laden. It portrayed the "unique" position of bin Laden as the greatest enemy of the United States, using phrases such as "One name" and "One of FBI's Ten Most Wanted Fugitives." bin Laden was characterized by CNN as "exiled Saudi millionaire," "the enemy," "terrorist," "crazy killer," Islamic fundamentalist," "prime suspect," "Saudi dissident," "fugitive al-Qaeda leader," "terrorist mastermind," "evil Osama bin Laden," "exiled Saudi dissident," "murderer," "against civilization," and "not someone to be admired." CNN was mainly dependent on archival pictures of bin Laden and al-Jazeera exclusives. CNN tended to air pictures showing bin Laden in the training camps, surrounded by guns, and in front of the Muslims' holy book, the "Qur'an."

Coverage by CBS of the September 11 attacks differed little from CNN's coverage in its emphasis on the American dominant discourse and its view of bin Laden as prime suspect, although it offered some diversity. Starting from September 12, 2001, CBS began to include bin Laden in its coverage. Like CNN, CBS covered the celebrations in some parts of the Arab and Muslim world, especially in the Middle East region. They aired clips of Arabs and Muslims, men, women and children, civilians celebrating by setting off fireworks and waving their hands as a sign of victory. On the other hand, they showed many scenes of mourning in America. bin Laden was characterized by CBS, as by CNN, as the "Most Wanted Terrorist," "suspected mass murderer," "terrorist," "unindicted coconspirator," "mastermind behind the bomb attack," and so on. To show him as a villain, CBS gathered evidence about his involvement in various terrorist attacks and killings around the world, including assassination and explosions.

The New York Times represented the "Self"—Americans—in a state of shock, horror, and grief: "Washington struggled to regain a sense of equilibrium"; whereas the "Other"—Muslims—were represented as terrorists, attackers, hijackers, perpetrators of evil acts, and the like. It conveyed to the readers the idea of war against terrorism: "Bush commits U.S. to hunt down both terrorists and their supporters." From the very beginning it portrayed the attacks as evil acts: "Bush: The search is underway for those who are behind these evil acts." In the first day after the attack, September 12, it conveyed suspicion of bin Laden: "Intelligence officials said they strongly believed that Osama bin Laden's terrorist organization was behind the attacks." It increasingly blamed him after that day: "Federal authorities: The hijackers who commandeered commercial jets that attacked the World Trade Center and the Pentagon were followers of Osama bin Laden, the Islamic militant who has been blamed for some of the bloodiest attacks against Americans." On September 14, Judith Miller wrote of bin Laden: "With his gentle eyes, skeletal frame, long black beard and habitual kalashnikov, Osama bin Laden has become the world's most reviled symbol of terror." *The New York Times* put forward the idea of Jihad as an explanation for the attacks: "Laden has mobilized hundreds of Muslim militants in far-flung countries to fight and die in a borderless jihad. . . . His goal has been consistent for a decade: victory in a self-proclaimed jihad, or Islamic holy war, against the United States and its allies."

MASS MEDIA OF THE ARABIC SIDE

While the American administration was trying to isolate bin Laden rhetorically, Edwards (2002) explained, there were also reports that the al-Qaeda leader was viewed very differently by many in the Middle East and South Asia. News reports made it clear that many saw bin Laden as a hero on horseback, intent on righting wrongs committed against the Muslim people. Edwards argued that bin Laden's death will in all likelihood not mean what leaders in the United States might want it to, no matter how many spin doctors are assigned to the case. And although the producers at al-Jazeera tap sources unavailable to the West, the ultimate disposition of bin Laden's legacy is beyond their control as well.

In the case of bin Laden, the group of Arab and Muslim people who gather around him and make him their hero, act under a key motivation. They hate Israel and America for many reasons. This hostility has roots. Hamdi (1998) interviewed the Sudanese Islamic leader, Dr. Hasan Abdullah al-Turabi, in 1987, 1994, 1996, and 1997, and obtained some good answers regarding this. Dr. al-Turabi said, "In this context, America has significant experience." He talked about Iran, and how America sided very closely with the Shah, as a result of the international power intrigues of the Cold War. The Americans considered the Shah sincere even if he was a traitor to his own people, but by ignoring other considerations their policy in the region was a shambles and they lost control of the situation. Eventually, they had to abandon the Shah completely as if he had never been their most trusted ally. Furthermore, they became embroiled in a confrontation with the new rulers.

Lesch (2002) further clarified the picture. The main issues raised by the Islamic militants resonate throughout the Middle East and the Islamic world, where there is widespread condemnation of the U.S. military presence, its sanctions following the war against Iraq, its support for a hegemonic Israel and its apparent endorsement of repressive regimes. Even so, the Islamic scholars reject the violence. Reducing Islam to Jihad seriously distorts the faith, Lesch explained. It is noteworthy that the spiritual leader of Lebanon's Hizballah movement, Shaikh Muhammad Hussain Fadlallah, condemned the attacks on the United States as "not compatible with Shariah law" or with the real meaning of Jihad. Jihad, in his view, could not involve killing innocent people in a distant land and could not mean "aggressive combat." Similarly, the respected Egyptian theologian Shaikh Yusuf Abdallah al-Qaradawi stated:

> Islam, the religion of tolerance, holds the human soul in high esteem, and considers the attack on innocent human beings a grave sin. Even in times of war, Muslims are not allowed to kill anybody save the one who is engaged in face-to-face confrontation with them. Killing hundreds of helpless civilians is a heinous crime in Islam.

Similarly, Cornell (2002) confirmed that Arab and Muslim political activists tell us that American support for Israel created the hatred that led to the attack on the Twin Towers. Talking heads from the Israeli government tell us that America has finally tasted the terrorism that Israelis have long experienced. Cornell mentions a popular Arab song about the al-Aqsa Intifadah which asks, "Where is the anger of the Arabs? Where is Salah al-Din (Saladin)?" (p. 326).

The Arabic mass media that work in such environments are also influenced by their communication capabilities and opportunities. In Arab countries, "whether newspapers are government owned or private, they are subject to considerable influence, and even censorship, by authorities. This is also true of broadcasting, through more stations are government-owned or -controlled than private throughout the region" (Ogan, 1995, p. 202), and despite the fact that the Middle East is coming online in increasing numbers, many governments are hoping to control access to sensitive political and religious discussion (Sorensen, 1996), and many have adopted various means to restrict the flow of information online. In recent years, the Arab world has witnessed the development of a large number of international television services (Amin, 1996). Every Arab country has a television service that can be seen in the Arab world. Egypt, for example, has several services available; others, such as Jordan, have satellite services that simply rebroadcast a domestic television channel. Egypt, Dubai, and Tunisia have moved television beyond the Arab world. These services can be seen in Europe, North

America, and even Latin America (Boyd, 1999). Since the late 1960s, the Arab states have been using different international (private and governmental) satellite systems, mainly for international traffic ("Telecommunication policies," 1996). The link between civil society and satellite broadcasting in the Middle East is becoming clearer and more significant with two simultaneous and related developments: first, the growing importance of satellite broadcasting in the region; and second, the growing awareness of the people of the Middle East of civil society issues (Amin, 2000). Whether newspapers are government owned or private, they are subject to considerable influence, and even censorship, by authorities.

The *Arab Press Freedom Watch* has been established to play an active role in defending freedom of the press, human rights, and promoting democracy. The Egyptian press is taking the lead among others in the Middle East. "Cairo is the largest publishing center in the Arab world and also in Africa. It is home to 17 dailies, 30 weeklies, and more than 30 other publications that publish less frequently. The environment for publishing in Egypt is quite competitive" (Ogan, 1995, p. 192). al-Ahram newspaper, according to Thussu (2000), has defined "the Arab journalism for more than a century" (p. 24). The Middle East News Agency (MENA), which is located in Egypt, is defined by Hachten (1996) as one of the best second-tier agencies after two great news organizations, "DPA" in Germany and "Kyodo" in Japan. As with newspapers, so with broadcasting, as more stations are government owned or controlled than private throughout the region. Perhaps no country is more explicit in its censorship than Saudi Arabia. In every nation of the Arab World except Lebanon, the national broadcasting systems used to be entirely government owned. The old and former socialist regimes, including Egypt, Syria, and the Sudan, continue to maintain dominant state ownership of the media. However, beginning in the 1990s, many Arab countries decentralized and liberalized their broadcasting systems. Although nearly every Arab country has its own state-funded channel on one satellite or another, the explosive growth of channels has mostly come from the private sector, namely, from the pay-TV companies. The most famous private Arabic television channel, especially in terms of the high coverage of "al-Qaeda or bin Laden news, is al-Jazeera." al-Jazeera, the Qatar-based network, played a key role in bin Laden's hero image representation. al Jazeera is an independent broadcasting voice in the Arab world, watched by 35 million people. It has been a vital source of information about a-Qaeda because its reporters have had access to al-Qaeda leaders and tapes of bin Laden. It was the only source of recent and "fresh" information about him, although he was the one who decided to air his statements through its cable. Being based in the Middle East, al-Jazeera included different types of news stories, starting with the sensational ones about bin Laden (i.e., his current statements, documentaries about his life, personal life, family and origins, whether he is alive or not), to other types of news stories such as bin Laden's debate with the American point of view and his revolutionist ideas, which affected to a great extent the Arabic public sphere more than the official or public opinion. al-Jazeera was indeed very fortunate in bin Laden's selection of it, although the American media then categorized al-Jazeera as a "channel for the terrorist" and its credibility was weakened, at least in Western countries. Basically, al-Jazeera's coverage of bin Laden's involvement in the September 11 attacks could be described as "very intensive" as it made use of both full and debate styles of reporting in almost every form of broadcast (i.e., news stories, news briefs, comments, debate programs, talk shows, interviews, analysis, and so on). al-Jazeera emphasized personal facts about bin Laden's life, which affected some people especially in the way they emotionally relate to him (i.e., as one who has achieved what they hope to achieve in their lives).

More interestingly, this effect was very obvious in some Arabs and Muslims carrying his picture in anti-Western/American demonstrations. News included bin Laden's family background as a very wealthy young symbol or leader. He was an "orphan" boy who aroused sympathy because he lost his father at the age of 9 years. He was represented as a highly educated person, having received a Bachelor's degree in public administration and economics from the University of King Abdul Aziz, an elitist educational institution. al-Jazeera reported from the English newspaper *The Sun* that an English teacher who instructed bin Laden in an English private school in Saudi Arabia said that he was a quiet and shy student. He added that bin Laden was a normal student, not too religious, he always submitted his work on time and he made no trouble at all. He was wealthy, the tallest of his colleagues, and very handsome; he had high self-esteem and was remarkably decent and polite. This teacher thinks that the Western education of bin Laden cultivated the seeds of violence in his personality. bin Laden's relationship to Jihad, which is a highly appreciated concept in Muslim life, was first observed in December 1979 during the Russian invasion of Afghanistan, where he was a hero, leading al Mujahedeen (militant Muslims), gaining renown among them, especially during the Jalal-Abad fight, which forced the Russians to retreat from Afghanistan.

Palestine is another case that has caused bin Laden's statement to reverberate through the Middle East. The continuous Israeli violations against Palestine during the Intifadah have increased the publicity of bin Laden as a leader seeking revenge for the plight of the Palestinian people and the victims of this conflict. There is an obvious connection between bin Laden and his revolutionary ideas of justice and freedom for sacred Islamic land, and the great depression in the Arab public sphere where people are pessimistic about their leadership and political position in relation to American imperialism. All these circumstances have contributed to the making of bin Laden as a hero for a group of Arab-Muslim people.

Another way to identify bin Laden as an Arabic Muslim hero is by his demand in the 1980s to boycott American goods in the Arab countries as a kind of protest against its policies toward Muslims generally, and Palestinians particularly. bin Laden was described on an al-Jazeera program, "al Itigah al-Moaakess" or "the Opposite Direction," as the "conscience of the Arab-Muslim nations," especially after accusing the Arab leaders of being agents/alliances of American imperialism and domination. Interviewers saw bin Laden's heroic leadership as "socially constructed," as a direct result of the American hegemony in the Arab region. Evidence of the leadership of bin Laden is a poll conducted by a Kuwaiti newspaper "al-Ra'ay al-Aam" or "public opinion," which shows that 82.7% of Kuwaiti, Egyptian, Syrian, Lebanese, and Palestine respondents from the ages of 25 to 44 voted for bin Laden as "Mujahid." Interestingly, 76% of them said they would be "sad if Americans catch bin Laden." To present himself as a religious hero, in the first aired program (pre-recorded) bin Laden described the important stages in his life, making a point of constructing his "leadership" and "true Muslimship." He said that his father was "honored" to be one of the builders of the holy mosque and a contractor who refused to derive any benefit from its construction—which represents a very high degree of Islamic faith. bin Laden's principles are human freedom, equity, and justice. His enemies are basically two: Israeli Jews and Americans. bin Laden swore to take revenge on Americans because of the sanctions on the "innocent" Iraqi children, of whom millions died as a result of the injustice.

When asked about his health, he replied that he was very healthy and enjoying his life in Afghanistan. At the same time, he could live in tough circumstances such as extremely cold and hot weather. Also, he said he liked to ride horses for up to 70 kilometers without rest. For the actual public sphere in many Arab nations, bin Laden represented the ultimate "hero" and the only "solution" to American imperialism. bin Laden was the only "challenger" of America and its policy around the world; he comes after a phase of "disappointment" in the Arab world, especially during the continuous Israeli occupation of the Palestine land. To globalize his heroism, al-Jazeera reported on September 28 that an American citizen living in Oregon had been arrested because he had a bin Laden tattoo on his chest. On the same day, al-Jazeera reported from Mexico that there had been an enormous interest in buying tee-shirts that had bin Laden's picture with the logo of "bin Laden Our Hero." A Mexican company manufactures both bin Laden and Bush facemasks. Women also were admiring bin Laden. On September 27, al Jazeera showed a picture of a Pakistani woman, wearing hejab, hiding her face, but holding a photo of bin Laden with "Hero" written on it in English during one of the demonstrations against the American attack on

Afghanistan. The same scene is represented in different demonstrations in Jakarta-Indonesia, Afghanistan, Palestine, and many Arab countries. Another interesting picture is that of a young Pakistani man who is reading a book about bin Laden in one of the Pakistani libraries.

Looking at the nonverbal aspects of communication, we notice that bin Laden, during one of his pre-recorded videotapes, was using his right hand in swearing that "USA will never have rest or peace," like a professor lecturing to his students. On the same tape, he gestured with a pursed hand. As nonverbal communication theorists describe this hand gesture, "the fingers and thumb of one hand are straightened and brought together in a point facing upwards. Held in this posture the hand may be kept still, or moved slightly" (Morris, Collett, Marsh, & O'Shaughnessy, 1979, p. 44). This hand movement has several meanings in the nonverbal analysis. It can be used, for instance, to ask about something, to emphasize an idea, as a tool of threat, and so on. What might be relevant in this discussion of bin Laden and his heroic representation is the use of his hand movement for both criticism and emphasis. On different occasions, he addressed his enemies and threatened them. At the same time, when addressing his followers, he emphasized his standpoint and defended his ideas. A study of Arab use of this specific hand movement and its significance suggests that it often indicates threat (Morris et al., 1979).

al-Dustor, a Jordanian newspaper, was a good channel for news stories about the September 11 attacks. In the first few days after the attacks, it published news stories about bin Laden, characterizing him as "decent," "shy," and "nonviolent." At the same time, there was some suggestion of the involvement of Saddam Hussein in the attacks. Also they published justification for bin Laden in his statement "I didn't do it, Mullah Omar wouldn't allow me to do this kind of action." *al-Dustor* selected its stories about bin Laden very carefully. Although international news agencies published the same news about bin Laden, it is clear that *al-Dustor*, among other Arab newspapers, selected what was convenient for some of its audiences, public opinion, and the public sphere. It quoted from Reuters some news stories indicating that bin Laden might not be responsible for the attack—that he might be "innocent." Moreover, these were news stories about the refusal of religious leaders to accept bin Laden's involvement in the attack, saying that the "U.S. is not right in accusing and blaming bin Laden. It is an American political game." There were various news stories about demonstrations in Arab and Muslim countries where the people were denying bin Laden's guilt and refusing to bring him to American authorities. Representing the idea of the "Other," *al-Dustor* quoted from the American Internet site "Hot Box." A poll result showed that 20% of the visitors to this site visitors said that the Israeli Musad was behind this attack; another 6% said that they might be Americans extremists. Again, the "Other" for the Jordanian newspaper, as for many Arab newspapers, is "Israel." In another news story, *al-Dustor* said that many Arab analysts are sure that "Israel is the only one capable of invasion of American security systems."

An immediate reaction to the September 11 tragedy was published in *al-Jazirah*, a Saudi newspaper, by bin Laden's family, one of the most prestigious families in Saudi Arabia, expressing their shock and sadness at what had happened in the United States and offering condolences to American victims. At the same time, they denounced the actions of Osama bin Laden, describing him as a "non-member of our family." Moreover, Awad Aboud bin Laden announced, "This criminal action is totally refused in our true Islamic faith." Osama bin Laden was described by *al-Jazirah* as the "refugee", "the first suspect." Moreover, *al-Jazirah* interviewed the Saudi foreign minister who said that bin Laden was not a Saudi citizen anymore, that they had taken his Saudi citizenship from him because he did not deserve it. He added that bin Laden was a bad representative for Arabs and Muslims.

In the first few days after the attacks, bin Laden was the focus of *al-Itihad*, a United Arab Emirates newspaper. *al-Itihad* reported neutrally about bin Laden, quoting from many sources, such as Arab newspapers, various analysts and regional and international news agencies. It tried, as many Arab newspapers did, to correlate their "Other," Israel, with the accusations of bin Laden. In many articles and comments, *al-Itihad* criticized bin Laden's statement accusing the United States, asking about whether he was a good Muslim or not, especially in relation to his statement of defending Islam and the Palestinians. *al-Itihad* said that because of bin Laden's position and accusations, Ariel Sharon, the then Israeli prime minister, had a chance to prove that Muslims and Arabs are terrorists.

In contrast to many Arab newspapers, who indirectly sympathize with bin Laden, the Iraqi newspaper, *al-Thawra*, covered bin Laden stories with admiration for what he did to the United States on the one hand, and intensive criticism of American imperialism and domination in the Arab countries and the Middle East on the other. Although the newspaper expressed condolence for American victims, it also criticized American policies and "the evil American administration." The "Other" for *al-Thawra* was "Israel" as well as "America." It justified bin Laden's involvement in the terrorist attack (if it is true) as a "natural response to the unfairness and injustice of American policy." Israel was "evil," "the first terrorist" but not bin Laden, who was indirectly described as a "hero" and portrayed as the one who took revenge for Palestine and Iraq and every "victim" of America, which is "evil," "hateful," "offensive," "enemy," "devil," and "mean," all over the world. America was also "unjust," "prejudiced," and a "violator." *al-Thawra* showed pictures of demonstrations throughout the Arab countries against the United States, the crowded public in the streets happily celebrating the "great victory" of bin Laden against America. bin

Laden, in *al-Thawra's* estimation, was not "afraid" of America, but a "challenger" of its policies, a "powerful" character, and one who holds "principles" and "values."

In *al-Ahram*, bin Laden was described as the "terrorist," "first suspect," "leader of al-Qaeda," and "international terrorist." On the official level, *al-Ahram* blamed bin Laden for the critical situation into which he put both Arab and Muslim nations. It quoted the Egyptian president Hosni Mubarak, who said, "Egypt suffered a lot from terrorism." It should be noted here that Egypt, like Saudi Arabia, tried in their government-controlled media coverage to criticize and accuse bin Laden in an effort to avoid or clean up the negative image that resulted from the American claim that most of the attackers and bin Laden followers were Egyptians and Saudis. This point was emphasized in many ways through different types of coverage in *al-Ahram*. It again quoted Mubarak, this time saying, "If America can catch bin Laden, we [Egyptians] will clap our hands for her." In addition, *al-Ahram* said, "bin Laden is not representative of us, as Arabs and Muslims"; "Bin Laden is negatively affecting the Palestinian–Israeli conflict." On the public sphere level, *al-Ahram* reported from universities, schools, and different educational institutions all over Egypt the demonstrations protesting against the American policy and attacks on "innocent" Muslims and Arabs.

CONCLUSION: THE TWO FACES OF BIN LADEN

bin Laden as Evil

In his public statements, President George W. Bush routinely referred to bin Laden as "the Evil One" and "the Evildoer," and has used phrases like "wanted dead or alive" and "we'll smoke him out of his hole" to indicate the administration's resolve to bring bin Laden to justice (Edwards, 2002). Also, in his annual report to Congress, director of Central Intelligence George J. Tenet told the U.S. Senate Select Committee on Intelligence on February 7, 2001, that the "highest priority" threat facing the United States today is international terrorism; and within that category, Osama bin Ladin's global network is "the most immediate and serious threat" (Tenet, 2001, p. 83).

Mandel (2002) described bin Laden as an instigator of collective violence. Compared with perpetrators of collective violence, Mandel explained, instigators are more powerful and less interchangeable, and they tend to rely on some form of nationalism to rally support. The growing conflict after the attacks between the United States and its allies and Islamic militant groups has been framed by both sides as a struggle against the forces of evil by the forces of good. These overly simplistic construals of "the other side as evil" and "our side as just" have contributed to an escalation of international violence and threaten us with the possibility of a long-term conflict. Mandel examined conflict from a social psychological perspective by considering the distinction between instigators and perpetrators of collective violence. He examined briefly how bin Laden, as a key instigator of terrorism over the last decade, used religious nationalism to rally support for his cause; and how the leaders of both sides—bin Laden and Bush—used the notion of "good versus evil" to frame the present conflict. Mandel determined that the function of instigators is not to carry out the acts of violence themselves but to tune and transmit the messages that will effectively motivate others to cause harm and to provide perpetrators with the requisite resources for accomplishing their tasks. Compared with perpetrators, instigators tend to have greater social influence and a wider range of power. Whereas perpetrators may have access to weaponry or other forms of low-grade power, the power of instigators often derives from control of wealth (medium-grade power) and information (high-grade power), which usually provides the requisite conditions for control of weaponry. An important feature of instigators is that they act as catalysts of collective violence, often by conveying a vision for a better life or by identifying a perceived source of threat in times of social unrest. Currently, for Mandel, the main instigator of terrorism by Islamic militants is bin Laden.

Furnish (2002) claimed that bin Laden aspires to be the "Mahdi" for Muslims because he cannot be the Caliph as long as he does not have a territorial base. Operating without a territorial base, as a virtual fugitive, bin Laden could resort to claiming the most powerful, yet most hazardous, title in Islam: the Mahdi. The Mahdi, or "Rightly-Guided One," is one of two positive eschatological figures who, according to Islamic teachings, will appear at the end of time—the Prophet Jesus being the other. Together, these two will combat unbelievers and the forces of evil: the antichrist-like Dajjal, or "Deceiver"; the *Dabbah*, or "Beast"; and the murderous, rapacious hordes of Ya'juj wa-Ma'juj, who appear earlier in the Bible as "Gog and Magog." Furnish claimed that bin Laden acts as "Mahdi" because he has the characteristics ascribed to him in the Islamic traditional texts. In addition, Furnish claimed that some Western commentators have already observed that bin Laden may consider himself Saladin reborn, at least in terms of his desire to expel the new "Crusaders"—the Americans and Israelis—from the Abode of Islam (*dar al-Islam*), just as Saladin defeated the real Crusaders in the year 1187.

bin Laden's overall objectives, Murphy (2002) believes, are to get rid of pro-Western governments in the Middle East, to remove U.S. military forces from the region, and to bring about an Arab–Israeli peace settlement. Murphy wrote that, on October 4, 2001, the United Kingdom released a document entitled "Responsibility for the Terrorist Atrocities in the United States, 11 September 2001." The document provides background on bin Laden, al-Qaeda, and their relationship to the *de facto* government of Afghanistan, the Taliban. The document also noted that al Qaeda virulently opposes the United States, and that bin Laden urged and incited his followers to kill American citizens, in the most unequivocal terms. On October 12, 1996, he issued a declaration of Jihad as follows:

> The people of Islam have suffered from aggression, inequity and injustice imposed by the Zionist-Crusader alliance and their collaborators.... My Muslim brothers: your brothers in Palestine and in the land of the two Holy Places [i.e. Saudi Arabia] are calling upon your help and asking you to take part in fighting against the enemy—the Americans and the Israelis. They are asking you to do whatever you can to expel the enemies out of the sanctities of Islam.

In February 1998 he issued and signed a "fatwa," which included a decree to all Muslims:

> The killings of Americans and their civilian and military allies is a religious duty for each and every Muslim to be carried out in whichever country they are until al Aqsa mosque has been liberated from their grasp and until their armies have left Muslim lands.

bin Laden as Hero

Much has been written about bin Laden, both before September 11 and after. Richard Curtiss (2002) tells of Osama's beginnings as a hero. During the Afghan war against the Russians, with American support and his family's resources, it was easy for Osama to acquire what was needed to turn the tide against the Russians and also to make a serious contribution. At age 23 he went to Afghanistan and stayed for a brief time before returning to Saudi Arabia. On his next trip to Afghanistan he brought funds and know-how, partly from employees in the family business. Soon he was bringing in trucks, bulldozers, and all the heavy construction material needed to make a serious difference in Afghan fortunes. The Afghans soon turned bin Laden into a folk hero. By then, Osama was called "the Sheikh." There was no question that he was brave. He also had become legendary for his generosity. While some transitions were taking place in Saudi Arabia, bin Laden's dreams were different. He wanted new worlds to conquer, but without devoting the years of preparation and hard work needed to make his country's dreams come true. Meanwhile, conspiracies and violence began to appear wherever he went. After several events had occurred it became clear that Osama was on a collision course with reality. He realized that he would have to leave his country. He went first to the Sudan, where he was welcomed for a time. After 5 years in Sudan, it was time once again for bin Laden to move on, and he returned to Afghanistan. He began setting up training camps for old Islamic militants. Those who showed promise were then encouraged to fight revolutions of their own. Thousands of young men were trained there for revolution.

bin Laden returned to Saudi Arabia as a kind of cult hero in 1989. His speeches at mosques were often recorded and eagerly passed around the Middle East. Some still consider him a hero of the anti-Soviet Jihad. Weinbaum (1991) explained that only when Muslims act as brothers can they hope to work together to overcome their adversities and adversaries. Believers must capture power from the unworthy, and institute the correct laws and values in societies that have been corrupted by adopting the ways of the West. Arab socialism, although incorporated into the rhetoric of Arab nationalism, is distinctive for its emphasis on economic justice and government responsibility to counter economic imperialism.

Among the survivors from the bases hit in Afghanistan who were linked to bin Laden, support for him was redoubled. Reeve (1999) narrated that Mohammad Hussain, an 18-year-old militant training in the camps when the bombs fell, was left with deep wounds in his back and chest. Six of his friends were killed. "I could smell perfume from the blood of those martyrs" (p. 202), he said. "We will take revenge from America and its president. They should not think we are weak. We will emerge as heroes of Islam like Osama bin Laden" (p. 202). The fanaticism of bin Laden's closest followers and soldiers is also unlikely to wither away. "We spent a lot of time waiting to see (bin Laden) which gave us a chance to really sit around and talk with bin Laden's soldiers" (p. 203), said John Miller of America's ABC News, one of just a handful of Western journalists to have interviewed the al-Qaeda leader. "They talked a great deal about the battles in Afghanistan, in Somalia, in other places where they've fought and their level of commitment to him. They regard him as almost a god" (p. 203). His influence within the militant Muslim world cannot be underestimated.

REFERENCES

Abdelkarim, R. Z. (2001). American Muslims to Osama bin Laden and co.: Don't do us any favors. *Washington Report on Middle East Affairs*, 20(9), 72.

al Sayyid, M. (2002). Mixed message: The Arab and Muslim response to "Terrorism." *The Washington Quarterly*, 25(2), 177-190.

Alexander, J. C. (1981). The mass news media in systemic, historical, and comparative perspective. In E. Katz & T. Szecskö (Eds.), *Mass media and social change* (pp. 17-51). Beverly Hills: Sage.

Amin, H. (1996). Egypt and the Arab world in the satellite age. In J. Sinclair, E. Jacka, & S. Cunningham (Eds.), *New patterns in global television: Peripheral vision* (pp. 101-125). New York: Oxford University Press.

Amin, H. (2000). Satellite broadcasting and civil society in the Middle East: The role of Nilesat. *Transnational Broadcasting Studies, 2,* 1-2.

Barry, D. T. (2001). Assessing culture via the Internet: Methods and techniques for psychological research. *CyberPsychology & Behavior, 4*(1), 17-21.

Bergen, P. L. (2001). *Holy war, Inc.: Inside the secret world of Osama bin Laden.* New York: The Free Press.

Bird, S. E., & Dardenne, R. W. (1988). Myth, chronicle, and story: Exploring the narrative qualities of news. In J. W. Carey (Ed.), *Media, myths, and narratives: Television and the press* (pp. 67-86). London: Sage.

Blythe, H., & Sweet C. (1983). Superhero: The six step progression. In R. B. Browne & M. W. Fishwick (Eds.), *The hero in transition* (pp. 180-187). Bowling Green, OH: Bowling Green University Popular Press.

Bodansky, Y. (2001). *bin Laden: The man who declared war on America.* New York: Random House.

Boyd, D. A. (1999). *Broadcasting in the Arab world: A survey of the electronic media in the Middle East.* Ames: Iowa State University Press.

Brawley, E. A. (1983). *Mass media and human services: Getting the message across.* Beverly Hills: Sage.

Browne, R. B. (1983). Hero with 2000 faces. In R. B. Browne & M. W. Fishwick (Eds.), *The hero in transition* (pp. 91-106). Bowling Green, OH: Bowling Green University Popular Press.

Carrier, R. (1997). Global news and domestic needs: Reflections and adaptations of world information to fit national policies and audience needs. In A. Malek (Ed.), *News media and foreign relations: A multifaceted perspective* (pp. 177-194). Norwood, NJ: Ablex.

Cornell, V. J. (2002). A Muslim to Muslims: Reflections after September 11. *The South Atlantic Quarterly, 101*(2), 325-336.

Curtiss, R. H. (2002). Osama bin Laden: From hero to renegade. *Washington Report on Middle East Affairs, 21*(5), 33.

Davis, R. (2001). *The press and American politics: The new mediator.* Upper Saddle River, NJ: Prentice-Hall.

Edwards, D. B. (2002). bin Laden's last stand. *Anthropological Quarterly, 75*(1), 179-184.

Ferrell, W. K. (2000). *Literature and film as modern mythology.* London: Praeger.

Fishwick, M. W. (1983). The hero in transition. In R. B. Browne & M. W. Fishwick (Eds.), *The hero in transition* (pp. 5-13). Bowling Green, OH: Bowling Green University Popular Press.

Furnish, T. R. (2002). bin Ladin: The man who would be Mahdi. *Middle East Quarterly, 9*(2), 53-59.

Giselinde, K. (2002). Media culture and Internet disaster jokes: bin Laden and the attack on the World Trade Center. *European Journal of Cultural Studies, 5*(4), 450-470.

Hachten, W. A. (1996). *The world news prism: Changing media of international communication*. Ames: Iowa State University Press.

Hamdi, M. E. (1998). *The making of an Islamic political leader: Conversations with Hasan al-Turabi*. Boulder, CO: Westview Press.

Karim, K. H. (2000). *Islamic peril: Media and global violence*. Montréal: Black Rose Books.

Karlberg, M., & Hackett, R. A. (1996). Cancelling each other out? Interest group perceptions of the news media. *Canadian Journal of Communication, 21*(4), 1-9.

Lesch, A. M. (2002). Osama bin Laden: Embedded in the Middle East crises. *Middle East Policy, 9*(2), 82-91.

MacDonald, S. (2002). Hitler's shadow: Historical analogies and the Iraqi invasion of Kuwait. *Diplomacy & Statecraft, 13*(4), 29-59.

Mandel, D. R. (2002). Evil and the instigation of collective violence. *Analyses of Social Issues and Public Policy*, 101-108.

Morris, D., Collett, P., Marsh, P., & O'Shaughnessy, M. (1979). *Gestures: Their origins and distribution*. London: Jonathan Cape.

Mowlana, H. (1997). The media and foreign policy: A framework of analysis. In A. Malek (Ed.), *News media and foreign relations: A multifaceted perspective* (pp. 29-41). Norwood, NJ: Ablex .

Murphy, S. D. (2002). Terrorist attacks on World Trade Center and Pentagon. *American Journal of International Law, 96*(1), 237-255.

Norris, P., & Inglehart, R. (2002). Islamic culture and democracy: Testing the "Clash of Civilizations" thesis. *Comparative Sociology, 1*(3-4), 235-263.

Ogan, C. (1995). The Middle East and North Africa. In J. C. Merrill (Ed.), *Global journalism: Survey of international communication* (pp. 189-207). White Plains, NY: Longman.

Reeve, S. (1999). *The new jackals: Ramzi Yousef, Osama bin Laden and the future of terrorism*. Boston: Northeastern University Press.

Rivers, W. L., & Schramm, W. (1969). *Responsibility in mass communication*. New York: Harper & Row.

Rollin, R. R. (1983). The Lone Ranger and Lenny Skutnik: The hero as popular culture. In R. B. Browne & M. W. Fishwick (Eds.), *The hero in transition* (pp. 14-45). Bowling Green, OH: Bowling Green University Popular Press.

Sorensen, K. (1996). Silencing the net: The threat to freedom of expression on-line. *Human Rights Watch, 8*(2), 1-24.

Special report: Fighting terrorism. (2001, September 22). Osama bin Laden's network: The spider in the web. *The Economist*, 17-19.

Stocking, S. H., & LaMarca, N. (1990). How journalists describe their stories: Hypotheses and assumptions in news making. *Journalism Quarterly, 67*(2), 295-301.

Telecommunication policies for the Arab region "the Arab book." (1996, November 11-15). *Regional telecommunication development conference for the Arab states 'Lebanon.'* ITU: Telecommunication Development Bureau.

Tenet, G. J. (2001). Osama bin Laden as America's most serious threat. *Middle East Quarterly, 8*(2), 83.

Thussu, D. K. (2000). *International communication: Continuity and change*. London: Arnold.

van Dijk, T. A. (1991). *Racism and the press*. London: Routledge.

Wedgwood, R. (2002). al Qaeda, terrorism, and military commissions. *American Journal of International Law, 96*(2), 328-337.

Weinbaum, M. G. (1991). Arab opinion, U.S. foreign policy, and the Persian Gulf. *Southern Illinois University Law Journal, 15*, 501-527.

White, S. H., & O'Brien J. E. (1999). What is a hero? An exploratory study of students' conceptions of heroes. *Journal of Moral Education, 28*(1), 81-95.

Wikan, U. (2002). My son—A terrorist? He was such a gentle boy. *Anthropological Quarterly, 75*(1), 117-128.

Yanay, N. (2002). Understanding collective hatred. *Analyses of Social Issues and Public Policy, 2*(1), 53-60.

Chapter 8

FEMALE "HEROES" AT GROUND ZERO

Verbal and Visual Accounts
Reconceptualize the "Heroic"

Valerie J. Smith
California State University, East Bay

Courage and valor characterized the immediate on-the-scene reactions to the tragedy of 9/11. The news was full of acts of heroism as many tried to rescue and aid those in the doomed Twin Towers. Yet, the reporting on the heroes at Ground Zero was primarily male-oriented and consequently obscured the heroic acts of women. This chapter explores hero-gender differences and focuses on two female New York City police officers who were in the middle of the rescue mission.

U.S. citizens and people worldwide watched the news in stunned shock and utter disbelief as every television station repeatedly aired scenes of four hijacked commercial planes crashing into the World Trade Center in New York City, the Pentagon in Washington, DC, and in Pennsylvania's rural farmlands. The terrorist attacks on September 11, 2001, and their horrific aftermath claimed more than 5,000 lives. The World Trade Center complex suffered the worst casualties, with 2,823 civilians and rescue workers confirmed missing or dead. New York Mayor Rudolph Giuliani (2001) declared about the rescue workers and volunteers: "Their courage, selflessness and professionalism saved more than 25,000 lives that day—making it the most successful rescue operation in our nation's history" (p. 8).

In the days and weeks that followed the attack, rescue and recovery efforts by both heroic men and women were unrelenting in the rubble pile of what had been the World Trade Center and was now referred to as "Ground Zero." Yet the news media's coverage of Ground Zero often praised the heroic deeds of New York's "firemen" and "policemen," making daily references to the "brotherhood"—while virtually ignoring similar heroic actions of women. Although their voices largely went unnoticed, thousands of female rescue workers and volunteers also heroically participated at the scene of the disaster, risking and even giving their lives. After reviewing a wide range of scholarship that reveals the typically male characteristics within definitions of hero—perhaps the reason for the media's serious oversight—this chapter studies in-depth verbal and visual texts of two female rescue workers at Ground Zero to discover the actual characteristics they embody. Drawing from Tannen's (1990) genderlect theory, this chapter considers ways in which females can be understood as heroic and then suggests redefining and recognizing the term *hero* in a manner inclusive of both male and female deeds.

HERO LITERATURE

In mythology and religion as well as in contemporary books, films, and television programs, heroes have traditionally been represented as men with typically male traits. Although women have served in heroic roles throughout the ages (Fayer, 1994), these female heroes have often been portrayed as if they were in lesser roles—if they were even represented at all. Fayer reasoned that the most widely recognized heroes reinforce Western culture's values by having taken actions consistent with "courage, command, and conquest in conflicts—typically a male domain" (p. 24). Similarly, Edwards (1984) stated: "Western culture has represented heroes typically as military leaders: commanding, conquering, and above all, male" (p. 4). These male characteristics dominate in definitions of hero.

The word *hero* and its original definitions are Greek, with heroic concepts first framed in myths (Fishwick, 1985). Joseph Campbell (1988) defined heroes as being self-sacrificing, acting to redeem society. Campbell's (1973) monomyth suggested that all myths, which may include both factual and fictional elements, follow the same pattern in which the hero goes through formulaic rites of passage: separation, initiation, and return. Fierbaugh (1998) explained: "The hero is called to adventure, faces obstacles, and then transforms. Popular culture and Campbell's work suggest this is a process primarily for males" (p. 2). Greek myths in most instances "either excluded or assigned lesser roles" to women (Fayer, 1994, p. 27). Since ancient times, heroes have been recognized and studied as males.

The "predominance of males in religious systems" has also continued to contemporary times (Fayer, 1994, p. 28). The liturgical calendar of the Roman Catholic Church is an example: With 212 saint days of celebration designated, 77% are for male saints and 34% for female, with 29% of those for the Virgin Mary. Joanne Turpin recently began a much needed revision of Christian history by "focusing on the lives of one woman in each century who made significant contributions" (p. 28). A similar revisioning of military history is underway, with *The Warrior Queens* chronicling the "lives and deeds of women rulers who have led their countries in battle" (p. 29).

Overall, the "biased recognition of males and their achievements continues in general books about heroes and heroism" (p. 30). As an example, Dixon Wecter's (1941) lengthy volume, *The Hero in America: A Chronicle of Hero Worship*, does not include female heroes in the discussion nor does it consider the possibility of a female hero. Wecter's list of heroes ranges from Captain John Smith to Henry Ford and Charles Lindbergh among others. As late as 1976, McGinniss, taking his definition of hero from *The American Heritage Dictionary of the English Language*, stated that heroes are men (Fayer, 1994, p. 32). In 1985, Fishwick defined heroes as superior men in the book *Seven Pillars of Popular Culture*. He summarized: "In classic times, heroes were god-men; in the Middle Ages, God's men; in the Renaissance, universal men; in the eighteenth century, gentlemen; in the nineteenth century, self-made men" (p. 32).

In the 1980s and 1990s, some authors reinterpreted heroes in history from nonsexist perspectives, bringing overdue recognition to the numerous heroic roles of women through the ages. In *The Hero Within* (1998) and *Awakening the Heroes Within* (1991), Pearson revised Campbell's monomyth to include women. Meanwhile feminist writers and critics, such as Carol Christ, Annis Pratt, Maureen Murdock, and Melodie Mackey, postulated emerging versions of a female monomyth (Mackey, 1998).

Representation of female heroes in film and television programs has been largely absent, although exceptions do exist. Rickey (1991) contended that males get the major roles in movies because it is "commercially safer" (p. 14). However, having female heroes featured in contemporary television programs and films has occurred relatively recently. Edwards (1984) described the female hero as "a primary character" who "inspires and requires followers," and "possesses vision, daring and power: to charm; move; break with the past; endure hardship and privation; journey into the unknown; risk death and survive—at least in spirit" (pp. 5-6). "Heroines," on the other hand, whose femininity is often signified on screen with the youthful attributes of "innocence, powerlessness, and childishness," have existed since film and television were invented (Walsh, 1989, p. 73). Although the "cult of youth and masculinity continue to dominate the American popular imagination" (p. 90), Walsh's study showed that a minority undercurrent of elder movie actresses who possess a more "autonomous and empowering imagery of aging" (p. 76) have also existed throughout American cinema. A minority of films and television programs feature women in leading, heroic roles.

The female hero may often be excluded from recognition in mythology, religion, and contemporary books, films, television programs, and news media, but she is real. In an attempt to correct the literature that has largely remained gender-biased and thus missed seeing the particular emergent structures of women's experiences in heroic acts, this chapter discusses gender and heroism by focusing on the visual and verbal accounts of two of the female rescue workers at Ground Zero. This discussion leads to a reconceptualization of heroic to include female experiences, which may then allow for fuller recognition of female heroes by news media and others.

VISUAL COMMUNICATION

The events of September 11 immediately received extensive visual media coverage, including thousands of color photographs. Many of these images have since been compiled into vivid and heartbreaking photo essays, preserving their representation for future generations.[1] Because pictorial accounts such as these photographs are typical of our visual culture, scholars have become interested in studying visual images. Over the past two decades, a renewed "philosophical concern with the visual" termed the *pictorial turn* has arisen, focusing on the ontology and epistemology of photography and the cinema (Griffin, 2002). In the 1970s, key figures in making visual communication a subfield within American communication research were Sol Worth, Larry Gross, and their students in the Annenberg School for Communication at the University of Pennsylvania. Worth and Gross clarified important conceptual distinctions that relate to this study. They used interpretive strategies to study "how meaning is communicated through visual images" (e.g., see Griffin, 2002; Gross, 1981; Worth & Gross, 1974). They differentiated between photographs representing natural sign-events and symbolic sign-events. For natural sign-events a natural cause is assumed (Griffin, 1995). Photographs taken of female rescue workers in action at Ground Zero, such as the two photographs in this chapter, would be natural sign-events. In contrast, posed photographs would likely be symbolic sign-events in which the photographer or director intended a particular meaning while the photograph was being taken. Worth and Gross described the "interpretation of natural sign-events as attribution," where we "attribute existence to these events and respond according to our familiarity with related life experiences" (p. 446). I suggest that when a photograph is a natural sign-event featuring a human subject, rather than attempting to relate the photos to our own experiences, the photographs may be best understood in their natural setting by understanding the subjects of the photographs themselves from their own perspectives. In the case of the two photographs of female police officers in action, Officers Carol Paukner and Tracy Donahoo, by attributing significance to their viewpoints the audience may gain new insights about ways of living in the world that may not directly relate to their personal life experiences or previous understanding of heroic. The photographic images provide instantaneous access to the nonverbal experiences of both women, thus enriching and contextualizing their stories as well as inviting viewers to interact with the symbolic action presented. By interpreting the photographs of these real-life female heroes in the natural setting of this crisis, a more accurate conception of the heroic—inclusive of females—can be attained.

VERBAL AND VISUAL ACCOUNTS
OF GROUND ZERO

How did New York City Police Officer Carol Paukner and her rookie partner, Officer Tracy Donahoo, participate in Ground Zero? The lived experiences of these two women on September 11 may be constructed from their verbal and pictorial accounts. The reader is thus invited to understand what it might have been like to serve as a female rescue worker at Ground Zero. Extensive quotations are used to provide a sense of immediacy. The accounts are synthesized and summarized from a formal and an informal interview I conducted and from various other documents, particularly the book *Women at Ground Zero* written by Susan Hagen and Mary Carouba (2002). Paukner and Donahoo's experiences serve as representative examples of the 30 narratives in the book. Further evidence of the extent of female involvement in the rescue efforts at Ground Zero is included.

Officer Carol Paukner

"That morning," Paukner recalled, "a call came over the radio for an unknown condition at the World Trade Center. My rookie partner, Tracy

Donahoo, and I went upstairs, and we saw the streets covered with debris" (Hagen & Carouba, 2002, p. 5). After realizing that the World Trade Center had been hit by an airplane, Paukner and Donahoo "ran to the base of the second building where the bookstore was located and immediately started evacuating people" (p. 5):

> [The people] were running through the doors, and we were trying to calm them down. Meanwhile, there was stuff falling off the building, and we tried to keep everybody under the overhang. We were telling them, "Please stay under the shelter! Move to the left, go up Church Street, and get out of here!" (p. 5)

She continued, "A lot of people did listen to me, and I assisted many people who were injured out of the building" (p. 5). "One woman had multiple sclerosis," she recounted; "I carried her up the escalator and carried her up to Broadway, one block away, where they were setting up a triage center" (p. 5). "At that time, I knew there were more planes coming," Paukner related. "The FBI and the federal marshals were there, and they said, 'You're not a coward if you want to leave. There are more planes coming. This is terrorism'" (p. 6). "'How could I leave all those people?' I said to another officer, 'I'm going to die today.' I just looked at the building and said, 'This is my day'" (p. 5).

In a short time, the jet fuel from the first plane came down the elevator shaft, causing a huge explosion. The impact blew Paukner into the glass partition of the bookstore and knocked her to the ground. Two police officers yelled to her, "Get up! Run!" She was able to get up and run into a small doorway with them. "We stayed there until the explosions stopped . . . then we all ran back and continued evacuating people from the building" (p. 5). In about 20 minutes, Paukner heard a huge plane getting dangerously close and then hitting the building. She was blown through the exit, but was able to catch the door of the building as she came out; she was barely able to hold on. She vividly recounted the chaotic scene:

> There was so much smoke and soot that I couldn't breathe . . . people were blowing past me, particles were flying, people were flying. . . . I held on with one hand, and the wind force was so strong that I couldn't get my other hand up to the doorway to pull myself through. Then my hand hit a leg. I pulled on the leg and it was a man. He was alive, and he was screaming to me because it was so loud, "Grab my hand! Grab my hand!" So I grabbed his hand, I pulled myself to him, and we huddled in this corner. . . . We were lying on bodies and trying to hold on. (p. 6)

After it became silent, they could hardly breathe; they were choking, and could not see because of debris in their eyes. As they attempted to crawl out, they called for people, but a lot of individuals were already dead. Because of the debris, they found it difficult to crawl so they stood up and felt their way along the wall as they kept vomiting (p. 6).

When they saw trees, they realized they were outside. Paukner saw that the man she was with was Richie Vitale, a police officer. They both still felt they were going to die as the area was not safe and so many dead bodies — parts of people — were around them. They tried to help anybody they saw who was still alive. A woman standing near them was holding her hands open and saying with bewilderment, "I lost my pocketbook. I lost my pocketbook." They took her arm and said, "We have to get out of here. Come with us." The picture was taken at this point, with Paukner on the left (and an unidentified man behind her, to her right), Vitale in the center, and the woman who lost her pocketbook on the right (personal communication, August 19, 2003). Paukner's ordeals for the day were hardly over, however, with several more incidents that are not recounted here, before they reached safety (e.g., see Hagen & Carouba, 2002).

After being released from the hospital early that evening, Paukner and Vitale went to his precinct to watch coverage of the attacks on television. Paukner stated, "We couldn't believe we had been there. We couldn't believe we were alive. We couldn't believe how many people had died. But we also knew that we had saved a lot of people" (p. 8). Paukner later reported:

> I have a torn rotator cuff in my shoulder, and my knee is torn in three places. I'm going to need surgery on both. I also threw my neck out, hurt my right foot, and burned my eyes. I still have a lung infection. I feel like somebody's sitting on my chest. I can't get rid of this cough or sleep lying down. I've been treated for it, but it won't go away. (p. 9)

Paukner's recollection of events then takes a personal turn, focusing on her own identity and how it developed. She stated:

> There's not one cop I know, or one firefighter, who has not thought about leaving the job. . . . But I think going back on patrol would be a good thing for me. I always wanted to be a cop, all my life, since I was a little girl. I didn't want Barbie dolls. I wanted police action figures. I have that in me. I'm able to help people, and that's what I did that day. I know I did my best, but I wish I could have done more. (Hagen & Carouba, 2002, p. 9)

Now, a few years after the incident, Paukner has had several surgeries and is still recovering from her injuries. She has been forced to take early retirement because of the extent of her disabilities (personal communication, February 28, 2004).

Officer Tracy Donahoo

Donahoo remembered, "September 11 was my second day on patrol. I graduated from the academy in May, then did 3 months of training, so this was only my second day as a real police officer" (Hagen & Carouba, 2002, p. 120). "I was excited because it was my first day working with a senior partner who had time on [e.g., experience]," Donahoo continued:

> I was like, OK I'm going to learn something. It was a female officer and I thought to myself, "This is great. I'm going to see how she handles herself. How she interacts with people." Then when we were a block away from the Trade Center we saw the terrified people coming out of the building. I felt like, "This is why I wanted to become a cop because I'm actually helping people. I'm doing something like a doctor or a nurse." (personal communication, August 17, 2003)

She went up to Five World Trade with her partner, Paukner, before they were separated. Donahoo described her early moments as a rescuer on that tragic day:

People were going down to a sublevel from the North Tower and coming up through Building Five, and we were trying to get them across the street. They were taking it very slow. They were saying, "Oh, I just walked down 70 flights. Don't make me walk any faster." We were trying to keep them under the roof, because there was still debris coming down from where the first plane hit. (Hagen & Carouba, 2002, p. 120)

Fifty minutes after the second plane hit the South Tower and it began to collapse, Donahoo yelled to the people still coming out of Five World Trade: "Get back in the building! Get back in the building!" She thought it was some type of avalanche and recounted, "You could see the fear in people's faces. . . . Just when I got in the building myself, the South Tower came all the way down." Donahoo flew about 20 feet through the air when the debris of the World Trade Center hit the ground (p. 121). Donahoo later wrote in a published letter, "It was so dark and I couldn't breathe. I had to stick my hand in my mouth to remove the dirt that was sealing it" (Donahoo, 2003, p. 2). Everyone was screaming in the building. She decided she was not going to die in there and she shouted, "Shut up! Shut up! Shut up! I'm a police officer!" and then they were quiet (Hagen & Carouba, 2002, p. 121). She said, "We're going to get out of here!" (p. 121). Donahoo remembered that the bookstore in the lobby of the building had glass all around and told the firefighter next to her. After she and the other rescue personnel turned on their flashlights, this firefighter then walked ahead and broke the glass (which had somehow remained intact) (p. 122). She described the frightening scene: "There were steps in the middle of the store, and people were tripping as they were coming through, so I stayed behind with my flashlight to get them safely down the steps. . . . I was the last person to walk out of there" (p. 122).

On the street, in her stunned state, Donahoo encountered chaos and confusion. After walking down one block to Broadway, she came across her sergeant from her command. She recalled, "He said, 'Oh my God, you've got to call the command. They've been calling your shield number for an hour'" (p. 122). The pay phones were swarmed with reporters and when she said, "I have to use the phone." They said, "In a minute." She persisted, "No, you have to get off the phone. I have to call my command." Another reporter insisted on using the phone next until he realized Donahoo was a police officer and then he apologized, "Oh, sorry, officer" (p. 123). Donahoo was surprised that he could even tell she was an officer because she was covered completely in white. She described herself in these words: "I had all this debris on me, and my hair was totally saturated with the stuff" (p. 123).

While Donahoo was on the phone with an officer from her command, the North Tower came down. She vividly depicted the scene:

"We walk into the lobby and she's right there with the front desk man and we're like, 'Thank God.'" (personal communication, August 17, 2003)

> I heard a *Bang!* And then this black smoke came at me so fast. I saw ambulances flying down the street and people running and screaming, and I dropped the phone and ran to the next corner and jumped behind a building. All the smoke and debris went past me. (p. 123)

When she finally was able to contact her command again, about 30 minutes later, the officer she had previously been talking with was distraught. He anguished, "Oh my God. I thought you were dead. I thought you were killed when you were on the phone with me" (p. 123).

A few hours later the people at the CVS Drug Store down the block from the World Trade Center had their doors open. They invited her and the police officers she was with to wash with their soap and towels in the back room: "Come in. Get whatever you need." Donahoo stated, "I took some stuff to clean my eyes because I had debris in them." After they had cleaned themselves and were walking back to her command, this picture was taken about five blocks from the Trade Center. Donahoo's hair was sticking up from all the debris in it. In the background over her right shoulder is where the Trade Center was. In the photograph, she and the officers who accompanied her were talking with two plain clothes police officers who needed a flashlight for a civilian rescue. Although exhausted, they all turned around and went to rescue a little girl trapped on the 22nd floor of a building without power and in an area that was closed off to the public. Donahoo recounted, "I'm pretty tired at this point, but I'm prepared to walk these 22 flights to see if this little girl is alright" (personal communication, August 17, 2003).

Because Donahoo's physical injuries were minimal she only took 1 day off. She and her colleagues then worked 16-hour days into October and 12-hour days after that (personal communication, August 17, 2003). About her experiences of September 11, she reflected: "I think I was calm during the whole thing because I was stunned. I didn't realize what a terrible situation I was in. I wasn't hysterical" (Hagen & Carouba, 2002, p. 123).

Donahoo's dangerous experiences only deepened her commitment to the profession. She explained:

> Before this I wasn't sure if I wanted to be a cop. The process of deciding whether or not I wanted to be one was a long one. But during and after September 11, I knew that this is what I'm supposed to be doing. (p. 124)

She wrote in a published article:

> We are all stronger than we think. I know that the women who served at Ground Zero didn't think they had such strength before September 11, 2001. I found my calling. . . . The helping aspect of being a police officer is what I like about it. I'm glad I was there. We saved thousands of people. Thousands of people got out of those buildings. (Donahoo, 2003, p. 3)

Other Female Rescue Workers

Paukner and Donahoo's verbal and visual accounts provide two in-depth examples of the many women heroes serving in a self-sacrificing manner to save others' lives at Ground Zero. Captain Brenda Berkman of the New York City Fire Department and her colleagues also worked resolutely during long, hard shifts despite being "consumed with grief, disbelief and exhaustion" (Willing, 2002). Although Berkman is one of only 25 female firefighters out of 11,500 firefighters in New York, women are more represented in other human service occupations in the state. At least one third of the paramedics and emergency medical technicians are women, and of the "NYPD's 38,000 uniformed [police] officers, more than 6,000," or about 16%, are females (Hagen & Carouba, 2002, pp. xiv-xv). The Port Authority, which had jurisdiction over the World Trade Center, employs about "1,350 police officers" of whom 99 or about 7% are women.

Not only were a significant number of female emergency workers and volunteers at the site immediately and for days afterward, they came from all across the country (Hu, 2002). Women professionals were "part of search-and-rescue and other firefighter teams. Women nurses and doctors, women construction workers, women chaplains, military women, Red Cross women—women were volunteering in every capacity" (Berkman, 2001, p. 5). As a noteworthy example, Eileen Shulock, the volunteer director of an organization for women interested in using the Web, immediately e-mailed its members after the attacks and brought more than 3,000 "webgrrls" and other volunteers to Ground Zero, many specializing in direly needed organizational and technical skills (Dollarhide, 2001b). Along with thousands of courageous men, these many brave women working in numerous capacities risked their own safety to try to save others. Three uniformed women lost their lives on that first day, and many more women were injured in their heroic attempts to save others (Berkman, 2001, p. 5). Clearly, females were heavily involved with the rescue efforts at Ground Zero.

In the vast majority of instances, the news media overlooked the efforts of women, focusing instead on male acts of heroism. Hagen and Carouba (2002), authors of *Women at Ground Zero*, noticed this disturbing omission: "New York's 'firemen' and 'policemen' emerged as the new American heroes. The media presented story after story about the 'return of the manly man' and made daily, unapologetic references to 'the brothers' and 'our brave guys'" (pp. xi-xii). Gradually, Berkman (2001) noticed this tendency as well. She reported the following:

> It began at funerals. Speaker after speaker would talk about the men, the guys, and the terrible pain of the men. "Firemen" this and "firemen" that—totally ignoring the dozens of women firefighters and police officers in attendance from all over the country. (p. 5)

As a result, she noted, "Over and over, the women firefighters were saying to me how upsetting this was to them" (Willing, 2002). Then Berkman also began to receive a "lot of calls, emails, letters [asking] were there any women there [as rescue workers]?" (Hu, 2002). She answered that "women were there, working right alongside men," although this was not evident in media coverage (Hu, 2002). Three months after the attack, the "predominant image" of rescue workers remained male, even though "hundreds of female Red Cross volunteers, police officers and emergency technicians were at the scene every day" (Dollarhide, 2001a).

RECONCEPTUALIZING THE "HEROIC"

The idea and existence of female heroes is not new, but throughout the ages heroic women have rarely received the same level of visibility and recognition as male heroes. With conceptions of the self-sacrificing hero often represented by typically "male" characteristics—such as commanding, conquering, strong, and aggressive—and much of history being written by men, discussions of female heroes have been largely muted.

With the news media's coverage of heroes at Ground Zero focusing almost exclusively on the contributions of men and phrasing their stories in gender-biased language, Tannen's (1990) gender communication studies offer insights into the underlying construction of the media's focus on the masculine. Her research claims that many men routinely interpersonally engage the world as individuals in a "hierarchical social order" in which they are either "one-up" or "one-down" and concerned about status (p. 24). People often communicate within this perspective to "achieve and maintain the upper hand if they can, and protect themselves from others' attempts to put them down and push them around" (p. 25). Life is generally focused as a "contest to preserve independence and avoid failure" (p. 25). Although many exceptions among individuals exist to the general gender categorizations that Tannen introduced, the dominant perspective in mass-mediated society is constructed along such patriarchal lines. This construction favoring typically masculine traits seems to exist particularly during times of sudden large-scale crises when images of heroes are called for, perhaps because emotionally based decisions are more likely to be made by news personnel and because the image of the larger-than-life male hero brings feelings of a power advantage and thus safety.

Both male and female heroes engaged in self-sacrifice at Ground Zero, but the media viewed the sacrifices in such a way to reinforce societal beliefs of man as a larger-than-life protector and woman as powerless. The result was that female heroes were largely invisible to media audiences, as is typically the case. Apparent exceptions to the media providing visibility to female heroes seem manufactured by the press and trivialize the true nature of heroes. During the Iraqi War in 2003, U.S. Private Jessica Lynch fell victim to Iraqi soldiers, became a prisoner of war, and was given outstanding treatment at the local Iraqi hospital in Nasirayi. Dr Harith a-Houssona who treated her stated that she had a few broken bones, but no bullet or stab wounds as the U.S. media had reported (Kamfner, 2003). Rather, Lynch was a victim and her rescuers were the ones who had the heroic qualities. Yet the media mislabeled her powerlessness as heroic, trivializing the sacrifices that others have made and suggesting that female heroism is in essence victimization. In contrast, Browne (1987) explained that women who exhibit heroic qualities have consistently been treated as invisible because men fear they would otherwise overpower them. Although the media lauds attention on a powerless female, the powerful ones at Ground Zero were ignored. Edwards (1984) stated that the "woman hero is an image of antithesis" in the patriarchal and hierarchical context within which men and women are assigned unequal positions; "different from the male—her sex her sign—she threatens his authority and that of the system he sustains" (p. 4). Thus, to Edwards, the female hero has a "fugitive existence," with her presence overlooked as she represents a marker of "patriarchal instability and insecurity" for society (p. 4). If media representations engage the world hierarchically, then the masculine hero is the powerful one at the top rung—perhaps a reassuring and familiar figure to the world in a time of terrorist attacks, but also an inaccurate portrayal of the actual rescue efforts at Ground Zero.

Drawing on Foucault (1970), Foss (1996) suggested that for submerged groups to have their voices heard in the dominant culture, the group's members must first develop their own authentic voice. Likewise, Ferguson (1984) claimed that women must present their perspectives and experiences in terms other than those of the dominant male structure (p. 154). By analyzing the verbal and visual texts of Paukner and Donahoo's experiences at Ground Zero, examples of an authentic female voice describing alternative heroic characteristics emerges. Tannen's gender studies are again useful: She described a typical female orientation to the world as exhibiting qualities of equality, support, and interdependence. I suggest that Paukner and Donahoo as well as others—both male and female—exhibited such qualities in contrast to the media's emphasis on the "manly man."

Equality

Tannen (1990) explained that many women approach the world as people in a "network of connections" who are concerned about equality (p. 25). Paukner and Donahoo clearly demonstrated this approach. By heroically remaining at Ground Zero in the face of danger while others were fleeing, they showed the great value they place on other human beings, with the value of others' lives equal to or even greater than their own. Foss and Griffin (1995) highlighted a feminist principle that illustrates this value: "[E]very being is a unique and necessary part of the pattern of the universe and thus has value" (p. 4). This sense of worth is "not determined by positioning individuals on a hierarchy so they can be ranked and compared" (p. 4). Paukner carried the woman with multiple sclerosis up the escalator and down the block because she believed that even though the woman had a debilitating infirmity, she was just as valuable and necessary as others in this world. Paukner chose to enact this selfless caring for another human being, finding emotional and physical strength within herself to carry out an act that would be difficult for anyone to do alone. When the FBI and the federal marshals told her, "You're not a coward if you want to leave," she felt she could not leave the others. Her decision to stay and her resolve, "I'm going to die today," indicate her dedication to the value of all of human life (Hagen & Carouba, 2002, p. 5). In the visual of Paukner, everything is white or ashen gray, eliminating any markers of competition or status and visually illustrating at the surface the values of human equality already embedded within the rescue workers. Similarly, Donahoo personally believes that "a hero is someone who cares more about another human being than about themselves" and their own welfare (personal communication, August 17, 2003). Paukner and Donahoo showed civilians how to survive. They took charge in their service to others, but not from a motivation of hierarchy or status. Rather, by equally valuing the importance of all human existence, Paukner, Donahoo, as well as many other rescue workers—both female and male—saved thousands of lives that day.

Support

Within this framework of equality, Tannen (1990) contended that individuals interacting with others are trying to give and seek support. Both Paukner and Donahoo exhibited nurturing and helping qualities from the time they arrived at the base of the Twin Towers. Paukner stated that they tried to calm people down as they ran through the doors and that she "assisted many people who were injured out of the building" (Hagen & Carouba, 2002, p. 5). When the explosion from the jet fuel rushed down the elevator shafts, Paukner's own life was gravely threatened. She and Officer Vitale found support in each other and eventually escaped outdoors. Although still afraid for their own lives, they tried to help anybody they saw who was still alive, including the woman in shock who "lost her pocketbook" (personal communication, August 19, 2003). In the photograph of Paukner and Vitale, both made careful, deliberate steps with their eyes focused on the ground, in contrast to the bewilderment of the lady they were assisting to their left. Typical heroic strength and determination were certainly part of their quest to live, but so also were the qualities of nurturing and support.

Similarly, Donahoo's motivation for becoming a police officer was to help people on a daily basis. Although at the entry-level rank as a new officer, she did not have to prove herself to her colleagues or civilians as she normally might to achieve status and respect. Rather, she worked in a concentrated, methodical fashion, first with her partner and later with two other female officers, to fulfill her role in rescuing others. Her first solo directive in her new position as an officer was shouting to others, "Get back in the building" and her second was "Shut up! I'm a police officer!" when they had been buried under debris in Five World Trade Center after the South Tower fell. Although these are commands perhaps typical of masculine heroic images, Donahoo spoke them from a nurturing orientation. Revealing her feminine perspective, she speculated later that "maybe males do it as sort of a macho thing too whereas females may just want to help people" (personal communication, August 17, 2003). In her self-sacrifice to help others, she was the last person to walk out of the destroyed and unstable bookstore. As the photograph of Donahoo illustrates, she agreed to return to an unstable building to ascend 22 flights to save a child, even though the instance occurs at the end of a long, exhausting, and dangerous day of ongoing search and rescue. She supported other officers by leaving the colored, living world of safety and returning to the black, white, and gray destruction of Ground Zero. Day after day, thousands of heroic men and women willingly returned to the site to offer support and to care for each other, in their diligent quest and fading hope to find other equally valuable family, friends, colleagues, and strangers still alive.

Interdependence

Tannen (1990) described a female orientation to the world as a "community, a struggle to preserve intimacy and avoid isolation," with people existing in a network of interdependent relationships with each other (p. 25). Although the news media did acknowledge the community of the "brotherhood," this recognition isolated females. Yet the life-threatening seriousness of the events of September 11 acted to eliminate competition and build interdependence among the rescue workers—of either gender—at least for that day and often during the ensuing months as they focused on their shared goal of rescue and recovery. When two police officers yelled to Paukner, "Get up! Run!" she was able to run to a small doorway with them (Hagen & Carouba, 2002, p. 5). They were together during the explosion, forming a transient community of interdependence that helped them to survive and afterward to continue assisting others. Twenty minutes later, Vitale screamed to Paukner, "Grab my hand! Grab my hand!" So she grabbed his hand, pulled herself to him, and huddled in a corner—trying to hold on to him while the force of the plane hitting the tower was blowing past them (Hagen & Carouba, 2002, p. 6). In the photograph, the linked arms of Paukner, Vitale, and the woman who lost her pocketbook show camaraderie and mutual commitment to survive, a vital network of connections during this crucial moment. The fortitude and determination held by Paukner and Vitale in this human-created blizzard of white was strengthened by their companionship.

Donahoo's experience also shows interconnectedness. For example, she told the male firefighter next to her about the glass in the bookstore lobby, and then he proceeded to break it as a way of escape. In general, the attempts at coordination and maintained phone contact of the rescue workers further demonstrate the interdependence among these heroes. Paukner and Donahoo also participated as members of the larger United States and world community, as can be seen in the visual of Donahoo. The cloud of smoke in the background where the Twin Towers stood as well as Donahoo's used mask, debris-saturated hair, and remnants of white or gray ash on her clothes illustrate her direct involvement at Ground Zero. Yet, the U.S. flag flying in the breeze symbolizes the outpouring of broad community support that was with her and rescue workers like her.

SUMMARY AND CONCLUSION

Thousands of women and men assisted in the rescue and recovery efforts at Ground Zero after the horrific terrorist attacks of September 11, 2001. Traditionally in mythology, religion, books, television programs, and movies, as well as in real life, heroes have been defined as self-sacrificing, recognized as male, and described as possessing masculine characteristics—although alongside men many females have quietly performed what most people would consider heroic deeds. History and the events of September 11 reveal that although female heroes have existed throughout the ages, oral and written heroic stories have largely ignored them. As a result, to be recognized for their heroic acts, women heroes often must overcome additional obstacles and invisible barriers because their very presence creates tension and seeming unbalance in a patriarchal society. The problem is not in the ability to be heroic but in being recognized as heroic and sometimes being allowed to serve in heroic roles. Yet without doing these incredible deeds of heroism, these women cannot attain a sense of their authentic selves as full human beings.

In the ways that a heroic woman resembles the male hero, "she questions the conventional associations of gender and behavior," such as men being strong and aggressive and women being weak and passive. Females of course may possess such strength and aggression, as these qualities are not inherently masculine. In the ways she differs from the male hero, however, "she denies the link between heroism and *either* gender *or* behavior" (Edwards, 1984, p. 5), showing that male heroes may also possess typically feminine qualities. The female hero demonstrates that characteristics of equality, support, and interdependence, are inherently human, not specifically female.

While illustrating that the inherently human qualities of heroes may threaten the current power structure, it allows a reconceptualization of hero to include qualities typically associated with females and not just those characteristics usually identified with masculinity. Whether the rescue workers and volunteers on September 11 viewed the world in a controlling and hierarchical manner or in an interdependent way emphasizing support and equality, at Ground Zero both men and women engaged in similar heroic acts of self-sacrifice to protect others from harm. This chapter has provided a contrast to the news media's portrayal of Ground Zero heroes as larger than life, conquering and male. I suggest that at Ground Zero the qualities these front-line heroes of both genders embodied also included an interdependent community, nurture and support among the rescue workers, and a sense of equality toward the value of all human life.

ENDNOTE

1. Photographic essays published about September 11 include *Above Hallowed Ground* (Sweet, 2002), *New York September 11* (Photographers, 2001), *One Nation: America Remembers (from LIFE)* (Sullivan, 2001), *What We Saw: CBS News, with an Introduction by Dan Rather* (CBS Worldwide, 2002), *September 11: A Testimony* (Glocer, 2002), *The New York Times: A Nation Challenged—A Visual History of 9/11 and its Aftermath* (Raines, Lee, Schlein, & Levitas, 2002), *Here is New York: A Democracy of Photographs* (George, Peress, Shulan, & Traub, 2002).

REFERENCES

Berkman, B. (2001). Celebrating the many roles of women: Remarks of Lt. Brenda Berkman. Remarks presented at the National Women's Law Center's 2001 Awards Dinner. Retrieved August 1, 2003, from http://www.wfsi.org/BerkNWLC.html

Browne, P.E. (1987). *Heroines of popular culture*. Bowling Green, OH: Bowling Green State University Popular Press.

Campbell, J. (1973). *The hero with a thousand faces*. Princeton, NJ: Princeton University Press.

Campbell, J. (1988). *The power of myth*. New York: Doubleday.

CBS Worldwide, I. (2002). *What we saw: CBS news, with an introduction by Dan Rather*. New York: Simon & Schuster.

Dollarhide, M. (2001a). Firefighter Berkman is two kinds of a hero. *Women's Enews*. Retrieved August 1, 2003, from http://www.womensenews.org/article.cfm?aid=769

Dollarhide, M. (2001b). Using e-mail list, Shulock finds 3,000 volunteers. *Women's Enews*. Retrieved August 1, 2003, from http://www.womensenews.org/article.cfm/dyn/aid/708

Donahoo, T. (2003, Summer). On the job on 9/11. *Q*, pp. 2-3. Retrieved August 1, 2003, from http://www.qc.edu/nis/qmag/qmag_su03.pdf

Edwards, L.R. (1984). *Psyche as hero: Female heroism and fictional form.* Middletown, CT: Wesleyan University Press.

Fayer, J. (1994). Are heroes always men? In S. J. Drucker & R. S. Cathcart (Eds.), *American heroes in a media age* (pp. 24-35). Cresskill, NJ: Hampton Press.

Ferguson, K.E. (1984). *The feminist case against bureaucracy.* Philadelphia, PA: Temple University Press.

Fierbaugh, J.L. (1998). *The quest of the female hero: Mary Cassatt, Paula Modersohn-Becker, Georgia O'Keeffe.* Unpublished master's thesis, California State University Dominguez Hills, Dominguez Hills, CA.

Fishwick, M.W. (1985). *Seven pillars of popular culture.* Westport, CT: Greenwood Press.

Foss, S.K. (1996). Judy Chicago's "The dinner party": Empowering of women's voice in visual art. In *Rhetorical Criticism.* Prospect Heights, IL: Waveland Press.

Foss, S.K., & Griffin, C.L. (1995). Beyond persuasion: A proposal for an invitational rhetoric. *Communication Monographs, 62,* 2-18.

Foucault, M. (1970). *The order of things: An archeology of the human sciences.* New York, NY: Pantheon.

George, A.R., Peress, G., Shulan, M., & Traub, C. (2002). *Here is New York: A democracy of photographs.* New York: Scalo.

Giuliani, R.W. (2001). Introduction. In R. Sullivan (Ed.), *One nation: America remembers September 11.* Boston, MA: Little, Brown.

Glocer, T.R.C. (2002). *September 11: A testimony.* New York: Pearson Education.

Griffin, M. (1995). Between art and industry: Amateur photography and middlebrow culture. In L. Gross (Ed.), *On the margins of art worlds* (pp. 183-205). Boulder, CO: Westview.

Griffin, M. (2002). Camera as witness, image as sign: The study of visual communication in communication research. In W. B. Gudykunst (Ed.), *Communication yearbook* (Vol. 24). Thousand Oaks, CA: Sage.

Gross, L. (1981). Introduction. In L. Gross & S. Worth (Eds.), *Studying visual communication.* Philadelphia, PA: University of Pennsylvania Press.

Hagen, S., & Carouba, M. (2002). *Women at Ground Zero: Stories of courage and compassion.* Indianapolis, IN: Alpha Books.

Hu, S. (2002). Documentary celebrates the women of Ground Zero. *CBS Broadcasting, Inc.* Retrieved August 1, 2003, from http://beta.kpix.com/news/local/2002/09/05/ Documentary Celebrates the Women of Ground Zero.html

Kampfner, J. (2003, May 18). Saving Private Lynch story flawed. *BBC News.* Retrieved February 12, 2004.

Mackey, M. (1998). *The female hero.* Unpublished master's thesis, California State University Dominguez Hills, Dominguez Hills, CA.

McGinniss, J. (1990). *Heroes.* New York: Simon & Schuster.

Pearson, C. S. (1991). *Awakening the heroes within: Twelve archetypes to help us find ourselves and transform our world.* San Francisco: HarperSanFrancisco.

Pearson, C. S. (1998). *The hero within: Six archetypes we live by* (3rd ed.). San Francisco: HarperSanFrancisco.

Photographers, M. (2001). *New York September 11.* New York: PowerHouse Books.

Raines, H.I., Lee, N.P.E., Schlein, L.P.E., & Levitas, M.T.E. (2002). *The New York Times: A nation challenged—A visual history of 9/11 and its aftermath*. New York: The New York Times.

Rickey, C. (1991, March 24). Too male & too pale. *The Philadelphia Inquirer Magazine*, pp. 14-16, 32-35.

Sullivan, R.E. (2001). *One nation: America remembers September 11*. Boston, MA: Little, Brown.

Sweet, C.E. (2002). *Above hallowed ground: A photographic record of September 11, 2001 by photographers of the New York City Police Department*. Harmondsworth, Middlesex, England: Viking Studio.

Tannen, D. (1990). *You just don't understand: Women and men in conversation*. New York: Ballantine Books.

Walsh, A. (1989). "Life isn't yet over": Older heroines in American popular cinema of the 1930s and 1970s/80s. *Qualitative Sociology, 12*(1), 72-95.

Wecter, D. (1941). *The hero in America: A chronicle of hero worship*. New York: Charles Scribner's Sons.

Willing, L. (2002). Beyond Ground Zero: Six months later. *Women in the Fire Service, Inc.* Retrieved August 1, 2003, from http://www.wfsi.org/Berkman2.html

Worth, S., & Gross, L. (1974). Symbolic strategies. *Journal of Communication, 24*(4), 27-39.

Chapter 9

HEROES IN A GLOBAL WORLD

An Examination of Traditional Folkloric
and Mythic Formulae for Heroes and Contemporary
Iterations

Susan Duffy
California Polytechnic State University

In this chapter, Duffy argues that there are traditional folkloric and mythic formulae by which heroes have been constructed across time, geography, and religions. She identifies current heroes of 9/11 and war to explore hero construction in relation to martyr heroes, fantasy heroes, anti-heroes, and villains, and considers the blurring distinctions between them. She concludes by returning to the continued importance of the traditional hero of myth and folklore in a global world.

Since September 11, 2001, the use of the term *hero* has become ubiquitous in the American media. In the years since, rarely can one open a newspaper, magazine, or hear a news broadcast without a reference to a national, regional, or local "hero," April 2003 brought another highly visible event that was loosely tied to the events of September 11. The U.S. military campaign in Iraq resulted in a new proliferation of real and mediated heroes. The

American heroes of 2001 were epitomized in the images of the New York firefighters, and the ordinary individuals who banded together on the doomed airplanes leaving a brave and poignant "Let's roll" whisper in the memory of a nation. The term was applied to Rudolph Giuliani who stood resolute and stalwart as he oversaw the response to the worst attack by outside forces ever on American soil.

The American heroes of 2003 share the same common roots of the ordinary citizens of 2001, and the same essence of the divine. Their youth, their dedication, their physical trials, and their courage in overcoming fear, captivity, and foreign resentment created a new gallery of heroic icons that include helicopter pilots, generals, cooks, mechanics, and even embedded journalists. The image of the two American soldiers pulling down the statue of Saddam Hussein becomes a scene as memorable as the planting of the flag at Iwo Jima, but given to us in "real time." These men and women—models of selfless sacrifice, compassionate responses and noble sentiments—become inspirations to us.

The nobility of the images, which in themselves constitute a kind of high iconographic art, tend to readily percolate down through cultural spheres until they land awkwardly in the realm of popular culture and here are manifested in our society in myriad ways from the philosophical to the commercial. Resonant images continue to emerge, running the gamut from the profound designs for the Twin Towers memorial to the more profane fashion designs that incorporated fireman chic in apparel. After September 11, 2001, there was a marked increase in the purchase of firefighter action figures produced by toy companies. A new found fascination with all things military, with special operations, and the lexicon of military jargon remains evident in toy stores and video games.

Half a world away, those who we call "liberators" are called "invaders" by an opposing press corps: Those who have been dubbed "heroes" within their specific cultural circles are those who we call "terrorists" and "evil ones." Yet, they too have become models—deemed worthy of emulation by young people. A recent article in the *San Francisco Chronicle* noted the increase in Palestinian parents who have begun actively seeking counseling for their children, and in many cases reporting their own children to Israeli and Palestinian authorities because of the willingness of their children to emulate suicide bombers. Clearly, the concept of the martyr hero has become a potent image in our contemporary world. More than merely an "image," the martyr hero has become a dangerous international role model. Unlike heroes of the past whose exploits and heroic actions were conveyed through word of mouth, through bardic interpretations, and through epic stories, today's "men of action" (for clearly there is a question as to whether they are all heroes) receive instantaneous recognition through media coverage, which repeats their stories daily for weeks on end. In effect, their continual presence in the home through mediated sources of television, magazines, and newspapers not only increases exposure to the stories of individuals, but acceptance of the stories whether honorable or repugnant, and establishes them as models for good or ill. Extending the analysis to other kinds of heroes in today's world leads to some disturbing examples that blur the line between fantasy heroes, their emulation by young people, and subsequent real action with real consequences in today's society.

Questions arise: "Are the media creating both heroes and anti-heroes?" "What is the difference between a 'hero,' an 'anti-hero,' and a 'villain' who becomes the featured character in a film, series, or novel?" "Who are today's heroes?" "Are there sufficient positive heroes to offset the influence of what many would consider an anti-hero, and/or a villainous character who becomes a model for aberrant behavior?" In 2001, a Harris Poll of 1,022 Americans reported that more than 50% of those polled could not name any figure they considered heroic. One in six polled had "no hero at all." One in four had recently removed a former hero from their list due to "unethical conduct" (*U.S. News*, 2001).

For the sake of definition, a *hero* in the most secular of terms is one who is a central figure in an important event or period who is subsequently honored for outstanding qualities; usually qualities of nobility, courage, and self-sacrifice. An *anti-hero* is a decidedly modern conception in literature who lacks the noble characteristics of the "hero," and is identified with a lack of courage, honesty, and an ambivalence toward commonly held mores and virtues of the society. An anti-hero walks a crooked line and at times deviates among roles ranging from comic, to rebellious, to psychopathic. The anti-hero is not necessarily an evil character. Anti-heroes can have positive elements when, by rejecting the values evident in a corrupt society, they enter into conflict with the powers that be within the corruption. But another anti-hero may be fundamentally corrupt, yet retains a place of prominence in the event/story being related. Anti-heroes are not entirely unsympathetic, nor are they governed by the moral code of the dominant society. Lists of anti-heroes in literature and film tend to categorize these protagonists using classifications that label the character as comic, emotionally disturbed or deviant. The anti-hero may also serve as a defiant challenger to the social norm, or the hero who is an outsider to the dominant social group. Literary and filmic anti-heroes mentioned most often in each category include any of Woody Allen's protagonists, Don Quixote, Tom Jones or Forrest Gump in the comic classification; *Midnight Cowboy, Rainman, One Flew Over the Cuckoo's Nest*, or even Elliot's J. Alfred Prufrock provide striking examples of anti-heroes who fall under the emotionally disturbed category; *Look Back in Anger* and *Clockwork Orange* provide examples of the defiant anti-hero as does the James Dean portrayal of Cal in *East of Eden*. The characters of Nora and Hedda Gabler in the plays of Ibsen, Willy

Loman in *Death of a Salesman*, Yosarian in *Catch 22*, and the reviled protagonists of *Phantom of the Opera*, *Kiss of the Spider Woman*, and *Native
Son* are outsiders to the dominant class or controlling social group.

But what about the villain; the antisocial, sociopathic character who
creeps into the popular mind-set through literature, film, news, or television
series and who generates a following, for whatever reasons? Has popular
culture sanitized the role of villain and allowed it to usurp the position of
anti-hero? Traditionally, the villain is the unprincipled or evil character capable of committing great crimes. Are Hannibal Lector, Earl Turner, Nicolae
Carpathia, Tony Soprano, Lestat, or even Darth Vader villains whose actions
should be repugnant to civilized people, or does our society dilute the
heinousness of their actions with a concoction of pop psychology and a perverse interest in the aberrant? How is it that murderers such as Richard
Rodriguez, Ted Bundy, John Wayne Gacy, or Jeffrey Dahmer, achieve notoriety bordering on celebrity status. Today, one of the most disturbing
aspects of popular culture is the extent to which the distinction between the
noble hero is blurred with the ignoble villain. Professionals in the fields of
psychology and sociology try to determine causal links between actions of
these heroes, anti-heroes, and even villains and the actions of alienated youth
and adults in today's world here and abroad.

The average American finds incomprehensible cultures that produce
political terrorists, suicide bombers and assassins, and soldiers who use
women and children as human shields in war. On the other side of the world,
citizens in European and Asiatic countries find it equally incomprehensible
that children in the United States have opened fire in schools with semi-auto-
matic rifles, that Black men have been dragged to their deaths behind cars,
and that snipers randomly picked off victims in Virginia suburbs. What
prompts these expressions of despair, anger, political, or religious fervor?
Where are the heroes? Does the cult of celebrity created by the media give
rise to inappropriate heroes—or anti-heroes? Are the terms *role models* and
heroes used synonymously, if not mistakenly?

Of immediate concern to parents, teachers, and those who study culture
are the mediated images in film, television, literature, news, and current
events that offer sharp and sustained attention to individuals who quickly
become objects of imitation by others. In another day and time, such imitation would be labeled *hero worship*, and it would not be cause for concern.
More and more sociologists, psychologists, and scholars of popular culture
recognize that there are increasing incidents in our own society whereby
individuals real or fictional, reached a certain level of recognition, notoriety,
or respect; acquire an interested following; their actions are then imitated—
but with intentional horrific results.[1]

When one considers contemporary examples of the last decade that
include Oklahoma City bomber, Timothy McVeigh, Columbine shooters,

Dylan Klebold and Eric Harris, Palestinian and Iraqi suicide bombers, and the many other young people who made local or national headlines for embarking on a course of action prompted by underground novels, song lyrics, and the restive stirrings of political writers and artists, one wonders about the nature of heroes in today's global world. Is it even possible to use the term *hero* when the heroic actions imitated whether real or fictional, leads to the killing of innocent people? Are children, youth, young adults, here and around the world given the necessary literary and media skills required to recognize the difference between a hero, an anti-hero, and a villain in the guise of an anti-hero or protagonist in a literary or world story? Are there a series of cultural inoculations that prepare individuals to recognize the hero from the monster, the divine from the deviant? If so, how are they provided? Through family or cultural values? Religious traditions? Literary and artistic exposure? This chapter examines some traditional hero motifs found in world literature and looks at how the hero is interpreted and re-interpreted in the modern world. Primarily, this chapter raises questions addressing the construction of contemporary "heroes" and whether they provide acceptable or unacceptable models for children. The answers should lead to lively debate.

THE ROLE OF THE HERO

The traditional hero is the embodiment of cultural values of a specific society and the actions of the hero are the core components of cultural myths and folktales. Cross-culturally and cross-generationally, the values presented in these stories are the same: compassion, kindness, courage, and perseverance in the face of obstacles. Appropriately, these are the values embodied in the contemporary American firefighter hero and the American soldiers who made their way to Baghdad and whose paths we charted on the evening news, partaking in sandstorms, enemy fire, and medical assistance for civilians and wounded opposition. In a study of heroes, one comes quickly to understand that an individual's character is equally important as noteworthy action. Ironically, it is the Babylonian/Sumerian hero of Gilgamesh—the national epic hero of what is modern Iraq—who provides one of the earliest examples of a hero worthy of emulation. Gilgamesh wants to know how to become immortal, and sets out on an epic journey filled with battles, forests, deserts, monsters and the discovery of a true friend. Despite the grand nature of the journey, the moral of Gilgamesh is beautiful in its simplicity. He discovers that one achieves immortality when one is remembered for the "good deeds" done in a life well lived. In her introduction to *World Mythology*, Donna Rosenberg (1999) asserted:

The hero myths examine the relationship between the individual's desires and his/her responsibilities to society. Often the choice is crucial but uncomplicated; whether or not to risk death to save the community. . . . Heroes define themselves by how they relate to external circumstances. They acquire lasting fame by performing deeds of valor, but they acquire even greater heroic stature by winning an inner battle against their desires. (pp. xvii–xviii)

From Gilgamesh, to Quetzaquatl, to Moses, to Luke Skywalker, to Harry Potter, the heroes of world mythology have remarkable similarities that have been noted by many experts in comparative literature from Otto Rank to Joseph Campbell.

Rank's (1957) hero pattern is as follows:

1. Hero is child of distinguished parents usually son of a king
2. Origin preceded by difficulties such as continence or prolonged barrenness, or secret intercourse of the parents due to external prohibition or obstacles
3. During the pregnancy there is a prophecy in form of a dream or oracle cautioning his birth and usually threatening danger to the father
4. As a rule after the birth, the child is put in a box or basket and put in water
5. He is saved by animals or lowly people and suckled by a female animal or humble woman
6. When he grows up he finds his distinguished parents and may seek revenge on his father, or be acknowledged as a rightful heir.

Both Thomas Carlyle (1884) in his famous essay on "Hero Worship" and Campbell (1968) in his book, *The Hero with a Thousand Faces,* provided classifications for types of heroes found in world literature, mythology and iconography.

Carlyle's	*Campbell's*
Hero as divinity	Hero as warrior
Hero as prophet	Hero as lover
Hero as poet	Hero as emperor and as tyrant
Hero as priest	Hero as World Redeemer
Hero as man of letters	Hero as saint
Hero as king	

To distill all that Carlyle or Campbell said about the role of the hero in society, and the identification of the individual with the hero figure in a short chapter is impossible. Yet, each has an overarching consideration that informs the entirety of his discussions. For Carlyle, the primary character-istic of a hero is that "he is sincere: . . . a deep great, genuine sincerity, is the first characteristic of all men in any way heroic. . . . Such sincerity as we named it has in very truth something of the divine. . . ." (pp. 276, 285, 372). For Carlyle, the divinely touched/guided hero is a "Great Man," "the ablest Man," who in turn becomes the model for moral behavior for the generation from which he sprang. Carlyle believes that "all dignities of rank on which human association rests are what we may call a heroarchy (government of heroes)—or a hierarchy, for it is sacred enough withal" (p. 245). Moreover, he believed that society is founded on hero worship, which he believed to be a transcendent admiration of a Great Man. For Carlyle, hero worship ". . . cannot cease till man himself ceases. . . ." (p. 246). Ironically, the mid-19th century in which he wrote was not unlike our 21st century and suffered from what he called a spiritual paralysis that stemmed from skepticism.

> I am well aware that in these days hero-worship professes to have gone out and finally ceased. For reasons which it will be worthwhile some time to inquire into is an age that as it were denies the existence of great men; denies the desirableness of great men. . . . Scepticism (sic) means not intellectual Doubt alone, but moral doubt; all sorts of infidelity, insincerity, spiritual paralysis. . . . For the scepticism [sic] . . . is not intel-lectual only; it is moral also; a chronic atrophy and disease of the whole soul. A man lives by believing something; not by debating and arguing about many things. . . . It seems to me you lay your finger here on the heart of the world's maladies when you call it a Sceptical World. An insincere world; a godless untruth of a world. (pp. 246, 394, 396-397)

The crux of Carlyle's lecture series on the hero and hero worship revolves around reverence for the "sincere" man who seems to have acquired this gift of sincerity from a divine source and thus stands apart from other men as one spiritually and morally distinct.

Campbell's title, *The Hero With a Thousand Faces* alludes plainly to his thesis that we all have the potential to be heroes; it is the deed, whether physical or spiritual, that gives rise to the hero in individual cultures. For Campbell, we are all potential heroes in our own lives, progressing on the path from birth to death and finding our bearings among the Jungian arche-typal symbols that provide the clues to meaning. For Campbell, the tradi-tional hero's journey is marked by three stages:

1. Separation/departure.
2. The trials and victories of initiation or fulfillment.
3. Return/reintegration with society.

It is an inward journey taken by all of us as we come to realizations about our role as members of a humane society. It is in the return that Campbell divined the function of the hero: "to teach the lesson he has learned of life renewed" (p. 20). Yet even for Campbell, whose heroes within us have the potential to transcend the trappings of human existence, all is not well with how contemporary society looks at hero figures, if they exist at all.

> The problem of mankind today is precisely the opposite to that of men in the comparatively stable periods of those great co-ordinating mythologies which now are know as lies. Then all meaning was in the group, in the great anonymous forms, none in the self-expressive individual; today no meaning is in the group-none in the world; all is in the individual. But there the meaning is absolutely unconscious. One does not know toward what one moves, one does not know by what is propelled. The lines of communication between the conscious and the unconscious zones of the human psyche have all been cut, and we have been split in two. (p. 388)

HEROES TODAY

Analysts from multiple disciplines address the psychological need for the heroes of folklore and mythology, make the argument that these stories and heroes help us to find models of right behavior and allow one to discover a meaning to life. In his book, *The Uses of Enchantment: The Meaning and Importance of Fairy Tales*, a book unique for its hygienic premise that children need these stories in order to grow up with a sense of psychological well-being, Bettelheim (1975) speaks to the value of this particular literature and art form. "The child needs . . . and this hardly requires emphasis at this moment in our history—a moral education which subtly and by implication only, conveys to him the advantages of moral behavior, not through abstract ethical concepts but through that which seems tangibly right and therefore meaningful to him" (p. 5) He explained:

> The child identifies with the good hero not because of his goodness, but because the hero's condition makes a deep positive appeal to him. The question for the child is not 'Do I want to be good?' but "Who do I want to be like?" The child decides this on the basis of projecting himself wholeheartedly into one character. If this fairy-tale figure is a very good person, then the child decides that he want to be good, too. (p. 10)

If Campbell's hero, or Carlyle's "great man" or Bettelheim's fairytale figure are to provide the model for society's values and by extension behaviors, and because their actions have traditionally been passed down through the telling of tales . . . what stories today are children hearing that allow for the kind of hero worship that Carlyle said is needed by society and who do children and adolescents identify as heroes?

A Swedish study published in 2000 compared adolescent ideals at the beginning and the end of the 20th century. The study examined multiple studies conducted worldwide on children from 1898 to the 1990s and found that despite the diversity of populations surveyed, there still was a remarkable similarity in the responses of children, and similarity in responses based on gender. The earliest studies found that the youngest children chose personal acquaintances and parents, but as the sample increased in age, "public characters," particularly famous people from national history, became more prominent as the "ideal." Interestingly, religious figures of "god, and Jesus" received a large response in the early part of the century. In the years following World War I, contemporary heroes such as Charles Lindberg, and celebrities such as silent film star Clara Bow were mentioned as leading hero figures for children, and a 1935 study found that for boys, the most often mentioned public figures were contemporary athletes. As the studies progressed through the 1940s and 1950s, researchers found that historical heroes such as Lincoln and Florence Nightingale were being replaced by the glamorous adult whom children identified as "the person you would most like to be when you grow up." Movie stars, athletes, and imaginary characters like Superman replaced historical figures. Studies in the 1960s through the 1980s, posed a slightly different question: "What sort of person would you like to be like?" . . . rather than asking children to identify a specific person. This sample also included the possibility that children could answer, "may be yourself." And researchers account for the increased number of responses with this answer to a new ideology of self-acceptance prevalent in this time period. A study in 1990 asked 11- to 15-year-olds to list three individuals they would most like to be like if they could. Of the boys, 75% named a media figure like Rambo, Arnold Schwarzennegger, and Superman, followed by pop stars, and 45%–63% of the girls (proportion increased with age) preferred pop stars, models, and film stars. In this same 1990 study, children were asked to list three individuals whom they would "Least like to be like." What had been the norm in the early part of the century was now completely reversed. Nearly 75%, and more as the age increased, indicated they would least like to be like a personal acquaintance (parent, etc.) and media figures were mentioned only 25%–35% of the time. The conclusion reached was that "media figures have 'taken over' as the prime source of ideal models and that in comparison personal acquaintances are viewed less positively." In the 1914 studies, a majority of the historical figures chosen

were from national history or poets and writers. These were the most popular answers among boys. In the 1994 study, only 1 out of 2,000 respondents
mentioned a writer. The most popular answers were sports heroes, movie
stars, and pop artists. By 1996, literary/historical figures were completely
replaced by media figures. However, the 1996 study posed the following:

1. Who would you most like to be like?
2. Which qualities in a human being do you value most highly?
3. Mention a person you know about who has some or all of these
   qualities.

Although media figures did remain the first choice for Question 1, in looking at a correlation between who they wanted to be like, and qualities that
were valued, "boys preferred their ideals because of their skills, where as
more girls chose model figures because of their physical characteristics—
mainly their good looks." However, regarding highly valued qualities, "girls
more frequently mention moral qualities, whereas talents and skills are only
mentioned by boys." A 1998 study provided some glimmer of hope in that
it found that adolescents, although they did identify glamorous media figures as people they would most like to be like, also listed the traditional values of honesty, loyalty, friendship, and helpfulness as qualities they wanted
to possess (Teigen, Normann, Bjorkheim, & Helland, 2000).

PROBLEM MEDIA ROLE MODELS

Continuing with a brief historical recounting of studies of heroes, one needs
to consider John Shelton Lawrence and Robert Jewett's (2002) book, *The
Myth of the American Superhero*. In it, the authors provided an overview of
several contemporary "heroes" and how they served as models for aberrant
action. But before discussing the models they identified, one needs to consider another section of their book that looks at when heroes arise in a society. Lawrence and Jewett labeled the decade of 1929–1939 as the "axial
decade" in the evolution of the American superhero.

> In 1929 we enter what we choose to call the axial decade for the forma-
> tion of the American monomyth. Here the unknown redeemer on a
> horse becomes the masked rider of the plains; his sexual renunciation is
> complete; he assumes the uniform and the powers of angelic avengers
> and thus he grows from mere heroism to super heroism. The develop-
> ment of the sexually renunciatory superhero, the most distinctive fea-
> ture of the monomyth, accelerates to its climax soon after the 1929

release of the sound-film version of Gary Cooper's *The Virginian* (p. 36). Following the phenomenal success of Superman comics in 1938, the axial decade closed with a proliferation of superheroes. The masks, uniforms, miraculous powers, and secret alter egos combine with sexual renunciation and segmentation to complete the formation of the monomythic hero. Batman, Sandman, Hawkman, and the Spirit all spring to life in 1939. The Green Lantern, The Shield, Captain Marvel and the White Streak followed in 1940 and Sub-Mariner, Wonder Woman, Plastic Man and Captain America were born the following year. (pp. 43-44)

A question for consideration before we move on might be: Whether the contemporary hero figure emerges in times of economic crisis. The parallels between the economic collapse in the United States in 1929 and the stock market catastrophes of 2001–2003 both seemed to have allowed heroes to emerge in their mythic and folkloric grandeur. Ironically, too, the comic book characters of the 1930s were resurrected in films of the 1990s and into the 21st century.

Historical background aside, the focus of Lawrence and Jewett's study ultimately rests on the contemporary characteristics of the American superhero and how the American interpretation of this figure has moved away from the classical model of initiation, to a peculiar Americanized hybrid of violence and redemption:

> Our concern lies with these ritualized mythic plots because they suggest important clues about the tensions, hopes and despair concerning democracy within the current American Consciousness (p. 5). . . . Whereas the classical monomyth seemed to reflect rites of initiation, the American monomyth derives from tales of redemption. It secularizes the Judaeo-Christian dramas of community redemption that have arisen on American soil, combining elements of the selfless servant who impassively gives his life for others and the zealous crusader who destroys evil. (p. 6)

Of particular interest to these authors are specific characters from film that have taken on superhero status in contemporary America, and how emulation of those characters has not always resulted in laudatory action. *The Matrix,* which achieved cult status among young filmgoers, as did the violent film roles of Stallone, Schwarzennegger, Norris, Eastwood, and Seagal, comes under scrutiny not only for the "apocalyptic redemption" they promote, but also for the similarities of the hero figures that become formulaic when considered over a large number of films. The characters of Neo and Trinity of *The Matrix*, like the characters in the other films alluded to are, in Lawrence and Jewett's estimation:

lonely, selfless, sexless beings who rescue an impotent and terrorized community. . . . Trinity and Neo behave as chastely as do the terminal loners Dana Scully and Fox Mulder of *The X-Files*, the investigators of *CSI*, the characters in *Smallville*, and any other popular series in which the iconoclastic hero, working alone or with a small team, working tirelessly, and ethically, tries to improve the situation in which he/she finds themselves. (p. 5)

The book tries to answer questions posed by the authors that touch on the paradoxes associated with American superheroic fantasies. These are as follows:

1. Why, in an era of sexual liberation, do we still have heroes marked by sexual renunciation?
2. Why, amid so many signs of secularization, do large audiences entertain so many fantasies of redemption by supernatural powers?
3. Why, in a country trumpeting itself as the world's supreme democratic model, do we so often relish depictions of impotent democratic institutions that can be rescued only by extralegal superheroes?
4. Are these stories safety valves for the stresses of democracy or do they represent a yearning for something other than democracy?
5. And why do women and people of color who have made significant strides in civil rights continue to remain almost wholly subordinate in a mythscape where communities must almost always be rescued by physically powerful white men? (pp. 7-8)

Continuing on, it becomes evident that the superheroes of the axial decade responded to specific villains clearly drawn as villains. Both the superheroes with super powers and the classic cowboy heroes lived in a world that lacked ambiguity between good and evil. Good and evil, right and wrong are as evident in these stories as they are in the classic folk fairytale. However, as one moves through the 1970s and 1980s, the media present a different evil—one within our midst even in the midst of trusted governmental institutions. Stallone's *Rambo* series, Eastwood's *Unforgiven*, Gibson's *Braveheart* and *the Patriot,* and *The Left Behind* series, and the earlier, although nonetheless influential *Turner Diaries* of 1978, play on this theme of undetected evil among us.

The undetected evil among us was a primary news emphasis of the two years prior to September 11, 2001. We were a nation besieged with images of internal violence of school shootings, murders carried out to what were deemed "satanic" lyrics, and domestic violence at the hands of religious extremists, bigots, and jingoists. We were a nation continually wringing our hands, asking where we had gone wrong, and wondering what had happened to our children. In short, we were the national embodiment of a line in Bertolt Brecht's play *Galileo*: "Unhappy is the land that needs a hero" (Polster, 1992, p. 182).

Whereas Bettelheim discussed the child's willingness to identify with the hero, and its prosocial benefits, other analysts noted the propensity for some individuals to "go over to the dark side," to use contemporary hero terminology. For these individuals, identification with the figure of the hero fills a psychological need, but one that is not universally prosocial. In his writings, Otto Rank (1957) explored what he called the "remarkable similarity between the career of certain anarchist criminals and the family romance of hero and child . . ."

> Where the paranoiac in conformity with his passive character has to suffer persecutions and wrongs which proceed from the father . . . the anarchist complies more faithfully with the heroic character by promptly becoming the persecutor of kings and finally killing the king precisely like the hero. . . .
>
> The true hero of the romance, is therefore, the ego, which finds itself in the hero, by reverting to the time when the ego was itself a hero, through its first heroic act i.e.: the revolt against the father. . . . This explanation of the psychological significance of the myth of the birth of the hero would not be complete without emphasizing its relations to certain mental diseases . . . the hero myths are equivalent in many essential features to the delusional ideas of certain psychotic individuals, who suffer from delusions of persecution and grandeur—the so-called paranoiacs. Their system of delusions is constructed very much like the hero myth . . . for example the paranoiac is apt to claim that the people whose name he bears are not his real parents . . . that he is the son of a princely personage. . . . Besides the paranoiac, his equally a-social counterpart must also be emphasized. In the expression of the identical fantasy contents, the hysterical individual who has suppressed them, is offset by the pervert, who realizes them, and even so the diseased and passive paranoiac—who needs his delusion for the correction of the actuality which to him is intolerable . . . is offset by the active criminal who endeavors to change the actuality according to his mind. In this special sense, this type is represented by the anarchist. The hero himself as shown by his detachment for the parents, begins his career in opposition to the older generation; he is at once a rebel, a renovator and a revolutionary. However, every revolutionary is originally a disobedient son, a rebel against the father. . . . The truly heroic element than consists only in the real justice or even necessity of the act, which is therefore generally endorsed and admired; while the morbid trait, also in criminal cases is the pathologic transference of the hatred from the father to the real king, or several kings, when more general and still more distorted. (pp. 81-94)

Add to this the psychological phenomenon of the "Werther Effect." A phrase coined in 1974 by sociologist David Phillips to describe imitative antisocial behavior, specifically suicidal behavior, transmitted via the mass media. Lawrence and Jewett drew heavily on the research on the Werther effect to provide a perspective on which to come to some understanding of seemingly random violence enacted by young people in the United States over the last decade. Early in their book, Lawrence and Jewett took pains to explain the Werther effect, which takes its name form a character in Goethe's novel of 1774, *The Sorrows of Young Werther*. This was a classic story of unrequited love and Werther, in his desperation, commits suicide. This book, they maintained, became an important landmark of popular culture in the first era of mass-produced literature and purportedly caused hundreds of copycat suicides. They asserted that evidence supports the claim that all over Europe large numbers of young people committed suicide with a copy of the book clutched in their hands or buried in a pocket. Using Phillips' and their own definition and explanation of how this phenomenon works, one begins to formulate plausible explanations for the propensity of violent actions among America's youth following the examples of contemporary fictional heroes both moral and a-moral, and the contemporary fascination and emulation of the anti-heroes (villain?) of *The Turner Diaries* and the *Left Behind* series. Lawrence and Jewett described the Werther Effect as a voluntary change in behavior produced by "interaction with a powerful artifact of popular culture" (p. 9). Film images tend to provide the most significant examples that researchers are able to identify in contemporary society.

> A Werther Effect characteristically embodies a redefinition of the boundary between fact and fantasy. When an artifact enters the arena of popular culture and assumes its own existence in the imagination of fans, a powerful through elusive process begins. We can hardly sort out the causal and motivational influences in the Werther related suicides. However, they begin to illustrate an interesting interplay between fantasy and reality that begins to obliterate any clear distinction between mere entertainment and seriously contemplated life purposes. . . . In the Werther effect an audience member:
>
> 1. Experiences a work of fantasy within a secular context that
> 2. Helps to shape the reader/viewer's sense of what is real and desirable in such a way that
> 3. The reader/viewer takes Actions consistent with the vision inspired by the interaction between his own fantasy and that popular entertainment. (pp. 9-10)

The blurring between fantasy and reality is an element that comes into play when one begins to emulate one's chosen hero. Does this suggest that

Americans are suffering from a national mental illness? Or does it indicate that Americans witness reality with a fantasy perspective? Consider media coverage of the recent war in Iraq and the war response directed at Afghanistan for the 9/11 attacks. From their livingrooms, viewers took part in sorties vicariously. Through technological wonders of satellites, mounted cameras, and embedded journalists, viewers were placed in the tanks and planes, they saw bombs hit, and they moved cautiously with the camera as their eyes through streets and caves, and took cover when shelled by marauding rebel fighters, and Iraqi Republican Guard units. The media created a sense of immediacy, an intimacy to a reality that was half a world away. Does the same blurring of reality exist when individuals participate repeatedly in the stories created by film? Does Coleridge's "suspension of disbelief" stay permanently suspended for some individuals so much so that their reality becomes a dreamscape or nightmarish compilation of images created to tell a story from which they are unable to escape?

Lawrence and Jewett (2002), as well as other researchers in media violence, point to the same examples etched indelibly in public consciousness: Oklahoma City bomber, Timothy McVeigh, and Columbine shooters, Dylan Klebold and Eric Harris. McVeigh's association with extremist groups advocating violence against the state, was fueled, it appears, by an infatuation with violent fantasy characters. His prison interviews with Lou Michel and Dan Herbeck revealed his admiration for the Rambo character of Stallone films, and Chuck Norris' *Missing in Action* series. "These were men's men in McVeigh's eyes and he wanted to be like them" (p. 157). The type of violent hero McVeigh found attractive was consistent and supported by letters McVeigh wrote from prison to journalist Phil Bachrach in which he commented repeatedly that Clint Eastwood's *Unforgiven* was the best film ever made. In their independent study of the Oklahoma City bombing, Elizabeth W. and Jay Mechling (1995) discovered additional parallels between *Braveheart* and the Oklahoma City bombing. They were struck by the similarity between the rhetoric of the American militia movements and the Scots' "freedom fighters." "The movie's message so congruent with the Patriot movement with which McVeigh associated himself, legitimates violence against the state" (Lawrence & Jewett, 2000, pp. 157-164).

We know from media reports that Klebold and Harris, the two students responsible for the shootings at Columbine High School, filmed themselves discussing their planned attack on the school. The conversation contained several references to the controversial film, *Natural Born Killers,* whose ironic rendering of sociopaths was taken literally by some as a model course of action. The black trenchcoats of the two students during the attack was not considered coincidental by analysts trying to make sense of the carnage at Columbine.

In *The Basketball Diaries* . . . Leonardo Di Caprio character enters a classroom wearing a trench coat and blasts away with a shotgun....*The Matrix*, released in 1999 has a redemptive climax featuring a pair of shooters dressed in long black coats, lugging bombs and guns into a building for a destructive raid . . . and [Klebold and Harris were] also devotees of two violent videogames. *Doom* and *Quake*, which had been featured on *Computer Gamin World's* cover depicting a flying gunman wearing a long black coat. (pp. 202-203)

Do the contemporary tragedies of life imitating art (of which these are but a few) provide evidence of an ever-increasing Werther Effect that must be recognized and addressed by educators, analysts and media executives, or has Brecht's line of theatrical dialogue, "Unhappy is the land that needs a hero," become a tautology?

ADDITIONAL PROBLEMS TO CONSIDER IN DEPICTIONS OF CONTEMPORARY HEROES

Put simply, where are the role models—the heroes for women? In virtually all the books examined for this chapter, the predominant image of the hero has been male and action-oriented. Although many analysts recognize the absence of women as members of a heroic cultural pantheon, none has treated it so directly as Miriam Polster (1992) in her book, *Eve's Daughters, The Forbidden Heroism of Women*.

Our modern mythologists, the media, still perpetuate the standard heroic stereotypes. . . . The media favor slick and quick presentations of heroic deeds. Television and movies, newspapers and magazines BYPASS THE HEROISM OF WOMEN BY CONTINUING THEIR HABITUAL SKEW TOWARD THE FLAMBOYANT AND SENSATIONAL. . . . An emphasis on direct physical action usually means that the courage of articulate but nonviolent objectors is ignored. . . . Female heroism is rooted in the particular circumstances and values of women's lives, where connection and relationship may not be quickly settled in adversarial terms. It should come as no surprise that women have been in the foreground of reform movements protesting burdensome taxation, worked to form labor unions, etc. . . . Women's heroism has been equally brave and equally original as men. But because in some of its forms it differs from the traditional pattern of heroism, it has often gone unrecognized. . . . Women's heroic choice differs from that of the classic male hero who has throughout legend physically separated himself form home and family in order to follow his heroic path. . . . The woman hero . . . does not separate herself. (pp. 16-20)

Postler addressed the psychological component of female heroism, noting that the heroic responses of women are often very personal, and that women are generally moved by compassion for people rather than by abstract principles. She reiterated what others have found to be true, that the circumstances that arouse women's heroic response are often intensely personal, and that women tend to be self-disclosive about abusive incidents, personal failures, hurts, painful histories. "Such public disclosure is heroic—and costly in loss of public approval and support" (p. 32). Popular media figure, Oprah Winfrey, comes to mind as a contemporary embodiment of these attributes and is often listed among the most admired women in public opinion polls. But is she portrayed as a hero? "Our concept of heroism has traditionally valued the exploits of heroes who distance themselves from home and family. We have not recognized the heroism of women who did not unravel kinship ties" (p. 137).

One of the most interesting sections of Polster's book relates to what she identified as the extraordinarily narrow footing given "Women's Heroic Terrain—The Pedestal." In contrast to the statues erected of men that depict the deeds of actual historical personages of military and political renown, public statuary—public art depicting women have been by and large allegorical symbols of virtue and noble sentiments meant to inspire men to greater moral and spiritual heights. Examples can be culled from across generations of artistic depictions: the muses, the three graces, blind justice, victory, and the Statue of Liberty. But particularly interesting is Polster's observation that "more often than not the types that stood for national values were female in form" (p. 108).

Her own analysis of the psychological studies that look at young people's perceptions of heroes considers the four overarching characteristics that one finds in a multitude of studies:

1. Determinance—courage, generosity, etc.
2. Depth—stand the test of time.
3. Distance—child feels close to the hero, sense of heroic presence.
4. Domain—arena in which the hero excels.

But Postler added a fifth characteristic that helps to shape the idea of "hero" in the mind's eye and imagination of the child:

5. Database—where people have learned about heroes, school, books, film, TV.

It can be easily asserted and convincingly argued that the idea of the hero today is a mediated image; constructed through television and film. There are few, if any, women presented as heroes either of the prosocial or antisocial ilk, and female criminal behavior conducted in imitation of a "hero" figure or action is not as common as it is in male hero emulations. The line becomes more blurred in consideration of the hero for women and people of color when one tries to make a distinction between a hero and a celebrity. Is the professional athlete a hero, a role model, or an icon of financial success? What happens when celebrities fall from grace and are accused of criminal actions? Is there a difference between the "heroes" of boys and girls? Do Venus and Serena Williams, Oprah, Beyonce, or Condalezza Rice serve the function of role model or heroes to young African-American girls? When considering diversity in America, who are the heroes for members of the Hispanic community? The deaf community? How are the role models for this group presented? Do Selma Hayak and Jennifer Lopez stand as individuals who have achieved "heroic stature" . . . and if so why? Is it because of their beauty, their accomplishments, their intellect, their altruism, and their selfless devotion to improving society, or is it a more base fascination with sex appeal and money?

An article in the *Boston Globe* in 2001 considered the growing celebrity of Asian athletes in American sports venues and the effect this has had on Asian American men. Although the figures of Hideo Nomo, who made his professional debut in America with a no-hitter; Lee Bong Je, who won the Boston Marathon; or Wang Zhizhi, who plays for the NBA generate pride within adolescent Asian men, "Asian parents are reluctant to hold up sports stars as role models for their sons, fearing it brings aspects of American life they don't want, such as valuing short-term fun over long-term academic investment. . . . They see education as the primary route to success" (Wen, 2001). In a nation that scorns the intellectual, that produces movies in which "intellectual" children and adolescents are ostracized as "nerds," "geeks," "losers," and social misfits, why would young people want to emulate them as heroes?

An issue of political correctness regarding heroes came to the foreground when a statue was proposed to commemorate the firefighters in New York who raised the flag on the rubble of the World Trade Center buildings. The ethnicity was changed to represent multiple groups, rather than the actual ethnic groups of those who had planted the flag. Is this proper poetic license with the idea of "hero"—that it transcends ethnicity? Or were those protesting not sure that despite their lack of ethnic diversity, the individuals to be depicted in bronze represented the heroic in all of us . . . the humane in all of us and the compassion in all of us.

CURRENT TRENDS

In looking for the heroes of children today, one can turn to various forms of evidence. Certainly there are the academic surveys—studied, tallied, and legitimized statistically—that continue to indicate that sports figures, movie stars, and pop stars head the list of those children seem to admire. Then there are the commercial pieces of evidence: the blockbuster films, the toys children request, and the styles worn. The line blurs again between the idea of role model and hero. One of the most interesting "heroes" of the last few years has been Harry Potter. It is all the more astounding in that Harry Potter started as a literary phenomenon in a visual age. Children around the world were reading voraciously.

The British Harry Potter phenomenon counters the anti-intellectual trend so prevalent in American film, but only because it fits the traditional hero formula precisely. Harry Potter is an orphan, raised by abusive relatives. He is actually a "special" person because of his birthright, which he discovers through a series of revelations, adventures and, with the assistance of others (animal, human, and superhuman), his true nature comes to light. With modest changes one finds the same formula in the *Star Wars* trilogy and the *Wizard of Oz*. Film trends through the 1990s and the early years of 2000–2003 presented a renewed interest in the superhero characters. It is uncanny that so many were resurrected in the last decade: Batman, Zorro, The Shadow, Spiderman, Dick Tracy, and animated in the characters of Buzz Lightyear and Howdy in *Toy Story*. Of interest, too, are the film renditions of contemporary video game characters: Mortal Combat, Street Fighter, Tron, and Laura Croft. The quintessential "man of action" has been captured in the *Indiana Jones* trilogy.

Can a correlation be drawn between the increase in films with "action-hero presidents," and the presidential rhetoric of the last 20 years that echo the ultimatum of the cowboy hero: Reagan warning terrorists that "you can run, but you can't hide," and George W. Bush announcing that he wanted Osama bin Laden "dead or alive," and defining terrorists and other rogue political forces in the moral syntax of "the evil ones," and "the axis of evil."

What is it in our society that has resonated deep within us to become fascinated with the characters in *The Matrix, Rambo, Lethal Weapon, Braveheart, The Patriot, Dances with Wolves, Rocky, The Turner Diaries,* or *The Left Behind* series? Are the disturbing parallels in case studies of McVeigh, Bernard Goetz, T. Kyzinski, Klebold and Harris that indicate their violence was imitative of fantasy characters, a dark coincidence, or do they point to something more sinister about who have become the role models in today's culture? What help or assistance do we seek in our fascination with television shows such as *Touched by an Angel, It's a Miracle,* and others of that ilk that look to divine intervention or supernatural aid in these trying times?

Why have we become fascinated with the image of the New York firemen, the U.S. Marines, and a 19-year-old female soldier saved by special operations forces? Why have they become our national symbols of heroism?

It is not because they wear an identifiable uniform, or engage in dangerous exploits or rescues. Some have been identified by the media, but most remain nameless to us, their selfless efforts an inspiration to us, their simple planting of a flag, the toppling of a statue of a dictator, moving to us. They have been absorbed back into a community, but we know they will appear again when needed. They do not seek celebrity or notoriety when others appear on cereal boxes or talk shows, or march in parades merely because they survived a terrible event. They are not merely survivors like the miners in Pennsylvania. The New York firemen and the American soldiers in Iraq have come to symbolism heroism. Like Gilgamesh, they will be remembered for their good deeds. It is this element of the hero that resonates across the millennia and continues to provide hope for the ordinary citizens of the world who cherish those moments when individuals rise up through exemplary behavior and provide inspirations to others to move forward with compassion, kindness, and the courage and perseverance to overcome obstacles.

There is an inherent veracity in the traditional folkloric and mythic formulae that construct heroes across time and cultural divisions of religion and geography. The virtues of compassion, courage, and perseverance embodied in actual and fictional depictions of the traditional hero are a necessary antidote in a culture that struggles to explain copy-cat crimes while its children and adolescents play video games where the object is to win by stealing cars, shooting police officers and kidnapping and killing prostitutes. The traditional hero of myth and folklore, the national hero of service and personal sacrifice, the civic hero of hard work and generosity and the personal hero of commitment and love are needed in this global world. They remain the models of humanity at its best—of the ordinary man or woman doing extraordinary things. If the only thing ever taught to our children in schools is to have compassion and courage, the world will change. It is imperative that our children find role models, find heroes who possess these virtues so that we can forever lay to rest Brecht's admonition, "Unhappy the land that needs a hero."

ENDNOTE

1. Several full text articles by contemporary scholars are readily available via Internet searches. See essays by David P. Phillips on the Werther effect, http://pespmc1.vub.ac.be/Conf/MemePap/Marsden.html; Susan L. Hurley, www.warwick.ac.uk/staff/S.L.Hurley on Imitation and media violence, and Jan E. Ledingham, C. Anne Ledingham and John Richardson on the effects of media violence and children www.hc-sc.gc.ca/hppb/familyviolence/html/nfntseffemedia_e.html; Joanne Cantor on the psychological effect of media violence on children www.joannecantor.com/montrealpap_fin.htm.

REFERENCES

Bettelheim, B. (1975). *The uses of enchantment; the meaning and importance of fairy tales.* New York: Vintage Books.

Campbell, J. (1968). *The hero with a thousand faces* (2nd ed.) Princeton, NJ: Princeton University Press.

Carlyle, T. (1884). Heroes and hero-worship. In *Carlyle's Works.* Boston: Dana Estes and Charles E. Lauriat.

Lawrence, J. S., & Jewett, R. (2002). *The myth of the American superhero.* Grand Rapids, MI: William B. Erdmans.

Polster, M. F. (1992). *Eve's daughters: The forbidden heroism of women.* San Francisco, CA: Jossey-Bass.

Rank, O. (1957). *The myth of the birth of the hero: A psychological interpretation of mythology.* New York: Robert Bruner.

Rosenberg, D. (1999). *World mythology: An anthology of the great myths and epics* (3rd ed.). Lincolnwood, IL: NTC Publishing.

Teigen, K. H., Normann, H-T. E., Bjorkheim, H. O., & Helland, S. (2000). Who would you most like to be like? Adolescents' ideals at the beginning and the end of the century. *Scandinavian Journal of Educational Research, 44*(1), 1–17.

U.S. News & World Report. (2001, August 20). *131*(7), 26, 28–29.

Wen, P. (2001, April 27) Finding new heroes: Asian-Americans take a quiet pride in successes in the athletic arena. *Boston Globe* archives. www.bostonglobe.com.

Chapter 10

A RETURN OF THE "REAL?"

Discussions with Children Ages 5 to 13 About the Contemporary Hero

Cheryl Harris
University of South Carolina

Alison Alexander
University of Georgia

Since September 11, 2001, the authors of this chapter argue, there has been a resurgence of superheroes as well as media coverage of courageous acts. Children are avid consumers of mass media content. Among the images they see are heroes who embody courage and self-sacrifice as well as superheroes who possess special powers. Harris and Alexander ask how, among the vast number of characters to whom they are exposed, some are elevated to the status of hero? By conducting interviews with children, Harris and Alexander seek to identify the characteristics children view as heroic.

✧ ✧ ✧

The post-9/11 "return to values" theme has resulted in a virtual avalanche of resurrected and highly nostalgic heroes throughout American popular culture: Spiderman, He-Man, Scooby-Doo, and even the Lone Ranger have made comebacks in television, movies, comics, toys, books, and on the Internet. In the new storylines, narratives focusing on patriotism, loyalty, justice, and the elevation of the everyday person by a heroic act are common. Compared with children's fare from just a few years ago, where very stylized concepts of superpowered adventure, supercharged action, and individuality were strongly emphasized, this is a marked change.

This shift is certainly not coincidental. Heavy media coverage of courageous acts by firemen, policemen, and everyday citizens in the aftermath of the World Trade Center terrorist attacks suggested that the average person can become a hero, not just those given other-worldly superpowers by a genetic accident or alien birth.

The influx of heroic but "average Joe" character revivals led *Curious Pictures*, the New York City-based entertainment and production company, to develop a new division called the "Character Spa," where "classic characters can come to freshen up." Executive Vice President Richard Winkler was quoted as saying, "There's a lot of equity built up in a number of [old] characters—and that's value that can be re-exploited . . . the idea came to us a couple of months before NATPE." Among the "antique" characters that Winkler is thinking of resurfacing is the "Captain Crunch" figure used in advertising the cereal of that name some two or three decades ago. The Character Spa is currently conducting tests to determine whether children will consider Captain Crunch a heroic character, and what associations a new generation—along with their parents—might have with the reconstructed figure of a portly, bumbling ship captain given to almost accidental acts of bravery (Connell, 2002, p. 84).

From infancy, American children are immersed in a sea of images typically dichotomized simply as "good" or "evil," as many studies have confirmed. Among these, how are some characters elevated to the "heroic"? In 2001, a Harris Poll of 1,022 adults "reported that more than half of those polled could not name any figure they considered heroic" (Harris, 2001). If adults are having difficulty identifying people to admire, how, then, are children attaching meaning to the concept of the "hero"? From whom or what are they learning to define the "heroic" ideal? When many adults are disillusioned about the inherent goodness of others, but the news media are trumpeting the "return of the hero" almost daily, and the culture industry is reviving somewhat tired figures considered heroic in an earlier, and much different era, it presents a complicated environment in which children are asked to identify key role models and aspirational figures. Arguably, being able to do so is an important rite of passage in child development.

METHODOLOGY

With these problems in mind, we conducted a series of discussions with children in North America between October 2002 and September 2003. The study utilized a dual-methodological approach.

The first wave of interviews was conducted online in Fall 2002. Families with children under the age of 16 who were members of research panels owned by two online research companies, Northstar Interactive, Inc. and eSearch, Inc., were contacted and asked to participate in the initial study, which required logging on to a secured online survey containing several open-ended questions and a brief demographic section. Parents were given the opportunity to examine the questionnaire and obtain more information from the researchers. Parents were asked to assist younger children if they needed help inputting their responses through the keyboard. Informed parental consent was also obtained for a possible follow-up discussion, expected to be conducted by an online focus group procedure. About half of the children and their parents agreed to be re-contacted for the follow-up study.

Seventeen children between the ages of 5 and 13 participated in the initial discussion. Of these 17 participants, 4 were girls (23.5%) and 13 were boys (76.5%.) Nearly 60% were between 5 and 7 years old, with a few (23.5%) between 8 and 10 years old and the balance (17.6%) between 11 and 13 years old. Although one participant was Canadian, the remainder were distributed across the country, from states including California, Florida, Indiana, Kansas, Massachusetts, Michigan, Minnesota, Missouri, Nevada, New York, Ohio, Pennsylvania, and Texas.

The decision to employ an online interviewing methodology for this wave was prompted, first, by a desire to include children from many locations in North America. A face-to-face interviewing strategy alone would have precluded us from including broadly dispersed geographic locations in the sample. Second, by 2002, more than 60% of children between ages 6 and 8 in U.S. families had internet access; 35% of children between ages 2 and 5 have Internet access and have used the Internet; and the number is even higher for children over age 9: 77% are Internet users. Half of the children between the ages of 7 and 12 are reported to go online four or more times a week, with 20% going online daily (*North America Online: Demographics and Usage*, 2003, and *America Online/Digital Marketing Services*, 2003). Therefore, we felt comfortable that access to the Internet was now a common trait among U.S. children and would likely not introduce undue bias within the sample.

The second wave of interviews replicated the questionnaire from the earlier study but altered the delivery of the survey to paper and pencil. This time, the participating children were members of a Girl Scout troop in Athens, Georgia. Eleven girls between the ages of 9 and 11 participated. Data were gathered from this group in September 2003, and completing the questionnaire was included as part of a regular troop meeting, although it was not mandatory. The final sample of 28 children, combined from both waves, contained the characteristics cited in Table 10.1.

TABLE 10.1. Sample Characteristics

ATTRIBUTE	SAMPLE %
Gender	
Girls	53.6
Boys	46.4
Age	
5—7	42.9
8—10	42.9
11—13	10.7
Geographic Location/Region	
Northeast	10.7
South/southeast	42.9
Midwest	25.0
Southwest/west	17.9
Canada	3.6

DISCUSSION OF RESULTS

The focus of both waves of interviewing was identical: The children were asked to talk about who their heroes are, what constitutes a hero, what happens when a hero *isn't* a hero anymore, and how they talk about their heroes to friends and family.

Because the sample is small, these results should be considered preliminary and exploratory. We intend to follow up this initial study with a more comprehensive qualitative discussion, returning to the same participants to gather more in-depth information on the formation of their perceptions and ideas on this topic.

When asked, "What is a hero?" the children had a variety of responses:

A person who you look up to and a person who is special to you (Girl, age 8-10)

A hero is somebody who helps you and encourages you (Girl, age 8-10)

A hero is brave (Girl, age 11-13)

A hero is a person that does something brave (Girl, age 8-10)

A hero is a person that is brave and responspil [sic] (Girl, age 8-10)

A hero is a person who can do extraordinary things. Also the person is brave. (Girl, age 8-10)

A hero is someone who helps you (Girl, age 8-10)

A person who is a couragise [sic], honest, modest and heroic person (Girl, age 8-10)

somebody who saves the day (Boy, age 5-7)

A person who can save people or somebody who inspires you or you look up to. (Girl, age 8-10)

someone who you look up to (Boy, age 8-10)

someone to look up to (Girl, age 11-13)

a person that saves other people (Boy, age 5-7)

a person who helps you and beats evil (Boy, age 5-7)

Somebody that saves you (Girl, age 8-10)

a person who does good things and saves people (Boy, age 5-7)

superman (Boy, age 5-7)

someone who saves people. someone who teaches people (Boy, age 8-10)

Someone like Superman, who helps people in need (Boy, age 5-7)

A person who shows compassion for others and does good deeds (Boy, age 8-10)

someone that is a role model, that a person looks up to, is a "good" person, someone that you may want to be like (Girl, age 14-16)

someone who is brave (Boy, age 5-7)

A hero is a person that did something that was heroic (Boy, age 8-10)

someone you look up to (Boy, age 5-7)

someone you admire and want to be like (Boy, age 11-13)

I don't know! (Girl, age 8-10)

Batman (Boy, age 5-7)

A hero is a fireman, a policeman, and an ambulance driver (Boy, age 5-7)

The next question was: "Can anybody be a hero?"

Yes, because anybody can be your hero (Girl, age 8-10)

Yes, because anybody can encourage and help others (Girl, age 8-10)

Yes because they can always be brave (Girl, age 11-13)

Anybody can be a hero they don't have to so something great to be one (Girl, age 8-10)

Yes, all it takes is kindness and courage (Girl, age 8-10)

Almost anybody can because we can all do great things. Also you can be a hero just by helping people (Girl, age 8-10)

Yes, if you admire them (Girl, age 8-10)

Yes, because it takes a pinch of courage and a bit of knowledge (Girl, age 8-10)

yes cuz if they wanna they can (Boy, age 5-7)

Yes, all it takes is to be looked up to (Girl, age 8-10)

yes anyone can be (Girl, age 8-10)

yes if they do hero things (Boy, age 8-10)

yes because u don't have to be a famous person to be a hero (Girl, age 11-13)

yes, because they are strong (Boy, age 5-7)

No. Because not everybody can save people (Boy, age 5-7)

yes anybody can be nice and help somebody (Girl, age 8-10)

Yes, anybody can (Boy, age 5-7)

yes, because anyone can save anyone at anytime. People can teach people new things all of the time (Boy, age 5-7)

Yes, anyone can help another (Boy, age 8-10)

yes anyone can be. If someone looks up to you and likes the person that you are and tries to be like you then I would consider you a hero in their eyes (Boy, age 5-7)

yes because anyone can be brave (Boy, age 5-7)

Yes you can. You could be a hero to your mom if you help her around the house, you could be a hero to your dad if you help him with the yard work, you could be a hero to a little kid if you do something for them, but to be a real hero you like have to save a country or the earth or something like that (Boy, age 11-13)

yes, because if you look up to your mom then she is a hero too (Girl, age 8-10)

yes. because anyone can be a role model for little kids (Boy, age 5-7)

just hero guys (Boy, age 5-7)

of course, firemen are heroes (Boy, age 5-7)

Yes, if they wish to (Boy, age 5-7)

In the responses to these questions as reported earlier, it is clear that children see an opportunity to be heroic in the everyday, and in people known to them as well as in media portrayals.

We asked the children who their heroes are and why they became important to them. The question read, simply: "Who are your heroes? And, why is that person a hero to you?"

My mama because I look up to her!!!! (Girl, age 8-10)

My mom is my hero because she helps and encourages me (Girl, age 8-10)

My sister because she stands up for me, and helps me, and I know I can talk to her (Girl, age 11-13)

My mom is because she cares about me, my babysitter too and my dad (Girl, age 8-10)

Britney Spears is a hero to me because she can sing and so can I (Girl, age 8-10)

My parents are my heroes because they help me if I'm hurt or sad (Girl, age 8-10)

My Mom, because I love her and I look up to her. Also family and friends, because they are nice to me (Girl, age 8-10)

superman, he has eye vision batman, he has batman bombs green lantern, he has lantern powers (Boy, age 5-7)

My younger brother, he is the only boy in the family and he is special. My mom, she takes care of all 5 of us kids (All by herself). My grandmother, she works in a hospital and takes care of people (Girl, age 8-10)

my mom is my hero cause she is my mom (Girl, age 8-10)

my parents because they helped me through life with problems i've had. my teachers because they've taught me all the things that i want to learn (Girl, age 11-13)

1. spiderman . . . because i like his web and he defeats villians 2. batman . . . because defeats his nemisis 3. yoda because he is wise and strong 4. my daddy . . . because he helps me, he plays with me, he lets me help around house (Boy, age 8-10)

My mom, dad and police. Because they help me stay safe (Boy, age 5-7)

my grandma cause she helps me all the time since my mom died (Boy, age 5-7)

batman because he's cool. superman he saves people from danger. spiderman gets bad guys (Boy, age 5-7) my hero is my mom. she teaches me how to read and use the computer, and she is a good person (Boy, age 5-7)

Mommy and Daddy (Boy, age 5-7)

Superman, because he fought for peace and freedom (Boy, age 8-10)

My Mom. Because she has held on to her beliefs and continued to do so through some very tough times. No matter what she keeps pushing forward (Girl, age 14-16)

firefighters because they are brave and go into fires to save people and houses police because they might get shot doing their job catching the bad guys soldiers because they are protecting us and our way we live (Boy, age 5-7)

My mom and my dad, they have helped me though the years I have lived. My big brother, he has helped me though hard times, and hugged me when I needed a hug. My neighbor, I enjoy my time over at her house. She is a really good artist, and when I go over there she teaches me things that I never would have known if she hadn't told me (Boy, age 11-13)

my mom, because she teaches me how to be good, she buys me everything, and she is a great person (Boy, age 11-13)

my dad. he works hard to take care of our family and loves us all a lot. my grammie kathy. she's fun to do things with and she always makes me pancakes and spaghetti. she's very talented and helps lots of people (Boy, age 11-13)

the hero guy from PBS kids. . . . (Boy, age 5-7)

Buzz lightyear (Boy, age 5-7)

My hero is a fireman because they help people from fire (Boy, age 5-7)

Numerous earlier studies concluded that "media figures have taken over as the prime source of ideal models" for children (Duffy, 2002.) In a 2001 study of 500 families classified as "non-television viewers" conducted by Barbara Brock (2001) of Eastern Washington University and published on the "TV Turnoff Network," Brock asked these children to name their heroes. Presumably unaffected by television portrayals of who or what heroes should be, Brock was still surprised to see that although parents, teachers, and coaches were sometimes mentioned as heroes, figures such as Harry Potter, Michael Jordan, Winnie the Pooh, Robin Hood, and Laura Ingles from the 1980s series (and earlier novel) *Little House on the Prairie* received multiple votes.

In study after study of children and their role models from the 1980s through the 1990s, children named role models from the ranks of super-heroes, characters who received special powers from mysterious or unknown sources, and who were able to save people because they were, in fact, "superhuman." The idea of a fireman or policeman or a businessman in a dusty gray suit joining the ranks of the "super hero" is rarely or never mentioned.

However, these data begin to suggest that we may be seeing a change in attitude toward the "everyday hero." This contradicts a rather wide range of sources that assert that celebrities and fictional characters are much more likely to be named as heroes and role models than people who are known to them, by even very young children. A relatively recent Swedish study (Teigen, Normann, Bjorkheim, & Helland, 2000) looked at a century of data on "adolescent ideals" and found that the youngest children might name acquaintances and relatives as personal heroes, particularly parents, but older children were more likely to choose "public characters."

Cutting across the wide age range of ages 3–16 included in this study, we instead see a rather consistent pattern of citing personal acquaintances or people with local functions (firemen, policeman) described as primary heroes. It may be, as Bruno Bettelheim (1989) said, that the child responds to specific individuals as role models based on a "deep positive appeal," one not limited to "goodness" alone but also psychological well-being.

An interesting question then becomes: "What happens when an 'every-day hero' is knocked off the heroic pedestal?" Does that happen, and when it does, could the effect be more devastating than if the hero is a distant, fictional character or other "public person"?

We asked: "If you ever had a hero and later decided they weren't your hero anymore, what happened?"

> They might have done something wrong or betrayed me (Girl, age 8-10)
>
> They started to be mean (Girl, age 8-10)
>
> My 14 year old sister, because she is doing bad things and causing trouble (Girl, age 8-10)
>
> you are disappointed and let down (Girl, age 8-10)
>
> maybe they were lying about helping (Boy, age 8-10)
>
> Well, my other older brother used to be but he started to be mean and run away when ever he could so now I don't really like him (Girl, age 8-10)

Although a short-term, exploratory study such as this cannot answer questions about long-term impact of "hero disappointment," it appears that children do understand that heroes can let one down, and that the withdrawal of "hero worship" is a possibility.

Children do communicate with family and friends about heroes, their qualities, and their deeds. We asked: "What kinds of talks do you have with your friends about your heroes?"

> We talk about if they might have done something brave or cool (Girl, age 8-10)
>
> we talk about how why we choosed [sic] our hero and why (Girl, age 8-10)
>
> how cool they are. What special things they do (Boy, age 5-7)
>
> we have talks in school (Boy, age 5-7)
>
> not much but we play fire fighters and police (Boy, age 5-7)
>
> i tell my friends that my mom is the best mom in the world (Boy, age 5-7)
>
> most of my friends have heroes like spiderman, but they're not real people so they're not real heroes (Boy, age 5-7)
>
> how strong they are and their powers (Boy, age 8-10)
>
> We talk about them saving people. (Boy, age 11-13)

"What kinds of talks do you have with your parents about your heroes?"

> That the fighting part is bad (Girl, age 8-10)
>
> I had to write an essay about heroes in school (Girl, age 11-13)
>
> we talk about what makes a good hero (Girl, age 8-10)
>
> We talk about I thought yoda was great in star wars (Girl, age 8-10)
>
> I pretend that I'm batman and save them (Boy, age 5-7)
>
> I asked what was a hero for school one time (Boy, age 8-10)
>
> My Mom knows that I look up to her and respect her (Boy, age 5-7)
>
> that any person can be brave and save a life or even just help you out when it might be dangerous (Boy, age 5-7)
>
> I don't have talks with my parents about my heros (Boy, age 8-10)
>
> i tell my mom that she is my hero, and i love her very much (Boy, age 5-7)
>
> we talk about what makes a hero and how anybody can be a hero if they do the right things and are good people and love god (Boy, age 5-7)
>
> All kinds of stories (Boy, age 8-10)
>
> We talk about them saving people and about them going in the ambulance and they fix people up (Girl, age 14-16)

We wanted to ask explicitly about heroes derived from popular culture products. How common are they, and can children articulate what qualities they admire in this type of heroic figure? We asked: "Who are your heroes on the television programs you watch . . . or in movies, video games, books, comics? And why?"

Hilary Duff, I want to be just like her (Girl, age 8-10)

My hero in music is Britney Spears because she is a good singer. My hero in television is Hilary Duff because she is cool (Girl, age 8-10)

Raven Symone, because she cares about the community (Girl, age 11-13)

Hilary Duff, she is so nice (Girl, age 8-10)

Scooby-Doo, he is funny and he scares monsters away from my brothers bedroom. Superman, he is strong and helps people. Batman, He beats the Joker and all the bad guys (Boy, age 5-7)

spiderman because he is the best he trys hes best to save everyone! tobey maguire, because hes cute and hes a very nice person (even though i've never met him) :) (Boy, age 5-7)

1. he-man..he beats skelator, because skelator is evil 2.power rangers..they defeat the forces of evil 3.spyro because he beats warriors who are bad (Boy, age 8-10)

Bugs Bunny because he always helps everybody (Girl, age 8-10)

spiderman, because he saves people and chases the bad guys (Boy, age 5-7)

Spiderman, because fights against evil (Boy, age 5-7)

Well, the only hero I have in these categories, is in video games. His name is Link, and I play lots of video games with him in it. There are 3 that I can think of, there is, Link to the Past (the first one I played), and there is The Ocerina of Time (this one is my favorite), there is Majora's Mask (this is very good!), and then there is Super Smash Brothers (it is kinda cool) (Boy, age 8-10)

scooby doo and shaggy, because they are really funny and they are always there for each other (Boy, age 8-10)

i like buzz lightyear and tarzan because they always win with the enemy and they are funny (Boy, age 5-7)

captain planet he saves the environment (Boy, age 5-7)

Rescue Heroes because I like the show and because they save people (Boy, age 11-13)

Kids could name quite a few heroes from the media, as might be expected, and were clear that these media heroes "defeat evil," "win over the enemy," and "save people." "Helping people" was also an essential quality, similar to the values expressed in the earlier questions.

Finally, we wanted to ask about another special category of hero: The "superhero." The prefix "super-" is frequently used to describe any number of phenomena: "supermodel," "superstar." Do children conceptualize a "superhero" as one who deserves the hyperbole because of some extraordinary essentialized quality, different from those they had been naming so consistently in their other responses?

We asked the children to describe: "What is a superhero, in your opinion?"

Nice, always helpful, and polite (Girl, age 8-10)

Someone who has special powers (Girl, age 8-10)

A person who is nice and does brave things (Girl, age 11-13)

A person who is always reliable (Girl, age 8-10)

can do all kinds of special things (Girl, age 8-10)

a super hero to me tries to be very best person and saves and gives advice! (Boy, age 5-7)

a super hero has super powers and super strength (Girl, age 8-10)

like spiderman . . . a pretend person (Girl, age 8-10)

somebody that does really really good stuff (Boy, age 8-10)

someone who helps save people from bad guys (Girl, age 11-13)

someone who can fly (Boy, age 5-7)

A hero who is famous. (Boy, age 5-7)

Well the first thing that comes to mind is cartoons . . . someone with special powers (Boy, age 5-7)

someone that has powers like super man and spider man (Boy, age 5-7)

One who is very strong, and can save the world in a second (Boy, age 8-10)

someone that never lets you down (Girl, age 14-16)

someone who really loves people and helps others (Boy, age 5-7)

Based on these responses, a "superhero" is a title set aside mostly for people with "special powers" and who might also be "famous" or "a pretend person."

SUMMARY

In this sample, the participating children seemed to agree that heroes "save others," are people to be admired, "someone who is a good person" and "does good deeds." Parents, teachers, and people they might know were equally as capable of heroism as the superhero characters familiar from TV, film, comics, and the Internet. Is this a sign of a reversal of former trends where heroes were almost universally described as those taken from fiction? Perhaps the 9/11 crisis, after which hundreds of stories of "average person" heroics flooded the media, somewhat altered children's perceptions of what constitutes heroism?

Although more research would be required to prove the point, this preliminary study suggests that kids are capable of seeing heroic acts and heroes among their everyday surroundings. Furthermore, they have an understanding that the elevation to the status of hero must be earned and maintained—it is not conferred without personal sacrifice.

It remains to be seen if the "antique" but in some ways more "ordinary" fictional heroes being brought back to life by television, comics, toy makers, and others will continue to emphasize their quotidian roots. However, even if just a momentary blip, they stand in contrast to the increasingly outrageous super-enhancements of recent heroic superheroes dreamed up in production houses around the world over the past 15 years.

Are the new fictionalized heroes—particularly the resurrected and reconstructed ones—in children's culture playing out this theme in any discernible way? Perhaps the return of relatively simple characters from a presumably "gentler era"—such as "Captain Crunch"—and without the cynical edge of many 21st-century cartoon superheroes, reinforce the sense of safety and simplicity that children require.

A question to be pursued in further research might be "what function is served by heroic 'everyday' characters" for children consuming these media portrayals? Do children somehow require the reassurance—in order to feel safe in a very dangerous world—that the seemingly ordinary people around them can suddenly become extraordinary if circumstances require it?

ACKNOWLEDGMENTS

Special thanks to Janet Westergaard at Esearch.com for contributing online panelists. Panelists were also derived from the "Netkids" panel maintained by Northstar Interactive, Inc.

Thanks also to the Girl Scouts of Athens, Georgia, their parents, and the troop leaders who made the second wave of interviewing possible.

REFERENCES

America Online/Digital Marketing Services. (2003). *Survey of children ages 7-12 on internet usage.* http://news.earthweb.com/stats/article.php/3089701

Bettelheim, B. (1989). *The uses of enchantment.* New York: Vintage Books.

Brock, B. (2001). TV-free families: Are they Lola Granolas, Normal Joes, or High and Holy Snots? Retrieved October 25, 2001, from http://www.tvturnoff.org/brock7.htm

Connell, M. (2002, April). Reload and rewind. *Kidscreen,* p. 84.

Duffy, S. (2002). *An examination of traditional folkloric and mythic formulae for heroes and contemporary iterations.* Unpublished working paper, California Polytechnic University, San Luis Obispo, CA.

Harris Interactive. (2001). *Harris Interactive Annual Report on America's Heroes.* http://www.harrisinteractive.com/news/allnewsbydate.asp?NewsID= 343

North America Online: Demographics and Usage Report. (2003). *eMarketer,* New York. Also see http://www.emarketer.com.

Teigen, K. H., Normann, H-T. E., Bjorkheim, H. O., & Helland, S. (2000). Who would you most like to be like? Adolescent's ideals at the beginning and the end of the century. *Scandinavian Journal of Educational Research, 44*(1), 1-17.

Part III

CASE STUDIES

Chapter 11

DEFINING THE HEROIC IN A CONTEXT OF ARAB-ISLAMIC VALUES

A Case Study of Sheikh Zayed
bin Sultan Al-Nahyan of the UAE

Susan Z. Swan
Zayed University

All cultures, all religions, all communities have heroes but those heroes vary from one to the other. The word hero comes from the Greek meaning "embodiment of composite ideals," so the heroes chosen or created reflect and may shape specific ideals. Communities require heroes as well as leaders. The relationship between the two are explored in this chapter. The nature of Arab-Islamic heroes and heroic leadership is examined in this chapter by Susan Swan through the case study of Sheikh Zayed of the United Arab Emirates (UAE) and his role in the formation and development of the UAE over the past 33 years.

✧ ✧ ✧

I dreamed when I was little that I would stand before Sheikh Zayed and he would place his hands on my head and say "bless you, my daughter." Later when I was older and I knew that this would not happen, I saw

him on television. He spoke to us and told us as women we had an impor-
tant role in our new country—that we were important and we needed to
study and do well and earn our higher degrees and make a difference.
Then I felt blessed by him. He is our father, you know . . . not just our
leader. We call him Baba.

—Alia Yousuf

THE NATURE OF HEROES

Saturdays. The early 1960s. The flickering screen of a small black-and-white
television: *Rocky and Bullwinkle, Shock Theatre, Saturday Afternoon at the
Movies.* It was a portal to the sublime and the ridiculous, the pathetic and
the ironic, the romantic and the heroic. The cartoons were funny; the zom-
bies and werewolves just scary enough to be exciting. But it was the "feature
events" that kept me hoping for a rainy afternoon, free to sprawl on the
floor, mesmerized by the swash-buckling of Errol Flynn as Geoffrey Thorp
and Captain Peter Blood; thrilled by the jungle adventures of Tarzan and
Jungle Jim. I was part of the rough bravery of the wild west, the daring
adventures of Tonto and the Lone Ranger, the wartime heroics of the Dirty
Dozen and Audie Murphy, the epic struggles of Spartacus and Ben Hur.

These figures were, for the most part, creatures of imagination. A few
real-life heroes were tossed in the mix, although I'm not sure I knew who
was real and who was not for a long time. What caught and held me were
the actions of the characters—moving forward in the face of danger; being
tempted, falling, rising back up; sacrificing for the right and the good. I was
heart-broken the first time I realized that heroes died (the film *Beau Gest*
carries forever the taint of that moment) and yet, I was reassured to know
that some things were worth dying for.

Fast-forward 40 years. It is now the 21st century. 9/11 has come and
gone. The world seems awash with fear, war seems commonplace, and
would-be heroes are crushed beneath sensationalism and cynicism. My early
heroes seem to be mere echoes from a distant past. Drucker and Cathcart's
(1994) volume, *American Heroes in a Media Age,* examines this unheroic
turn and suggests that our heroes and their heroic deeds may indeed have
been destroyed through overexposure and invasive reporting, replaced by
media "figures" and media "events." The very innovations in media that we
hoped would make fundamental changes for the good have become the tools
of their destruction, so altering the relationship between public figures and
audiences that we no longer seem to understand the distinction between
celebrity and heroism.

Perhaps, however, the death knell has been sounded too soon. Is it possible that the arguments presented hold only within the idiosyncratic boundaries of American culture? Is it possible that the model of media development presented by Strate (1994) and Cathcart (1994), and by extension McLuhan (1964) and Ong (1982), is not the Genesis model they imply, with each new medium redefining message simply by coming into existence? Could our experience be but one result of a Darwinian process, with different cultural contexts producing different species of mediation? Is it possible that Gumpert's (1994) wrinkle theory holds when irony dominates the zeitgeist of a people, but not when other aspects of the psyche dominate? What if, by changing the cultural context, we change the mode of heroic development? What if, by compressing the historical context, we alter the sequencing of media development and hence the media practices? What if, by altering the values and norms, we open a door to an heroic figure who still serve as the "center that holds" in a milieu as fully mediated as that of 21st century America, yet radically different in its psyche?

Imagine, then, a place where, at least in the popular mind, one man is credited with single-handedly turning a dry barren landscape into a paradise; transforming the lives of pearl divers and camel drivers barely eking out an existence into lives filled with luxury and pleasure; engineering the only country in the 20th century to be formed as a result of peaceful union rather than war or disintegration; and, setting into place in a mere 40 years all the advances of the 14th through 20th centuries. Even more, imagine that this man carried with him a rags-to-riches narrative, a frontiersman's ethos, and a philanthropist's portfolio; that he was widely adored and respected, admired for his religious devotion, and held up as the model for future generations. Such a man would seem to carry all the markers of "hero." Is it possible?

It is possible . . . if we are transported out of the United States to the United Arab Emirates (UAE), a small federation sitting as the "rhinoceros horn" of the Arabian peninsula. The hero is perhaps an unlikely one to American minds caught up in post-9/11 stereotyping, for he is both Arab and Muslim, and yet, he offers an heroic figure who can be seen sympathetically by Americans and whose media imaging directly challenges the assumed norms of hero creation in 21st-century America. This hero is His Highness Sheikh Zayed bin Sultan Al-Nahyan,[1] the late head of the Al-Nahyan family and the Bani Yas tribe, ruler of the emirate of Abu Dhabi, and president of the UAE.

Because Sheikh Zayed and even the UAE are unknown to many people, an introduction is necessary to set the context. Against that backdrop, I discuss (a) the nature of the heroic in an Arab-Islamic context and then analyze (b) how well the heroic images of Sheikh Zayed held by the Emirati fit the criteria for being heroic and (c) how the images are created through media messages in the UAE. Finally, I use Northrup Frye's (1957) schema of the modes of the heroic in literature to explore the differences in the imaging of the heroic between the United States and the UAE. This analysis aims for a more global understanding of the nature of media, stepping outside bounds that are unwittingly ethnocentric to a broader understanding of the impact of culture on communication processes.

SETTING A CONTEXT: THE COUNTRY AND THE MAN

The United Arab Emirates

On December 6, 1971, the UAE was born. The federation, which celebrated its 30th anniversary in 2001 with great pomp, represents a remarkable achievement. In a time when countries are formed mostly from civil war or ethnic cleansing, this union was for the common good; it was voluntary, without armed conflict, and developed entirely through dialogue and diplomacy. To the few Westerners familiar with the region, these tribal states (emirates) were know as the Trucial States, dubbed so by the British, who were the dominant force in the area from the early 1700s until they began their withdrawal from the region in the 1960s. The emirates, which were essentially small independent kingdoms, included Abu Dhabi, Dubai, Sharjah, Ajman, Umm al Quwain, Ras al Khaimah, Fujairah, Qatar, and Bahrain. Although ultimately only seven of the emirates signed onto "the Union" (Qatar and Bahrain went their own ways), the unification of such fiercely independent tribes is unprecedented.

Unification, or at least mutual cooperation, was a concept suggested by the British in 1952, in the face of growing resistance to British (as well as French and American) influence in the region and rising nationalism (Wilson, 1999). This resulted in the creation of the Trucial States Council. The local impetus came in late 1961 when Sheikh Rashid bin Saeed Al-Maktoum, Ruler of Dubai, began discussions of a possible union within his *majlis* (open council) and between himself and other sheikhs of the region. Progress was halting, blocked by old rivalries and fears of losing individual power. The strongest resistance came from Sheikh Shakhbuut of Abu Dhabi and Sheikh Saqr of Sharjah, the emirates located on either side of Dubai. In 1964, Rashid approached Sheikh Zayed in hopes that he could influence his brother Sheikh Shakhbuut. Rashid's dream was enthusiastically picked up by Zayed, but it took until 1966, with Shakbuut's abdication and Saqr's overthrow, for the balance to shift seriously toward unification. With the power given him as ruler of Abu Dhabi in 1966, Zayed began to work as a

full partner with Sheikh Rashid toward uniting the various small tribal powers of the northern peninsula into a loose federation with Dubai, Abu
Dhabi, and Sharjah. They saw this as the best approach to individual and
collective success, particularly in light of the full withdrawal of the British
from the Trucial States, to take effect by late 1971 (Al-Fahim, 1995). Their
fear that the sudden absence of the British would leave the area without military protection and with few financial resources outside of Dubai and Abu
Dhabi gave new energy to their endeavor.

It is clear that the country came into being only because of the dedication and commitment of these two men. Agreements were made, fell
through, made again, collapsed, and rebuilt. When the documents of unification were finally ratified in 1971, their vital role was recognized. Zayed
was elected by the Supreme Council as the country's first president and
Rashid its first vice-president and later prime minister. Their creation,
although small at 83,000 sq km (about the size of Maine; CIA, 2005), opened
the door for transformation that has been dubbed repeatedly a "miracle in
the desert" (see, e.g., Fernando, 2001; Swidey, 2003).

Prior to unification, nothing can be said to have been "developed," even
though the emirate of Dubai was slightly better off than the rest of the country as a result of its growing role as a port city and commercial center. The
population had grown little from that in 1900, when there were about
100,000 people in the region, with a 1 to 10 ratio of urban-dwellers to Bedu
(Wilson, 1999). "As late as 1957, there was not a single doctor in the
sheikhdom of Abu Dhabi" (Al-Fahim, 1995, p. 64) and little other health
care, with only a British Royal Air Force clinic in Sharjah for acute care.
Infant mortality stood at 145 per 1,000 and life expectancy at 53 (Kawach,
2003a). As recently as 1960, there was no electricity beyond the few small
generators in the rulers' compounds, no running water, no paved roads, no
telephones, no printing presses, no radio, no television. Water was scarce
and brackish; the first taste of sweet water by the residents of Abu Dhabi
came with the building of a desalination plant in 1961 (Al-Fahim, 1995). The
first mud road in Abu Dhabi was not built until 1961. There were fewer than
five schools other than the *mutawa*[2] and illiteracy stood at about 98% (Al-
Fahim, 1995) . Most people lived in palm frond huts called *areesh*. There
were a few mud houses, owned by the rulers and a few "wealthy" merchants
in Dubai, and only a single eight-room hotel in the entire country. There was
a single nonpaved airstrip, mostly for the use of the British military,
although a few 8- or 15-seat commercial flights left each week (Wilson,
1999).

The situation is vastly different today. Richard Curtiss (1995) of the
Washington Report on Middle East Affairs summed it up as a move "from
bold dream to spectacular reality in one generation." The official population
at the end of 2001 was at 3,488,000 (*UAE Yearbook*, 2003) with 85% of the

people living in urban areas. The current per capita gross domestic product (GDP) of $43,400 closely parallels that of Western Europe (CIA, 2005a). There are a host of other indicators of change (*UAE Yearbook*, 2003). There are 1,173 government and private schools, 2 government universities, 4 full-program private universities, and 11 technical colleges. Literacy is at 93% for 15- to 45-year-olds and 80% for the entire population, with equal rates for males and females. (This compares with Yemen, with 50% literacy, 70% for males and 30% for females; CIA, 2005b.) There are 38 airports (6 international) that, in 2001, served more than 20 million passengers, many of whom stayed in one of the 258 hotels in one of the three largest emirates, including the landmark Burj al Arab, advertised as the only seven-star hotel in the world and whose striking sail boat design has become an icon for the city of Dubai.

There are 30 hospitals and 115 primary care facilities. The quality of health care in the UAE has been classified by the World Health Organization (WHO) as having achieved the highest level of international health standards in terms of quality and access. This quality is reflected in the most recent figures on infant mortality (now only 8 in 1000) and life expectancy (now at 75; Kawach, 2003a). In terms of telephone access, there are more than 1 million "land" lines, 2.3 million mobile phone users (65% penetration), and 1 million Internet users (30% penetration). The UAE is first in the Arab world in e-governance and 21st of the 190 UN member countries. It has the largest information technology complex in the Middle East. There are now 9 television stations, 4 cable/satellite services, 14 radio stations, 9 daily newspapers (6 with online editions), and numerous weekly and monthly magazines. Media access is offered in Arabic and English, with lesser access in Hindi, Urdu, and Malayalan. Dubai hosts the regional headquarters of CNN, Reuters, and Middle East Broadcast Company (MBC).

It would be easy to lay the success of the venture at the feet of the oil fields of Abu Dhabi and the commercial districts of Dubai. In the minds of the people of the UAE, however, the success rests directly at the feet of Sheikh Zayed himself. In popular memory, the dream realized in 1971 was Zayed's. Virtually any UAE citizen will enthusiastically tell the stories of Zayed's diplomacy, his willingness to travel tirelessly by camel, horse, boat, and Land Rover from emirate to emirate, sitting in *majlis*, talking and listening. They will argue that it was Zayed's leadership that guided the negotiations and then guided the young country into its place among the most developed in the world. To his people, it was—and is—his leadership, his charisma that holds his people together. And in 2003, it was still his hand that nominally guided the tiller of the country; he was in his sixth five-year term as president of the federation, elected each time unanimously by the Supreme Council of Rulers of the UAE.

SHEIKH ZAYED BIN SULTAN AL-NAHYAN

Sheikh Zayed was born the fourth son of Sheikh Sultan bin Zayed in about 1916.[3] Sultan had ruled Abu Dhabi from 1922 to 1926, following in the footsteps of his father, Zayed bin Khalifa, known as Zayed the Great, who ruled from 1855 to 1909. They are of the Al-Nahyan family of the Bani Yas tribe; their family has ruled the territory and people of the Abu Dhabi region for three centuries. They have roots in the tribes of the central hills of the Arabian peninsula and have followed a pattern of succession that has often been bloody and fratricidal (Van der Meulen, 1997). Zayed grew up in a climate harsh by any standards. Most of the country is desert waste-land with temperature averages of 98 to 100° F from May to December, soaring regularly in late summer to 110 to 120° F, with humidity in the 80% to 90% range. Fresh water is scarce and, in the past, there was little to eat beyond dates, imported rice, fish, coffee, camel milk, and yogurt. Sheep, camel, and goats were common herd animals, although used more for transportation, wool, and milk than for meat. During Zayed's youth and early adulthood, the Al-Nahyan family had resources no greater than what others had. They often lacked basic food and water, and certainly had no access to (or even conception of until mid-century) plumbing, refriger-ation, modern transportation, or air conditioning. During the relatively pleasant winters, they moved to temporary camps on the coastal plains, near present-day Abu Dhabi, with access to fresh fish and a modest sea trade. During the summers, they retreated to the inland oasis of Al Ain (Buraimi), where there was some escape from the heat and humidity. The "summer palace" was a walled complex of simple mud and clay buildings with separate quarters for the many men and women of the family. The *majlis*, or meeting place, for the men was under a tree at the entrance to the compound.

As the youngest son, Zayed had grown up mostly in the desert. He served first publicly as a guide for the surveyors of oil companies in the 1930s and then in 1946 became ruler's representative (governor) in Al Ain, drawing admiration for his traditional accomplishments in horse and camel riding, hunting, and falconry, and building a reputation for diplomacy and honesty—the account of his turning down a $42-million bribe from the Saudis in 1952 to turn over the Buraimi Oasis is not atypical (Al-Fahim, 1995). Zayed's elder brother Sheikh Shakhbuut, who ruled from 1928 to 1966, "was a conservative leader with a cautious, fugal style" (Rashid, 2001, p. 9). By 1966, however, it was clear that the British were leaving the Gulf and the vast resources of oil reserves were coming in, setting the scene for leadership responsive to such changes. Shakhbuut would not adapt and so in traditional Bedu fashion, the family met in council and decided to replace

him with Zayed. (Fortunately this power change did not follow tradition to
the letter. Rather than being subject to the bloody coup that had typified
most changes of power in the family for centuries, Shakhbuut consented to
the change, accepting exile gracefully and lived peacefully in Iran and
Lebanon until his death in 1990.)

Zayed's accession day as ruler in Abu Dhabi is the annually celebrated
August 6, 1966. His first acts were to initiate infrastructure improvements in
Abu Dhabi and Al Ain with money stockpiled by his brother, building
roads, desalinization plants, mosques, hospitals, and schools. Money and
resources were shared widely throughout the emirate in the form of comfortable housing with plumbing and electricity, start-up grants for businesses, and civic donations. Additionally, Zayed directed billions of dirhams to
humanitarian aid, with money to build hospitals in less developed countries
and to aid war refugees and victims of natural disasters. The money had been
accumulating since the first oil concessions were sold in the late 1930s and
then began pouring in with the first export of crude oil in 1962. The policy
of spending on general improvements, sharing the wealth with the tribe, and
generously engaging in humanitarian aid was a radical departure from that
of Sheikh Shakhbuut and from the model found in neighboring Saudi, where
income to the royal family is kept for the royal family and general living
standards drop each year. Indeed, Zayed was the third richest head of state
in the world, with assets of $20 billion, according to Forbes ("Arab rulers,"
1999) and yet his policies of sharing the wealth have allowed him to garner,
as far as I can tell, no resentment from his people as a result. Emirati, as well
as many non-Emirati, know that if they are in need, all they have to do is
what they would traditionally have done—approach the leader of the tribe
and ask for help.

Zayed's leadership has been progressive in many ways and has been rec-
ognized in a variety of awards. Some of them highlight his environmental
vision, others recognize his work as statesman, whereas others recognize his
commitments to and demonstration of his faith. Among them are the 1995
Appreciation Award and Gold Medal from the International Food and
Agricultural Organization (FAO), the 1997 World Wildlife Foundation's
Gold Panda award (given for the first time to a head of state), 1997 Gulf
Business Award for Environmental Action awarded by the Gulf
Cooperation Council (GCC), the 1998 Most Prominent International
Personality of the Year award from the French people, and the 1999 Islamic
Personality of the Year award. Clearly, His Highness Sheikh Zayed bin
Sultan Al-Nahyan was a remarkable man and showed visionary leadership
for his country and his people. Does this make him a hero? In order to
determine this, one must look at what being a hero means to the people of
the Arabian Gulf as a prelude to an examination of the perceptions of Zayed
by his people as heroic.

DEFINING THE HEROIC
IN AN ARAB-ISLAMIC CONTEXT

Heroic Elements Based in Culture and History

Understanding the heroic in any given culture requires an understanding of daily life, cultural values, stories and legend, and history. The origins of these heroic elements in the Middle East, as in any culture, do not lie in a single source. In the Gulf region, they emerge from two distinct, yet interwoven sources—religious and ethnic. The religious centering provided by Islam is the soul of thought and belief in the Gulf, whereas the ethnic grounding provided by the history and experience of the Bedouin is the heart.

Islam as a Base for Defining the Heroic

Religion provides the point of greatest cultural commonality across the Middle East and North Africa, bringing together Arabs, Persians, and Turks, as well as smaller ethnic groups. The Qur'an (along with the *hadith*, teachings based on the sayings and life of Prophet Mohammad, and the *shariah*, the law based on the Qur'an) offers a comprehensive guide for life and is built atop the guidelines of Judaism and the early Christian church, for the Qur'an is, to Muslims, not a replacement narrative, but an extensional one, delivered through the archangel Gabriel to the Prophet Mohammed in 609 CE. This means that the heroic narratives of prophets like Moses, Abraham, and Solomon belong in the tapestries of all three sister religions and thus the value systems underlying them are familiar to all believers of "the one God." Unlike in the West, however, where religion often has become separated from daily life, for Muslims even today, religion *is* daily life, establishing the very rhythms of the day.

Muslims are called to a progressive "perfecting" of one's self (as are Christians), ever striving toward an "assimilation of divine attributes" (Sharif, 1963–1966, 1983, p. 145). Getting to perfection is impossible, but to strive toward it is a responsibility of each Muslim aiming to please God. Some Muslims—who we might call heroic—are called to the highest striving and highest responsibility. These most dedicated (literally *al-muHsineen*, the dedicated)

are those who are not only on the right path themselves, but in addition by their good example and magnetic personality lead others to the way of righteousness and help in establishing a social order based on peace, harmony, and security. Complete power, wisdom and knowledge, true guidance from the Lord, prosperity, rise in worldly position, power and

knowledge are the by-products of their life of graceful righteousness
(*ihsaan*). (Dar, 1983, p. 177)

What are the traits these most dedicated would have, traits that are the basis
of *taqwa* (piety)? In the *History of Muslim Philosophy,* Dar's work is helpful with this, summing up key attributes in nine categories: life, eternity,
unity, power, truth, beauty, justice, love, and goodness. These can be further
distilled into three dimensions: (a) a balance of focus on earthly and eternal
life; (b) the noble virtues; and (c) the responsible use of power toward unity.

Balancing Earthly and Eternal Life. The first dimension calls for a balancing of earthly life and eternal life. One is not to turn away from the joys
and blessings of life, nor to turn away from wealth and prosperity that might
come one's way, but rather to find happiness in the beauties of God, nature,
and fellowship. But one must not lose sight of the divine in the face of
"things momentary." Fulfilling the five pillars of Islam helps to achieve this
balance (Smith, 1986). Acceptance and repetition of the creed, "There is no
God but Allah and Mohammed is his Prophet" (the first pillar), and regular
prayer, the second pillar, help keep one's eyes on God. The third and fourth
pillars, charity (*zakat*) and fasting during the month of Ramadan, are
reminders to set aside the blinders of self-absorption and to be sensitive to
those in need. The fifth pillar is the once-a-life pilgrimage (*hajj*) to Mecca, a
mark of sacrifice and dedication as well as a reminder that one is part of the
larger community of Islam, joining together as it does, equal under the eyes
of God, men and women of all ranks, races, and countries.

The Noble Virtues. The second dimension identifies three primary
virtues of the dedicated Muslim: love, justice, and wisdom. Love and justice
are, of course, shorthand for a host of other virtues, such as compassion,
mercy, patience, forgiveness, humility, gentleness, fairness, generosity, and
truth. Wisdom stands for humanity's "search for knowledge or truth" (Dar,
1983, p. 161) and resides in (a) pure reasoning (dialectic), (b) scientific and
historical knowledge (gained through observation, experimentation, study
of nature and history, and travel), and (c) ultimately through intuition or
moral reasoning, the "knowledge by the heart" (p. 150).

Power and Unity. The third dimension explains the responsible use of
power toward achieving unity. Unity is the "presence of moral order" (p.
157). Internal order requires the "coordination of reason, will, and action"
(p. 157) to act with dignity and self-control. External order requires joining
together for the common good, first in the family and then at larger levels of
social organization. Both types of order require power. Power begins with
undertaking action of one's own accord and taking responsibility for one's

own physical, spiritual, and emotional development. Power may also be granted over the natural world and over others, but this must be accepted with great care. As one's power increases, so does one's responsibility and the level of accountability in the eyes of God. A leader of a State, just as a father in the home, is called to demonstrate perseverance, patience, firmness, courage, and trust in God in order to build a state/family based on "peace and freedom of thought, worship, belief, and expression" (p. 160). The good leader would be a guide, not a dictator, and should exert power with love, kindness, and an eye toward harmony. Inertia (a refusal to take up the responsibility given one) and abuse of power (seen through oppression of others and denial of truth/justice to them, arrogance, over-blown pomp, self-glory, and vanity) are disvalues and anathema in the eyes of God.

The Bedu Tradition as a Source of Heroic Values

The second source of values for Emirati, and for the heroic model, is ethnic tradition. The archetype of the Arab is grounded in the soul of the Bedouin, the nomad of the deserts. Even for Arabs in countries where the nomadic life has almost disappeared, the values represented in the traditions and customs of the Bedouin people are of great importance.[4]

The Bedouin predated the coming of Islam by at least 1,600 years, being first referred to specifically as Arabs in 854 BCE (Patai, 2002), although, of course, they existed earlier as Semites, a race that split at the time of Abraham into the Arabs, descending from his son Ishmael, and the Israelites, descending from Isaac. Their life was harsh, and tribes and family groups migrated with the seasons to follow supplies of water and pasturage. Their belongings were few and foodstuffs limited mainly to camel milk and dates, with meat and fish an occasional supplement. Survival was the primary goal, and customs that enhanced chances of survival were prized. Protecting one's blood kin came first—and all traditions evolved toward this end. Three clusters of qualities served to protect one's tribe best and thus are key to understanding the Bedu ethos (Patai, 2002): bravery/courage, hospitality/generosity, and honor/self-respect.[5] Bravery and courage are vital for immediate survival while the nobility of hospitality and generosity and the dignity gained via honor and self-respect are more related to smoothing social organization and thus serve long-term survival.

Courage (khamaasa). The first of these clusters is courage. This in part reflects a need to endure pain and deprivation with fortitude, because both were part of daily life. It also means boldness and willingness to risk one's life to gain resources for the tribe, which often involved raids on neighboring tribes (or passing ships) as well as courage and determination when called on to exact revenge in the face of a blood debt or honor violation. In addition to a fierce loyalty, one needed the ability to use arms (e.g., the short knife or *jambeea*, sword, and, later, rifle), to ride camel and/or horse, to navigate across the desert, and to plan and execute a raid. Manliness demanded high-skill levels in these arts of the warrior and the readiness to use them for survival and sport. Such values also lead to devaluing more sedentary, agricultural lifestyles, and so, in a conflict similar to that found in the American west between ranchers and farmers, the Bedouin traditionally resisted as dishonorable more settled ways of life.

Hospitality and Generosity (deeyafah and karam). The hospitality of the Bedu is legendary—stories abound of blood oaths put on hold in the face of an enemy's petition for the mandated three days of hospitality, of extraordinary hospitality at marriages, burials, and other great life moments, of the gentleness of a village toward a stranger.[6] Such hospitality helps mitigate the harshness of the desert life, ensuring the sharing of resources within one's tribe and aid for desert wanderers who are temporarily outside the protection of their own tribe and thus at the mercy of the elements. The head of a tribe has additional responsibilities in terms of hospitality and generosity, being required to share his "wealth" and to be available personally to his family, clan, or tribe to consult for advice, to listen thoughtfully to the concerns and opinions of his people, and to serve in the highly prized role of mediator to resolve tribal conflicts without bloodshed (Patai, 2002).

Honor and Self-Respect. The concepts of honor and self-respect are probably the most complex of the traits of the Bedu. Honor is the "collective property of the entire tribe" (p.100) and is tightly bound up with notions of face (*wajh*). Self-respect is the internalization of honor and exists through active self-monitoring and self-control. This leaves one ever-vigilant and one may go to great lengths to avoid exposing one's "inner self with all its errors and weaknesses" (p. 107) or exposing the weaknesses of another, leading to a premium on respect of other as well. "Shame," the public side of the private matter of guilt, results from threats to one's own, or one's family's, reputation and honor. It is to be avoided at all costs, even if shading the truth is required. Maintenance of honor is bound up with many aspects of life and may be increased through purity of blood; virility (producing many children, especially sons); modesty and humility (especially of one's daughters and wife[s]); and respect of one's parents and elders. Demonstrations of courage, hospitality, and generosity also accrue honor to self and tribe. Even raids must be done within the dictates of honor; raids on poor tribes is dishonorable, raids on equal or stronger tribes honorable.

The Bedu Ethos

The Bedu ethos, ultimately, is driven by a fierce clannishness paired with a fierce independence, counterbalanced by a lavish sense of hospitality and generosity, and mediated by an exacting code of honor. It is an ethos derived from life in a context of extremes — times of quiet and lethargy interspersed with bursts of energy and emotion, times of plenty interrupted by times of want and deprivation. Being able to respond bravely and with dignity in the face of such extremes is what makes one heroic in the Bedu world. This is an ethos which is quite different from the Islamic ethos. The cultural balancing of the inward-directed heroic model of the righteous and dedicated Muslim with or against that of the outwardly focused, active and honorable Bedouin adds significant complexity to the Arabian culture, but makes the search for the heroic model all the more interesting.

Current Perceptions of the Heroic Elements

Gathering Perceptions

To analyze how UAE nationals define the heroic and perceive Sheikh Zayed, 21 students in a basic research methods class participated in focus groups on these topics and then interviewed 151 Emirati. The convenience sample was designed to include four distinct groups: females under age 40, females over age 40, males under age 40, and males over age 40.[7] Gender and age were considered because gender is a significant cultural dimension in the Gulf, with most of life spent within gender-circumscribed groups, and age offers a way of tapping in the differences in life experience between those who were adults before unification and those who came after. At least 30 interviews were conducted in each category, with additional interviews in the female under age 40 group.

The ages of those interviewed ranged from 15 to "around 80." The average age of the under-40s was 21; of over-40s, 49. Almost all were born in the UAE (93%); all were Muslim (97% Sunni; 3% Shi'a); 60% were from Dubai with 36% from Sharjah, Ajman, and Umm Al Quwain (the emirates served by Zayed U-Dubai campus). Although the households they live in ranged from 2 to 18, most shared quarters with 9 to 10 relatives (young people remain in the family home until they marry). All the over-40 participants were married as were 40% of the under-40s.

Education is new to the UAE and thus there are, as yet, few influences on cultural values from formal schooling. Of those interviewed, 32% were students; of the remainder, 25% had no education, or none beyond the *mutawa*; 25% had attended 6 to 12 years of school; 25% graduated from high school; and the remaining 25% graduated from an undergraduate,

graduate, or professional school (females outnumber the males at this level, which fits with overall statistics on post-high school education in the UAE). Their parents had even less opportunity for education. For the under-40s, 46% of their parents had no schooling or attended a *mutawa* only; for the over-40s, this holds for 88% of their parents.

Arabic was the first language for 90% of the participants. The other 10% have Ajami, Hindi, and Farsi as their first language, but have also spoken Arabic most of their lives. About 25% of the interviews were conducted fully in Arabic; 50% in a combination of English and Arabic; and 25% fully in English. Although the questions were crafted in English, Arabic equivalents were provided for all key terms and students practiced with one another in both languages before doing real interviews.

Defining Hero

Participants were asked to define a *hero* and to identify the traits of a hero. The responses ranged from the cynical: "a hero is an idiot who saves a stupid girl" to the more sublime: "a strong man who did things that were impossible and has a perfect personality." The results are strongly reminiscent of the traditional definitions of the hero in the west. Of the 151 individuals interviewed, 5 felt that anyone could be a hero, 3 felt no one could be, and 3 felt heroism was circumstantial. As one older man put it: "There are no rules to be a hero; it is a matter of fate and circumstance. Some are heroes in our eyes, but for others they are criminals."

In all, six elements dominated the definitions. They indicated that a hero must, in order of precedence:

1. Do the extraordinary, the unique, or the impossible.
2. Sacrifice self and protect others.
3. Accomplish/do something.
4. Be famous.
5. Show courage.
6. Demonstrate power.

The *uniqueness* might come from having especially high morals, being able to create and achieve a great vision that no one else could achieve, or do something unexpected or "impossible." This unique hero is *other-directed*, helping, protecting, and saving others. He or she is one "who loves people and the people love him" and is "willing to give all that one has" to "benefit the community." This turn toward the other calls for inner strength, in that the hero must be *courageous*, "not afraid of death," and "steadfast in front of everything that comes for him." It also calls for one to *exhibit power* "in the right way," using it "in the right time and position" and being the one who can exert "control over a situation." This power must be used to *take action*, "to achieve," "take responsibility," "lead the people to victory," or to be the "person capable of doing hard tasks and accomplishing them." A hero must be a *"known hero,"* so as a result a hero is liked, loved, respected, an object of pride—someone "you cannot forget all your life."

Not surprisingly, the traits identified for a hero are consistent with these six elements. For the Emirati, the most important trait for a hero is *courage*, with 65% of those interviewed giving courage or bravery as an heroic trait. *Power and strength*, given by 44% of respondents, seemed the next most important trait. A third complex of traits related to *"nobility of character,"* with 33.3% listing such traits as just, fair, honest or true, forgiving, patient, respectful, gentle, equal, and self-controlled. Close behind this, with 27% of responses, are traits that show the hero as *other-focused*. This includes helping others, doing good, having a big heart, being loving, kind, and self-sacrificing, and bringing peace to "heal the world." The last important trait given is *wisdom*, with 21% of respondents listing wisdom, intelligence, logic, and cleverness as key traits for a hero. It would seem that the cowardly, the power hungry, the ignoble, the selfish, and the unwise need not apply to be hero in the UAE.

Identifying Heroes

Respondents were ask to name up to three people they would consider to be a hero. Eighty-two different people or categories of people were nominated. One name dominated the polls: Sheikh Zayed. He was noted as a hero by 62% of those interviewed. Four others also received significant mention: Sheikh Mohammad bin Rashid Al-Maktoum (20%), Osama bin Laden (19%), Prophet Mohammad (16.5%), and Gamal Abdul Nasser (12.5%).

All of these men are political figures in one way or another. Sheikh Mohammad is now the ruler of the emirate of Dubai, the vice-president and prime minister for the UAE, and a prime mover for a high tech infra-structure and high-end commercial ventures in Dubai. He is a man who conveys vigor, energy, and power. Prophet Mohammad was not only an instrument of God's voice, bringing the Qur'an to the world, but he was also a political leader of some success (and was a model Sheikh Zayed followed in his own political career: www.zayedprize.com). Gamal Abdul Nasser was the leader who brought about the final expulsion of the British from Egypt and remains one of few leaders to have successfully ejected an unwilling colonial power from Arab soil. Perhaps the most confusing result of this list is the high ranking of Osama bin Laden. This is a bit more understandable if one can see that for many Arabs, his actions are a stand for Palestine in the face of continued Israeli terrorism. There is an element of the anti-hero value too as his actions are seen as thumbing the nose to a superpower often seen overseas as a bully, particularly in the Middle East where 20th-century colonial powers have wreaked havoc politically and socially.[8]

Once one moves beyond the "top 5" heroes list, four categories of heroes emerge: the Companions of the Prophet, other local and international leaders, personal heroes, and societal heroes. Popular culture heroes barely make an appearance and sports heroes not at all; only three pop figures are identified, all of a fictional or quasi-fantasy nature: Superman, Hulk Hogan (for his physical strength), and Michael Jackson.

The Companions. A sign of how much of life in the Gulf is grounded in religion is that 50 respondents named Prophet Mohammad and his Companions as heroes. The Companions parallel the Apostles and were the colleagues and contemporaries of the Prophet who supported the beginnings of Islam.[9] The adherents to the pagan religions that dominated the Arab world, as already established powers, objected strongly to the newly rising religion, and many of the Companions had to fight in defense of themselves and their families in the name of religious freedom. The need to defend one's self as a Muslim and Arab has not disappeared and modern-day equivalents of the Companions, typically Muslims under attack, are also considered heroic. This is reflected in the naming as heroes the Muslims in India (left over from the still contested partitioning of British India into India and Pakistan), the Palestinian people, and Mohammad al-Doorah, a 12-year-old Palestinian murdered by Israeli forces.

Leaders Against Oppression. Other leaders—local, Arab, and international—were named, although most were listed only once out of the 388 "candidates" for hero. The exceptions who are mentioned more frequently include Sheikh Rashid, late ruler of Dubai and co-founder of the UAE, and Sheikha Fatima bint Mubarak, wife of Sheikh Zayed and strong advocate for women's rights in the UAE. A series of heroes from Muslim North Africa are also featured, including Salah Al-Din (Saladin), the great Muslim leader against the Crusaders and ruler of Egypt in the 12th century; Omar al-Mukhtar, leader of the resistance movement in Libya against Mussolini's forces; and Anwar al Saddat, assassinated president of Egypt. Ghandi, instrumental in freeing India from the British yoke; Nelson Mandela from the South African apartheid movement; and Martin Luther King, Jr. from the American Civil Rights Movement are also identified, showing a strong bent toward those who stand up against oppression.

Personal Heroes. Heroes are not always world or political leaders. For many of us, it is someone close to us who gives us our most personal sense of heroism, setting the standard for how we live our lives. This is true for 42 of the Emirates interviewed. The family members listed included "my ances-tors," mothers, children, brothers, and cousins. The most common person-al hero though was the respondent's father or husband (given by 28 people), an identification that fits given the role of the father/husband in traditional Islamic society as the one responsible for bridging between the family and the outside world, providing for and protecting the family, and providing the example or model of how to live life. He is seen a warrior of sorts, whether actual or economic, and is called on to show publicly the traits of virtue, courage, and generosity.

Societal Heroes. In the United States, it is not uncommon to see people who fill particular social service roles accounted as heroes. The prominence of attention given to fire fighters and police officers following 9/11 is a notable example of this. In the Emirates, police officers, firefighters, soldiers who protect, teachers, and doctors are those most often named in this cate-gory. Appreciation for such people makes especial sense given that 40 years ago no one existed in the entire country to fill these roles and so those who were the first to provide protection from physical harm, disease, and igno-rance surely seemed heroic.

An Overall Schema of the Heroic

Between the schema of heroic traits derived from religious and cultural sources and those defined directly by the modern Emirati, a highly similar set of heroic characteristics emerges, as shown in Table 11.1. This suggests fairly high consistency between the traditional and modern values. These characteristics should feel relatively familiar to Americans, with the require-ments of religious heroism approximating that seen in the Christian mission field and the remaining characteristics approximating the heroism of the American frontier. Two things unique to the Gulf experience are that (a) these values are not those of unique subcontexts of experience, but rather they typify norms of common expectation and (b) the religious dimension must not be isolated from the other heroic dimensions, but rather must be wholly integrated with them.

THE HEROIC NATURE OF SHEIKH ZAYED

He has changed my life. I want to do something to my country and for Sheikh Zayed who gives us all that we need. So I work hard to protect my country from any enemy. And about me, I promise Sheikh Zayed to be as he wants us to be.

—Ahmad

TABLE 11.1. Comparison of Arab-Islamic values and modern hero traits

TRADITIONAL

ISLAMIC VALUES	BEDU TRADITION
Appreciation of life	Bravery/courage (strength/power)
Aim to the eternal life	
Love	Hospitality/generosity (nobility of spirit)
Justice	
Wisdom	Honor/self-respect (dignity)
Use power for unity	

MODERN

DEFINING QUALITIES	HERO TRAITS
Do the extraordinary	Courage
Sacrifice self/protect others	Power/strength
Accomplish deeds	Noble character
Be famous	Other-focused
Show courage	Wisdom
Demonstrate power	

THE PERCEIVED CHARACTERISTICS OF SHEIKH ZAYED

When the Emirati were asked to name examples of heroes, 62% named Sheikh Zayed. When later they were asked directly if they "would consider Sheikh Zayed a hero," the figure skyrocketed to 98.6%.[10] Indeed, only two individuals gave a "no" response; both were males under 40 who felt Sheikh Zayed was not adventurous enough to be a proper hero (perhaps not surprising for a youth looking at an 87-year-old man). Respondents were also asked whether Sheikh Zayed deserved the admiration that many felt for him. Again, the response was 98.6%. The dissenters here were both females over age 40; to one, "only our God deserves admiration," and to the other, "All his traits indicate that he is a person who should be admired, such as wisdom, courage, justice, and honor, but he is a simple person and would not, I think, want us to admire him so." When asked how well he provided an example for their children to follow, 86.2% rated him as 5 (or 6!), with 5 being the "perfect model" and 98% rated him at least 4 out of 5. When asked if he had been a good model for living the Islamic life, 74.5% rated him as a perfect model (5 of 5), whereas 96.6 % rated him at least 4 out of 5. The reasons given for scores of 4 suggested that only Prophet Mohammad gave the perfect example; that no human could be perfect given human nature leads to error; or that Zayed was too tolerant in allowing unIslamic practices (such as drinking alcohol) in the country.

Most of those interviewed not only described Zayed as a hero, but repeatedly expressed great affection for him. Many were distressed when asked how he might compare to other Arab or world leaders, indicating the questions were "improper." The primary reason? To suggest that Zayed even *could* be compared with others was an insult, implying he was at the same level as other leaders, something they saw as simply ridiculous. Many sent messages back to me (as the instructor) expressing their hope that I would truly come to understand how great and how loved their *"Baba Zayed"* was (*baba* is an affectionate term for father or grandfather).

Given that virtually all the Emirati interviewed consider Zayed to be a hero, one might ask how well the traits that they ascribe to him fit with those identified as proper for a hero. The first question to address this asked respondents to describe Sheikh Zayed. Generosity and hospitality were given by 48.7% of the respondents, with this being especially salient for females over age 40 (72.4%) and less salient for males under age 40 (34.4%). Wisdom, love, courage, and "our father" were each given by more than 30% of those interviewed. For males, courage was listed as a descriptor most often by the youth (44.1%) and least often by their fathers (18.8%). He was considered to be a leader, kind, helpful, and just by around 20% of the respondents.

When descriptors were clustered, out of the 744 possible items given, five clusters of traits emerged. The most important cluster was that capturing nobility of character, with a total of 44% of the responses, including love and its byproducts (22%), justice (12%), and wisdom (10%). A second cluster capturing the concept of leadership and accomplishment (including "father") accounted for 19% of the responses. The remaining three clusters were nobility of spirit (generosity and hospitality) accounting for 13% of the total responses; courage, 10%; honor/respect/dignity, 7%. Only 7% of the items did not easily fit into these clusters, demonstrating a strong parallel of descriptors with the characteristics of heroism already established.

The Emirati were also asked what important values Zayed learned from growing up in the Bedouin life. The three categories defined by Bedu traditions emerged as important for Zayed. Generosity, hospitality, and nobility of spirit (magnanimity) were noted by 50% of those interviewed. Courage, strength, and power were noted by 22.2% and honor, respect, and dignity by 15.3%. In addition, patience and love were additional important components. Patience was noted as an important learning by 44% of the Emirati. This they noted was especially important due to the hardships of the life. And, 11% remarked that what/who he learned to love was crucial for making him who his was: love of his people, love of his traditions and customs, and love of his desert land (including the animals and plants that are his heritage).

When asked how they felt about Sheikh Zayed, four concepts dominated: love (74% of the respondents), respect/honor (41%), father (36.5%), and pride/admiration (35%). Those interviewed emphasized that their love for him was like that for a father and that this love was a companion to his clear and abiding love for them, for their country, and for anyone in need. They respect and honor him for who he was, for his great achievement in building their country, his transformation of the desert into a "green oasis," a "paradise," and for his ability to maintain traditions even as they made rapid progress to first-world status. They refer specifically to his ability in the past to live on hunting, with rifle and falcon, to ride both camel and horse, and to live "the simple life."[11] They also respect him for living the Muslim life, living by the rules of Islam, building Islamic institutions, and providing resources for people to learn to read the Qur'an and to make the pilgrimage. It is clear to them that "he wants to win the paradise and thinks of it all the time. The proof is what he is doing for Islam and Muslims." They say without hesitation that they are proud of him and admire him beyond all bounds. They are proud of his ability to transform the hard and difficult desert life into the most modern of lives, with luxury undreamed of 30 years ago. They detail how he facilitated this with housing grants, a marriage fund to offset rising bride prices (by Muslim law, a man provides money at marriage to guarantee the bride with resources should he die or the relationship end in divorce), free education through the university level (and beyond if warranted), and grants to start businesses.

A final question to sum up "in one word" what Sheikh Zayed means to them was revealing. The most frequently occurring word, given by 44% of the Emirati, was "father." This is a concept that recurred throughout the interviews and ultimately every single person referred to him as "father" at least once. Given that "father" is an ultimate term for Bedu and Muslim alike, this is a high compliment. Some students have told me they even thought he really was part of their family when they were young because of his picture in their homes and because they heard him called "Baba Zayed" so frequently—discovering he was not blood kin did nothing to alter their respect and love for him. A remarkable range of superlatives were also given. He was "my everything" or "every good or great thing" (7%); he was the "perfect model" or "best example" (5%); he was "rare," "special," "a gem," and "my hero" as well as the perfect, the best, and the greatest (12%). He was "our love, our heart, our spirit, our life, our soul, and the soul of the UAE" (10%). Some (7%) summed him up through traits: wise, loyal, brave, noble, just, clever, loving. The fact of his leadership, personalized as our lovely, dear, and best leader, appeared for 8%. His contributions to the country formed the final 7% of responses: safety, improvement, beautiful world, source of peace, living in luxury, a country completed, and paradise. One young woman declined to sum up her feelings in a single word, claiming that "if said, all the words in the world will still not describe my feelings about Sheikh Zayed."

THE MEDIA IMAGING OF SHEIKH ZAYED

Shaping the Media Images

It is clear from these findings that Sheikh Zayed is definitely considered a hero by his people, presenting heroic qualities from traditional and contemporary Emirati expectation. Many of these images come directly from the families, as Zayed is talked about in the homes and is a part of the consciousness of each child from an early age. Children are taught songs about Zayed, see pageants of his life and the birth of the country, and participate in the Accession Day and National Day festivals each year. There is considerable media input as well. Once television stations arrived in the UAE, he received considerable television coverage, with his speeches at events featured, his appearances in the community, and the conversation and advice-offering from his regular majlis. This almost disappeared when he was in declining health, occurring only on rare State occasions, on his return from trips abroad, or serendipitously when coverage was provided for an event and he showed up unexpectedly, to the surprise and delight of all (such as celebrations of local soccer championships or the finals of a chess tournament). These latter occasions may have involved no more than a few minutes of shaking hands through the open window of his car, but to the people there and to those who caught the vignette on the news that night, it was highly meaningful. Having only small amounts of television coverage, however, does not mean there is a dearth of other media. As a resident of Dubai, my experience suggests that media coverage of Sheikh Zayed was dominated by three primary domains: public artifacts, print media, and the Internet.

Public Artifacts

One cannot be in the UAE more than a few minutes without encountering at least one of the many "monuments" to Sheikh Zayed. His portraits are an ever-present element of life, both in public and in many homes, Emirati and expat alike. Every government office, building, and school features his portraits. This is not surprising. What is surprising (especially as there are no laws requiring the posting of his image) is the presence of his portrait in every other place imaginable—from hotels, banks, and groceries to shopping malls and coffee shops. Banner portraits 20 stories high show up on the sides of tower buildings in Dubai and Abu Dhabi and larger-than-life "poster statues" proliferate on roadsides and in parks. Various portraits are used, but the most common pose is a smiling Sheikh Zayed with hand extended in a wave of welcome. Any artist of note (or not) does at least one portrait of Zayed to display his or her talent and show respect. When he was alive, some would get presented personally to the Sheikh himself and others were displayed prominently in shops, art galleries, shopping centers, and public buildings.

The range of images does not end here, however. Sunscreens in the back windows of cars feature Sheikh Zayed, mostly alone against backdrops of the UAE flag or map, but occasionally in smiling connection with Sheikh Rashid or Sheikh Khalifa (Zayed's eldest son). In book shops and *souk* stalls, gas stations and groceries, vendors sell all manner of items with Zayed's image, from posters to postcard sets, from stickers and buttons to carpets and calendars. The range and stock goes up at festival times, especially for Accession and National Days. On campus, the favored carry-all is a canvas bag bearing Zayed's image encircled by the Arabic Z (the logo for Zayed University). These items come from no central government agency bent on blanketing the country with Zayed's image, but are the product of many small trading and novelty companies, and even students doing projects, who want to demonstrate sincere regard for the president and patron saint of the UAE.

Print Media

The print media present images of Sheikh Zayed in two main avenues: newspapers and books. In 2004 there were six major daily newspapers: *Al Ittihad*, *Al Bayan*, *Al Khaleej* (Arabic) and *Khaleej Times*, *Gulf News*, and *Gulf Today* (English). Until his illnesses began a few years ago, Sheikh Zayed was a front-page feature daily in all the papers. After his illness, he appeared less often but still every few days when he was in-country. These photos are typically of him sitting in formal reception of other sheikhs or international dignitaries or sitting in the passenger side of his car, visiting project sites, community events, or talking with his people. The first reinforced important images of Zayed as statesman, meeting with such people as the King of Bahrain or the prime minister of France, other ruling sheikhs or with ambassadors and envoys. The second reinforced Zayed's concern for the events and people of his country, conveying that although he was not as able as he once was, he still cared.

Content of the articles created and maintained Zayed's image as well. A selection of articles from a few weeks in Summer 2003 offers representative glimpses of the Sheikh's character. They variously reported his pledge to pay the health care costs of the 2-year-old sole survivor of a Sudanese plane crash ("Boy survivor," 2003), the opening of a women's care hospital in Ramallah, completed with funds from Sheikha Fatima (his wife) ("Fatima hospital," 2003), the gifting of $40,000 to save a California elementary school from closing ("Zayed gift," 2003), the success of his far-visioning creation of Sir Bani Yas island, a significant "nature preserve and agricultural research station" ("Sir Bani Yas," 2003), the gratitude of Bedouin for his support of their traditional lives, by gifting them with all of his own camels and subsidizing markets for camel meat and milk products (Murshed & Hafi, 2003), the progress of a housing project paid for by him in Gaza to replace war-destroyed homes (Kawach, 2003b), his call for "quick restoration of Iraq's sovereignty by setting up a legitimate government and mitigating the suffering of its people" ("Zayed calls," 2003), and his support for a controversial change in Crown Prince of Ras al Khaimah (Al-Baik, 2003).

In just this small sampling, he was established as generous (even beyond his own country and religion), concerned (here through his wife) about the welfare of women, far-visioning, preserving of tradition, and as a statesman who supports other Arab countries. This was typical of the daily information on Sheikh Zayed, in addition to regular press releases that journal Zayed's sending and receiving of cables, phone calls, and letters between himself and other world leaders, which conveys a sense of continuing regional and international involvement.

Another important source of print imaging of Sheikh Zayed is books. Some of the books are commemorative, such as a series from the Zayed International Centre for Coordination and Follow-up to document the celebrations for Zayed's safe return home after his kidney transplant: *Gratitude, love and sincerity parade; Nation's jubilation over leader's safety;* and *Zayed's noble deed (Pardoning 6000 prisoners)*. These are in Arabic, although some commemorative books are in English and widely available. These include *Zayed: Man of the environment* (Al-Qubaisi, 2001), published to coincide with the first Zayed Environmental Award in 2002 and to highlight via photographs and quotations, the environmental rhetoric and policies of Sheikh Zayed. A similar book, *Zayed: The Advocate of Peace and Noble Deeds* (n.d.), brings together photographs of Zayed with heads of state of more than 60 countries with short statements of praise from these notables. *Feminine issues in the United Arab Emirates: Perspectives of A Visionary Leader* (2000) offers his progressive views on women's issues, in Arabic and English, to coincide with the Arab Women's Summit in Cairo.

Of greatest value are four coffee table books, in Arabic and English editions, that capture, mostly in photographs, the history and personality of Sheikh Zayed. These photo books are wildly popular with locals and expatriates alike and form the heart of displays on Zayed and the UAE in virtually every bookstore. Three of these are by Noor Ali Rashid, photographer of the sheikhs and people of the region for more than 40 years: *Abu Dhabi: Life and Times* (1996), *The UAE: Visions of Change* (1997), and *Sheikh Zayed: Life and Times* (2001). The photographs reflect the nature of a simple man who became a great leader and capture Zayed's role in The Early Years and on The International Stage as well as Founder of a Nation, A Visionary Ruler, Man of Traditional Values, and Father of the Nation. He is seen in posed and informal shots and in many moods. We see the traditional (Zayed hunting with his falcons, dancing at a Bedouin wedding, or astride a pure white Arabian) and the modern (admiring skyscrapers in Abu Dhabi or stepping onto a jetway). We see him at the signing ceremony to unite the emirates and being welcomed by Queen Elizabeth II, laughing with Sheikh Rashid and cozying up with his grandchildren. We see him at prayer in a mosque in Abu Dhabi and as a pilgrim in Mecca. In *Abu Dhabi* and *The UAE*, especially, pains are taken to show that while the modern is being built, the traditional is being retained. The images of "before and after" are an important feature of these books, showing vividly the transformation from desert flats to high-rise towers, from barasti to brick and mortar. He is also photographed with the other ruling sheiks, an important technique to convey a sense of cooperation and unity.

The newest of the books, *Zayed: A Photographic Journey*, is the most striking. Its frontpiece is the earliest—and most famous picture of Zayed. Taken in 1948 by Sir Wilfred Thesiger, the photograph shows Zayed at age 30, astride a horse with only a blanket as saddle, holding a falcon on his extended arm. The image conveys tradition, confidence, power, and simplicity. This work, which blends photographs with inspirational quotations from Zayed about responsibilities, visions, and beliefs, covers a wider range of topics than the other three and includes a section on women. We see images of a man from humble beginnings dedicated to "greening the desert," a man concerned for the greater Arab nation and committed to a role as "peaceful statesman," a man of generosity and charity. We also see his concern for the future, "nurturing the youth," ensuring education for all, and "recognizing the role of women." Several photographs are especially captivating: reading the Qur'an by flashlight while on a hunting trip, shaking hands with Queen Noor of Jordan, laughing with his granddaughters, praying with a grandson, and playing volleyball on the beach.

The Internet

The young Emirati are an online group, connected through home computers, Internet cafes, and sophisticated mobile phones. My students quickly pointed me to the major Web sites on Sheikh Zayed, rattling off the URLs from memory. They frequently pull images from these sites to use as wallpaper for their computers. A look at the images of Zayed created via the Web then is especially important to get a sense of the images seen, and generated, by the younger generation. There are dozens of Web sites that feature Sheikh Zayed. Some sites are formal, official sites, giving the facts of Zayed's life and formal portraits. Some are corporate sites, giving a nod to the President by posting his photograph and perhaps a brief bio.[12] Many sites, however, are homage sites, built by students, faculty, and homesick expatriate UAE nationals.

Most of the formal sites are from governmental agencies or foundations. These are primarily text-based, such as the biographies posted by the Emirates Center for Strategic Studies and Research, www.ecssr.ac.ae/00uae.zayed.html; the central government site, www.uae.gov.ae/Government/sheik_zayed.htm; and www.zayedprize.org (the site for the Zayed International Prize for the Environment, a $1 million bi-annual prize for environmental achievement). Headings suggest consistency in presenting an heroic image of a man of goodness, generosity, and justice; a statesman; an advocate for the advancement of women; a man of faith; and a visionary who gets things done. A more interesting site is for the Ministry of Information and Culture, which publishes the on-line version of the *UAE Yearbook*. In each edition up to 2004, the first chapter is on Sheikh Zayed; however, remaining chapters lay credit for all advancements, cultural and economic, at his feet. The lead chapter, http://uaeinteract.com/uaeint_misc/pdf/English/Sheikh_Zayed.pdf, contains biographical information and a collection of photographs. The lead portrait, taken in his late 50s or early 60s, shows Zayed as strong and decisive. The other shots move from an early photo posed in front of an old truck, with him wearing traditional garb (*dishdasha*, *guttra*, and *jambeea* or knife) to one joining Sheikh Rashid to walk with a boy scout troop; from a "deep" conversation with little girls through meetings with international figures and, finally, to the now familiar image through the window of his car.

A far more dynamic site is an homage site created at the behest of Sheikh Mohammed bin Rashid al Maktoum, Crown Prince of Dubai: www.sheikhzayed.com. This flash site, available in either Arabic, English, French, German, or Japanese, begins with a series of water droplets rolling from a leaf into a pool, adds the recitation of a poem of dedication to Zayed backed by Arabic music, and segues through graphics of the desert to a city skyline with the image of Sheikh Zayed and the UAE flag ghosted on it. A whirling arc of images leads one to pages on his life, his leadership, his poetry, and UAE history plus a gallery of 25 photographs.[13] The guest books (in Arabic and in English) are also testimony to a deep affection for Zayed.

Other homage sites vary widely in quality and many are less than original (cheerfully borrowing text and photographs from other sites); still they offer direct insight into how people see their ruler and president. The most extensive of these are www.uaezayed.com and www.alshamsi.net/zayed. On all of them, visuals dominate text and much creativity is expended appropriating and recasting photographs of Zayed with Arabic design elements into postcards. The choice of photos also shows clear preference, with several showing up on site after site: four by Thesiger showing the Zayed of 1948; several of the middle-aged Zayed on hunting expeditions, often with falcons; and a series of specific photos of him riding a white horse, sitting under a palm surrounded by baskets of fresh dates, chatting with his granddaughters, praying with a grandson, laughing with Sheikh Rashid, walking through the tall grass, watching the flow of newly piped-in water into an ancient *falaj* (aqueduct), and several of the formal portraits. Few of the gallery images feature him with other rulers or dignitaries, Arab or international. These are instead personal images, images that show why he is loved, why he is of their world and yet still slightly beyond as their leader and life's model.

FINDING MEANING IN THE MEDIA IMAGES OF SHEIKH ZAYED

Analyzing the media imaging of Sheikh Zayed using the conceptual model that has driven recent work on changing media and the heroic would be difficult. Media practices in the United States are built atop centuries of developing literacy, with the shift from dominant oral cultures to a typographic media base having occurred long ago. Even the shift to electronic media, with the advent of radio and television, predates the existence of the UAE. In addition, the cultural norms for sharing information and for defining public and private are vastly different between the United States and the UAE (Walters & Quinn, 2003). We must search for another model to make sense of a context where all modern contributions to culture from the 14th century onward have occurred in less than 50 years, where a culture dominated by orality suddenly made a headlong leap into written literacy, digital television, and the Internet.

Northrup Frye offered a means of explaining multiple models of media development as well as the development of the heroic as part of the same process. Frye was not especially interested in media practices. He was interested in the nature of criticism, the best practices of which ought to be flexible enough to account for media development. In *Anatomy of Criticism,* Frye (1957) was attempting specifically to understand the nature of critical theory in terms of modes of literature, symbols, archetypes, and rhetorical genre. His essay on the theory of modes is particularly relevant. In it, Frye builds on Aristotle's *Poetics* to craft a model of the heroic in literature. Because rhetoric was the real-world analog of literature and the *Poetics* was considered by Aristotle as a companion work to the *Rhetoric,* the extension of Frye's work from literature to the real politic seems natural.

As Frye outlined five modes of the heroic, he argued that these are not absolute: whereas one mode may characterize a given age, the other modes still have a presence and cannot be discounted if one is to fully understand the literature in or the multiple trends of thinking within any given era. The modes that he outlines are the mythic, romantic, leader hero, commoner hero, and ironic. Each of these modes carries with it a unique type of poet or narrator, responsible for creating and maintaining the heroic narratives of an age.

Mythic Heroes

The first literary model of hero, according to Frye, is the mythic hero, "superior in kind" to people and the environment. This hero is a divine being, bound closely with the cultural identify of a people, and represented in their national (but not nationalistic) epics. These heroes are the gods and goddesses of the Greeks and Romans; the nature gods of indigenous peoples; the God of Judaism, Christianity, and Islam. The poet of the mythic hero is more oracle than mere journalist; examples include the Hebrew prophets, Native American shamans, and Brigham Young. The resulting accounts tend thus, according to Frey, to be encyclopedic, being collections of accounts, poetry, and sayings rather than ordered narratives with plotlines driving the shape of the text.

These heroes are not ones with whom people would interact directly, except through vision, divine revelation, or prayer. They are often present by reference, being used to legitimate the actions and beliefs of lower-order heroes. For American culture, the mythic ideals are primarily Judeo-Christian along with the nature gods of the Native Americans. For Islamic culture, Allah emerges as the monolithic mythic ideal. And, in its account of the revelation of the Qur'an (which parallels the revelations of the 10 Commandments and the gospels), Islam provides a "clear historical instance ... of the mythic mode in action" with the Prophet Mohammad as an archetypal example of the union of prophet, oracle, and poet (Frye, 1957, p. 55).

Romantic Heroes

The second level of hero is that of romance,[14] legend, and folktale, in which the hero is "superior in degree" to others and to the environment. These humans do "marvelous" acts in which the "ordinary laws of nature are slightly suspended," where extraordinary courage, conversations with animals, and enchantments are typical fare. This is the realm of "chivalry and knight-errantry" as well as the "legends of the saints" (p. 34). The context of the romance is almost a character itself. If the plot is comic and results in reintegration of hero and society, the setting may be "idyllic" and pastoral, "idealizing a simplified life in the country or on the frontier" (p. 43). If the plot is tragic and leads to disintegration, the setting may be hellish as the hero's failure is paid for by the whole of his people and his land (as with the dying land of the Fisher King in *Parsival*). The poets of this mode, as are its heroes, are of a "nomadic age" (p. 57) and offer the archetype of the troubadour, gifted rather than inspired, moving from place to place, collecting, preserving, and teaching the histories, stories, and traditions of a people. They are vital in an oral culture and bring news of other places and peoples in times of limited contact.

There are few heroes in this mode outside of fiction. They include the prophets of the mythic heroes (such as Moses, Jeremiah, and Mohammad). Those who enact true miracles also qualify, such as Joan of Arc, Francis of Assisi, Mother Teresa and the Dahli Lama. Other people may be described as knights or saints, but this tends to be metaphoric. The most important contribution of this mode for most real-world heroes is the concept of context as character. The image of Sheikh Zayed draws power from his placement against the vast canvas of the Arabian desert, a setting that only through nostalgia (or transformation) becomes "idyllic." He parallels in this the image of the cowboy, living on the vast plains and wastes of the American west. Neither Sheikh Zayed nor the American cowboy qualify as a romantic hero, but their settings add cache to their images.

Leader Heroes

The third level of hero, the leader hero, more closely resembles lived experience than does that of mythic or romantic hero. Still, there is a sense of elevation above the norm of humanity. As Frye put it:

> If superior in degree to other men [sic] but not to his natural environment, the hero is a leader. He has authority, passions, and powers of expression far greater than ours, but what he does is subject both to social criticism and to the order of nature. This is the hero of the high

> mimetic mode, of most epic and tragedy, and is primarily the kind of
> hero that Aristotle had in mind. (pp. 33–34)

This hero is associated with the "cult of the prince and the courtier in the Renaissance" (p. 35). In the tragic mode, this hero becomes isolated or distanced from society and experiences a fall as a result of a tragic flaw (e.g., Bill Clinton). In the comic mode, the hero eventually triumphs to "construct his (or her) own society in the teeth of strong opposition" (p. 43). Unlike the nomadic age of the romance, the leader hero typifies a time of settling down. The theme of these epics thus becomes nationalistic in tone and focus; distant quests are replaced with "symbols of convergence, the emblems of prince, nation, and national faith" (p. 57). As the gaze shifts inwardly to the king, court, or high council, the role of the poet shifts also, as he or she comes to serve the court and support the heroic leader.

This is a role legitimately ascribed to George Washington and Thomas Jefferson, Mohandas Ghandi and Martin Luther King, Jr., Nelson Mandela and Eleanor of Aquitaine. This is a role that requires participation in an epic life, with achievements of a sublime nature (and, occasionally, failures of epic proportions). Not all leaders, then, are leader heroes; only those who are elevated above the norm, who push beyond the mundane, become heroic (e.g., the dedicated, *al-muHsineen*). This is the mode that best captures the role of Sheikh Zayed. He is very much "a central figure who constructs his (or her) own society in the teeth of strong opposition, driving off one after another all the people who come to prevent or exploit him, and eventually achieving a heroic triumph, complete with mistresses [in this case, wives], in which he is sometimes assigned the honors of a reborn god" (p. 43).

Because the poet of the leader hero is charged with supporting the hero and using narratives of him or her to illustrate heroic leadership, a natural protection from exposure of one's wrinkles exists (at least in the comic form). This certainly fits with Sheikh Zayed, living in a context where public challenges of leaders is just not done. This reluctance to criticize him is not just the result of statute though, but also of deeply engrained norms that call for one to not shame another in public—challenge and criticism do in fact occur, but it is in private, in the *majlis* or through intermediation. In Zayed's case, where genuine affection and admiration dominated the feelings of his people, every citizen seems vested in maintaining his image as heroic, even to the point of setting aside whispers of fallibility on the basis that humans err and as such are subject to the judgment and forgiveness of Allah, not themselves. Zayed's narrative was until 2004 an epic of ascendancy; it offered birth without the parallel of death. It was a story without its last chapter, substituting an envisioned future to give an artificial sense of completeness. Curiously, the very concept of Zayed's death was considered literally unspeakable and was a topic about which there was mass denial.

People prayed for his long life, even offering their own life's energy to Allah for him; fearing that no leader could be to them what this most heroic of leaders was, they hoped against hope that he would somehow become the romantic hero who would not die.

Common Heroes

The action of the next heroic mode is centered in "common humanity" (p. 34). Here the lead character is in a narrative that insists on a level playing field. The hero, if he or she could be called that, represents one who is neither superior to others nor to the environment. Frye claimed that this quasi-heroic figure is a result of the emergence of a middle-class ethos, with an unwillingness to see any other above one's self and thus searching for heroes based on similarity in order to validate one's own place in life. This generates a continual tension between the urge to individuate and the urge to conform to the established norms of society. The tales are episodic rather than epic; short stories as well as serialized radio and television dramas and comedies are well suited to this form. This is the realm of domestic tragedy and melodrama, with pathos resulting from attempts to rise "above" one's self or from being excluded from the society to which one is entitled. The comic turn parallels "Cinderella" and "Beauty and the Beast" narratives where one is brought low (deservedly or not) or does not "fit" into society; circumstances eventually change, and the "hero" is either returned to his or her rightful position or finds a new place in a more comfortable setting ("Thumbelina"). The tragic turn introduces sensationalism and the pitifulness of characters who become isolated rather than individuated. So, the world hungered for every sensational detail of Princess Diana's life (and death), but the tale ended up as much about pity as admiration.

The poet of a tale of the common hero emerges as one of the most "intensely individualized" figures of a nominally individualistic society. Frye even argued that the poet of common humanity edges toward the status of the romance hero—a singular character offering "acts of individual creation," living "in a higher and more imaginative order of experience" (p. 59). Hence, we can see the elevation of the journalist, the bestseller novelist, and the actor, all of whom seem a bit higher than the common person, taking on the role of presenting us with images of ourselves.

This mode is the source of the everyday hero, the firefighter, the teacher, the baseball player, the personal heroes of one's family. In this realm, Rosa Parks, Charles Lindbergh, Helen Keller, and Jackie Robinson are all rightful heroes, normal people called by circumstance to step outside a society that did not "fit" to build something better, a something that eventually defined a new status quo. We look up to those who found or created a place to "fit" and call them heroes, perhaps because we too feel alienated and alone. Or, tragically, we find representations of ourselves who pay a terrible price. Some prices are exacted by external forces (Anne Frank); others by internal forces that lead one to "pretend or try to be something more than he is" or to exploit the sensationalism of fear or arrogance in order to avert pity (Mike Tyson) (p. 39). Cultural reactions to this latter type of "hero" begin to edge toward the ironic in our compulsion to expose imposters, to "cut them down to size." And, so we begin to dethrone heroes such as Thomas Jefferson for having lived as flawed humans, in his case owning slaves and having a relationship with Sally Heming. Such a situation invites a wrinkle theory approach (Gumpert, 1994). In pointing out someone else's wrinkles, we may no longer be threatened by someone who may be "better than me." The dark side of the strong individualistic bent of American culture thus may be to invite unwarranted scrutiny in order to insure that ultimately we are all equal, even if it is an equality of mediocrity. The tension then between wanting representatives of our selves elevated (thus to feel empowered) and wanting to see representatives of our selves deflated (in order to feel equal, or even superior) opens the door to a mediaocracy that can feed both desires.

In the UAE, there is clear evidence of the valuing of the common hero. Perhaps this is newly emergent, appearing with increased prosperity or even increasing exposure to mediated narratives on television, in film, and in print media. Or perhaps it has been present all along as a natural element of Bedu and Islamic culture, a tool to level out status for peaceful existence in small groupings. It may result from a life that demands everyday heroism simply in order to survive the harshness of life and which punishes the hubris of any individual putting him or herself above another. They have not escaped the dark side, however, and non-Emirati are often scapegoated for the ills that have come with progress. Ironically, the image of Sheikh Zayed may well gain power from the local concept of common heroism. Indeed, in a culture in which by tradition tribal leaders are chosen by consensus from among the adult males and are simply the first among equals, it is the emergence of Sheikh Zayed as a leader hero that is unusual. It may be the nation building required in the creation of the UAE at this time and in this place that has created a need for an heroic leader—and that part of the admiration and love for Zayed comes because he filled this role without violating the sense of being first among equals.

Ironic heroes

The final mode of the heroic for Frye moves beyond the quasi-heroic figure to the deposed or anti-heroic figure. This is the realm of the "ironic hero," a figure inferior to others and embedded in a narrative of "social revenge" (p. 45). In this intensification of the dark side of the commoner hero mode, narratives of scapegoating emerge allowing society to shift its collective guilt onto scoundrels who have tried to fit into proper society. The plotline involves exposing the impostor or revealing treachery from someone thought to be socially and morally acceptable or even honorable (O.J. Simpson). There is an element of savagery and brutality in this mode, according to Frye; the lynch mob is waiting just out of sight. The tendency to madness is accentuated when the object of revenge is someone who rose high in position or trust (Richard Nixon). There are dangers to this mode. A mob who suddenly finds itself the guilty party can be doubly dangerous, which can happen if we find ourselves gulled into targeting the wrong party or taking aim at a fool rather than a true scoundrel (Frye cites Charlie Chaplin as providing telling examples of this). Also, there is a danger of confusing the identity of the heroic figure—is it the person who exposes the "bad guy" or the "bad guy"? Is Luke Skywalker the hero? or is it Darth Vader? The popularity of brutal crime novels and horror films, featuring such horrific characters as Hannibal Lecter and the infamous Jason, are an example of where this ambiguity dominates.

The "poet" of the ironic tale can be a fearsome creature, with yellow journalism and witch hunts the norm. The hunt for details on which to hang a potential hero, often offered under the guise of the "search for truth," becomes the apotheosis of this mode. Bill Clinton can be impeached for a sexual dalliance while Jerry Springer makes millions by exposing (or imitating) social deviance. Everyone is open to exposure. Our failings are no longer part of the human condition, but we are open to attack for being too common, "all too human" (p. 317). Satire and ridicule become normal modes of operation, and the standards for behaving badly begin to blur—if the whole world is fallen, what does it matter if we are just one more in hell. Poetry becomes parody; fear and pity become terror; and "terror without an object, as a condition of mind prior to being afraid of anything, is now conceived as angst or anxiety" (p. 66), the generalized condition of us all in an ironic mode. It seems that the poet of the ironic mode may, in fact, aid and abet terrorism, making attacks and counterattacks the norm, a turn that easily invites the emergence of the anti-hero, the Osama bin Laden figure who responds against terrorism in one place with terrorism in another.

In these post-9/11 days, the turn toward the ironic is especially dramatic. The American Patriot act is scapegoating in its very nature, threatening key liberties and freedoms held by Americans in an attempt to gain control of an ambiguous situation. Words (unhappily) uttered by Stephen A. Douglas during in the American Civil War: "there can be but two parties— the party of the patriots and the party of traitors" have been brushed off and used to intimidate those whose take is different from the government's. Even the pop culture icons, the Dixie Chicks, have felt the hammer of "social revenge." For simply stating that they were "ashamed the president of the

U.S. is from Texas" (for the invasion of Iraq), they have been branded traitors, had their music boycotted by entire radio networks, had their CDs
burned, their belongings vandalized, and have received death threats
("Chicks defiant," 2003). This is scapegoating at its "finest"—non-thinking,
knee-jerk reactions, yet with the perpetrators of attacks on those who would
believe differently being held up as heroes.

The turn to the ironic seems to be slow to arrive in the UAE, with the
exception of press on Palestine. Searching out personal details of others is
neither polite nor legal. Attacking others through media outlets is inappropriate and bad form. (Not even comparative advertising is allowed because
it is considered rude!) Some people do stand in favor of bin Laden, in part
because they believe the West is scapegoating Arabs and Muslims, yet others worry that the ironic choices are not the good choices, that the only way
to step back from the precipice is to come to understand one another and to,
indeed, come to see ourselves in one another.

CONCLUSION

Current work in understanding the mediation of public heroes has led many
to hold that the inevitable product of an explosion of media technologies is
a world in which celebrity is more important than heroism, anti-heroes
thrive, and heroes are short-lived creatures, with their time in the public eye
determined by breadth of exposure and depth of invasion into their private
lives (Strate, 1994). This chapter challenges those assumptions, arguing
instead that the results of media are more complicated than simple presence.
Frye's model of the heroic modes gave a tool to help understand the significant differences in mediation of heroic images in the United States and the
UAE. It became clear that because of cultural norms, religious sensibilities,
and legal statutes that the media in these two countries functions very differently. It appears then that while the two countries are comparable in
terms of media technologies available, the result of the mediation is quite
different.

In the United States, where little privacy from the media remains and
where media workers freely dig for information, Gumpert's (1994) argument for the wrinkle theory holds. Through overexposure, audiences see
cracks in the image of a potential hero quickly and discard them just as
quickly, making it necessary to cycle through many heroes if one is to have
a hero at all. So although at least a few heroes may start out at the leader hero
level, media exposure quickly reveals their flaws and reduces them to commoner hero or ironic hero. In the UAE, however, there are still many social
and legal protections for individual privacy. And, although a potential hero

may make him or herself available to the media (and indeed must do so to be realized as a hero), it is the media that must be circumspect. This means that potential heroes may, if they possess the appropriate characteristics for hero-dom, reach that status; a leader hero may emerge and be maintained effectively in the public eye for a long time.

This approach to mediation of heroes also helps one to understand the phenomenon of "*Baba* Zayed." In a media environment that discourages the exposure of wrinkles, a man such as Sheikh Zayed can rise to a peak of public regard and adoration—and remain there. The images created of Zayed also seem to be images of extraordinary power in that they merge elements from three of the five heroic modes. He is placed within the setting of the romantic hero, having grown up in the desert (idyllic through nostalgia) while yet actively building, literally, toward a scene that is pastoral (idyllic in fact). He governed within the context of the leader hero, demonstrating nobility of spirit, nobility of character, and deep faith. And, yet, he maintained the touch of the commoner in a way that is heroic, being available to his people in *majlis* and out, joining in their joys and sorrows, and being integrated through representation in the very fabric of their daily lives. He represented the best of themselves, holding onto the traditions and character of the Bedouin, the "purest" of Arabs, grounding his personal and political will in the values of Islam, and using these qualities to guide his people into a new time of prosperity and peace, a time that offered to them a bit of paradise on earth. In the words of one of those interviewed, he was "the very best of us," a hero for his time and a legend for the future.

ADDENDUM

On November 2, 2004, Sheikh Zayed bin Sultan al Nahyan passed away. In keeping with the Gulf culture's norms that grant privacy to public figures (and perhaps a keen desire to work out quietly any last-minute political struggles that might have disrupted a transition of power), not a single word was leaked into the media during the 10 days Sheikh Zayed spent in the hospital critically ill. However, also in keeping with local traditions that give priority to face-to-face connections, it was clear that, of course, everyone in the country knew of his condition. We held our collective breath and waited for the end. Within a few hours of the announcement of his death, the entire country turned inward. Everything except essential services shut down for 3 days of deep mourning. Even the construction sites that provide the 24-hour background to life in Dubai and Abu Dhabi were silent, creating an eerie stillness. The government, schools, and most businesses remained closed for a full week—music was stilled, play areas were closed, even conversations were quiet, subdued, and often tearful. Official mourning continued throughout the 40 days traditional to Islam, with concerts cancelled, cinemas closed, and conferences rescheduled.

The media silence preceding Sheikh Zayed's death was replaced afterward by a media explosion. All radio and television stations, including satellite feeds, switched from regular programming to readings of the Holy Qur'an; these continued for a full week. Day after day, newspapers documented his life and accomplishments. Pages and pages were given over to letters from the community and to poems and stories from school children. Papers and magazines were also filled with full-page advertisements from companies and individuals expressing their prayers for his soul, their grief at his loss, and their condolences for his family and his people. Web sites were altered to carry memorials. Screen names for online chatting were revised to express sadness and respect. Cars and trucks displayed photographs of Sheikh Zayed and became an important site for unity in collective grief.

Coverage of Zayed's death internationally was widespread, but overshadowed by news of election returns in the United States and then by the death of Yasser Arafat, both much different models of a statesmanship of power and wealth. While *The New York Times* could not resist highlighting the "celebrity" aspect of what they called Zayed's "flamboyant" life, its November 3 obituary otherwise stands with a host of obituaries from around the world—from the *New Zealand Herald* to the *Pak Tribune*, from Al-Jazeera to the BBC—as testaments to both the heroic accomplishments of Sheikh Zayed and to the deep affection with which he was regarded. In the best tradition of romantic heroism, his death has secured his role as a public icon. The spirit in which this has occurred is perhaps captured best in the closing lines of the November 3 *Gulf News* editorial: "We say goodbye to our father Zayed. We remain steadfast in our love and loyalty for him. Zayed will stay etched in our hearts forever."

ACKNOWLEDGEMENTS

My thanks are extended to the 19 students in COM 205 Information Gathering, Fall 2002, and to 2 independent study students: Aisha, Alyaa, Amani, Amena, Amina, Asmaa, Ayesha, Dina, Fatema, Fatima, Huda, Maitha, Nada, Naema, Nawal, Noura, and Rawdha. Thanks especially to Hend, Sadiyah, Shaima, and Suaad, who went above and beyond; and Dahlia Abdul-Khaliq, whose translation skills helped make this happen.

ENDNOTES

1. Pronounced ShÇke Zi-ɔd bin sul-Tân al Nâh-hâ-yân.
2. The *mutawa* were religious schools children could attend to learn to read (or memorize) the Qur'an. No other subjects were covered. A student who completed the Text, which typically took 2 to 5 years, was considered graduated.
3. Obtaining biographical facts in the Gulf region is not always straightforward. Birth dates are difficult to determine because there were no official birth or death records kept before the 1960s and differences between Islamic and Gregorian calendars create variability in dating events. In addition, personal information falls under the realm of the private and thus is conscribed tightly. Custom and tradition literally and figuratively pull a veil over the parts of life that involve women. Statute disallows the publishing of most personal information as well as public criticism of rulers and policy (Walters & Quinn, 2003).
4. There are parallels in the American experience, which may increase understanding of the Bedouin ethos. This includes those Native American tribes that are traditionally nomadic as well as in the "frontier spirit," still arguably alive in the Dakotas, Montana, and Wyoming.
5. Patai's (2002) *The Arab Mind* is considered a standard work in mideast cultural studies. Based on extensive conversations with Emirati and Yemeni, I judge his schema of Bedu qualities to capture the *facts* of the characteristics well. His interpretations of their meaning and impact though are highly ethnocentric and racist and should be read with a shaker of salt.
6. Examples abound even today. At a Bedouin wedding in Dubai, I was told that "no one is ever turned away" and that many of the hundreds of guests inside the women's tent and outside in the men's area were not directly invited, but no less welcome. Any left-over food would be boxed for the poor as a mark of generosity. In Yemen, young men of the northern tribes told me tales of hospitality that give a new face to kidnappings that have front-paged the region. They told me of the French who were fed meat during their "stay" by a tribe itself too poor to eat meat, of a youth taking English lessons at great expense so that the American he was negotiating with (yes!) to kidnap would not feel lonely, and of the Germans sent home with gifts of honey and silver as a mark of the regard with which they were held by their "hosts." Kidnappings in Yemen are part of a millennia long practice of mutual hostage holding to prevent raiding from other tribes; to be honorable no harm must come to the hostages. Modern ones have been to pressure the government to provide such basics as water and schooling. Deaths occurred the single time the government decided to not "play by the rules," using force to gain the hostages "release"—they were actually shot by the government troops.
7. Students at Zayed University are female UAE nationals. There are many social restrictions that govern what they can or cannot do and to whom they can or cannot speak. This makes anything but a convenience sample impossible if one goes beyond the walls of our closed campus. Approaching strangers, male or female, and approaching males outside one's immediate family is out of the question. Males interviewed have to be close kin (fathers, brothers, grandfathers,

uncles, or husbands). A few students in progressive families were allowed to interview males outside the family, but with chaperones. Virtually all interviewed were family members, friends of family members, and school mates; these are the people with whom our students are allowed to interact. Given that this is a tight community with high degrees of similarity from family to family, the findings are probably still fairly representative. I am sure they even underestimate the overall sense of regard in which Sheikh Zayed is held as only 4% of those interviewed come from Abu Dhabi, his home emirate.

8. Just as many respondents expressed a negative view of bin Laden's behavior, concerned that he is unwise, choosing violence as first resort and against innocents. They worry that his actions, which many feel are anti-Qur'anic and *haram* (forbidden), paint the whole of Islam with the brush of radicalism. Opinions about bin Laden are polarized and highly controversial throughout the Middle East.

10. The specific Companions listing included Khaleed bin Al-Waleed (a Muslim general, know as the "Sword of Allah), Abu Bakr Al Sadeq (an early convert and first Khalif or successor to Muhammad), Salman al-Farisy (known as Salman the Good, a scholar and later governor near Baghdad who completed the first translation of the Qur'an into another language (Persian), Omar bin al-Khattab (the second Khalif or successor to the Prophet; he was martyred, stabbed during prayer), Bilal bin Rabah (a slave turned warrior for Islam and the originator of the formal call to prayer, still heard from every mosque five times a day), Hamzeh bin Abdul Mutalib (uncle to Muhammad and martyr, killed in battle to protect the faith), and Saad bin Abi Waqas (founder of the first Arab city beyond Medina dedicated to Allah, a city in what is now Iraq). In addition, two Imam's are identified. Imams are successors to Muhammad who claim descent through his son-in-law, Ali bin Abi Taleb, who was the second convert to Islam (after Mohammad's wife, Fatima) and a Companion. Imams are heroes for Shi'a Muslims; the disagreement over succession is the source of the split between Shi'a and Sunni. Imams listed include Ali himself as first Imam and Hussain bin Ali (Ali's son and second Imam).

10. The first question was asked following a series of items on personal values/traits and came before Sheikh Zayed was introduced as a topic. The second was one of the last questions asked and followed questions about memories of, feelings toward, and traits of Sheikh Zayed.

11. Until his illness and kidney transplant in 2000, Zayed spent a significant part of each year in the remote desert, living the simple life of his youth and practicing the hunting, falconing, and riding skills that are traditional to the Bedouin people and teaching these skills to his sons. This endeared him to his people, although the judgment of the effect on his sons (of which there are at least 19) is mixed. All but the oldest few grew up wholly in luxury and wealth. One wonders what impact this may have on the next generation of leadership for the country—even nationals (when one can get them to speak of it) fear what may happen when the inevitable occurs.

12. A look at the site for the Emirates Bank Group illustrates the use of portraits of the sheikhs that dominate public imaging: http://www.ebgannualreports.ae/2001/sheikhs.htm

13. This must-see site is highly evocative emotionally, even if it requires patience. Some flaws make the site frustrating. It is difficult to control the speed of visuals, one cannot skip the opening sequence on re-entering, and the back function does not work.
14. "Romance" here is in the sense of "an imaginative story," what today would equate with the fantasy genre. It is not used in the sense of a love story. The hero of today's romantic film and novel, if heroic at all, is heroic at the commoner level rather than at the romance level.

REFERENCES

Al-Baik, D. (2003, June 18). Exclusive: People will have governance role. *Gulf News*. Retrieved July 16, 2003, from http://www.gulf-news.com/Articles/news.asp?Article ID=90494

Al-Fahim, M. (1995). *From rags to riches: A story of Abu Dhabi*. London: London Centre of Arab Studies.

Al-Qubaisi, M.K.bin K. (2001). *Zayed: Man of the environment*. Abu Dhabi: Al Karawan Advertising and Publishing.

Arab rulers top "rich list." (1999, June 22). BBC News-internet. Retrieved April 15, 2002, from http://news.bbc.co.uk/2/hi/middle_east/374776.stm

Boy survivor of Sudan air crash flown to London. (2003, July 12). *Khaleej Times Online*. Retrieved July 16, 2003, from http://www.khaleejtimes.com/Displayarticle.asp?section=theworld&xfile=data/theworld/2003/july/the-world_july258.xml

Cathcart, R. S. (1994). From hero to celebrity: The media connection. In S. J. Drucker & R.S. Cathcart (Eds.), *American heroes in a media age* (pp. 36-46). Cresskill, NJ: Hampton Press.

Chicks defiant with interview, nude cover. (2003, April 25). *CNN.Com/Entertainment*. Retrieved July 20, 2003, from http://edition.cnn.com/2003/SHOWBIZ/Music/04/24/dixie.chicks/

Central Intelligence Agency (CIA). (2005a). United Arab Emirates. *World Factbook 2005*. Washington, DC: U.S. Government Printing office. Retrieved October 30, 2006, from http://www.cia.gov/cia/publications/factbook/geos/tc.html

Central Intelligence Agency (CIA). (2005b). Yemen. *World Factbook 2005*. Washington, DC: U.S. Government Printing office. Retrieved October 30, 2006, from http://www.cia.gov/cia/publications/factbook/geos/ym.html

Curtiss, R. H. (1995, December). The UAE: From bold dream to spectacular reality in one generation. (pp. 48-50,112). Retrieved April 15, 2003, from http://www.washington-report.org/backissues/1295/9512048.html

Dar, B.A. (1983). Ethical teachings of the Qur'an. In M. M.Sharif (Ed.), *A history of Muslim philosophy* (pp.155-178). Karachi, Pakistan: Royal Book. On-line: http://www.al-islam.org/historyofmuslimphilosophy/11.htm

Drucker, S.J., & Cathcart, R.S. (Eds.). (1994). *American heroes in a media age*. Cresskill, NJ: Hampton Press.

Fatima hospital set to open in Ramallah. (2003, July 10). *Gulf News*. Retrieved July 16, 2003, from http://www.gulf-news.com/Articles/news.asp?ArticleID=92231

Feminine issues in the United Arab Emirates: Perspectives of a visionary leader. (2000, November). Abu Dhabi: Zayed Centre for Coordination and Follow-up.

Fernando, N. (2001, December 6). Role models for all time. *30 years: Dream to reality. Gulf News Special on the 30th anniversary of UAE National Day*, p. 47.

Frye, N. (1957). *Anatomy of criticism: Four essays*. Princeton, NJ: Princeton University Press.

Gratitude, love, and sincerity parade. (n.d., prob. 2001). Abu Dhabi: Zayed International Centre for Coordination and Follow-up.

Gumpert, G. (1994). The wrinkle theory: The deconsecration of the hero. In S. J. Drucker & R.S. Cathcart (Eds.), *American heroes in a media age* (pp. 47-61). Cresskill, NJ: Hampton Press.

Kawach, N. (2003a, July 7). UAE in top spot on lowest Arab infant mortality rate. *Gulf News*, p. 6.

Kawach, N. (2003b, June 28). Zayed City taking shape in Gaza. *Gulf News*. Retrieved July 16, 2001, from http://www.gulf-news.com/Articles/news.asp?Article ID=91262

McLuhan, M. (1964). *Understanding media: The extensions of man*. New York: McGraw-Hill.

Murshed, M., & Hafi, M. (2003, July 6). Sheikh Zayed worked wonders. *Gulf News Tabloid*, p. 9.

Nation's jubilation over leader's safety. (n.d., prob. 2001). Abu Dhabi: Zayed International Centre for Coordination and Follow-up.

Ong, W. J. (1982). *Orality and literacy: The technologizing of the word*. New York: Methuen.

Patai, R. (2002). *The Arab mind* (rev. ed.). Long Island City, NY: Hatherleigh Press.

Rashid, N. A. (1996). *Abu Dhabi: Life and times through the lens of Noor Ali Rashid*. Dubai: Motivate Publishing.

Rashid, N. A. (1997). *The UAE: Visions of change*. Dubai: Motivate Publishing.

Rashid, N. A. (2001). *Sheikh Zayed: Life and times: Through the lens of Noor Ali Rashid*. Dubai: Motivate Publishing.

Sharif, M.M. (1983). Philosophical teachings of the Qur'an. In M.M. Sharif (Ed.), *A history of Muslim philosophy* (pp. 136-154). Karachi, Pakistan: Royal Book. On-line: http://www.al-islam.org/historyofmuslimphilosophy/10.htm (Original work published 1963–1966)

Sir Bani Yas: One Man's Vision: Mideast Magazine rpt. (2003, July 8). WAM/ Emirates News Agency. Retrieved July 10, 2003, from http:// www.wam.org.ae/2003 /Jul/08/909459.htm

Smith, H. (1986). *Islam. The religions of man*. New York: Harper & Row.

Strate, L. (1994). Heroes: A communication perspective. In S. J. Drucker & R.S. Cathcart (Eds.), *American heroes in a media age* (pp. 15-23). Cresskill, NJ: Hampton Press.

Swidey, N. (2003, April 5). Miracle in the desert: Dubai: Is this the new Middle East? *Halifax Herald Limited*. Retrieved July 8, 2003, from http://www.halifaxherald.com/ stories/2003/04/05/fJournal130.raw.html

United Arab Emirates yearbook 2003. (2003). Abu Dhabi, UAE: Ministry of Culture and Information. London: Trident Press. Online: http://www.uaeinteract.com/uaeint_misc/pdf/index.asp#year

Van der Meulen, H. (1997, May). *The role of tribal and kinship ties in the politics of the United Arab Emirates.* Unpublished doctoral dissertation, The Fletcher School of Law and Diplomacy, Tufts University, Medford, MA.

Walters, T., & Quinn, S. (2003). *Bridging the Gulf: Communications law in the United Arab Emirates.* Dubai: IdeasLab.

Wilson, G. (1999). *Father of Dubai: Sheikh Rashid bin Saeed Al-Maktoum.* Dubai: Media Prima.

Zayed: A photographic journey. (n.d.). Abu Dhabi: Emirates Heritage Club and Zayed Center for Heritage and History, United Arab Emirates.

Zayed calls for swift Iraq government formation. (2003, June 26). *Gulf News.* Retrieved July 16, 2003, from http://www.gulf-news.com/Articles/news.asp?Article ID=91262

Zayed gift saves California school from closing down. (2003, July 9). *Gulf News*, p. 7.

Zayed: The advocate of peace and noble deeds. (n.d.). Abu Dhabi: United Arab Emirates Committee of Public Culture and Improvement.

Zayed's noble deed (pardoning 6000 prisoners). (n.d.). Abu Dhabi: Zayed International Centre for Coordination and Follow-up.

Chapter 12

ORALITY VERSUS MONOTHEISM OR MEDIA VERSUS NARRATIVES

Biblical Heroes and the Media Environment of the Spoken Word

Eva Berger
School of Communication,
College of Management, Israel

Heroes are the products of specific eras of communication. The earliest heroes emerged from a media environment of the spoken word. In this chapter Eva Berger explores Jewish Biblical heroes Abraham, Moses and David. She asserts heroes of the Bible are essential to the fiber of the Jewish being, and considers these heroes with regard to narratives and their differences, including their distinct relations between man and G-d. To more fully consider the nature of "oral heroes," a comparison of oral heroes is offered by comparing the heroes of Ancient Greece with Jewish Biblical heroes.

❖   ❖   ❖

One of the commonplaces of our time is that the world's problems stem, at least in part, from a lack of fitting leadership; from a poverty of heroes deserving of the title. In his analysis of the place of America and the American Idea in the stream of history, Francis Fukuyama (1992), for example, described the triumphant West as facing the sheer ennui of normal life, ennui that manifests itself in an eccentric taste in heroes. Along the same lines, Charles Krauthammer wrote (1997), in an essay entitled "The End of Heroism": "Hard heroes are hard to come by today. When you are estranged from the experience—the very idea—of heroism as Americans are, you improvise" (p. 72). And he illustrated what he meant by improvisation. He provided a sample of some of the historical figures being lionized at U.S. theaters at the time of the writing of the article: one fascist (*Evita*), one Nazi agent (*The English Patient*), and a pornographer "with a penchant for sadistic misogyny" (*The People vs. Larry Flynt*). And he attributed this kind of unlikely heroism to the fact that Americans were living not in an antiheroic time (like the 1960s when it was important to make G.I. Joe into a scoundrel) but rather in a merely unheroic time. "These are inconsequential times, times of tranquility at home and abroad for Americans," he wrote, and inconsequential times do not require hard heroes.

If Fukuyama and Krauthammer are right, then the opposite of their thesis should also be true. In other words, in consequential, stormy times, hard heroes should be easy to find. And in today's America—years after the war in Iraq, six years after the September 11 attacks on the World Trade Center and The Pentagon—they are not. It is true that at one point, President George W. Bush, as well as General Tommy Franks, seemed to have the potential of rising, in the eyes of Americans, to heroic status. After all, the victory over Iraq was fast and effective and Saddam Hussein's regime was overthrown. The pictures of Saddam's statues being brought down in Baghdad and other cities and more so—the picture of Saddam's capture and humiliation—are the kind of pictures with the symbolic power to elevate presidents and generals to hero status. But criticism from home as well as from Europe and the UN is ongoing, and the proverbial "smoking gun" in the form of clear evidence of chemical weapons is still to be found. All of this, combined with the fact that bin Laden is still at large (at least by the time these lines are being written), and that pictures of looting, chaos, and dead American soldiers in Iraq are also quite prevalent, points to the fact that, despite it all, Americans are left, again, with no real heroes.

One exception to this absence of heroes is what may be called "category heroes," by which is meant organizations, institutions or groups of people (and not specific individuals) that, in the context of some historical event, are respected, admired, and elevated to hero status. Exceptions of such abstract category heroes are hundreds of "unknown soldiers" in all wars throughout history; millions of victims of the Holocaust; prisoners of war (POW); or the New York police and fire departments generally, and in the context of the September 11 attacks.

Because they are part of a group, these category heroes are faceless and abstract. Sometimes, television and other visual media, which are concrete and "all about faces," choose a specific individual out of the group, tell their stories, and make their heroic traits more tangible for the audience, like the girl painted red in the black-and-white *Schindler's List,* or Shawna (Johnson of El Paso, Texas), a POW captured by Iraqi forces, or the specific firefighter at the center of the first film about September 11 (with Sigourney Weaver). But these specific heroes are very local and temporary, and the categories of which they are part always prevail in the minds of the audience over their individuality. And so, as previously claimed, there are no real heroes in America today.

And the same is the case with today's beleaguered Israel. Six years have passed since the beginning of the El-Aqza Intifadah—the Palestinian uprising and subsequent Israeli military actions—that all but buried the hopes engendered by the Oslo Peace Agreements, and no breakthrough is in sight to put an end to the cycle of violence. The nightly news on television, as well as the hourly news reports on Israeli radio, are constant reminders that tranquility is not what characterizes the times in Israel. Despite the Palestinian authority's election of new prime minister (Abu Mazen) and his replacement with Abu Allah and U.S. pressure on both sides to adopt its "road map to peace," suicide bombers are still exploding in Israel's streets and train stations, the Israeli Army is still deep in the occupied territories, Chairman Arafat's quarters at the Muqata'a have been torn down, and the U.S. attack on Iraq brought back memories of more than a decade ago and fears (fortunately not materialized) of an Iraqi attack on Israel, this time using chemical or biological weapons. In other words, these are very consequential times. They require courageous decisions, intelligent moves, and heroic actions. These are heroic times—but where are the heroes?

This is the question at the heart of this chapter. For the purpose of trying to answer it, two ideas—that are in a certain sense opposites of each other, or at least partially contradictory—have been brought together. The first idea is that the medium by which a story is told, influences its content. In other words, we experience heroes through stories, and not all stories are alike. They can be told, or written down, or be made into a movie or a television program. Each one of these forms of communication (the spoken word, writing and print and electronic media) have changed the way in which we disseminate information and tell stories. This has changed the stories themselves, and the heroes in them. Heroes become famous through the dominant medium of communication of their culture, so that when the dominant medium of communication changes, so does the nature of the hero.

The second idea used here is that all cultures have heroes, but the heroes themselves vary from culture to culture, and cultures are different from each other in more ways than their modes of communication. As Lance Strate (1985) said:

> The hero can best be understood as an aspect of culture, a part of a society's collection of symbols or totems. The hero is a human figure that

serves as an object of admiration, aspiration, and at times, worship. The
story of the hero's life is a codification of a culture's values, beliefs and
prescribed behaviors. (p. 47)

The second idea is, in other words, that although codified in written,
spoken or broadcast form, the hero may get his characteristics not from the
language or symbol system used to tell about him, but from the values,
needs and beliefs of those who tell about him.

The lack, or at least relative poverty of heroes in Israel, may be
explained by the first idea. Israel is a modern, industrialized, technological
society, similar, at least in this way, to many other Western countries, where
technological innovations generally, and new media of communication
specifically, have altered people's ways of thinking, acting and communicat-
ing. With the introduction of private stations and cable, and a general move
toward privatization and a free market economy, television has become an
integral part of Israelis' life. Alarming numbers and statistics of literacy rates
(similar to those in the United States) flood the scholarly literature in education; prime ministers began, in 1996, to be elected through direct-person-
al elections (and not by their party as before—although this law has now
been revoked); and missionary media-rabbis can be found on tapes, videos,
and television. It may be, then, that regardless of a culture's character, when
television and other visually oriented-entertaining media are introduced,
changes take place in that culture's psyche that impose themselves and make
old values, beliefs, and heroes obsolete. It may be, on the other hand, that
Israel's rich history, tradition and heritage, filled with hard, deep, interesting
heroes, cannot be erased, even by television, and the answer to the question
of lack of such heroes today, is found somewhere else. This is where the second idea comes in, and where a need for an historical analysis of heroes past
becomes apparent.

For the purposes of such an analysis, Strate's (1991) study has been used,
and his classification of heroes based on eras of communication is applied to
Jewish history and culture. The scope of this chapter does not allow for an
analysis of Jewish heroes throughout all of Jewish history. And so, Biblical
times (Jewish culture at the point of its very inception), and the Bible—its
narratives and its heroes—have been selected as the database for analysis and
discussion of their characteristics in relation to the media environment of the
spoken word.

Daniel Boorstin (1978) defined a hero as a human figure admired for
courage, nobility, or exploits, and he emphasized intrinsic greatness and
achievements as essential qualities. The definition in this chapter, too,
emphasizes admiration over any specific qualities, so that human beings
who are the object of worship, admiration, or imitation are regarded as
heroes. The selection of the specific heroes for analysis, however, was not a

simple one, as the vast majority of figures in the Bible fit this general definition. The period in question is, after all, the time when the Jews had the most
profound and lasting influence on world civilization. In the end, the Biblical
heroes were selected on the basis of an internal division of the period into
the different stages in the dialogue between God and the people. Inherent to
these stages are types of heroes: the patriarch, the leader, and the king. And
Abraham, Moses, and David represent them, respectively. There are two
more types of heroes in the Bible: the judge and the prophet, examples of
which are important figures such as Samuel and Jeremiah. However, under
the considerations for selection here, they seem less central.

The first purpose of this chapter is to find out whether Biblical heroes
are typical oral heroes. In other words, to assess the weight of the spoken
word and the oral media environment it creates in comparison to the subjective cultural conditions of life during Biblical times in the definition of the
conception of heroes and heroism. The second, more general purpose of the
chapter, is to try to make some generalizations regarding the question of the
weight of cultural contexts and the needs and values of people in those contexts, in comparison to media environments generally, in defining heroes.
Such generalizations may provide a glance into what we may expect in terms
of heroes in the midst of the turmoil that characterizes these consequential
times, our global environment, and our changing cultures.

BIBLICAL TIMES

The term *Biblical Times* encompasses a long period, characterized, at different stages, by very different historical events, lifestyles, and figures.
Moreover, the Bible, the document that tells of Biblical times is, itself, the
product of writing over a period of more than 1,000 years. Nevertheless, the
existence of the term suggests that there are certain generalizations that can
be made about Biblical times, and that the period has been marked as having
a beginning and an end, all of which provides the basis for a discussion of
specific aspects of the era, and in this case, of its central figures or heroes.

The description of Biblical times begins with Genesis, the first Book of
the Bible, which opens with an account of Creation, describes the origins of
humankind, and ends with the close of the patriarchal age. The account of
Israel's history begins in the Book of Exodus: the liberation from Egyptian
bondage molds the Hebrews into a people, the Revelation at Mount Sinai
lays the foundation of their religion, and the erection of the Tabernacle gives
them their first national shrine. For 40 years, the Israelites continue to wan-
der in the wilderness and finally conquer parts of Transjordan. The
Pentateuch concludes with the death of Moses. Apart from its narrative sec-

tions, the Bible contains large amounts of legislative material. The Former Prophets are historical works. They describe Joshua's conquest of Canaan, the troubled times under the Judges, the work of Samuel, the inauguration of the monarchy under Saul, its consolidation under David and Solomon, the partition of the country into two kingdoms, and the history of the divided monarchy until the destruction of the northern kingdom of Assyria (722 B.C.) and of Judah by Nebuchadnezzar (586 B.C.). The Later Prophets include the books of Isaiah, Jeremiah, Ezekiel, and the twelve (Minor) Prophets. The Hagiographa is a literary mix, including devotional poetry, aphorisms, lamentations and reflections, as well as historical descriptions and accounts.

This is an outline of the traditional story. There are, of course, multiple interpretations of this story, and of the book that gives these times their name. The traditional account of the story of the Hebrews embodied in these historical books of the Jewish Scriptures is viewed by some as a literal, faithful and exact account of the events and lives of people at the time. Others (who subscribe to the modern critical view) do not, like radicals do, question the veracity of the traditional story in every detail, but accept it as an outline, and study it using the tools of modern day disciplines, such as archaeology, anthropology, and comparative literature and history. For these latter critics and writers the question of authorship in the Bible is a very central one. They see the works of the Bible as literary texts composed by fallible humans with a point of view (and not as the received Bible of the normative traditions). It is only within such a paradigm and based on such assumptions that a book titled *Who Wrote the Bible?* (Friedman, 1987) could have been written. In this book, its author, Richard Friedman, explains that the effort to discover who wrote the Bible began and continues because the answer has significant implications for both the traditional and the critical study of the Bible. The questions at the heart of Friedman's book are those such as: When did the author live (the eighth or the fifth century B.C.)? Did the author witness the events in the story? If not, how did the author come to have an idea of what happened? Was it through written sources, old family stories, divine revelation, or completely fictional composition?

Similar questions are at the basis of yet another book—*The Book of J* by Harold Bloom and David Rosenberg (1990). Here, Bloom, the interpreter among the authors (Rosenberg is the translator), assumed that the Bible, which has formed the spiritual consciousness of much of the world ever since its writing, was written by a woman (J), living at the court of Solomon's son and successor, King Rehoboam of Judah. According to Bloom, the author was also not a professional scribe, but a member of the Solomonic elite, writing for her contemporaries. Furthermore, Bloom believes that the Torah is not "any more or less the revealed Word of God than are Dante's *Commedia*, Shakespeare's *King Lear*, or Tolstoy's novels"

(p. 11). Rather, he regarded the Bible as a library of literary texts, and Yaweh, in the Book of J, a literary character. Thus, for Bloom, as for Ralph Waldo Emerson whom he quoted, the place which the Bible holds in the world, it owes not to miracles, but to the fact "that it came out of a profounder depth of thought than any other book" (p. 16).

This chapter takes this modern, critical approach. It does not see the central figures described in the Bible as necessarily having existed exactly when and as described, but it assumes the existence of real figures, upon whose deeds and lives those of the figures told about by the text were based. For example, there are those who question whether Abraham ever existed. And it may be that, if he did exist, it was simply as an outstanding personality, to whom many of the shrines of Palestine traditionally owed their foundation, and not as the ancestor of the Hebrew people. Isaac and Jacob, too, are regarded sometimes as semi-symbolic figures, perhaps representing a tribal motif (Roth, 1961). In this sense, the Bible is similar to the *Iliad* and the *Odyssey* where many stories and themes may be older than the heroes they are attributed to. One thing is certain: Whether true historical figures, mythical heroes or composite characters denoting entire tribes in a story true only in its most basic outline, the heroes of the Bible are part of the fiber of the Jewish being. They are admired, quoted, imitated and followed even to this day. They are thus heroes under the definition used in this book and probably under most other definitions. And the question is then, what are these heroes like? Do they follow a pattern? Do they have any characteristics in common?

On the most basic, surface level, and at least in the latter sense, they seem to be very much like oral heroes, such as the heroes of Ancient Greece. But in order to go deeper into their characterization, a characterization of both oral environments and of oral heroes must precede so that a comparison is possible.

THE KEY CHARACTERISTICS
OF AN ORAL MEDIA ENVIRONMENT

In an oral media environment, all information is stored only in the human-biological memory. The ability to retain this information is achieved through practice and repetition. What this means, among other things, is that it is hard to preserve the information over time. Therefore, oral societies are conservative, or traditional (Ong, 1982). In other words, they value the old over the new, and transmit it from generation to generation to preserve the social heritage and the culture. Because it is preserved only in the human memory, the information comes out differently in each performance: details are added or omitted, the order of events is changed, the end of the narrative is altered, and so on. Thus, preservation in oral cultures is done through variation (or in spite of it, in our literate terms). And this includes the omitting of information no longer relevant to the present. Oral cultures are economical. Many stories and themes are condensed into one and the deeds of many figures attributed to one.

What all of this means is that, in oral societies, the ability to store information over time is limited. And so is its transmission over space. The latter is dependent on the former. Without electronic media that separate the concept of communication from that of transportation, messages must be physically transported over space and must be stored during the period of transportation. The messages must be cast in mnemonic formulas so that they are preserved in the messenger's mind for delivery. Transmission also depends on the means of transportation available. And without writing, messages can only be transported orally by a messenger by foot, on a horse's back or by ship. (And even if there are early forms of writing systems in Ancient Greece or in later Biblical times, there are not yet significant supplies of light, easily transportable writing surfaces like papyrus).

Other characteristics of oral media environments are the slow speed or slow rate of diffusion of information (stemming mostly from the previous two limitations: storage over time and transmission over space), and the small quantity of information that can be made accessible due to the limited preservation ability of the human memory. (This, of course, despite the fact that, compared to our own, literate memory, oral memory is stronger. We can depend on printed and otherwise stored information, which atrophies our memories).

Although the volume of information in oral cultures is relatively small, the information itself is very accessible. To decode information in such cultures, all one needs is competency in the language used. Therefore, by around the age of seven, all members of the culture have full access to the information. Accessibility is further increased by the fact that the techniques used for memorization, composition and performance (such as repetition, formulas and cliches), are also helpful in its reception. Limitations of access, when they exist, are due to the fact that certain kinds of information may be regarded as the exclusive property of certain groups (such as men or women, authority figures, priests or medicine men or women, leaders, judges, or the old).

The special form of presentation of the information is one last characteristic of the oral media environment. The form is characterized by various elements but it can generally be referred to as retention-centered (because memorability is key). The oral tradition includes short sayings, songs, and poems, as well as epic narratives. The latter is regarded as the highest form of oral composition and is studied extensively. One of its major features is its narrative form. This form allows the inclusion of large amounts of information that are also easy to repeat. The epic song is formulaic and is often a stitching together of many sentences, verses and themes. Short songs are also combined to form longer narratives. (This may be the reason why they lack tight plotting). The oral epic is episodic, not linear, so it disregards temporal sequence. This is easy to understand if one thinks of how often in conversation, we go back to tell of something we forgot. On the other hand, this does not happen as often in writing (except for in cases when flashbacks are used as a stylistic choice).

Knowledge in an oral culture must be conceptualized in a form that is "close to the human life-world" (Ong, 1982); that is situational and not abstract; that comes out of the context of the experience of the people listening to it, and not in the form of lists and categories, or abstract rules or theories. The narrative form provides this necessary context and, again, makes the events memorable.

The action described in oral narratives is filled with conflict and struggle. It is agonistic (Ong, 1982). Combat and verbal conflict, physical contest, and name-calling are all central elements, as well as the exchange of proverbs and insults. And because combat and struggle are generally cooperative activities, the agonistic quality of the narrative action is complemented by the presence of strong positive feelings such as loyalty and friendship. But both conflict and cooperation are taken to extremes (again for the sake of memorability). The form that information takes in oral cultures, then, is a product of the oral mindset.

THE KEY CHARACTERISTICS
OF THE ORAL HERO

A media environment of the kind described here, brings about heroes of a certain kind, with various identifiable characteristics. These are characteristics of the heroes of eighth century B.C. Greece, as presented by Strate (1991). Strate claimed that they can be regarded as traits characteristic of oral heroes generally, as he describes these as being characteristics not only of the cultural conception of the hero in eighth century B.C. Greece, but "in oral media environments in general" (p. 78). And whether this is so is, of course, the question at the heart of this chapter.

According to Strate (and to Ong, 1982, and others before him) oral heroes are, first and foremost, characterized by their abilities. These mythical and legendary heroes have a greater power of action than our own. They have extraordinary if not fantastic abilities. They are exceptional individuals, apart from any identification with the divine. Some have the gift of superhuman strength or might, whether or not it is balanced by artifice. Other heroes display their knowledge of strategy, others their courage, and others still are known for their wisdom (usually stemming from experience and advanced age).

As for their moral character, it is closely related to their abilities. Cowardice and immorality, for example, very often go together. Moral errors generally are punished, and even without divine retribution, they are the cause of strife and unhappiness among mortals. These moral errors include unfaithfulness, lasciviousness, pride, and arrogance. Morality, on the other hand, is represented by traits and virtues such as hospitality, loyalty (marital, filial, or of a servant), patience, and chastity.

The appearance of oral heroes (at least the heroes of Ancient Greece) also plays a role in their characterization. Ugliness, for example, is characteristic of villains and monsters. Physical beauty is associated with women, and is not valued for its own sake among men. Moreover, for a man, vanity about one's appearance is vilified. Male heroes may be described as handsome, but this is derived from their might and social status. Generally, descriptions of appearance in oral epics are stereotypical, with very little detail (aside from descriptions of the unusual and the bizarre).

The heroes' social status is of kings or princes. They are generally aristocratic and they value symbols of status such as spoils and prizes from contests. They are honor-sensitive and are concerned with both concrete objects and wealth, as well as with titles. As for their occupation, they are usually political and military leaders. They are also athletes and masters of other trades such as sailing and singing of tales. They possess extraordinary abilities and qualities. They are superior in might, stature, good looks, artifice, wisdom, morality, leadership, and eloquence. The acts performed by these heroes are consistent with these abilities and qualities. Physical action is stressed to demonstrate their abilities, whether it is performed in battle or in other contexts such as travel, exploration, navigation, and athletic contests. Physical acts are complemented by speech acts, so that physical contest is very often preceded by verbal conflict in the form of insults, taunts, and statements of blame. And speech acts are also positive, as is the case with accomplished singers of tales.

The scene in which oral (or at least Ancient Greek) heroes perform their acts is varied. It is a mixture of local and foreign, known and unknown settings. The places are combinations of imagination and fact, of the real and the supernatural worlds. And there are places such as Sacred Mountains that are common mythical symbols and represent the bridge between heaven and earth. Although the scenes vary, the heroes themselves are local to the culture in which they are admired (under certain conditions this can be transcended to some degree). And although local in terms of space, the heroes are distant from the society in which they are admired in terms of time. In other words, oral heroes are figures from the past.

These are, then, the main characteristics of the oral media environment and of the oral hero. What follows is a detailed description of the heroes of the Bible and a comparative analysis of their characteristics to those presented earlier.

THE HEROES OF THE BIBLE

Abraham

Abraham is the first patriarch. And the term *patriarch* must be clarified, as it is a current conception that is not quite correct (Buber, 1963), although it is used here as it is in most sources. Patriarch implies a certain kind of leadership, and no true rulership or leadership is exercised at this time, as there are as yet no people to lead. The conception indicates a way along which the people are to be led beginning with these men. They are Fathers. It is for them to beget a people. They are those from whom this tribe proceeds. When God speaks to them or blesses them, the same thing is always involved: conception and birth, the beginning of a people. With Abraham and the other patriarchs, we are at the peculiar point in biblical history where God narrows down his original plan for all of mankind and causes a people to be begotten (called to do the work toward the completion of the creation, the coming of the kingdom).

Abraham is, then, the first Father. The Father, one must add, of three great Semitic religions—Judaism, Christianity, and Islam. He is the ancestor of the Hebrew and Arabic peoples, referred to or described in different places and on various occasions as seminal prophet (Gen. 20:7), model of holy obedience, believer in and recipient of a personal covenant with his single, eternal God, and repository of all wisdom and science. Abraham is the symbol of humility, hospitality, and kindness (Gen. 18).

Until the 18th and 19th centuries, most people assumed that Abraham really existed. The stories of the Bible were accepted with faith. Then philosophers such as Hegel began to rationalize the lives of the patriarchs, imposing contemporary concepts on age-old tales. But later, archaeological digs at Abraham's birthplace (the city of Ur on the banks of the River Euphrates near the Persian Gulf), and the discovery in recent years of ancient tablets corroborating many of the names of his relatives, friends and enemies, appeared to confirm his history. Ruins exposed confirm that he was a sheik of a group of nomads or outcasts called the Habiru (later the Hebrews). This was a group of non-city dwellers, who wandered from place to place, settling for short periods, and who served as mercenaries and traders. Wherever they roamed, they kept their language and beliefs. Their religion was portable, thus Abraham was the first wandering Jew. The Bible records his moving around the Middle East, from his birthplace near the Persian Gulf, through the land of Canaan, to Egypt and back to Hebron. Along the way, he negotiated treaties with local kings, acted as hired soldier, and purchased burial plots from the Hittites. As a pilgrim he made his progress across deserts and mountains, and he did not immediately become the great prophet of legend. His wanderings exposed him to personal danger and hardship. He was first called Abram, and later Abraham, as he was transformed by his experiences and faith into a new man.

Abraham's tale first made clear the delicate nature of Jewish life through the ages: While the Canaanites prayed to their old God El for a good harvest and a long life, Abraham expanded such worship to include the concept of a land promised forever to one people. This novel covenant-as-lease and not as a perpetual gift (unique to the Jewish religion) may be revoked if God's laws are not carefully followed. Heavenly grace and favor are won only after an anxious existence, which includes multiple tests (the supreme test of Abraham's faith in God being the command to sacrifice his son Isaac).

The scriptural narrative of Abraham's life begins with the call of God received by him at the age of 75, instructing him to leave his homeland and proceed to an unknown destination that later proved to be the Land of Canaan (Gen. 12:1-5). Midrashic legend, in Aramaic, however, provides dramatized accounts of his early years and tells, for example, of how he smashed his father's Terah idols exclaiming, "They have mouths, but they speak not. They have ears, but they hear not. Noses have they, but they smell not. They have hands, but they handle not. Feet have they, but they walk not!"

Abraham was a dissenter from the start, and found no intellectual encouragement in his environment. And it is this dissent and the wrath it provoked in his contemporaries that eventually forced him to go into a life of hiding and wandering with his family. His skepticism persisted and set him ever farther apart. Other stories about his formative years point to this same trait: precocious unwillingness to accept ideas without questioning. His disputes culminated, when he matured, in a new theory of life and the universe—a theory of an invisible God. This was a revolutionary idea for that ancient era. The natives of Ur were polytheists and they had a variety of theories about the world's creation. They had rituals around all of the gods and all of the theories—from fertility to human sacrifice and Abraham was opposed to them all. To set himself apart, he finally initiated all the male members of his household into a formal acceptance of a new concept of the sacredness of the human body and of its functions. By this symbolic act of circumcision, the clan was set apart through a physical sign. This was his covenant with God.

The Jewish chronicles describe Abraham as a soft-spoken, gracious man, friendly host to wanderers who appeared at his home, devoted husband, father, and uncle. He is described, too, as capable of indignation, when the honor and safety of his family were at stake. When he was quite an old man, he set out with an untrained army of 318 domestics in pursuit of marauders who had abducted his nephew and, after a bloody battle, brought the nephew back alive.

Abraham's wandering continued until, finally, he and his family began to feel at home in Canaan. No matter where they journeyed, they always tried to reach back for that land, where Abraham died at the age of 175, and was buried in the cave of Machpelah.

Moses

Abraham's covenant with God was personal. Moses' covenant, however, reached a new level of sophistication as it was a covenant on behalf of an entire people. Unlike Abraham who, as aforementioned cannot be considered a real leader, Moses was the prototype of a leader and a lawgiver. In the ancient Egyptian language, Moses, or Mosheh, means "born of" or "is born"; the Hebrew masheh translates as "drawn of." Whatever the origins, Moses' life story dominates the Bible. He was the most exemplary of the Hebrew prophets and probably the most influential Jew in all history. As either a model or a real man, he brought to human life a concern for the downtrodden, an idealism, a hope, a system of laws by which people can survive each other. Through Moses, God directed mankind.

Moses, son of Amram and Jochebed of the tribe of Levi, was born at the height of Egyptian persecution, when Hebrew male infants were drowned at birth. After a period of hiding, Moses' mother placed him in a casket among the Nile reeds. He was rescued by Pharaoh's own daughter and brought up in the royal palace. When he grew up and learned of his origin, he became interested in his enslaved brothers, and one day, he killed an Egyptian taskmaster he had caught beating a Hebrew. He fled across the Sinai Peninsula, past the wilderness of Paran, to the northwest Arabian Desert, into the land of Midian. There, he became a cattle breeder working for the local priest Jethro, and married his daughter Zipporah, with whom he had two sons. When he was 80, he witnessed God in the Burning Bush at Mount Horeb and he sensed a "call" to return to Egypt and lead out his people. Moses, as the ancient scroll describes him, was a devout Hebrew, and he sensed his call as God's will, as Divine command. In other words, he looked upon himself (despite his natural humility) as an emissary summoned by God to forge a nation out of the descendants of Abraham. So he returned to Egypt and there, with the help of his brother Aaron (who was his assistant and interpreter as Moses, we are told, spoke sluggishly and ineloquently), he appeared before Pharaoh and demanded in the Lord's name "Let my people go!" Ten plagues reinforced his demand and the

Hebrews were released. Pharaoh then changed his mind and set out to pursue them, but his whole army drowned in the Red Sea. Moses had the courage, know-how, and strategy to lead the oppressed in such a revolt. And it is the Jews' flight from Egypt, the Exodus, rather than the Creation, that defined the Jewish people.

The next major event in Moses' life was the giving of the law at Sinai. There would have been no point in leading his people out of Egypt, Moses reflected, without an objective other than their physical freedom, without a way of life that would set them apart from Egyptian religious practice, from blind superstition, and from brutal barbarism. So Moses retired solitarily to the mountains to prepare for a constitution that would weld his people together. The Decalogue (or Ten Commandments) and other laws (613 primary prohibitions and mandates, statutes, judgments, and testimonies) were given by God directly to Moses (and not conceived by him), and Moses, as the agent for their transmission, bound the people in a Covenant to the Lord. These laws (regarding private property, human life, sexual morality, filial relations, the honor of neighbors, etc.) were partly inscribed on clay tablets and papyrus rolls, and much of it, we are told, was transmitted orally to the elders. Thus, these laws—the Sinai Covenant—are known in Hebrew as Torah and Halakhah (written and oral law). Simple justice and respect for life were established in Sinai as the controlling forces of humanity.

Along with this Covenant, Moses also built the Tabernacle or "Tent of Meeting," which was to serve as a symbol of God's presence among them; he expounded sacrificial practices, and organized a judicial system. During the first period of wandering, Moses often clashed with some of the people. One such case was brought about by the sin of the Golden Calf, when upon his descent from Mount Sinai, he found some people in a drunken idolatrous frenzy around the calf. This led him to shatter the tablets of the Covenant but, more importantly, to understand that it would not be easy to purge them of the superstitions they had accumulated in a land where people always thought in graphic forms. (Thus Moses' second injunction forbidding any "graven images.")

Moses led Israel for 40 years through the desert until the old generation died and a new generation that could be brought into Canaan had grown up. He was himself forbidden to come into Canaan (as punishment for an act of disobedience). And so, before his death, he appointed Joshua as his successor and in a public farewell address that inspired a feeling of spiritual separatism in the hearts of his people, summarized the past 40 years and the laws laid down at Sinai. He blessed the people, gave them guidance for their life in Canaan, and died at the age of 120 and was buried at a place unknown "unto this day" (Deut. 34:6).

Moses was a prince in Egypt, then a killer, an outcast, a shepherd, a liberator of slaves, a receiver of God's laws, a judge, a conqueror, a prophet.

He was versed in Egyptian science and philosophy (having been educated at the officers' academy), and he understood warfare (for he had successfully conducted an Egyptian campaign against the Ethiopians). His every act had rich, symbolic meaning: The burning bush that is not consumed, for example, manifests God's omnipotent control over nature. (It has also been seen as a symbol of Jewish survival and of the visionary wisdom of Moses.) And the Golden Calf marks the end of worship of animals. The calf itself and anyone who bows down to it are condemned and destroyed in fury.

Moses was, above all, a prophetic lawgiver, preparing his people for a new and unique religion, the basis of which is complete monotheism and loyalty to God. (This concept was, of course, nurtured by Abraham, but Moses gave it form and substance.)

Moses, who is portrayed by the Bible as the greatest of all prophets; as the one who, alone among men, knew God "face to face," is revered by Christians and Moslems, too. The traditions established by him defined the Jewish people (as he transformed them from a horde of slaves into "a treasured people") and formed the basis of the other two great monotheistic religions: Christianity and Islam.

Despite all his greatness, however, Moses always remained a mortal, fallible human being. He was a man with faults like other men, never a minor god. He represents the passionate and self-sacrificing leader, liberator and teacher—the first faithful shepherd of God's flock.

David

David was the second king of Israel (reigning around 1010–970 B.C.). He was the most successful and popular king Israel ever had, the archetype king and ruler. David was the youngest son of Jesse, of the tribe of Judah. His name may be derived from the term *davidum*, which signifies a military marshal. He was born in Bethlehem where, like Abraham and Moses, he herded sheep. He is described as "skillful in playing and a mighty man of valor and a man of war, and prudent in affairs and a comely person and the Lord is with him" (I Sam. 16:18). At the age of 25, he became armor-bearer to Saul, friend of his son Jonathan, and, after displaying his military prowess in war with the Philistines, husband of Saul's daughter, Michal. At the age of 30, he was crowned king after Saul's death in the battle of Gilboa, and he proceeded to conquer Jerusalem, which he made the capital of his kingdom. (David's kingdom was, at first, two separate national entities with separate contracts with him personally, and only later a coordinated nation.) Of immense importance to the future course of history was David's placing of the Ark in Jerusalem, signifying a cultic unification emphasized later by the erection of Solomon's Temple. Jerusalem became the "City of David."

During David's reign, the kingdom expanded considerably. He crushed armies and broke military powers (such as the Philistines, Ammon and Moab, and Aram) and annexed large tracts of territory. Internally, he made preparations for building a central temple and organized the national administration. With this centralized national government, the tribes coalesced into one homogeneous political unit. His reign gave coherence and an international resonance to Jewish affairs. Shapiro (1994) explained that by David's example, God's covenant with the Jewish people, ". . . was channeled into everyday life through a humane method of governing, the enlightened rule of a constitutional monarchy" (p. 49) or as Johnson (1987) called it: "theocratic democracy" (p. 59).

As a monarch, David did not dictate to his subjects absolutely, and he listened to their will. He despised oppression and believed in the concepts of justice, freedom, and responsibility, all of which served as models for constitutional government in later eras and in other places. He was a popular king, and a model leader of fighting men, but he could not control his own family or his own passions, which often led to disastrous consequences (such as the death of his son Absalom, committing crimes of passion in open revolt against the established order, or his own shipment of Bathsheba's husband to die in battle after failing in his other attempts to legitimize her adulterous pregnancy).

This and many other examples fill the biblical record of David's life story. It portrays his complex character in great detail. He is described as shepherd, mercenary, bandit, statesman, warrior, conqueror, slayer of Goliath and empire builder; lyric singer, poet and ritual dancer; friend, lover, polygamist, and adulterer; as father and as king. He is presented in high as in low tide of fortune, sinning, ruled by his passions, and repentant. The Bible depicts both his virtues and his vices.

Tradition ascribed to him the composition of many psalms and also the organization of Temple music. In later generations, his qualities became the ideal of Israelite kingship. Agaddic (legendary) treatment of David is copious and in the main, highly laudatory; it has also found its way into the Koran, and Christianity regards David as the ancestor of Jesus. His personality fired the popular imagination: A Rosh Hashanah adage says "David king of Israel lives forever." And the traditional site of his tomb has become the object of pilgrimages.

ARE BIBLICAL HEROES TYPICAL ORAL HEROES?

As previously mentioned, oral heroes have various identifiable characteristics. These are characteristics very clearly present in the heroes of ancient

Greece but, as also mentioned before, Strate (1991) explained that they can be regarded as traits characteristic of oral heroes generally. Whether this is true of the heroes of oral-biblical times, is this chapter's central question, and it can now be answered on the basis of the discussion to this point.

In Strate's (1991) analysis, their abilities are what most significantly characterize oral heroes. And based on this characteristic, biblical heroes seem to be influenced by their oral environment, as are Greek mythical and legendary heroes. Abraham, Moses, and David are all described as having a greater power of action than our own. Abraham was a substantial chief and a mercenary (with the petty king of Sodom, Gen. 14). He dealt with the major authority of Egypt (Gen. 12) and was a man familiar with cities, complex legal concepts and religious ideas. David was a great warrior who, still as armor bearer for Saul, slew giant Goliath. And his military successes were rounded off by diplomatic alliances and dynastic marriages. He was a man of capacity and experience, of knowledge, travels and grasp of economic factors. And Moses even had extraordinary if not fantastic abilities: He was a leader and served in a human way as a tool for the act pronounced by God: "I bore you on eagles' wings and brought you onto myself" (Exodus 19:4). Moses saw visions and epiphanies and apocalypses, and he is presented as a giant conduit through which the divine radiance poured into the hearts and minds of people. All three heroes were exceptional individuals, apart from their identification with the divine. They did not have the gift of superhuman strength or might, but they displayed their knowledge of strategy, their courage, and their wisdom.

The moral character of oral heroes is closely related to their abilities. Oral heroes' morality is represented by traits and virtues such as hospitality, loyalty, patience, and chastity, and biblical heroes seem to be typical oral heroes in this sense, too. Abraham is the supreme example of the good and just man. He was peace-loving (Gen. 13:8-9), although also willing to fight for his principles and magnanimous in victory (14:22), devoted to his family and hospitable to strangers (18:1), concerned for the welfare of his fellow men (18:23), and above all God fearing and obedient to divine command (22:12; 26:5). He was always faithful and carrying of God's instructions.

Moses, too, was a man of extraordinary moral character. He was a man of intense spirituality, loving solitary communion with God or alone, yet not a hermit. He was an active spiritual force who hated injustice, and sought

> to translate the most intense idealism into practical statesmanship, and noble concepts into details of everyday life . . . he was a lawmaker and judge, the engineer of a mighty framework to enclose in a structure of rectitude every aspect of public and private conduct-a totalitarian of the spirit. (Johnson, 1987, p. 26)

David's moral character is also central in his biblical description. And he, too, was an oral hero, although more than Abraham and Moses, for his moral errors. The moral errors of oral heroes are generally punished, and even without divine retribution, they are the cause of strife and unhappiness. These moral errors include unfaithfulness, lasciviousness, and pride, all of which seem to fit King David at different points in his life. However, although described as vindictive, he was also magnanimous; he hated his enemies, but also loved his friends; he was prone to sin, but quick to repent; he was deeply pious by nature and thus the symbol of Jews' undying faith.

As for the description of appearance of oral heroes, it is usually stereotypical, with very little detail (aside from descriptions of the unusual and the bizarre). And such is the case with oral biblical heroes as well. Among the men preceding him and contemporaneous with him, only Abraham appears prominently in the ancient chronicles. His personal affairs, social relations, and even economic relations, are dramatized in detail. We know quite a lot about him, but we do not know what he looked like. The narrator did not describe his appearance. We can only draw upon our imagination, from the incidents of his life. Or we can conjure up an image from certain tablets unearthed in his native region by archaeologists, some of which show his Semitic contemporaries on caravan route. The Jews never set up a monument to him as did other peoples such as the Egyptians, Babylonians, Persians, and Greeks. And the same is true of Moses and David, whose charisma can be felt in their artistic representations, such as Michelangelo's marble statue of David, but not described in the text.

The biblical heroes' social status and occupations are comparable with those of oral heroes, too: They are kings (like David) or even Abraham (who according to Hellenistic legends was king of Damascus) or prophets and leaders (such as Abraham or Moses) although it seems, generally, that they are more humble and self-conscious than the oral heroes of Greek mythology, and less honor-sensitive or concerned with wealth and titles. They are political and military leaders; men of decisive actions and electric presence; and masters of other trades such as singing. Their acts (whether physical or speech acts) are consistent with these abilities and qualities: Physical acts are complemented by speech acts, and often preceded by verbal conflict in the form of insults, taunts and statements of blame (as is the case in the description of David's slaying of Goliath). Goliath dared the Hebrews and said

> Why are ye come out to set your battle in array? Am not I a Philistine, and ye servants to Saul? Choose you a man for you, and let him come down to me. If he be able to fight with me, and to kill me, then will we be your servants: but if I prevail against him, and kill him, then shall ye be our servants, and serve us. . . . I defy the armies of Israel this day; give me a man, that we may fight together. (1 Samuel, 17:8-10)

And to this David replied:

> What shall be done to the man that killeth this Philistine, and taketh
> away the reproach from Israel? For who is this uncircumcised Philistine,
> that he should defy the armies of the living God? (1 Samuel, 17:26)

Like with Greek oral heroes, the scene in which biblical heroes perform their acts seems to be made up of places that are combinations of imagination and fact, of the real and supernatural worlds. In the Bible, for example, as in Greek epics, there are places such as Mount Sinai, which are mythical symbols and represent the bridge between heaven and earth. It is there that Moses goes to receive the Ten Commandments from God and from there he descends back to the people.

It is clear, then, that there are many similarities among the oral heroes of Ancient Greece and biblical heroes. This is not entirely surprising, as the archetypically oral heroes of eighth century B.C. Greece are either contemporaries of some biblical heroes, or they come later than others (like the ones analyzed here), making the latter necessarily oral too, at least chronologically speaking. The age of the patriarchs, and of Abraham's wanderings in the land of Canaan (2000 to 1200 B.C.), was the time when the Egyptian Empire was extended; Moses led the Jews out of Egypt and they settled in Palestine around the Age of Achilles and the Siege of Troy (1200 to 1100 B.C.); and the time known as the Age of the Judges (1100 to 800 B.C.) when David and Solomon are kings, is the time immediately preceding the Age of Homer (800 to 700 B.C.), when the Greeks became known as Hellenes. In other words, covering a period of time exceeding 1,000 years, the Bible reflects several of the most significant epochs of ancient civilization. The nomadic existence of tribes living in the desert and the trade routes and the Middle East are the background to the Pentateuch. The shadows of the Egyptian, Phoenician, Babylonian, and Assyrian empires fall across the historical and prophetic books. And the Persian period, with the advent of Greece in the horizon, covers the last works of the canon. And all of these epochs belong, in terms of media environments, to the oral era.

However, despite their being contemporaries or predecessors of Greek oral heroes (and thus oral in terms of their media environment), and despite their oral-hero characteristics, some differences can be found between Greek and biblical oral heroes.

These differences are clearest in the descriptions of Moses, and his history that is filled with much failure in between his great successful actions. If we set the individual events that made up his history side by side, we see that his life consisted of one failure after another, through which runs the thread of his success. Each stage of his leadership in taking the people out of Egypt was a failure. Whenever he came to deal with them, he was defeated by them, and had to let God interfere and punish them. And this is true not only in the story of the exodus, but also in the history of the wandering in the desert. The personal history of Moses' own life, too, does not point back to his youth and to what grew out of it but

> . . . it points beyond, to death, to the death of the unsuccessful man, whose work, it is true, survives him, but only in new defeats, new disappointments, and continual new failures-and yet his work survives also in a hope which is beyond all these failures. (Buber, 1963, p. 125)

Moses is a great figure but in no sense a superhuman one. Biblical heroes generally are not half-gods, although they have special abilities, including hearing God's voice. Johnson (1987) explained that Jewish writers and sages, fighting against the strong tendency in antiquity to deify founder-figures, often went out of their way to stress the human weaknesses and failings of Moses. The fighting against (instead of naturally succumbing to) the tendencies of a time, itself, may point to the fact that perhaps the role of a media environment of any given age may differ, in a more significant way than believed to this point, from culture to culture (and this is part of the central question of this chapter). But Johnson also added that there was no need for this fight, as it is all in the record. Moses is presented in the Bible as

> hesitant and uncertain almost to the point of cowardice, mistaken, wrong-headed, foolish, irritable and, what is still more remarkable, bitterly conscious of his shortcomings. (Johnson, 1987, p. 28)

Moses confessed: "I am slow of speech, and of a slow tongue," in a way atypical of oral heroes, especially lawgivers. In general, Moses' image is of an isolated, rather desperate and inefficient figure, struggling with the burdens of a huge role he reluctantly accepted but grimly sought to discharge. This, in itself, does not take away from his hero status. But it does make him a rounder oral hero, different from the typical oral heroes of Ancient Greece such as Odysseus who, like Moses, exhibits might, courage, artifice, leadership and morality, but lacks Moses' individuality. Odysseus was a king, soldier, sailor, singer, athlete and beggar, but he was not an individual personality. He is a generic hero, a type character. Unlike Odysseus, Moses is a mixture of the heroic and the human, making great decisions and doing great acts in a seemingly brave and relentless manner, while concealing all kinds of doubts and sometimes, sheer bewilderment.

Despite these shortcomings and less-than-heroic traits (in an oral culture's sense), Moses remains the most central figure in Jewish history, the creative force and molder of the people, and a figure of great impact on the ancient world. The Greeks conflated him with their own gods and heroes, especially Hermes and Musaeos; he was credited with inventing Hebrew writing, seen as the prelude to Phoenician script and so of Greek. Eupolemus said he was the first wise man in the history of mankind. Artapanos credited him with organizing the Egyptian system of government and inventing all kinds of warlike and industrial machinery. Aristobulus thought that both Homer and Hesiod drew inspiration from his works, and there was a general view among many ancient writers that mankind as a whole, and Greek civilization in particular, owed much to his ideas.

It is true that these are all characteristics of Moses only. But David's representation, too, as previously mentioned, is filled with descriptions of his very human character (vindictive, sinful, etc.). Despite all these traits (more characteristic of literate than of oral heroes), he too remains a great king with grand military successes, an artistic imagination, and a central position in Jewish history.

There are some other differences yet between Greek and biblical oral heroes. Greek heroes are sometimes supernatural heroes, whereas biblical heroes are not (although the events surrounding them sometimes are, like the burning bush). Moreover, abstract phenomena are not personified or anthropomorphized in the Bible the way they are in Greek oral epics. In these epics, historical processes and sociological phenomena, as well as concepts such as justice or love, are situationalized as agents performing actions. The authority of Zeus as described in the Iliad, for example, represents the political and social order (Strate, 1991). But Abraham, Moses, or David cannot be summed up as representing anything as specific as this. They are exemplars, but not of concrete patterns of behavior to be imitated, as the Bible does (and Greek epics do not), include abstract instructions to be followed (as in the Ten Commandments) and not only personifications of such abstract ideas and instructions.

Greek oral heroes generally lack moral development over time, whereas such development can be found in biblical heroes. Among the figures analyzed here, this is clearest in the portrayal of Abraham who underwent great moral development and became a whole new man through his faith. And, as previously mentioned, this development was even captured symbolically in the change in his name—from Abram to Abraham.

Biblical heroes, generally, seem to be rounder and less generic characters than the flat or "type" characters of oral Greece. Abraham, David, and Moses are not identified with particular characteristics like Achilles is with might, Odysseus with artifice, or Nestor with wisdom. Biblical heroes incorporate many characteristics, sometimes even opposites of each other. This is usually true of later literate characters, and of real and complex humans, always.

Characteristics are, then, personified by Greek oral heroes, and so are other abstractions. Rain, for example, is conceptualized as an action (and not a process or an event) and an action requires an agent. In other words, there must be a rainmaker. Not so in the case of biblical heroes. It is the one and only God who is responsible for the rain and every other event. It was God, and not Moses, who provided the Israelites with food, in the form of manna, as they wandered through the desert.

To try to understand these differences between Greek and biblical heroes, it is useful to apply the popular distinction between legendary heroes that are human, and mythic heroes that are gods, to the discussion here. Biblical heroes are legendary, of course, and not mythic, and this distinction is more significant in the case of Biblical heroes than it is in that of Greek oral heroes. Strate (1991) also used Northrup Frye's distinction between a mythic hero (who is superior in kind to other men), and a romantic hero (who is superior in degree to other men). And here, too, it is clear that Greek heroes are of both kinds, whereas biblical heroes are mostly romantic. In other words, biblical heroes are fallible and mortal. As opposed to Greek heroes, they are never given the same epithets as God, they are never considered offspring or descendants of God, and God never disguises himself as a human. In the Bible one cannot find mortals and immortals facing each other in combat, and mortals cannot become gods (all of which is possible for Greek oral heroes). And this is because heroes are also defined by a culture's relationship with God. The conception of gods in Greek literature assumed several gods that, like humans, have flaws, whereas the Bible tells of one, monolithic God that, unlike humans, is flawless.

It is clear from all of this then, that biblical heroes are oral heroes. But they are like Greek oral heroes in some ways, and different from them in others. There are a few possible explanations of these differences. One possible explanation is that when it comes to Israelite literature, orality and literacy should not be pictured as strict opposites or alternatives but as ends of a continuum, as Niditch (1996) suggested. Her study of this literature approaches the idea that large, perhaps dominant, threads in Israelite culture were oral, and that literacy in ancient Israel must be understood in terms of its continuity and interaction with the oral world. In this oral world, the vast majority of people lived in villages, they worked the land, they were led by elders, told stories, preserved custom and law, and cited proverbs orally. Yet, this does not mean that no one in the villages could write or read or that writing was not used in commercial transactions and letters, or found upon commemorative stones, or that writing was unfamiliar to people. In other words, in this generally oral world, writing for pragmatic purposes was quite common. The oral and the written interplay in this traditional culture. And like in other oral cultures, here too there is repetition, formulas, epithets and special patterns of content, but "the contextual 'writing world' concerns of writers influence the forms of traditional-style works preserved in the Bible" (Niditch, 1996, p. 45).

Another possible explanation of the differences between Greek and Biblical oral heroes is inherent in the theories about the relationship between media environments and culture themselves. These theories include the idea that the oral media environment should be understood as having the same type of effect on cultures as the natural environment has on the evolution of species. Thus, Strate (1991) said:

> the oral media environment would favor certain forms over others, make it easier for certain forms to survive. . . . The media environment sets up parameters, and variation among those parameters . . . would be related to other sociological or cultural factors. (p. 135)

In other words, biblical heroes generally fall under the parameters set up by the oral media environment to which they belong. But the sociological, cultural and religious factors related to a moral code, new and revolutionary as was the one necessary to create a people who believe in one God, required a clear distinction between humans and that God. And one way to begin to achieve this distinction was through the lowering of the status or the humanizing of the heroes that made up that people's narratives. A vivid and realistic depiction of the heroes, with an emphasis on their human failures and faults clearly sets humans apart from God, no matter how righteous and able the humans are. As Johnson (1987) argued:

> The real purpose of the Bible narratives [is] the depiction of individuals, the ancestors of the people, in a moral context and, still more important, the origin and development of their collective relationship with God. (p. 15)

CONCLUSION: ORALITY VERSUS MONOTHEISM OR MEDIA VERSUS NARRATIVES

Although the oral media environment of which they are part is palpable or recognizable in some of the biblical heroes' characteristics, it seems that an idea—monotheism—is stronger in defining them (or at least in setting them apart from other oral heroes) than the media environment. Although both biblical heroes and Greek heroes lived in a time when the spoken word was the main medium of communication; and although writing, beginning to spread, was still in the hands of a chosen few, the distinction between the mythic and the romantic characterizes one culture and not the other. It characterizes Jewish culture and does not characterize Greek culture, as this is a logical categorization associated with abstract monotheism, where even the greatest heroes are superior in degree, but not in kind, to other men.

Of course, no generalizations can be made yet about the heroes of later periods in Jewish history in comparison to their contemporaries in other cultures. Further research is currently being conducted to ascertain whether the idea presented here is a viable one: that abstract ideas, group narratives, or ideological/cultural contexts are stronger definers of conceptions of the hero than media of communication. If the idea of monotheism defines (more significantly than the spoken word) who shall be considered a hero in Biblical times, perhaps the ideas of "survival as a people" and "nationhood" define who will be a hero in later times in Jewish history, and not the advent of print (or at least not as centrally as believed hereto). And maybe the idea of yearning to become normal — "a nation among nations" in yet later times in Jewish history (modern Israel) defines who is a hero then, more centrally than television. In other words, such research has the potential of, if not eliminating, at least balancing the determinist view that sees media environments as almost omnipotent. One may find that the content more than the structure, the message more than the medium, people's stories and narratives more than their tools of communication, their interpersonal relationships more than their symbolic existence in front of a screen, can be the sources from which new, real heroes (and not celebrities), so desperately needed in our ever more connected global environment, may arise. If this is found to be true, real life and our retelling of it, and not its mediated version, may help us reach what Drucker and Cathcart (1994) long for: the requisite consensus on societal ideals and morals for bestowal of the title of hero, in spite of the watchwords of the day — fragmentation, heterogeneity, pluralism, and multiculturalism.

The political, social, cultural, and economic conditions of a specific culture, with its dreams and aspirations embedded in them and in the stories it tells itself about its life, may, in spite of television and the computer, and in spite of the power we have for so long assigned to them, bring back inspirational models of human greatness to us as Americans or Israelis or as citizens of the globe.

REFERENCES

Bloom, H., & Rosenberg, D. (1990). *The book of J*. New York: Grove Weidenfeld.

Boorstin, D. J. (1978). *The image: A guide to pseudo-events in America*. New York: Atheneum.

Buber, M. (1963). *Israel and the world: Essays in a time of crisis*. New York: Schocken.

Drucker, S.J, & Cathcart, R.S. (Eds.). (1994). The hero as communication phenomenon. In S. J. Drucker & R. S. Cathcart (Eds.), *American heroes in a media age*
(pp.1-15). Cresskill, NJ: Hampton Press.

Friedman, R.E. (1987). *Who wrote the Bible?* New York: Summit Books.

Fukuyama, F. (1992). *The end of history and the last man.* New York: Avon Books.

Johnson, P. (1987). *A history of the Jews.* New York: Harper Perennial.

Krauthammer, C. (1997, February 10). The end of heroism, *Time,* p. 72.

Margolis, M., & Marx, A. (1958). *History of the Jewish people.* New York: Meridian.

Niditch, S. (1996). *Oral world and written word: Ancient Israelite literature.*
Louisville, KY: Westminster John Knox Press.

Ong, W.J. (1982). *Orality and literacy: The technologizing of the word.* New York:
Methuen.

Roth, C. (1961). *History of the Jews.* New York: Schocken Books.

Shapiro, M. (1994). *The Jewish 100: A ranking of the most influential Jews of all time.*
New York: Citadel Press.

Schwarz, L.W. (Ed.). (1956). *Great ages and ideas of the Jewish people.* New York:
Random House.

Strate, L. (1985). Heroes, fame and the media. *Et cetera, A Review of General
Semantics, 42*(1), 47-53.

Strate, L. (1991). *Heroes and humans: An examination of the relationship between
media environments and conceptions of the hero.* Doctoral dissertation, New
York University, New York.

Chapter 13

MENACHEM BEGIN

A Hero's Guiding Vision

Sondra M. Rubenstein
University of Haifa

Adam Ehrlich*

Menachem Begin's story and rise to prime minister parallels that of the establishment of Israel as the Jewish state. This chapter examines the rise of this controversial statesman and makes the case for Begin, as Israel's political hero, based on a theoretical montage that includes a theory of charisma. The circumstances of situational charisma are explored and the authors make the case that Begin as hero is the result of vision, personality, and defining moment.

Although Israelis on the right will have no difficulty agreeing with the choice of Menachem Begin as a political hero, those on the left will, at the very least, agree that Begin was a "heroic" figure with a vision. For non-Israelis, however, the choice of Menachem Begin as a "hero" may seem sur-

---

*Adam Ehrlich is a freelance writer. He graduated from Haifa University.

prising. Their obvious question is why not David Ben Gurion, Israel's first prime minister (who served from 1949 to November 1954 and again from 1955 to 1963), or Yitzhak Rabin, the much mythologized prime minister, whose assassination succeeded in obscuring the memory of General Rabin's inability to function (as a result of shock) during the most dangerous opening hours of the Yom Kippur War of 1973. Or, why not any of a number of other brave Israeli military leaders? More will be said about Ben Gurion as the ideological nemesis of Menachem Begin. As for Rabin, his assassination was, indeed, a great tragedy for Israel, and no one can deny his contributions, in a positive sense, to the failed Oslo peace process. And, Israel has had and has many extraordinary military heroes, whose love of, and sacrifices, for their country can never be negated.

However, the case made to support the choice of Menachem Begin as a "political hero," framed from a personal perspective, rests on his extraordinary leadership abilities, unyielding commitment to the Jewish nation, and his enduring vision of Israel as a free, democratic, and progressive Jewish state.

A THEORETICAL MONTAGE

It is difficult to determine who is a "hero" because the word is hard to define. However, the great man theory of history may be helpful because it focuses on the power of a single individual to change the course of history. In comparison, Karl Marx's economic-based analysis of the inevitability of spontaneous revolution ignores the impact of individual political leadership on historic change. One advantage of the great man theory is that it can coexist with, and enhance, other theories useful in identifying who qualifies as a hero. There are many different types of heroes, but our focus is on political heroism.

In this study of Israel's Menachem Begin, the justification of identifying the late prime minister as a political hero will include a theoretical montage consisting of the great man theory, combined with theories relating to charisma and leadership. Connected to the belief that one individual can be the catalyst for great change and leave an important legacy is the axiom that some are "born to greatness." This concept assumes the individual has long displayed talents and abilities that distinguish greatness from mediocrity, the extraordinary from the ordinary.

The great man theory ignores conventional religious notions of predestination. But, for some, the expression "born to greatness" assumes a degree of predetermination and help from a higher being, a deity. We believe any emphasis on personal characteristics that are dependent on the intervention of a deity should be replaced by the more earth-bound concept of a "guiding vision" as a distinguishing attribute of a political hero. In the case of Menachem Begin, his guiding vision evolved as a result of his cumulative life experiences, the influences of key individuals and specific events. As BBC's Gerald Butt (1998) said:

> Begin was committed throughout his life to the cause of fighting anti-Semitism. In his view, this struggle justified the creation and defence of the Jewish state by any means necessary (even if this meant ordering an air attack on an Iraqi nuclear reactor, as he did in 1981).

As we will see, beside his life-long commitment to the Jewish state and his impressive organizational and analytical abilities, Begin was so gifted rhetorically that he quickly came to the attention of Vladimir Ze'ev Jabotinsky[1] and rose in the ranks of the *Betar* organization, the popular Jewish pioneering youth movement founded by Jabotinsky. While it is not always easy to identify the specific attributes people perceive in someone they are willing to follow, German sociologist Max Weber (1974, pp. 245-252) identified what he called "a gift of grace," or charisma (p. 252). Weber believed that it was charisma that enabled someone to be perceived as having a credible vision, one worth following.

Expanding on his initial theory, Weber (1974) describes the phenomenon of the "routinization" and "depersonalization" of charisma. He claims charisma exists in its pure form only upon its moment of inception. Being transitional by nature, charisma must eventually develop into either the traditional, rational-legal form of authority or dissolve itself through inertia. In either case, charisma must change and, by doing so, according to Weber, it loses its compelling and enigmatic characteristics.

This phenomenon is addressed in Michael A. Toth's (1982) "Theory of Two Charismas," in which the author distinguishes between "charisma of the outer call" and "charisma of the inner consolidation." He states that in most social movements, following the passing of the original leader (the charisma of the outer call), through martyrdom, demise, or whatever the reason for replacement, a second leader (the charisma of the inner consolidation) arises from among the inner disciples of the movement. The "double occurrence" of charisma, according to Toth, appears to reconcile problems of the "routinization of charisma."

Toth noted that both leaders must be charismatic, but their charismas are of a different nature. The first possesses a charisma in the classic sense of "a gift of grace," enabling him to attract initial followers who accept his vision and who assist in the founding of the organization. The second leader has a more "down-to-earth" charisma, enabling him to maintain the organization through responding to change and distress. It also enables him to challenge and to transform a revolutionary social movement into an institution capable of governing.

As seen here, Toth's (1981) theory helps to explain the successive charismatic impact of Jabotinsky and Begin. The latter, soon after his arrival in Palestine, would assume the mantle of leadership of *Betar*'s successive organization the *Irgun*. Begin's unique combination of charismatic leadership, spellbinding rhetoric, personal courage and steadfastness[2] would enable him to reorganize and consolidate the *Irgun*, while institutionalizing the original Betari vision and the moral beliefs of Jabotinsky, *Betar*'s former leader, at a time of enormous distress and instability (Toth, 1981)

This concept, then, begins to approach Robert C. Tucker's (1970, pp. 69-94) "situational charisma," which explains why under certain extraordinary circumstances (such as a war, an economic crisis, a political power vacuum, etc.), a new leader emerges and quickly attracts a following. In such times of distress and insecurity, Tucker explained, an individual with specific gifts of mind and spirit can more easily be perceived as charismatic, while the same individual in other settings might not even be noticed. Tucker disputed Weber's critics, who claimed that charismatic leadership was a thing of the past, belonging to the "magico-religious ambiance" of primitive societies that believed in mythology, witchcraft, and magic (Loewenstein, 1966, pp. 79-90; also see Loewenstein on the influence of Weber's theory of charisma, p. 74).

To counter those criticisms, Tucker spoke of the "usefulness" of Weber's concept of charismatic leadership as meeting a "vital theoretical need," which was "virtually indispensable, particularly for the student of revolutionary movements of various kinds." As seen here, because of Menachem Begin's vision of a Jewish state, its timing, and how it would come about, he was seen as a revolutionary. In this regard, Tucker provided a theoretical foundation on which we can build. He wrote:

> Charismatic qualification may, on the one hand, consist in extraordinary powers of vision and the communication of vision, especially when this vision relates to the possibility and way of overcoming distressful conditions. Alternatively, it may consist in unusual powers of practical leadership of people along the way to such a goal.

Begin had both "extraordinary powers of vision and communication of vision" and "unusual powers of actual leadership." The concept of vision is important because it replaces notions of a higher being who will guide us and take care of us. The conviction behind the vision must be strong, completely dedicated to the goal, whereas the goal itself must be presented as achievable. Begin was totally dedicated to the goal, and his followers believed in its achievability. Rhetorical skills are crucial in explaining the necessary strategy, tactics, and sacrifices and in persuading potential followers to fulfill their role in attaining the vision. Without vision there is only the fleeting charisma of an actor on the screen, an empty vessel.

Our examination of Begin's life focuses on the evolution of his ideas and his vision of a Jewish state. His guiding vision and ideology were more political, although intertwined with religion; more pragmatic, although containing idealistic strands; more capable of compromise though firmly based on ethical principles.

IDEOLOGICAL FOUNDATIONS

Ze'ev Dov Begin, Menachem's father, was a passionate Zionist and a great admirer of Dr. Theodore Herzl (1860–1904), the founder of modern Zionism. Ze'ev instilled in his son a strict moral code, which was a meld of Jewish traditions, religious tenets, and his belief in the right of the Jews to "return" to their Jewish homeland in the land of Israel. As Begin (2002) wrote in *The Revolt*:

> From my early youth I had been taught by my father—who, as I was later told, went to his death at Nazi hands voicing the liturgic declaration of faith in God and singing the Hebrew national anthem, Hatikvah—that we Jews were to return to Eretz Israel [literally, the land of Israel]. Not to "go" or "travel" or "come"—but to return. That was the great difference, and it was all-embracing. (p. 3)

He and his siblings were involved in Zionist youth movements from an early age, beginning with *Ha'Shomer Ha'Tzair* (The Young Guard), which Menachem joined when he was 12 years old, in 1925. *Ha'Shomer* began as a scout movement but adopted the Marxist ideology as its guiding light about one year after Menachem joined. Believing a Jew must "first . . . fight for [his] own freedom," before fighting for "the freedom of the world," Ze'ev and his family abandoned the left-wing, Marxist ideology of the movement (Silver, 1984, p. 10).

At 15, Menachem joined the *Betar* youth movement, which represented, for him, the "total Zionism" necessary to achieve "the ideal of *Eretz Yisrael* as a Jewish State in our time" (Silver, 1984, p. 10). In *Betar*, Menachem found the "true expression," the ideological basis of all that he and his family had long accepted.

Although both *Ha'Shomer* and *Betar* advocated the return to Zion, *Ha'Shomer* saw it as a necessary step in the creation of a Jewish proletariat. The Kibbutz system, with its communal style of living and agricultural-based economy, would provide the perfect gateway for that transformation.

Consistent with the Marxist assumption that revolution against capitalism was inevitable, *Ha'Shomer* believed that the Jewish proletariat would join the international class struggle. *Betar*, however, saw the return to Zion as the critical step in the creation of the Jewish state, an end in itself. BBC's Gerald Butt (1998) commented that the "movement abhorred the socialist ideology behind other wings of Zionism, and advocated strong leadership and discipline." Thus, by adopting *Betar*'s tenets, Begin chose the ideology that conformed to his own vision. We believe that this pivotal decision marked the direction in which his vision was evolving.

His first exposure to political charisma occurred at the age of 17 when he heard Ze'ev Jabotinsky, *Rosh Betar* (Leader of *Betar*), speak. Of Jabotinsky (1880-1940), Begin would later write:

> The greatest influence in my life I attribute to Jabotinsky. I was won over by his ideas. . . . My entire life has been influenced by him, both in the underground and in politics: the willingness to fight for the liberation of the homeland, and the logical analysis of facts in political matters. (Silver, 1984, pp. 10–11)

Betar offered Begin the opportunity to hone his emerging leadership skills and provided a direct outlet for the expression of his ideology. He quickly rose through the organization's ranks, becoming the *Betar* commander for the Brest district while in high school. He received his law degree from the University of Warsaw in 1935, and in April 1939, Jabotinsky appointed him *Betar*'s chief organizer in Poland. Accepting a position as a law clerk with a Warsaw law firm, Begin rented a room, and on May 29, 1939, he married Betari member Aliza Arnold.

He "toured the length and breadth of the land, speaking, cajoling, mobilizing recruits" (Silver, 1984, p. 7). The 70,000 members in over 700 branches throughout Poland spoke volumes about his skills as a recruiter and his commitment to the party as a vehicle to achieve his vision. All this coincided with the rapid deterioration of the Jewish condition in Europe.

FROM WARSAW TO VILNA

The outbreak of World War II found Begin in Warsaw, following his return from a frustrating trip to escort 1,000 *Betar* members to the Romanian border, from where he had hoped, consistent with Jabotinsky's and his vision, they would make their way to Palestine.[3] Until then, the border with Romania had been open, but with the signing of the Molotov-Ribbentrop Pact, Romania closed its border. *Betar* members were dispersed to their hometowns, from which most were sent to Nazi death camps, where they perished.

With the Germans closing in on Warsaw, Menachem and Aliza fled. After 7 weeks of traveling by foot, wagon, horseback, and train, the Begins and the rest of the Polish *Betar* leadership found themselves in Vilna, capital of "Free Lithuania." There, they continued their mission to save as many Jews as possible from Europe and to send them to Palestine, despite growing British objections and determined efforts to halt what they considered illegal immigration.

"Free Lithuania" could not remain disengaged from the war raging throughout Europe. Begin was informed of the Soviet advance while speaking at Vilna's Polish University on the anniversary of Theodore Herzl's death. In the midst of the meeting, Begin was handed a note: "Russian tanks have entered the city" (Silver, 1984, p. 24). Before panic could overwhelm the audience, Begin led them in singing *Hatikva*, the Zionist anthem. Only after they had finished singing did the audience leave the building.

Begin and the *Betar* leaders knew it was only a matter of time before they would have to confront the notorious NKVD, the Soviet secret police. The Russian secret police in Lithuanian was known as hostile to Zionism, considered a "national deviation" from the Socialist revolutionary path. After receiving, and ignoring, a summons to the Vilna town hall regarding an "application" Begin had not filed, he relocated to a small town on the outskirts of Vilna. However, shortly after arriving:

> [A] black sedan drew up outside the house and discharged three husky men . . . the biggest asked why he (Begin) had not responded to the municipality's invitation. . . . Begin put on a great show of innocence, claiming that since he had not applied for anything, it must be a mistake. . . . The police had no warrant, but they made it clear that unless Begin came willingly, he would be taken by force. (Gevasi, 1979, p. 108)

Begin took leave of his chess game, polished his shoes, and only after showing his "guests" out, parted from his wife and left. He would not see Aliza again until 1942. In the interim he would be confined to labor camps in Siberia and elsewhere until 1941.

SOVIET INCARCERATION

Following a short stay in NKVD headquarters, Begin was transferred to the notorious Lukishki Prison in central Vilna. The NKVD accused Begin of "serving the interests of British imperialism" and declared him "a dangerous element in society." The monotony of his 9-month stay in Lukishki was broken only by near ceaseless interrogations. Begin treated them as an "intellectual exploration, a deadly game of chess. . . . [He] would not agree that Zionism was a bourgeois national deviation" (Silver, 1984, pp. 29-30). In his book *White Nights*, Begin (2002) wrote: "[I]t was my faith against his faith. . . . I had something to fight for. . . . I fight therefore I am." He spoke of the devastating effects of solitude and isolation, of the "wall of silence," and its impenetrability.

On what later turned out to be his last night of interrogation, he signed a statement reading: "I admit that I was chairman of the *Betar* of Poland" (Silver, 1984, p. 29). However, this statement was agreed to only after he bravely argued and refused to sign an earlier version, reading: "I admit I am guilty of having been the chairman of the *Betar* organization in Poland. . . ." Admitting guilt, for Begin, was tantamount to denouncing his vision in the face of Soviet intimidation.[4]

Shortly thereafter, he was sentenced to 8 years of hard labor and transferred by train north-eastward, where he and his fellow prisoners were forced to work on the Trans-Siberia railway. Begin described the harsh conditions of life in the labor camp. Unless one has survived such a camp, perhaps the closest one can come to understanding would be to read Alexander Solzhenitsyn's (1962) *One Day in the Life of Ivan Denisovich*, or Menachem Begin's (2002) description of how one learns to forget about "civilisation." He tells of the phrase that conveys the philosophy of survival, "You'll get used to it," and he explained:

> You need a bed to rest on? Nonsense. You will lie on boards, on a floor, in the snow, on the earth, and you will sleep.
>
> No, civilisation is not essential. You shake it off quickly if you are forced to. Yet, strangely enough, the less civilisation in your life, the greater your desire to live. Just to live, to live, to live. Man is a vigorous animal. Even when he is reduced to semi-bestial circumstances, his will to live is elemental. He gets used to everything, except death. (p. 15)

A second transfer took place before the harsh northern winter set in. Begin (2002, p. 22) described the boat trip north, towards a sub-polar region:

> Darkness. Filth. Stench. Fleas and lice. Seven hundred half-bestial Urki. A few Jews. A handful of dreamers of Zion. . . . What help could they hope for?

While sailing toward a destination on the Arctic Sea, an order arrived to liberate all Polish citizens. General Sikorski[5] and Stalin had signed a pact that allowed the release of all Polish citizens held by the Russians. They were to join the Free Polish Army, which was to be trained in Palestine and then sent to fight the Germans.

In the transit camp, waiting for passage southward to the Caspian Sea, Begin found his sister "by pure chance" and some *Betar* friends. He sent his first telegram to Eretz Israel and received one, bearing several signatures, among which was that of Aliza's.

BEGIN'S "RETURN"

Begin finally reached the eastern bank of the Jordan River, via Iran and Iraq, and crossed into Eretz Israel in early May 1942. He wrote about his thoughts as he "drank in the odour of the fields of my Homeland":

> I had been arrested, charged, sentenced and exiled as an "agent of British Imperialism." What became of this British agent? Arriving in Eretz Israel with the Polish Army he soon had on his head the largest of the rewards offered by the British police for the capture of those who were trying to smash British rule in Eretz Israel. (This is the only "record" I have ever achieved and I shall always be very proud of it. (Begin, 2002, p. 25)

Begin cited "two fundamental facts" as the immediate causes of the Hebrew Revolt in Eretz Israel: The ongoing Nazi extermination of Europe's Jews and Britain's locking the gates to survival. The British *White Paper*, published in September 1939, so heavily restricted Jewish immigration to Palestine, it—in effect—closed off escape. Citing the Balfour Declaration (November 1917), which "viewed with favor the establishment in Palestine of a national home for the Jewish people,"[6] Begin (2002) stated:

> British policy . . . was ready to back a great ideal which would enable Britain to take over control of Palestine without seeming to. The ideal was at hand: the Jews to whom the Bible had promised Palestine, were persecuted and needed a home. The ideal was very appealing. Britain would promise the Jews a Home—in Palestine. Not Palestine as a Home, but a Home in Palestine. Britain would have Palestine, and the Jews would have a Home in it. (p. 31)

He also explained British motivation for then controlling Jewish immigration:

One cannot say that those who shaped British Middle East policy at that
time did not want to save the Jews. It would be more correct to say that
they very eagerly wanted the Jews not to be saved. The average
Englishman was probably as indifferent to Jewish lives as any other
non-Jew in the world. But those who ruled Palestine and the Middle
East were not in the least "indifferent."[7] They were highly interested in
achieving the maximum reduction in the number of Jews liable to seek
to enter the land of Israel. (Begin, 2002, p. 28)

Begin and others cited "outcomes" of the British policy to obstruct the use
of Palestine as a "haven" for the Jews of Europe attempting to flee Hitler's
gas chambers. The *Struma, Milos, Pacific,* and the *Patria* were ships carrying
hundreds of Jewish immigrants that were either sunk or sent back to their
points of departure. In both instances, the human cargo was murdered.

THE REVOLT

Begin's intention on arrival in Palestine was to join the *Irgun Zvai Leumi*
(IZL),[8] which he found in dire straits. Brutal British reprisals against the
Irgun had followed their violent reaction to publication of the *White Paper.*
Only 600 *Irgun* activists survived,[9] and only small amounts of arms and
explosives remained following British confiscation and Arab raids.

The death of David Raziel, during a secret mission for the British in
Iraq, and British incarceration of most of the IZL leadership, left the *Irgun*
much weakened. However, the heaviest blow was the split with Raziel's sec-
ond-in-command Avraham Stern, whose faction, the "Fighters for the
Freedom of Israel" (FFI)[10] became known as the extremist Stern Gang. With
this split, Raziel's successor Ya'acov Meridor, although an able and respected military commander,[11] apparently "did not relish the awesome task of
reorganization" (Gervasi, 1979, p. 143) dictated by the imperative of expelling
the British from Palestine.

David Niv, an *Irgun* veteran and official historian, cited the disappointment in Meridor's leadership abilities, which rallied support for his replacement. Niv explained that many believed a leader was needed who could revi-
talize and rekindle the spirit of the *Irgun.* He stated:

At the end of 1943, it was not only a question of military operations, but
a question of taking a stand. It was a time for a man of politics rather
than a professional military commander. All the decisions needed political sensitivity. (Silver, 1984, p. 42)

Thus, the movement clamored for capable leadership. Such circumstances are consistent with Tucker's theory of situational charisma. As one can conclude from what Niv wrote, it was not just capable leadership that was needed, but rather a specific mixture of political sensitivity, motivational, and organizational skills. Begin, with his vision, fortified ideology, legal education, integrity, organizational, and political experience was perceived as perfect to fill the power vacuum in an extremely distressful situation. However, still a private in the Polish Army, he refused to desert. Following frenzied bureaucratic scrambling, he acquired a release and became the IZL commander toward the end of 1943.

In February 1944, the *Irgun* declared war against the British administration. Begin (2002) spoke of the heroism of *Irgun* members whose attacks against government, military and police installations were meant to draw attention to the demand: "Immediate transfer of power in Eretz Israel to a Provisional Hebrew Government." The Irgun Declaration proclaimed the following:

> Our people is at war with this regime—war to the end. This war will demand many and heavy sacrifices, but we enter on it in the consciousness that we are being faithful to the children of our people who have been and are being slaughtered. It is for their sake that we fight, to their dying testimony that we remain loyal. (p. 43)

Begin's steadfast commitment to the vision of a Jewish state endured throughout the years. During that time, *Irgun* members, after issuing warnings to the British to evacuate the premises, blew up the King David Hotel in Jerusalem, where British government offices and their military headquarters were located. They also attacked British stations and fortresses, humiliated the government by stealing supplies from their stores, and forced the British police and soldiers to stop harassing Jewish worshippers and intimidating them to stay away from the Western Wall.

The campaign to overcome the British prohibition against the centuries' old Jewish custom of praying and blowing the Shofar at the Wall,[12] was difficult and bloody. But the symbolic importance of restoring the right of Jews to pray at what they considered their sacred Wailing Wall was a huge psychological victory. Hunted by the British for these and other acts of rebellion, the *Irgun* went underground. Begin (2002) commented:

> It never occurred to the British that we lived . . . as we did: almost openly. . . . [W]e had made a virtue of necessity. . . . In Eretz Israel there was neither mountain nor forest for the rebels to hide in. We were completely exposed to the enemy's eyes. [Yet], we saw but were unseen. We naturally had a variety of names, we used a selection of identity docu-

ments, usually home-made. . . . We were not surrounded by body-guards, we carried no arms for our own defence. We were teachers and students, real or imaginary. We were real or imaginary merchants or bookkeepers . . . engineers and mechanics . . . indistinguishable from other citizens. (pp. 105-106)

Although Begin memorialized fellow *Irgun* members who bravely sacrificed their lives, his own bravery and heroic acts can only be interpreted from his actions. Rumors and legends spread, including the one about his having agreed to meet and speak "enemy to enemy" with General Barker, the commanding officer of the British Occupation Forces. In one version, Begin had set the condition that they meet alone at a café, in civilian dress. Breaking his word, Barker came with a contingent of soldiers who surrounded the café. Thinking Begin was already inside, the general entered and looked around, but the only person there was a Catholic priest reading a newspaper. As he waited for Begin, Barker started a conversation with the priest. Minutes passed; Barker decided Begin was not coming and left. The following day the general supposedly received a letter from Begin (2002) noting that while the *Irgun* always keeps its word, the General had broken his by not coming alone. The rumored letter concluded: "The priest with whom you had such a friendly chat was I" (pp. 119-120).

THE YISHUV'S INTERNAL CONFLICT[13]

Begin and the *Irgun* faced strong opposition in their struggle to achieve their vision of a Jewish state in *Eretz Yisrael*. This included the Arabs who also claimed Palestine as their homeland; the British who, under a League of Nations mandate, had taken upon themselves the task of controlling immigration and governing the country until it was deemed fit for self-rule; and, perhaps most disturbing, the internal struggle between the right-wing *Irgun*, led by Begin, along with *Lehi* (the Stern Gang), and the left-wing *Mapai*,[14] the official representative of the Jewish Agency, led by David Ben Gurion.[15]

Aside from the standard ideological and economic differences that usually exist between left- and right-wing parties, there existed between these two camps a schism that seemed unbridgeable. Although both parties were faithful to the Zionist vision of *Eretz Yisrael*, the two camps clashed on the issue of armed revolt against the British. The *Irgun* advocated the immediate commencement of operations, regardless of the war in Europe. However, *Mapai* advocated "patience," a restrained approach, working through legal channels, at least while the British were still fighting the Nazis in Europe.

Attempts were made to unify the two armed parties, but Begin refused any unification with Ben Gurion so long as the latter refused to join the revolt against the British. Of the attempts at unification, Begin (2002) wrote:

> ... the fact is that the official Zionist leadership wanted us to stop our struggle immediately after we launched it. First they tried to cajole us. When cajolery failed, threats followed. And the "deeds" that came next would have brought about civil war *had we not determined that the greatest menace to the future of our people was internal conflict.* (p. 135, italics added)

Having made this determination, Begin was adamant that his people take no part in the spilling of Jewish blood. Contrary to his "extremist" reputation, he consistently advocated restraint during the collaboration of the *Haganah*[16] with the British against the IZL and *Lehi*, and even during outright attacks by the *Haganah* against the IZL that led to *Irgun* deaths. For Begin's vision to be fulfilled, there could be no civil war between the Jews.

In September 1944, Begin held meetings with Moshe Sneh, head of the *Haganah* General Headquarters, and Eliyahu Golomb, *Haganah* leader, to discuss relations between the *Irgun* and *Yishuv* leadership. On the question of national authority, Sneh said the *Haganah* had received a mandate from the Jewish people and that if the *Irgun* continues its activities, "a clash will result." Golomb demanded cessations of *Irgun* operations against the British and warned, "we do not want a civil war . . . but we will be ready for that as well." Begin responded as follows:

> We have no intention of seizing power in the *Yishuv*. We have said this on many occasions. We have no ambitions. . . . [W]e think that Ben Gurion is the man who can lead our youth into battle today. . . . We have no party or administrative interests. We pray for the day when we can proclaim the end of the *Irgun*'s task and disperse it. And the moment that you go out to war—we will all rally under a united leadership, in which you will constitute the decisive majority. But as long as you have not done this, we will conduct our battle. (www.etzel.org.il/english/index/html).

In November 1944, about 2 months after the *Haganah–Irgun* meeting, two *Lehi* members assassinated Lord Moyne, Britain's minister of state for the Middle East, in Cairo. Moyne had been responsible for implementing the *White Paper* policy, which led to the deportation of Jewish immigrants and, in many cases, to their deaths when they were forced to return to their point of origin in Nazi-controlled Europe. They died when their pitifully unsafe ships sank during the return voyage, or in front of Nazi death squads, or in Hitler's gas chambers.

Moyne's two assassins were executed following their trial, and the British police in Palestine launched retaliatory strikes against the Stern Gang and the *Irgun*. The Zionist quasi-government quickly denounced the assassination and hastened to assist the British police. This set off what Begin called "the open season" and others called "the hunting season" against Stern and *Irgun* members. During this time *Palmach*[17] volunteers kidnapped and tortured about 100 *Irgun* members and handed them over to the British. Norman Weinstock cited Begin's remark that *"Ha'Shomer Ha'Tzair showed a zeal worthy of a better cause in helping Ben Gurion hand over members of the Irgun to British repression"* (www.marxists.de/middleast/weinstock/notez.htm#11-54).

UNIFICATION AND DISTRUST

The end of the war in Europe ended the schism and brought about a unification of the Jewish factions within the *Yishuv*. Under the leadership of Ben Gurion, the factions fought together for the end of the British Mandate. However, Ben Gurion's distrust of Begin endured, despite Begin's repeated assurances that he sought no power for himself. Following negotiations, it was decided that all factions would retain their political and organizational independence but that the factions would forego independent operations and would fight together to bring about the Jewish State.

Sadly, Ben Gurion's continued mistrust led to the greatest test of Begin's resolve to avoid a civil war. This occurred with the destruction of the Altalena,[18] by the Provisional Government, which claimed the IZL intended to launch an "armed revolt" that would bring it to power. The *Irgun* ship was carrying 900 soldiers, thousands of air-combat bombs, and enormous amounts of other hard-to-come-by war material. And, according to Begin, the Provisional Government "knew about the arms ship sailing towards our shores. . . . And . . . decided to bring the 'Altalena' in during the truce period. Otherwise she would not have come."

Writing about the tragedy years later, Begin continued to lament "that night in 1948" when the *Altalena* "went up in flames. . . and the ship became the common grave of a number of the brave men who had come as volunteers to fight for their people." He spoke over the radio about the ship, its arms and its dead, and admitted that he was moved to tears.

Despite enduring memories of this painful incident, Begin never doubted his conviction that the shedding of tears, instead of fratricidal blood, brought salvation. He concluded his graphic description of the Altalena incident, saying: "And so it came to pass that there was no fratricidal war in Israel to destroy the Jewish State before it was properly born. In spite of everything—there was no civil war!"

FROM FREEDOM FIGHTER TO POLITICIAN

With the establishment of the State of Israel, the *Irgun* transitioned into the *Herut* (Freedom) political party, opposing David Ben Gurion's *Mapai* party. Menachem Begin conducted the *Irgun*'s transition from an "underground resistance" organization, which had operated under an unwritten code of behavior, into a legitimate political party with a clear political agenda.

In accordance with Toth's "Theory of Two Charismas," mentioned earlier, Begin possessed the charisma and organizational skills needed to succeed Jabotinsky, who had died at a *Betar* summer camp in America in 1940. A significant point is that Begin's style of charisma and innate talents also enabled him to transform himself from the leader of a revolutionary group into the leader of a valid political party, thereby institutionalizing Jabotinsky's vision and beliefs at the center of his party's moral code.

In the early years of state building, there were many controversial issues and serious problems to resolve. However, in the early 1950s the one issue, in particular, that stirred the most painful memories and the deepest passions was the acceptance of German reparations.[19] This involved a highly emotional and complex blending of domestic economic, political, and psychosocial concerns with strong foreign policy implications. Because it stood in opposition to his vision of a tough, strong, independent, and dignified Jewish state, Begin campaigned with all his heart against accepting "blood money" from the murderers of 6 million Jews. Thus, Weber (1974, p. 247) was on to something when he wrote:

> [C]harisma, and this is decisive, always rejects as undignified any pecuniary gain that is methodical and rational. In general, charisma rejects all rational economic conduct.

The acceptance of this money was also anathema to various left-wing groups, the many apolitical survivors of Hitler's death camps, religious groups, and the *Herut* coalition, which actively demonstrated against what they saw as a German attempt to wash away its sins (Weber, 1974). However, the determining factor in the government's acceptance of German reparations was the practical needs of the infant Jewish state struggling to survive.

From the advent of the State, Begin was prepared to join a national unity government, just as he had put aside animosities that would have incited others to civil war. However, with Ben Gurion's refusal to accept him and his *Herut* coalition as partners in government, Begin led the parliamentary opposition.

In the years that followed, Begin's reputation as a gifted orator, writer, and political leader continued to grow. Lenni Brenner (1984, chap. 14; also at www.marxists.de/middleast/ironwall/09-mebegey.htm), associated with the "radical left," has been an articulate and severe critic of Begin. In contrast to Begin's admirers, Brenner notes: "If chauvinism was Begin's prime crowd-pleaser, pandering to ultra-Orthodoxy was an integral component of his parliamentary strategy."[20] It is worth noting that Brenner's "worldview" and political leanings are far to the left, much removed from the political beliefs of Begin's.

In 1965, Begin played a key role in the creation of the *Gahal*[21] faction that consisted of Herut and the more progressive Liberal Party. This was an important step, helping to legitimize his right-wing views among Israel's middle class and to enlarge his constituency. On the eve of the Six-Day War in 1967, he was finally asked to join the National Unity Government of Prime Minister Levi Eshkol.[22] According to Brenner (1984, chap. 13), "the 1967 war finally brought complete respectability to Begin and Herut."

In the aftermath of that war, the government of Israel accepted a U.S. proposal that signaled Israel's willingness to consider withdrawing from some of the captured territory. Begin and his *Gahal* colleagues opposed the government's decision, and Begin resigned from the unity government. In those years, Begin's vision of a "Greater Israel" was uncompromising. *Gahal* was strengthened in 1973 by joining with several smaller right-wing parties to form the *Likud* (Unity) opposition block headed by Begin.

Perhaps anticipating a run for the U.S. presidency, Jimmy Carter and his wife Rosalynn traveled to Israel in May 1973, as official guests of Prime Minister Golda Meir. Writing about his conversations with the Israeli prime minister, Carter noted that Begin's *Herut* party had 22% of the Knesset seats,[23] and commented:

> Neither Mrs. Meir nor I realized it then, but a member of one of the larger minority parties was destined to play a major role in her country's history, and much of his political strength would come from his deep fundamentalist convictions, based on a rigid interpretation of the scriptures. . . . Within four years he would be Prime Minister of Israel. (Carter, 1985, p. 30)[24]

Attempting to explain *Likud's* stunning victory over the party that had governed Israel since its founding, Carter cited the growth in the Oriental (Sephardic[25]) Jewish community, which had a significantly higher birthrate than the *Ashkenazim*.[26] He noted that by 1977, the *Sephardim* gave the *Likud* coalition a two-to-one margin. However, regarding the major factor for Begin's victory, Carter concluded:

But the *character* of Menachem Begin was a major factor in the victory. A *charismatic leader* and *spellbinding speaker*, he was able to convince many Israelis of his *personal courage* and his *steadfastness* in pursuing the political goals for Israel from which he had never deviated. . . . Begin's messages were easy to understand. He had a clear idea of when he might yield and what he would not give up in negotiations with his Arab neighbors and the United States. . . . (Carter, 1985, p. 41, italics added)

THE DEFINING MOMENT

History consists of certain defining "moments," in which all that was prelude and all that followed is identifiable as "pre-" and "post-." In the long history of humankind, a historical moment can therefore be seen as an era, during which a profound change (for better or worse) occurred. It is in those "moments" in the course of history that a "great" individual accepts the challenge of leadership, and all that preceded in that person's life is seen as preparation, process, evolution; and, all that follows in his or her life pales by comparison. This is particularly true when considering the life and work of a political hero. Winston Churchill, for example, suffered many failures, despite his enormous abilities and rhetorical skills. Yet, in his defining moment at the start of World War II, he rose to the challenge, inspiring millions of people in Britain and elsewhere across the world to "fight on" through years of horrific tragedy.

In the case of Menachem Begin, his achievements before the outbreak of war, his imprisonment by the Soviets, his years leading the *Irgun*, and his years of frustration leading Israel's parliamentary opposition, were all prelude to his electoral victory in 1977, which initiated a new era in Israeli politics, and ultimately led to the Camp David Peace Accords. On June 21, 1977, Begin's first day in the prime minister's office, he summoned his aide, Yehuda Avner. Telling Avner that he received a letter of invitation to Washington from President Jimmy Carter, Begin then said: "I will prepare the reply, and you will Shakespearize it." Avner (2003) related that Begin then gave him an encouraging smile and added in English: "Polish my Polish English. Stylize it. Give it a touch of Shakespeare."

Within the next few minutes, Begin received a phone call from Ezer Weizman, his new Defense Minister. Weizman reported that overnight two PLO Katyusha attacks launched from southern Lebanon hit northern Israel and a Muslim militia had slaughtered civilians in a northern Lebanese Christian Maronite village. The prime minister, with a pained expression, said that these attacks may represent a test of his will on his first day in office. According to Avner, Begin then suggested "a commensurate response," and added:

And as for the Muslim attack on the Christians, the policy of our new government is clear. It is our moral duty as a Jewish state to come to the aid of the Lebanese Christian minority. We shall come to the aid of any persecuted minority in the Middle East. The Christian world has abandoned the Maronites. We shall not abandon them.

Avner wrote that he was "dumfounded." He explained:

Begin had just turned Israel's Lebanese doctrine on its head. Yitzhak Rabin, his predecessor, never permitted Israeli forces to become so directly entangled in the Lebanese bloodbath for fear of being sucked into its infernal civil war.

Assessing the new prime minister, Avner (2003) stated:

No other premier before—or since—has possessed his cozy acknowledgement of God, his deep reverence for the Jewish heritage, his innate sense of Jewish kinship, his familiarity with ancient customs. None has had his infectious, Jewish common touch, which made Jews everywhere feel they really mattered. . . . Jews everywhere sensed that Prime Minister Menachem Begin was the quintessential Jew.[27]

Begin gave voice to the Sephardic communities who had been mostly ignored by successive Labor governments led by Israelis of European origin (BBC News, 1998). He also soon proved to be far more pragmatic than many political observers, both domestic and foreign, had predicted. To some extent, Begin's media style was not fully appreciated by the press in Israel or abroad, where preconceived prejudices against him long endured. Examining the semantic trick of influencing public opinion by choice of words, it is clear that Begin was considered by many in the media and among the Israeli public as the "quintessential outsider" in Israeli politics (Maoz, 1998).

Jason Maoz cited various reasons why Begin was "reviled by the Israeli media." These included his leadership of the underground *Irgun* during the 1940s, the reputation of the *Irgun* as a "terror militia," his far-right politics, and even "his very dress and demeanor," which was more formal and set him apart from first-generation Israeli leaders who tended to dress casually in open-necked shirts and even shorts on the hottest of days.[28] In addition, Begin's political opponents and the media in Israel and abroad were often uncomfortable with his forthright references to Jewish history, the Holocaust, world "indifference" to what was happening, and Jewish "destiny."

As Maoz pointed out, even Israel's American supporters were uncomfortable with his rhetoric. In short, he touched a nerve, reminding them of their Jewishness and, perhaps, awakening in them an undesirable sense of connection. "Disbelief" would best characterize the reaction of the American media to Begin's political ascent. This was followed by an enduring hostility. Maoz noted that the "media in Western Europe were, if anything, even more critical than their American counterparts."

During his first year in office, Prime Minister Begin invited Egypt's President Anwar Sadat to Jerusalem and 2 years later, in March 1979, they signed a peace treaty,[29] for which they were awarded the Nobel Peace Prize in December 1978. Carter (1982, pp. 319-403) commented:

> From Begin's point of view, the peace agreement with Egypt was the significant act for Israel. . . . With the bilateral treaty, he removed Egypt's considerable strength from the military equation of the Middle East. . . .

President Carter's well-known frustration with Begin surfaces from time to time in his writing, such as when he noted: "Begin spent the best part of his energy on the minute details of each proposal, the specific language of each sentence or phrase" (p. 43). No doubt, Begin was legalistic and pedantic, taking no chance on even a misplaced comma. He understood the deep significance of what he was doing; he knew that much was riding on this treaty.

Facing strong opposition from his own right-wing supporters, Begin set about fulfilling the treaty's difficult provisions, which ultimately included the forceful dismantling of the Sinai settlements. Carter acknowledged the following:

> Some of the concessions made by Begin were highly unpopular with his closest political associates . . . but he went forward courageously to gain Knesset approval for the withdrawal of all Israelis from the Sinai. (p. 45)

Unmentioned by President Carter in this context of difficult concessions for Begin and Israel was the courage it took to give up the strategic depth Israel had gained after defeating Egypt by controlling the Sinai, or the oil fields it had discovered and developed, which met a very large percentage of its oil requirements.[30]

However, even the peace treaty did not bring better press for Begin. He was still portrayed as the "intransigent" stumbling block to Anwar Sadat's "noble quest for peace" (Maoz, 1998). For example, Flora Lewis, the late *New York Times* correspondent, wrote an op-ed piece on the prime minister, voicing an attack usually heard from Jewish left-wing critics such as Noam Chomsky. Ms. Lewis wrote:

Menachem Begin's continuance in power would be too much of a risk
for the world at large. . . . Mr. Begin is a stubborn, narrow-minded man.
. . . Menachem Begin has one great achievement to his credit—peace
with Egypt. . . . Even the peace with Egypt was wanting, flawed in the
stingy focus on legalisms and failure to match the courageous initiative
of Anwar Sadat with a gesture of spirit . . . (www.letterfromgotham.
blogspot.com/2002_09_29_letterfromgotham_ archive)

On the issue of Judea and Samaria,[31] Begin's obsession with the Land
of Israel, the land of his forefathers, meant that he could not agree to divide
it, to cut it up, to give pieces of it away. The Begin government funded
archeological digs at many sites, seeking and finding evidence of ancient
Jewish ties to the past; and, when it came to Jerusalem, Begin committed
himself to safeguarding its reunification. Thus, after giving up the Sinai,
which had been used as a staging base from which the Egyptians had previously attacked Israel, he was never able to bring himself to give up anything more.

Beyond the issue of the West Bank territories, there was the national
security issue raised by the Iraqi nuclear reactor. Iraq had never been reti-
cent in showing its antagonism toward Israel, and as Maoz (1998) stated,
"While the world media were preoccupied with Menachem Begin's threat to
peace," Saddam Hussein, with French and Italian help was assembling a
nuclear bomb factory. As the French refused to desist from arming Hussein
with nuclear weapons and continued to insist Iraqi intentions were purely
peaceful, for Begin the question became when to launch the raid to destroy
the reactor. Although worried about the American reaction and expecting
the United States to join in the predictable UN condemnation, he felt certain that U.S.–Israeli relations would remain strong. He also felt certain that
President Ronald Reagan and his Secretary of State, Alexander Haig, would
remain Israel's warmest friends.

Facing a close re-election race against Shimon Peres, leader of the opposition Labor Party, Begin informed him of the plan to destroy the reactor.
Peres opposed the plan, and Begin realized that if he went ahead with the
raid, the media and his political opponents would accuse him of creating a
dramatic event to win votes. He also knew a harsh reaction, domestically
and internationally, would follow. However, his fear of a Peres victory, and
his conviction that Peres would lack the courage to launch such a raid, motivated Begin to act quickly, before the election. According to a Begin aide, the
prime minister "couldn't bear the thought of Israel living in terror of an
Iraqi bomb" (Maoz, 1998).

Thus, on June 7, 1981, Israeli pilots were sent to destroy Iraq's Osirak
nuclear reactor, then nearing completion. Israelis were elated by the news,
and Peres and his supporters, realizing how strongly the typical voter felt
about the destruction of the reactor, toned down their criticism. Addressing

representatives of the world press, Begin's defense—true to his usual rhetorical style—was direct and emotive:

> The Iraqis were preparing atomic bombs to drop on the children of Israel. Haven't you heard of the one-and-a-half million little Jewish children who were thrown into the gas chambers? Another Holocaust would have happened in the history of the Jewish people. Never again, never again. Tell your friends, tell anybody you meet, we shall defend our people with all the means at our disposal. (Maoz, 1998)

While the press dutifully reported the prime minister's words, they also reported the Soviets' characterization of the Israeli action as "an act of gangsterism." The late Moshe Dayan simply said:

> Not one Arab would shed a tear were Israel to vanish off the face of the map. . . . To me, the raid was a positive action. Iraq was producing nuclear weapons against Israel, and we were obliged to defend ourselves. (Maoz, 1998)

The international media played up the United Nations' condemnation, but Begin encoded his letter to President Reagan with the holocaust theme:

> A million and half children were poisoned by Ziklon gas during the Holocaust. Now Israel's children were about to be poisoned by radioactivity. For two years we have lived in the shadow of the danger awaiting Israel from a nuclear reactor in Iraq. This would have been a new Holocaust. It was prevented by the heroism of our pilots to whom we owe so much.[32] (Brenner, 1984, p. 387)

Begin's emotive vocabulary flowed from his life experiences and painted pictures that resonated in the hearts of his supporters. Although President Reagan temporarily halted delivery of some fighter planes, he privately assured Begin of his continued support. Despite the firestorm of criticism reported by the international media, Begin won re-election. A decade later, during the 1991 Gulf War, informed public opinion in America would view the bombing with greater understanding and relief.

Re-elected as prime minister one month later, in July 1981, Begin would soon respond to another national security threat, this time emanating from Israel's northern border. The incursion into Lebanon in June 1982, to end terrorist infiltrations and the continuous cross-border PLO Katyusha attacks into northern Israel, ultimately turned out very badly. Initially, "Operation Peace in the Galilee" halted assaults by Muslim Militias against the Christian

Maronites in Lebanon, saw an end to terrorist attacks against Israelis, and led
to the forced departure of most PLO fighters to Tunisia and other Arab
countries. But, it also led to a disastrous massacre of Palestinians in the Sabra
and Shatila refugee camps. The massacre was perpetrated by the Christian
Phalangists, Israel's allies, who were seeking to avenge the murder of Bashir
Gemayel, their leader and newly elected President. Begin was extremely distressed by the news of what the Phalangists had done and by the condemna-
tions of the world press, reflecting the assessment of their governments.

Then, in November 1982, came the death of Aliza, while he was in the
United States for various speaking engagements. Begin quickly returned to
Israel, and from then on, life became more difficult for him. He grew
increasingly depressed over his personal loss, the ongoing war in Lebanon,
the escalating number of casualties, the growing anti-war sentiment within
Israel, symbolized by a mass peace demonstration on the streets of Tel Aviv,
and, ultimately, the feeling he was no longer able to continue. His health failing, he resigned in September 1983 and spent the last decade of his life with
family and friends, away from the public eye.

IN RETROSPECT

One could never accuse Menachem Begin of being "indifferent." He spent
his life fighting for causes in which he believed, often against incredible odds
of physical and political survival. Consistent with his inner strength as a
leader, he was pugnacious. Although curious about what was said of him,
when it came to the British press he had consistently low expectations of ever
achieving their understanding. Yehuda Avner mentioned a telephone conversation Begin had with Lord Isaac Wolfson, which began: "So tell me, Sir
Isaac, the British press, do they have a good word to say about me on my first
day in office? Or am I still their favorite fiend?" Begin listened, "clucked his
tongue, wagged his head, and in a tone huffy with disdain, shot back":

> So *The* [London] *Times* is at it again, preaching Middle East appease-
> ment just as it preached German appeasement in the Thirties. That's the
> newspaper, remember, which dismissed the atrocities of Hitler's
> Brownshirts as mere "revolutionary exuberance." Bah!

Begin continued to listen to Sir Isaac, and then in a tone of resignation said:

> So there are people who still think of me as the ex-terrorist, eh? After all
> these years they are still blinded by their prejudices. But you know the

> truth Sir Isaac. You know we were never terrorists. . . . We were freedom fighters. We fought bravely, fair and square, man-to-man, soldier-to-soldier, against the British. Never did we deliberately hurt civilians . . . (Avner, 2003)

Ask any number of Israelis if they think Menachem Begin was a hero and these are some of the comments you will most likely receive:

- He showed courage and took risks to make peace with Egypt.
- In retrospect, he showed courage in ordering the raid that destroyed the Iraqi nuclear reactor.
- Given the risks to national security and the personal political costs. . . .
- I don't know if he was a hero, but he did many heroic things. . . .

Ask whether Begin was wrong to react to the attacks against the Christian Maronite community in Lebanon, or whether the cross-border attacks and the Katyusha rockets that hit northern Israel justified Begin's reaction, you will most likely hear that "something had to be done." In the end, even those who consider themselves on the political left will most likely agree that, "but for Lebanon," Begin looks better in retrospect than he did at the time.

CONCLUSION

When asked about Menachem Begin, almost no one mentions or considers his many heroic acts throughout his life, and it is clear that for many Israelis, the single act of signing a peace treaty with Egypt was enough, if not to call him a hero, at least to call him "heroic."

To Gerald Butt, Begin was:

> a hard man, who brought the Right in Israel to power for the first time. He was stern in manner, with the appearance of a schoolteacher rather than a statesman. But it was Begin's hard streak that gave him confidence to start the process of making peace with the Arabs. (BBC News, 1998)

However, in the this statement, substituting words like "brave" and "courageous" for "hard" reflects a more accurate picture of Menachem Begin. While a single extraordinary feat of courage could easily determine heroism on the part of other types of heroes, a political hero is a different breed of "hero." In today's world, only when the defining moment places the media spotlight on a particular accomplishment, does it enable people to focus their attention. Only then do they discern a single act of heroism, while missing the hero. To be clear, we think political heroes are not "tested" in or by a single event. We believe their intermittent or ultimate political demise (as was as true for Churchill as it was for Begin) distracts public attention.

Sadly, the extended view gets missed when studying political heroism. Such great individuals ought, instead, to be judged through the study of their consistent and enduring commitment to their people, their vigilance and acts of self-sacrifice, their intelligence and conviction in the "rightness" of their vision. A retrospective view of Begin's lifetime experiences leads to the conclusion that he was a great and charismatic man, a political hero who loved and made sacrifices for his people.

He was passionate in his beliefs and enjoyed meeting and speaking with young people in Israel and abroad. On a visit to address Jewish students at a California university, a young woman asked him what she could do to help Israel. He smiled and told her to learn to speak Hebrew and also to encourage her friends to do so. She then said: "Oh, but that will make us seem different." The prime minister's spontaneous response was completely true to his values: "There is nothing wrong with being 'different.' The problem is with being *indifferent*" (italics added).[33]

ENDNOTES

1. Jabotinsky was the founding leader of the *Betar* Zionist youth movement.
2. These are the qualities President Jimmy Carter (1985, p. 46) attributed to Menachem Begin
3. Jabotinsky had denounced the Jewish agency's stand opposing illegal immigration. He advocated mass immigration, exploiting all means, legal and illegal, and believed it was the solution to the Jewish problem in Europe.
4. This was an example of one of Begin's enduring characteristics, what some people (including President Jimmy Carter) might have called "nitpicking." Begin's legal training to demand "precision" served him well all through his life, especially later, in his negotiations as Israel's prime minister.
5. General W. Sikorski, who was the prime minister of the Polish government in exile, had been encouraged by British Prime Minister Winston Churchill to create the Polish Brigade (Churchill, 1950, pp. 108, 391).
6. For one analysis of British "fears, motivations, and perceptions" regarding the issuance of the Declaration, see Rubenstein (1985).
7. Take note of the word *indifferent*. To Begin it was a word that signified an important value: Jews must be aware, care about the world around them. They could never afford to be "indifferent."
8. Hebrew for "National Military Organization." Sometimes IZL is also referred to as Etzel, based on its Hebrew initials.

9. It is difficult to determine the total number of *Irgun* members before the British reprisals at that time; figures vary depending on the author.

10. The FFI was also called *Lehi*, based on the initials of their Hebrew name, *Lohamei Herut Yisrael.*

11. Begin spoke very highly of Meridor's ability, bravery, and commitment to the cause, as evidenced by his repeated escapes from British captivity. "Barbed wire fences could not hold him," Begin stated and cited Meridor's (1985) book, "Long is the Way to Freedom" (Begin, *The Revolt*, pp. 62-63).

12. The Shofar is a ram's horn once sounded in war and on solemn occasions. It is still blown on the Jewish New Year and Day of Atonement. The Western Wall is the surviving wall of King Solomon's Temple, dating back to the tenth century, B.C.E.

13. *Yishuv* is the Hebrew word used to describe the Jewish community in Palestine.

14. Hebrew acronym for Eretz Israel Labor Party.

15. Born in Russian Poland, Ben Gurion immigrated to Palestine in his youth. An ardent Socialist, he was the leader of Mapai and for many years chairman of the Zionist Executive. Following the British withdrawal, he became Israel's first prime minister.

16. *Haganah* is the Hebrew word for defense; this was the military wing of the *Mapai* and the Jewish Agency.

17. The *Palmach* is cited by Begin (2002) as "The more thoroughly trained section of the Haganah."

18. *Altalena* was Jabotinsky's pseudonym, with which he signed all his reports and articles.

19. The idea that Jews be compensated for their material losses may have grown out of a speech made by Kurt Schumacher, the post-war leader of the German Social Democratic Party. Schumacher, addressing an American Federation of Labor meeting in San Francisco in October 1947, spoke about the moral necessity of the Germans admitting their crimes against the Jews. See Rubenstein (1985, pp. 319-321).

20. In 1993, Abraham Foxman, the ADL's National Director, identified Brenner as a "member of the radical left." The debate over Foxman's and Brenner's opinions is accessible on the web through the Anti-Defamation League's website and through editors@fantompowa.net for Brenner's side.

21. Gahal is short for the Hebrew name Gush Herut-Liberalim.

22. In 1963, Eshkol succeeded Ben Gurion, whose government's involvement in the espionage and sabotage operations associated with the mid-1950s Lavon Affair ultimately destabilized his government. See J. L. Talmon (1961, pp. 22-30). Also see Seidenwerg (1976), the controversial account of Avri El-Ad, the former Israeli officer and intelligence operative involved in the effort to establish an Israeli spy network in Egypt.

23. Thus, Begin's Herut party controlled 26 of the 120 seats in the Knesset, Israel's Parliament.

24. Jimmy Carter, *The Blood of Abraham: Insights into the Middle East* (Boston: Houghton Mifflin Co., 1985, p. 30). Actually President Carter never really understood the deep impact the British policy of keeping Jews from entering "the land of Israel" and the horrors of the holocaust had had on Menachem

Begin. Although Carter did understand Begin's charismatic leadership abilities, his relationship with Begin might have been different (better) had President Carter been more perceptive and more knowledgeable about the Middle East, at the time he was finding it so difficult to "deal with" Menachem Begin.

25. "Oriental" Jews, whose families came from Africa and Asia, were called *Sephardim* (from the Hebrew word for Spain, *Sephard*). As a result of the Spanish Inquisition, the Jewish community in Spain dispersed and many resettled in Africa and Asia.

26. Those who fled Spain and settled in either western or eastern Europe and Russia became known as *Ashkenazim*.

27. Yehuda Avner went on to a distinguished diplomatic career, serving as Israel's ambassador to England and Australia.

28. Israelis generally dressed for their own comfort in a country with a subtropical climate. However, since the 1990s, with Israel's tremendous advancements in the high-tech area, many Israelis (who work in high-tech companies, banks, government, academia, etc.) have begun to dress more formally than they once did.

29. For a personal perspective on the Camp David negotiations, see Carter (1982)

30. In the earlier context of his 1973 visit to Israel, the then governor of Georgia attended a public forum and recorded some "private and public comments," that included: "Israel receives 90% of its oil needs from the Sinai and Iran." (See Carter, 1982, p. 29.) However, in the context of the 1977 Peace Treaty, Carter failed to include the loss of Sinai oil as a major concession on Begin's part.

31. Begin always referred to the West Bank territories by their biblical names. Originally, these territories were designated by the UN in their 1947 Partition Plan to become part of the new Palestinian state. However, they were annexed by Jordan in 1950 and then occupied by Israel after the Jordanians attacked Israel in 1967.

32. PalestineRemembered.com (1999–2000).

33. This incident was related to one of the authors during a telephone interview with a friend of the Begin family.

REFERENCES

Avner, Y. (2003, March 14). The quintessential Jew remembered. *The Jerusalem Post*.

BBC News. (1998, April 21). Publ. at 10:21 GMT 11:21 UK, *BBC Online Network*.

Begin, M. (2002). *The revolt*. Israel: Steimatzky Group.

Brenner, L. (1984). *The iron wall*. London: Zed Books.

Carter, J. (1982). *Keeping faith: Memoirs of a president*. New York: Bantam.

Carter, J. (1985). *The blood of Abraham: Insights into the Middle East*. Boston: Houghton Mifflin.

Churchill, W.S. (1950). *The second World War: The Grand Alliance, Vol. III*. Boston: Houghton Mifflin.

Gevasi, F. (1979). *The life and times of Menachem Begin*. New York: G.P. Putnam's Sons

Loewenstein, K. (1966). *Max Weber's political ideas in the perspective of our time.* Amherst, MA: University of Massachusetts Press.

Maoz, J. (1998, January 1). The day Israel saved the world: Israel's destruction of Saddam Hussein's nuclear reactor. *The Jewish World Review.*

Meridor, Y. (1985). *Long is the way to freedom.* Tujunga, CA: Barak Publishers.

Rubenstein, S. M. (1985). *The Communist movement in Palestine and Israel, 1919-1984.* Boulder, CO: Westview Press.

Seidenwerg, A. [El-Ad]. (1976). *Decline of honor.* Chicago: Henry Regnery.

Silver, E. (1984). *Begin.* London: Weidenfeld & Nicolson.

Solzhenitsyn, A. (1962). *One day in the life of Ivan Denisovich.* (Many different publishers).

Talmon, J.L. (1961, March–April). Lavon affair—Israeli democracy at the crossroads. *New Outlook.*

Toth, M. A. (1982). *Theory of two charismas.* Lanham, MD: University Press of America.

Tucker, R. C. (1970). The theory of charismatic leadership. In D. A. Rustow (Ed.), *Philosophers and kings: Studies in leadership.* New York: George Braziller.

Weber, M. (1974). The sociology of charismatic authority. In H.H. Gerth & C. Wright Mills (Eds.), *From Max Weber: Essays in sociology.* New York: Oxford University Press.

Chapter 14

HERO OR VILLAIN, BUT ALWAYS A CELEBRITY

John Paul II

Maria Way
University of Westminster,
Harrow, UK

In 1896, Pope Leo XIII was filmed by the Lumière Brothers. In 1921, the Catholic dioceses began to run radio stations in the United States. The development of media technology is reflected in the history of the Catholic Church. Today, the pope is both a celebrity and a hero and the Vatican a center for world-wide media. This chapter provides a historical and analytical portrait of the pope as hero and the media institutions that support him.

He is a man of contrasts. Contemptuous of modern consumerist culture and yet he is a master of the consumerist media, and he is a celebrity because of it.

—Comment on voice over of
John Paul II: The Millennial Pope

Even to Catholics, John Paul II was for some a hero and for others a villain. The opening quote is very true. He was a celebrity worldwide. He appeared on television screens and in newspapers and magazines. There was a seemingly endless market for news of him. Why is this?

We live, we are told, in an increasingly secularized age. In the Western world, attendance in places of worship is decreasing (UK Christian Handbook 2004/2005, 2005). There is a crisis of vocations to the Catholic priesthood which will, it is expected, be exacerbated by the spate of sexual abuse cases that have been reported in the last few years. Religious orders are in trouble. The average age of members of both male and female orders is increasing and this has caused financial problems as there are no longer enough younger members to provide for the older ones. The Roman Catholic Church is seen by many as antiquated and divisive in its ideas on morals, the family, women, homosexuality, and yet its leader was received around the world as if he were the answer to all problems. His use of the media, both at home in the Vatican and in his travels around the globe led to the development of a "Popecentric" Church and to what Garry Wills (1980) called *papolatry* from the media. Although others may speak, others may travel, he *was* the voice and face of the Catholic Church.

John Paul II was not the first pope to appear in the media. The Roman Catholic Church has a long history of taking up media in order to spread the Word as She understands it. There were pictures from as early as the first century—perhaps surprising in view of proscription by the Jewish faith against using pictorial representation, and statues and stained glass soon appeared. The Church's personnel were responsible for saving Latin and Greek scholarship for posterity because they produced sometimes stunningly beautiful hand-copied versions of them along with prayer books, books of Hours, Missals and Bibles, as well as the writings of religious thinkers. Printing and lithography were taken up as cheaper and speedier means of producing such material. During the reign of Pius IX (reigned 1846–1878) portrait photographs of the pope appeared and combined with the possibility of lithography made him, according to Duffy (1997), the most recognizable pope ever, despite the fact that since Italian unity in 1870 he had been, in his own words, "a prisoner of the Vatican." Leo XIII (reigned 1878–1903) asked the Lumière brothers to go to Rome to film him in 1896, just a few months after the first commercial film was shown at the Catholic University of Louvain, Belgium. Leo was 86 years old, but on celluloid at least he could escape this prison. There was sometimes a feeling in the Church that the cinema was "dangerous" (Molhant, 2000), but Church institutions soon began using films either as a tool for evangelization or in order to show edifying material to the young. The first "parish cinema" was founded in Milan as early as 1904. As early as 1921, Catholic dioceses began to run radio stations in the United States and in

1931 the Vatican opened its own radio station, free of Mussolini's fascist state. By a piece of serendipity, the film of its opening was the first film made with a live outside broadcast soundtrack. Newsreel films of popes became almost commonplace. Pius XII had already been filmed for French Television in 1949, a film in which he blessed the people of France and, somewhat strangely, delivered a talk on the importance of mass communications. Today's more sophisticated audiences may be amused by film of Pius XI opening Vatican Radio—he had evidently no knowledge of how to best appear on film and often had his back to camera, for instance, but there is an air of "naturalness" in such films. Pius XII was given to overblown hand and arm gestures, which probably looked good from the distance of St. Peter's Square, but look over–theatrical on film. John XXIII managed to take the media in his stride, despite the fact that he was in his late 70s when he became pope in 1958. In fact, his speech to the crowd gathered in St. Peter's Square after the first day of the Second Vatican Council in 1963 was a *tour de force*. Even now, this speech can move the viewer to tears with its statement that "even the moon has come out to join us on this night," and that they should each return to their home, find a child to caress and tell that child that this was a caress from the pope (a pope who knew that he was dying). Paul VI followed John's lead and began to travel outside the Vatican, not only in Italy but also in other countries. However hard he tried, he was not a media natural, perhaps due to his coloring and physique, as Cardinal Bea (1964) suggested. With each pope of the mass media age, the media have increased in power and availability and it is perhaps with John Paul I that that power was most strongly demonstrated. He reigned for only 33 days, yet he is remembered warmly as "the smiling pope" because television film of his short reign had gained such wide distribution. Thus, John Paul II was not the first pope of the mass media, a title usually given to Pius XII by writers such as Marchione (2002) and Eilers and Giannatelli (1996). Given that it was Leo XIII who was the first filmed pope and the first Encyclical on the mass media, specifically on film, *Vigilanti Cura*, was published in the reign of Pius XI and "ghost written" by Fr. Daniel Lord, S.J., who had started the League of Decency in the United States, this might seem to be an unjustified title for Pius XII.

The mass media, which Paul VI described as "*a most powerful means of social transformation*" (Apostolic letter—*Octagesimo Adveniens* 20), have enabled a globalization of communication unparalleled at any other time in history. We can watch simultaneous broadcasting from any part of the world. Add to this that John Paul II had his own radio station (Radio Vaticana), his own television station (Centro Televisivo Vaticano—[CTV]), his own newspaper (*Osservatore Romano),* his own Web site (www.vatican.va), that he made bestselling CDs and wrote a number of books, and that there were arrangements made with local broadcasting stations wherever he traveled to broadcast, and we begin to realize that it is not only Silvio Berlusconi who is a broadcasting mogul in Rome. CTV has a firm hand on the images we see of the pope(s). Originally started for the 1950 Jubilee Year (4 years before television started in Italy), the television station was dismantled at the end of the year to be restarted in 1983/1984. Through the last 20 years or more there have been contracts with RAI (the Italian state broadcaster) that enable simultaneous broadcasting of major papal events in Italy. The resultant programming is also broadcast on the 40 Catholic television stations in Italy and on 40 Italian "friendly" stations (interview with E. Milano, Director, SAT2000, 2002). One of these stations is SAT2000, a digital station set up by CEI (the Italian Bishops' Council) in 1998. In addition, the images are relayed around the world to interested stations. These may be those like the Eternal World Television Network (EWTN), based in Alabama, now said to be the largest religious television network in the world, which not only broadcasts all major papal events on television but also streams them on the Internet, or terrestrial national channels. Suffice it say that in the 2000 Jubilee Year, 122 countries took all of the images of papal events and many other countries took some of them. Through his travels, John Paul II was no longer just shown on religious television slots; he also appeared on prime-time news broadcasts. Although popes before John XXIII had appeared on news broadcasts from time to time, the decision of John XXIII to leave the Vatican and to travel, and later Paul VI's decision to travel abroad, visiting the Holy Land (a much lower key visit than that of John Paul II in 2000) and India, among other places, laid the foundation for the high media profile of John Paul II.

Although, by the nature of the position they hold, popes have always been "celebrities," their audience was limited to those who could see them in the flesh or who could see the statues or pictures (at first painted, then printed and photographed). The reach of the mass media has, however, meant that John Paul II had one of the most easily recognizable faces on the planet. Not only did the people of the world see the images of him taken "at home" in Rome, but he travelled to the far corners of the world. This has meant that many more people have seen him in the flesh than have seen any other pope, and television and radio stations in those countries filmed and recorded him and put him on their TV screens and radios.

Talking to media industry leaders while visiting the United States in 1987, Pope John Paul II said:

> Yours is indeed a profound influence on society. . . . Hundreds of millions of people see your films and television programs, listen to your voices, sing your songs and reflect on your opinions, it is a fact that your smallest decisions can have global impact. (*Wavelengths*, 1995, p. 13)

Media's ability to penetrate the private and cultural space of anyone at any place on the planet,[1] combined with John Paul's use of the media, made him a star worldwide. Through the years of his papacy his "image" changed from that of the "man's man that women could love," through the "benevolent grandfather" to the "suffering servant." It has been suggested that he gloried in this suffering (Zamoyski, 1998).

Fore (1896) suggested that those in the media can woo the viewer or listener by:

> . . . taking their own genuine needs (to be safe, to be liked, to be comfortable) and using them to create other needs which make them not only willing but quite eager to agree to what is being said, to buy what is being sold . . . (p. 128)

Other religious leaders have used the media to better or worse effect. In the United States one thinks particularly of Billy Graham and of Bishop Fulton Sheen (whose own case for beautification was put forward in 2002). While Sheen's program is one of the few religious programs, perhaps the only one, that has run at a profit, the Vatican showed a fiscal loss of 41,895,000,000 Lire in 2001 (the last year that accounts were to be shown in Lire). As the media are one of the major ways by which the Vatican evangelizes, there is little likelihood that this part of the organization will be closed down. For Dayan and Katz (1992), John Paul II used *televised trips to turn virtual power into effective authority.* Yet, as the author Arias (1986), who viewed John Paul II as an absolutist monarch, said, his style was not diplomatic. Mussolini is said to have suggested that the crowd was like a woman—it needed a strong man. John Paul, particularly once he was infirm, had a sheer doggedness that, despite the hands shaking from Parkinson's disease, the really bad days when his speech (in any language) was almost unintelligible, and the shots of him very obviously dribbling, showed a strong man totally secure in his faith. He had also been pope for a long time. In September 2002, he became the fifth longest reigning Pope ever, and he thus became something of a treasured icon. At his death in 2005, he had reigned for almost 27 years, the third longest papal reign. People who were then 30 years old (and some who are older) really had not known any other Pope.

HOW HE CAME TO BE

During the last years of his life, Paul VI is said to have been aware that he was not popular, in part due to the outcry against his encyclical *Humanae*

Vitae (1968). He felt increasingly isolated. In 1978 he died and a new, very different pope was elected. Albino Luciani was first and foremost a pastor. With a style more like that of John XXIII than of Paul VI, he endeared himself to the world and began to be called "The Smiling Pope." His ability to communicate, his apparent simplicity and modesty charmed even the most hardened critic of the Vatican. After only 33 days as pope, he died suddenly and rumors began that he had been murdered. Viewing his media appearances, one becomes aware of just how much this man did not want to be pope. He appears fragile, as he proved to be, and yet he made an impact on the world in only 1 month.

When the Conclave met to elect his successor, it was felt that someone stronger and perhaps younger should be elected. The man they elected, Karol Wojtyla, was 58. Not only had he been a university professor, he had been a manual laborer. Not only had he been a cardinal, he had also been an actor. Not only was he a priest, he was also a poet and writer. A philosopher rather than a theologian, he was portrayed as a sportsman and, as Cambridge University's Eamon Duffy said, as a "Bishop with Balls" ("Absolute Truth," 1998). He was also able to communicate with people, even if, on a visit to Poland shortly after the fall of Communism, he was able only to communicate his rage at the ways in which the Poles had taken up the evils of capitalism so soon after Communism's fall. In unedited film (Centro Televisivo Vaticano) of his visit to Mexico in 2002, he banged the arm of his chair with his hand when it became apparent that those being presented to him were not moving on fast enough. Not just balls—he had a temper, too. Neil Ascherson said that on the Pope's first visit to Poland as Pope, in 1979, it was noticeable that people felt that he was talking to each of them personally ("John Paul II," 1999). At large events—audiences, masses, and so on—it was one of his strengths that this happened. An Australian university lecturer, nominally Catholic, visiting Rome in 2002, went to an audience only because he felt it was an opportunity to add value to his holiday. He said that he found himself in tears and felt that this man's message was aimed at him directly, despite the fact that he was far from being a fan of John Paul II (I. Barnabas, personal communication, August 2002). According to Don Roberto Giannatelli SDB (personal communication, August 10, 2002), John Paul II developed this style, certainly in person-to-person contact. When he first became pope, he did not look at the person in front of him, but over that person's shoulder. Soon, however, he began to look them in the eyes.

The constant travels of John Paul II put him on TV screens in a way that previous popes could only have imagined. His use of the media in his work of evangelization has been noted. In a September 5, 1999 interview on Channel 5 in Britain, the actor Leslie Grantham said: *"It doesn't matter if you have a face like a Baboon's bum, if you are on television often enough you become a star."*

As written elsewhere (Way, 2002), John Paul was a star. We live in an age where celebrity, whether in "reality" television, crime stories, or the lives of the famous/infamous, sells media products. A celebrity, but was he a hero or a villain?

HERO

When John Paul was elected, he was for many an unexpected choice as pope. The first non-Italian for more than 400 years, he came from a Communist country. Poland may be a country whose identity is formed by Catholicism, but it was nevertheless Communist. Many, including ex-President Gorbachev of the former USSR, believe that it was because of John Paul's influence that the Communist bloc fell ("Absolute Truth," 1998). Since 1917, the Roman Catholic Church has seen Communism as its greatest enemy, to the extent that many feel that the Church was too favorable to Fascist regimes. There is no need to go into this further in this chapter as more than enough has been written about the attitudes of the Church and, more particularly, Pius XI and Pius XII in the period leading to World War II, during the war and in the post-war period (see Blét, 1999). Much of what has been written is ill-informed and biased either for or against this thesis. Those in the West who lived through the Cold War, whether Catholic or not, were led to believe that Communism was a great ill and an enemy to democracies everywhere. So, for the people and governments of democracies (and for some in the former dictatorships), John Paul became a hero in this regard.

John Paul was a man of faith in what is seen as an increasingly secular world. His type of faith may have been neither yours nor mine, but it was very evident. He was seen to practice what he preached—whether as the sportsman that he was when elected, as the benevolent grandfather or as the ailing, infirm, dogged man we saw before his death. He had a form of charisma that attracted many people, young and old, but perhaps particularly the young. At any event where there were young people, he seemed to feed on their energy. Often, he seemed stronger at the end of a long event than at the beginning. When he travelled to Israel and Palestine in the Jubilee Year 2000, it was part of a quest that he had long desired to undertake. As he arrived, a CNN reporter questioned the likelihood of the pope making it through the afternoon, let alone a gruelling visit. As he left, the same reporter remarked on how much stronger John Paul seemed than when he arrived. That he could attract many to the Church from groups that are seen as distanced (the young, the lapsed, those outside the Church by reason of being from other faiths), also made him a hero.

In his 80s, he showed clearly the signs of infirmity, not just through age but also because of the accidents he suffered. He had a broken hip, he had been shot, and he suffered from Parkinson's disease—yet he continued. Previous popes have, since the loss of the Papal States in 1870, mainly stayed in Rome—some such as Benedict XV, the pope during World War I, actually stayed within the Vatican being, as Pius IX is said to have called himself, a prisoner of the Vatican. John XXIII and Paul VI began to travel, John within Italy, and Paul both in Italy and overseas. John Paul II travelled more than any other pope in history. He visited many European countries (even those where the Orthodox are in the majority); North and South America, Africa, Asia, and Australasia. He undertook the 96th trip of his papacy in May 2002 and eventually made more than 100 overseas visits. He said that he would continue with his workload as long as he could physically because he believed that if he, in his infirmity, could continue, others who are sick or otherwise enfeebled would be given the strength to continue with their own lives. To many of these people and to their caregivers, he was a hero. Foucault (1989) wrote that the sick and dying are increasingly institutionalized. John Paul used his institution to bring sickness and death back into the public arena. He spoke often of what he described as the present day's "culture of death." In using his own sickness and vulnerability, he attempted to counteract this by proving that he had a usefulness and strength beyond and despite his weakness.

John Paul was a man of contrasts. Very conservative in some ways, for instance in regard to sexual matters, he was yet a keen advocate of ecumenism. In an age where there was unrest and even war blamed on religion, this was indeed a strength. He worked on dialogue with the Orthodox and Protestant churches in an attempt to draw the Christian churches together. At the October 6, 2002 canonization of St. José Maria Escriva de Balaguer, he included the Orthodox in the ceremony and on October 13, celebrated a mass in St. Peter's Basilica in the presence of the Orthodox Patriarch of Romania. He reached out to the Jews and was the first pope (since St. Peter, perhaps) to enter a synagogue to pray with the Jews there. He invited Muslims, Hindhus, Sikhs, Buddhists, and those of other faiths into dialogue with the Church. Gilbert Levine, the conductor, said that it was through his meeting with John Paul II that he came back to his Jewish faith. Levine (in "John Paul II: The Millennial Pope," 1999) believes that the pope was more interested in people's faith than in their sectarian loyalty. I personally do not believe this and think that his aim was to evangelize (a view endorsed by Ugo Moretto, then director of CTV, in a personal interview, November 2000). However, that he was able to encourage this interfaith dialogue in difficult times did make him a form of hero.

He worked unceasingly for peace. Throughout his reign, he prayed for peace, pleaded for peace. Although it was Paul VI who started the World

Days for Peace, which occur each January 1, it was John Paul II who brought these days to the notice of the world by holding what can only be described as "Peace Extravaganzas" in 1984 and 2002, as well as other more minor events. Using the backdrop of Assisi, a place associated throughout the world with St. Francis (one of the patron saints of Italy, along with St Catherine of Sienna), he called together spiritual leaders from all faiths to pray together for peace in the world. Christ is sometimes called "The Prince of Peace" and for at least the last 100 years, popes who are the representatives on earth of that Prince of Peace, have been calling for peace in the world. John Paul II gave these pleas a marked media presence throughout the world and in all faiths. Who else could call together the Free Protestant Churches, the Catholics and Lutherans, the Jews, the Muslims and the Hindu, the animists and the humanists, together with many other faiths, on the same platform, witnessing both their faiths and their desire for peace. For this also he was a hero.

ALWAYS A CELEBRITY?

Mark Silk (1998) wrote that the media in America tend to think of religion as "a good thing" (although the 2002 reporting on abuse cases related to the Catholic Church may have changed this view). Yet it is the media who set up "celebrities" and then knock them down again if possible. There have been cases where scandal involving "televangelists" in the United States have been seized on with some glee. Wills mentioned the "papolatry" that seemed to seize the media in the United States during the pope's visit. It is not only in the United States that this happened. When the pope visited the United Kingdom in 1982, there was considerable speculation as to how his visit would be accepted in a country where the Catholic hierarchy had been reinstated less than 150 years before and which, in some places, still has a tendency to anti-Catholicism (e.g., it is only recently that Glasgow Rangers and Celtic football teams have had players from outside their own faith groups). However, wherever John Paul went he was greeted like a long-lost son and he filled Wembley Stadium with people, something in the manner of many pop stars who have played there.

Even those who were not Catholic turned out to see the visiting Pontiff who was, as he said himself, the first Bishop of Rome to set foot on British soil (John Paul II, Address at Mass in Westminster Cathedral, 1982). After his visit to Britain (his 13th visit abroad) he toured the world. In Ireland, 25% of the country's population attended mass in Phoenix Park, Dublin. In Manila, 10 million people attended mass. It was not just his religious position that drew the crowd. He had become a media personality. John Paul played to the crowd. He wore Native American head dresses; South American ponchos; imitated Charlie Chaplin by waving his walking stick in tune to the music at events; made his hands into spectacles to look at the crowd; sang along (sometimes off key) with the crowd. Most of all, he had a sense of timing that many actors would envy. He could work a crowd in the manner of seasoned performers. It would seem that had he not become a priest, he might have been a considerable success as an actor. He certainly used his abilities in this regard in a way no other Pontiff had.

John Paul also "worked" the entertainment and media industries. Although Pius XI, as long ago as 1934, addressed the film industry, this was a semi-private event. When John Paul spoke at the Registry Hotel in Los Angeles, on September 15, 1987, not only did 1,200 American communicators attend the event, but many of them were moved to tears (Trasatti, 1988). The event was televised and filmed. He made a number of addresses about the media industry (see, e.g., Foley, 2000). Katz and Dayan (1992) suggested that he used the media to promote his authority. He certainly did this, but he also promoted himself as a celebrity, a celebrity in what Sorohan (1979) called (in the case of Ireland) "a broadcasting miracle." To add to his celebrity status, he attracted other celebrities. Not only did he meet politicians, heads of state, and religious leaders, but he also met film and pop stars. He appeared on stage with Bob Dylan, he gave audiences to Bono and U2 (and tried on Bono's sunglasses), and the cover of Trasatti (1988) shows him shaking hands with Charlton Heston (perhaps this should have a caption "Pope meets Moses"). As written elsewhere, during his papacy, he had a long career as a star, one full of reinvention (Way, 2002). As he changed physically, so he changed his media image and built on his celebrity status.

Despite this emphasis on John Paul II as a celebrity, it must be said that other popes, although they were not perhaps quite so visible, also drew crowds. Anyone who has watched films of the crowds in St. Peter's Square in February 1939, as Pius XI was dying ("Pio XI," n.d.), will know that popes have been able to draw crowds for a long time, sometimes, as in the case of Pius IX, because by the time of their death they were so disliked. In Pius IX's case, it was only without difficulty that the crowd was stopped from throwing his coffin in the River Tiber.

The Catholic Church has its own celebrities other than popes—saints. To be a saint one has to be dead, Catholic, and have drawn a following (either in life or after death) that has been sufficiently strong so that it can push a cause for canonization. Sometimes canonization has been relatively fast (indeed, at one time many saints were made by popular acclamation— which was suggested at the death of John XXIII by some of the participants of the Second Vatican Council), in other cases it takes centuries. Marco d'Aviano, a 16th-century Cappuchin monk known for his diplomatic work for the Church, was beatified only on April 27, 2003. Mother Teresa, who died in 1997, was beatified on October 19, 2003. John XXIII was beatified in 2000, but has yet to be canonized. Apart from a following, to be made a saint there has to have been an attested miracle before beatification can be considered. Popes, of course, are not always saints. The Borgia pope, Alexander VI (the father of Lucrezia Borgia), is unlikely to be a candidate. Of 20th-century popes only one, Pius X (1903–1914), has been canonized to date, although the cause for the beatification of John Paul I was started in 2002 and others are being considered alongside John XXIII. To be a saint is to be a type of hero, although some saints are more heroic than others. St. Thérèse of Lisieux might, by some, be considered heroic for her refusal to listen to pleas from her superiors to desist from praying in the cold when she was suffering from tuberculosis—perhaps for the other nuns in her convent she was a problem. The obvious way to be both a hero and a saint is to be a martyr. Although most people think of martyrs as those who died in the early church under Roman persecution, there are the 40 martyrs of England and Wales, who were martyred by the Protestants in the 16th century, as well as many others, particularly in the developing world, who have since died for their faith. One thinks of those like Archbishop Romero in El Salvador, who was murdered for his stance, or the deaths of six Jesuit priests, their housekeeper, and her daughter, who were killed in the same country. Even today, many religious and lay workers for the Church work in conditions that put their lives on the line. These are truly heroic people. Outside the Church there are, of course, those who think that these people are merely troublemakers. For those without faith, they are perhaps just considered rather stupid. In a post-colonial age, those religious who went to the new world that was opening up to bring the word of the Gospel may be seen as having been instrumental in destroying the culture of the indigenous peoples they went to "save." One wonders whether in years to come the media presence of John Paul II will be seen in a similar way.

John Paul's celebrity status did wonders for his book sales as well. He wrote extensively (it should be noted that encyclicals are not necessarily written by the pope—they usually are not.) He had been published before his accession to the Throne of Peter, but reissues of his books have sold in the millions. One must wonder whether the people who buy these books either read or understand them since they are heavily philosophical. It was his celebrity that sold them, not their content.

Just as Lévi-Strauss (1978) wrote of the making of myth, "*there are histories that are highly repetitive, the same type of event can be used several times. . . . But they don't take place in the same spot, they don't affect the same people and, very likely, they are not in exactly the same historical period,*" papal events and, even more so, papal travels, are to an extent repetitive. They always have masses. Where possible, they always visit major shrine sites. Major religious and political figures are always involved (and sometimes other celebrities), but they do not affect the same people. Each country treats the visit as its own. Each person reacts differently to that visit. The historical period is different and this affects the nature of the discourse, although the basic narrative (the story of Christianity and the Catholic Church) is always the same. The mythic quality of Christianity underpins the myth that is the pope. "The Day I Saw the Pope" itself becomes a mythical story, much as stories of the Queen Concert at Wembley Stadium or of Elvis Presley's Las Vegas appearances do. The celebrity angle almost overwhelms the religious reason for John Paul's presence. Whether we believe John Paul to be a hero or a villain, he was certainly always a celebrity.

CONTROVERSIAL ISSUES

Sexual Teaching

For the traditionalists in the Church John Paul was both a hero and a villain. He supported the idea of "traditional" morality at a time when society seemed to be bent on assisting its breakdown. In many Western countries, the number of marriages each year is decreasing and the number of marriages that do take place, but then end in divorce, is increasing. Many Catholics who divorce feel that they are no longer wanted in the Church. There is a supposition that a Roman Catholic annulment is something only given to the rich and powerful. Although annulments are not easy to obtain (they make civil divorces look ridiculously easy), it is possible for the "ordinary person" to go through the process if there are sufficient grounds that are canonically acceptable. The Church has made statements about homosexuality that seem to many to be confused. Although the Church accepts that a homosexual orientation is something that is not chosen but inborn, it does not accept the physical practice of that homosexuality. Thus, the divorced (those who have not received an annulment) and the homosexual Catholic either have to go against the teaching of the Church if they wish to enter into a sexual relationship, or they have to live a celibate lifestyle.[2] This is a difficult choice. Those who, like the pope, have taken Holy Orders, have chosen a celibate lifestyle and have done so of their own free will. Even they are not always successful in keeping these vows although, despite publicity to the contrary, the majority seem to. Quite a number of priests have left the active ministry to marry (or sometimes to "come out"). This is surely better than living a lie. Many of these men would be good, perhaps even better, priests in their new lives. Laicization, the process by which priests are returned to lay status, is possible within the Church, but is nowadays very rare. It seems to be an even more difficult process than annulment and is frequently much more unpleasant. Thus, it is easier not to bother. This not only means that men are lost to the ministry, but also that they have to remain outside the Church, and must marry outside the Church. The story of Archbishop Milingo, who through his healing ministry was gaining considerable congregations, first in Africa and then, when moved to Rome, in Italy, caused considerable adverse publicity. Milingo undertook a marriage (at 71) with a follower of the Reverend Moon, then not only dropped his wife, but also wrote a book about the experience (I confess that I have not read the book). After a period of time in South America, he returned to Rome and was accepted back into the fold. There has been a certain frisson attached to the story (elderly celibate celebrity marries—disappears—returns to the fold), but the fact that the Church accepted him back, apparently with some ease, angered many on both wings of the Church. Would he have been accepted back had he been merely a parish priest? (Probably, yes, if he had finished with the woman.) Where is the justice to the woman involved? (There is still a tendency to blame the woman in such cases.) If such a thing is acceptable why can the Western Church not accept a married clergy when the Eastern Church has one? (The likelihood of a married clergy in the Western Church under John Paul was nil.) In the second week of October 2002, a committee refused the idea of deaconesses, although in September 2002, the pope had made a statement encouraging the ordination of married men as deacons (see www.zenit.org for the texts of these statements). The coda to this story is that in 2006 Milingo returned to his wife and was finally excommunicated.

In addition, there were the various statements on abortion and contraception. Paul VI's encyclical *Humanae Vitae* was seen to be the result of his inability to make a decision. The Committee that had been called together to discuss the issue, which included married couples, had come to the conclusion that contraception should be accepted by the Church. Curial intervention seemed to have caused Paul VI not to accept their view.[3] The result of the encyclical was that many couples for the first time ignored the Church's teaching and began, or continued, to use artificial contraception to limit their families. Considered a matter of conscience, some priests could not find it in their hearts not to pardon those who, in the confessional, admitted to using contraceptives. Other priests simply left the Church. John Paul did nothing to change the Church's ruling. At a time when AIDS had become a plague of incredible proportions in some countries, he had advised continence rather than the condom. Although continence may be the only surefire method to stop AIDS from spreading, we are here talking about real people with real feelings. Abortion is, quite simply, always wrong. Only a woman who has carried a child that is possibly handicapped severely; whose birth might endanger her life and her ability to care for other children; or who is perhaps in a marriage where the male partner is incapable of supporting her and their children, or who has actually left her to care for her family alone, can understand the possible reasons that make women consider, or actually have, an abortion. I could not personally do this and did have problems in one of my pregnancies, but the heartache I suffered makes me quite aware of the problems that other women might have in continuing with such a pregnancy. A priest told me that in the pope's own Poland, many people are fanatically against contraception, yet the abortion rate is very high, abortion being treated almost as a lesser evil. This is surely a wrong emphasis. That a celibate leader seeks to advise the laity on their intimate lives in such a way made him a villain to many—and yet he made these statements from a commitment to faith that is hard to fault. For many women and men, his statements on sexual matters were anti-women. It was also an exercise of power over the laity who have chosen a different path, often one that seems to be denigrated as being a vocation "lower" than that of the priest or religious. As Hebblethwaite (1995b) said:

> The difficulty of loving the church—or loving anybody—is that love is incompatible with power relationships. So it is when the hierarchical church appears intent chiefly on imposing its power. . . . Power drives love out.

This is a Mother Church headed by a male leader many in the Western world consider to be an autocrat. Küng went so far as to call him "the last of the European dictators" (Hebblethwaite, 1995b). Küng (a priest as well as a professor) was stopped from teaching in a Catholic University. Although there are still more women than men in most congregations in Western Europe, the sexual teaching of the Church is often a reason for women (and some men) to vote with their feet and to stop attending. The recent publicity about pedophilia in the Church and the feeling within the Church that there should be more openness in the future in regard to these cases is worthy, if rather late. The Church should be considering not only the healing of the victims of pedophiles and their abusers (and I do not feel that money is ever an answer or a salve in such cases except in a perhaps symbolic way), but should also look at those who feel outside the Church because of their sexual orientation or marital status; those who have had abortions. God is a forgiving God. The Church, we are often told, is without fault. The Church is, however, made up of human beings and they are often neither forgiving nor do they show as much love to their fellow humans as they might. That John Paul could reach out to people in a crowd and make them feel that he spoke to them, did make him something of a hero in a world where people feel increasingly isolated in a society and where there seems to be a trend toward the demise of the stable family.

Mary

John Paul II often chose Marian shrines as places to visit during his media pilgrimages around the globe. Czestochowa, Monserrat, Fatima, and Lourdes in other countries; the Madonna del Parto and Madonna del Divin'Amore in his own Diocese of Rome. He spoke a great deal about the Virgin and more and more emphasis has been put on Mary's part in Christianity. His Virgin is an accepting woman. Her place is to be the mother of the Saviour. Some have said that his close attention to the concept of the Holy Mother may be a result of the early loss of his own mother. Certainly, the content of some of his published poetry would bear this out. He had a view of womanhood that was in some ways idealized. If one watches enough film of papal events, one sees that he paid attention to children, the young, the sick and to those with children. Many of my own contacts pointed out that he paid little or no attention to the single woman or man. If they were single women of childbearing age, they lacked a child. If they were middle-aged women they should have had a child. If they were single men, there was a sense that they had chosen the wrong path. Either they should have become a priest or, perhaps, they were gay. At a time when, certainly in Britain, the number of single-person households was increasing rapidly,[4] these people may also be lost to the Church through such an attitude. They certainly feel somewhat outside the fold of the Shepherd of Christianity. Many have pointed to the story of the Annunciation and the choice that Mary was given to accept or refuse this "job position" as Mother of the Saviour. The choice is something often forgotten and is certainly not something that John Paul II emphasized.

 With some of these decisions, the pope, whose media presence led to the "popecentric" Church mentioned earlier, made himself a villain to both the conservative and liberal wings of the Roman Catholic Church. Being the center of attention all the time and the victim of the "papolatry," Wills suggested, had its downside. John Paul II was the person at whom the buck stoped. His was the focus of the Church's presence and any problems could be blamed on him, even though Hebblethwaite (1995a), writing in 1994, pointed out that John Paul had had more than enough time to put his own stamp on the Curia and so, in fact, the Curia was likely to be made up of people who followed his line. John Paul II followed his own feelings rather than those of others in the Church. A Vatican official (who shall remain anonymous for obvious reasons) described John Paul II to me as being headstrong and sometimes difficult. As I said earlier, the episode in Mexico and his visit to Poland after the fall of the Communist bloc also showed him to be a man with a temper, one who it would perhaps have been better not to cross.

AND NOW FOR SOMETHING
COMPLETELY DIFFERENT?

John Paul II, pope, hero, villain, celebrity. . . . As I said earlier, the media build up a celebrity and are then quick to knock them down. During his reign, there were attempts to talk to women who knew him as a young man (see "John Paul II: The Millennial Pope," 1999), to discover any scandal there might have been. Inquiry has been made into his attitude toward the Nazi regime in Poland and then to the Communist regime that followed. Rather, as Monty Python would say, "nobody expects the Spanish Inquisition," nobody expected him to be Pope. A man from a far, Communist country, who was credited with bringing down the Communist bloc. A man of contrasts, who did not like Communism and could not cope with Capitalism. A media star throughout the world. Upon his death the media got onto the celebrity bandwagon and tried to demystify the myth. Perhaps we should begin to think of the next man in the job. He has a hard act to follow. Hero or villain, he is the successor not only of John Paul II, but of a 2000-year line of men, good or bad, heroes or villains who have led a multinational company whose message he will have to carry around the world and on the world's media. Not only does he have to be religious leader to 20% of the world's population, to be the leader of a massive institution, to be a person beyond scandal, he also has to become a celebrity in his own right, a media star and, preferably, also a hero in an increasingly secular world. As Archbishop Foley said (personal communication, May 2002), he will have to be, as popes have always had to be, a man for his time. The time is the present and his main stage will be the media.

A NEW MAN

Since this article was written, John Paul II has died. In 2005 it became evident that his life was drawing to a close. The illnesses and his age had caused a visible decline in his health and, eventually, in spring of that year he was unable to carry out the Easter services. The world's media began to gather and take up the places they had previously agreed to rent with a view to getting a good position—terraces, rooftops, windows, wherever a good vantage point could be taken. At Easter, there are always many media companies around the Vatican's perimeter, but this time there were more. On Easter Sunday, John Paul II came to his study window, but was unable to speak to the world. His Easter message was read by someone else. By April 2 he was dead, and not just the media, but also the people of the world came to Rome to say their goodbyes. Vatican Radio staff (personal communication, June 2005) estimated the number of visitors at 4 million, to a city that only has a population of just over 2 million. They came because John Paul II was the pope, the only one that many of them had ever known. They came because they loved him (he was their hero), because they hated him (he was a villain), but mostly they came because he was a celebrity.

On April 8, the world watched his funeral in Rome, either in person or on their television screens. The Vatican Television Center's images were taken up by broadcasters in 220 countries (personal information from Archivist at Centro Televisivo Vaticano, June 2005). The main celebrant was Cardinal Ratzinger. Ratzinger was already known to the world because he had been making headline news during his time at the Vatican. At the Conclave, it was he who was made the next pope; another non-Italian took up the post. Newspaper headlines greeted his election with far less respect than those published at the election of the Polish pope—"The Panzer Pope" and "Papa Ratzi" from the British press are two that spring to mind. Again, the media searched into his history, trying to find scandal. The most they could come up with was that he had been in the Hitler Youth. Because this was obligatory at the time, it is hardly scandalous.

Benedict XVI, the name Ratzinger took, is a shy man. In personal conversations with those who know him I have been told this, and also that he is a kind and caring person who listens to people. To take on the media mantle of John Paul II must be an enormous cross to bear for a shy person, but he has taken on the task with some aplomb. His style is different—he seeks the camera less often, for instance. In a personal conversation with a Swiss bishop, a friend of mine who has known Ratzinger for many years, the bishop said that he had worried about his friend, but that Ratzinger seemed to have flowered into this role. So far, his travels have not been so frequent as John Paul II's, but they seem to have been successful. His visit to Germany for the World Youth Days in August 2005 drew just as much attention as did the Youth Days attended by Wojtyla. In May 2006, a contact at the Vatican Press Office told me that Benedict XVI, far from being overshadowed by his predecessor, was actually drawing in bigger crowds— at least 20% bigger than those who had come to see John Paul II in person. He has, therefore, already been a villain, due to his previous reputation as a conservative; a hero, because he has been well-known since he attended the Second Vatican Council (1962-65) as one of the theology experts (he was then known for his liberality in theological thought), and because he is now the pope. Already he is a celebrity—a headliner on TV, radio, newspapers and magazines, and the Internet. Could it now be possible that we will ever have a pope, hero or villain, who is NOT a celebrity? I very much doubt it.

ENDNOTES

1. "In some cases, the media is controlled by powerful political, economic and ideological forces, since the mass media can sometimes be a means of cultural invasion, undermining the traditional, religious and family values in Asia, education and formation as to their use is very important" John Paul II. Letter to the Delegates of the Federation of Asian Bishops' Councils Vth Plenary Assembly, Bandung, 1990.
2. See, for instance, the statement of the Bishops of Switzerland. www.zenit.org October, 2002
3. See, for instance, interviews in *Absolute Truth.*
4. A recent report on housing in London showed that 50% of the housing in London sheltered one-person households.

REFERENCES

Films

Absolute Truth. (1998, September). BBC TV.
John Paul II: The Millennial Pope. [1999] *Pope—A Pope for the Ages at the Crossroads of History.* (1999) A Frontline co-Production with Helen Whitney Productions in association with ARTE. Produced by Helen Whitney.
The Opening of Vatican Radio (1931). Paramount Sound News [Filmoteca Vaticana & CTV].
Le Pape et le naissance de la television. (1950). Un film de J.P. Chartiers [Montage de René Guerin.CTV.]
Pio XI: il Papa della Conciliazione. (n.d.) In the series Testimonianze: Cultura Religiosa. Milan: Sampaolo Film.

Books

Arias, J. (1986) *Giovanni Paolo II: Assolutismo e misericordia.* Milano: Sperling & Kupfer Editori.
Blét Pierre, S. J. (1999). *Pius XII and the second world war according to the archives of the Vatican* (L. T. Johnson, Trans.). Mahwah: Paulist Press.
Dayan, D., & Katz, E. (1992). *Media events: The live broadcasting of history.* Cambridge, MA & London, England: Harvard University Press.
Duffy, E. (1997). *Saints and sinners: A history of the popes.* New Haven, CT & London: Yale University Press in Association with SC4.
Eilers, F.-J., & Giannatelli, R. (Eds.). (1996). *Chiesa e Comunicazione Sociale: I documenti fondamentali.* Torino: Editrice Elle di Ci.
Foley, J. P. (Ed.). (2000). *Giovanni Paolo II e il Cinema: Tutti I Discorsi.* Roma: Ente dello Spettacolo.

Fore, W. F. (1986). Communication and religion in the technological era. In *The myth of the information revolution: Social and ethical implications of communication technology*. London/Beverly Hills & Newbury Park/New Delhi: Sage.

Foucault, M. (1989). *The archaeology of knowledge*. London/New York: Routledge.

Hebblethwaite, P. (1995a). *Pope John Paul II and the church*. Kansas City, MO: Sheed and Ward.

Lévi-Strauss, C. (1978). *Myth and meaning*. London/New York: Routledge.

Marchione, M. (2002). *Pio XII: Attraverso Le Immagini*. Vatican: Libreria Editrice Vaticana.

Molhant, R. (2000). *Catholics in the cinema: A strange history of belief and passion — beginnings: 1895-1935*. Brussels: OCIC.

Silk, M. (1998). *Unsecular media: Making news of religion in America*. Chicago/Urbana: University of Illinois Press.

Trasatti, S. (Ed.). (1988). *Il Papa a Hollywood: Il Discorso di Giovanni Paolo II. 25 Commenti Italiani a cura di Sergio Trasatti*. Rome: Ente dello Spettacolo.

UK Christian Handbook 2004-2005. (2005). London: Christian Research.

Encyclicals

Humanae Vitae: Encyclical of Pope Paul VI on the Regulation of Birth. July 25, 1968.

Vigilanti Cura: Lettera enciclica di papa Pio XI sul cinema. June 29,1936.

Articles

Bea, Cardinal A. (1964). Preface. In J. Walsh, S.J., *The mind of Paul VI: On the church and the world*. London: Geoffrey Chapman.

Hebblethwaite, P. (1995b), Why I love the church. *National Catholic Reporter, 6*.

Sorohan. J. (1979) Pulling off a broadcasting miracle with nine weeks' notice. *Irish Broadcasting Review*, pp. 46-47.

Wavelengths (1995, June). *XLVIII*(13).

Way, M. (2002). Pope as media star: A long career full of reinvention. Paper presented at the IAMCR Conference, Barcelona.

Wills, G. (1980) The greatest story ever told' *Columbia Journalism Review, 19*, 25–33.

Zamoyski, A. Interview in John Paul II: The Millenial Pope.

Chapter 15

GODS IN ALL THINGS

Media, Culture and Cycles
of Heroic Construction in Japan

T. J. M. Holden
Tohoku University

The hero in Japanese is ingrained into the history of Japan. This chapter examines the changing concept of heroism in Japan, tracing an evolutionary path from the "mythic" to the "mundane." The intimate link between gods and heroes and the religious ethos of Shintoism in the development of Japan is a contrast to a more secular perception of the American hero, particularly in the creation of the nation.

✧ ✧ ✧

WHAT IS A JAPANESE HERO?

Ask that question in 1945, and the answer would likely have been a member of the Divine Wind Special Attack Force—*Shimpu Tokubetsu Kogekitai*—or, what has come to be popularly (although erroneously) known as *kamikaze* fighter pilots. These intentional suicides—who aimed their flying incendiaries at American ships in the hopes of exchanging one life for hundreds—were labeled "gods without earthly desires",[1] men whose unflinching sacrifice for nation marked their deaths as "heroic."[2]

Ask the question in 1995 and the answer would have more likely been a batter in a baseball game who smacked a *sayonara* single, scoring the winning run. That man would be smothered by teammates as the opposing team slinked off the field in defeat. He would be slapped on the head and back and butt, pushed up on a platform, cheered by 200 remaining fans as he was accorded the so-called *"hero interview,"* broadcast nationwide on TV. The following night, time permitting, another hero—perhaps a pitcher or a rival batter—would be accorded the same moniker. Or, if fortune so deemed, the previous night's star might once again play the present hero.

In the new millennium, Japanese heroes must no longer crash and burn. They can live for another day. They can perform a second act of heroism, thereby further securing their place in history, gaining another rung on the ladder toward cultural immortality. And more so than in the past, Japanese heroes are popular figures, celebrities whose deeds and images owe much to communications media that construct and sustain them for profit and popular pleasure.

That, in a nutshell, is the thrust of this chapter. On the following pages I trace this sea change in the conception of heroism in Japan. I explore, as well, the underlying reasons for this change, as well as the manifestations and implications of such transformations. To a large degree, the answer lies in profound structural changes: in polity and economy; as well as significant cultural changes: in technology, morality, and lifestyle. The answer also lies in the increasingly central position of media in Japanese society, the powerful links between capitalism, communication, and entertainment, as well as social forces bearing on and flowing through media—forces such as individualism, nationalism, globalization, and celebrity.

At the same time, and not without contradiction, the answer lies in a certain stasis that has pervaded the depiction of heroism from time immemorial: a repetitive pattern that threads from earliest myth, through national consolidation, embracing phases of war-making, and epicureanism. Surveying cultural history, what we find are alternate periods of martial activity, followed by pleasure-seeking, each period serving to determine the interpretation and perception of heroism. Bouts of social cataclysm are followed by periods of restructuring, economic prosperity, a certain moral licentiousness, and political quiescence. This trend, as is seen here, has delivered us to a present in which celebrity, leisure, and globalized sport export are the fulcrum of society's definition of heroism.[3] Which is another way of saying: To look at the historical, technological, economic, and political contingencies that bear on Japanese conceptions of heroism may only take one so far. Another important dimension inheres in continuities—certain logics of culture and rhythms of history. Undergirding it all stands a basic heroic archetype: "god." It is out of this universal type that a limited number of incarnations have flowed. These incarnations have been expressed over the course of Japanese history, through an array of media forms. Let's now turn to a brief consideration of each.

JAPAN'S BASIC HEROIC ARCHETYPE

It would be a mistake to regard the two conceptions of hero introduced at the outset as Japan's only types. They are, however, emblematic of the basic archetype: *kami* ("god"). Subsumed within that type are numerous kinds that can be located in contrasting spheres, which I label the *mythic* and the *mundane*. Surveying some 14 centuries of recorded Japanese history, among the most important mythic variants include *nature, kamikaze,* and the *fantastic;* the mundane manifestations include: *samurai, corporate warriors,* and *entertainers and celebrities.* Before considering each of these, the central archetype from which all others flow is discussed.

Gods As Heroes

Unlike the United States, which can point to a revolution and a written document as its points of conception, Japan starts with a creation myth. This myth was actually written in the late seventh century and sent to all corners of Japan by political emissary-settlers (Hunzinker & Kamimura, 2002). It was likely crafted by astute politicians, cognizant of the importance of legitimizing their claim to power. It cleverly played on the human desire to hear tales of one's uniqueness. For the creation myth asserted that Japanese possessed exalted status; they descended, it was said, directly from heaven.

Specifically, the myth explains how two gods—one male, the other female—were sent from the sacred realm to create and rule over the earthly world. As the gods stood on the celestial bridge, regarding the swirling fog below, the male suggested that "they should try . . . stirring up the brine with their spear. So saying he pushed down the jeweled shaft and found that it touched something. Then drawing it up, he examined it and observed that the great drops which fell from it almost immediately coagulated into an island, which is, to this day, the Island of Onokoro" (Shibukawa, 1999) or Japan.

Creation of the remaining islands of Japan soon followed (then, as an afterthought—and quite a while later—the remainder of the world). So, too, did an unending procession of *kami* result. First were those taking the form of nature's elements: land, sea, mountains, rivers, trees, and herbs. The sun goddess, *Amaterasu*, proved especially important in this account. First, because she presides over the Plain of Heaven, and shines on Japan; but, second, because she bore a divinity-child, *Ninigi*, who, in turn, gave birth to *Jimmu Tenno* (or *Kamu-Yamato*), the first emperor and founder of the imperial dynasty.[4] In the words of one commentator, it is through this natural divinity—from god to human—that the hegemony of the Yamato House is mythically legitimized."[5] This, of course, has repercussions later in modern history, as the Japanese empire installed the notion of divine accession to assert its superiority over other nations and ethnic groups and justify Japan's subjugation of them. The "state Shinto" that resulted created a deity out of the emperor. Common people were not to peer at the ruler directly, his pictures were treated as holy relics in schools and, if possible, they were housed in separate shrines. What's more, all Japanese citizens were instructed that they lived merely to repay their emperor's benevolence; their job was to die, if necessary, to achieve his nation's objectives (Reischauer, 1978).

Pursuing the mythological thread, one sees that in Japanese folklore—and then later instituted in Shinto religion and wedded to the State—gods, nature and humans are not clearly distinguishable. They are often cut of the same cloth and their exploits are often presented as bound together—as in the case of a suicide bomber who pens a *haiku* about the purity of the ephemeral cherry blossom, before boarding his aircraft and serving the heroic function of defending the divine, serving as one of the "emperor's shields" (Matsuo, cited in Morris, 1975, p. 314).

Defense of cultural beliefs and societal institutions, then, qualify as heroic acts. And, indeed, *kami*, as spirits, often serve this protective role. They stand sentinel over Japan—the nation, its natural environs, its human population—guarding it against enemies and calamity. Thus, one repeatedly hears of tales such as the famous *kamikaze*—or "divine wind"—episode of the 13th century, in which a sudden typhoon swept across the archipelago, causing more than 100,000 of Kublai Khan's invaders to perish just off the coast. So, too, do Japanese make it an annual ritual to visit a shrine, offer coin, and pray for good fortune in work, health, and for family. However, *kami*s are not exclusively beneficent, meaning that *kami*s are not always heroes. Indeed, as in the case of the unanticipated wind, *kami*s can be capricious, vengeful, audacious, beguiling—even evil.

So, where, then, is the link between gods and heroes that might prove more substantial and enduring? It resides in the religious ethos of Shinto, an indigenous religion that, over the course of centuries, ascended to cultural supremacy throughout Japan. Reischauer (1972) explained:

> Shinto . . . "the way of the gods" . . . was based on a simple feeling of awe in the presence of any surprising or awesome phenomenon of nature—a waterfall, a mountain crag, a large tree, a peculiar shaped

stone, or even some lowly thing awesome only in its capacity for irrita-
tions, such as an insect. Anything awe-inspiring was called kami, a word
usually translated as "god" but basically meaning "above," and by
extension "superior." This simple Shinto concept of deity should be
borne in mind in trying to understand the deification in modern Japan
of living emperors and of all Japanese soldiers who have died for their
country. (pp. 12–13)[6]

As this chapter develops, we see how Reischauer's admonition applies not
only to representations of the Emperor and war, but throughout history: in
the depictions of warriors, artists, corporate workers, fantasy characters, and
celebrities. In fact, no matter what incarnation the Japanese hero takes, no
matter what environmental circumstances give birth to them, no matter the
medium through which they are depicted, heroes in Japan all assume the
character of *kami*: Japanese heroes are those whose special talents or status
is sufficient to place them above the average person.[7]

If one suspects, then, that there might be a rather limitless supply of
gods, one would be correct. As the popular saying goes: There are as many
as 800 deities.[8] One can still see remnants of this in daily life—encountering
people whose family names are, literally, "Stone God," "North God,"
"Village God," "River God," and "Forest God," among others. It is this
polytheism, along with its companion cornucopia of incarnations, that may
account for the rather large number of manifestations of heroic types that
have surfaced during the course of Japanese history. It may also account for
why contemporary Japanese media seems to exhibit an insatiable appetite—
a peripatetic restiveness—for newer, fresher, progressively more excessive,
celebrity heroes.

MYTHIC HEROES

Nature as Hero

What is the most famous Japanese painting? At least in popular conception
it is almost certainly *Hiroshige*'s view of Mount Fuji—often simply called
"The Great Wave" (Fig. 15.1). In this picture two powerful objects—a vol-
cano and a *tsunami* (or tidal wave)—are depicted. The only sign of humanity is a boat, swallowed in the well of the wave. Conveyed is the overwhelming force of nature—an earthly supernatural presence.

As has been seen, nature plays a leading role in Japan—not only in life,
but in myth. The cluster of islands comprising the nation is the progeny of
Gods. The original *kamikaze*—the divine wind from which World War II
fighter pilots derived their name—sprung from the typhoon that miracu-

Figure 15.1

lously swept away an invading army and saved the nation from certain defeat and subjugation.[9] And this perception of nature as divine ripples through Japanese media over the centuries: from folklore, to woodblock prints, from poetry to cinema, novels to advertising. For instance, nearly every writer of import has at least one title referring to the natural world: Akutagawa (*Autumn, The Garden*), Kawabata (*Snow Country*), Tanizaki (*Some Prefer Nettles*), Mishima (*The Sound of Waves*), Dazai (*The Setting Sun*), Abe (*Woman in the Dunes*). Nature often serves as metaphor for the lives of human protagonists—whether mundane or tragic, the prototype or explanation resides in nature.

So too in *ukiyo-e*—the dominant visual form of the 18th and 19th centuries, "the world's first true mass art and the forerunners of the picture postcard" (Reischauer, 1978, p. 76). Although the environment was not the sole genre in woodblock prints, when depicted, it evinces a striking tendency: Most often it dwarfs any human present. This is effected either via sheer scale or by overwhelming force. For instance, in Fig. 15.2a, although humans work along the banks of the river, they appear as mere specks, nearly impossible to discern. In Fig. 15.2b, the great Mount Fuji looms high above a village, casting its glorious reflection in the adjacent bay.

Figure 15.2a

Figure 15.2b

In cases when nature was not overwhelming humans, it was containing them: framing their actions or defining their existence. In Figs. 15.3a and 15.3b, we witness human agents bounded (and battered) by nature: villagers trudging through drifts of snow or laboring across the span of a bridge, braving a deluge from the heavens. In such cases it is human existence on nature's terms.

Rendered in Chinese characters the word "nature" (*shizen*) means "from itself, thus it is." In effect, nature is a *mode of being*, not a state of simple existence. Nature possesses the power of spontaneous development; it is an entity capable of acting, of producing effect, of achieving. The things that it achieves are so much more powerful than those accomplished by human hands. And in Japanese mediations—from the telling of the *kappa* (Fig. 15.4a) myth, to the photography of cataclysms such as the Great Kanto Earthquake of 1923 (Fig. 15.4b) or the reportage of the Hanshin Earthquake of 1995 (Fig. 15.4c), this is true. Nature proves time and again that it is a force defying human comprehension and control.

The heroic, awe-inspiring status accorded to nature, has meant that even today the natural emerges as humanity's equal, at the very

Figure 15.3a

Figure 15.3b

Figure 15.4a

Figure 15.4b

Figure 15.4c

least. It is a common to preface written correspondence with a salutation that refers to prevailing weather conditions. There is something about the commonality of humans constrained within a universe of "natural" forces, as well as the attempt to communicate the bounding conditions under which the correspondence was drafted. Moreover, in popular (and pervasive) communications such as news, entertainment, and advertising, nature is accorded a central position. A random sample of television ads, for instance, will bear out the fact that in cases where actors are posed in the natural environment, the latter receives as much or more visual and significatory attention as the former. This is true even when the person depicted is a famous person or celebrity (see Fig. 15.5). Significantly, when the human (in the form of a celebrity or entertainer) appears in natural settings, the latter is emphasized as much or more than the former.

As one can see in Fig. 15.6, advertisements employ nature as a frame for human action that is highly reminiscent of *ukiyo-e*. Beyond serving as a simple frame, the natural is often employed to define the human actor. Thus do nearly identical tropes of signification and nature-based code creation appear in advertising that earlier were present in *ukiyo-e*. In a word, the pervasive, insuperable, heroic status of nature has not dissipated with time in Japanese media.

Figure 15.5

Figure 15. 6

The Kamikaze as Hero

Nature is not only heroic, of itself; it has served to assist in the construction of heroic types. This is true, to a certain degree, in the case of the *samurai*, whose adoption of Zen in the 12th century resulted in reverence for and harmony with nature. The embrace of nature not only worked to reinforce asceticism, it found its way into the samurai's artistic creations: representations of landscapes in simple monochromatic painting and highly stylized rock gardens. Perhaps the most significant wedding of nature with the "way of the warrior," however, was the adoption of the *kikusui*—or floating chrysanthemum—as crest for the 14th-century samurai, Masashige Kusunoki. His status as national hero lay in the willing sacrifice of his life (and that of his 600 men) at the behest of and on behalf of the emperor in the face of superior opposition forces. For these efforts, Kusunoki's heroic tale was promoted by the Imperial household during the *Meiji* era. So, too, was the heightened use of his half-flower symbol. Kusunoki signified selfless human sacrifice for the emperor and, beyond, the nation.

The invocation of natural symbols among the warrior class descended to the *kamikaze* pilot of the Pacific War. Appropriating Kusunoki's crest for their planes, and employing *kikusui* as labels for their missions, the young suicides often cited Kusunoki's sacrifice as a model for their endeavors. Beyond the chrysanthemum, however, they also invoked the cherry blossom as a natural metaphor. Like the famous flower, life is evanescent; precious, short-lived, it blooms all too quickly, sparkles spectacularly, then is snuffed out in an all-too-brief span. The medium for commemorating their act of heroism was the poem. Following their sacrifice, the names and artifacts of these "earthly gods" were installed in national shrines: war monuments adjoining Shinto temples.

Of course, the *kamikaze* were appropriating more from the past than simple romanticized naturalism. Like Kusunoki, they accepted the idea— later installed in the *Hagakure* that "the way of the warrior is (finally) revealed in the act of dying." In the words of another warrior: "one's way of dying can validate one's entire life" (cited in Morris, 1975, p. 13).

Like Kusunoki, the *kamikaze* were serving their emperor. This seemed natural because it was how the pilots had been socialized over the course of their brief lifetime.[10] As Kapur (1999) has explained:

> During the *Meiji* period, educational reformers resurrected the legend of Masashige Kusunoki and enshrined him as a national hero who epitomized loyalty, courage, and devotion to the emperor, the ultimate samurai warrior who represented everything the samurai code of *bushido* stood for. The story of Kusunoki's noble sacrifice became part of the national curriculum that all young Japanese studied in the years prior to the war, such that by 1944 every Japanese knew the legend.

The linkage between samurai, self-sacrifice for nation and heroism was further forged as pilots prepared for their final mission. Numerous authors have explained that: "The cadets would then hear a spiritual Moral Lecture from their commanding officer on the great heroes and battles of the past, Japan's divine mission to free Asia from the decadent Western powers, and the samurai code of *bushido*" (Warner, Warner, & Seno, 1982, p. 40).

Millot (1971) indicates that "such lectures would focus on legendary heroes such as *Yoshitsune*, the famous *Minamoto* warrior who chose death over dishonor, *Yamato-Takeru*, another legendary figure who died for the Emperor and was turned into a great white bird, the wandering samurai

Figure 15.7.

Miyamoto Musashi, or the famous 47 *Ronin,* who avenged their murdered
master and then chose to follow him in death by committing suicide" (p. 6).
Contemporary heroes were also mentioned in speeches: the men who lost
their lives in Shanghai in a 1932 uprising, sailors who perished in midget
submarines during the Pearl Harbor attack, Sakio Komatsu who crashed his
plane into an American torpedo to save the aircraft carrier *Taiho,* Shigeo
Nobe, who rammed a B-29 bomber, and Rear Admiral Masabumi Arima,
commander of the 26th Air Flotilla in the Philippines, whose effort to convince the Imperial Navy to adopt crash-diving tactics, resulted in his personally leading a kamikaze-style suicide mission in October, 1944.[11]

The heroism that all this speech-making loosed is commemorated at
Yasukuni Jinja, the shrine that houses a war memorial. The monument, constructed in 1869, is a medium in which heroism is consecrated and preserved
and through which heroism is communicated and reproduced. Although the
shrine is home to the souls of some 2.4 million Japanese soldiers killed in
service of their emperor since the Meiji era began, the great majority of the
dead belong to those who fought in the Pacific War. The physical remains of
many warriors are buried there, including those of *Hideki Tojo,* general and
wartime prime minister of Japan, who was convicted of alleged war crimes
and then executed in 1948 by the U.S. Occupation tribunal. At *Yasukuni*
two rooms are devoted to the *kamikaze* fighters. One is for the survivors of

the special tactical squadron; the second is devoted to some 6,000 men, age 17 to 30, who crashed their planes and manned torpedoes into the U.S. fleet.[12]

Almost every year for the last decade of the 20th century (and halfway into the new millennium), a succession of Japanese prime ministers managed to infuriate regional neighbors as well as draw wide-spread media attention by visiting *Yaksune* shrine on the day commemorating the end of the Pacific War. Invariably, these leaders have sought to mollify angry Asian neighbors demanding apologies:[13] They have claimed that the visit is ventured as private citizen, rather than national figurehead. There is never any dispute, though, about the intention of their visit: to honor fallen Japanese heroes.

What is the cultural significance of these war dead? In his historical exploration of Japanese heroes, Morris (1975) opined:

> The myth of the failed hero . . . is the Japanese equivalent of the universal concept of a fallen god who is resurrected so that he may survive in a transcendent world—a world representing the perfection of those ideals for which he struggled on earth. . . . While the Japanese hero is promised no paradise or Elysium where he will receive compensation for his earthly travails, he does survive in the memory of his nation. (p. 65)

In this way, Morris concluded, "The failed heroes of Japan may thus be regarded as demigods" (p. 65)

The Fantasy Action Hero

In 1954, a dinosaur long in slumber beneath the ocean was awakened by atomic fallout and, thence, transformed into a mutant monster, terrorizing humankind. In his first incarnation, Godzilla was the enemy—a cinematic warning against human's reckless development of technology (Fig. 15.8). Subsequent movies, however, reinvented the beast as humanity's savior—rescuing earthlings time and again from an unending stream of other-worldly monsters: Mothra, King Kong, King Ghidorah, Destroyah, Ebirah, the Smog Monster, Gigan, Megalon, and Mechagodzilla.[14] Whichever form he took—whether as friend or foe—however, Godzilla was reprising the ancient *kami* archetype. He was the power capable of dwarfing humans and freezing them in awe. In true *kami* fashion, while he began his career as a vengeful force, he was reborn as a friend of humankind, a defender of the earth.[15]

Godzilla (Fig. 15.9) was on the cusp of the superhero era in contemporary popular culture, part of a lineage that includes the mighty tyke *Atomu*,

Figure 15.8

Figure 15.9

the extraterrestrial Ultraman, the computer-generated, parallel-universe-dwelling Gridman, and the human-sized (but not always human) *Dai Renja* (or "Great Rangers"). Gill (1998) provided a concise analysis of these heroes, exposing threads that can be traced to earliest aspects of Japanese culture, as well as providing passing, but illuminating, contrast to heroes in American society.

In all of these representations of hero, women are conspicuously absent. The *Dai* Rangers have always had at least one token female, but never a majority. By contrast, villains are quite frequently female—witches and goblins—capable of casting spells and marshalling the allegiance of an array of creatures: gnomes and the like.

To some degree, the woman-as-evil antagonist exists in *animé* (animation) and *manga* (comics), however, there is also greater presence of positive images: girls and young women who possess occult powers of telepathic communication, telekinesis, the ability to confer eternal life. According to Napier (1998), a number of these so-called *shôjo* heroines "hav(e) . . . virtually godlike powers" (p. 102). In the case of one, in particular,[16] "there is the explicit equation . . . with a godlike figure from ages past who will come to save the world" (p. 102).

Such is the case, as well, for the much ballyhooed *Sailor Moon* (Fig. 15.10). This heroine is just an average junior high school girl—clumsy, dipsy, cloying, and cute—or, so she thinks, until she encounters a talking cat, which reveals the truth about her identity: She is actually the human manifestation

Figure 15.10

of the extraterrestrial Princess, Serenity. Serenity is one of the last survivors of the Moon Kingdom, which was destroyed by the evil Queen Belial. Serenity, who now calls herself "Sailor Moon," becomes Earth's guardian, supported by her band of "Sailor Scouts."[17] Throughout the television series, Serenity and her partners engage in an ongoing struggle with the forces of Queen Belial, who take possession of ordinary mortals in their attempts to control the Earth. The scouts never kill the evildoers, opting, instead, to change them back to their human incarnations.

In the view of one analyst, the *Sailor Moon* series was significant in that:

> it established the lucrative genre of portraying schoolgirls and boys as having double lives and secret identities. . . . Comics like Sailor Moon offer pure escapism, a world in which every Junichiro and Keiko can secretly be a dimension-busting superhero, and so neatly avoids contemplation of the mind-numbing routine they are trapped within. (Catton, 2002)

MUNDANE HEROES

The Samurai as Hero

To the Western mind, the word samurai conjures images of a master fighter. The word, itself, means "servitors," but the images that might have once been conjured among Japanese might have been something other than mere faithful subjects. Quite possibly, the image would have been more of oppressor. After all, the samurai were functionaries who served as a buffer between the aristocratic and the commoner; holders of a position in a rigid, caste-based social order. Their job was to defend those above from those below. They were often ruthless in performing their task. What they more often did was act out of their own class interest in ways that were often quite abusive to those beneath their rank.

This is quite at odds with the modern conception of the samurai. "The Japanese samurai is the archetypal warrior-hero," it has been written, "the creation of history, legend, and myth. His story is the story of Japan from the early feudal period to the present as the spirit of the samurai's code of discipline, loyalty, and honor."[18] In short, it has been only with the passage of time that the retainer-warrior has been recast as heroic. The modern tendency to view the samurai's "way" of bravery, honor, self-discipline, asceticism, and a fatalist acceptance as virtuous and rather selfless is only, in part, the result of the prism of historical development. Such perceptions have also been greatly due to the activity of media such as *ukiyo-e*, literature, and cinema. Through these instruments, the image of the samurai as noble and tragic, as the uncompromising, uncomplaining defender of Japan, has been continually reproduced. In such a way, the samurai has become one of the paragons of Japanese heroism.

Mouer and Sugimoto (1990) maintained that individualism lays at the heart of hero-construction in Japan. They pointed to "popular heroes" such as Miyamoto Musashi, Ishikawa Goemon, Kogarashi Monjiro, Nemuri Kyoshiro, and Zato Ichi—samurai all—as exemplars. "None were hermits, but each moved through society on his own . . . in each case the hero is a strong individual who stands by himself" (p. 197).[19] Supporting this assertion, Reischauer (1981) observed that "contrary to the picture of the modern Japanese as merely group oriented 'economic animals,' many Japanese prefer to see themselves as fiercely individualistic, high-principled, self-disciplined and aesthetically sensitive modern day Musashis" (p. xii).

As a class of hero, the samurai has been remediated in scores of *ukiyo-e* prints, books and film.[20] To provide a sample of how these figures have been reconstructed over the years, consider the media treatments presented in Fig. 15.11.

Miyamoto Musashi was a brilliant swordsman, an outlaw, a skilled artist, a philosopher. He was a study in divided selves, tormented by spiritual disharmonies and hounded by rivals seeking to defeat him and thereby claim the title of Japan's greatest warrior. His life has been told in numerous media, but not better than in Eiji Yoshikawa's *Musashi*. This prodigious tome was originally published in serialized form in the newspaper *Asahi Shimbun* during Japan's militarist heyday, 1935 to 1939. The resulting book has been called Japan's *Gone with the Wind* (Reischauer, 1981), not only because of its setting of civil war, but also because of its scale. It has been reprinted more than 14 times, has spawned seven films, has given rise to countless stage productions, and been rendered as mini-series on three national networks.

Although *Musashi* is the best-known and most widely mediated samurai, he is far from the only one. Between the mid-1950s and the 1970s, a torrent of samurai films spewed from film studios. This great output followed a decade-long lull in production, due to the American Occupation ban on a genre that was deemed an instrument of prewar and wartime feudal culture and militarism. Akira Kurosawa's masterpiece, *The Seven Samurai*, revived interest in the genre, not only because of its artistic achievement, but also because of its theme. Depicting Japan's era of civil war, masterless samurai are depicted as weary of war, but scornful of injustice. These compassionate, courageous warriors will, for the mere price of rice, spring to the defense of the less fortunate or defenseless against bands of marauding bandits.

Perhaps the most successful series among these period pieces was that depicting the adventures of Zato Ichi.[21] His film series, which ran from 1962 to 1989, included 26 titles. It centers on an actual (although by now nearly mythic) figure, a blind vagabond, who is both masseur and swordsman.[22] Similar to Kurosawa's samurai, during the course of his extensive travels, Zato assists the poor and downtrodden, often in the face of imposing numerical disadvantage. The secret to the popularity of these films may inhere in the "blending (of) the pathos and humor of Chaplin's 'Little Tramp' with the action-hero authority of a Robert Mitchum or Clint Eastwood."[23]

Figure 15.11

The overall effect of such films was not only to romanticize the samurai but to glorify their exploits, as well. These independent, no-nonsense fighters became heroic figures—especially for a nation of workers increasingly tethered and beholden to newer masters: the corporation, foreign occupiers, the redeveloping state.

Of course, film was not the first medium to treat the samurai. Neither, for that matter, was literature. In fact, the theater and *ukiyo-e* were earlier fertile sources for depicting the world of the warrior and, in that way, installing the samurai as a hero-object in the culture. As one recent exhibition argued:

> the Japanese have over time meticulously observed and interpreted events, major and minor. Among others, these have included the violent rise of the military class to power in the twelfth century, the schism between two competing courts in the fourteenth, the chaos of the warring states period in the sixteenth, and the great vendetta by the forty-seven masterless samurai (*ronin*) in the eighteenth. These events have helped to generate a host of heroes and villains that the Japanese featured on the kabuki and puppet stage and glorified in woodblock prints.[24]

They were also heroic images that were remediated in poetry, the reprinting of *Hagakure*,[25] and literature during the early 20th century. Such constructions of heroism served to underscore Japan's noble warrior tradition, in turn serving as pillars of justification and projections of strength for an expansionist, globalizing State.

The Corporate Warrior As Hero

A recent *Time Asia* article about contemporary Japanese heroes linked sport celebrity with the economically deflated Japanese ego. In the words of reporter Tim Larimer:

> Joe Salaryman—once a blue-suited samurai who made factory workers in Detroit tremble—has been stripped of his dignity and his wealth by Japan's perennially stagnant economy. Headlines of layoffs and bankruptcies remind Japanese men so incessantly of their shortcomings that even alpha males are dizzy with self-doubt.[26]

The American fad of the 1980s—born of desperation and paranoia—of businessmen mining Miyamoto Musashi's *Book of Five Rings* for insights into the "samurai business mentality" notwithstanding, the notion of organization man as warrior is far from a Western invention. According to Yoshihiro Yonezawa, "when Japanese adults became avid *manga* readers in the mid-1970s, it was the white-collar employee ("salaryman") who was more and more the comic book hero."[27] This had much to do, of course, with Japan's rising economic clout worldwide. After decades of relative seclusion and international quiescence, it was increasingly extending its global presence. The media—and in particular *manga*—helped reinforce this sense of heroic ascension.

Manga is not a trivial media form in Japan.[28] According to one author, its annual aggregate circulation in 1989 was 1.16 billion, or 27% of the total books and magazines (Lent, 1989). Another author claims that in 1995 it was 2.25 billion, or 47% of published material. *Shonen Jump*, a popular weekly magazine for boys, sold more than 6 million copies a week.[29] A statistic reported in 2001 on Japanese television claimed that in excess of 5,480,000,000 comics are printed in Japan each year, a figure that averages out to nearly 1.5 million a day. Although accurate figures are difficult to pin down, Lent has averred that "the hugeness of the Japanese comic art industry has no parallel in the world. A number of magazines top 1 million circulation, and cartoonists are among the highest-paid individuals in the nation" (Lent, 1989, p. 230).

Within the *manga* form, scores of consumption sectors exist: from those targeted for young girls to those focused on sports, from those centering on science fiction to those depicting gay love. Just as in the case of Superwoman or Batman, many *manga* feature a central character whose activities are presented in serialized form. During the 1990s, a number of *manga* about salarymen began to appear. The most famous of these was probably Hiroshi Motomiya's *Salaryman Kintaro*. Its breakaway popularity has led to remediation as movies, television series, and even in commercials.

In addition, there was Kenshi Hirokane's manga-depicted Section Chief Shima Kosaku at the end of the 1980s; other entries included Juzo Yamasaki and Ken-ichi Kitami's *Tsuribaka Nisshi* (Fishing Fool, Nisshi) and Norio Hayashi and Ken-ichiro Takai's *Somubu Somuka Yamaguchi Roppeita* (See Fig. 15.12).

Figure 15.12

These manga were far from identical. Shima was a middle-aged section manager, whereas Nisshi was a middle-echelon employee. As opposed to Shima's hard-driving style, Nisshi was laid back: more interested in fishing than in work. Shima's activities were dramatic: He would often travel overseas or engage in corporate in-fighting with rivals. Nisshi's quiescent, unassuming hobby was often the magical spur that surprisingly resolved problems in the corporate milieu. Whereas Shima was a dramatic hero, Nisshi was off-beat and Yamaguchi unassuming. Kintaro's character is, by far, the most volatile. He is known to retreat into the demeanor of his biker past and shout, shove, kick, or throw punches. In the early series, one of his stock phrases was akin to: "don't fuck around with a salaryman, dude." In one scene he screams at the board of directors: "Everything you do is to main-tain your image! All Japanese companies cover themselves with lies and produce nonsense results!" Kintaro's creator acknowledged that his hero would not survive even one day in the corporate world. Nonetheless, con-sumers have taken to him as a projective fantasy-object. As one bookseller asserted, "Most of our buyers are salaried workers in their 40s who would like to do the things Kintaro does in the story. I think he encourages work-ers that they can be successful without a certain education or background" (Prusher, 2002).

Considering the range of characters who have struck positive chords among the *manga* consumer, it is hard to assert the existence of a singular heroic type. Kintaro can be a lone wolf and a bully, but always in railing against the traditional approach taken by his rigid, conservative company. Shima, too, goes his own way, but does so in confronting the petty villains and game-players within his organization. Yamaguchi, by contrast, was good-natured, a seeker of harmony. His aim was to resolve personal con-flicts and petty troubles within the company; whether in aggregate or alone, these characters serve as heroes for harried commuters burdened by an unending life on the organizational treadmill.

All in all, one analyst concluded, "'Salaryman' *manga* depict everyday situations readers can identify with. They suggest how we might solve our own problems, and offer a release for negative, pent-up emotions" (Yonezawa, 2002). At the same time, "the adventures and idealism of such heroes give readers an opportunity to escape from mundane reality." In Yonezawa's opinion, *manga* white-collar workers "may seem like ban-tamweights" when placed alongside the comic book superheroes of other spaces and times, "but they achieve something valuable for their companies, triumph over rivals, and remain true to their ideals—taking on heroic pro-portions for readers today" (Yonezawa, 2002).[30]

Global Celebrity as Hero

In 2002, *Time Asia* ran a cover story on "Asian Heroes," which were defined as "the men and women whose lives and work have had a profound impact on the world around them."[31] Among their choices for heroism: a young child guarding a herd of water buffalo along the Thai border, a South Korean airplane crash survivor who rescued fellow passengers, and activists of numerous stripes—for religious tolerance in India, for increased AIDS awareness in China, against sexual slavery in Thailand. Twenty heroes in all were spotlighted—from countries as diverse as Japan, Afghanistan, Taiwan, Tibet, the Philippines, Indonesia and Myanmar, and the region of Kashmir. The e-zine also featured an online poll to enable readers to vote for their favorite hero.[32] Although the results were less than scientific,[33] for our purposes they are telling: Four of the top eight Asian heroes were Japanese. And although other countries tended to boast religious leaders, politicians and activists, Japan's heroes were of a different kind: sports stars, film directors, performers, and even a cartoon character. Entertainers all. Figures, in addition, whose careers began locally, but whose greatest success has come on stages and fields, in arenas and livingrooms outside national boundaries. Japan's heroic incarnations are very much the product of Asia's most technology rich, economically advanced, politically stable, leisure-oriented country.

Japan's contemporary era, which begins with postwar reconstruction, was decidedly (and understandably) devoid of the martial. Sure, the occasional text would be published by cultural icons like Sadaharu Oh (see Fig. 15.13), baseball's all-time home run king, drawing parallels between their life and the way of the warrior;[34] in the main, however, this quiescent era was pure entertainment. As seen previously, genre movies about *samurai* were more often statements against war, rigid social class, and inequality; so, too, science fiction films were often fables that argued against the ills of technological development associated with militarism. Comic superheroes have most often encountered enemies who do not originate from rival nations or in support of opposing ideologies; rather they emanate from extraterrestrial domains.

Figure 15.13

Thus, is it that the contemporary era has mirrored the *Meiji* moment: just as 100 years before—when *samurai* were displaced as a class of visible, oppressive regulators—in the 1950s the martial organization receded and a more libertine milieu prevailed. There, entertainment as a dominant cultural discourse came to the fore. Part and parcel of this change, as it was 100 years before, a different approach to heroism emerged. Back then, Allen Hockley (2002) asserted, "the popular arts struck a balance between the heroic ideal and the ethos of the people for which they were made." In a society in which the separation between god and human was not explicit, and where the military no longer held sway, "Japan's definition (was) . . . diverse enough to include writers, warriors, lovers, monks, and prostitutes." So, too, after the Pacific War, heroes were drawn from the cultural categories of writers, athletes, singers, actors, and radio and television hosts.

Comparing these eras, then, one perceives a kind of rough equivalence. Indeed, as we shall reprise in closing, there appears to be a sympathetic relationship between what Mannheim (1936) has called the "socio-political, historico-cultural context" and the social construction of heroism. On such an account, the heroes of martial eras were drawn from the ranks of public affairs (i.e., politicians, warriors), whereas the heroes of more quiescent times derived from the realm of entertainment and everyday life. In support of this, one can quote Kato (1989) who observed that in the Meiji era, although the merchants' "major concern was money-making . . . in their value system leisure activities had great importance" (p. 303). A tradition, he asserted, that "has been continued in contemporary Japan" (p. 303). It is not a surprise, then, that arts and entertainment, and their purveyors, artists and entertainers, were elevated in sociocultural stature by virtue of an active system of production and consumption — both then and now.

To take a recent example, consider the way news programs treat Japanese athletes in overseas markets. In the mid-1990s when the first Japanese baseball player went to America, the local reaction was relatively antagonistic. How could this player, Hideo Nomo, have the audacity to leave the comfort of his home, to abandon his team, to work for himself in a foreign country? Did he really think he could match up against the giants on the other side of the Pacific? But after Nomo began to win — to prove that he was actually capable of competing on an equal footing, the media embraced him. His games were televised live via satellite; hordes of viewers amassed outside *Shinjuku* station to cheer his every pitch on the megascreen overhead. Every strikeout and victory was recorded on the front pages of the sports newspapers. His rookie of the year award became a point of pride for the entire, bubble-burst, economically flagging, politically scandal-ravaged nation. This maverick, trail-blazing athlete was dubbed an authentic contemporary hero.

Just after the turn of the century, with 14 players in the major leagues, 7 of whom are "position" (or everyday) players, American baseball is broadcast not every fourth or fifth day, but virtually every day of the week. Always a team featuring a Japanese player is highlighted. Every night of the week, sports programs feature reportage on "today in the major leagues." These 30- to 60-second capsules feature highlights of every Japanese player in action that day. Rarely are exploits of other (i.e., foreign) players spotlighted—unless a significant event (such as Barry Bonds' record breaking 71st home run) occurs. Most often, as was the case when Shawn Green tied the major league record by hitting four home runs in one game, the foreigner's achievement follows the recap of the Japanese player's day. Although the results of the contest are generally reported in the corner of the screen in written script, it is rare that the actual flow of the game is reported. This stands in stark contrast to the coverage of domestic baseball contests, where a story-based, inning-by-inning approach is generally adopted.

This same pattern holds in the case of Japanese soccer players in European leagues. When Japanese golfers or marathon runners compete in foreign tournaments, the news frame is always on them. The tournament winners—generally American, African, or European—are almost always reported, but as often as not, the results are written on the screen. By contrast, the footage is of Japanese competitors. To give one example, in the 2002 Chicago Marathon, the videotape shown was of the third-place Japanese male finisher, then of the bronze female medalist. This, despite the fact that the British competitor on the women's side (not shown cutting the tape) set a new world record. The aggregate effect of such an approach to "news" presentation is to valorize the Japanese entrants. Incessantly, it is the Japanese who are foregrounded; Japanese nationals are established as objects larger than life on the global stage.

The current information environment—structured by 24-hour news cycles, constituted by multiple media forms, and characterized by high-volume, highly perishable data consumption—almost necessitates the endless production of heroes. Absent acts of heroes and figures of greater than normal proportion, very few social moorings would exist for the workaday salaryman and woman, confronted by a litany of escalating concerns: a stagnant economy, a declining birthrate, increasing graying of the population, spiraling crime.

Heroic construction, then, is not only needed in Japanese society, it is pervasive. Beyond that, it is a communication approach well suited to the Japanese historico-cultural context. In her fine discursion on the social construction of celebrity in Japan, Stefansson (1998) speaks of how contemporary "idols (are) somewhat like gods in the polytheistic mythologies . . . " (p. 155). There, then, is intimation of the larger phenomenon being described here. It is not only in the realm of celebrity that the practice of multiple hero-construction transpires; rather, it resides as well in the deep-seated, less accessible or perceptible realm of culture.

At the same time, there are any number of tangible factors that have affected this phenomenon of contemporary heroic construction. Bestor (1989) cited a few, among them: a high rate of urbanization, high education, well-developed media, mass marketing, and mass consumption. Above all, institutional forms such as department stores, production companies, music and literary publishers, and private radio and television stations have all worked—independently and, at times, in concert—to play central roles in the construction of contemporary heroes.

This harmonizes well with (pop)media theorizing of the McLuhan/ Warhol variety. In a globally wired village that has become one interlinked economy, where everyone is accorded 15 minutes of fame, everyone has the chance to play hero. It is proven every day on the "wide-shows" and tabloid newspapers, where even the rather mediocre baseball player, Shinjo, will have each of his fly-outs, strike outs, and "aw shucks," happy-go-lucky, "I'll get 'em next time" quips for the press presented on the nightly news. Shinjo's daily underachievements do nothing to diminish his standing as cultural hero, however. His return from the states is duly captured on film for replay on the evening news; he appears in commercials; he models clothing in local fashion shows; he is quoted in daily news reports; during the season he is shown spitting sunflower seeds or joshing with teammates as he sits on the bench. One economic analyst even pronounced that he was a "role model" for Japanese to emulate. Rather than striving to be Ichiro, who is beyond reach for the general Japanese public, he argued that Japanese in these depressed times should aim to be more like Shinjo: a hard-pressed, middling minion who somehow manages to muddle through. In short, one does not have to be built of epic proportions to be heroic nowadays. Gods come in all shapes and sizes.

DISCUSSION: UNDERSTANDING HEROIC CONSTRUCTION IN JAPAN

Having surveyed a number of the important types of heroes resident in Japanese culture, I now consider the question of construction: How have the stories of heroism been distributed through the culture? Of course, the short answer is media, itself, connected with the prevailing political and economic configuration of the society. For, although heroic types can span media, each epoch has had its own particular medium through which to communicate tales of heroism. In turn, it is the technical, social, sensual, and emotional dimensions of these media that have served to determine the power of the stories, their place in the society, if not the endurance and impact of the heroes themselves.

To give an example, absent the (controversial) war memorial, *Yakusune Jinja*, there would be little in the way of media to glorify the *kamikaze* pilots of the Pacific War. Aside from the random movie,[35] there is very little contemporary acknowledgment of the historical role and cultural position of

these heroic national demigods. Nor is there much in the economic or popular climate that points to this class of hero as "heroic." Between the time of
penning and publishing this chapter, Clint Eastwood's *Letters from Iwo
Jima* was released. This movie transforms Japanese soldiers making a desperate last stand against a numerically overwhelming American side into heroes.
What this theatrical release suggests is that the claim here may be subject to
amendment, as the years pass.

Genre Spanning

By contrast, the story of the legendary *samurai*, Miyamoto Musashi, has
been "remediated"[36] any number of times. It has been depicted in *ukiyo-e*,
in literature, in numerous movies and television dramas. We even saw
Musashi invoked in the autobiography of the legendary home run hitter,
Sadaharu Oh, to help account for his success. So, too, has been the career of
the epic tale of the 47 *ronin—samurai* who, following the loss of their master, battle impossible odds to avenge his death. The effect of constant remediation of tales such as these is to underscore the qualities, personalities, and
conditions qualifying as heroism. In the modern media environment—
where comics beget anime, which beget tie-in goods, or where TV broadcasts are remediated as daily sportscasts, player interviews, and capsules,
newspaper columns, mass-produced biographies, and public appearances
centering on "life overseas"—the ability to magnify rather mundane events,
transforming them into acts of grand heroism, is immense.

Mediating Heroism

To a large degree, heroes in virtually every society are artifacts of the institutions of communication. Absent the oral historian, the painter, the poet,
the journalist, the record company or web page designer, the exploits that
come to be deemed heroism would not be recorded, pondered, extolled. In
the Japan of the past this meant literature, poetry, painting, war monuments
and song, above all. In the contemporary era this has meant film, *manga*
(comics), television, and popular music. One element of this chapter has
sought to draw the link between media form and heroic content. It has
sought to demonstrate that in the Japan of today constructions of heroism
are increasingly dominated by the rhetoric of celebrity, pop art, and sport.
What I hope is also clear is that such constructions stem from developments
in the economy, polity, cultural rhythms, and mores. Importantly, because
these factors differ from conditions in the past, constructions of heroism do,
as well: not only how heroes are created and delivered, but also *who* is being
packaged and labeled "heroic."

Context

One dimension of mediation is context. Whether physical, psychological, or situational, fora for heroic acts are essential in order to construct heroism; a certain milieu is required. Of course, this can be accidental, as in the case of nature or the sudden up-cropping of terrorism. It can also be structural— and to some degree by design—as in the case of scheduled athletic competition, or the existence and enforcement of rules by an unfeeling or unbending state. These are the conditions that often frame heroic acts and select or enable the manufacture of heroes.

Milieus change. Not only the structural features that determine who can be a hero and what qualifies as a heroic act, nor the media that helps create heroes, but also a culture's perception or definition of heroism. This certainly appears to be the case if one believes, along with Morris (1975), that *Saigo Takamori* was "the last true hero of Japan" (p. 275). *Saigo* was the *Meiji*-era reformer who committed suicide in the final stages of an abortive rebellion he encouraged (but did not approve) in 1877. His acts of premeditated political protest stand in stark contrast to those of the comic heroine *Sailor Moon*, who, week in and week out, saves the world from extraterrestrial evil doers, or salarymen whose major heroic deeds are securing overseas contracts (thus maintaining the financial solvency of the corporation) or standing up to the resident office bully (thereby maintaining precious organizational harmony).

As we have seen, however, it would be a mistake to view these changes as simply evolutionary. Seen in static terms—in isolated moments—one might be able to allege that the hero has undergone a significant transformation: from a tragic figure who chooses or is chosen for inevitable defeat—as in the case of the *samurai* Kusunoki—to an individually centered, empowered person who pursues paths that are perhaps collectively less profound, but more positive in terms of personal result—such as an Ichiro Suzuki or Hidetoshi Nakata. However, a closer scrutiny of heroes through the ages discerns a certain recurrence at work; a pattern that we consider more closely in conclusion.

(Media) Form and (Heroic) Content

The content that has defined heroism has changed, most assuredly; but to no small degree, such shifts may be due to changes in the nature (or form) of communication by which heroism is conveyed. For instance, it may very well be that transformations in perceptions of heroism are the result of shifts in media preference among consumers: from early written forms to the visual arts, then finally electronic- and digital-based information and entertainment. Thus, whereas Japan's earliest heroes were depicted in painting, literature and poem, today Japanese more often encounter representations of heroes in cinema, comics and, increasingly, televisual and computer media.

On this account, whatever changes have transpired in the composition of heroes have been cultivated by changes in technology. In the most recent years this has included the development of the World Wide Web, networks of instantaneous transmission via satellite, the mass production of DVDs and CDs—as well as the rapid expansion of economic networks (television companies, record labels, Internet providers) to support such expansion. To take just a couple of ready examples, prior to Hideo Nomo's historic trek overseas to ply his trade in America's "big leagues," Japan's NHK limited its broadcasts of American baseball to divisional playoffs and the World Series. After Nomo joined the Dodgers in 1995 NHK broadcasts became a weekly affair. And when Ichiro Suzuki and Tsuyoshi Shinjo became position players on their respective American clubs, daily broadcasts of American baseball was born. A second example is how a story about a particular personality—a recording or film star, even the prime minister—will appear on the morning infotainment programs, then be broadcast throughout the day on the various "wide shows" on every major television channel throughout the nation. So, too, will the story be reported in daily tabloid newspapers and weekly celebrity magazines. The effect of such treatment is to magnify the people and events they are associated with until they have grown well out of proportion to their actual social import or "natural" cultural significance.

Beyond technology and routines in information dissemination has been a transformation in the characteristics of the Japanese hero. The content of heroism can be traced to changes in the structural features of society: matters of polity and economy, above all. What has not much changed, I argue, is the cultural continuity—the fact that heroism still apparently derives from or emulates a basic prototype: the gods. Specific manifestations may differ over time, yet they manifest a curious tendency to reappear every so often. This claim finds support in the studies of popular culture that we considered earlier—Gill's and Napier's, above all. As the former author asserts "a look at the programs reveals recurrent themes which, in some cases have their roots in supernatural beliefs dating back to antiquity" (Gill, 1999, p. 33).

Evolutionism or Cycles of History

Surveying the media canvas that ranges from 10th-century myths to 11th-century literature to 17th-century *ukiyo-e* (woodblock prints) to mid-20th-century *haiku* (poetry) to 21st-century newscasts, it may appear as if there is a variegated career to heroism. It was first defined in terms of a culture governed by powerful supernatural forces and mystical beliefs; growing into a society demarcated by rival clans of self-sacrificing warriors; giving way to a unified, but insular nation, defined by clearly segregated castes; this, in turn, succumbed to an increasingly externally focused nation of militarists in service of one supreme lord, the emperor; only to give way to a phoenix-like entity in which workers strove to serve company (and possibly, therefore, economy); finally, giving way to a nation of self-satisfied self-aggrandizers. In that milieu heroes are no longer self-sacrificers, but self-seekers: individually centered entertainers who ply their skills in service of self and their own personally (or corporate) cultivated fan base who consume them for their own private satisfaction.

Yet, perhaps what appears to be a succession of distinct heroic epochs is misleading. Perhaps there is a certain repetitive quality to them. Gill and others have asserted a certain primordial mysticism that has never disappeared. Reischauer and Mouer and Sugimoto and even Mishima allege that considerable individualism has been present through the ages. Unlike cultural theories that maintain that Japan is governed by a singular, uniform, all-encompassing groupishness, we must view Japanese events and cultural production through the prism of individual actors.

CONCLUSION: THE ENDS OF HEROISM

As witnessed in this chapter, the heroic reflects the context within which heroism arises and operates. At least with regard to Japan, conceptions of heroism represent a relatively narrow, repetitive discourse; a discourse that, although restricted, is also dependent on and attuned to cultural values, societal structure, developments in technology, and means of communication. Ultimately, however, what this chapter demonstrates is the strategic position and uses of heroes in a society. The Japanese case indicates that a hero is a form of god. Moreover, these gods are invoked at particular moments for specific purposes.

In his oft-cited book, Morris (1975) claimed "the failed heroes of Japan may . . . be regarded as demigods" (p. 65). In fact, however, this chapter suggests that all heroes are gods of some kind. Moreover, as seen here, the Japanese hero is not confined merely to those who have failed. Nor are heroes limited to the class of warriors. The god-heroes who persist in national memory include nature, fantasy-characters, entertainers, and even a category of societal service. In fact, hero is a mixed bag of social objects— people and things—whose achievements and image are constructed and communicated to serve specific purposes. Their likenesses, stories, achievements, words, and character, are appropriated by "marketers," who then transmit them, via media, to information consumers in the public sphere. For marketers, the motive may simply be the desire to turn a profit (economic production) or sell a political program (State-promoted, ideological production). For consumers, the reception may be a better means of defining one's place in the human order or simply making life fuller. Japanese identity is implicated in either process, although the difference may be between class and individual definitions; between national identity, in the case of the State, and individual or reference group identity, in the case of personal image consumption.

This insight leads in a number of directions at once. First, if heroism in contemporary Japan is defined either as comic figures repelling aliens or else as the simple act of departing the protection of the home shores and excelling in the larger foreign realm of athletic endeavor, then heroism is not only quite a trivial thing, but also an indicator of how insular the Japanese have historically been. A look at their heroes tells us a great deal about the impoverished nature of the Japanese psyche.

Second, the motives underlying heroic production and the meanings derived from reception and use may greatly differ. This is what Hall (1979) has shown in outlining his model of the "cultural circuit." The values that enter into the production of news can often differ from the interpretations that are extracted in the process of news consumption. We see this in Japan today, where, in providing viewers with the kind of information they think will enhance viewership, all news stations provide a recap of Japan's baseball and soccer exports' achievements overseas. Whether the newspackagers are trying to create messages of heroes achieving in "hostile" foreign lands, the aggregate effect of this uniform approach to reporting social "reality" may be otherwise. The meanings derived by news consumers may be of heroic global Japanese.

Finally, in thinking about the mediation of heroism in Japan, we must ask ourselves whether this is a pattern we have encountered before. Not the part about participating in "Major League Baseball" or "Serie A" soccer; rather the part about how, following a bout with the martial, comes the mundane; first politics, then the popular. Following external relations do internal issues swell to matter most. This is true, I argue, even though the most recent heroes are popular entertainers whose achievements are measured in terms of the global (i.e., external) stage. In point of fact, their activity—as reported back home by the media—are actually discourses about self; they serve as mediations about national efficacy; they are missives sent by Japanese to themselves about their identity. As such, these communications about Japanese heroes are basically inner-directed.

The main point here, however, is that following such quiescence comes discord. That is, if a pattern is in play. And if so, it is a pattern that has been in existence for hundreds of years. Studying it, one discerns the kind of dualism installed at the heart of Mannheimian sociology of knowledge (Mannheim, 1936).[37] On this version, Japanese heroic forms appear to manifest a cyclical logic, in which, above all, competing conceptions appear to take turns dominating public discourse. This is true whether the heroic type represented in the media frame is a warrior or a fantasy figure, a force of nature or a celebrity. Whatever the specific incarnation, the base polarities seem to be martial versus epicurean.

If this is so (and were the notion of historical patterning to continue to hold true), it becomes less certain that the Japanese vision of heroism in "noble failure" or of selfless, unflinching service to the State is entirely buried in the past. Certainly, the heroes of today are less self-sacrificing and less bent on personal destruction. Nonetheless, like the entertainers and artisans who were deemed heroic in the 19th century, yet gave way to *kamikaze* fighters and corporate warriors, this fashion may, too, pass. Is it possible that Ichiro and *Doraemon* will yield to nationalists seeking to defend the motherland against the likes of China, North and/or South Korea or America? This is certainly one reason—though not the only one—why we should concern ourselves with the matter of Japanese heroism in an increasingly mediated, globalizing world.

ENDNOTES

1. The words are from a speech by Vice Admiral œnishi Takajirÿ prior to the first organized (and most successful) *shimpu* attacks from the Philippines. The words are quoted by his senior staff officer, Inoguchi Rikihei (1958), in his memoir (with Nakajima Tadashi) entitled *The Divine Wind: Japan's Kamikaze Force in World War II.*
2. This label is the characterization of a would-be *kamikaze* pilot, himself. Forced to turn back to base due to foul weather conditions he wrote: "To plead that I could not sight the American ships is merely an excuse. People will say that I preferred humiliation to a heroic death. Shame on me!" (Nagatsuka, 1972, pp. 258–259).
3. For sustained attention to this phenomenon see Holden (2002). Also viewable at the following: http://www.tiger.intcul.tohoku.ac.jp/~holden/Presentations/ Sport_ Exports.files/frame.htm.
4. Historically, however one is hard-pressed to find women among the ranks of Japan's heroes, this is *not* the case in the realm of the gods. Not only are special roles accorded to women in national and imperial creation, as sentinels of water, women appear continuously in commercial text and other artistic communications, as Fig. 15.14 demonstrates.
5. See the online course entitled *Japanese History: Exploring Japanese Feudalism* at http://www.variable.net/hidden/japan/toc.html.
6. Shintoism arose in nascent form in prehistoric times, then following a period of displacement by the Chinese-inspired Buddhism, was installed via the promulgation of formalistic legal codes and the formation of state-sponsored offices at the end of the ninth century. Its societal position was further secured during the

Figure 15.14

Meiji restoration via its association with the state. The proliferation of Shinto meant that certain ritual forms were validated and reproduced; in particular, practices that sought to conjure and pay homage to the spirit of the gods became ubiquitous. In practical form this meant that the *tama*, or efficient force, of the gods was called out; this eliciting became a fixture of all religious ritual. The forces that served to support all life were singled out for praise, provided with offerings in hopes of appeasement or else nurturing, then ushered back to their realm. This notion of calling out is ensconced in numerous cultural forms, particularly *sumo* (wrestling), *kabuki* (theater), and *taiko* (drumming); as Gill (1998) suggests, it even appears in children's television shows.

7. This interpretation seems well founded based on history. To cite but two examples, from opposite ends of the historical spectrum: The earliest recorded writings about clan elders sometimes accorded them the title "god of the clan"; so, too, in the 1990s sports news often referred to the National Basketball Association's Michael Jordan as *kami sama* (literally "Mr. Exalted").

8. The appellation translates as "800 myriads of deities." It is intended more as an indicator of profusion, rather than serving as a term of precision and specificity.

9. In his account "Divine Wind and Ancient Heroes: Reconstructing the Kamikaze Ideology" (http://www.stanford.edu/~nickpk/writings/Kamikaze.html, page last accessed 9/09/02), Nick Kapur discusses the tales associated with ritual suicide in service of country.

10. Yukio Mishima (1978), in his disquisition on *Hagakure*, admitted: "I suppose some people will say that the *kamikaze* fighter pilots, despite their high sounding name, were forced to die. And certainly these youths not yet out of school were forced by the national authorities to proceed to their death against their will. Even if they went of their own will, they were rounded up into attack forces almost by coercion and sent to certain death, and certainly this is true" (p. 101).

11. This incident came 1 week before suicide tactics were officially adopted by the military. Thus, Arima came to be regarded as the *father of the kamikaze*.

12. Source for much of the previous passage: Sherman (1991).

13. In fact, in 2002, some 800 people (mostly South Koreans) filed suit against Prime Minister Koizumi, claiming that his two visits to Yakusuni shrine violated the constitutional separation between church and state.

14. This was true, that is, until declining audience receipts led Toho Studios to once again recast Godzilla as villain. Scores of web pages have been constructed in honor of Godzilla. A nice one in terms of movie credits and plot summaries is

All Kaiju Movies, at http://www.fortunecity.com/roswell/argento/44/allmovies2
.html.

15. However, in his third, post-1985, incarnation, Godzilla was the heroic villain that humanity could not revere, given his overwhelming, supernatural evil.

16. Nausicaä is the heroine of Hayao Miyazaki's feature-length film anime film, *Nausicaä of the Valley of the Wind*. Miyazaki is the creator of an endless string of films that have been successful both in Japan and abroad—all of them featuring strong, lead female characters. A few titles include: *Tottoro, Princess Mononoke, Sen and Chihiro*, and *Laputa, the Castle in the Air*.

17. Interestingly, in the original, there was a "gang of five" super-heroines, a species of heroic formation, according to Gill (1998). In subsequent years, however, the team of Sailor Scouts expanded to 7, then 9 and finally 10.

18. http://www.aems.uiuc.edu/HTML/ChalkGuides/Samurai.html

19. The authors contrast this with a host of American heroes, who have sidekicks or assistants. They also point out that popular dramas of the 1970s and 1980s tended to depict individualists dissatisfied with the organization or group within which they function. Unlike the popular ensemble TV shows in the United States, the Japanese characters were forever challenging superiors who hid behind their authority and acted unfairly.

20. The word has been coined by Bolter and Grusin (1999), referring to any work that appears in one form of communication that is then appropriated by or rendered in the form of another.

21. This according to the martial arts web site: *Budo Kai*, http://www.concentric. net/~Budokai/chambara/zatoichi.htm.

22. In some ways, Zato bears a certain resemblance to another character popularized on film during this era: *Tora-san*. This loveable, itinerant peddler, with a heart of gold, traversed every corner of Japan, in pursuit of a variety of cockeyed, get-rich-quick scams, yet always ended up affecting the lives of those he encountered. The film series, *Otoko wa Tsuraiyo* [It's Tough Being a Man], was the longest running series in any country, ever: spanning 27 years and 48 movies. For a fine capsule about this character, see Catton (2002).

23. From: "Return of the Japan Outlaw Masters," an announcement of *The American Cinematheque* at the Egyptian Theatre, May 6–16, 1999, http://www. egyptiantheatre.com/japanoutlaw21999.htm.

24. "The Floating World of Ukiyo-e: Shadows, Dreams, and Substance," an exhibition presented by The Library of Congress, September 27, 2001–January 19, 2002, and now reproduced on-line at http://www.loc.gov/exhibits/ukiyo-e/.

25. The 18th century treatise detailing the "way of the warrior."

26. Found at http://www.time.com/time/asia/features/heroes/nakata. html.

27. http://www.jinjapan.org/nipponia/nipponia12/see.html.

28. In fact, it is a medium of long-standing, well-established social practice, and deep-seated cultural significance. The originator of *manga* was the renowned *ukiyo-e* artist, Hokusai, a painter with more than 30,000 pieces to his credit. He employed the term (which literally means "whimsical pictures") to "refer . . . to his method of drawing a picture according to the way his brush or drawing materials glided across the page at random" (Sanchez, 2002).

29. According to Kenshi Hirokane, delivered at a manga symposium at Georgetown University, August, 1995. These figures are reported on the following web page: http://www.hoboes.com/pub/Comics/Conventions/DC/Georgetown%20Mang a%20Symposium (date last accessed; October 7, 2002). Frederik Schodt (1996) lists this figure as closer to 40%.

30. It should be noted that beginning in the early 1990s this heroic figure soon experienced denigration in popular media. For instance, television commercials began replacing the image of armies of workers conquering foreign climes with depictions of armies of ants scattered maliciously (and gleefully) by frustrated corporate minions. Similarly, the salaryman soon became represented in the form of worker bees buzzing home or monkeys mindlessly carrying out repetitive tasks. All too soon, the once-widespread representation of salaryman as bold, proud, conquering hero had all but vanished from public view in lieu of depictions of overworked, harried, slovenly, even unsympathetic louts.

31. This article can be found online at http://www.time. com/time/asia/features/ heroes/index.html.

32. Poll results were found at http://www.time.com/time/asia/features/heroes. The total number of votes was 809,364.

33. Voters could cast preferences more than once. Furthermore, the voting period also has not been specified, thus it is unclear whether any maturation effect is present. Finally, there is no indication where voters reside, thus one cannot adduce whether circulation is influential in the choice of heroes. Scanning *Time Asia*'s circulation figures, one notes that Japan has the largest circulation of all Asian countries, while Afghanistan has no listed circulation. This might account for why Japan has four entries in the top 10 and Afghanistan's lone candidate for "heroic" status (their post-Taliban president) checks in at number 16. Interesting to note is that his paltry 119 votes is not even half of that given to a virtually anonymous numbers runner in the Philippines. China, as well, which has four heroes on the list (although only two receive votes)—and the eleventh most popular choice overall—has no listed circulation. On the other hand, Malaysia boasts circulation figures superior to Taiwan, Thailand, and Indonesia, yet offers no heroes for the top-20 list (while these others do). If Internet access is one potential explanatory factor, then consider that Singapore is a highly connected webworld, ranked fifth on the circulation list and yet features no heroes on *Time Asia*'s list.

34. In his 1985 autobiography, Oh wrote: "There have been two figures who have been a constant inspiration for me throughout my career. Lou Gehrig and Miyamoto Musashi . . . Musashi the legendary Japanese samurai, beat his archrival Kojiro with more than strength and technique—it was also spirit-discipline."

35. The most recent was *kimi wo wasurenai* [I will never forget you], released in 1995. It cast a number of young "idols" in the role of sacrificial suicides, but died a rather quick death at the box office. Importantly, it failed to generate any imitation or follow-up cultural products (a sign of social impact in Japan). Moreover, whatever small amount of public discussion about its theme that attended its release was all too soon forgotten.

36. The term "remediated" belongs to Bolter and Grusin (1995).

37. On this view, a dominant way of thinking (ideology) gives rise to a rival vision (utopia), which eventually can ascend to a position of dominance. This process of ascension to superiority, resistance and replacement as dominant ideology can, like the operation of a pendulum, swing back and forth between generations over an extended period of time in any given culture or society.

REFERENCES

Bestor, T. (1989). Lifestyle and popular culture in urban Japan. In R. Powers & H. Kato (Eds.), *Handbook of Japanese popular culture*. Westport, CT: Greenwood.

Bolter, J., & Grusin, R. (1999). *Remediation: Understanding new media*. Cambridge, MA: The MIT Press.

Catton, J.P. (2002). "Sailor Moon" big in Japan. Accessed October 10, 2002, from http://www.metropolas.co.jp./biginjapanarchive349/304/biginJapaninc.htm.

Gill, T. (1998). Transformational magic: Some Japanese superheroes and monsters. In D. P. Martinez (Ed.), *The worlds of Japanese popular culture: Gender, shifting boundaries and global culture*. Cambridge, UK: Cambridge University Press.

Hall, S. (1979). Encoding/decoding. In S. During (Ed.), *The cultural studies reader*. London: Oxford University Press.

Hockley, A. (2002). *Heroes and heroines in Japanese popular art*.

Holden, T.J.M. (2002, July). *Sports exports/Media imports: How Japan engages a globalizing word*. Paper presented at the 23rd general assembly and annual conference of the IAMCR, Barcelona, Spain.

Hunzinker, S., & Kamimum, I. (2002) *Kakue Tanaha: A political biography*. Accessed October 1, 2002, from http://www.rcrinc.com/tonaka/index.html.

Kato, H. (1989). Japanese popular culture reconsidered. In R. Powers & H. Kato (Eds.), *Handbook of Japanese popular culture*. Westport, CT. Greenwood.

Lent, J. (1989). Japanese comics In R. Powers & H. Kato (Eds.), *Handbook of Japanese popular culture*. Westport, CT: Greenwood.

Mannheim, K. (1936). *Ideology and utopia: An introduction to the sociology of knowledge* (L. Shils & E. Shils, Eds. & Trans.). New York: Harcourt, Brace Jovanovich.

Millot, B. (1971). *Divine thunder: The life and death of the Kamikazes* (L. Bair, Trans.). New York: McCall.

Mishima, Y. (1978). *On Hagakure: The samurai ethic and modern Japan* (K. Sparling, Trans.). Tokyo: Charles E. Tuttle.

Morris, I. (1975). *The nobility of failure: Tragic heroes in the history of Japan*. New York: The New American Library.

Mouer, R., & Sugimoto, Y. (1990). *Images of Japanese society*. London: Kegan Paul.

Nagatsuka, (1972). *J'etais un Kamikaze*. Paris.

Napier, S.J. (1998). Vampires, psychic girls. Flying women and sailor scouts: Four faces of the young female in Japanese popular culture. In D.P. Martinez (Ed.), *The worlds of Japanese popular culture: Gender, shifting boundaries and global culture*. Cambridge, UK: Cambridge University Press.

Oh, S., & Falkner D. (1985). *Sadaharm Oh: A zen way of baseball.* New York: Vintage.

Prusher, I.R. (2000). Dilbert with an attitude: Japan's new "salaryman." *The Christian Science Monitor.*

Reischauer, E.O. (1978). *The Japanese.* Tokyo: Charles E. Tuttle.

Reishauer, E.O. (1981). Foreword. In E. Yoshikawa, *Musashi* (C. S. Terry, Trans.). New York: Kodansha.

Rikihei, I. (1958). *The divine wind: Japan's Kamikaze force in World War II* (R. Pineau, Trans.).

Sanchez, F. (2002). *History of Manga: The early days: pre-manga history.*

Schodt, F. (1996). *Dreamland Japan: Writings on modern Manga.* Berkeley, CA: Stone Bridge Press.

Sherman, G. (1991, December 7). Japan's war heroes have their shrine. *The Globe and Mail.*

Shibukawa, G. (1999). Tales from the *Kojiki.* In P. Brians et al. (Eds.), *Reading about the world* (Vol. 1). New York: Harcourt Brace Custom.

Stefánsson, H. (1998). Media stories of bliss and mixed blessings. In D. P. Martinez (Ed.), *The worlds of Japanese popular culture: Gender, shifting boundaries and global culture.* Cambridge, UK: Cambridge University Press.

Warner, D., Warner, P., & Seno, S. (1982). *The sacred warriors. Japan's suicide legions.*

Yonezawa, Y. (2002). White-collar workers are heroes too, with manga.

Chapter 16

SHREK AS A TEST OF THE UNIVERSALITY OF THE HERO'S QUEST

Steven C. Combs
Hawaii Pacific University

Heroes embody social values but are those values universal or culture-specific? In this chapter Steven Combs considers Joseph Campbell's concept of the archetypal hero, opposing this while arguing that the hero is a culture-bound construct that reflects and reaffirms particular values of significance to the community. Therefore, the hero in one culture can be the villain in another. He contrasts Western and Eastern views by applying Daoist teaching, important in Chinese culture to the notion of hero through an extended analysis of the motion picture Shrek.

For as long as humans have told stories, we have talked about great individuals who have performed with remarkable skill and valor. These "heroes" are notable not only for their reputed feats of conquest but also for their symbolic function. The hero functions symbolically as a role model or possible self that embodies particular social values. We are induced to identify with the hero, seeing ourselves in the hero's trials and triumphs. Hence, the rhetorical form and function of hero stories is to illustrate how heroes look and act. The attributes of heroes themselves and the solutions of successful heroes to their challenges suggest the traits that individuals should aspire to in order to be positive influences on the community. The stories of heroes are thus symbolic inducements that suggest possibilities for action in a world of conflict and choice. Hero stories use princesses, dragons, and magic as metaphors for the problems that beset us and the pathways for our triumphs.

In his monumental work, *The Hero With a Thousand Faces*, Joseph Campbell (1949) first put forth the idea that the story of the hero is universal, representing basic patterns of human existence found in every culture:

> And whether it was *Finnegan's Wake* or the Navaho material, or the Hindu material, or Heinrich Zimmer's, it was all the same material. That was when I realized—and nobody can tell me any differently—that there's one mythology in the world. It has been inflected in various cultures in terms of their historical and social circumstances and needs and particular local ethic systems, but it's one mythology. (Campbell, cited in Cousinesau, 1999, p. 126)

Campbell believes that hero stories are universal because the hero is an archetype of the human psyche. Hero stories represent basic psychological issues that face us all. The challenges the hero faces, and the appropriate responses, are keys to the basic human condition. Thus, although there can be many variations of the hero myth, as suggested by titular reference to "a thousand faces," Campbell maintained that there is one basic hero story or monomyth.

Because the hero story is a monomyth, the path the hero travels to resolve the various issues of the human psyche is also invariant. Campbell presented the solutions to our problems as universal, thus celebrating certain paths of transcendence as correct for all of us. Given the symbolic function of hero stories, to promote identification with the hero, Campbell suggested that the monomyth allows individuals to see possibilities in their own lives for navigating the universal problems of human existence.

I take issue with Campbell's notion that the hero is an archetype of the subconscious mind and the implication that the key conflicts in our lives, and their solutions, can be framed as universal. I argue, in contrast, that the hero is a culture-bound construct that reflects and reifies particular values held important in the community. In other words, an individual can be termed a *hero* based on the values of one culture and deemed a villain by the standards of another. I justify this claim by examining the film *Shrek* (Adamson & Jenson, 2001). The analysis indicates that the ogre Shrek is a hero according to the standards of Daoism,[1] but fails to achieve the status of universal hero by Campbell's criteria. *Shrek* thus offers a competing version of the hero, one that is grounded in Asian philosophy and not universal human psychology.

Daoism is a fitting test for Campbell's claims because it is a significant perspective that differs greatly from Western views. I. Lu (1986) observed that the influence of Daoism has been so pervasive that "it is difficult to name a single facet of Chinese civilization that has not been touched by it in some way" (p. vii). X. Lu (1998) noted that Daoist teachings "have permeated every area of Chinese life: its culture, thought patterns, and state of mind" (p. 228). Daoism remains a significant component of Chinese culture (Lu, 1998) "and it is a key to understanding many phases of Chinese life, including religion, government, art, medicine, even cooking" (Nagel, 1994, p. 8). Daoism also continues to affect all Asian countries influenced by China (Chan, 1963; I. Lu, 1986; Sun, 1995). Given the significance of Daoism to Asian culture, Campbell's inability to assimilate the Daoist hero would obviate his claim that heroes are universal. Furthermore, some of my previous work points to the value of using Daoism as a lens for communication criticism (Combs, 2002a, 2002b).

Shrek, awarded the Best Animated Film award for 2001 from the Academy of Motion Picture Arts and Sciences, is a particularly appropriate choice for this analysis because of several aspects of the story. As discussed here, *Shrek* is a fairytale. It is a paradoxical fable of an ugly, hideous creature who manages to find true love and happiness. X. Lu (1998) identified these very aspects—paradox, fables, and glorification of the ugly and handicapped—as central characteristics of the rhetoric of the Daoist sage Zhuangzi. Zhuangzi also believed that the humblest person and the simplest things, including toads, insects, snakes, and birds, can give insight because they live with nature. Shrek is an unassuming soul who lives in a swamp and is integral with his natural world. *Shrek*, through paradox, fable, and central character, is a study in Daoist cultural values. It offers an alternative vision of the hero with which audiences are invited to identify.

The first section of this chapter juxtaposes Campbell's theory and Daoist thought, outlining the basic question of whether heroes are universal or cultural. Next, it situates Shrek as a Daoist, in order to examine the nature of the Daoist hero. The second section applies Campbell's theory of the hero story to *Shrek* in order to test the applicability of Campbell's archetypal hero to the Daoist hero. The final section discusses the findings and implications of this study. It concludes that *Shrek*, although not conforming to Campbell's archetype, is a hero from a Daoist perspective. The analysis of *Shrek* reveals that Campbell's theory is grounded in a masculine, Western view that is perhaps centralized in our culture, but is far from universal in the values it celebrates and developmental processes it postulates.

UNIVERSAL VERSUS CULTURAL HEROES

Campbell viewed the hero as an archetype of the psyche, following C. G. Jung's notion that an archetype is an image or idea that is part of the collective unconscious. Hence, "the symbols of mythology are not manufactured; they cannot be ordered, invented, or permanently suppressed. They are spontaneous productions of the psyche, and each bears within it, undamaged, the germ power of its sources" (Campbell, 1949, p. 4). Archetypes thus transcend culture because they are situated in the unconscious minds of all individuals.

According to Campbell (1949), the Jungian archetype theory explains why the hero myth transcends culture. The "ubiquitous myth of the hero's passage" serves "as a general pattern for men and women, wherever they may stand along the scale" (p. 121). The hero represents every individual embarking on a quest or journey of self-discovery. "The individual has only to discover his [sic][2] own position with reference to this general human formula, and let it then assist him past his restricting walls" (p. 121). The motivation for this struggle is personal development—the search for identity, the individual's need to find meaning and purpose in life.

The quest for meaning is a process of enlightenment that requires the hero to attend to two primary tasks. The first is a process where one identifies core, underlying issues of the psyche, as opposed to those that are manifest, battles the demons attendant to these core issues, and makes a breakthrough that engenders transformation. The second task is to give the insight derived to others, "to return then to us, transfigured, and teach the lesson he has learned of life renewed" (Campbell, 1949, p. 20). The hero's victory or transformation is only complete if it benefits the community. Thus, "the happy ending of the fairy tale, the myth, and the divine comedy of the soul, is to be read . . . as a transcendence of the universal tragedy of man" (p. 28).

Although Campbell believes that the hero provides transcendent responses to universal issues, he glossed over the fact that his view makes assumptions that are not held in all cultures. These differing assumptions affect basic views of reality and core values. They condition behavior by celebrating certain modes of conduct over others. Ultimately, these differences play out in differing conceptions of the hero.

At a cosmological level, the dominant Western worldview is dualism. Western thought presupposes a permanent real world that stands behind appearance. This view is starkly exemplified by Plato's distinction between the true world of forms and the seductive pseudo-reality of the sensual world, and later by the Christian distinction between heaven and earth. The West venerates rationality and sees the individual as a distinct and vital entity. Individuals use their faculty of reasoning to "solve" life's puzzles and penetrate the perceived world in order to apprehend the underlying reality. In Daoism, there is one world, and it alone constitutes reality. There is no independent agent, such as a god, to provide order and life. The world's order results from a continuous interaction of the opposing forces of *yin* and *yang*. *Yin* is passive energy—motionless and still, sometimes described as feminine, earthy, or dark. *Yang* is active and overt energy—male, fiery, or light. According to Laozi, the Dao is the source of these two elements and everything is formed and harmonized by the interaction of the two. The order in the universe is not created by a grand design but is the natural consequence of the dynamic interaction of all life forms—"the many making one."

Dao has been literally translated as "way" or "path." The Dao is both the "mother," or creator, of all things and the order that stands behind the creation of the universe. The Dao created a natural equilibrium where everything blended perfectly. To Daoists, the constant flux and transformation of nature signifies the universal process that makes everything as one. Hence, one does not act on nature but remains within nature, thereby remaining within the Dao (Blofeld, 1985; Chan, 1963). Yet humans have the ability to follow what is natural or defy the Dao and be governed by human conventions. As a guidepost of what is natural, Daoists look to the state of nature that exists apart from humans. Nature moves slowly and is best adapted to with minor changes made early and often. Life is affirmed by being soft and flexible, like new vegetation, whereas hardness and rigidity move us toward death.

Those who are in harmony with the Dao move with the spontaneous and effortless flow of nature. A key term that embodies these concepts is *wu-wei*, or non-action. It refers to "the kind of unpremeditated, nondeliberative, noncalculating, nonpurposive action (or more accurately, behavior) that dominates Taoist discourse" (Schwartz, 1985, p. 188). *Wu-wei* is the natural, spontaneous movement that harmonizes everything (X. Lu, 1998). To be with the Dao one must surrender having an effortful life "by engaging in the activities which are actionless" (Parrinder, 1983, p. 333).

The key to effortless action is to avoid acting with conscious intent, but instead to be true to one's nature and move with the Dao. When one is aligned with the Dao it is possible to move like a leaf on a stream of water. When one knows well "the principles, structures, and trends of human and natural affairs" then "one uses the least amount of energy in dealing with them" (Watts, 1975, p. 76). Hence, *wu-wei* combines comprehensive and innate intelligence "with taking the line of least resistance in all one's actions" (p. 76). The result is that one's actions are effortless yet perfect.

Kryder (1997) noted that "human action that is harmonious with Tao is spontaneous, effortless, and inexhaustible," and "that the perfected individual is a sage, free from desire and strife." Spontaneity, effortlessness, desirelessness, and freedom from strife follow naturally from the Dao. The hero recognizes that the purpose of life is to find what is inside oneself and enact the elements of destiny that have been conditioned by the universe.

Spontaneity flows from the recognition that one does not need to rehearse to be oneself. One need merely follow the way. Mair (1994) observed, "above all, Master Chuang (Zhuangzi) emphasized spontaneity" (pp. xliii). By being spontaneous the sage "could climb the high places and not be frightened, could enter the water and not get wet, could enter the fire and not get burned" (Watson, 1964, p. 73).

Daoism upholds the connection and importance of all things in the one world. It values unity and recognizes the underlying perfection of the natural world. It promotes consonance with one's fate or destiny, because acting within oneself is the most natural way for a self to act. Furthermore, it upholds the values of balance and harmony, which result from the inherent order of the natural way. One must not strive to achieve external, human goals, but move in accordance with nature.

Whereas Campbell's hero strives to reconcile internal conflict by conquering the dangerous and barbaric natural world, the Daoist hero is not a warrior but a peaceful sage who avoids conflict and lives simply and in consonance with nature. The Daoist hero does not slay dragons and villains, but intrudes minimally upon the world, and only to restore its balance. The question at this juncture is whether Shrek is a Daoist. I argue that, by noting fundamental elements of Daoism and applying them to the film and its central character, Shrek is readily seen as a Daoist figure—and a potential hero from a cultural perspective.

Shrek is clearly positioned by its producers as a hero story, complete with a dragon, princess, and a happy ending; it is thus ripe for analysis of the extent to which it upholds the hero archetype. The film establishes itself as a fairytale,[3] although an irreverent one, in the opening scene. The film begins with a shot of a book; the page opens to a classic fairytale about a lovely princess who had a spell on her that "could only be broken by love's first kiss." The basic plot line is that Lord Farquaad wants to marry a princess in order to raise his social standing. By marrying a princess and making her his queen, Farquaad believes that DuLoc, his realm, "will finally have the perfect king!" He chooses to wed Princess Fiona, who is imprisoned in a castle guarded by a ferocious dragon. Farquaad puts together a tournament so that the finest men in DuLoc can compete to determine the knight most capable of rescuing the princess on Farquaad's behalf.

Shrek enters the picture by virtue of a decree made earlier by Farquaad designed to promote perfection in his realm. Farquaad's forest is populated by a number of fairytale creatures, including the Three Little Pigs, Snow White and the Seven Dwarfs, the Three Blind Mice, Pinocchio, and the Big Bad Wolf. Farquaad believes that the "fairytale trash" are poisoning his beautiful world. He has decided to have the creatures physically relocated—to the swamp that is Shrek's home. The invasion of the numerous, clamorous creatures destroys Shrek's peaceful solitude, and this forces him to seek out Farquaad to demand his swamp be returned to its previous state.

Donkey, a talking donkey who has "glommed on" to Shrek in order to be protected from Farquaad's goons when they were rounding up the fairytale creatures, accompanies Shrek in his journey to DuLoc. Once in DuLoc, Shrek and Farquaad make a deal. Shrek gets his swamp back if he rescues Princess Fiona for Lord Farquaad.

Shrek and Donkey make their way to the castle, battle a ferocious dragon, and rescue the princess. On the trip home, Shrek and Fiona realize that they are attracted to each other. A crucial misunderstanding leaves them unrequited and unable to tolerate each other. We also learn the secret of Princess Fiona. She is a beautiful woman by day, but beginning each sunset she turns into an ogre. A witch cast an enchanted spell on her as a little girl: "By night one way. By day another. This shall be the norm until you find true love's first kiss and then take love's true form."

Shrek returns to Farquaad with the princess and is granted the title to his swamp. He returns to his now quiet home but is very sad that he will no longer be with Fiona. Donkey clarifies Shrek's misunderstanding with Fiona and tells him that she loves him. Shrek decides to go to DuLoc and tell Fiona how he feels about her. With a ride from the flying dragon, who has returned to the scene, Shrek and Donkey arrive just in time to stop the wedding. The dragon eats the evil Lord Farquaad, Shrek and Fiona confess their love for each other and kiss, and the princess turns into her true form—that of an ogre! Everyone lives happily ever after.

Shrek's Daoist tendencies are evident throughout the film. His moves are entirely spontaneous; planning never seems to go beyond the moment, yet he manages to acquit himself quite well in whatever he does. Shrek is also fearless, although he displays prudence in all of his deeds. For example, when Shrek and Donkey make their way inside the dragon's castle to rescue Fiona they see piles of the bones of knights who have tried to slay the dragon. Suddenly, the dragon appears. Shrek grabs the dragon by the tail, just as the dragon is about to eat Donkey. Shrek is swung back and forth wildly. He lets go of the tail at the precise moment and the momentum sends him flying high in the air, across the castle and through the roof of the princess' chamber.

Shrek exhibits his spontaneity and adherence to *wu-wei* as the rescue scene continues. As Shrek flies off to rescue Fiona and spirit her out of the castle, Donkey is left alone with the dragon. He discovers that the enormous beast is female and very susceptible to flattery. Donkey has made a friend, but Shrek continues with the business at hand and hurries Fiona out. Suddenly, the dragon roars and appears down the hall. "You didn't slay the dragon," Fiona cries out in disbelief. "It's on my to-do-list," replies Shrek. "Now come on!" "But this isn't right!" protests Fiona. "You were meant to charge in, sword drawn, banner flying. That's what all the other knights did." "Yeah," notes Shrek wryly, "right before they burst into flame." "What kind of knight are you?" asks Fiona. Shrek replies, "one of a kind."

Shrek takes the path of least resistance. He is aware that the goal is not to display bravery but to rescue the princess. By not battling the dragon he avoids the fate of other knights, who failed to rescue Fiona. Furthermore, by not killing the dragon, Shrek keeps intact a vital savior who will reappear later in the film.

Living spontaneously, effortlessly, without desire, and focusing on the self and not the control of others enables one to minimize conflict and strife. Although fame, wisdom, and fortune may seem to promote happiness, Zhuangzi suggests that transcending the mundane affairs of life is a key to being healthy:

> If you abandon the affairs of the world, your body will be without toil. If you forget life, your vitality will be unimpaired. With your body complete and your vitality made whole again, you may become one with Heaven. (Watson, 1964, p. 118)

Living with the Dao is a prescription for health, longevity, and satisfaction. Finding the Way may be difficult, but having found the path, life becomes very simple.

An example of how Shrek attempts to avoid unnecessary strife is found in a scene where Shrek and Donkey have embarked on their quest to save the princess. Donkey confronts Shrek with the irony that Farquaad had no right to relocate the fairytale creatures in his swamp in the first place, and now Shrek must do an additional duty, rescue of the princess, in order to get his swamp back. Donkey maintains that Shrek should not have to perform the rescue, and wonders why Shrek doesn't just stand up to Farquaad: "I don't get it. Why don't you just pull some of that ogre stuff on him? You know. Throttle him. Lay siege to his fortress. Grind his bones to make your bread. You know, the whole ogre trip." Shrek replies, mockingly, "Maybe I could have decapitated an entire village and put their heads on a pike, gotten a knife, cut open their spleens and drink their fluids. Does that sound good to you?" The donkey doesn't think so. Shrek realizes that he must not draw attention to himself or it will lead to further trouble.

In every way imaginable, Shrek lives a dignified life, despite being alone and situated in a swamp. He is quite adept at living in the natural world, maintaining a balance that stems from his effortless and parsimonious approach to life. Shrek lives simply and comfortably, apart from society. He satisfies his appetites, but does so in modest ways. He avoids planning, acts only when necessary, and when he does act it is the minimum effort needed to accomplish his objectives. Consequently, Shrek is a Daoist.

SHREK'S HEROIC QUEST

Although Shrek is a Daoist, it remains to be seen how his actions conform to Campbell's basic hero story. In order to further analyze the story, I examine Campbell's theory of the stages and functions of the mythic journey and apply it to the film. Campbell referred to the one single myth that is the core of the hero quest as the *monomyth*. The monomyth has a standard path or formula that breaks the rite of passage into three major phases: separation, initiation, and return. The three phases are further divided into stages, beginning with "The Call to Adventure." This stage "signifies that destiny has summoned the hero and transferred his spiritual center of gravity from within the pale of his society to a zone unknown" (Campbell, 1949, p. 58). The call may be seen psychologically as "the awakening of the self." It is an indication that "the familiar life horizon has been outgrown; the old concepts, ideals, and emotional patterns no longer fit; the time for the passing of a threshold is at hand."

The call is frequently announced by a "herald," whose appearance marks the "call to adventure" (Campbell, 1949, p. 51). The form of the call includes typical circumstances such as "the dark forest, the great tree, the babbling spring, and the loathly, underestimated appearance of the carrier of the power of destiny" (p. 52). The hero does not always answer the call, and may instead enact the second stage, "Refusal of the Call." This amounts to "a refusal to give up what one takes to be ones' own interest" (p. 60).

These sequences are evident in *Shrek*. The herald is Donkey, who crashes into Shrek as he attempts to escape Farquaad's guards, who are trying to remove him from the forest along with the other fairytale creatures. The guards run off, scared of Shrek, who then turns and walks away. Shrek's challenge is foreshadowed. Despite Donkey's flattery, charm, and humor, Shrek insists that Donkey "go away." Shrek thereby refuses the call by not accepting the challenge of interaction. Because Donkey has nowhere to go, Shrek allows him to sleep outside on the porch.

Shrek's initial refusal, however, is soon overridden. It seems that all the fairytale creatures that have been rounded up were relocated to Shrek's swamp, where they eventually found his house and warm fire. Shrek tries to shoo away the creatures, but there are too many of them and they protest that they have nowhere to go. Pinocchio and one of the Three Pigs tell Shrek that Lord Farquaad has forced them to go to the swamp. Shrek finally answers the call by announcing that he will demand that Farquaad rid the swamp of the creatures. He realizes that he will not be left alone until he responds to the call. It is clearly in his perceived self-interest to answer.

When the hero answers the call, he or she has an encounter with some-one or something that provides assistance. This "supernatural aid" is given by "a protective figure . . . who provides the adventurer with amulets against the dragon forces he is about to pass" (Campbell, 1949, p. 69). In the case of Shrek, the supernatural aid is a gift from Donkey. It is not prototypical, however, in two respects. First, the supernatural aid comes from the herald, instead of the usual crone or old man. Second, the gift is not a magical abil-ity or an amulet but a personal relationship. Donkey has the ability to pen-etrate Shrek's tough exterior, provide amiable companionship, and confront him with honesty and compassion. Donkey is the key to Shrek's challenge — overcoming his fear of being hurt by people who don't understand and appreciate him.

The next part of a hero's journey is "Crossing the First Threshold." This is where the hero, accompanied with "the personifications of his destiny to guide and aid him," encounters the "threshold guardian," custodian of the new territory (Campbell, 1949, pp. 77-78). The threshold represents the foray outside the protection of the old way of life.

The castle DuLoc is the first threshold in Shrek's journey, and Farquaad is its guardian. The opening shot of the scene where Farquaad is introduced shows him walking proudly, stridently, and menacingly down a long hall-way while a hooded torturer pours milk into the empty glass. When Farquaad arrives at the doorway to the dungeon, where the torturer and the glass of milk are waiting, it becomes clear that Farquaad is only half the size of the two guards waiting outside the doorway. Inside, the "Gingerbread Man" is whimpering, as the torturer abuses him by dunking him head first into the glass of milk. Throughout the scene, Farquaad is portrayed as cruel, petty, and narcissistic.

The final stage in The Separation is to enter the "Belly of the Whale." Here the hero is prepared for transformation by killing the former self. The hero dies (is annihilated) and emerges a new person. The passage is "a mag-ical threshold" or "transit into a sphere of rebirth" that "is symbolized in the worldwide womb image of the belly of the whale" (Campbell, 1949, p. 90). The two sets of teeth at the entrance (whale's mouth) and the ordeal of the belly force the self to break through the ego barriers that protect the former self.

> One by one the resistances are broken. He must put aside his pride, his virtue, beauty, and life and bow or submit to the absolutely intolerable. Then he finds that he and his opposite are not of differing species, but one flesh. (Campbell, 1949, p. 108)

The ordeal forces a confrontation of the self where the hero "discovers and assimilates his opposite [his own unsuspected self] either by swallowing it or by being swallowed" (p. 108).

Shrek must venture out of his swamp (safety zone) and into the excessively stylized and heavily populated castle. There, Shrek must defeat Farquaad's best knights and confront the tiny tyrant. Entering DuLoc, and crossing the threshold, takes Shrek into the "Belly of the Whale."

As Shrek and Donkey enter the castle, which looks like a storybook castle one might find at Disneyland, except that it is incredibly phallic, they walk toward some noise, and end up in the arena where the knights are about to begin the tournament. Shrek interrupts Farquaad, who then decides that the champion will be the knight who kills the ogre. Shrek, with Donkey's able assistance, defeats all the knights and displays his tremendous strength, agility, and cunning. Shrek has spontaneously and effortlessly acquitted himself as a champion, thereby positioning himself for a fortuitous meeting with Fiona. Shrek's bargain with Farquaad to rescue the princess represents the annihilation of his former self because Shrek has engaged the world outside his swamp, and must venture out further still.

The self-annihilation of the hero is an important part of the preparation for personal growth. But "the original departure into the land of trials represented only the beginning of the long and really perilous path of initiatory conquests and moments of illumination. Dragons have now to be slain and surprising barriers passed—again, again, and again" (Campbell, 1949, p. 109). The hero now enters the "Initiation" phase, which involves a series of further trials (Road of Trials) that represent "a deepening of the problem of the first threshold." The question remains: "Can the ego put itself to death?" (p. 109). In the second phase, the hero will confront the feminine form (goddess, temptress), the masculine form (father), and the deity (gods, goddesses). Having mastered the tests or issues attendant to these three forms, and received the gifts of insight derived from these confrontations, the hero is prepared for the final phase of the quest—the return.

Before Shrek encounters the feminine, which in this case is Princess Fiona, he must rescue her from the dragon's lair. Shrek and Donkey set out for the dragon's castle and arrive 2 days later. Once inside the dragon's lair, Shrek rescues the princess, outwits the dragon, and escapes across the bridge as the dragon incinerates it right behind them. Shrek and the others climb to safety while the dragon looks on, unable to give pursuit. The dragon seems far more upset at losing her new found love, Donkey, than at having let Fiona escape.

One of the important encounters in this stage of the journey is "Meeting with the Goddess." The hero encounters the feminine, the "Queen Goddess of the World" (Campbell, 1949, p. 109). The relationship between the two establishes the distance the hero must go in the quest for transformation.

> Woman, in the picture language of mythology, represents the totality of what can be known. The hero is the one who comes to know. As he progresses in the slow initiation which is life, the form of the goddess undergoes for him a series of transfigurations: she can never be greater than himself, though she can always be more than he is yet capable of comprehending. She lures, she guides, she bids him burst his fetters. And if he can match her import, the two, the knower and the known, will be released from every limitation. (p. 116)

The woman as knower, hero as the one who comes to know indicates a superior–subordinate relationship. The hero's task is to become an equal and then a master.

What enables the hero to learn what she or he needs to know is that the woman presents herself not only as a goddess, the Madonna, but also as a sinner. It is the further meeting of "Woman as the Temptress" that is crucial. The woman confronts the hero with contradiction—the mother's love and the seducer's lust. She "is the guide to the sublime acme of sensuous adventure. By deficient eyes she is reduced to inferior states; by the evil of ignorance she is spellbound to banality and ugliness. But she is redeemed by the eyes of understanding" (Campbell, 1949, p. 116). If the hero can see the woman as she is in roles such as mother, grandmother, seducer, and wife, then he has mastered the gift of love and understands the "total mystery of life; for the woman is life, the hero its knower and master." The hero is now equated with the father figure: "he is in the father's place" (p. 121). The seeker becomes the master: "The seeker of life beyond life must press beyond her, surpass the temptations of her call, and soar to the immaculate ether beyond" (p. 122).

Shrek's meeting with the goddess and temptress are pivotal and well-detailed elements of the film. As he and Donkey first approach the castle gate, Donkey asks, "So where is this fire-breathing pain in the neck anyway?" "Inside," says Shrek, "waiting for us to rescue her." "I was talking about the dragon Shrek."

Once rescued, Fiona insists on knowing the identity of her rescuer. "The battle is won. You may remove your helmet, good Sir Knight." Shrek is reluctant to reveal himself, but Fiona persists and he finally relents. It is obvious from Fiona's face that she is disappointed. Instead of the handsome prince she expected, she sees a huge green head with large ears that stick out like fat antennae. Fiona is upset that her true love, who she thinks is Farquaad, did not care enough about her to rescue her himself. They then set out on their journey back to DuLoc. As nightfall approaches, Fiona is visibly agitated and demands that they make camp for the night and she be provided with shelter. She knows the sundown will mark her transformation to an ogre and she does not want anyone to know her secret.

The next morning, Princess Fiona is up and in a very good mood. This day is remarkable because we see some of her unique talents. For example, while Shrek and Donkey lay asleep on the ground the princess comes upon a beautiful blue songbird, nesting in a tree. She begins singing to the bird, which answers back with its song. They continue singing back and forth in turn until Fiona emits an incredibly high-pitched note that the bird then tries to imitate. The note, however, is well beyond the bird's range, and its chest swells from the effort until it pops and explodes. There are three eggs in the nest. The next shot shows the eggs frying sunny-side-up on a rock. Fiona is cooking the eggs for Shrek and Donkey. Later, as they continue the journey and are walking in the woods, Shrek belches, which he says is a compliment to the breakfast. Donkey scolds Shrek for acting that way in front of a princess. Fiona then burps herself and says that she appreciates the compliment. Donkey observes, "She's as nasty as you are." Shrek says, "You know, you're not exactly what I expected."

As they continue walking back to DuLoc, Shrek and Fiona flirt and play constantly. As they cross a meadow, Shrek is annoyed by hordes of flies. Fiona breaks off two sticks holding a big spider web, and uses the web to snare the flies. She ends up with a wrapped up ball of web and flies on a stick, which she then gives to Shrek, who eats it like cotton candy. Shrek grabs a frog and blows into it until it pops up and floats like a living balloon. He ties a string to it and presents it to Fiona. Fiona grabs a snake, blows it up, twists it like a balloon poodle, strings it, and gives it to Shrek. They are laughing, giggling, and falling in love.

Shrek thus meets the goddess. He seems to have found a soul mate, a *yin* for his *yang*. Fiona is in a bind because of her circumstances, but her heart tells her to tell Shrek her secret and hope that he still loves her. Unfortunate circumstances, however, further test Shrek as the goddess because a witch.

That night, Donkey goes into the windmill in which Fiona is staying for the night and inadvertently discovers Fiona's secret. She explains that she has always been an ogre, beginning each sunset. Meanwhile, Shrek makes his way back to the windmill, carrying a sunflower and practicing a conversation with Fiona where he professes his love for her. Just as he steels himself to knock on the door, he overhears the conversation going on inside. "I can't just marry whoever I want. Take a good look at me, Donkey. I mean, really. Who could ever love a beast so hideous and ugly? 'Princess' and 'ugly' don't go together. That's why I can't stay here with Shrek." Shrek is crestfallen, thinking that Fiona is referring to his looks when, in fact, she is bemoaning hers. He throws down the flower and walks away, not hearing Fiona continue, "It's the only way to break the spell." "You at least gotta tell Shrek the truth," says Donkey. "No! You can't breathe a word. No one must ever know." Fiona makes Donkey promise never to tell.

The next morning Fiona tries to tell Shrek her secret and feelings for him. But Shrek is too hurt and angry to listen. Fiona doesn't know that Shrek is caught in a misunderstanding, and is taken aback by his anger and stern words. Just then Farquaad and a contingent of soldiers arrive, and both Shrek and Fiona have seen enough of each other for the moment. Farquaad gives Shrek the deed to his swamp and then proposes, saying, "Will you be the perfect bride for the perfect groom?" Fiona accepts the proposal and they make plans to marry that day, "before the sun sets." Shrek shuffles back to his swamp, crestfallen and angry.

Shrek ultimately reconciles his anger for Fiona through Donkey. In fact, throughout the movie Donkey confronts Shrek's inability to express his feelings and connect with others. Donkey follows Shrek back to his house in the swamp and tries to be supportive of the sad and angry ogre. Shrek finally tells Donkey to go away. "There you are, doing it again," says Donkey. "Just like you did to Fiona. All she ever did was like you, maybe even love you." "Love me? She said I was ugly, a hideous creature. I heard the two of you talking," Shrek confides. "She wasn't talkin' about you," urges Donkey. "She was talkin' about, uh, somebody else." Shrek decides to crash the wedding and confront Fiona. Donkey whistles for his girlfriend, the dragon, who has returned to the scene, and they all fly to DuLoc. The trio land outside the castle, and Donkey tells the dragon he will whistle for him if needed.

Shrek and Donkey break into the chapel just before the couple's first kiss. Shrek implores Fiona not to go through with the marriage. He begins to confess his feelings for her. The sun has now set, and Fiona reveals her ogre form to Shrek. "That explains a lot," remarks Shrek. Farquaad is appalled. "Ugh! It's disgusting!" He calls for his guards to take Fiona and Shrek away.

As large and powerful as Shrek is, the dozens of guards are able to over-power him and begin to cart him off. Shrek breaks his arm free and whistles for the dragon. Farquaad rants among the chaos, "I will have order! I will have perfection! I will have . . ." Just then, the dragon bursts through the large window overhead and reaches down and eats Farquaad. Shrek then tells Fiona he loves her and she tells Shrek she loves him. They kiss, and there is more fog and magic dust sparkling about. We hear Fiona's voice: "Until you find true love's first kiss and then take love's true form." Fiona's body emits giant beams of light, as her true form is manifest. It turns out that "love's true form," the form Fiona takes, is that of an ogre. Shrek, her res-cuer, is also her true love. Fiona is a bit dazed. "But I don't understand. I'm supposed to be beautiful." "But you are beautiful," says Shrek. Donkey, perched atop the dragon's back, tearfully says, "I was hoping this was going to be a happy ending."

As a coach carrying Shrek and Fiona drives off down the road, the cam-era pulls back, framing the scene in the book of fairy tales that opened the movie. The last full line in the story is "And they lived ugly ever after." The next page proclaims "The End," and the book closes to end the film.

Shrek's final confrontation with the feminine is out of sequence with Campbell's hero pattern. It occurs toward the end of the film during the wedding scene. It is also unclear if the confrontation leads to a reconciliation of the duality of the feminine. Further, the remaining elements of the hero pattern are not evident in the film. What are left undone is the confrontation with the masculine figure (Atonement with the Father), the transcendence of the masculine–feminine duality (Apotheosis), the communion with the gods and the gift of their transcendence (The Ultimate Boon), and the entire return stage.

Although there is no explicit "Atonement with the Father" or "Apotheosis," it is possible to give a sympathetic reading of *Shrek* to tease out what may be implied. A basic issue in the atonement with the male is resolving the father figure's god-like and sinful nature. The father sins with the temptress, but is more importantly a source of evil power. Interestingly, Campbell (1949) often referred to the father as an "ogre" (see p. 130). Campbell also referred to ogres as barriers of the hero or things that must be overcome (see pp. 109, 121).

The father then is two dragons to be slain: "the dragon thought to be God (superego) and the dragon thought to be Sin (repressed id)." The idolization of the father seals off "the potentially adult spirit from a better balanced, more realistic view of the father, and therewith of the world" (p. 130). "Atonement (at-one-ment)" "requires an abandonment of the attachment to the ego itself," which leads to "the abandonment of the self-generated double monster—the dragon thought to be God (superego) and the dragon thought to be Sin (repressed id)" (p. 130). Hence, the hero must reconcile the false image of the father as all-powerful and interact with the father as a peer rather than subordinate.

When the hero successfully confronts the dualities of the feminine (goddess–temptress) and masculine (god–ogre) then another aspect of transcendence occurs. Campbell refers to this as "Apotheosis." Apotheosis is the elevation of oneself to the status of a god. This occurs because the hero has mastered the feminine and masculine. Furthermore, this mastery leads to the realization of our androgyny. The conflict with the feminine and masculine is with those elements within ourselves. The hero becomes the androgynous god: "Male–female gods are not uncommon in the world of myth. They emerge always with a certain mystery; for they conduct the mind beyond objective experience into a symbolic realm where duality is left behind" (Campbell, 1949, p. 152). The hero masters the dualities among and between the feminine–masculine through love (p. 158). Love is the corrective for ignorance and fear.

Although not explicit in the film, one could read *Shrek* in this way: The father figure is the ogre—Shrek himself. The task is to see that he is not all-powerful and that he can be emotionally needy. Shrek becomes at one with himself when he accepts the desirability of a relationship with Fiona. He thus achieves apotheosis. His transcendent love, acceptance of himself and another irrespective of form, is the final result of the film.

Because the film ends at this point Shrek neither receives "The Ultimate Boon" nor engages in the third, and final, phase—"The Return." In Campbell's view, this is a crucial element. The return entails a "reintegration with society" that is "is indispensable to the continuous circulation of spiritual energy into the world, and which, from the standpoint of the community, is the justification of the long retreat" (Campbell, 1949, p. 36). The return is a difficult task, for "the returning hero, to complete his adventure, must survive the impact of the world" (p. 226). It is important to understand what Campbell thinks happens in The Return in order to assess Shrek's failure to complete this phase.

The final trial of the hero is to reconcile her or his mortality. "The Ultimate Boon" is a gift from the gods. The hero ascends to the heavens and interacts with the gods and goddesses in order to obtain the gift of immortality.

> As he crosses threshold after threshold, conquering dragon after dragon, the stature of the divinity that he summons to his highest wish increases, until it subsumes the cosmos. Finally, the mind breaks the bounding sphere of the cosmos to a realization transcending all experiences of form—all symbolizations, all divinities; a realization of the ineluctable void. (Campbell, 1949, p. 190)

The grasp of the universal gives the hero a sense of immortality. The hero is able to see the boundless and realize that there is a place there for all of us. The hero is released from the ego-driven focus of the mortal body. "Immortality is then experienced as a present fact: 'It is here! It is here!'" (p. 189).

The annihilation of the former self is now complete and the enlightened, transcendent self is ready to engage in the third phase of the process. "The Return" is an essential element of the monomyth:

> The full round, the norm of the monomyth, requires that the hero shall now begin the labor of bringing the runes of wisdom, the Golden Fleece, or his sleeping princess, back into the kingdom of humanity, where the boon may redound to the renewing of the community, the nation, the planet, or the ten thousand worlds. (Campbell, 1949, p. 193)

Not surprisingly, this phase of the quest also has its risks and challenges, and so the hero's journey remains perilous.

The first issue is whether the hero will return at all. Sometimes there is a "Refusal of the Return." Assuming the hero does not get caught up in some element of narcissism or self-focus, the hero begins to return. The journey home is termed the "Magic Flight," because supernatural forces often aid it. Sometimes there is a need for intervention in order to escape the guardians of the return threshold, and the hero receives "Rescue from Without." Had Shrek accomplished his tasks and returned with the gift from the gods and goddesses, then the dragon's assistance in killing Farquaad would exemplify "Rescue from Without." But Shrek's was not a return and the dragon's act could not be termed as assistance in the return.

The hero's return is marked by "Crossing the Return Threshold." This can be seen as a return from the spirit world or heavens. It is a crossing from one world to another. Yet the mystery that is discovered is that the divine and human worlds are not distinct:

> Here is a great key to the understanding of myth and symbol—the two kingdoms are actually one. The realm of the gods is a forgotten dimension of the world we know. And the exploration of that dimension, either willingly or unwillingly, is the whole sense of the deed of the hero. The values and distinctions that in normal life seem important disappear with the terrifying assimilation of the self into what formerly was only otherness. (Campbell, 1949, p. 217)

The individual is left behind at this crossing point. But in its place is the sense of the ultimate and boundless. The individual becomes one with the universe, making the loss of self a discovery of something far more important. The burden of the quest is now clear: overcoming the fear of losing the self. That is why this is the domain of heroes: "the hero-soul goes boldly in—and discovers the hags converted into goddesses and the dragons into the watchdogs of the gods" (Campbell, 1949, p. 217).

Crossing the final threshold enables the hero to be "Master of Two Worlds." The hero is able to pass freely between the divine and human. The hero's mastery is the ability to move back and forth without "contaminating the principles of the one with those of the other, yet permitting the mind to know the one by virtue of the other" (p. 229). The hero "has been blessed with a vision transcending the scope of normal human destiny, and amounting to a glimpse of the essential nature of the cosmos" (p. 234). This perspective gives one the "Freedom to Live." Dwelling in the mortal and immortal makes it possible to live without fear of death. The hero's actions are released from worry because of "a realization of the passing phenomena of time to the imperishable life that lives and dies in all" (p. 234). The hero is released from annihilation and, thus, the fear of death.

DISCUSSION AND IMPLICATIONS

Obviously, Shrek's failure to work through the process of the return is significant. What must be considered is whether the analysis suggests that
Shrek is a flawed hero, because he fails to complete his initiation and does
not return to society with the gifts of his transcendence, or whether, instead,
Shrek exemplifies a different kind of hero altogether, one who would not be
expected to follow Campbell's pattern. If Shrek is flawed, then Campbell's
claim of universality remains intact, and this fairytale supports the pattern.
On the other hand, if the story of the ogre is the story of a different kind of
hero with a unique purpose and narrative form, then it mitigates Campbell's
claim of universality. Campbell admitted that different cultures have variations in their hero stories; the issue here is the significance of the variation.
Ultimately, the test for the significance of the variations is whether the story
makes more sense as a flawed hero story or a Daoist tale.

I am disinclined toward the first view, a flawed story, because what happens in the film is more omission than failure. Of course, it is always dangerous to interpret what is "not there." Yet the nature of the omissions, and
the overlay of Daoism, make a better accounting of what is and is not present in the story than simply to say, it fails because it is incomplete. I claim
that the story is complete. *Shrek* succeeds as a Daoist tale.

Closer examination of the form of the monomyth reveals that the hero's
trials revolve around one essential idea: overcoming the ego or self in order
to transcend dualities through divine love or grace. The purpose of the call
is to awaken the hero to the sense that things must change. The individual,
with supernatural help must cross the threshold and annihilate the ego. This
prepares the hero to resolve several important dualities: the female, the male,
the male–female, and mortality–immortality. The hero must then return and,
again with supernatural rescue, transcend the human and divine worlds and
the individual and the universal. The result of all of this is freedom. One's
unique identity is discovered. The annihilation of the former self and communion with the divine signifies immortality.

For a Daoist, this process and its functions are nonsensical. The Dao
knows of no distinctions. There are no dualities; hence they do not need to
be overcome. Seeing the female as either goddess or temptress, seeing male
as god or ogre, is incongruent with Daoism. Even the male–female dichotomy, which is seen in *yin* and *yang*, is only marginally compatible with Daoist
thought. All things are created by the dynamic interaction of *yin* and *yang*,
and the feminine and masculine exist in varying degrees in all things. The
mingling of the two is the essence of creation and the nature of all things.
The end point for Campbell's hero, androgyny, is the starting point for a
Daoist.

Daoist views of mortality–immortality and divine–human are also similar but crucially different. Campbell clearly maintains a two-world focus, Heaven and Earth. Daoists are monists. There is no deity in Daoism and immortality does not come from mastering a two-world dichotomy but from recognition of the one that is all. Dichotomy is an illusion. It should never be postulated in the first place; it does not need to be overcome. By resisting the tendency of some humans to dichotomize we avoid the need to transcend a false perception of distinctions. Finally, freedom does not come from mastery of the dualities of the universe. It comes from submission to the natural way, surrendering to the flow that is the undivided universe. Freedom is the goal, but it is achieved by release from effort, not slaying dragons.

For these reasons, it makes sense that Shrek does not complete the work of Campbell's hero. Shrek begins the film as a Daoist, and his only reason for leaving his hermitage is to restore it to its natural state. Farquaad is a metaphor for the meddling of men such as Confucians who attempt to impose human values, such as beauty and perfection, on a universe that is naturally balanced. Although Shrek must come to terms with his pain from thinking he had been scorned by his love, he does not do so by transcending the duality of the goddess–temptress. He simply acquires more information: the truth about Fiona's feelings. Shrek never had a problem with either of the forms Fiona takes in the film. He suspects that a beautiful princess will not be attracted to him, but only because that is how he is usually treated by others, who do not really know him. He is content with who he is. His lack of confidence is not in himself but in her sagacity. He is clearly thrown off by his misunderstanding about Fiona's feelings toward him, which he likens to a betrayal by Fiona, but he is hurt because he believed Fiona raised false expectations. He was content with not liking her until she showed interest in him. His response when she reveals her ogre self is matter of fact. Shrek accepts Fiona in both of her forms. He fails to reconcile dichotomies because he does not see them in the first place. He has no need for growth. His views are situated in the here and now, and he has no duality to overcome. Shrek is a sage, a Daoist hero.

What makes the story a Daoist tale is that there is a message for Daoists. Namely, do not be so successful in your detachment from others that you miss out on the rare individual who might be compatible with you. It is understandable that Daoists feel the need to retreat from society to be themselves. Nonetheless, there may be occasional individuals that the universe puts in one's path who should be embraced. Fiona and Donkey prove their alignment with the Dao because they refuse to let Shrek's form, his unusual appearance and habits, detract from his overall wholeness. The message for Daoists is do not shut out everyone. Remain open to whatever the universe presents. By overcoming his inclination to live as a hermit, Shrek learns a valuable lesson.

Shrek is the story of someone who lives as a Daoist. He has no desire, until his solitary and natural life is shattered. He does not transcend or bring back boons for the good of society. He returns to his prior state. The difference in Shrek is not a transformation, but a revision of circumstance. His quest or restoration gives him the opportunity to connect with another being like himself. He meets a counterpart who is just like he is. He is no longer alone, and he has learned a valuable lesson about trusting his feelings to select others, but he is otherwise the same.

A major implication of this study is that Campbell's claim that the hero is an archetype is an overstatement. This study suggests that concepts of the hero are more products of culture than the unconscious mind. Moving from universal to cultural explanations of heroes enlivens the possibilities for finding meaning and value in our lives. Rather than maintain that we are all the same, based on Campbell's Western modernist values, cultural approaches validate the different answers humans have found for vital questions regarding how one should live. Modernists and Confucians might not see Shrek as a hero, preferring more scrupulous planning, the elevation of the hero above the natural world, and an outcome where the hero improves the community by sharing the insights of rational "enlightenment." Yet some of us, including those who do not consider themselves to be Daoists (and few do!) may nonetheless appreciate the actions, outcomes, and values that are celebrated in the film.

Similarly, *Shrek* becomes a vehicle by which Westerners can thoughtfully engage Chinese cultural beliefs and values. X. Lu (1998) noted, "Western scholars of this century still labor under the assumption that Western culture is at the core of universal values, civilization, and progress. Eastern culture, in contrast, is viewed as subordinate and inferior" (p. 16). By uncovering the traditions of Chinese culture "we gain new information about rhetorical theories and practices, challenging the Eurocentric views of rhetoric and expanding our knowledge of the history of rhetoric in the process" (p. 1).

Shrek also demonstrates the viability of animated films to move beyond entertainment and be lenses for critiquing social standards and practices. *Shrek* induces audiences to identify with a new vision of the hero's form and function. It challenges the traditional Western notion of hero by valorizing the individual who focuses on being content, living simply, and avoiding conflict. It celebrates living harmoniously with nature and using the natural flow of the universe to accomplish one's objectives. The film thus illuminates non-Western perspectives on society and vividly demonstrates the possibilities for alternative visions not only of the hero but also the individual in the world at large.

ENDNOTES

1. Also Taoism. There are two different systems for rendering Chinese characters to English. The traditional system, created by British scholars, Wade-Giles, uses "Taoism" and "Tao" and typically refers to its chief proponents as "Lao Tzu" and "Chuang Tzu." The more contemporary approach, created by Chinese scholars and referred to as the pinyin system, uses "Daoism," "Dao," "Laozi," and "Zhuangzi" respectively. There are also additional spellings of these and other key words, but they are fairly close to those provided above and easily understood.

   Note that when I refer to Daoism I mean the seminal perspectives offered by Laozi and Zhuangzi that are sometimes referred to as "philosophical Daoism." There is a version known as "religious Daoism," which includes rituals and worship of deities.

2. Note Campbell's usage. Whenever he speaks of a person in the singular it is "he," "him," or "his." His refers to an individual or person as "man," and generally pluralizes with "men," and an occasional "they."

3. The archetype of the hero's journey can be manifest in myths or fairytales (Campbell, 1949, pp. 37-38).

REFERENCES

Adamson, A., & Jenson, V. (Directors) (2001). *Shrek* [Film]. DreamWorks Pictures.

Ames, R. (1993). *Sun-tzu: The art of warfare*. New York: Ballantine.

Blofeld, J. (1985). *Taoism: The road to immortality*. Boston: Shambala.

Campbell, J. (1949). *The hero with a thousand faces*. New York: MFJ Books.

Chan, W. (Ed. & Trans.). (1963). *A sourcebook in Chinese philosophy*. Princeton, NJ: Princeton University Press.

Cleary, T. (1999). *The Taoist classics: The collected translations of Thomas Cleary* (Vol. 1). Boston: Shambala.

Combs, S. C. (2002a). The dao of communication criticism: Insects, individuals, and mass society. *Social Semiotics, 12*, 183-199.

Combs, S. C. (2002b). The dao of rhetoric: Revelations from *The Tao of Steve*. *Intercultural Communication Studies, 11*, 117-136.

Cousinesau, P. (Ed.). (1999). *The hero's journey: Joseph Campbell on his life and works*. Boston: Element.

Kryder, R. P. (1997). A modern way of the eternal tao. In Lao Tsu, *Tao Te Ching* (G. Feng & J. English, Eds. & Trans.). New York: Vintage.

Lu, I. (1986). In C. Po-tuan, *The inner teachings of Taoism* (T. Cleary, Trans.). Boston: Shambala.

Lu, X. (1998). *Rhetoric in ancient China, fifth to third century B.C.E.: A comparison with classical Greek rhetoric*. Columbia: University of South Carolina Press.

Mair, V. H. (Trans.). (1994). *Wandering on the way: Early Taoist tales and parables of Chuang Tzu*. New York: Bantam Books.

Nagel, G. (1994). *The tao of teaching*. New York: Primus.

Parrinder, G. (Ed.). (1983). *World religions: From ancient history to the present* (rev. ed.). New York: Facts on File Publications.

Schwartz, B. I. (1985). *The world of thought in ancient China*. Cambridge, MA: The Belknap Press.

Sun, K. (1995). How to overcome without fighting: An introduction to the Taoist approach to conflict resolution. *Journal of Theoretical and Philosophical Psychology, 15*, 161-171.

Watson, B. (1964). Introduction. In *Chuang Tzu: Basic writings* (B. Watson, Trans.). New York: Columbia University Press.

Watts, A. (1975). *Tao: The watercourse way*. New York: Pantheon.

Chapter 17

THE MEDIATED SPORTS HERO

Susan J. Drucker
Hofstra University

Are "sports heroes" true heroes? In this chapter, Susan Drucker claims it is the mass media's celebrification of athletes and sporting events that creates the illusion of heroes emerging from sports. She examines the features of the traditional concept of hero and provides an explanation for the illusion that a sports hero is a real hero. She demonstrates the ways that stadia, photography, news, publicity, radio, and television play a part in constructing this myth and points out that it is the celebrification process at work making athletes into pseudo-heroes.

PROLOGUE

Since the publication of *American Heroes in a Media Age*, sports heroes have been elevated to ever greater heights in terms of salaries, media exposure and marketability. Multimillion dollar packages and celebrity product endorsements beckon. Name recognition and respect for on-field accomplishments have led to careers in acting and to elected office.

If athletes are actually heroes (a discussion found later in the chapter), they have increasingly been revealed as flawed. Doping scandals have rocked many sports. Performance-enhancement drugs abound. Barry Bond's pursuit of the coveted major league baseball homerun throne has been tainted by his alleged connection to the steroid scandal.

Sports figures have always been in the spotlight and involved in some scandals, but certainly the astronomical rise in salaries of professional athletes has made scandal-prone athletes further susceptible to media scrutiny. Sports figures are implicated in cases of domestic abuse, charged with rape, driving under the influence, tax evasion, illegal gambling, betting on their own sports, and even murder. News media cover the stories, entertainment media dramatize, fictionalize, and further propagate the flaws of the modern sports "hero."

The international fame and adoration increasingly enjoyed by sports figures has grown in the past decade. Any local sports heroes may be transformed into nonlocal global sports figures. Local sports marketed internationally has created sports heroes (or pseudo-heroes) recognized around the world. NBA basketball and the New York Yankees franchise merchandise is ubiquitous, especially the knockoffs. For soccer fans, World Cup champions, Euro Cup victors, and fan favorites like David Beckham have created a lucrative sports memorabilia market worldwide. Foreign audiences started tuning into American pro sports, especially basketball, in previously unheard of numbers. Teenagers snapped up player jerseys and stayed up until all hours of the night to watch games on live television. They began imitating moves on their own courts and fields. According to David Goldiner, a reporter for the *New York Daily News*:

> More than any single athlete, Jordan, the magnetic and charismatic Chicago Bulls superstar, transformed American sports into a global phenomenon. Jordan's soaring dunks and graceful athleticism made him a worldwide poster child for the American dream. Starting in the late 1980s, he drew hundreds of millions of dollars into the sport and became one of the most recognized persons in the world. (Goldiner, 2003)

American sports are beamed around the world. At the same time, foreign stars have been welcomed onto the fields, courts, and rinks of the U.S. professional leagues. Chinese basketball center Yao Ming, high-scoring forward Dirk Nowitzki from Germany, and Brazilian Nene Hilario have emerged as stars in the NBA. Satellite radio and television, along with coverage provided via the Internet, mean following one's "home team" does not depend on remaining home. Immigrant communities around the world retain home team allegiance religiously following their sports legends. The sports club or café that offers a live satellite feed often serves as a central meeting point in immigrant enclaves.

Some sports have been exported, creating international sports heroes. The adoption of baseball in Japan, although not a recent innovation, has changed with the exportation of legends to U.S. franchises. Player "heroes" are both welcomed in their new homes and followed faithfully by fans "back home." A few of these include, Ichiro, Hideo Nomo, Hideki Matsui, Hideki Irabu, Sasaki Kazuhiro, and Masato Yoshii.

The first player exchange was in 1964 between the San Francisco Giants and the Nankai Hawks that brought Murakami to the majors, but since the 1990s, the exchange has had a more noticeable impact. The global media environment enables up-to-the-minute fan following. In Japan, legions of fans tune in at odd hours each day to watch their chosen hero take on North American adversaries. For example, with Suzuki on the Seattle Mariners, Japan's NHK network broadcasts each Mariners game back to Japan and, between innings, focuses on Suzuki as he jogs, stretches, tosses a warm-up ball (Pearlman, 2001).

America's "national pastime" has become internationalized. By 2000, both top rookie honors went to foreign born players (Seattle Mariner's Kazuhiro Sasaki from Japan and Dominican Republic-born shortstop Rafael Furcal of the Atlanta Braves). By 2003, major league players in the United States came from 31 different nations (Vass, 2003). In 2006, baseball had global all stars with players from all over Latin America (including Cuba, significantly from a political standpoint). Chan Ho Park joined the Los Angeles Dodgers in 1994 and became the first Korean player in major league history. The "beisbol" players of Latin American countries like Venezuela, Panama, and, especially, the Dominican Republic, now supply sports "heroes," including homerun hitter Sammy Sosa. For decades, a few Latin American stars excited U.S. baseball fans and ignited interest at home, as epitomized by Mexican pitcher Fernando Valenzuela and Dominican curve-baller Juan Marichal, but now more than 25% of all Major League Baseball players are born outside the United States (Goldiner, 2003). Volumes have been devoted not only to significance in terms of sports but the cultural importance of the exported sports "hero" exemplified by Robert Whiting's (2004) book *The Meaning of Ichiro*, which focuses on Japanese who play baseball in the American major leagues.

Whether genuine hero, ersatz hero, or authentic celebrity, the sports figure has remained a recognized, celebrated personage with an increasingly distant significance.

THE SPORTS DILEMMA

I faced a great dilemma. I had the opportunity to take the trip of a lifetime to the Amazon, or I could spend a weekend in a small town in upstate New York where I would attend a 1-hour ceremony honoring a man I have spoken with directly for a sum total of 3.5 minutes in my life. I rearranged my plans and made reservations for Cooperstown. Tom Seaver, alias "the Franchise," alias "Tom Terrific," star pitcher of the New York Mets, entered into baseball's Hall of Fame. I had planned to attend since I was 12 years old. I have watched him age. I cried with him when he was traded. I ran out in the middle of college classes to call sports phone when he was pitching. I remembered his anniversary, his birthday. I've seen his children grow. I've seen his wife not age a bit in 23 years. I've seen his 300th major league victory, shared the moment when his uniform number was retired, and even listened to Yankee broadcasts. I ultimately attended the induction ceremony. I was not disappointed. It is a relationship of intensity, durability, one that has passed the test of time and is marked by loyalty and fidelity. This brings me to the task of attempting to unravel the nature of the relationship between the professional sports hero and the fan.

All cultures have heroes, but the hero and the heroic varies from culture to culture and from time to time. What is considered heroic is a function of cultural priorities and values and, equally significant, is related to the communication medium utilized for presenting and preserving information about heroes (Cawelti, 1985; Strate, 1985). This chapter explores the nature of "hero," the notion of "sports hero," and the way they function in society as a communication phenomenon whose scope and use has been and is being altered by the rapid advance of electronic media. Despite the cries of social commentators noting the lack of "real heroes," we continue to see endless titles relating to "sports legends and heroes" and we can even purchase "hero series trading cards." It is the thesis of discussion that the nature of modern sports fosters the illusion that heroes emerge from professional sports; however, these so-called "sports heroes" are actually products of the celebrification of the pro-athlete rather than the creation of a hero.

THE SPORTS PSEUDO-HERO

Why do modern-day sports seem so naturally to offer candidates for heroes, and are these athletes really heroes in the classical sense of the word? An examination of traditional features of the concept of *hero* provides some explanation for the illusion that real heroes emerge from professional sports.

There are so many definitions of hero that one is tempted to simply draw on Justice Potter Stewart's observations regarding censorship and say "I know it when I see it" and conclude that it is not often seen in sports. There have been many competing definitions of hero including the following:

> A central personage taking an admirable part in any remarkable action or event; hence, a person regarded as a model. (Webster's Collegiate Dictionary)

> The hero is a mass symbol, a "vehicle for the imaginings of thousands" who is transformed by imputation and abstraction more and more into what people want of public figures. (Klapp, 1962, p. 14)

The professional athlete performs, acts, and is said to be a role model. Critics have argued that sports heroes constitute a subtle form of social control when they "become the personifications of certain kinds of values and the interpretation of performances and the conduct of spectators becomes part of a wider process whereby particular kinds of life styles, values and ideas are 'sold'" (Hargreaves, 1982, p. 128).

The appearance of heroism in professional sports may also be fostered by the publicness of the acts. If "heroism is a public drama" (Edwards, 1988, p. 48), the real hero does not merely enjoy fame as a fleeting character on the public stage, but is a figure who endures the passage of time. According to Carlyle (1908), "A hero can be poet, prophet, king, priest or what you will, according to the kind of world he finds himself born into." Today's world is a "wide world of sports" with many of those figures ever increasingly appearing on a public stage being heralded as our modern heroes. Libraries devote shelves and shelves to volumes on the "legends": The Great Ones, The Hall of Famers, Boys of Summer, and the Summer of 49 in which some of them played. Bookstores are filled with everything from Iron Mike to the more cerebral works of the late A. Bartlett Giamatti—Renaissance scholar, baseball commissioner, sports fan. Once there were merely The Champions, Monday night baseball, Saturday night wrestling, Sunday Golf, Sunday afternoon football, and Monday night football. We now have *Sports Extra*, *Sports Update*, *Sports Central*, 24-hour sports radio, Sportschannel, and ESPN. Need a break? Go to the movies to see *Field of Dreams*, *Bull Durham*, *The Natural* or *Babe Ruth*. Still not satisfied? Rent a tape, settle in, and turn on *Brian's Song*, *North Dallas Forty*, *The Lou Gehrig Story*, and so on.

Achievement in modern professional sports is anything but a private act. Heroes are also creations of a common will, of combined action, of collective expression (Edwards, 1988; Fishwick, 1972; Lipsky, 1975). To Robert Penn Warren (1972), no true hero can exist in the absence of a communal soul, and Michael Lever asserted that sports is an institution that holds people together (Wenner, 1990). "We" have something in common, "we" share more than physical proximity, "we" share a sport's history, a tradition, a team, a standard of excellence, records held and broken, and our heroes. Shared sports heroes can cross economic, social, linguistic, racial, and geographic barriers. The concepts of communal interest and community itself, traditionally place-based notions, have been altered by the modern world in which the electronic media of communications permit, indeed encourage, a sense of the communal based on interest rather than place. Modern professional sports has been called an interest-based community (Gumpert, Lehman, & Drucker, 1990). All communities need heroes. Communities form around heroes, and interest-based communities are no exception.

The traditional hero emerged by acting within the larger social, political, religious, and economic realm. The hero has been alternatively positioned as saint, world redeemer, emperor (Campbell, 1968), leader, lover, politician (McGinniss, 1990), writer, mythic or literary character, and warrior. The modern sports hero restores civic pride, serves as role model, plays a role in often-repeated sports legends, is followed by groupies, writes autobiographies, runs for public office, but most often "leads the troops into battle" as teammates take the court, ice, or field. With these notions, it is a small step toward equating talented athletes with heroes.

The marriage of organized professional sports and the concept of hero is natural as the traditional requisite ingredients for hero creation appear to be present. The hero is one who makes an archetypal journey. According to Joseph Campbell (1968), the hero's story is composed of elements common across time and culture:

> The standard path of the mythological adventure of the hero is a magnification of the formula represented in the rite of passage: separation–initiation–return: which might be named the nuclear unit of the monomyth. A hero ventures forth from the world of common day into a region of supernatural wonder: fabulous forces are there encountered and a decisive victory is won; the hero conies hack horn this mysterious adventure with the power to bestow hams on his fellow man. (p. 30)

The journey for the professional athlete runs from the sandlots to the little leagues, school sports, amateur leagues, minor leagues, professional competition, and finally retirement. The "hero" acts; the athlete performs. The hero is brave even if called on to make the "supreme sacrifice." Within seconds, the athlete may tear cartilage, rip a tendon, break a bone, or sustain a blow to the head resulting in a career-ending injury. When the risks of unfolding action are replaced by memories of victory, sacrifice, or survival, the athlete is venerated by nostalgia, uniform numbers are retired, Oldtimer's games are attended, restaurants are opened to house memorabilia, life stories are written, and the Hall of Fame beckons. The hero performs acts of significance: "Sports are said to reflect and reaffirm such cultural values as achievement, hard work, discipline, teamwork, loyalty, and tradition" (Trujillo, 1994, p. 222). According to Wenner (1989), spectator sports also serve a therapeutic function as they can be pleasurable, heighten attachment to place, offer "a fantasized extension of self," and "provide a sense of being part of something" (p. 224).

The illusion of heroism is clearly fostered by these delineated characteristics. Yet, on close examination of the hero-creation process, the resemblance to modern-day celebrities is startling. Twentieth-century mass media made available in the United States an unending stream of celebrities, and Americans in return responded with adulation and devotion. The evolution of a media relationship based on identification without interaction can be traced to the establishment of the Industrial Revolution in America and the rise of the mass-circulation daily newspaper. The persistent presentation of "news" about individuals enabled large numbers of people to identify with them, carefully following their dramatic triumphs, their emotional setbacks, and their personal idiosyncracies, drawing ever closer toward a new form of relationship with public characters. "News" of stars of the sports world is not relegated to the sports pages alone. When reading or hearing reports on entertainers or other well-known individuals, the sports "star" is often found dining at the next table, dancing at the same club, making a cameo appearance on television or film, or promoting the same product as the celebrity.

The varied definitions of celebrity include the following:

- A famous or well-known person. *(Random House)*
- State of being renown; State of being celebrated (i.e. to perform publicly and with appropriate rites; to proclaim or publish abroad). *(Webster's Collegiate Dictionary)*
- The state or quality of being celebrated, *i.e.* having *been* made famous. *(Funk & Wagnalls)*
- The celebrity *is* a person known for his/her "well-knownness." The celebrity is created and maintained by media. (Boorstin, 1961)

The celebrity's fame is molded, created, and prefabricated. The professional athlete's fame and status are created through an updated process of hero-making.

THE MEDIA AND THE CELEBRIFICATION
OF THE PROFESSIONAL ATHLETE

Dreaming, we are heroes. Waking, we invent them. (Edwards, 1988,
p. 48)

The process of hero construction has been a function of the communication
process that has undergone radical change due to developments in communication technologies. Heroes were created through the ritual retelling of the
story of their great deeds. The narrative, the story, the myth, or the epic,
embodying the heroes' deeds, was, to oral cultures, the means of hero creation and perpetuation (Campbell, 1968). According to Ong (1967), there
exists considerable evidence that the dominant medium of the communication of a culture affects the notion of hero:

> The figures around whom knowledge is made to cluster, those about
> whom stories are told or sung, must be made into conspicuous person-
> ages, foci of common attention, individuals embodying open public
> concerns. . . . These figures, moreover, cannot be too numerous or atten-
> tion will be dissipated and focus blurred. (p. 204)

Print and electronic communication technologies have provided new mechanisms for hero-making, which in turn have changed the end product and its
functions.
    The ancient hero's deeds often reflected acts of physical strength and
courage on a naturally occurring stage. Contrasted with the naturally occurring challenge (offered by dragons, monsters, wars, and famines), we find
sports to be a rule-bound autotelic or self-contained activity. Were gladiators
the first sports heroes? Were ancient Olympians? When the stage for the
heroic deed is limited or intertwined and dependent on technology, one of
the few fields remaining for testing a human against a challenge is the carefully planned, constructed, and groomed sports arena. Hero creation has
been modernized; heroes changed. In an oral culture, the heroic is oriented
toward contests and combat. Heroes are closely associated with well-known
and widely remembered events such as slaying the dragon or saving the village through moral courage and individual sacrifice. The ephemeralness of
spoken discourse serves to limit the number of figures selected and sharpens
the focus on those figures to be remembered. Heroes' actions in an oral culture are more readily remembered because they are portrayed as having a
marked influence on the outcome of events, and they must serve as inspiration to those who feel they have little control over natural forces. It is significant to note that modern-day "hero making" is a multimedia phenomenon.

THE STADIUM AS COMMUNICATION MEDIUM

The sports arena, stadium, amphitheater, or complex is a public place. From Greece and Rome to the Superdome, that venue serves as a place of interaction. Public places were and are a medium of communication, that is, they are essential carriers of communication (Rykwert, 1978).

The stadium is a place of communal activity; the team and players "represent" a place that provides a sense of identification for fans. Professional sports take place in spaces that yield community affiliation and contact. Modern culture is populated with citizens who live their lives behind locked doors and darkened car windows, individuals who shield themselves from contact in public with others. Yet, the very same people shout, converse, pass the hotdogs, discuss the latest managerial blunder, and sing the National Anthem in unison. In this context, games are won and saved, sports stories are retold, and legends are created. This context has become increasingly mediated as the announcer supplements the images appearing on diamond vision that are carefully orchestrated to evoke the response desired by team management. Communication in the stadium plays a part in the creation of the sports hero. Stadia offer finite capacity with access ruled by barriers of financial means and distance, but the modern micro and mass media place no such limitations on fans as functions of the arena have been augmented, if not displaced, by allsports talk radio, ESPN, *Sports Illustrated*, and sports phone.

PHOTOGRAPHY

Sports figures, great and small, find themselves in team pictures, in news photos, and in the homes of millions. Posters are marketed, photographs are autographed, pictures with fans are posed for, and trading cards are sold. Posters are sold at the stadium and in malls alongside those of the hottest rock star du jour. Teams sponsor "Photo Days," providing photo opportunities for their fans. Some encourage players to make themselves available to fans before games for this very purpose. According to Al Harazin, former general manager of the New York Mets (personal communication, May 9, 1990), "everyone wants to touch the ballplayers, and I have found out that through enough camera days and other promotional days at ball parks that if you don't have a lot of people coming through the gate you can do a lot of things."

According to Tim Nolan (personal communication, October 10, 1991), proprietor of Classic Hobby Nostalgia, a sports memorabilia shop on Long

Island, posters are the province of the kids, whereas adults specialize in collecting and coveting photographs and autographed posters. Possessing photos and posters is, according to Sontag (1977), a symbolic form of control of personal relationships with others. Having photos and posters indicates "possession" of the other person, and they are an aid in maintaining a relationship by bringing closer the person in the photo. Is it possible that the ubiquitous celebrity poster is now the counterpart of the statue of the hero in the public square? The memorial statue erected to honor and remember the hero has long been a feature of the hero-creation and preservation process. Statues, dedicated by the public, were placed in public places, including halls of fame.

Images adorn the face of trading cards. Baseball trading cards were introduced in the later part of the 19th century and became an institution with the emergence of Topps bubblegum cards in 1951. By 1984, trading cards were transformed from a childhood hobby into a multimillion dollar business (Nolan, personal communication, October 10, 1991). A 1952 Mickey Mantle baseball card can fetch as much as $50,000. There are many lines of trading cards as Topps is no longer alone in the field. Different companies offer distinctive series, each with players striking a distinct pose. Fourteen different companies produce football trading cards, the sport for which cards are least popular. Why would football cards be less popular? One suggestion has been that people relate to players when they are covered in helmets and built up in shoulder pads, therefore, the close-up photos on the cards destroy the illusion (Nolan, personal communication, October 10, 1991).

Promoters organize shows. There are monthly shows at which on average 30 to 40 dealers attend, and there are larger shows drawing as many as 100 to 500 dealers. "In some areas one could attend a different card show each night of the week" (Nolan, personal communication, October 10, 1991), and these trading card shows provide a forum for conversation based on common interests. A child's hobby has become a big-money industry with monthly price guides, magazines, price lists, and international trade associations. Nolan, owner of a sports trading cards shop said "If I had to rely on kids I'd be out of business" (Nolan, personal communication, October 10, 1991).

WRITING

Writing and print have revolutionized sports and the creation of the sports hero as well. According to Guttman (1978), to the ancients, the game on the field was a repetitive ritual or ceremony. Sports records have existed since the ancient Greeks and have been a significant means for creating the sports hero. With writing came inscriptions, poems, and recordkeeping as a means for preserving and recreating the very transitory achievement of the sports act (Giamatti, 1989). The sports record, the "record book," in and of itself may not make what has commonly been called the sports hero. Although according to traditional notions, a hero's deeds, in the record book, might be enough to create a hero, in order to be placed on the pedestal reserved for the most revered, the modern sports figure must visit the sick hospitalized child, serve as spokesperson for a charity, and answer fan requests for photos and autographs. These activities are approved of by the front office, but are not generally required. According to Gregory Bouris (personal communication, July 16, 1990), formerly of the New York Islanders Hockey team, the personality and attitude of a player is considered when evaluating future players. Fan relations and community relations are part of the profile of an Islander. A personality system has developed in professional sports.

Like trading cards, autograph collecting has become commercialized. The collection of celebrity autographs is not new, but the formalization of the sports star autograph show is a recent innovation. Shows are organized with sports figures of the past and present paid by the hour. Interaction with fans is limited as the more signatures that are signed, the more money that is made. Conversation with fans who seek the autograph to keep, cherish, or sell at a profit is limited by financial motive. Autographs can bring large sums. A baseball autograph of Monte Irvin is worth $75 as are Carl Hubble's and Lefty Gomez's, but Ralph Kiner's is worth only $25.

Sports heroes are also created through the omnipresent sports biography and autobiography. Autobiographical narratives are now the method by which public figures communicate the myths that audiences identify as heroic for their particular situation. Narrative analysis of these popular forms of communication reveal these new myths as hero-making strategies (McLennan, 1994). Autobiographies of sports heroes collaborating "with" or "and" professional writers abound. One can read *Audibles, My Life in Football* by Joe Montana and Bob Raissman (1986); *Martina* by Navratilova with George Vecsey (1985); *Billyball* by Billy Martin with Phil Pepe; *Throwing Heat, The Autobiography of Nolan Ryan*, by Nolan Ryan and Harvey Frommer (1988); and *The Perfect Game* by Tom Seaver and Dick Schapp. One will find "along withs" such as Dick Schapp, Pete Axthelm, and Neil Amdur on such works. Add to the list the works of Yaz (Carl Yastrzemski), Dave Winfield, Michael Jordan, Dwight Gooden, Jose Canseco, Wade Boggs, Roger Clemens, and "before and after" stories of Pete Rose and one begins to get the sense of enormity of the professional athlete autobiography genre. Coaches, managers, and sportscasters, and celebrities (if not heroes all) can be added to the list. According to McLennan (1994), personal narratives enable these public figures to meet the ever-increasing demands placed on them to account for their behaviors and provide their own interpretation of events. In so doing, they create a public image and position themselves as heroic persona. The genre formed is one in which the individual may fashion an image beyond that of the record book or repair a damaged image by presenting himself as a hero, which is often accomplished by recounting the heroic journey or quest.

Sports pages, sports magazines, and the sportswriter all provide weekly, daily, and up-to-the-minute fuel for the celebrification process. Each move, play, decision, pout, frown, and temper tantrum is recounted, retold, analyzed, and criticized. The long-established and ever-growing genre of sports writing has contributed greatly not only to the celebrification of the professional athlete, but to the myth of the sports hero as well.

RADIO, TELEVISION, TELEPHONE

The electronic media have proved the most powerful tool in the creation of the pseudo-hero of sports. The celebrated athlete grew along with the electronic media and helped provide a seemingly endless source of content for media that consumed programming at a great rate. In 1922, even before the advent of commercial radio, WEAF broadcast in New York a University of Chicago–Princeton game, taking place in Chicago (Barnouw, 1975). In 1939, two baseball games were telecast by an experimental NBC television—a Princeton game and a Brooklyn Dodger match (Barnouw, 1975).

Although initially viewed with some skepticism by team owners who feared the loss of revenue from game attendance, the economic and marketing benefits of selling broadcast rights quickly became apparent. Total revenue from television for Major League Baseball, for example, rose from $15.8 million in 1960, to $40.7 million in 1970 (Horowitz, 1974), to the $1.1 billion for CBS network rights alone during the 1990-1993 seasons (Jassem, 1990). In 2006 Fox Sports completed the last year of a six-year, $2.4 billion deal with major league baseball, and in July of that year, a new agreement was announced between Major League Baseball and Fox Sports said to guarantee baseball more than the $400 million it received from the network's previous 7-year contract. The agreement extends the relationship with Fox through 2013 (Sessa, 2006).

The sportscaster has become friend, critic, and a major voice through which a team presents itself. According to Al Harazin (personal communication, May 9, 1990), the men in the booth are team spokesmen, ambassadors, and salesmen, as well as interpreters of events on and off the field. The sportscaster walks the line between journalism and ambassador for a sport or club. For many fans, there is daily contact with the sportscaster. They may even correspond with the announcer (McCarver, personal communication, June 8, 1990). The radio call-in format offers yet another opportunity to interact with the specialist prepared to highlight, praise, elevate, and venerate the sports professional. The familiar voice is presented as expert (i.e., either professional broadcast journalist or former participant). With some degree of credibility, the sportscaster helps celebrate the athlete by calling the action, placing accomplishments in the context of the omnipresent record, and instantaneously providing the enormity of a feat in terms of endless statistics. According to sportscaster Brent Musburger, "the announcer works with the action itself, presented live on television the picture is more important than the announcer . . . the announcer is secondary to the output of the truck" (cited in Verna, 1987 p. 64). The mediation of the sport itself goes a long way in explaining why professional sports has celebrities or pseudo-heroes.

The nature of broadcasting, television in particular, also contributes to the making of the celebrity athlete. The live, the unpredictable, the dramatic "are the core of TV . . . they are the one thing TV [in particular] can do that no other medium can match" (Verna, 1987, p. 41). Television coverage personalizes and creates "stars" we know on and off the field. To sportscaster Tim McCarver (personal communication, June 8, 1990), "Television takes you into the heart and soul of the players." The audience sees each bead of perspiration, each grimace, each tension-filled expression as the camera zooms in as a basketball is shot, a baseball is hurled, a football is passed, or a tennis ball is served.

As the sound quality from the playing field has been improved, the audience can hear the crack of the bat. Managers, umpires, and players have even been miked, which closes the psychological distance between fan and participant as the fan becomes even more intimate with the player. Graphics provide player identification, history, statistics, and constant reminders of "heroic deeds." The actions of the pseudo-heroes are retold via high-tech means. Replays and stop-action shots explain why things happen and provide cause and effect (Verna, 1987).

Both mass and micro media provide means for getting to know the professional athlete. The telephone allows fans to "reach out and touch" players when they appear on radio or television call-in programs or gives fans the privilege of paying large sums to dial a 900 number to hear a prerecorded message from the likes of Jose Canseco discussing what he ate for breakfast. The ability to directly contact the player brings the sports figure closer to the fan and promotes the relationship of celebrity–fan rather than hero–worshipper.

Athletes now have agents and are seen endorsing everything from sports equipment to jockey shorts. Can any of us forget Jim Palmer's underwear? Are we not expecting all Super Bowl victors to be going to Disney World immediately after the game clock runs out? The images of Joe Montana downing a Diet Coke, Bo Jackson running downcourt in his Nikes, Hulk Hogan hawking Right Guard stick deodorant, Nolan Ryan praising Advil, Magic Johnson selling subscriptions to *Sports Illustrated*, and World Series champs adorning cereal boxes are endless. The commercialization of the sports figure further "de-heroizes," as it enhances the fame and celebrity status of the athlete.

It is not merely the tremendous amount of information that modern media furnishes about professional athletes that makes them celebrities rather than heroes. The rise of personal information, the "up close and personal view" of the individual, leads to the demise of the all-powerful sports pseudo-hero.

THE NATURE OF THE SPORTS HERO–FAN RELATIONSHIP OR "ARE THEY REALLY HEROES?"

In a culture in which one may determine how often a hero is seen (we can always go to the videotape); may own unflattering photos; may see the sweat or hear grunting and cursing, may view the majestic swing, throw, run, dunk, pass, fumble, error, or foul instantly replayed over and over again, what is the nature of the relationship between sports figure and fan?

As Boorstin (1961) contended, heroes have been replaced by celebrities.

> Before we had celebrities we had heroes. . . . Now what these types all share, of course, are admirable qualities—qualities that somehow set them apart from the rest of us. They have done things, acted in the world, written, thought, understood, led. Celebrities, on the other hand, needn't have done—needn't do—anything special. Their function isn't to act—just to be. To a large extent, celebrity has entirely superseded heroism. . . . Celebrities are passive objects of the media-created whole out of "ordinary" newspaper print, or film, or broadcast airwaves. (Monaco, 1978, pp. 6-7)

The hero is known for deeds, the celebrity for "well-knownness" (Boorstin, 1961). The celebrity hero need only be a presence, need only be the focus of media attention, someone with whom the audience can readily identify. Because we all need something to satisfy our expectations of human greatness, we produce our celebrity heroes everyday by watching them on either the big or small screen, by reading and talking about them, by buying recordings and posters, and so on. The sports figure, although performing deeds, certainly performs the function of celebrity as well. The sporting contest may foster the impression of heroic deeds, all the while presenting an ordinary person with extraordinary athletic prowess and media attention.

The "heroic" nature of sports activities is questionable when held up to traditional measures. When held under the scrutiny of the modern star system it is difficult to imagine the illusion of heroism being maintained. According to Donald Ohlmeyer, head of Ohlmeyer Communications:

> The biggest thing that sports can do right now—the biggest thing the three networks can do to try to protect themselves . . . is to rediscover the hero. We live in an era where there are no more heroes. All of our heroes are being convicted for reckless driving or for taking cocaine, for raping girls and getting thrown in jail! That's what's wrong with sports right now. . . . The heroes are gone. (Verna, 1987, p. 66)

Pete Rose, Len Bias, Otis Nixon, Lenny Dykstra, and Mike Tyson follow in the tradition of the hard-drinking, gambling sports figures of old. On and off the field, court, or ice, behavior is examined carefully. Unlike the hero, the fall of these sports figures does not become part of the hero-making process. It is, however, a part of the celebrification process.

The word fan, a term derived from *fanatic,* characterizes a relationship based on an intimate knowledge of a personality created and sustained by the mass media industry and maintained by the personality's ability to control media attention rather than to control or shape events. (The athlete is never completely in control of his or her talent, the events in the game, injuries, or outcomes.) The fan relationship with the celebrity or media personality is a symbiotic one—a relationship that appears to fulfill an important need in the public psyche.

Caughey (1986) pointed out that the celebrity's appeal is linked to the fan's daily social relationships. It is taken for granted in our present culture that everyone knows of great numbers of celebrities including sports figures. According to Caughey, "Pseudo mutual acquaintances of this kind often provide American strangers . . . with the basis for socializing" (p. 220). This goes well beyond linking American strangers, as Michael Jordan has in capturing the imagination of children around the world.

What we see evolving from our dependence on the new relationships forged with celebrities is a shift from the traditional notion of the hero as a transcendent character dominating events through great deeds to a more ordinary but highly talented and well-publicized person who reflects our desire to escape ordinariness and gain some recognition in an impersonal, technological world. In Cathcart and Drucker (1986), we argued that the reliance on the celebrity in the establishment of self and the involvement with celebrities to help create a place for ourselves in a modern world in which traditional concepts of place and community have been altered by electronic media (see Drucker & Gumpert, 1991; Gumpert, 1987; Meyrowitz, 1985) would seem to argue that "solitary identification" is an important and widespread person–media personae relationship (Drucker & Cathcart, 1989).

The modern sports hero is actually a misnomer for the sports celebrity. Critics have noted true sports heroes are an endangered species, whereas sports celebrities are as common as Texas cockroaches (Trujillo, 1989). On the surface, professional sports seem to offer a natural source for heroes, but on closer examination they offer celebrated sports figures shaped, fashioned, and marketed as heroic.

REFERENCES

Barnouw, E. (1975). *Tube of plenty: The evolution of American television* (2nd rev. ed). New York: Oxford University Press.

Boorstin, D. (1961). *The image: A guide to pseudo-events in America.* New York: Atheneum.

Campbell, J. (1968). *The hero with a thousand faces* (2nd ed.). Princeton, NJ: Princeton University Press.

Carlyle, T. (1908). *Sartor resartus: On heroes and hero-worship.* New York: E.P. Dutton.

Caughey, J.L. (1986). Social relations with media figures. In G. Gumpert & R. Cathcart (Eds.), *Inter/Media: Interpersonal communication in a media world* (3rd ed., pp. 219-252). New York: Oxford University Press.

Cawelti, J.G. (1985). With the benefit of hindsight: Popular culture criticism. *Critical Studies in Mass Communication, 2,* 363-379.

Drucker, S., & Cathcart, R. (1989, November). *The celebrity and the fan: An exploration of a media relationship.* Paper presented at the Speech Communication Association Convention, San Francisco, CA.

Drucker ,S. & Gumpert, G. (1991). Public space and communication: The zoning of interaction. *Communication Theory, 1*(4), 294-310.

Edwards, L. (1988, Spring). The labors of psyche. *Aperture,* pp. 48-55.

Fishwick, M. (1972). Prologue. In R.B. Browne, M. Fishwick, & M.T. Marsden (Eds.), *Heroes of popular culture* (pp. 1-8). Bowling Green, OH: Bowling Green University Popular Press.

Giamatti, A.B. (1989). *Take time for paradise: Americans and their games.* New York: Summit Books.

Goldiner, D. (2003). Games for the whole world. http://usinfo.state.gov/journals/itsv/1203/ijse/goldiner.htm

Gumpert, G. (1987). *Talking tombstones and other tales of the media age.* New York: Oxford University Press.

Gumpert, G., Lehman, G., & Drucker, S. (1990). *Sports and the media community.* Paper presented at the Speech Communication Association convention, Chicago, IL.

Guttman, A.(1978). *From ritual to record.* New York: Columbia University Press.

Hargreaves, J. (1982). Sport and hegemony: Some theoretical problems. In H. Cantelon & R. Gruneau (Eds.), *Sport, culture, and the modern state* (pp. 103-140). Toronto: University of Toronto Press.

Horowitz, I. (1974). Sports broadcasting. In R. Noll (Ed.), *Government and the sports business* (pp. 275-323). Washington, DC: Brookings Institution.

Jassem, H.C. (1990, November). *American sports and the media dollar.* Paper presented at the Speech Communication Association convention, Chicago, IL.

Klapp, O.E. (1962). *Heroes, villains, and fools.* Englewood Cliffs, NJ: Prentice-Hall.

Lipsky, R. (1975). *Sports world.* New York: Quadrangle.

Martin, B., & Pepe, P. (1987). *BillyBall.* New York: Doubleday.

McGinniss, J. (1990). *Heroes.* New York: Simon & Schuster.

McLennan, D. B. (1994). The autobiography, cultural mythology, and the modern hero. In S. Drucker & R. Cathcart, (Eds.), *American heroes in a media age* (pp. 111-133). Cresskill, NJ: Hampton Press.

Meyrowitz, J. (1985). *No sense of place: The impact of electronic media on social behavior.* New York: Oxford University Press.

Monaco, J. (1978). *Celebrity: The media as image makers.* New York: Dell.

Montana, J., & Raissman, B. (1986). *Audibles: My life in football.* New York: Wm. Morrow.

Navratilova, M., & Vecsey, G. *(1985). Martina.* New York: Alfred A. Knopf.

Ong, W. J. (1967). *The presence of the word.* Minneapolis: University of Minnesota Press.

Pearlman, J. (2001, June 11). Ichiro the hero: U.S. baseball fans are now on a first name basis with the Japanese outfielder who is tearing up the league. *Time Asia. 157*(23). http://www.time.com/time/asia/arts/magazine/0,9754,129011,00.html

Ryan, N., & Frommer, H. (1988). *Throwing heat: The autobiography of Nolan Ryan.* New York: Doubleday.

Rykwert, J. (1978). The street: The use of its history. In S. Anderson (Ed.), *On streets* (pp. 15-28). Cambridge, MA: MIT Press.

Seaver, T., & Schapp, D. (1970). *The perfect game: Tom Seaver and the Mets.* New York: Dutton.

Sessa, D. (2006, July 11). Baseball expands TV coverage with Fox, Time Warner contracts. Retrieved October 15, 2006, from Bloomberg.com.

Sontag, S. (1977). *On photography.* New York: Dell.

Strate, L. (1985, Spring). Heroes, fame and the media. *Et cetera, 42*(1), 47-53.

Trujillo, N., & Vande berg, L.R. (1994). From wild western prodigy to the ageless wonder: The mediated evolution of Nolan Ryan. In S. Drucker & R. Cathcart (Eds.), *American heroes in a media age* (pp. 221-240). Cresskill, NJ: Hampton Press.

Vass, G. (2003). The wide world of baseball: Foreign-born players are filling major league rosters, showing the true measures of global talent in the American pastime Baseball Digest. http://www.findarticles.com/p/articles/mi_m0FCI/is_2_62/ai_95915320/pg_2

Verna, T. (1987). *Live TV: An inside look at directing and producing.* Boston: Focal Press.

Warren, R. P. (1972). Dearth of heroes. *American Heritage, 23*(6), 4-7.

Webster's Third New International Dictionary. (1964). Springfield, MA: G. & C. Merriam.

Wenner, L. A. (1989). *Media, sports, and society.* Newbury Park, CA: Sage.

Wenner, L.A. (1990). Therapeutic engagement in mediated sports. In G. Gumpert & S.F. Fish (Eds.), *Talking to strangers: Mediated therapeutic communication* (pp. 223-244). Norwood, NJ: Ablex.

Whiting, R. (2004). *The meaning of Ichiro: The new wave from Japan and the transformation of our national pastime.* New York: Warner Books.

Part IV

THE BUSINESS OF HEROES

Chapter 18

FROM HERO TO CELEBRITY

The Political Economy of Stardom

Philip Drake
University of Sterling

The blur between hero and celebrity has increased over the years, particularly linked to the role of the mass media as means of image production. To a great extent, today's celebrity has replaced the former hero, the latter a figure connected with deed rather than production. This chapter is a political economic analysis of the celebrity/star juxtaposed with prior conceptions of the hero.

✧ ✧ ✧

The hero was distinguished by his achievement, the celebrity by his image or trademark. The hero created himself; the celebrity is created by the media. The hero was a big man; the celebrity is a big name.

—Daniel J. Boorstin (1961, p. 70)

The professional celebrity, male and female, is the crowning result of the star system of a society that makes a fetish of competition.

—C. Wright Mills (1956, p. 74)

In 2003, during the war on Iraq, the British newspaper *The Times* (2003) devoted the cover of its supplement to a picture of a soldier wearing aviator shades and smoking a cigar, with the title "Heroes, And Why We Still Need Them." The story centered on British Lieutenant Tim Collins and, suggesting that heroes are made under conditions of adversity, argued that his "chiselled good looks, his military bearing and a stirring address" (Morrison, 2003, p. 4) had made him a hero even before the war had started. The assumption of such writing on heroic figures is that their everydayness is overcome by extraordinary deeds—deeds of bravery or leadership, or more quietly, of courage or resilience against adversity. Heroes, according to these accounts, are made by history, brought reluctantly into the public eye through their achievements. Heroes are deserving of media attention, ennobled by their acts, and through them gain public visibility, functioning as inspirational figures for the rest of us. By contrast, celebrities are not usually known for their achievements, but first and foremost by appearances in and across the mass media. Theirs is a phenomenological presence that accumulates visibility through its increasing media circulation. Take, for example, Maria Fe Sotelo, a shopping mall security guard in Manila who became a media story for returning a bag containing 500,000 pesos to its owner in January 2003. Her deed was regarded as heroic precisely because it was a noble act—placing others before self, honesty before greed—and she gained a certain media visibility from it, even momentary celebrity. Her media circulation, however, was short-lived and so her celebrity status eventually waned.

The contrasting of the hero with the celebrity is most notably and clearly examined in the works of C. Wright Mills (1956) and Daniel Boorstin (1961). They argued that celebrities are created by the media rather than by achievement, by access to power and notoriety rather than through their heroic deeds. As the opening quotations indicate, these critics regard the mass media and the development of consumer capitalism as responsible for the shift from the celebration of heroes to that of celebrities. Clearly, this division does not allow for heroic public figures that subsequently become celebrities—most obviously sports stars—or for celebrities whose fame has been hard-won through years of labor and achievement. However, their arguments are useful for several reasons. First, they acknowledge the role that the mass media has taken in blurring the two categories. Mass media has made distinguishing achievements from their presentation in mediatized form increasingly difficult. Although one might counter this claim by recognizing that heroes have always relied on their acts being reported in the mass media, such as the news press, it is arguably the media themselves that are now central to the construction of celebrity. Traditionally, heroes are recognized for their heroic deeds, then achieve media visibility subsequently. Second, there is an assumption in such writing that "true" heroes are those untouched by the hand of the media, that they are known for their deeds rather than their media visibility, or what Boorstin famously called their "well-knownness." This assumption will be examined as it points to certain moral arguments about the recognition of particular deeds as especially worthy and valued. In the mediated public sphere the distinction between heroes and celebrities has become almost impossibly blurred. Public events in the contemporary age are predominately experienced by audiences in their mediatized form. Making the distinction between heroes and celebrities, therefore, becomes a judgment about intention: heroes as reluctant public figures, celebrities as publicity seeking. Furthermore, it also becomes a question of genre: heroes are primarily figured through news discourse, celebrities through entertainment genres.

The aim of this chapter is to examine how celebrities have been able to co-opt qualities traditionally associated with heroes to argue for a stronger right of control over their images. It argues that legal rulings continually make the assumption that fame is achieved through individual deeds rather than publicly conferred through media circulation. Put differently, celebrities have been able to claim that their public visibility is due to private endeavor and thus argue they should have exclusive control of the property rights of their images. The assumptions bound up in this allocation of rights are examined in greater detail below.

THE RISE OF CELEBRITY CULTURE AND THE DECLINE OF THE HERO

Analysis of the apparent decline of the hero is hardly recent. In "The Triumph of Mass Idols," published in 1944, Leo Lowenthal (1944/1961) examined the evolution of the popular biography. By surveying the articles that appeared in *The Saturday Evening Post* and *Colliers* between 1901 and 1941, he argued that there had been a shift from "idols of production" such as industry leaders and politicians to "idols of consumption" such as film and sports stars. From 1901 to 1914, 74% of the subjects in his survey came from traditional "heroic" professions such as politics and business; however, after 1922 more than 50% came from entertainment and sport (stars such as Babe Ruth, Gloria Swanson, and Charlie Chaplin). Following this work, and that of Mills and Boorstin, it has been claimed that the latter half of the 20th century saw an overwhelming rise of the celebrity in contemporary Western culture and a subsequent decline of the traditional hero. John B. Thompson (1990), for instance, argued that it is now celebrities (rather than heroes or role models) who operate as a "source of motive power in putting ideas across of every kind—social, political, aesthetic, moral" (p. 163).

Since Mill's examination of the power of celebrities as a new "power elite" (subsequently revised by Francesco Alberoni [1972], who argued that their "institutional power is very limited or non-existent"), a number of critics have drawn attention to the ideological function of stars and celebrities. It is worth noting that the terms have been used interchangeably; however *stars* and *stardom* are invariably used to examine film celebrity, whereas *celebrity* tends to be used to discuss the extra-textual aspects of the star, predominant in sociological studies (see Gamson, 1994).

In his important research on film stardom, Richard Dyer (1979) argued that stars resolve ideological contradictions for audiences by naturalizing certain values and myths. For example, Hollywood stars can offer the appeal of attainable fame and extraordinary wealth at the same time as they are desired for their unattainability and impossible glamour. Barry King (1986), examining the labor market for film stars, suggested that media visibility confers on actors a substantial monopoly power over their own labor, and which they are able to exploit in collaboration with the major media conglomerates, creating a circle of escalating costs and salaries for a celebrity elite. Star power in the media industries is, of course, primarily gauged in economic rather than cultural terms, but the two are importantly interwoven.[1] In his classic analysis of the culture industries—and one that clearly influenced Boorstin's thinking—Theodor Adorno (1991), writing in the 1940s saw this power exclusively as a means of *pseudo-individualization*; he argued that the industries themselves have the power to create stars, and stars were simply a way through which capitalism can maintain its ideological luster.

Boorstin's (1961) argument, like Adorno's, is that celebrities exist only in relation to their conditions of production; that "in themselves" they are devoid of meaning. Boorstin suggested that celebrities are figures in the public sphere who function as a "nationally advertised trademark" (p. 162) and by doing so constitute a "new category of human emptiness" (p. 58). The assumptions of manipulation evident here are derived from the critiques of the mass culture industries by the Frankfurt school, who argued that the processes of mass cultural production corrupted the authenticity of works of art. Adorno (1996) posited that the celebrity/star system is central to this process, as stars absorb the contradictions between cultural production and individualistic art:

> Its [the culture industry's] ideology above all makes use of the star system, borrowed from individualistic art and its commercial exploitation. The more dehumanized its methods of operation and content, the more diligently and successfully the culture industry propagates supposedly great personalities and operates with heart-throbs. (p. 26)

Here the star system, borrowed from legitimate art, works to efface the standardized and alienated mode of production in mass culture. Thus, Adorno's notion of "authentic" art is one that is autonomous from the conditions of mass production, allowing it a distance from and hence an ability to critique social contradictions and structures. "Heart-throbs" and "supposedly great personalities," for Adorno, appeal to emotional rather than critical instincts, feeling rather than thinking.

Adorno used the concepts of *standardization* and *pseudo-individualization* to elaborate his theory of the operations of the culture industry as a form of ideological deception. He regarded celebrities/stars as one of the most important ways through which standardized culture was pseudo-individualized—in contrast with traditional heroes produced outside of mass culture. He argued that the drive toward profit maximization leads to part interchangeability, where products will vary only superficially, requiring individualization through means such as advertising and publicity (aspects that Adorno clearly saw as a surface deception, hence his preface *pseudo* to the term). The marketing of stars, then, is seen as a way of reconciling the contradictions between capitalist mass production and art—stars being in an ideal position to resolve this contradiction as they exist in both public and private spheres.

Stars, argued Adorno (Adorno & Horkheimer, 1979), are thus an affective device in the operation of a capitalist hegemony:

> Not only are the hit songs, stars and soap operas cyclically recurrent and rigid invariable types. . . . The details are interchangeable . . . they never do anything more than fulfil the purpose allotted to them in the overall plan. (p. 125)

It is this pseudo-individualization that deceives, for Adorno (1990), and endows "cultural mass production with the halo of free choice or open market on the basis of standardization itself" (p. 308). For such critics, ultimately celebrities are interchangeable, individuated only by type, and predictable in the response they effect. These claims are strong, and continue to resonate in many critiques of celebrity. However, the pseudo-individualization charges leveled by Adorno and Boorstin are reductive and ultimately unhelpful in examining the power of celebrity. The consumption of celebrities by audiences is far more complex than such analysis suggests. Instead, I wish to focus on the allocation of property rights around celebrity, and suggest that this—rather than deception—is at the center of the political economy of the contemporary star system.

Celebrities then, are deeply implicated within a capitalist system of exchange, and accumulate value through media circulation. As John Ellis (1992) noted, they are paradoxically both ordinary and at the same time extraordinary, individualistic yet always mediated by and through mass culture. Celebrity must at the same time seem obtainable (unlike, say, membership in the aristocracy) yet maintain a distance necessary to continue the aura of stardom. Dyer's (1979) analysis of the concept of the "individual" is useful in examining this paradox (and is central to his study of stars), drawing on Weber's formulation of charisma. Weber outlined how the ideology of individualism is central to Western culture, even if that individual in the late 20th century might be characterized by an unstable, shifting identity. The notion of the individual, argued Dyer, helps to smooth over contradictions in ideology, and in this vein celebrities embody the public individual in the media age. Herein lies the paradox. Celebrities embody individualism at the same time as they constitute a para-social experience, available for collective consumption (via the media) but removed from everyday, personal interaction.[2] Similarly capitalist economics promotes itself on the basis of its individualistic libertarianism, its consumer-sovereignty, the law as a guarantor of individual freedom, while circumscribing such freedoms within social, legal and moral norms, and hegemonic frameworks. How, then, can these paradoxes illuminate our understanding of celebrities and heroes? We shall now turn to an examination of Hollywood stardom.

THE RISE OF CELEBRITY: THE CASE OF THE NEW "FLEXIBLE" HOLLYWOOD STAR SYSTEM

Celebrity and stardom has often been synonymous with Hollywood cinema, although as should be clear it is by no means exclusively its domain. Celebrities exist outside of Hollywood in television, sport, music, and politics; however, the evolution of the Hollywood star system offers a useful case study for the phenomenon of celebrity. Although there is a popular perception that Hollywood has seen the end of the "star system"—certainly it no longer functions as it did during the 1930s to 1950s when stars were contractually tied exclusively to studios—the last two decades have seen substantial reinvestment in celebrity-driven media and ancillary businesses. The major film and television studios no longer directly control stars under exclusive contracts, but the economic pre-eminence of both still depends on their collaboration. The economic scale and scope of a major film or television production almost invariably necessitates the casting of stars. Astronomical increases in star salaries—topping $20 million plus gross percentages per role by the start of the 21st century for "A" list movie stars—reflect the movement from production as the primary focus of the media industries toward a much wider conceptualization of a major feature film or television series as a "franchise" that relies on the publicity value of stardom to attract public interest. The high profile of a film or television series is used as a major leveraging device to access other markets. For example, the enhancement to revenue for a major film from distribution channels such as television, cable, video, and DVD rentals and sales often dwarfs the initial amounts returned in domestic theatrical rentals. The casting of a star usually guarantees certain minimum returns and thereby offsets exposure to risk, as well as extends the longevity of revenues accruing from a particular film or television franchise. Furthermore, Hollywood stars function as global celebrities, enabling product pre-recognition in remote markets. They exemplify the global–local status of the industry: remote, glamorous, and "other," yet at the same time familiar, reassuring and "known" all around the world. This new autonomy of celebrities can be usefully related to theories of post-Fordism, addressing some of the weaknesses of the Frankfurt school's deterministic analysis.

Post-Fordism and Celebrity

The term *post-Fordism* has often been simultaneously equated with a set of changes in the dominant mode of production, in aesthetic forms, and in patterns of consumption. Murray Smith (1998) suggested that post-Fordism constitutes:

> a shift from a largely undifferentiated mass market served by a limited array of standardized, mass-produced commodities, to that of a more heterogeneous range of specific markets to which more specialized products can be profitably sold. (p. 7)

Questions about periodization are central to the post-Fordist debates. As Ash Amin (1994) noted, post-Fordism is usually used to describe a "putative transition from one dominant phase of capitalist development in the post-war period to another thirty to fifty year cycle of development based upon very different economic, societal and political norms" (p. 3). There is clearly an attempt in this work to address shifts in ways that develop our understanding of the capitalist economy as something dynamic and changing rather than static and monolithic. Most conceptualizations of post-Fordism orientate themselves around one of three theoretical approaches, loosely defined as the "regulation approach," the "flexible specialization/accumulation approach," and the "neo-Schumpeterian approach" (Amin, 1994, p. 6). For reasons of space, I concentrate on the second, arguably most influential, of these and consider its usefulness in examining the political economy of celebrity.

The flexible specialization thesis is most notably associated with sociologists Michael Piore and Charles Sabel (1984) in their ground-breaking book, *The Second Industrial Divide*, and later in varying formulations with the work of Paul Hirst and Jonathan Zeitlin (1991),and numerous articles by Susan Christopherson and Michael Storper (1986, 1987, 1989, 1994). This work has been extremely influential in contemporary political economy and economic development. Unusually, flexible specialization theorists have also developed a particular interest in analyzing the structure and organization of the contemporary media industries, seeing in them "meta"-evidences of just-in-time production techniques, "lean" organizational structures, backward and forward networking between service companies, detailed division of labor, and external economies of agglomeration rather than internal economies of scale. I briefly summarize the main points of the flexible specialization thesis before considering how it can be applied to analysis of contemporary media celebrity.

Flexible specialization theories make a distinction between mass production as a mode of production, and flexible specialization. Mass production, Piore and Sabel (1984) argued, involves the standardization of goods produced by product-specific machines and semi-skilled workers, as in the archetypical Fordist assembly-line. Flexible specialization, on the other hand, produces customized goods through skilled workers, involving a division of tasks between different specialisms. Their analysis tended toward conceptualizing macro-economic change and relating it to industrial practices—for example, they attempted to explain the stagnation of the global economy in the 1970s as the start of a new "industrial divide." This, they argue, was typified by the rise in new manufacturing technologies (in particular computer-related processes), the introduction of flexible work practices, and the change in scale economies that enable small firms to compete effectively with larger organizations through the implementation of new production techniques, and as part of an inter-firm and inter-sectoral network of firms.

The package-unit system in Hollywood is used by Storper (1994) as a good example of flexible specialization. We might then see celebrities as newly "flexible" forms of capital, no longer tied to the studios with exclusive contracts, as had usually been the case until the 1950s. One tangible result of this has been an increase in the cost of celebrities/stars, who have gained a new flexibility in production and benefited from developments such as the introduction of profit participation contracts. As Storper (1994) describes: "in exercising their newly found market power, stars shifted distribution of the rents to specific assets in their favour" (p. 207). Another result has been an increase in horizontal integration and less formal linkages (alliances, joint ventures, distribution-chain partnerships) across different media. Celebrities offer an important branding function whereby different products across different divisions may be grouped within a particular franchise. For example, the cross-marketing of a major Hollywood film usually involves the licensing of star images for a range of merchandising and product tie-ins.

There are substantial flaws in the flexible specialization models described above, partly a result of changes since the publication of this work.[3] Flexible specialization theorists have a tendency to idealize the upsides of flexibility, described in terms of collaboration between firms and external agglomeration economies, and ignore the downsides—the gate-keeping over distribution networks, the continued oligopoly power held by the studios, the strategic behavior conducted by the majors. I suggest that celebrity functions as an important means of regulating these relationships. Although stars initially appear to be an example of a "flexible" factor of production, they are in fact an example of "flexible integration." The interests of stars and the industry are *interdependent*, they are both required in order to continue the hold that Hollywood has over global distribution channels. Stars, with the ability to underwrite blockbuster scale economics, are an important means through which Hollywood has secured its global competitive advantage. Without celebrity, Hollywood would be less able to control global distribution; without the distribution networks of the majors, stars would be less able to accumulate the publicity value that accrues through this distribution. Despite their apparent independence, then, I am arguing that there is an incentive for celebrities to *strategically cooperate* with the majors, as it is to the advantage of both parties. Organizations such as the Screen Actors Guild (SAG) and the Association of Talent Agents, despite not always agreeing with the industry, recognize this interdependence with the studios.[4] A key factor in this interdependency is the legal enforcement of the celebrity "right of publicity."

OWNERSHIP OF THE IMAGE:
THE RIGHT OF PUBLICITY AND THE RISE
OF THE CONTEMPORARY CELEBRITY

Publicity assumes in part the role formerly held by ideologies: to clothe, dissimulate and transform reality. (Lefebvre, 1971, p. 97)

To gain a fuller understanding of the political economy of the contemporary media industries it is important to examine issues of property rights. Henri Lefebvre's (1971) comment suggests that publicity operates as an almost invisible regulator of cultural property. The right of publicity, as a property right held by stars, is at the very center of this economic control. The management of property rights (through copyright, trademark, and intellectual property law) is big business in the creative industries. Acquisition of film and music libraries for hundreds of millions of dollars demonstrates the importance of the allocation of property rights over cultural goods. Licensing distribution rights in overseas markets operates as an important

means of sustaining global reach and dominance in the entertainment industries. Able to cover costs within the domestic market, overseas licensing
allows Hollywood's products, for instance, to impose high-cost barriers to
entry in overseas theatrical markets. Each new format or technology introduced (video, laserdisc, DVD, video-on-demand) offers the potential to
extend revenue streams as old films are repackaged as new "content." New
formats therefore dramatically increase the value of content libraries, as
those who are able to control the property rights to content are able to
increase prices in response to the increased demand for their products. The
economic power of celebrity is crucial to this process. Media libraries accumulate value as stars build up a body of work that can be marketed as a series
(as for instance in the DVD releases of Clint Eastwood's "Dirty Harry"
series). These franchises depend on properties of celebrity, in particular its
"joint-ness" characteristic in consumption. In overseas markets, stars provide a pre-recognized brand around which multiproduct franchises can be
built. Understanding the *allocation* of these rights is therefore central to an
analysis of the political economy of celebrity.

Surprisingly, few cultural critics have tackled questions of intellectual
property rights. Useful research in this area has been undertaken by Jane
Gaines (1991), who draws upon critical legal studies, in particular the
Marxist critique of legal doctrine by theorist Bernard Edelman. Edelman's
work, exemplified particularly by his book, *Ownership of the Image* (written in 1973 but not translated from French until 1979), powerfully argues
that legal doctrine, in its attempt to remove ambiguity, takes its meaning
through continual citation and appeal to discourses of "common sense"
(Edelman, 1979). Edelman suggested that copyright and other intellectual
property rights operate as a means through which the law confers monopoly power. He provides Gaines with an important starting point in her critique of intellectual property law in *Contested Culture: The Image, the
Voice and the Law*. Drawing upon the Marxist (and post-Marxist) intellectual tradition associated with British Cultural Studies, Gaines' thesis, developed through case studies of legal rulings around cultural properties, is that
legal doctrine works to uphold a set of discourses that assign ownership to
goods in a way that appears inevitable, yet often appeals to value judgments
such as originality. She suggests that the appeal to "common sense" in legal
discourse overwhelmingly favors dominant interests, working to secure a
hegemonic understanding of how things "are." Law, through its policing of
property rights, operates thereby as an institution that determines who can
assign meaning to particular cultural products, such as celebrity images, and
who is able to circulate them for direct economic benefit. Although a U.S.
newspaper is able to print photographs captured of a celebrity on holiday,
for instance, by arguing that this falls under a newsworthiness privilege, it is
unable to sell a poster adorned with this image. This would be considered a

violation of their rights as it allows the newspaper to directly profit from the celebrity status of the star.

Most accounts of U.S. publicity rights trace their development back to the "right of privacy." This was introduced in law through a highly influential article written by Samuel Warren and Louis Brandeis in 1890. They defined it as "the right to be let alone." A full account of the flaws of this "right" is beyond the scope of this chapter, however, important to note is that the right of privacy is a personal right designed to defend against personal intrusion, rather than a property right designed to defend an individual's economic interests.

The relationship between privacy and publicity rights is complex and developed from the engagements between celebrities and commercial interests. Courts began to rule as early as 1903 that unauthorized use of a person's photographic image was a violation of the right of privacy. When applied to noncelebrities the defense of one's identity from commercial exploitation clearly constituted a privacy right. However, as Michael Madow (1993) points out, the making of this argument was rather more problematic in the case of celebrities as through their fame they were often deemed to have waived their right to privacy. It was this problem that led to the introduction of the right of publicity. Non-stars could plausibly claim that unwanted publicity was an intrusion of their right of privacy, but such an accusation was difficult to sustain for famous individuals whose images were publicly circulated. As stars lacked the grounds to complain about public exposure, their legal argument shifted from a complaint about *unwanted* publicity to one about *uncompensated* publicity. This is a crucial distinction as it shifts the law away from a *privacy right* toward a *property right*—that is, the right to economic control over the commercial circulation of star images. In effect, this might be understood as the privatization of the public celebrity image.

Further reasons for this shift can also be discerned. The right of privacy was an individual right and therefore not *descendible* or *assignable* (Madow, 1993). The lack of descendibility obviously meant that the right was relinquished upon death. The nonassignability of the right of privacy meant that although stars could license their image to be used for commercial purposes (as did many Hollywood stars), they were unable to enforce this right so as to prevent another commercial interest from also using it, thus they were unable to exclusively capture the monopoly power inherent in their valuable public images. The right of publicity, then, enforced property rights over star images and addressed the perceived shortcomings of the right of privacy in controlling such images as property.

INTERROGATING THE RIGHT OF PUBLICITY

The right of publicity is the right of an individual to control the commercial use of his or her name, likeness, and other identifying characteristics as private property. The recognition of the right of publicity can be aligned with the needs of the media industries who wished the courts to recognize the right in order to control use of identity in exclusive commercial deals. The right was first acknowledged by U.S. courts in a ground-breaking case in 1953 between two chewing-gum manufacturers over the exclusive use of the image of a professional baseball player to promote their product (see *Haelan v. Topps*, 1953; for a discussion of this case, see Madow, 1993). In resolving the dispute, the court ruled that an individual has the right to control the circulation of his or her image for economic purposes, such as product endorsement. It argued that:

> This right might be called a "right of publicity". For it is common knowledge that many prominent persons (especially actors and ballplayers), far from having their feelings bruised through public exposure of their likenesses, would feel sorely deprived if they no longer received money for authorizing advertisements, popularising their countenances, displayed in newspapers, magazines, buses, trains and subways. This right of publicity would usually yield them no money unless it could be made the subject of an exclusive grant which barred any other advertiser from using their pictures. (*Haelan v. Topps*, 1953, at 868)

This new intellectual property right was developed by Melville Nimmer (1954) in his seminal article "The Right of Publicity." Nimmer, perhaps not coincidentally, was a legal counsel for Paramount Pictures at the time, and lobbied hard to make the case for the extension and recognition of the right. He did this through appealing to a number of "common-sense arguments"; in particular those who achieved stardom did so through substantial personal investment, skill, and effort. This "labor argument" was reinforced by the construction of stars by the studios as hard-working but ordinary individuals elevated to fame through extraordinary effort and talent. In describing the right Nimmer explicitly referred to the needs of Broadway and Hollywood, effectively suggesting that stars required particular consideration in law. His success—and that of right of publicity advocate J. Thomas McCarthy[5]—can be measured by the fact that the right of publicity is now explicitly recognized by common law or statute in over half of all American states, including most importantly for the entertainment industries, the states of California and New York. Other states implicitly recognize this law under the right of privacy, which protects against "appropriation of name of likeness," or unfair competition law, which protects against misappropriation and unfair endorsement.

Like trademark and copyright law, the right of publicity involves a recognizable property interest, protecting against the unauthorized use of a person's identity—identifiers such as name, likeness, idiolect (the recognizable elements of performance) or voice—for commercial gain. This means that publicity rights are far more extensive than the laws that protect against false endorsement. Publicity rights are a form of property right that allows celebrities to control who profits from the commercial value of their public images. The right of publicity, as a property rather than privacy right, is descendible and assignable, making it commercially available for exclusive licensing.

What, then, are the consequences of the right of publicity? Is it simply a matter of economic control? On the contrary, the right of publicity has important implications for the circulation of stars as *symbolic* resources. Madow (1993) argues that the right of publicity is an unwarranted privileging of celebrity property rights over those that consume their famous images—in effect the propertizing of a public good. Clearly, this view considers the right of publicity as an unwarranted privileging of celebrity property rights over those that consume celebrity images—in effect the propertizing of a public good. Those who define the right present two main lines of argument. First, the "incentive effect" of stardom created by the assignment of property rights. Second, the "allocative efficiency" argument that suggests that assignment of property rights creates market efficiency.

The first argument follows the logic of copyright law. Here the right of publicity ensures exclusivity and hence creates an incentive for individuals to achieve fame through the expenditure of time, skill, and effort that is ultimately of benefit to society through their artistic works. It is argued that without the incentive effect provided by the right of publicity, performers would have less reason to strive for stardom. This argument is tenuous in the extreme. Very many attempt fame, but very few achieve it, and the distinction between these two groups cannot easily be accounted for in terms of talent (Adler, 1985). Stars who command vast salaries dramatically skew the labor market for performers. Most members of the SAG, for instance, are sporadically employed at minimum union wages. The incentive effect attributable to the right of publicity then, over and above the incentive to achieve the direct benefits of stardom is likely to be marginal at best.

This points to an important distinction between *performing rights* and *publicity rights*. The direct economic benefits of celebrity are already protected through copyright law, which defends the star's primary means of income against unlicensed distribution. The performing rights of stars are already protected under law, and this covers all performers, whereas publicity rights impact only on those who are famous (i.e., already have publicity value). Furthermore, countries such as the United Kingdom and France do not recognize the right of publicity, but instead have an array of less extensive legislation to deal with issues such as false endorsement, libel, and copyright infringement, and retain significant celebrity industries.

The second argument put forward to justify the right of publicity is that of *allocative efficiency*. Here publicity must be conceptualized as a private good to promote efficient use of scarce resources. This argument suggests that products that present opportunities for "free-riding" (the unpaid for consumption of associated benefits) prevent the market from valuing that product at the correct price. However, the application of such a theory to celebrity is not easily justified. The publicity value of stars increases through circulation, and it is far from clear that privatizing some aspects of their image will lead to increased publicity value.

In summary, then, the efficiency arguments used to defend the right of publicity are based on weak economic analysis and lack strong evidence to support their claims. I now consider other arguments used to advance the right of publicity, in particular those to do with "moral rights," often voiced, following Nimmer, in terms of the right of artists to "reap the fruits of their labors", an argument that importantly draws upon the discourses of heroic achievement and labor that we considered earlier.

Jane Gaines (1991) argues that moral rights involve a set of assumptions about authorship. The moral arguments put forward for the propertizing of celebrity publicity rights are that stars have earned their fame through hard work, effort, and investment in learning skills, and thus should be able to exclusively control the rewards of their fame, just as any other worker can enjoy the results of their labor. This argument is intuitively appealing, yet is faulty on several counts. The most obvious, as already stated, is that stars are not necessarily famous through talent or skill, but often through notoriety or connection with others who are famous. More significantly, labor arguments for the right of publicity ignore the massively skewed labor market caused by the publicity value added through stardom. Star images gain their immense value through public circulation, and thus most of the exchange value of stardom is publicly conferred rather than a direct result of the endeavors of a performer, however talented they may be. The celebrity's public image thus functions, as Dyer (1979) noted, as a polysemic sign. This takes on associative value through its cultural circulation, appropriation, and consumption—what Madow neatly calls the star's "semiotic freight" (1993, p. 127). These theoretical complexities tend to be lost in legal definitions, where a star's cultural meaning is usually unquestioningly assumed to emanate from the individual, and hence becomes their property. The notion that celebrity is potentially available to all is an important part of the discourse of fame in Western culture, and constitutive of its appealing mythology. Yet fame is clearly far from democratic, or indeed meritocratic, relying on some skill, much luck, often what culture defines as physical beauty, and access to social networks of gatekeepers in the celebrity industries.[6]

Thus, my argument is that assigning publicity rights to stars gives them monopoly power over meanings; in particular the ability to reinforce dominant meanings over oppositional readings. A case brought by Dustin Hoffman in 1999 against *Los Angeles* magazine offers an interesting balancing of First Amendment rights against the right of publicity. The magazine published a composite image of a publicity still of Hoffman from the film *Tootsie* (1982) which had been computer-enhanced, so that the character appeared to be dressed in designer clothes and high-heels, appearing in a fashion article entitled "Grand Illusions" (see *Hoffman v. Capital Cities/ ABC, Inc.*, 1999). Hoffman, who had not authorized the picture, sued on a number of grounds: the right of publicity, unfair competition, and the Lanham Act (which protects against false endorsement claims). The magazine defended its use of the image first by claiming it was a copyright issue, as the still was from a film. The court rejected this on the grounds that Hoffman's name, face, and persona were not works of authorship that fall under copyright law. The First Amendment defense—the often used newsworthiness privilege—was also rejected by the court, which argued that the article was lacking in any view of news, current affairs, or even a survey of fashion trends, and therefore the use of Hoffman's persona went beyond that necessary to convey any news angle in the article. Additionally, the court found that the use of Hoffman's image violated the Lanham Act, as it was deemed likely to confuse consumers as to his endorsement of the clothes and shoes he appeared to be wearing. Thus, the court awarded Hoffman $3 million damages, arguing that the magazine had violated his publicity rights.

The recognition of the right of publicity has, then, the effect of empowering stars, giving them control over the commercial potential of their images—effectively privatizing what had been a public cultural good. The commodification of image as property is used to justify its continued legal protection. The privatization of celebrity, as a phenomenon with public good characteristics, may have social costs by circumscribing the circulation of star meanings, as Madow (1993) claims. Clearly, the right of publicity— with its ability to enforce exclusive licensing deals—dramatically increases the importance of celebrities to the media industries, which propertize and license celebrity images.

NO MORE HEROES ANYMORE?:
SOME CONCLUSIONS

This chapter has argued, through political economic analysis of legal and economic frameworks, that celebrities have been able to license their public images as private commodities. In defending these rights, legal cases have made continual reference to moral rights arguments that draw upon traditional values associated with heroes, and efface the role of the media in the production of celebrity exchange value. Hence, the political economy of celebrity is one that firmly favors the rights of celebrities over their fans. Celebrities propertize themselves by drawing upon a discourse of achievement associated with traditional notions of the hero, in order to exclusively claim the intellectual property of their images, extending a former privacy right (available to all) to a property right (the right of publicity, available only to the famous). I have suggested that critiques such as that of Boorstin (1961) and the Frankfurt School, although useful in examining the imbrication of the celebrity system within a capitalist system of accumulation, ultimately say little about how celebrity power operates beyond castigating "pseudo-individualization." Using Hollywood as a case study, I have argued that celebrities have been able to exploit their monopoly power and maintain this both through accumulation (media circulation) and the ability to propertize their publicity value. It is significant that the first rulings for the right of publicity—in the mid-1950s—happened at the same time as the studio-based star system began to break-down, and critics such as Mills identified the new power and autonomy of celebrity.

So what becomes of heroes in a media age? The difficulty of separating celebrity from hero, mediated image from actuality, presentation from achievements, has itself left a popular cynicism about the ideals of heroism, intertwined as it is within an advanced capitalist system of exchange. The recent rise of reality television celebrity has only added to this perception. What is left, in effect, is the privatization of the heroic, and an increasingly close relationship between the media and construction of the hero. Furthermore, a loss of belief in the traditional institutions that had functioned as repositories of heroes—the military, the monarchy, the political arena—has left the very notion of heroes as tarnished. Our difficulty in making distinctions between real and manufactured heroism shifts the judgment increasingly to one about performance—of sincerity of motives, of intent, and of authenticity to past, nostalgic notions of heroism. Oddly, then, it may be that contemporary heroes are those unable or unwilling to propertize their media visibility (such as Maria Fe Sotelo), eschewing the celebrity system and viewing any publicity they receive as a public good. Increasingly, heroes are those closest to home, "untainted" by the media publicity machine, ordinary people who put others before themselves and never gain celebrity. This is a far more personal enactment of heroism than traditional notions of the public hero. Perhaps, in an age of ever-present mass media, the only heroes in which we still believe are those we can still reach out and touch.

ENDNOTES

1. See the *Star Power* surveys conducted by industry journal *The Hollywood Reporter.*
2. For a classic exposition of this argument see Horton and Wohl (1956).
3. See a critique of such work by Aksoy and Robins (1992) and Blair and Rainnie (2000).
4. For a consideration of SAG wage bargaining power see Paul and Kliengartner (1994).
5. McCarthy explicitly acknowledges his debt to Nimmer in McCarthy (1987).
6. In a study of 100 stars conducted by Jib Fowles, 67% were male, and in various top-10 star lists in the 1990s either all or nearly all of the top-10 film stars were male, and top male stars earned almost double that of top female stars. In the 1996 Academy Awards only one nomination out of 166 was to an African-American performer, leading to a protest by Rev. Jesse Jackson and his Rainbow Coalition. See Fowles (1992).

REFERENCES

Alberoni, F. (1972). The powerless "elite": Theory and sociological research on the phenomenon of the stars. In D. McQuail (Ed.), *Sociology of mass communication.* Harmondsworth: Penguin.

Adler, M. (1985). Stardom and talent. *American Economic Review, 75*(1), 208-212.

Adorno, T. (1990). On popular music. In S. Frith & A. Goodwin (Eds.), *On record: Rock, pop, and the written word.* London: Routledge.

Adorno, T. (1991). *The culture industry: Selected essays on mass culture.* London: Routledge.

Adorno, T. (1996). Culture industry reconsidered. In P. Marris & S. Thornham (Eds.), *Media studies: A reader.* Edinburgh: Edinburgh University Press,.

Adorno, T., & Horkheimer, M. (1979). *Dialectic of enlightenment* (J. Cumming, Trans.). London: Verso.

Aksoy, A., & Robins K. (1992). Hollywood for the 21st century: Global competition for critical mass in image markets. *Cambridge Journal of Economics, 16*(1), 1-22.

Amin, A. (1994). Post-Fordism: Models, fantasies and phantoms of transition. In A. Amin (Ed.), *Post-Fordism: A reader.* Oxford: Blackwell.

Blair, H., & Rainnie, A. (2000). Flexible films? *Media, Culture and Society, 22,* 187-204.

Boorstin, D. J. (1961). *The image.* Harmondsworth: Penguin.

Christopherson, S., & Storper, M. (1986). The city as studio, the world as back lot: The impact of vertical disintegration on the location of the motion picture industry. *Environment and Planning D: Society and Space, 4,* 305-320.

Christopherson, S., & Storper M. (1989). The effects of flexible specialisation on industrial politics and the labor market: The motion picture industry. *Industrial and Labor Relations Review, 42*(3), 331-347.

Dyer, R. (1979). *Stars.* London: BFI.

Edelman, B. (1979). *Ownership of the image* (E. Kingdom, Trans.). London: Routledge and Kegan Paul.

Ellis. J. (1992). *Visible fictions: Cinema, television, video* (rev. ed.) London: Routledge.

Fowles, J. (1992). *Starstruck.* Washington, DC: Smithsonian Institution Press.

Gaines, J. (1991). *Contested culture: The image, the voice and the law.* Chapel Hill & London: University of North Carolina Press.

Gamson, J. (1994). *Claims to fame: Celebrity in contemporary America.* London, Berkeley & Los Angeles: University of California Press.

Haelan Laboratories, Inc. v. Topps Chewing Gum, Inc. (1953). 202 F.2d 866 (2d Cir. 1953).

Morrison, R. (2003, March 24). Heroes: Are they really so hard to find. *Times,* 2, p. 4.

Hirst, P., & Zeitlin, J. (1991). Flexible specialisation versus post-Fordism: Theory, evidence and policy implications. *Economy and Society, 20*(1), 1-156.

Hoffman v. Capital Cities/ABC, Inc., Los Angeles Magazine. (1999). 33 F.Supp.2d 867 (C.D. Cal. 1999).

Horton, D., & Wohl, R. (1956). Mass communication and para-social interaction: Observations on intimacy at a distance. *Psychiatry, 19*(3), 215-229.

King, B. (1986). Stardom as an occupation. In P. Kerr (Ed.), *The Hollywood film industry.* London: Routledge & Kegan Paul.

Lefebvre, H. (1971). *Everyday life in the modern world* (S. Rabinovitch, Trans.). London: Penguin.

Lowenthal, L. (1961). The triumph of mass idols. In *Literature, popular culture, and society.* Englewood Cliffs, NJ: Prentice-Hall. (Original work published 1944)

Madow, M. (1993). Private ownership of public image: Popular culture and publicity rights. *California Law Review, 125*(81), 127-240.

McCarthy, J. T. (1987). Melville B. Nimmer and the right of publicity: A tribute. *UCLA Law Review,* 1703-1712.

Mills, C. W. (1956). *The power elite.* New York: Oxford University Press.

Nimmer, M. B. (1954). The right of publicity. *Law and Contemporary Problems, 19,* 203-223.

Paul, A., & Kliengartner, A. (1994) Flexible production and the transformation of industrial relations in the motion picture and television industry. *Industrial and Labor Relations Review, 47*(4), 663-678.

Piore, M., & Sabel, C. (1984). *The second industrial divide.* New York: Basic Books.

Smith, M. (1998). Theses on the philosophy of Hollywood history. In S. Neale & M. Smith (Eds.), *Contemporary Hollywood cinema*. London & New York: Routledge.

Storper, M. (1994). The transition to flexible specialisation in the U.S. film industry: External economies, the division of labour and the crossing of industrial divides. In A. Amin (Ed.), *Post-Fordism: A reader*. Oxford: Blackwell.

Storper, M., & Christopherson, S. (1987). Flexible specialisation and regional industrial agglomerations: The case of the U.S. motion picture industry. *Annals of the Association of American Geographers, 77*(1), 104-117.

Thompson, J. B. (1990). *Ideology and modern culture: Critical social theory in the era of mass communication*. Cambridge: Polity.

Warren, S. D., & Brandeis L. (1890). The right to privacy. *Harvard Law Review, 4*(5), 193-216.

Chapter 19

CELEBRITY LAW

Susan J. Drucker
Communication Landscapers

Whether hero or celebrity, the line between public and private life has become a more troubling divide when dealing with media coverage of public figures. Laws have been passed in numerous countries to protect the famous and new measures have been proposed. In this chapter, Susan Drucker surveys the legal landscape surrounding the love/hate relationship between heroes/celebrities and media attention.

✧　✧　✧

Tantalizing come-on promotionals, "play-by-play coverage,"and drama are no longer reserved for entertainment programming when the trials and tribulations of the famous and familiar media personae are available. The mass media relentlessly search out those who satisfy the public's appetite for super-star status and just as relentlessly portray their human faults and failings.

The public has always been fascinated by heroes, leaders, and the famous but the wall between public acts and private life has been replaced by a permeable divider. The boundary between public and private is blurred, as the private lives of public figures are served up for popular consumption. It is difficult to say whether the norms thus promulgated are more public, by virtue of their origin, or private, by virtue of their destination (Prost, 1991). The steps of public figure creation and deflation are interesting and intimately linked with the media of communication so important in the inflation/creation process. The medium invades privacy and sometimes does the famous in because the medium made them famous. Much has been made of this blurring of the public–private divide when dealing with media coverage of public figures. Laws have been passed in numerous countries to protect the famous and new measures, both of a self-regulatory and legislative nature, have been proposed in the United States. This chapter explores the symbiotic relationship of the press and modern-day celebrities and examines the legal landscape surrounding this love–hate relationship.

THE CONSTRUCTION AND DECONSTRUCTION OF THE CELEBRITY: THE SEARCH FOR THE FLAW

Media developments including the telegraph and photography fostered the emerging celebrification industry, which has been furthered in turn by film, television, video, and most recently, the Internet. The persistent presentation of "news" about entertainers enabled large numbers of people to identify with them, seriously following their dramatic triumphs, their emotional setbacks, and their personal idiosyncracies as they were drawn ever closer in a new form of relationship with public characters.

In our contemporary mass media culture the hero/celebrity is made and unmade by the same agency—media attention. The mass media relentlessly search out those who satisfy the public's appetite for super-status and just as relentlessly portray their human faults and failings. The studies reported here reveal that the means of telling the story and keeping it in the public eye determines what is heroic and who and what is to be celebrated. Performance rather than heroic deeds is what is celebrated now. A chronology of celebrity linked to the publicity industry (Gamson, 1994) supports the assertion that celebrity became systematized by the early 20th century. From developments in newspaper distribution, telegraphy, photography, through the early stages of sound recording, motion picture, and ultimately television, celebrity creation evolved into a powerful, professionalized, ultimately visible industry. It is an industry that produces fame and even manufactures sincerity through behind-the-scenes real-life glimpses taking the fan beyond the image, perhaps to glimpse blemishes and ferret out the "real" person of the back stage behind the front stage facade. The paparazzi become creators of art and audience voyeuristic tendencies are fulfilled by the print and electronic media. Discovery of the "real" person can result in uncovering flaws, imperfections, and errors in judgment. Now the phenomenon is not new, but its commercialization and development as an industry is intrinsically linked to two interrelated factors: (a) the development of media technology and (b) the changing conception of private and public affairs.

In the *Poetics,* Aristotle (1954) described the tragic hero as a great person who falls from "reputation and prosperity" through "some error in judgment," a flaw in his or her character.

> The perfect Plot, accordingly, must have a single, and not . . . a double issue; the change in the hero's fortunes must be not from misery to happiness, but on the contrary from happiness to misery; and the cause of it must lie, not in any depravity, but in some great error in his part. (p. 239)

Aristotle's protagonist is a person of such stature and nobility that his or her fall arouses in the audience the "tragic pleasure of pity and fear" (Aristotle, 1954, p. 240) (referring to the process of catharsis or purgation that purifies the spirit of that audience as they witness and learn from the downfall of that grand and majestic figure). The shift in the contemporary approach to the hero requires that not only must the hero share in our ordinariness, but that we discover the less-than-virtuous traits with which we can identify. Why the feeding frenzy seeking information as well as the flaw? Perhaps because the fame exceeds what the "hero" earned. The degree to which heroes can survive scrutiny becomes a central controlling factor. It is the technology and organization of the media of communication that promote scrutiny and that deter, alter, and facilitate the heroic relationship.

The paparazzi are a relatively new breed of independent photographers—the name is taken from a sidewalk photographer named Paparazzo who was a character in *La Dolce Vita,* the film directed by Federico Fellini. Although the paparazzi are linked to the medium of photography and characterized by a particular form of frenzy and competition, they are not the first group of fame hunters who have been linked to a particular medium. Because there is much to be learned from the past, the search for other combinations of medium and chroniclers of fame, sin, and flaw proves to be rather interesting: television—programs such as *Hard Copy, Inside Edition, Extra,* and *Entertainment Tonight*; newspapers—*The Star, The Globe,* and *Esquire*; radio—Walter Winchell, the reporters of the Yellow Press, the newspaper cartoonists who draw the famous and exaggerate their most obvious physical attributes. In the search for firsts, the work of William Hogarth stands out as the prototypical flaw hunter and moralist. "A

Harlot's Progress," "Marriage-a-la-Mode," "Rakes Progress," are devastating moral tales laid in six engravings in which detail after detail capture decadence, deceit, and duplicity.

The relationship of paparazzi and medium is important and fascinating. The paparazzi's medium is not merely photography, but the entire development of long lenses, fast film, flash attachments, high-speed cameras able to capture multiple moments in time. The paparazzi are able to intrude, capture the moment, get the viewer up close to the object of desire. At the same time, the paparazzi invade space, violate proxemic traditions and expectations. The long lens shatters expectation. Distance offers no protection against intrusion. The microscopic is transformed into the macroscopic.

Each medium of communication represents some modification of self— or more appropriately stated, the access of others to self and the loss of control of self to others. Proxemics represents cultural levels of appropriateness in relationship to others and allows for the command of intimate versus public distance—if the other person knows the rules. There is a paradox of proxemics in the age of the high-tech outfitted paparazzi who provide intimacy by reducing distance for the fan. Nonverbal communication researchers have identified eye movements as a means of overcoming psychologically the physical distance (Goffman, 1967). Edward T. Hall (1966) identified four major types of distances that relate to types of relationships: intimate, personal, social, and public, which are altered in the paparazzi-altered celebrity–fan relationship.[1] Hall defined public distance as ranging from 12 to more than 25 feet, in the United States, a phase in which a person is protected by space. At this distance, visual detail of face and eyes are lost but it is said to enable a person to assume a defensive position if he or she feels threatened. The personal distance, ranging from 1 1/2 to 4 feet provides a personal bubble and the intimate distance ranges from actual touching to a far phase of 6 to 18 inches at which the presence of others is known (Hall, 1966). Paparazzi-provided images alter these distances, often breaking the psychological and social rules associated with personal space by bringing fans into an intimate distance with the celebrity, a distance that reveals flaws, often in unguarded moments when the "telephoto presence" of others is unknown. Intimacy at a distance.

Techniques of observation throughout society have become increasingly prevalent, many originating in control in the workplace. Early industrial employers, in order to regulate and channel productivity, devised techniques to control and observe labor. Shoshana Zuboff (1988) noted the following:

> The French historian Michel Foucault has argued that these new techniques of industrial management laid the groundwork for a new kind of society, a "disciplinary society," one in which bodily discipline, regulation and surveillance are taken for granted. (p. 320)

Foucault's observations are linked to *panoptic power*, a form of power that displays itself automatically and continuously.[2] "Panoptic power lies in its presence; the Panopticon produces the twin possibilities of observation and control. It functions independently of the observer in the central tower and is meant to function effectively without an observing presence" (Zuboff, 1988, p. 321), an effect Jeremy Bentham called "universal transparency" (p. 320). Information systems, computers, and video screens record and display behavior in a media-age version of universal transparency "with a degree of illumination that would have exceeded even Bentham's most outlandish fantasies" (Zuboff, 1988, p. 322). The psychological effect of visibility creates a sense of supervision without direct engagement, which is accepted and taken for granted.

The law provides some protection when the boundary between intimate and public distance is breached through several legal causes of action, particularly those addressing wrongs collectively known as the invasion of privacy.

Privacy rights and communication freedoms are among those areas particularly intertwined with psychological and functional anticipation in using a given medium or instrument.

Intrusion includes the secretly recorded conversation, overly aggressive surveillance, or long-distance photograph taken with a telephoto lens. Intrusion is part of privacy law because intrusion violates a citizen's right to be left alone and to control information about themselves. This right is inferred in the constitution, although unstated and made actionable through civil tort law.

> Intrusion is a tort of information gathering, not a tort of disseminating information by publishing or broadcasting. Journalists gathering information with a secret camera or tape recorder may be liable for intrusion regardless of what they learn or whether they publish their information. "Where there is intrusion," a federal circuit judge said, "the intruder should generally be liable whatever the content of what he learns. An eavesdropper to the marital bedroom may hear marital intimacies, or he may hear statements of fact or opinion of legitimate interest to the public; for purposes of liability that should make no difference." (Middleton, Chamberlin, & Lee, 2005, p. 172)

Intrusion on privacy depends on the reasonable expectation of privacy. Many celebrity cases involve the distinction between public and private places. "What a person knowingly exposes to the public . . . is not a subject of Fourth Amendment protection" the Supreme Court has held (*Katz v. United States*, 389 U.S. 347, 351, 1967). In tort law, a private person has little expectation of privacy in public places. Common law decisions hold that people in public and quasi-public places must assume they might be pho-tographed or recorded.

PUBLIC FACES AND PRIVATE PLACES

The issue of privacy is of paramount importance in the developing field of celebrity law. In an editorial written at the time of the death of Princess Diana, Adam Phillips (1997) noted that "privacy has traditionally been the sign of privilege and power. The affluent have a lot to protect, the poor, however, are overexposed to everything—sickness, hunger, need. Indeed, it is part of the cultural legacy of the West to equate privacy with what we value most" (p. 17). Phillips continued:

> Today, privacy—that is, family life—is considered a haven in a heartless world. Indeed, it has become increasingly clear that our idealizing of private life is a sign of our despair about political life. We are addicted to publicity now because we have a lingering doubt that there may be no such thing as privacy; that the protection privacy affords might be a pro-tection racket for those who can afford it. It's as though we are not sure what privacy is anymore. (Phillips, 1997, p. 17)

Protection for invasion of privacy and the distinctions drawn between pub-lic and private spaces are very clear when comparing approaches interna-tionally. For example, the right of individuals to maintain some degree of privacy and be free from undue surveillance is embodied in various interna-tional human rights conventions including Article 12 of the *Universal Declaration of Human Rights,* which states that "No one shall be subject to arbitrary interference with his privacy, family, home or correspondence nor to attacks upon his honour and reputation. . . . Everybody has the right to the protection of law against such interference or attacks."

A similar statement is found in Article 17 of the Covenant of Civil and Political Rights (Koomen, 1993).[3] Laws reflect societal values. In the United States, privacy rights have been conceived of as the right to be left alone, which really encompasses protection of individual dignity and integrity by preventing the loss of individual freedom and independence (Hixson, 1987, p. 55), with protection from *government* invasion of privacy found within the Fourth Amendment, although the word "privacy" itself does not appear in the U.S. Constitution. In the United States, the protection against inva-sion of privacy has evolved since 1890.[4] However, France affords one of the strongest codifications of privacy protection. The French *Civil Code* has afforded a right to privacy for more than a century. Article 9 (i) states:

"everyone has the right to respect for his private life" (Koomen, 1993, p. 246). Under French law, a person can receive up to 1 year in jail and a fine of $50,000 for the violation of the privacy of another by "taking, registering or transmitting without consent the image of a person in a private place" (Privacy: France, 1998). In fact, following publication of photographs of Sarah Ferguson, then duchess of York, frolicking topless poolside with a friend, unsuccessful actions for invasion of privacy were brought in Australia, but the duchess and her companion successfully brought suit in France for breach of privacy based on the same publications and were awarded $139,000 and $58,000, respectively (Koomen, 1993).

Diverse civil and criminal laws currently exist that shape the legal arsenal celebrities have in seeking to protect their personal and pecuniary interests from unwanted media coverage, which go well beyond interests in privacy.

Not all news gathering in public places is permitted and overzealous reporting techniques may be subject to criminal and civil sanctions. Of course, the most famous case of this involved Jacqueline Onassis, which has long been used in journalism classes throughout the country to illustrate how aggressive journalism can cross over the barrier to illegal harassment (*Galella v. Onassis*, 358 F. Supp. 196; S.D.N.Y., 1972). Ron Galella, in pursuit of photos of Mrs. Onassis, guided children into glass doors, bumped the parents of Kennedy children's schoolmates, blocked passages, blinded people with flashbulbs, spied through a telephoto lens and trailed his prey for hours, chased her car, circled in a motorboat while Mrs. Onassis swam, and frightened a horse her son John was riding. The court ruled that Galella was liable for assault, battery, harassment, and infliction of emotional distress. A federal district court then enjoined Galella from taking pictures of Onassis from closer than 150 feet, but this was reduced to a 25-foot distance by a higher court.

Using privacy laws, the courts have recognized a person's right to solitude and have punished overzealous news reporters who tap phone lines, plant hidden microphones, use telephoto lenses, and break into homes and offices for stories. In general, reporters are free to pursue stories in public places, and when invited, in private places. Sometimes, the courts have had to draw the line between public and private places.

Overzealous surveillance or shadowing that falls short of harassment or assault may be intrusive. The New York Court of Appeals held that Ralph Nader could sue General Motors for hiring people to follow him very closely. The court held "mere observation" in a public place does not amount to an invasion of privacy, but that surveillance "may be so 'overzealous' as to render it actionable."

The Fourth Amendment protects citizens from unreasonable government intrusions, but it is tort law that protects citizens from intrusions by private citizens, including reporters. In the common law of privacy, intrusion is said to be a highly intrusive physical , electronic, or mechanical invasion of another's solitude or seclusion (Restatement [Second] of Torts, sec. 652B, 1977).

The evolution of the right to be left alone, or the right to privacy, and reasonable expectations of privacy often emerges from the nature of a particular geography location. Fourth and Fifth Amendment rights are implicated when considering search and seizure and freedom from self-incrimination associated with places in which there is a reasonable expectation of privacy. Courts have explored these expectations in physical spaces, ranging from cars to school lockers, and of course, homes and offices (LaFave & Israel 1986). Reasonable expectations of privacy are no longer restricted to the physical spatial realm. In *Katz v. United States* (1967), the Supreme Court found "the emphasis on the nature of a particular targeted area deflected attention from the issue of Fourth Amendment infringement" (*Katz v. United States*, 351). Media personnel therefore can photograph, film, and record what they can see or hear in public places as long as it is done without harassing, trespassing, or otherwise intruding. It is not an intrusion for a picture to be taken on a public sidewalk. Likewise, a picture taken of private property from a public sidewalk is not an intrusion. Courts are divided over what is a public place so that a restaurant may be a private place in which there is some expectation of privacy from an unwanted photographer or interviewer (Iowa Supreme Court), whereas a federal court in Maine ruled that a restaurant was a public place.

A cause of action for intrusion enhances the ability of the law to protect individuals in a private place from being the subject of surveillance and exposure. Many times, this involves an unconsented to trespass onto private property in order to gather information and images.

Trespass

Closely related to intrusion and often a claim that accompanies such a suit is a trespass claim, a claim based on physical invasion of someone's property. The trespasser enters private property or invites someone to enter private property without consent of the owner or "possessor" of the property. Going on the private property without permission may be a trespass whether or not any tapes, cameras, or other technological devices are used. The violation is the entering onto property rather than the publication that results from the trespass.

In the law of torts, the legal status of one who enters the land of another has been divided roughly into three categories: trespasser, licensee, and invitee. As the legal status changes, the obligations of protection owed the visitor by the possessor of the land increases; in other words, the categories have been used in determining liability for negligence. A *trespasser*, lowest on the scale, is defined as "a person who enters or remains upon land in possession of another without a privilege to do so, created by the possessor's consent or otherwise" (Prosser, 1971, p. 357) and generally no one has the right to enter without consent. Intruders have no right to demand protection from harm. A photographer or journalist who enters onto property with permission but who refuses to leave when asked is also guilty of trespass. When journalists misrepresent their identities or the reason for entry onto property, owners who gave consent for journalists to be on their property are deemed to have failed to actually give informed consent. Journalists may well be held to trespass if they enter a private place opened to the public lawfully but interrupt the normal activities of that place *(LeMistra Inc. v. CBS*, 402 NYS 2d 815 (1978).

A more recent interpretation of trespass has involved what can be called *mediated trespass*, such as when a photographer remains on a public street but uses a telephoto lens. While on private property, occupiers of land have the lawful right to exclude others and the tort of trespass to land has historically protected privacy from those who would enter onto land, observe, listen, and photograph. In fact, the tort is actionable without proof of publication or damage, damage being to the control and peaceful enjoyment of the land. Advances in the technology, the tools of paparazzi, enable private behavior to be recorded without a *physical* trespass by the photographer. To date, case law has not consistently extended *trespass* to the gathering of images via telephoto lens, however, it has been suggested that the law of nuisance may offer some protection to the occupiers of land against mediated invasion of privacy via photographing, filming, or surveillance where the activity constitutes a substantial and continuous interference with the plaintiff's right to enjoy land in his or her possession without having to prove harm to the property itself (Koomen, 1993, p. 240).

WHAT PRICE FAME?
RISK, FEAR, AND COMMERCIALISM

There are many existing tools applied to celebrities and used to protect their rights and interests, including criminal codes on the state and federal levels such as harassment, stalking, reckless endangerment, trespass, false imprisonment, intentional infliction of emotional distress, civil actions in defamation, invasion of privacy, and the right to publicity. A federal law specifically drafted to address the concerns of celebrities by creating both criminal and civil bases for liability was introduced in February 1998. These form the arena that could be called *celebrity law*.

The parameters of celebrity law seem to be stretching, no longer limited to sex, drugs, and rock and roll. Of course, there are still divorces, messy custody battles, spousal battery, drug charges, drunk driving sentences, breach of contract, tax evasion, and an occasional homicide charge. Defamation and copyright infringements are still popular civil cases. Today, drive-by shootings and date rape also find themselves on the celebrity criminal docket. These themes do not change. Although we can all think back to the top 10 lists of celebrity cases that might include anyone from William Kennedy Smith to O.J. Simpson, from Robert Downy Jr., and Mike Tyson to Kobe Bryant and Michael Jackson, the lives of celebrities are brought into legal battles. New dramatic, often private, storylines to cover are brought into a traditionally public forum. Throughout the frenzy of the pre-trial, trials and post-trial periods, there seems to be never-ending media coverage.[5]

Stalking and Harassment

The word *fan*, a term derived from "fanatic," characterizes a relationship based on an intimate knowledge of a personality created and sustained by the mass media industry, and maintained by the personality's ability to control media attention rather than to control or shape events (Boorstin,1961). Perhaps then, it should come as little surprise that as fans seek more intimate knowledge of celebrities and the press (of all varieties) seek to fulfill the demands of fans, celebrities increasingly report feeling hunted by both fans and paparazzi. Both fans and the press, aggressive paparazzi, in particular, each pose unique threats and suggest different legal recourse. The two types of risks are exposure to danger of physical harm, and exposure to harassing and annoying behavior that may lead to physical or emotional harm.

The first variety of risk is generally associated with behavior of the obsessed or persistent fan, "frequently due to a psychological disorder known as 'erotomania'" (Salame, 1993, p. 80). Erotomania "involves the pursuit of someone from a higher class or someone who is perceived as more successful [;] [t]he erotomaniac deludes himself into thinking it's love" (Lewin, 1993, p. B10). Recent years have seen a rise in the number of obsessed fans reportedly threatening the security of celebrities. Private security firms to monitor such threats have flourished. Celebrities such as Cher, Madonna, Michael Jackson, Michael J. Fox, Justine Bateman, Sarah McGlocklin, Belinda Carlisle, David Bowie, Whitney Houston, Vanessa Williams, Sharon Gless, Steven Spielberg, Johnny Carson, Jodi Foster, Kathy Lee Gifford, and even the on-air hosts of QVC (home shopping cable program) report experiences of being stalked. David Letterman's repeated brushes with a woman reporting to be his wife who kept finding her way into his secluded Connecticut home became the butt of countless jokes while generating very real fear. Of course, the most notorious of these cases is that of Rebecca Schaeffer, a popular young television actress co-starring in the sitcom, *My Sister Sam*. Schaeffer was stalked by obsessed fan Robert Bardo for a number of years and was ultimately murdered by him at the doorstep of her home on July 18, 1989. After this incident, the risks to celebrities appeared more real.[6] This incident led to the enactment of a large number of stalking statutes in rapid succession on the state level throughout the United States. These statutes were designed to protect victims of this behavior. California became the first state to pass such a law, making "stalking" a crime in 1991 and within 2 years the other 49 states had created similar laws. Stalking statutes provide law enforcement officials with a new way to respond to behavior that either stems from the relationship between strangers or mere acquaintances and public figures or that may involve people who have been in intimate relationships. It is reported that stalking in general has proliferated so that there are more than 200,000 stalkers in the United States (Gilligan, 1992, p. 286). Stalking statutes are most commonly invoked in cases involving women being stalked by their former husbands or boyfriends in domestic violence cases rather than by celebrities (Gilligan, 1992). Until the enactment of stalking statutes, law enforcement officers could do little because existing civil and criminal remedies failed to deter stalkers and only punished them after they committed some other illegal offense. Stalking laws make the act of stalking itself illegal.

Many of the state stalking statutes share common language typified by the California statute which reads[7] "Stalking is typically the willful, malicious, and repeatedly following or harassing of a person, usually along with a credible threat and intent to place that person in reasonable fear of death or great bodily injury or to place that person in reasonable fear of death or great bodily injury of his or her immediate family" (Gilligan, 1992). Many stalking statutes address circumstances where there is threat against the victim. Some states require stalking activities and the making of a threat (the minority of states take this approach), whereas more states require stalking activities *or* the making of a threat (Salame, 1993, p. 75).

Stalking as a *criminal offense* actually employs two common law tort theories (a) invasion of privacy and (b) intentional infliction of emotional distress. However, these tort claims have limited value in protecting victims because these civil actions may be difficult for some victims to afford, may have little deterrence value, and may require that a victim prove that the offense occurred when he or she was entitled to privacy. To bring a civil action for emotional distress, the victim must prove the stalker intentionally or recklessly committed an outrageous act that was calculated to cause and *did* cause severe emotional distress (Gilligan, 1992). But civil actions involve monetary liability, which may discourage some perpetrators but are less likely to hinder the obsessed stalker. Restraining orders form an alternative approach to money damages but these too are of limited actual usefulness.

Stalking laws have raised constitutional challenges with critics contending they may be overbroad or void for vagueness and thus infringe on constitutionally protected activities. However, many state legislatures have sought to avoid these challenges by excluding constitutionally protected activities. For instance, Arizona excludes "lawful demonstrations or assemblies" (Ariz. Rev. Stat. ANN '13-2921, 1992), Montana excludes those in demonstrations, assemblies, picket lines, peaceful protests, and the exercise of freedom of speech and press (Mont. Code. Ann '45-5), and Nevada excludes reporters, photographers, or employees of personalities, radio, or television within professional capacity gathering information (Nev. Rev. Stat. '200[5] [b] [2]).

Many statutes also address harassing behavior within the context of stalking statutes that under California penal law, is defined as follows:

> "harassment" means a knowing and willful course of conduct directed at a specific person which seriously alarms, annoys, harasses, or terrorizes the person, and which serves no legitimate purpose. The course of conduct must be such as would cause a reasonable person to suffer substantial emotional distress, and must actually cause substantial emotional distress to the person. "Course of conduct" means a pattern of conduct composed of a series of acts over a period of time, however short, evidencing a continuity of purpose. Constitutionally protected activity is not included within the meaning of "course of conduct." (Cal Penal Code '646.9 [e])

The statutory definition of harassment generally includes the knowing, willful course of conduct directed at a specific person that alarms, annoys, and reflects a *pattern* of conduct that in some states must rise to the level that would cause a reasonable person to actually suffer substantial emotional distress (Salame, 1993).

False Imprisonment

Although false imprisonment has rarely been applied to celebrity situations, in February 1998, two photographers were found guilty of falsely imprisoning Governor (then actor) Arnold Schwarzenegger and his wife, television news correspondent Maria Shriver in 1997. False imprisonment consists of the unlawful detention of the person by another, for any length of time, whereby the imprisoned person is deprived of his or her personal liberty. The unlawful detention of the occupant of an automobile may be accomplished by driving so rapidly that the person cannot alight. Criminal false imprisonment occurs with the unlawful arrest or detention of a person without a warrant, or by an illegal warrant, or when a warrant is illegally executed. The tort of false imprisonment is the nonconsensual, intentional confinement of a person, without lawful privilege, for an appreciable length of time, however short (*City of Newport Beach v. Sasse*, 9 Cal. App.3d 803).

In the Schwarzenegger case, the photographers were convicted of misdemeanor false imprisonment for detaining the Schwarzeneggers' Mercedes Benz, which was driven by Ms. Shriver who was taking their son to school. It was found that at one point, Giles Harrison and Andrew O'Brien forced the car to stop on a street and then swarmed the car when it stopped at a preschool. Mr. Harrison was convicted of reckless driving as well. Harrison was sentence to a 90-day jail term, while O'Brien received 60 days. Both were also ordered to pay a $500 fine and were placed on probation for 2 years ("Photographers convicted," 1998).

Reckless Endangerment

A person acts recklessly with respect to a material element of an offense when he or she consciously disregards a substantial and unjustifiable risk that the material element exists or will result from his or her conduct. The risk must be of such a nature and degree that, considering the nature and purpose of the actor's conduct and the circumstances known to him or her, its disregard involves a gross deviation from the standard of conduct that a law-abiding person would observe in the actor's situation (Model Penal code Section 2.02).

The tort (civil) and criminal actions noted throughout this chapter represent existing law that can be and has been applied to celebrity victim plaintiffs and defendants, but they have not been drafted to address celebrity concerns directly until recently. In a move that more directly responds to the struggle celebrities face in controlling their images, personal information, and private lives in public and private places, a federal law was proposed by Senator Dianne Feinstein (D-California) and Senate Judiciary Committee Chairman Orrin Hatch (R-Utah). On February 18, 1998, they announced legislation aimed specifically at curbing privacy abuses and harassment by tabloid media and paparazzi. The bill, known as the "Personal Privacy Protection Act," would make it a *crime* to persistently follow or chase a person in a manner that causes the individual to have a reasonable fear of bodily injury. The bill establishes a penalty of a year in federal prison and at least 5 years in federal prison if actions cause serious bodily injury and at least 20 years in prison if such actions cause death. The bill also allows *civil* actions against paparazzi who use high-powered lenses, microphones, or even helicopters to trespass for commercial purposes, providing for recovery of compensatory damages, punitive damages, and injunctive and declaratory relief. The bill also allows a civil action where paparazzi have trespassed or used visual or auditory enhancement devices to capture recoding that they otherwise could not have captured without trespassing, for commercial purposes. The bill does not criminalize the act of trespass but limits the remedy to trespass, by either a property owner or person photographed (Feinstein, 1998).

The law was drafted with the advice of the Screen Actors Guild and, in fact, the headquarters of this organization provided the location for the Senators to announce the proposed bill. Feinstein (1998) noted:

> Just because a person makes their living on television or in some other public arena should not mean they forfeit all rights to personal privacy. There is a line between legitimate news gathering and invasion of privacy. Between snapping a picture of someone in a public place and chasing them to the point where they fear for their safety. Unfortunately that line is crossed more and more frequently today by an increasingly aggressive cadre of fortune-seekers with cameras.

Senator Feinstein noted that "in today's world of tabloid journalism, paparazzi will go to great lengths to capture that rare or intimate picture that will be worth a fortune to the tabloids."[8] Unfortunately, some will cross not only the bounds of decency to get that winning shot, but the bounds of safety as well. The existing law alone was seen as being insufficient to protect the special needs of celebrities. Many argue there are constitutional flaws in this act, but others argue that staunch civil libertarians such as Professor Erwin Chemerinsky assisted in the drafting of the legislation in an effort to draw a narrow bill that would not interfere with news gathering or freedom of the press but would protect safety and address types of trespass (Joyce, 1997).

Defamation

Of course one of the most familiar legal mechanisms for the protection of celebrities has been the defamation suit. Given the nature of celebrity and the wrong that defamation claims seek to redress, this is a natural association. Celebrities, known for being well-known (Boorstin, 1961), by definition are concerned with the creation and maintenance of reputation, as that is the essence of their celebrity and its commercial value. Public involvement with celebrities is not entirely spontaneous, but results from the calculated dissemination of highly personal information (institutionalized as gossip columns and programming) (Gamson, 1992). Defamation—expression that injures reputation or words that expose to public hatred, scorn, shame, ridicule, and contempt—deprives one of his or her confidences and friendly intercourse in society. A cause of action for defamation calls into question falsehoods and only deals with statements of fact rather than of opinion.

Defamation involving the famous has dominated developments in this area of law since 1964 with the evolution of so-called constitutional limitations on libel law. In *New York Times v. Sullivan* (1964), the U.S. Supreme Court said that the First Amendment provides for the protection of false statements damaging the reputation of public officials suing the media for statements about their official conduct. The decision established the requirement of additional proof of "actual malice" (i.e., publication of a known falsehood or publication made with reckless disregard for truth). This additional proof was then extended to public *figures* by the decision in *Curtis Publishing v. Butts* (1967). The Supreme Court attempted to distinguish between the classifications of private person and public figure plaintiffs by varying the standard of proof for each. In 1974, in *Gertz v. Welch*, the court said that public figures are either persons of widespread fame or notoriety (celebrities) or people who have injected themselves into the debate about a controversial public issue for the purpose of affecting the outcome. Persons who became involuntarily involved in matters of public interest would not ordinarily be considered public figures, and would not have to prove *New York Times* actual malice (*Gertz v. Welch,* 1974). Public officials, public figures, and private persons involved in matters of public concern can collect presumed and punitive damages only if they prove actual malice. Presumed damages do not require proof of harm, whereas punitive damages are intended to punish a publication for false defamatory remarks. Public officials, public figures, and private persons involved in matters of public concern who do not prove actual malice must show actual injury in order to obtain damage awards. Actual injury is the proof of damage to reputation or mental anguish as well as actual monetary loss.

Celebrities embroiled in defamation suits have ranged from Carol Burnett and Shirley Jones to more recent cases of Tom Cruise, who sued publisher Bunte Verlag. Verlag published an interview that Cruise maintained never took place and that included allegedly fraudulent quotes saying the plaintiff is sterile and has a zero sperm count; $60 million in damages was sought ("Celebrity litigation," 1998). Clint Eastwood was awarded $150,000 from the *National Enquirer* for falsely suggesting he agreed to an interview with the tabloid. Steve Wynn received a $3.1 million award from a small book publisher for promoting a book suggesting he had ties to organized crime. In September 1997, Christie Brinkely sued the *National Enquirer* over stories she said described her as being mentally imbalanced and a "shop-aholic" and fearful of cows. Other suits include Lisa Marie Presley suing the same *Enquirer,* challenging a story reporting she had written "Nobody Loves Me, I'm Ugly" on her arms and Bruce Willis and Demi Moore also brought suit in July 1997 against the *Star,* which reported trouble in their marriage. Brooke Shields also sued the *Star* over a story claiming she had an eating disorder.

Many celebrities remain reluctant to file suit, particularly against tabloids, because this leads to further publication of the original allegation. Further litigation includes the pretrial discovery phase including depositions, legal mechanisms that open access to personal information about family and other private subjects (Higgins, 1997). The Libel Defense Resource Center compiles an annual report on trials and damages in defamation cases. In its report published in July 2003, they found that media defendants successfully defended four of the five verdicts in trials of libel, privacy, and related claims in 2002, a year marked by the lowest number of trials, and the highest media victory rate in any year since Media Law Resource Center (MLRC) began tracking trials in 1980 (Libel Defense Resource Center, 2003, http://www.ldrc.com/Press_Releases/bull2003-2.html).

The *American Bar Association Journal* (Higgins, 1997) reported that "celebrities now are fighting back on fronts other than the courtroom. In the past two years especially, they have taken their battle to the legislature in California, a state where a celebrity's good image can be worth millions" (p. 69).

> There, the Screen Actors Guild is backing a bill that would expose reporters and editors to huge personal liability for libels that come from paid sources. It would also allow the state to collect civil penalties of up to $250,000, for each proven libelous statement. In addition, the guild hopes to convince courts to reconsider case law that makes most celebrities all-purpose public figures. (Higgins, p. 70)

The Right of Publicity

Celebrities have sued successfully for another type of tort that has fallen under the rubric of invasion of privacy known as commercialization or appropriation and unauthorized publicity. This action is actually more aptly called the right of publicity. The right of publicity, recognized in more than 20 states, is the right of celebrities and public figures to financially exploit the commercial value in their names, likeness, photos, styles, voices, or other features and talents. Unlike the right to privacy, the right to publicity is a right to protect economic injury. It is once again related to control, in this case, control over unauthorized appropriation of celebrities' identities even if it does not cause mental distress. This is a tort action for the diminution of publicity value, particularly if the celebrity feels use of his or her image is inappropriate. Although the right to privacy does not survive the death of a celebrity, the right to publicity is a property right and does not necessarily die with the owner (Middleton, Chamberlin, & Lee, 2005). This right is "descendible" and several states have adopted statutes allowing people to bequeath the publicity value in their name or identity. In California, for example, a publicity statute prohibits, for 50 years after death, the commercial use of the name, voice, signature, photograph, or likeness of any "deceased personality" without prior consent of the person or his or her agent. However, it is not a violation of the California law or other state statutes recognizing the descedendibilty of publicity rights to use the identity of a dead person in news, public affairs, sports stories, or political campaigns, or in a book, magazine, musical work, film, or television program (Middleton & Chamberlin, p. 198).[9]

THE LOVE–HATE RELATIONSHIP WITH PAPARAZZI

Courtrooms and legal cases bring celebrities' lives into the public realm in an age when clearly defined boundaries separating public acts and private life keep shifting. Perhaps nowhere is this more clearly illustrated than by the culture of celebrity and the worldwide re-examination of the degree of privacy lost by public figures. A lead editorial in *The New York Times* discussed the "Cult of Celebrity," noting that it is at least as old as the industrial revolution. The editorial noted that the old days of "in-person" face-to-face celebrity press interviews had given way to a media-induced change in climate. *The Times* seemed to blame technology and the exploding number of journalists.

> there were only three [American] television networks, no hand-held cameras and no cellular phones ad modems that allow photographers to take and transmit pictures to their agents in seconds . . . that this makes a "qualitative change in the way famous people conduct their lives." (Celebrity, Then and Now, 1997, p. A28)

The death of Princess Diana brought both suppliers and consumers up short, demanding a re-evaluation and introspection on the part of the media with regard to the degree of privacy renounced in exchange for fame. Tabloids became easy targets. Who can forget Earl Spencer's accusation "I always believed that the press would kill her in the end . . . not even I could imagine that they would take such a direct hand in her death, as seems to be the case" (Lyall, 1997). Although the world mourned and sought solace in public places (filled with flowers and stuffed animals), or depended on television to watch, grieve, and come together or shared condolences and grief on the Internet, there was a calming sense of justness in the detention of seven photographers in Paris. Even after the paparazzi were released and fault and condemnation turned to a drunk driver, anyone associated with media coverage of celebrities continued to be suspect. Scarcely 4 months later, the public was privy to another media "feeding frenzy," this time presented "American Style." In the wake of the January 1998 allegations surrounding the Lewinsky affair, the American media, in all forms, joined in. Anti-press reaction came quickly. Newspaper and television Web sites were filled with irate e-mails complaining about coverage. The press turned on itself with programs like National Public Radio's "Talk of the Nation," which devoted 1 hour to "The New Rules of the Newsroom." Marvin Kalb, director of Harvard's Shorenstein Center for the Press, Politics and Public Policy noted, "I think it is perhaps one of the most sorry chapters in American journalism" (Goldberg, 1998).

The American public appeared to be torn between the desire to learn more and the fun of learning about the salacious details of our leaders' lives and its disapproval of the media turned gossip-monger. A CBS poll taken during the last week of January 1998 found that 62% felt there was too much coverage of the scandal (Goldberg, 1998). Subsequent revelations, presidential testimony, apologies, the delivery of the Starr report to Congress, and even the televised coverage of the House vote on impeachment hearings have not changed these figures significantly. But yet, there is some demand for more. In this context, there is heightened confusion about the delicate balance between the famous and the personal, between onstage and offstage, between public and private, between fair news-gathering practice and civil and criminal wrongdoing.

CONCLUSIONS

In the aftermath of the death of Princess Diana, social commentators sought to understand and explain our relationship to celebrities and our insatiable appetite for intimate details and authorized glimpses behind the curtain of celebrity. They consider our shared culpability in the death, which may have been caused by the partnership of paparazzi, celebrities, and fans. In an op-ed piece in *The New York Times*, Janna Malamud Smith (1997) suggested:

> With their basic human themes, stories about celebrities are one of our most powerful collective and personal ways of working out what we fell about our own lives. However hidden and covert the attention we pay them, however vocal our disdain, we follow the lives of celebrities because they allow us a complex psychic pleasure.

> We gratify impossible desires by identifying with celebrities, and at the same time, we confirm the worth of our more mundane lies by judging them. Why, we might ask, was Diana cavorting in St.Tropez with a new boyfriend . . . (Smith, 1997, p. A19)

Something is different. Celebrities are more prevalent and more accessible. Mainstream news media include lead stories devoted to the good, bad, and ugly of celebrity existence. Technological advances feed or meet the demand for ever more intrusive photos of celebrities as tabloids and magazines in print and electronic forms proliferate. Traditional photojournalists vie with paparazzi, traditional entertainment reporters and gossip columnists contend with gossips on line á la Matt Drudge and the Drudge Report.[10] Paparazzi have access to an array of lenses, cell phones, and digital cameras that can be hooked up to transmit to their publishers or over the Internet so that the whole world will see the fruits of their labor without developing a photograph.

We are spectators able to judge, we are empowered as we play a role in constructing and deconstructing those personages we have elevated. Perhaps our flaws appear minor by comparison. After all, we are not under the microscope being magnified. Traditional press law seeks to protect the rights of the media covering celebrities but diverse laws are being drafted and existing laws called into service as celebrities seek to control the forces that threaten the celebrity existence they sought. Celebrities are made by media, fans, and image management, the very same agents of destruction. This partnership produces celebrity as we know it today and the very same three way alliance has spawned diverse tensions, conflicting rights and interests that the evolving area of celebrity law seeks to address.

ENDNOTES

1. Hall noted that intimate distance ranges from the close phase of actual touching to the far phase of 6 to 18 inches, the presence of the other person is known. The individuals are so close it is considered improper for strangers in public in U.S. culture. Personal distance allows us to stay protected and untouched by others and ranges from 1 1/2 to about 4 feet. At this distance, we can physically touch. Social distance ranges from 4 to 12 feet, at which visual detail is lost. This is the distance in the United States in which business is conducted or we interact at a social gathering. Public distance ranges from 12 to more than 25 feet. In this phase a person seems protected by space (Hall, 1966).
2. The Panopticon was an architectural innovation developed by moral philosopher Jeremy Bentham and built by his brother Samuel in 1787. The structure consisted of a 12-sided polygon formed in iron and sheathed in glass to create an effect

called "universal transparency" by which a central tower with a wide window opened onto an inner wall of the surrounding polygonal structure. Each cell had a window on the inner and outer walls allowing for observation of workers or convicts from the central tower (Zuboff, 1988, p. 320).

3. Private at one point related to the Latin *privatus* and *privare* (to withdraw from public life). "Withdrawal" or "Seclusion" were replaced with private, meaning "independence" and "intimacy" and a sense of solitude appealing to the sense of decency and the dignified. There has been a successive progression to the point where the meaning of private life is associated with personal life and is seen in favorable terms, relating private with *privilege* or the Latin *privilegium*. A law or ruling in favor or against an individual implies special benefit.

4. Justices Warren and Brandeis first propounded the concept as an independent right in their *Harvard Law Review* article of 1890 (Warren & Brandeis, 1890). To them privacy is an "inviolate personality" that includes but reaches beyond ownership or possession.

5. Lawyers and legal commentators become celebrities, sportscasters and entertainment reporters assume the mantle of legal experts grappling with rules of evidence and nuances of procedure. In an age in which Court TV has met E! and ESPN, public knowledge and perception of the law is being shaped by celebrity cases. There has been a celebrification of the law with regard to public perception and knowledge of the law.

6. During a 6-month period in 1991, for example, the L.A.P.D. reported that their special "threat management unit" created after the Schaeffer murder, responded to 54 cases, including 29 dealing with high-profile celebrities, 13 with less well-known celebrities, 5 involving Hollywood executives, and only 7 involving ordinary citizens (Carr, 1991).

7. California stalking statute that has served as a model reads: '646.9 (a). Any person who willfully, maliciously, and repeatedly follows or harasses another person and who makes a credible threat with the intent to place that person in reasonable fear of death or great bodily injury or to place that person in reasonable fear of death or great bodily injury of his or her immediate family is guilty of the crime of stalking, punishable by imprisonment in a country jail for not more than one year or by a fine of not more than one thousand dollars ($1,000), or by both that fine and imprisonment.
(b) Any person who violates subdivision (a) when there is a temporary restraining order, injunction, or any other court order in effect prohibiting the behavior described in subdivision (a) against the same party, is punishable by imprisonment in a country jail for not more than one-year or by a fine of not more than one thousand dollars ($1,000), or by both that fine and imprisonment, or by imprisonment in the state prison.
(c) A second or subsequent conviction occurring within seven years of a prior conviction under subdivision (a) against the same victim, and involving an act of violence or "a credible threat" of violence, as defined in subdivision (f), is punishable by imprisonment in a county jail for not more than one year, or by a fine of not more than one thousand dollars ($1,000), or by both that fine and imprisonment, or by imprisonment in the state prison.
(d) Every person who, having been convicted of a felony under this section commits a second or subsequent violation of this section against the same victim

and involving an act of violence or "a credible threat" of violence, as defined in subdivision (f), is punishable in the state prison, for 16 months, two, or three years and a fine up to ten thousand dollars ($10,000) (Cal. Penal Code) (West, 1992).

8. Italian photographer Mario Brenna took the first photos of Diana embracing Fayed in a boat off Sardinia in July 1997 for which he earned $1 million for a single shoot.

9. Some states that do not recognize the right for people to bequeath publicity rights to their heirs emphasize the personal nature of the right of publicity and the difficulties in treating such rights as independent of the people themselves.

10. Matt Drudge is an online journalist publishing an electronic gossip newsletter called the Drudge Report. He is credited with being first to carry the Lewinsky scandal, scooping *Newsweek* in January 1998.

REFERENCES

Aristotle. ((1954). (I. Bywater, Trans.). *Aristotle's rhetoric and poetics*. New York: The Modern Library.

Boorstin, D. (1961). *The image*. New York: Vintage Press.

Carr, J. (1991, February 3). Coppola penning a Boston plot. *Boston Globe*, p. A35.

Celebrity Litigation. (1998). http://www.courtnews.com/lawsuits/celebs.htm.

Celebrity Then and Now. (Editorial). (1997, September 4). *The New York Times*, p. A28.

Feinstein, D. (1998, February 18). Personal Privacy Protection Act. http://www.senate.gov/-feinstein/paparazzi.html.

Gamson, J. (1994). *Claims to fame: Celebrity in contemporary America*. Berkeley: University of California Press.

Gertz v. Welch, 418 U.S. 323 (1974).

Gilligan, M.J. (1992). Stalking the stalker: Developing new laws to thwart those who terrorize others. *Georgia Law Review, 27*, 285-339.

Goffman, E. (1967). *Interaction ritual: Essays on face-to-face behavior*. New York: Pantheon.

Goldberg, C. (1998, January 30). Some journalists have met the enemy, and it is them. *The New York Times on the Web*. http://search.nytimes.com/search/daily/bin/fastweb?getdoc+site+site+8893+92+wAAA+paparazzi.

Hall, E.T. (1966). *The hidden dimension*. Garden City, NY: Doubleday.

Higgins, M. (1997, December). Public relief. *Journal of the American Bar Association*, pp. 68-71.

Hixson, R. (1987). *The right to privacy*. New York: Oxford University Press.

Joyce, J. (1997, November). Lost phot opportunities. *Journal of the American Bar Association*, pp. 36-37.

Koomen, K. (1993). Under surveillance: Fergie, photographers and infringements on freedom. *University of Queensland Law Journal, 17*, 234-246.

LaFave, W. R., & Israel, J. H. (1986). *Modern criminal procedure: Cases, comments and questions* (6th ed.). St. Paul, MN: West Publishing.

Lewin, T. (1993, February 8). New laws address old problem: The terror of a stalker's threats. *The New York Times*, p. B10.

Lyall, S. (1997, September 1). The press: Tabloids Diana used now loom as villains. *The New York Times on the Web*. http://search.nytimes.com/search/daily/bin/ fastweb?getdoc+site+site+18875+13+wAAA+paparazzi.

Middleton, K. R., Chamberlain, B. F., & Lee, W. E. (2005). *The law of public communication 2006*. Boston: Allyn & Bacon.

New York Times v. Sullivan, 376 U.S. 254 (1964)

Phillips, A. (1997, September 7). Grief on demand. *The New York Times*, 4, p. 17.

Photographers convicted in Schwarzenegger case. (1998, February 24). *The New York Times*, p. A14.

Privacy: France (1998, March 30). http://com.bu.edu/comnews/090497.html.

Prosser, W. (1971). *Handbook of the law of torts* 261 (4th ed.). St. Paul, MN: West Publishing.

Prost, A., & Vincent, G. (Eds.). (1991). *A history of private life: Riddles of identity in modern times* (Vol. V). Cambridge, MA: The Belknap Press: Harvard University Press.

Salame, L. (1993). A national survey of stalking laws: A legislative trend comes to the aid of domestic violence victims and others. *Suffolk University Law Review*, 27(67), 67-111.

Smith, J. M. (1997, September 8). Our celebrities, ourselves. *The New York Times*, p. A19.

Warren, S. D., & Brandeis, L. D. (1890). The right to privacy. *Harvard Law Review*, 4, 193.

Zuboff, S. (1988). *In the age of the smart machine: The future of work and labor*. New York: Basic Books.

AUTHOR INDEX

SUBJECT INDEX